PASCAL: STRUCTURE AND STYLE

Benjamin/Cummings Series in Structured Programming

R. Billstein, S. Libeskind, J. Lott, *MIT Logo for the Apple* (1985)

G. Booch, *Software Engineering with Ada* (1983)

D. M. Etter, *Structured FORTRAN 77 for Engineers and Scientists* (1983)

D. M. Etter, *Problem Solving with Structured FORTRAN 77* (1984)

D. M. Etter, *WATFIV: Structured Programming and Problem Solving* (1985)

P. Helman, R. Veroff, *Intermediate Problem Solving and Data Structures* (1985)

A. Kelley, I. Pohl, *A Book on C* (1984)

M. Kittner, B. Northcutt, *BASIC: A Structured Approach* (1985)

R. Lamb, *Pascal: Structure and Style* (1985)

S. Perry, *Beginning COBOL: An Interactive and Structured Approach* (1985)

W. Savitch, *Pascal: An Introduction to the Art and Science of Programming* (1984)

R. Sebesta, *Structured Assembly Language Programming for the VAX 11* (1984)

R. Sebesta, *Structured Assembly Language Programming for the PDP-11* (1984)

PASCAL
STRUCTURE AND STYLE

RICHARD LAMB

The Benjamin/Cummings Publishing Company, Inc.
Menlo Park, California ● Reading, Massachusetts ●
Don Mills, Ontario ● Wokingham, U.K. ● Amsterdam ●
Sydney ● Singapore ● Tokyo ● Mexico City ● Bogota ●
Santiago ● San Juan ●

Sponsoring Editor: Alan Apt
Production Supervisor: Larry Olsen
Book and Cover Designer: Rodelinde Albrecht
Artist: Robert Bausch

Designs at the opening of Chapters 1, 2, 3, and 5 by Robert Bausch.
Designs at the opening of Chapters 4, 6 through 19 by Jan Arthur Lee.
Cover drawing by Robert Bausch.

Photo Credits:
Figure 1.1 from Iowa State University.
Figure 1.2 from Intel Corp.
Figure 1.3 from IBM Corp. and Apple Computer, Inc.
Figure 1.6 from Historical Pictures Service, Chicago.

Library of Congress Cataloging-in-Publication Data
Lamb, Richard (Richard C.)
  Pascal structure and style.

  (Benjamin/Cummings series in structured programming)
  Includes index.
  1. PASCAL (Computer program language)   2. Structured programming.   I. Title.   II. Series.
QA76.73.P2L345   1986   005.13'3   85-18511

ISBN 0-8053-5830-7

CDEFGHIJ-DO-89876

The Benjamin/Cummings Publishing Company, Inc.
2727 Sand Hill Road
Menlo Park, California 94025

To my mother and father,
who have given me much,
especially a relationship with my Father,
who has given me everything.

Preface

Teaching computer programming has changed rapidly in the past few years, in large part because of the widespread availability and usefulness of computers in society. Scientists and mathematicians are no longer the only people who are using computers, and computer literacy is quickly becoming the most necessary skill that college graduates need to find a job. Many students who are not computer science majors are taking introductory computer classes in order to familiarize themselves with the field. In fact, many students have already taken computer programming courses in high school.

Unique Approach

This creates a problem. Most text books for the introductory programming course assume that students have had no experience in front of a computer and must learn everything for the first time. Other programming books assume the reader is fluent in one language and attempt to teach the reader in a minimum amount of time how to program in a second language. However, no current text book on the Pascal language assumes a mixed audience. This book assumes that the students using it will include students who have never studied any programming language before as well as students who have taken one or more programming courses in BASIC. This book does not assume that the student has a prior knowledge of BASIC, so the material will be easily understood by the novice. However, the BASIC programmer often starts with a disadvantage because of habits she or he has learned while programming with the limitations of BASIC, especially the unstructured dialects of BASIC. The book provides a Hints for BASIC Programmers section in each chapter to help encourage the good aspects and to help correct the bad aspects of prior programming experience in BASIC.

Emphasis on Examples

The current trend in computer science education focuses on teaching abstract problem-solving skills combined with the syntax and programming techniques of a particular language. The approach of this book follows this trend. Each chapter contains material that extends the student's knowledge of the syntax of Pascal as well as discussion about and complete examples of problem solving using the language elements covered in the discussion. The programming examples are interesting and are taken from common uses of the computer. The problems are discussed thoroughly; each is solved through rigorous application of the top-down approach to algorithmic development through the use of pseudocode. The problem is analyzed and developed in parts and then brought together, so the student is able to see each step in the process from problem statement to solution.

Important Features

Programming with Style: Chapter 5 is entirely devoted to development of a consistent and elegant programming style. This same consistent style is exemplified in the programs and program fragments throughout the text.

Common Errors and Debugging: Each chapter contains a discussion of syntax and execution errors that are commonly encountered after the introduction of the new material. This section also contains defensive programming hints to aid in program debugging.

Hints for BASIC Programmers: In each of the first 15 chapters, a section is devoted entirely to a comparison and contrast of the elements in BASIC that translate into Pascal. Often, the BASIC programmer's experience is a disadvantage, and bad habits need to be explicitly discouraged.

Writing Large Programs: Chapter 17, Writing and Documenting Large Programs, is a unique chapter on the issues involved in the development of large programs.

Programming Examples: Except for Chapter 1, 2, and 5, each chapter contains at least one and often two or more complete programming examples. These special sections give the problem statement, the initial main algorithm, algorithms for subtasks, and the individual procedures, often refined several times. The sections include the final program to be executed and actual input and output files.

Algorithmic Development: Each programming example illustrates fully the concept of top-down algorithmic development through the use of pseudocode. The pseudocode is informal English, allowing students to have a model of algorithmic development without being handicapped by unfamiliar formal structures.

Exercises and Self Tests: Each chapter contains many Self Tests at the ends of sections as well as Exercises at the end of the chapter. The answers to the Self Tests are given at the end of the book. The Exercises contain error-checking or analysis problems as well as a wide range of programming problems.

Instructor's Guide: Answers to Exercises and discussion about them are included in the *Instructor's Guide.*

All the programs and program fragments have been executed on a DEC-20 mainframe and are written in Standard Pascal as defined in the *Pascal User Manual and Report,* Second Edition (Jensen and Wirth, Springer-Verlag, 1975).

Organization

Each chapter is meant to contain enough material for one to three lectures in a normal semester or quarter course. (Usually, one-quarter courses will not finish the book.) The first chapter introduces computers and the need for programming languages. The second chapter introduces Pascal and the building blocks of the language.

The third and fourth chapters introduce variables and procedures, respectively. The first control structure taught is the procedure, in order to emphasize program breakdown and good design. The sixth chapter continues with the emphasis on procedural development as value and variable parameters are introduced. In this way, complete and consistent parameterization of procedures is emphasized and exemplified.

The fifth chapter, Programming with Style, is a detour from the introduction of the syntax of Pascal to the issue of *style.* This chapter collects many programming proverbs and motivates the student to write consistent, elegant code that is well commented and structured. Material in this chapter is referred to repeatedly throughout the text as a reminder.

Chapters 7, 8, 9, and 11 focus on other control structures and their use. The FOR loop, IF statement, REPEAT and WHILE loops, and the CASE statement are introduced, with particular emphasis on which control structure is most appropriate in particular situations.

Chapter 10 does for input and output issues what Chapter 5 does for the issue of style. It collects what has been mentioned up to that point and discusses how to use multiple input and output files.

Chapter 12 begins the discussion of data types and data structures. Chapter 12 introduces the notion of a type. Chapters 13 and 14 introduce arrays and multidimensional arrays. Chapter 15 discusses the concept of a record and illustrates the multipurpose data structure, the array of records. Optional Chapter 16 details the use of structured files and sets.

Chapter 17 provides a unique approach to the issue of writing large programs. It focuses on the trade-off between the complexity of the control structure and the complexity of the data structure needed to solve a large problem, and it outlines steps to make each of the control and data structures appropriate to the given problem. Chapter 17 considers a large problem, writing a database manager, and outlines its data structure and control structures.

Chapters 18 and 19 complete the discussion of the Pascal language with the topics of recursion and pointers. The disadvantages as well as the advantages of recursive control and data structures are presented.

Acknowledgments

Many individuals contributed to the development of this text. First, I am grateful to the members of the Department of Computer Science at Stanford University. Many of the ideas presented here came as a result of learning and teaching there. I would especially like to thank Denny Brown, Arthur Keller, Jock MacKinlay, Rich Pattis, and Stuart Reges for much of what I know about teaching computer programming. Arthur Keller and Stuart Reges were especially instrumental in my decision to write this book and its early development.

I would also like to express my gratitude to those who reviewed the manuscript and who gave very helpful comments at various stages in its development: James Gips, Boston College; Peter Flanagan, Boston University; Michael Main, University of Colorado; Tom Lynch, Northwestern University; Tom Bailey, University of Wyoming; Dave Lamb and Martin Widyono, Stanford University.

I also am indebted to individuals in Stanford Christian Fellowship who have played a part in the development of this text. Dave Lamb, Rob Perkins, and Martin Widyono have been helpful as teaching assistants and fellow instructors in developing examples throughout the text. Thanks also go to the many graders and other helpers with whom I have worked: Nate Bacon, Sue Dante, Ruben DiRado, Michael Dittmar, Kevin Gillette, Bill Glad, Curtis Gruenler, Mark Kennedy, Michael O'Brien, Rae Lee Olson, Katie Stock, and Kathy Wolfe. The text, like teaching itself, has been something of a team effort, and I am grateful to Sue Dante, Tom Nygren, Alissa Riper, Liz Argetsinger, and Mark Hornbostle for help in the typing of the manuscript. Greg Read provided helpful nontechnical advice throughout the development process. Finally, I am grateful for the prayers of the Christian Fellowships at Stanford University and University of California, Santa Cruz, as I began and completed this project.

Richard Lamb

Brief Contents

1. Introduction to Programming 1
2. Introduction to Pascal 21
3. Simple Number Crunching: Variables 39
4. Extending the Language: Procedures 71
5. Programming with Style 99
6. Procedures, Parameters, and Functions 119
7. Definite Repetition 151
8. Conditional Execution 195
9. Conditional Repetition 239
10. Input and Output 281
11. Conditional Execution: CASE 303
12. Extending the Language: Types 323
13. Storing Data: Arrays 345
14. Multidimensional Arrays 393
15. Storing Data: Records 419
16. More Data Structures: Files and Sets 473
17. Writing and Documenting Large Programs 497
18. Recursion 517
19. Pointers and Lists 541

Contents

1. Introduction to Programming 1

Adding Machines, Washing
    Machines, and Computers, 2
Computer Hardware, 5
Why Pascal? 7
Algorithmic Refinement and
    Pseudocode, 9
Program Execution, 12

SELF TEST, 17
Pascal and BASIC, 18
Hints for BASIC Programmers, 18
Summary, 19
New Terms, 20
Exercises, 20

2. Introduction to Pascal 21

Building Blocks, 22
    Reserved Words, 22
    Special Symbols, 23
    Numbers, 23
    Character Strings, 24
    Identifiers, 25
    SELF TEST, 26
    Separators, 26
Program Syntax, 27

SELF TEST, 28
Statements, 28
Empty Statements, 30
Common Errors and Debugging, 31
Hints for BASIC Programmers, 34
Summary, 35
New Terms, 35
Exercises, 36

3. Simple Number Crunching: Variables 39

Variable Declarations, 40
Assignments and Expressions, 42
    SELF TEST, 44

SELF TEST, 45
Writing Results, 45
    SELF TEST, 47

Constants, 48
    SELF TEST, 49
Reading Values from Input, 49
    SELF TEST, 53
Standard Functions, 54
Programming Example 3.1, 56

Programming Example 3.2, 60
Common Errors and Debugging, 63
Hints for BASIC Programmers, 65
Summary, 66
New Terms, 67
Exercises, 67

4. Extending the Language: Procedures 71

The Procedure Call, 72
    SELF TEST, 75
The Procedure Declaration, 75
Programming Example 4.1, 77
Programming Example 4.2, 84
Global and Local Variables, 89

Common Errors and Debugging, 91
Hints for BASIC Programmers, 92
Summary, 94
New Terms, 95
Exercises, 95

5. Programming with Style 99

Program Style, 101
    Indentation and Blank Lines, 101
    Capitalization, 102
    Identifiers, 103
    Constants, 104
    Comments, 104
    Procedures, 106
    Semicolons before ENDs, 107
Output Style, 108

Field Widths, 108
Files and Input/
    Output Procedures, 110
User Friendliness, 111
Common Errors and Debugging, 112
Hints for BASIC Programmers, 112
Summary, 112
New Terms, 113
Exercises, 114

6. Procedures, Parameters, and Functions 119

Value Parameters, 122
    SELF TEST, 125
Variable Parameters, 126
    SELF TEST, 128

Variables and Parameters, 128
    Local Versus Global, 128
    Parameters Versus
        Global Variables, 129

*Variable Versus
Value Parameters,* 132
Blocks, Scope and Activations, 133
SELF TEST, 135
Programming Example 6.1, 136
Functions, 140
Character Variables, 141

Programming Example 6.2, 142
Common Errors and Debugging, 145
Hints for BASIC Programmers, 146
Summary, 147
New Terms, 147
Exercises, 147

7. Definite Repetition 151

Repetition, 152
SELF TEST, 154
Compound Statements, 154
How Does It Work? 156
SELF TEST, 159
Nested Repetition, 159
SELF TEST, 162
Iteration, 162
SELF TEST, 163
Programming Example 7.1, 164

More on Character Variables, 167
Programming Example 7.2, 169
Programming Example 7.3, 174
Programming Example 7.4, 177
Common Errors and Debugging, 183
Hints for BASIC Programmers, 188
Summary, 190
New Terms, 190
Exercises, 190

8. Conditional Execution 195

IF-THEN-ELSE, 196
SELF TEST, 200
Nesting, 200
SELF TEST, 205
Assertions (Optional), 205
Boolean Operators
and Expressions, 207
SELF TEST, 210
Boolean Variables and Constants, 210
Boolean Functions, 214
SELF TEST, 216

Efficiency and Style, 216
Random Numbers and
Decision Making, 218
SELF TEST, 220
Programming Example 8.1, 220
Common Errors and Debugging, 229
Hints for BASIC Programmers, 232
Summary, 234
New Terms, 235
Exercises, 235

9. Conditional Repetition 239

The WHILE Loop, 241
SELF TEST, 242
Eoln and Eof, 242
SELF TEST, 247
Invariant Assertions (Optional), 247
Programming Example 9.1, 248
Programming Example 9.2, 253
The REPEAT Loop, 259
SELF TEST, 260

Comparative Advantages: FOR,
WHILE, REPEAT, 261
Programming Example 9.3, 263
Common Errors and Debugging, 271
Hints for BASIC Programmers, 273
Summary, 275
New Terms, 276
Exercises, 276

10. Input and Output 281

Multiple Input and Output Files, 283
SELF TEST, 286
Programming Example 10.1, 286
Programming Example 10.2, 289
Common Errors and Debugging, 295

Hints for BASIC Programmers, 297
Summary, 297
New Terms, 298
Exercises, 298

11. Conditional Execution: CASE 303

The CASE Statement, 304
SELF TEST, 307
Programming Example 11.1, 307
When to Use CASE or IF, 311
SELF TEST, 312
Increasing the Power of CASE, 312

Programming Example 11.2, 314
Common Errors and Debugging, 319
Hints for BASIC Programmers, 319
Summary, 320
New Terms, 321
Exercises, 321

12. Extending the Language: Types 323

Enumerated Type Declarations, 324
SELF TEST, 326

Use of Enumerated Types, 327
SELF TEST, 331

Subrange Types, 332
   SELF TEST, 335
Programming Example 12.1, 335
Debugging and Types, 339
   SELF TEST, 339
Types and Data Abstraction, 340

Common Errors and Debugging, 340
Hints for BASIC Programmers, 342
Summary, 342
New Terms, 342
Exercises, 343

13. Storing Data: Arrays 345

Introduction Arrays, 346
Array Declarations, 348
   SELF TEST, 351
Use of Arrays: Reading and
   Initializing, 351
Use of Arrays:
   Sequential Searching, 353
   SELF TEST, 354
Use of Arrays:
   Procedure ReadWord, 354
   SELF TEST, 356
Array Indexing, 356
Use of Arrays: Bubble Sort, 358

   SELF TEST, 360
Use of Arrays: Binary Search, 360
   SELF TEST, 368
Packed Arrays, 368
   SELF TEST, 371
Programming Example 13.1, 371
Programming Example 13.2, 376
Common Errors and Debugging, 385
Hints for BASIC Programmers, 387
Summary, 389
New Terms, 389
Exercises, 389

14. Multidimensional Arrays 393

Declaring Multidimensional
   Arrays, 394
Accessing Multidimensional
   Arrays, 397
   SELF TEST, 398
Programming Example 14.1, 398

Programming Example 14.2, 405
Common Errors and Debugging, 410
Hints for BASIC Programmers, 411
Summary, 413
Exercises, 413

15. Storing Data: Records 419

Declarations, 422
Usage, 424

   SELF TEST, 426
Arrays of Records, 426

SELF TEST, 429
Using Large Data Structures, 429
Sorting, 435
    SELF TEST, 436
Programming Example 15.1, 436
Variant Record Structures, 446

Programming Example 15.2, 449
Common Errors and Debugging, 467
Hints for BASIC Programmers, 468
Summary, 468
New Terms, 469
Exercises, 469

16. More Data Structures: Files and Sets 473

Files, 474
    Text Files Reconsidered, 475
    SELF TEST, 475
    Two Procedures: Get and Put, 476
    SELF TEST, 476
    File Parameters, 477
    SELF TEST, 477
    Files of Other Types, 477
Programming Example 16.1, 479

Sets, 482
    SELF TEST, 484
Programming Example 16.2, 485
Programming Example 16.3, 489
Common Errors and Debugging, 493
Summary, 494
New Terms, 494
Exercises, 494

17. Writing and Documenting Large Programs 497

Data Structure and
    Stepwise Refinement, 499
    SELF TEST, 502
Control Structures and
    Stepwise Refinement, 502
    SELF TEST, 504
The Trade-Off: Control and
    Data Structures, 504

Programming Example 17.1, 506
Common Errors and Debugging, 513
Summary, 515
New Terms, 515
Exercises, 516

18. Recursion 517

Single Procedure Recursion, 518
    SELF TEST, 520
    SELF TEST, 523

Programming Example 18.1, 524
Programming Example 18.2, 525
    SELF TEST, 527

SELF TEST, 529
FORWARD Declarations, 529
When Not to Use Recursion, 530
Programming Example 18.3, 531

Common Errors and Debugging, 537
Summary, 538
New Terms, 538
Exercises, 538

19. Pointers and Lists 541

Dynamic Versus Static Allocation, 543
   Declaring a Pointer Type, 543
Lists, 544
NEW and DISPOSE, 547
NIL and Initialized Pointers, 548
Fundamental List Procedures, 549
   Initialization, 549
   Stack Insertion, 549
   Queue Insertion, 550
   Deletion from the Head, 551

   Deletion from the Tail, 552
   Printing a List, 553
   SELF TEST, 554
Programming Example 19.1, 554
Other Pointer Structures, 560
Programming Example 19.2, 563
Common Errors and Debugging, 564
Summary, 565
New Terms, 566
Exercises, 566

Appendix 1: The
   GOTO Statement, A1-1
Appendix 2: Turbo Pascal, A2-1
Appendix 3: Character Sets, A3-1

Glossary, G-1
Self Test Solutions, S-1
Index of Selected Defined Identifiers, I-1
Subject Index, I-3

CHAPTER 1

INTRODUCTION TO PROGRAMMING

Adding Machines, Washing Machines, and Computers

The computer has become an object of mystery and veneration in our late twentieth-century society. Many of us stand in awe of a person who programs computers, and we feel ashamed if we cannot even turn on an office computer. While knowledge of computers seems like a priestly art only for the talented few, the ability to use computers has become almost as necessary as the ability to drive a car.

One goal of this book is to clear away the mystery and to teach the *art* and the *science* of using a computer to solve problems. A computer is simply a machine. It is not a simple machine, yet it is only a machine. Specifically, a computer is a machine with *at least* two capabilities: (1) the ability to store, process, and retrieve numerical data and (2) the ability to be programmed, allowing automatic control of the operations performed on the data.

An adding machine or electronic calculator is an example of a machine with the first capability. The adding machine stores data that are typed into the display. Numbers are processed (added) by hitting the correct operator key, and the result is retrieved by reading the display.

A simple adding machine is not a computer, however, because it cannot be programmed. The person using an adding machine must manually hit the add key every time an add operation is desired. There is no way to give the adding machine a list of numbers and tell it to add them all up or to determine which of several numbers is the largest.

A modern washing machine is an example of a machine that can be programmed. It can be instructed to use either hot, warm, or cold water in the wash cycle, to use either hot, warm or cold water in the rinse cycle, and to agitate normally or gently for a variable period of time. The washing machine is programmed by pushing buttons to control specific operations. A washing machine also is not a computer because it does not process data (although it could be said to process clothes).

A computer is a machine that can be programmed to perform logical and arithmetic operations. The first fully electronic machine that was able to do this was built by Dr. John V. Atanasoff, a professor of physics at Iowa State University. Atanasoff and an assistant, Clifford Berry, used Atanasoff's ideas to produce the **Atanasoff–Berry computer** (ABC). (See Figure 1.1.)

The ABC was little more than a calculating device for Atanasoff's students, but about the same time the government became interested in building a machine that could calculate missile trajectories rapidly. Building on the ideas and innovations of Atanasoff's computer, J. P. Eckert and J. W. Mauchly built ENIAC (Electronic Numerical Integrator and Calculator) in 1946 at the University of Pennsylvania (Figure 1.2).

ENIAC was a breakthrough for its day, but it was very large, very expensive, and very prone to breakdown. If electronic technology had not improved over the past forty years, the computer would be little more than a curiosity for most of us today. However, since the creation of the ABC and ENIAC, computers have tremendously increased in speed and dependability while decreasing in size and cost. The microcomputer revolution, which began in the mid 1970s, greatly increased the availability and usefulness of computers. The IBM PC and

Figure 1.1: The Atanasoff–Berry Computer

Figure 1.2: ENIAC

Apple's Macintosh computers, vastly more powerful than the dinosaur ENIAC, occupy only a fraction of the space. These two microcomputers are mainly responsible for the current widespread use of computers in schools, offices, and homes (Figure 1.3).

Figure 1.3: IBM PC and Apple Macintosh

Computer Hardware

The term **hardware** includes all the machinery involved in operating a computer. It includes the printer you receive results from, the terminal you sit at, and any other devices you use to enter, store, process, or transmit data. You don't need to know exactly how any of these things work to be proficient at getting the computer to work for you, any more than you need to have a mechanic's understanding of how a car works to be able to drive one. However, it is good to have a basic understanding of the different parts of any computer.

The muscle and the brain of any computer are its **central processing unit, or CPU.** It is the muscle of the computer because it is what gives the computer its power. Alone it has no ability to remember instructions, but when given instructions it can perform them with amazing speed and accuracy. It is the brain of the computer in the sense that it contains all the information about how operations should be carried out. The CPU controls the intake of data **(input)** as well as the production of results **(output).**

> **Central Processing Unit:** The part of the computer that recognizes and executes instructions and allows communication between the other parts of the computer.

The instructions that the CPU executes are provided by the program, or **software**, which is stored in the **memory** of the computer. The memory is much like a huge room of post office boxes, each initially empty but each with the capacity to store a small amount of information. The CPU is like the postal clerk who moves information from box to box, takes in new information for storage and processing, and produces results from the operations performed. (See Figure 1.4.)

> **Memory:** The part of the computer where instructions and data are stored for use and processing by the CPU.

Normally, when using a computer, a person will not even be aware of the CPU or the memory. The main elements of a computer that are the most visible are the input and output devices. The most common input/ouput **(I/O)** device is the computer terminal, which consists of a keyboard for input and a cathode ray tube (CRT) screen for output. When the computer is communicating, it sends its message (output) to the screen. The user responds by typing input at the keyboard. Other common I/O devices are punched card readers (input) and line

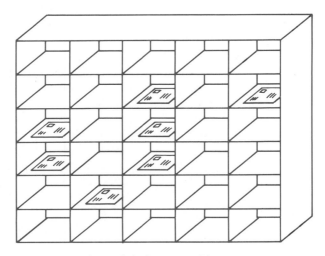

Figure 1.4: Computer Memory

printers (output). The different components of a computer and the relationships among its various parts are illustrated in Figure 1.5.

> **I/O device:** A component of a computer system that allows communication between humans and computers.

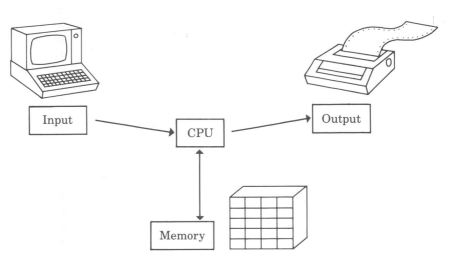

Figure 1.5: Components of a Computer

Perhaps this discussion leaves you a little dissatisfied. "Is that all?" Yes, that is all a computer is. Conceptually, it is a much simpler machine than a car. Furthermore, it is almost certain that you will never need much more understanding of how the computer works than what was just presented to make it work for you. The power of a computer lies not in its complexity but in the size of its memory, the complexity of the programs that operate it, and its speed.

Why Pascal?

Computers were first used to make many numerical calculations quickly. The first computers had only a small capacity to remember instructions given to them. Their memories were relatively small, and the computer instructions, written in a programming language such as FORTRAN or BASIC, needed to be compact and easily readable by the computer. FORTRAN was first introduced about 1957, and BASIC was introduced in the early 1960s. Both languages have been greatly modified since being introduced.

> **Programming language:** A set of vocabulary, symbols, and rules used to control the operations of a computer.

Computer memories have become larger and thousands of times less expensive since the 1950s. When memory space was expensive, the effort was made to minimize its use. Now, by contrast, programmer time has become relatively expensive. The past decade has seen a movement away from an emphasis on efficient and compact **programming code** (the programming commands used to direct the actions of the computer, so named because programs used to be very difficult to read) toward code that is easy to read, clear, and easily debugged.

Structured programming is a method of constructing and designing computer programs that emphasizes readability, modifiability, and ease of debugging. The term *structured* implies that there is an organized way in which a particular problem can be solved. Niklaus Wirth developed the Pascal computer language in 1971 with this concern as the design priority. The language was named after French philosopher and mathematician Blaise Pascal. (See Figure 1.6.) The Pascal language is designed to help or even at times to force the computer programmer to think and create in an organized way. Throughout this book, in the Hints for BASIC Programmers sections, Pascal will be compared with BASIC to show how structure decisions have been made in Pascal and other structured languages (such as Ada, Modula-2, and more recent versions of FORTRAN and structured BASIC). These sections will be very beneficial for students of BASIC who are learning Pascal; they may also be interesting to the new programmer.

Figure 1.6: Blaise Pascal

In a sense, the problems of computer programming are more like the problems of English or history than those of math, physics, or engineering. (That thought may be disconcerting to those who see themselves as out of their element in subjects such as English.) Programming is a great deal like writing an essay. In both cases there is an initial problem or task to be accomplished, a need for clear communication, and certain rules of grammar to be followed that allow clear communication to take place. Essays are not considered to be right or wrong solutions to questions, only relatively better or relatively worse solutions. (There is no one correct essay on Hamlet's fatal flaw, for example.) However, it is not entirely true that critical evaluation is merely subjective—there are objective criteria by which some essays are judged to be better than others, but the criteria are rarely quantifiable. Similarly, there are many different *correct* programs possible for any given problem, in the sense that many different programs will execute and produce the desired results, but some correct programs can be judged to be better than other correct programs, depending on the considerations that are used to evaluate them.

One goal of this book is to teach you how to write correct programs in Pascal. Of course, you can write an essay that is made up of grammatically correct sentences and yet does not accomplish your purpose or does so only in a limited and sloppy way (like essays that are typed from scratch at 2AM the night before they are due). A second goal of this book, then, is to do for Pascal what a good composition text or teacher would do for English—namely, discuss the mechanics of writing good programs that are well structured, well thought out, and clear.

We take as our basic assumption that computer programs should be inexpensive to write and use. We also assume that, over the long run, the most expensive part of computer programming is the time spent writing, debugging, and modifying the program. Although computer time is expensive, it is still probably less expensive to make the computer do more work if it will save programmer time (which is also expensive). The style of programming presented in this book may seem to be an extravagant use of computer time, but it enables the programmer to develop more quickly programs that will be easier to debug and modify.

Algorithmic Refinement and Pseudocode

Suppose you want to make a chicken dinner for a friend. You want to impress this friend, so you ask me for a good recipe. I know a great recipe, and so I tell you to write down the following things to do:

Buy 2 chicken breasts, 1/2 pint whipping cream, small can chicken broth, 1/2 lb. mushrooms, 1 onion, rice, broccoli.
Open chicken package.
Take skin off breasts.
Debone chicken breasts.
Put filets in lemon juice on plate.
Chop 1/2 onion.
Wash mushrooms.
Put 2 cups water in pan.
Heat water until boiling.
Cut mushrooms.
Put 1/2 tbsp. butter in frying pan.
Heat frying pan.
Put onions in pan.
Put mushrooms in pan.
Take mushrooms and onions out of pan.
Put 1 cup rice in boiling water.
Turn heat to low.
Put 1/2 tbsp. butter and 1/2 tbsp. oil in frying pan.
Put filets in frying pan.

How excited would you be about getting a recipe like this? Well, not very, I imagine. It is difficult to look at this list and figure out what is supposed to be happening or what this will finally produce. The task of making dinner no longer appears attractive to you, so you decide to take your friend out, instead. Suppose, on the other hand, I give you the following instructions:

1. Fry two chicken breast filets.
2. Prepare sauteed mushrooms and onions.
3. Prepare rice.
4. Prepare steamed broccoli.
5. Prepare cream sauce.
6. Serve chicken, sauteed vegetables, and sauce over rice; serve broccoli.

You might say, "Well, at least I know what we'll be having, although I don't know how to do all of *that*." You want me to be more specific. I could then elaborate on these directions to give you an idea of exactly what should happen in what order.

1. Buy ingredients: 2 chicken breasts, 1/2 pint whipping cream, small can chicken broth, 1/2 lb. mushrooms, 1 onion, rice, broccoli.
2. Filet chicken breasts.
3. Prepare 2 servings of rice.
4. Chop and saute mushrooms and 1/2 onion; set aside.
5. Fry chicken filets, set aside.
6. Clean broccoli.
7. Prepare cream sauce.
8. Steam broccoli, 8 minutes.
9. Add vegetables to sauce, heat 5 minutes.
10. Add meat to sauce, heat 5 minutes.
11. Serve chicken over rice; serve broccoli.

It is a lot easier to see what is happening in this case. In fact, as you read it, you decide that this sounds like a great meal, and you are no longer interested in going out to eat. But you still might say, "I don't know how to filet chicken, I don't know how to prepare 2 servings of rice," and so on.

I could then elaborate until I use only terms and commands that you already understand. Here's how I would expand two of the steps:

Filet chicken breasts:
a. Open package.
b. Peel off skin.
c. Hold breast at joint.
d. Carve meat off ribs.
e. Remove cartilage with knife.

Prepare 2 servings of rice:
a. Measure 1 1/3 cup water; put in pan.
b. Boil water.
c. Put 2/3 cup rice in water; turn heat to low.
d. Simmer 20 minutes; serve.

At this point, you would have no excuse for not producing a wonderful meal. This last list is somewhat like how fine recipe books are organized, with instructions for preparing parts of an entire meal in separate chunks.

The process that we have just gone through is called **algorithmic refinement.**

Algorithm: The systematic process or plan used to solve a problem.

Algorithmic refinement: The process of program design that begins with an abstract algorithm and successively refines the definition of the algorithm by defining in greater detail each of the subtasks of the algorithm.

The algorithm is the structure or outline of the solution to the problem of preparing a chicken dinner. The algorithm was refined twice as it went from five big tasks to ten smaller tasks to several three- or four-step jobs for each of the ten tasks given previously. The process of algorithmic refinement helps us to think about a problem in an organized way. (See Figure 1.7.)

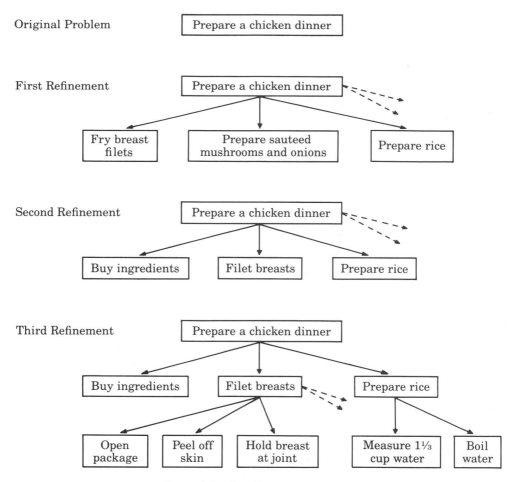

Figure 1.7: Algorithmic Refinement

When given a programming task, you are faced with two problems that need to be solved:

1. the problem of finding a clear specification of what the program must do (the program description).
2. the problem of finding a program that does what is specified by the program description.

If the program description is detailed enough, solving the second problem becomes easy, once we know the details of the programming language we are using. The process we will be using in this book to solve the first problem, that of writing a clear program description, will be algorithmic refinement through the use of pseudocode.

Pseudocode ("false code") is an abbreviated form of a solution to a programming problem. It includes programming language vocabulary together with English words in an informal structure. As in Pascal, indentation is a useful convention to help us understand what is supposed to be happening in the pseudocode statement of the algorithm. The pseudocode version of a program is analogous to an outline of an essay; both are used to help organize and refine the respective final products. Only after the pseudocode algorithm has been successfully refined will we attempt to convert the pseudocode into real Pascal code.

Other names for algorithmic refinement are *stepwise refinement* and *top-down programming*. These terms emphasize the fact that we think about a problem from the "top," breaking it down into its major constituent subtasks, as Figure 1.8 illustrates. Each of the major tasks is broken down yet further, until only very simple and straightforward tasks are left for the program to solve.

Program Execution

As you begin to learn the Pascal language, you will want to execute programs to use what you are learning. To do this, you will need to know how to execute a program on your computer. The first step in the interaction between your software and the computer's hardware is to enter the program you have written into the memory of the computer. You will need to use some kind of **editor** to do this. The memory is somewhat like a filing cabinet in which material is stored in the form of **files**. The program is stored in one file. Often the input and output will be stored in separate files as well. Figure 1.9 shows how all three files might be stored in the computer's memory.

> **Editor:** A program that allows programs or data to be entered into the computer's memory and allows the information stored in memory to be updated and corrected.

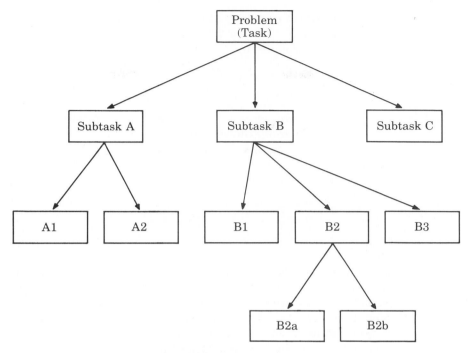

Figure 1.8: Top-Down Design

Once you have written a program and entered it into memory, you are ready to **compile** your program. You have written your program in a programming language (the **source code**) such as Pascal, but the computer cannot immediately execute your program. The **compiler** breaks each Pascal statement into instructions that are simple enough for the CPU to execute. These instructions

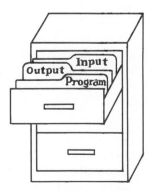

Figure 1.9: Files in Memory

are written in **machine language**, which is usually nearly impossible for a human to read. Notice that the compiler is a *program*, like those you will write, although much longer and not usually written in Pascal.

Compiler: A program that translates a source code program into a machine language program that can be executed by the computer.

Machine language: A computer programming language that specifies instructions that the CPU can execute.

Once you have written a program and compiled a machine language version of your program, you are ready to execute your program. Normally, the compilation and execution of your program will happen in two stages but with one command to the computer. The entire process, from the statement of the problem to the completion of a working program, is illustrated in Figure 1.10.

When you execute your program, you will normally operate in one of two execution modes—**batch** or **interactive**. Batch processing means that the entire program runs without any interaction with the user. A batch program is like a toaster: You put in the data (bread) and it produces the results (toast). If your toast is burnt, you may have to alter your program and try it again. With batch processing, you must have all the input ready at the beginning of the execution. Your input will be stored in a file, much like the file used to store your program. At first, your input files will usually be short, and they will probably be provided by your instructor. After you have programmed for a while, you may want to create your own input files, or perhaps another computer program may be used to create input files for your program.

The second mode of execution of your program is called **interactive** mode. In this case there is usually no initial input file. An interactive program requires the participation of the user, like a telephone. In interactive programs, the computer will ask the user at the terminal for the appropriate data and will display on the screen the calculated results. The program itself is written in such a way to indicate to the user the type and amount of data it requires to do its job.

Batch processing: The mode of program execution in which user interaction is not necessary. Input is from a file, and the output is written to a file.

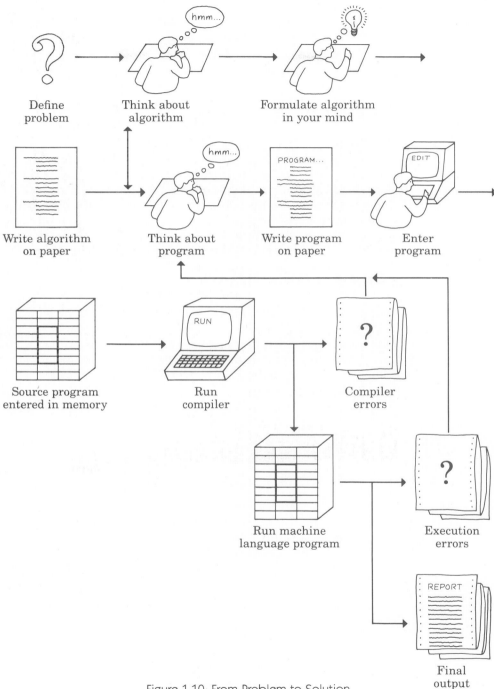

Figure 1.10: From Problem to Solution

> **Interactive processing:** The mode of program execution in which the user plays a role in the program's completion of the task given it. Input is gathered from the terminal keyboard, and output is sent to the user at the terminal screen.

There are corresponding advantages and disadvantages to each mode of execution. A batch-oriented program runs extremely quickly once the program is working and data have been entered to a file correctly. It is most useful when the quantity of input data is large and an input file already exists. The disadvantage of a batch-oriented program is that, if the data are improperly formatted in the input file, the program often will fail to execute properly. An interactive program is good for dealing with small data sets that the user can type quickly every time she or he runs the program. Because the program can tell the user what type of data it is expecting, it is more likely the data will be entered correctly. Furthermore, the interactive program can tell the user when the data have been entered incorrectly, and the user can reenter the data. Later we will discuss more completely combining terminal interaction and working with input files. Throughout this book, we will present examples of both interactive and batch programs to familiarize you with both modes of operation. You may be limited by your computer facility to one or the other mode; however, it is good to know how to use both. Figure 1.11 illustrates the difference between batch and interactive programs.

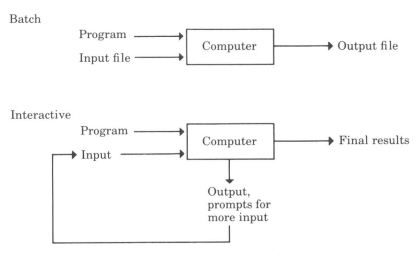

Figure 1.11: Batch and Interactive Programs

The following two programs do similar things, average a set of numbers. The first program, written to execute interactively, asks the user for two numbers and then prints their average. The second program, a batch-oriented program, reads 100 numbers from an input file and writes their average. The second program doesn't take noticeably more time to execute than the first because the computer can perform one or 100 operations in far less time than a second. At this point you are not expected to understand how these programs work; you are simply to notice stylistic differences between them.

```
PROGRAM InteractiveAverage (Input, Output);
(*This program asks the user for two real numbers and      *)
(*then prints their average.                                *)
VAR      First, Second, (* the 2 numbers given by the user *)
         Average : Real; (* the result computed and printed *)
BEGIN
         Writeln (Output, 'This program averages 2 numbers');
         Writeln (Output, 'Give me your first number.');
         Readln (Input, First);
         Writeln (Output, 'Give me your second number.');
         Readln (Input, Second);
         Average := (First + Second) / 2;
         Writeln (Output, 'The average of', First, ' and',
                          Second, ' is', Average);
END.


PROGRAM BatchAverage (Input, Output);
(* This program reads 100 numbers from an input file and   *)
(* prints their average to the output file.                *)
VAR      Num,           (* stores each number as it is read *)
         Total,         (* keeps a running track of the sum *)
         Average : Real;   (* the calculated average         *)
         Cntr : Integer;   (* the FOR loop index             *)
BEGIN
         Total := 0.0;
         FOR Cntr := 1 TO 100 DO BEGIN
                 Read (Input, Num);
                 Total := Total + Num;
         END;
         Average := Total / 100.0;
         Writeln (Output, 'The average of 100 numbers is',
                          Average);
END.
```

SELF TEST

For the previous two programs, answer the following questions:

1. What are the advantages of batch processing in this case?
2. Why was the first program written interactively?

Pascal and BASIC

It is likely that you did some BASIC programming before you began Pascal. If you didn't, don't worry, because the discussion in this book will help you begin from the beginning. If you have learned some BASIC, you will probably have some unlearning to do. It has been said that the surest way to ruin a programmer for life is to teach the person BASIC first. I don't subscribe to this view, as I myself learned BASIC first. However, the statement contains some truth. BASIC teaches a style that works well for short programs. In fact, it is probably easier and faster to write a five-line program in BASIC than it would be to do the same in Pascal.

Pascal was designed to facilitate good, readable, structured programs. A long Pascal program should not be significantly more difficult to read and understand than a shorter one. Longer programs are broken down into smaller and smaller subtasks, as the recipe was in the fourth section of this chapter. Normally, when we think of a solution to a problem, we can organize the solution into the solution of separate subtasks. Pascal helps us to think in an organized way and to write programs reflecting that organization. BASIC programs tend to be written using many GO TO statements, which hide any structure and organization a particular solution may have. This book will not teach you how to program in BASIC, but it will expose you to some of the differences between BASIC and Pascal and thereby reveal Pascal's superiority.

Hints for BASIC Programmers

Pascal programs are not handled by a computer in the same way BASIC programs are. Perhaps you didn't recognize the description of the compiler from your prior experience. That is because most BASIC programs are **interpreted**, not compiled. An **interpreter** does not produce a machine language program to be executed by the computer; rather, it looks at the BASIC code and executes the actions directly. With an interpreter, the distinction between compilation and execution vanishes because the interpreter actually executes the code itself— the process is a single step, not two steps as with compiled programs.

> **BASIC interpreter:** A program that takes a BASIC program as input and executes the statements as directed by the BASIC code.

Although it is possible to find a Pascal interpreter, your Pascal programs will probably be compiled, not interpreted. Because of the separation of compilation and execution, there are two fundamentally different types of errors in Pascal programs, compilation errors and run-time (or execution) errors. More discussion of these errors follows in the next chapter.

SUMMARY

Computers are machines that can be programmed to process numeric data. When computers were first invented, they were very large and very slow by today's standards, though still much faster than any previous calculating devices. In the past decade, the microcomputer revolution has brought the computer into the office and home.

Computers are machines (**hardware**) that are told what to do by programs (**software**). Any computer is composed of a **CPU** (central processing unit), a **memory**, and **input** and **output** devices. The CPU controls the intake of data to the memory, computes values within the memory, and sends results to the output device. The computer is conceptually a much simpler machine than a car; its power lies in the size of its memory, its ability to be programmed, and its speed.

The original restrictions on programming languages, that they be compact and easily read by computers, have been lifted because of the increased memory size. Computer time and memory space have become less expensive while programmer time has become more expensive. The programming language **Pascal** was developed to force programmers to write programs that were easily debugged and modified. This style of constructing programs is called **structured programming**.

When problem solving with a computer, often the most difficult step in finding a working program is deciding what you want the computer to do. Once you have determined the steps the computer must take to solve a problem, converting those steps into instructions written in Pascal is often not very difficult. The outline of steps toward the solution is called an **algorithm**, and the process we will use to design good and working algorithms is called **algorithmic refinement**. The algorithms we will use to write programs will not be written in a programming language. They will be written in **pseudocode**. A pseudocode algorithm operates for a complete program similarly to the way an outline operates for a complete essay.

Any computer you will be using has several different components that work together to allow you to **execute** programs on it. A handwritten program is entered into the memory of a computer by means of an **editor**. The program will usually be stored in a **file**, as will the input needed and the output produced. Once the program is in memory, a **compiler** translates the program into a **machine language** version of the program that the CPU can directly execute. Programs can be executed in two different modes, **batch** or **interactive**.

The programming language Pascal is superior to BASIC in its design because it facilitates good, readable, structured programs. If you have studied BASIC before, you may have some unlearning to do, though your familiarity with programming concepts will be helpful as you learn Pascal and structured programming. If you have never studied BASIC, you may find that language interesting since it is still the most widely used computer language.

New Terms

Atanasoff–Berry computer	memory	pseudocode
hardware	I/O device	editor
CPU	programming language	machine language
input	programming code	compiler
output	structured programming	batch processing
software	algorithm	interactive processing
	algorithmic refinement	BASIC interpreter

EXERCISES

1. Organize the following terms in chronological order from the initial problem to the final solution:
   a. editor
   b. pseudocode
   c. machine language program
   d. output
   e. problem refinement
   f. algorithm
   g. execution
   h. handwritten program
   i. problem statement
   j. program in memory
   k. compiler

2. Write a four-step algorithm for some task that you do every day, such as getting dressed, getting (or making) lunch, or preparing for bed. The size of each step should be approximately the same.

3. Take the four-step algorithm developed in the previous exercise and expand on each step with three or four smaller steps. Group the substeps and outline your algorithm in a systematic manner.

4. Categorize each of the following programming tasks, identifying whether each should be an interactive or a batch program. Try to identify what type of input would be needed and what the output of each program might be.
   a. a program to calculate the flight path of a rocket putting a satellite into orbit.
   b. a program to play a game of tic-tac-toe.
   c. a program to predict weather patterns from meteorological satellite data.
   d. a program to control the booking of airline reservations.

CHAPTER 2

INTRODUCTION TO PASCAL

Building Blocks

Before we can communicate in any written language, we must learn vocabulary and punctuation, the building blocks of grammar. However, it would be unreasonable to have to memorize all the words before even beginning to communicate. Indeed, the use of language at simple levels enables us to venture to more advanced levels of vocabulary and syntax. Consequently, you won't have to memorize all the words in Pascal's lexicon at the start.

The words and symbols that Pascal does understand automatically are few enough to warrant mention. These words and symbols are grouped into several classes that make up each program written in Pascal; a discussion of each class follows.

Reserved Words

In Pascal, **reserved words** have set definitions and uses that cannot be altered. Table 2.1 presents a complete list of reserved words in standard Pascal.

Table 2.1. Reserved Words in Pascal

AND	END	MOD	REPEAT
ARRAY	FILE	NIL	SET
BEGIN	FOR	NOT	THEN
CASE	FORWARD	OF	TO
CONST	FUNCTION	OR	TYPE
DIV	GOTO	PACKED	UNTIL
DO	IF	PROCEDURE	VAR
DOWNTO	IN	PROGRAM	WHILE
ELSE	LABEL	RECORD	WITH

Special Symbols

There are **special symbols** in Pascal, like punctuation in written language, that separate and organize the reserved words or act as abbreviations for certain computer operations. There are both one- and two-character special symbols. Never separate two-character special symbols with a space (: =). In the same way, the reserved word BEGIN should never be typed BEG IN. Table 2.2 lists all the special symbols in Pascal.

Table 2.2. Special Symbols in Pascal

+	–	*	/	=	<	>
[	]	.	,	:	;	^
(	)	<>	<=	>=	:=	..

Numbers

What programming language would be complete without a way to represent numbers? Numbers can be represented in several different ways, depending on how they are used. An **integer**, or whole number, is a sequence of digits. A + or – to denote positive or negative numbers is optional. An integer must be in the range [–Maxint, Maxint]. The value of Maxint is usually on the order of $2^{15}-1$ or $2^{31}-1$. Maxint is **implementation dependent**, which means that the numerical value will vary from computer system to computer system. If the representation of a number has a decimal point and a digit to the right of the decimal point, the number is **real**. Unlike an integer, a real number may have a fractional part, even if the fractional part is shown by a zero. A real number must have at least one digit on both sides of the decimal point. Therefore,

$$\left.\begin{array}{r} 5.00 \\ 0.5 \\ -0.925 \end{array}\right\} \text{ are legal real numbers}$$

whereas

$$\left.\begin{array}{r} 5. \\ .5 \\ -.925 \end{array}\right\} \text{ are not legal real numbers.}$$

Implementation dependent: Any feature of a language that is not fixed but varies with different computers. For example, larger computers allow larger ranges of numbers than personal computers or small systems.

Exponential notation can also express a real number. An exponential number is composed of three parts. The first is the **mantissa**. Following the mantissa is an "E", which stands for the word *exponent*, and then an integer. The integer shows the power of 10 that is multiplied by the mantissa. For example:

$$6.023\text{E}23 = 6.023 \times 10^{23} = 602300000000000000000000$$

$$-9\text{E}-9 = -9 \times 10^{-9} = -.000000009$$

It would be awkward to write the rightmost values in these examples; you can see the advantage of exponential notation. Note that the mantissa can be a real (with digits on both sides of the decimal point) or an integer (not written with a decimal), but the exponent is always an integer.

> **Exponential notation:** The method of expressing a number as a value (the mantissa) multiplied by 10 raised to the power indicated by the exponent.

Character Strings

Because computers must communicate with people, every computer language uses words to some extent. The computer needs a facility to print words or other nonnumerical symbols. These characters or words are called **character strings**. Define a character string by enclosing it within two single quotation marks. A character string may contain **alphanumerics** (letters and numerals), punctuation, and other symbols. For example:

```
'This is a legal character string.'
'So is this.'
'This isn't.'
'Neither is
this'
```

There is a problem with the third character string. Pascal reads the apostrophe for the contraction, which is the same as the single quote, as the end of the character string and does not include t.'. Therefore, to put a quote inside a character string, write it twice:

```
'This isn''t an illegal character string.'
```

Look again at the last character string in the group:

```
'Neither is
this'
```

This character string would create another problem because it spans two lines; a carriage return or carriage return-line feed (CRLF) lies between is and this'. Character strings must begin and end on the same line.

Identifiers

A computer language also needs the ability to use variables to define operations and to allocate new data storage locations. An **identifier** is the name of a value or operation. The user, the computer system, or the language may define an identifier.

> **Identifier:** A name given as any sequence of alpha-numerics. The first character in the sequence must be a letter.

The compiler can differentiate easily between integers and reals, which begin with a digit, and identifiers, which begin with letters. Table 2.3 distinguishes between some legal and illegal identifiers.

Some Pascal compilers allow the underline character in identifier names; you could use it to distinguish the different words as in this example: my_birthday. An easier way to accomplish the same thing is to capitalize the beginning of each new word in the identifier: MyBirthday or ThisIsALongIdentifierName. In Pascal, there is no length limit to identifiers, although the first eight characters (ten characters on some systems) in each identifier must be in a unique sequence. Therefore, these two identifiers are not distinguished in most implementations of Pascal:

ThisIsATest
ThisIsATrick

Table 2.3. Identifiers

Legal Identifiers	Illegal Identifiers
MyBirthday	My Birthday
X1	280Z
CS105A	C.S.105A
ThisIsLegal	(Illegal)

Capitalization is ignored in Pascal on most systems; BEGIN is the same as begin or Begin or BeGiN. (This book will use both upper- and lowercase in the text of programs. This is only a style preference, however, and not a specification of the language.) Some systems do not have lowercase.

SELF
TEST

Following is a list of elements that might be found in a program. Figure out what class of building blocks (reserved words, special symbols, numbers, character strings, identifiers) each is. If any is illegal, state why.

VAR	VARIABLE
'VARIABLE'	VAR.
123.	123.5
A123.5	A1235
'123.'	000.123
POBOX10106	P.O.Box10106
Number9	'Number'

Separators

The last type of building block may seem insignificant, yet it is by far the largest class of elements in a program. **Separators** separate each of the other building blocks from one another. Blanks, tabs, and carriage returns (which Pascal treats as blank spaces) are separators. This class also includes semicolons, which separate statements. Commas separate character strings, numbers, or identifiers in a list.

Separators impart order to a Pascal program. Other than the inclusion of separators, Pascal does not require that coding fall into a rigid layout. You don't have to indent or use carriage returns. A Pascal program does not have numbered lines.

Another type of separator, the comment, is also useful, but it is different in that it signals the human user, not the computer.

> **Comment:** A portion of the program ignored by the compiler but included to aid human understanding of the program.

The comment can occur anywhere a space or carriage return can occur; it doesn't need its own line.

```
PROGRAM(*This is a comment*)DoNothing; (*THIS is ONE TOO *)
BEGIN(*Another*)END.
```

The comment is enclosed by the special symbols (* and *). Curly brackets, { and }, can also enclose comments, but this book will use the two-character symbol because it is more visible.

The DoNothing program is legal, although not useful. In Chapter 5, we will see how comments actually expedite coding.

Program Syntax

The previous section discussed the building blocks of a Pascal program. Identify the elements in this program:

```
PROGRAM DoNothing:
(* This program illustrates simple program syntax *)
(* but really doesn't do anything.                *)
BEGIN
    (* The main program statements go here     *)
END (* The period ends the program.            *).
```

1. Reserved words: PROGRAM, BEGIN, END—these will, in this book, always be written in capital letters.
2. Identifier: DoNothing—the program name.
3. Special symbols: ; —separates PROGRAM header from the main program.
4. Separators: comments, spaces, carriage returns and tabs, which are overlooked by the compiler but useful to the reader.

Generally, a program is made up of two parts, a **declaration** and a **statement**. The dividing line between the two is the reserved word BEGIN, which begins the statement.

Figure 2.1: PROGRAM Syntax

```
PROGRAM <Identifier>;
    <Declaration part>
BEGIN
    <Statement part>
END.
```

Figure 2.1 demonstrates succinctly the **syntax** of a Pascal program. PROGRAM, BEGIN and END, and the period must be in every Pascal program. The definition of *syntax* is as appropriate to English as it is to Pascal:

> **Syntax:** The formal rules defining valid constructions in a language.

The structure of a Pascal program is simple and elegant. BEGIN and END are **delimiters**. Delimiters demarcate the actual executable statements of a program. Each BEGIN is balanced by an END. In the same way, the PROGRAM is balanced by the final period, which signals the end of the program.

Knowing the syntax of a language is not enough to derive meaning from it. In English, knowing that each sentence must contain a subject and a verb is only meaningful when we know what a subject is and what a verb is and how they relate. The rules that define how a syntactically correct construction is given meaning in a language are called the **semantics** of a language.

> **Semantics:** The formal rules defining how valid constructions in a language are to be understood.

SELF TEST
Each of the following English sentences contains an obvious error of some sort. Decide whether each error is a syntax error or a semantic error:

1. The blue boy wisely drove the duck off its head.
2. Wildly the ate rice.
3. Greg read but Bill glad.
4. Rachel heard wildly awesome apples clapping hands.

Statements

The task of learning Pascal can be separated into the tasks of defining *declarations* and *statements*. We will discuss declarations in Chapter 3. Let's begin here with statements. A statement is an executable Pascal instruction. The first type of statement we need is a statement that allows us to produce output. What good would a program be if the person running it could not determine the results of its execution? The statement in Pascal that produces output is the Writeln statement. For example,

```
PROGRAM IntroduceMyself (Output);
(* This program gives the user a brief introduction *)
(* to the author of the text.                       *)
BEGIN
    Writeln (Output, 'Hello, my name is Richard Lamb.');
    Writeln (Output, 'My friends call me Rich,');
    Writeln (Output, 'but my mother calls me Richard.')
END.
```

This program has some new features: (Output) in the first line (the program header or program declaration) signifies that an **output file** is going to be created. The effect of its position on the first line is implementation dependent, that is, different for different systems. The output file is the place in memory to which all the results will be sent. Writeln sends the quoted material to the file specified (almost always called Output). The above program would produce the following output:

OUTPUT
```
Hello, my name is Richard Lamb.
My friends call me Rich,
but my mother calls me Richard.
```

Some systems require a control character at the beginning of each line of output. The **control character** determines the amount of spacing before a printed line. If your system requires control characters, then you usually include a space before the first character in each output line. The following coding would produce disappointing results on a system that requires control characters:

```
Writeln (Output, ' This is a test.');
Writeln (Output, 'This is another test.');
Writeln (Output, '007 is my favorite spy.');
```

The output would be:

OUTPUT
```
This is a test.
his is another test.

07 is my favorite spy.
```

If your system requires control characters, you will probably use these codes, too:

- ' ' causes a single line feed before printing (the default)
- '0' causes a double line feed before printing
- '1' causes a begin new page before printing
- '+' causes no line feed (causes overprinting)

Notice as well that, in the `IntroduceMyself` program, a semicolon separates the first two `Writeln` statements. The semicolon acts as a statement separator and cannot be omitted between statements. If END followed the third statement, you could omit the third semicolon because END is a delimiter, not a statement. A carriage return is not sufficient to separate statements, although it is useful for the human reader.

```
PROGRAM DemonstrateSemicolons (Output);
(************************************************************)
(* This program illustrates the necessity and sufficiency *)
(* of semicolons as separators. As it stands now it will  *)
(* compile with errors.                                   *)
(************************************************************)
BEGIN
    Writeln (Output, 'Hello'); Writeln (Output,
                            'This is correct.');
    Writeln
            (Output, 'So is this.');
    Writeln (Output, 'This line will produce an error')
    Writeln (Output, 'because it didn''t have a semi-');
    Writeln (Output, 'colon. The carriage return is not');
    Writeln (Output, 'sufficient.')
END.
```

Think of semicolons as analogous to commas in a series of numbers. In the series (3,4,5,6), the parentheses are the delimiters BEGIN and END, and the commas act like the semicolons by separating adjacent elements. The series (3,4,5,6,) is improper because the final comma implies that another item or element follows. The list (3,4 5,6) is also improper because the second and third elements are not properly separated.

Empty Statements

Pascal has the capacity to handle an **empty statement.** An empty statement results from a superfluous semicolon that creates a statement that contains no instruction. In the following example, a semicolon separates a statement from a delimiter. Since the semicolon is superfluous, an empty statement exists between the semicolon and the delimiter.

```
PROGRAM EmptyStatements (Output);

BEGIN;      (* empty statement here because a semicolon
              is not necessary after a BEGIN, although
              it is not a syntax error.              *)
    Writeln (Output, 'This line has 2 empty statements.');;;
    Writeln (Output, 'This program will execute properly.');
END.
```

If we use the analogy of a series of numbers and denote the empty statements with letters, we can represent the program as:

$$(a,1,b,c,d,2,e)$$

There are two meaningful statements between BEGIN and END, with five empty statements. An empty statement lies wherever a semicolon is found but is not needed. The program will execute properly, without error. Semicolons belong only between statements. The following program contains two errors:

```
PROGRAM SemiColonErrors; (Output);
(* There's one, because of the extra ; before Output *)
BEGIN
    Writeln ; (Output, 'Here is another error')
END.
```

Common Errors and Debugging

Much of the time spent writing computer programs is spent **debugging.**

> **Debugging:** The systematic removal of errors from a computer program.

You will discover several different types of errors as you begin to write computer programs. **Syntax errors** occur when the rules that govern the construction of a program have been broken. Syntax errors are also called **compiler errors,** or **compile-time errors,** because the compiler spots them. Your program will not execute as long as syntax errors exist. They are easy to make and should be easy to fix once you find them.

Execution errors, or run-time errors, will become apparent while the program is running, after you have eliminated the syntax errors. Execution errors may be caused by faulty logic, by incorrect usage of Pascal constructs (**semantic errors**), or by data input errors.

A third type of error is the **intent error.** In this case, your program may execute without a hitch, but you find that it doesn't do what it is supposed to do. This situation can be avoided by careful programming strategy and adherence to the method of algorithmic refinement. Intent errors are often the most difficult to correct.

The goal of these Common Errors and Debugging sections is to decrease the amount of time you must spend debugging your programs. This goal will be achieved through **defensive programming.**

Defensive programming: The strategy of carefully and systematically writing programs to decrease the number of initial syntax, execution, and intent errors.

Defensive programming requires that you learn well the syntax rules of Pascal. It also requires that you learn how to spot and fix execution errors. Therefore, these sections will highlight the syntax rules mentioned in the chapter, especially those that a beginner is likely to forget. These sections will also discuss execution errors commonly seen with the topics presented in the chapter. Errors that are common at this point include:

1. **Not including a semicolon between statements.** If you get used to putting a semicolon at the end of every statement, you may have an extra semicolon before END, but the program should execute.

2. **Ending your program with a semicolon instead of a period.** The last END should be followed by a period (and just when you were getting in the habit of using semicolons!).

3. **Beginning a character string and not ending it with a quotation mark:**

```
Writeln (Output, 'Hello, My name is Richard);
```

The compiler finds the semicolon and the carriage return, but according to the coding, the string has not yet ended. The compiler complains with an error message such as string constant contains CRLF.

4. **Writing a character string across the end of a line:**

```
Writeln (Output, 'This is an
                 illegal character string.');
```

This error is the same as the previous error, as far as the compiler is concerned, and it will generate the same error message. Your intention is different, however. To correct this, do one of two things:

```
Writeln (Output, 'This is now a');
Writeln (Output, 'legal character string.');
```

or, if the output is to be on one line:

```
Writeln (Output, 'This is now a ',
                 'legal character string.');
```

Notice that the space between a and ' had to be included, or the text would have run together.

5. **Using a single quotation mark inside a command string.** A quotation mark inside a character string ends the string. Two marks are needed if one is meant to appear as part of the string:

```
'Isn''t this easy?'
```

6. **Writing malformed numbers.** It is an error to have commas or spaces in a number. Real numbers must have at least one digit (even if the digit is zero) on each side of the decimal point.

7. **Writing malformed identifiers.** It is an error to begin any identifier with a digit. Including a nonalphanumeric character in an identifier is an error.

8. **Failing to close a comment correctly.** One of the most difficult errors to spot is the failure to close a comment. The results can be disastrous or subtle. If the discovery of an error eludes you, look at the comments. For example:

```
PROGRAM CommentExample:
(* Forgetting to close this comment yields
                        several errors )
BEGIN      (* The parenthesis is sometimes
          mistaken for a closed comment     *)
        Writeln (Output, 'This line produces',
                         ' an error');
        Writeln (Output, 'So will this one.');
END.    (* Even this one will as well,
          because no BEGIN was seen.        *)
```

9. **Program header errors.** If the program is to produce output (and just about all are), then you must name the output file in the program header.

```
PROGRAM Example (Output);
```

If (Output) is not included, then an execution error will occur. This happens because you did not designate a place for the output. A syntax error in the program header is likely to cause major problems for the compiler, and it will probably look like dozens of errors have been made. For example, either leaving out the program identifier or the semicolon at the end of the line will cause the rest of the program to be misunderstood:

```
PROGRAM (Output);          (* this is an error *)
...
PROGRAM Example (Output)
BEGIN                      (* this is an error as well *)
```

10. It is not a syntax error to have a semicolon after BEGIN, although it is never necessary.

Hints for BASIC Programmers

Many of the building blocks of the Pascal language are similar in structure and usage to their counterparts in BASIC. BASIC has key words such as FOR, NEXT, and LET. The Pascal equivalent of a key word is a reserved word. Real numbers are the same in Pascal as they are in BASIC, and exponential notation looks exactly the same. Comments in Pascal and REMarks in BASIC are both ignored by the computer, though the format for comments in Pascal is much more flexible, as we'll see in later Hints sections.

The first chapter states that, for extremely short programs, BASIC is probably easier to write than Pascal. Let's compare two short programs that accomplish the same thing—one in BASIC, one in Pascal.

```
50   REM THE FIRST COMPARISON BETWEEN PASCAL AND BASIC
100  PRINT "THE FIRST THING TO NOTICE ABOUT PASCAL"
150  PRINT "IS THAT IT IS NOT AN ACRONYM, AND"
200  PRINT "THEREFORE NOT WRITTEN IN ALL CAPS,"
250  PRINT "LIKE BASIC IS."
300  END
```

```
PROGRAM ShortExample (Output);
(* This is a first comparison between Pascal and BASIC *)
BEGIN
        Writeln (Output, 'The first thing to notice about');
        Writeln (Output, 'Pascal is that it is not an');
        Writeln (Output, 'acronym, and therefore not');
        Writeln (Output, 'written in all caps,',
                         'like BASIC is.');
END.
```

Even in this simple example, it is evident why short programs are a bit more complicated in Pascal. It is necessary to declare the program as such with the reserved word PROGRAM on the first line, and then to mark the beginning of the execution with the reserved word BEGIN. In general, variables and other parts of the program must first be declared in Pascal before they are used in the program, so the introductory part of the program can be many lines long. Once we reach the statement part of the programs, the two languages look similar, at least at this point. Remember the flexibility of Pascal, however. An equally valid Pascal program might have all the Writeln statements on the same line. This cannot be done in BASIC.

Notice the absence of line numbers in Pascal. This may seem to create chaos, but you will soon find that this feature actually encourages better programs. References to parts of the program are by name, not by line number. A name is more meaningful and easily remembered than a number. As you will see, even long programs are easy to read.

SUMMARY

Reserved words, special symbols, numbers, character strings, indentifiers, and **separators** are the building blocks from which all Pascal programs are constructed. The set of rules governing how these building blocks are put together is called the **syntax**. The set of rules determining how syntactically correct statements are understood is called the **semantics**.

Pascal programs are comprised of **statements** and **declarations**. Between the declaration and the statement, as well as at the beginning and the end of the program, are **delimiters**, such as BEGIN, END, and PROGRAM. The first type of statement we need to use is the Writeln statement, which produces output. The semicolon acts as a separator to separate statements. A carriage return is not enough to separate statements, and single statements can span more than one line. A semicolon that occurs between a statement and a delimiter produces an **empty statement** but does not produce an **error**.

Debugging is the systematic removal of errors from a computer program. **Syntax errors** will be discovered by the compiler; **execution errors** will not usually be discovered until after all syntax errors have been eliminated. **Intent errors**, often caused by a faulty algorithm, are the most difficult to detect and to eliminate. We will use a strategy called **defensive programming** to minimize these and all other errors.

New Terms

reserved words	separator	syntax error
special symbols	comment	compiler error
integer	declaration	execution error
implementation	statement	semantic error
dependent	syntax	intent error
real	delimiter	defensive programming
exponential notation	semantics	PROGRAM
mantissa	output file	Writeln
character string	control character	BEGIN
alphanumeric	empty statement	END
identifier	debugging	

EXERCISES

1. Each of the words in the left column is related to or described by one or more of the terms in the right column. For each word on the left, identify the corresponding words on the right:

   BEGIN   compile-time error
   Writeln   separator
   PROGRAM   statement
   comment   run-time error
   execution error   reserved word
   syntax error   intent error
   END   special symbol
   semicolon   semantic error
                      delimiter

2. Each of the programs given in Exercises 2 through 5 contain two syntax errors. Find them.

   ```
   PROGRAM Example-1 (Output);
   BEGIN;
        BEGIN
            Writeln; (Output, 'I am very tired.')
        END;
   END.
   ```

3. ```
   PROGRAM AnotherExample (Output)

   BEGIN
        Writeln (Output, 'Why doesn't this work?')
   END.
   ```

4. ```
   PROGRAM AThirdExample (Output);

   (*Don't worry, we're almost done.
   BEGIN (*This is easy*)
        Writeln (Output, 'This also won''t work.'*)
   END.
   ```

5. ```
   POGRAM OneMoreExample (Output); BEGIN Writeln

   (Output, '''') END;
   ```

6. Categorize each of the following items as an identifier, character string, or number. Which would be illegal to have in your program as they are?

San Francisco	1985	.505805
SFO	1E9	232-4783
SF83	9e1	'(415)499-3131
St.Francis	E91	'IVCF'
Urbana'84	19E	IVCF
'Johnny Carson'	005	5/16/60
'Ain't Misbehavin'	005.	May1660
   ```

7. Write a program called `IntroduceMyself` in which you introduce yourself to the user of your program. Don't be too brief—tell your name, age or year in school, your major or occupation, and something interesting about yourself to convince the user that she or he isn't just hearing from a computer.

8. Write a program called `MakeLetter` that produces a short letter to a friend. Make the letter informative, clever, and brief. After finishing the program, execute it, then use the editor to change the name of the person who will receive the letter. Reexecute the program with the new name. (Correspondence made simple!)

SIMPLE NUMBER CRUNCHING: VARIABLES

Computers were first developed to perform large computations quickly and are still used primarily for numerical data processing and calculations. How can the computer process numerical data? Numerical computation is done through the use of variables, expressions, and assignments. This chapter introduces these concepts and adds the power of numerical computation to our limited knowledge of Pascal.

Variable Declarations

A **variable** is a location in memory in which information is stored and from which it can be retrieved. It is like a box or a cell that can contain items of the appropriate size. (See Figure 3.1)

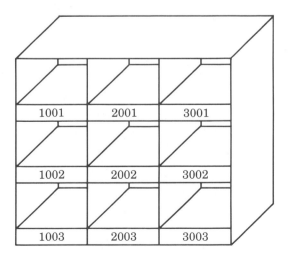

Figure 3.1: Identifier and Memory Cell

The **variable name** is the identifier that is associated with the location of the memory cell. When the programmer wants to store or retrieve a value, she or he refers to the variable name. In Pascal, every identifier used in a program must be declared or defined before it is used. (This stands in contrast to BASIC, in which most identifiers are recognized automatically; the programmer doesn't have to declare them.) In Pascal, every identifier must be declared and an identifier that names a variable is no exception.

A **variable declaration** consists of two parts: the identifier or variable name being declared and its corresponding **type**. Although we won't discuss all of them now, variables can be declared to be any of four simple types: **real**, **integer**, **boolean**, and **char.**

Table 3.1. Simple Types

integer	real
boolean	char

Notice that there is a distinction between integer and real variables. This is so because the information is stored differently, depending on the type of variable at hand. For example, the **machine representations** (the data in the machine's memory) for

```
255 (* the integer *)
```

and

```
255.0 (* the real number *)
```

are very different. In Pascal, if a variable or memory cell is declared to be an integer variable, attempting to store the value 255.0 in it will cause a compiler or run-time error to occur. The variable declaration helps the computer keep track of the differences between the intended usages of variables.

The variable declaration part of the program begins with the reserved word VAR and contains the declarations of all the variables that occur in the main program.

```
PROGRAM VariableDemo (Output);
VAR     Number : Integer;
        Rational : Real;
        A, B, C : Real;
        I, J, K : Integer;
BEGIN
        . . .
END.
```

The freedom you have in the formatting of variable declarations allows your own style and sense of aesthetics to influence your programming. Variables of the same type can be declared with commas separating them, followed by a colon and the type. Variables of different types must be separated by semicolons. More than one set of variables of each type can be declared. Notice that the reserved word VAR only occurs once in the whole declaration part. If it occurs again in the same set of declarations, the compiler will think you are trying to declare a variable named VAR, which is a reserved word—that is illegal.

The reason behind forcing you as the programmer to declare every identifier before it is used is to keep you thinking in precise terms about what you are doing and with what you are working. Pascal is a strongly typed language, meaning that every variable is declared as a certain type. It doesn't mean that every variable must have a known value at all times. Each variable type has set legal values that those variables can acquire.

Assignments and Expressions

Giving a variable a type does nothing about giving it a value. The type simply specifies what kind of values may be placed into the variable but doesn't specify any particular value. Variables must be given values after the end of the declaration part of the program, in the statement part. Practically speaking, there is no certain or useful way of predicting what the value of a variable is until it has been assigned a value. The **assignment** statement is used to put values into memory locations.

```
StudentID := 178297359;
Score := 97;
Ave := 95.2;
GPA := 4.0;
```

> **Assignment:** The act of storing a calculated or specified value in a memory location.

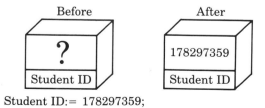

Student ID:= 178297359;

Figure 3.2: Variable Assignments

Notice that the value to be stored in memory is on the right side of the statement, and the identifier that names the location of the value is put on the left. The special symbol separating the two sides is : =. As with a reserved word, no spaces can occur between the semicolon and the equal sign. The : = was selected for use in Pascal because it really should not be read as a simple equality, =.

(The equal sign alone means equality in Pascal, which is used in boolean tests, a subject we discuss in Chapter 7.) The symbol should not be read as "equals," but as "is assigned to" or "gets equal to." Here are a couple of examples:

Example 1
```
StudentID := 178297359;
(* read as 'StudentID gets equal to 178297359' *)
```

Example 2
```
i := i + 1;
(* not i = i + 1, which is mathematically impossible *)
```

Example 2 illustrates one important reason why : = should not be read as an equality. The assignment statement works because the value on the right is calculated first and then deposited in the memory location on the left. No ambiguity results.

Look again at the examples of assignment statements above. Notice that StudentID and Score received integer values, and variables Ave and GPA received real values. Confusing the types of variables and values assigned to them can lead to a **type compatibility error**. In this case, a type compatability error would result from trying to put a real value into an integer variable. The reverse is not the case, however. When storing an integer value as a real variable, any Pascal compiler will do a type conversion automatically. This is because every legal integer is also a legal real value, although it is written differently. Every real value is not necessarily an integer.

Furthermore, we can assign the values of entire arithmetic expressions to a variable. Expressions in Pascal use standard binary infix operators: + (for addition), - (for subtraction), * (for multiplication), / (for real division), DIV (for integer division producing an integer quotient), and MOD (to produce the integer remainder of integer division where the second operand is greater than zero). DIV, MOD and / are undefined if the second operand equals zero.

> **Binary infix operator:** An arithmetic operator that occurs in an expression between two operands.

Standard arithmetic precedence rules apply in Pascal expressions.

> **Precedence:** An arithmetic hierarchy that determines the order of operations in an expression with more than one operator.

Table 3.2. Precedence Rules

( )	Parenthesized expressions first
–	Negation
*, /, DIV, MOD	Multiplication and division from left to right
+, –	Addition and subtraction from left to right

Without precedence rules, the numerical value of certain expressions could be ambiguous, perhaps dependent on the inclination of the computer at the time of execution. Remember that operations of equal priority are evaluated from left to right, unless parentheses are used to alter the order.

SELF
TEST

The following expressions are legal. Calculate their values according to the preceding rules.

1. -2 + 3 * 6 * 4 - 2
2. -(2+3) * 6 * 4 - 2
3. -2 + (3*6) * (4-2)

Integer division is like old-fashioned long division, where the quotient is an integer and the remainder is put over the divisor as the fractional part. Integer division, DIV, produces the quotient, and MOD, which is short for *modulo*, produces the remainder. Both have integer results.

```
20 DIV 3 = 6
20 MOD 3 = 2
38 DIV 5 = 7
38 MOD 5 = 3
```

When determining a modulo, if the first operand is less than zero, the result is the negative of the value of the operation if the operand were its absolute value.

```
-21 MOD 4 = -(21 MOD 4) = -1
-23 MOD 5 = -(23 MOD 5) = -3
```

Finally, MOD is not defined when the second operand is less than or equal to zero.

We can use these expressions in combination with an assignment to make simple calculations very quickly, as these examples illustrate.

Example 1
```
Pi := 3.1415926;
Radius := 3.5;                    (*measured in inches, perhaps *)
Circumference := 2 * Pi * Radius;        (* of a circle *)
Area := Pi * Radius * Radius;
Volume := 4 / 3 * Pi * Radius * Radius * Radius;(* sphere *)
SurfaceArea := 4 * Area;
```

Example 2
```
TaxRate := 11.5;                          (* in percent *)
NetIncome := GrossIncome - Deductions;
Tax := NetIncome * TaxRate;          (* simple calculations *)
```

SELF TEST

Calculate the values of the following legal expressions:

1. 80 MOD 2 DIV 3
2. 16 MOD 3/2
3. 3*(5 + 4) MOD 8
4. 2 * (3 * (5 * (7 - 1) - 1) - 1) - 1
5. -28 MOD 2

Writing Results

Once all the interesting results have been computed, they need to be written to some form of output. Otherwise the results are inaccessible to the person who wrote or is using the program. The Writeln statement produces output, as we have seen before.

Suppose the following program is executed. What will its output be?

```
PROGRAM Test (Output);
(*************************************************************)
(* This program demonstrates the difference between      *)
(* writing a character string and writing a number.      *)
(*************************************************************)
VAR     Number : Integer; (* the number we will write out *)
BEGIN
        Number := 10;
        Writeln (Output, 'Number');
        Writeln (Output, Number)
END.
```

This program illustrates the difference between writing a character string (`'Number'`) and writing a variable (`Number`). The output would be:

```
Number
       10
```

When a variable is written, the value stored in the memory location of the variable is retrieved and written to the output file. Writing to output does nothing to change or erase the value as it is stored in memory. When a number is written, it occupies a specific number of spaces, no matter how many digits it has. If it is a two-digit number, the first digit is usually preceded by ten spaces. The total allocated spaces are called the **field width.** Twelve spaces constitute a common field width. As we will see later, field width is one of the factors that a programmer can change.

If we wanted to calculate and print the results of one of the examples in the previous section, the complete program would be written as follows:

```
PROGRAM Geometry (Output);
(***********************************************************
* Calculates certain derived values for a circle and      *
* sphere each of radius 3.5 inches.                        *
***********************************************************)
VAR     Pi,       (* 3.1415926 *)
        Radius    (* 3.5 inches *)
                : Real;
        Circumference, Area : Real; (* of the circle *)
        Volume, SurfaceArea : Real; (* of the sphere *)
BEGIN
        Pi := 3.1415926;
        Radius := 3.5;
        Circumference := 2 * Pi * Radius;
        Area := Pi * Radius * Radius;
        Volume := 4 / 3 * Radius * Area;
        SurfaceArea := 4 * Area;
        Writeln (Output, Circumference, Area);
        Writeln (Output, Volume, SurfaceArea)
END.
```

Notice how this program writes more than one result per line. Another way to do this would be to use the `Write` statement, which works just like a `Writeln` but doesn't print a carriage return-line feed (CRLF) at the end of the line.

```
Write (Output, Circumference);
Writeln (Output, Area);
Write (Output, Volume);
Writeln (Output, SurfaceArea);
```

The output, for either of the two ways demonstrated, will look the same.

OUTPUT   2.199115E+01   3.848451E+01
          1.795944E+02   1.539380E+02

A way to produce output that is more readable and more understandable is to tell the reader of the output the significance of the printed values. The output would be much clearer if, in the place of `Writeln` in the previous program, the following were inserted:

```
Writeln (Output, 'A circle of radius', Radius,
        ' would have dimensions:');
Writeln (Output, '    Circumference = ',  Circumference);
Writeln (Output, '    Area          = ', Area);
Writeln (Output);
Writeln (Output, 'A sphere of radius', Radius,
        ' would have dimensions:');
Writeln (Output, '    Volume        = ',Volume);
Writeln (Output, '    SurfaceArea   = ', SurfaceArea);
```

Notice how clean the output looks:

OUTPUT   A circle of radius   3.500000E+00 would have dimensions:
             Circumference =   2.199115E+01
             Area   =   3.848451E+01

         A sphere of radius   3.500000E+00 would have dimensions:
             Volume   =   1.795944E+02
             SurfaceArea   =   1.539380E+02

You should also notice that `Writeln`, without anything other than the output file specification in parentheses (or a null or empty argument), produces a blank line on the output file. This is useful for separating chunks of output. Furthermore, the extra carriage returns in the middle of the two longer `Writeln` statements are accepted in Pascal, but the character strings must end before the CRLF and begin as a second string afterwards. Since it is now two strings, like any two items in a `Writeln` statement, a comma must separate them. A character string containing a CRLF will produce a compiler error.

SELF
TEST

What is the result of the following `Write` statement?

```
Write (Output, '5 * ', '4 - 3', ' * 3',
              ' = ', 5 * (4 - 3) * 3);
```

Constants

In the program on page 46, we declared Pi and Radius as variables. They received values at the beginning of the program, and the values never changed. Their values were constant and didn't depend on other values in the program. When values remain constant throughout a program, do not declare them as variables, but as Pascal constants.

> **Constant:** A memory location referenced by an identifier that stores a value that cannot be changed during a program's execution.

Constants are like variables in the sense that they must be declared before they can be used. If we declare Pi and Radius as constants, then we ensure that their values will not accidentally be changed, and it will be obvious to someone reading the program that they are not variables. The declaration of a constant contains the same information as the declaration of a variable and an assignment statement.

```
PROGRAM Geometry (Output);
(************************************************************
* Calculates certain derived values for a circle and      *
* sphere each of radius 3.5 inches.                        *
************************************************************)
CONST   Pi = 3.1415926;
        Radius = 3.5;                 (*  inches *)
VAR     Circumference, Area,          (* of the circle *)
        Volume, SurfaceArea : Real;   (* of the sphere *)
BEGIN
        Circumference := 2 * Pi * Radius;
        Area := Pi * Radius * Radius;
        Volume := 4 / 3 * Radius * Area;
        SurfaceArea := 4 * Area;
        Writeln (Output, 'A circle of radius', Radius,
              ' would have dimensions:');
        Writeln (Output, '    Circumference = ',
              Circumference);
        Writeln (Output, '    Area          = ', Area);
        Writeln (Output);
        Writeln (Output, 'A sphere of radius', Radius,
              ' would have dimensions:');
        Writeln (Output, '    Volume        = ', Volume);
        Writeln (Output, '    SurfaceArea   = ',
              SurfaceArea);
END.
```

Pi and Radius are declared as identifiers, and 3.1415926 and 3.5 are stored in their respective memory locations. Implicitly, Pi and Radius are real constants. The type of a constant is the same as the type of the value that it represents. The type of a constant is as important as the type of a variable. This means that constants are liable to create the same kinds of type conflicts in assignment statements that variables create. For example, with the following declarations, the second assignment is illegal:

```
CONST    Pi = 3.1415926;
VAR      Radius, Circumference : Integer;
BEGIN
         Radius := 3;
         Circumference := Pi * Radius;    (*error*)
END.
```

Constants differ from variables in that they cannot occur on the left side of an assignment because their values cannot be changed after they have been declared. Often when writing programs certain numerical maximum or minimum constraints are placed on your data, or certain physical constants, such as π or e, are used throughout. Rather than typing the values at every occurrence, declaring and using constants enhances the readability and modifiability of your program.

SELF TEST

Declare a real constant for the number of days in a year, and use it to write a program to print the number of days a person who is celebrating a twenty-first birthday has lived.

Reading Values From Input

Actually, in the program called Geometry, it doesn't really make sense to declare Radius a constant. Whenever we want to discuss a circle with a radius other than 3.5 inches, we must edit the program to give a new value to Radius. Unless we spent all the time we did just to write a program to calculate those values for one circle, we want a more general program.

The way to change the effect of the program and make it more general is to read the value of Radius in an **input file.**

Input file: A sequence of characters in memory that contains data needed to calculate or determine the results of a program.

If we use an input file instead of defining `Radius` as a constant, we can execute the program over and over and get different results from different data. The input file can consist of actual values stored in memory, in which case the program using it would be a batch program. It may, however, simply refer to the numbers that are typed by the user of the program, in which case the program is interactive.

In either mode of execution, batch or interactive, the statement that extracts a value from an input file is the same. It is simple and analogous to the `Write` statement

```
Read (Input, Radius);
```

In order to use this statement properly, several things must change in the program called `Geometry`. We must indicate that we are using another file, an input file, in the program header.

```
PROGRAM Geometry (Input, Output);
```

As a result of using an input file, `Radius` is now back to being a variable. Just as the value of a constant cannot be redefined, the value of a constant cannot be read from an input file. Essentially, `Read` acts as an assignment.

```
Read (Input, Radius);
(* Radius := The next value in the input file *)
```

It makes sense for `Pi` to be a constant because it really is a constant value that does not change from one execution to the next. `Radius` is now a variable; the program does not know what its value will be before it is executed.

```
PROGRAM Geometry (Input, Output);
(*************************************************************
* Calculates certain derived values for a circle and       *
* sphere where the radius is read from an input file.       *
*************************************************************)
CONST   Pi = 3.1415926;
VAR     Radius : Real;                (* measured in inches *)
        Circumference, Area,          (* of the circle *)
        Volume, SurfaceArea : Real;   (* of the sphere *)
```

```
BEGIN
        Read (Input, Radius);
        Circumference := 2 * Pi * Radius;
        Area := Pi * Radius * Radius;
        Volume := 4 / 3 * Radius * Area;
        SurfaceArea := 4 * Area;
        Writeln (Output, 'A circle of radius', Radius,
                ' would have dimensions: ');
        Writeln (Output, '    Circumference = ',
                Circumference);
        Writeln (Output, '    Area          = ', Area);
        Writeln (Output);
        Writeln (Output, 'A sphere of radius', Radius,
                ' would have dimensions: ');
        Writeln (Output, '    Volume        = ', Volume);
        Writeln (Output, '    SurfaceArea   = ',
                SurfaceArea);
END.
```

The Read statement doesn't require formatted data. The input file can have one or many values per line, with one or many blank spaces (or blank lines) between each value. When Pascal is asked to read an integer, it reads over blanks (including blank lines and carriage returns) and stops when, after reading a digit, it sees something that is not a digit. The input file may look like this:

INPUT   357.2

      21   19 32 29

64   117

If the first variable that is read is a real variable, it will be read properly, taking the value 357.2. If it is declared as an integer, it will be read as 357, with the .2 left over, ready to be read next. An error would probably result. If the next variable to be read from the input file were a character variable, Pascal would read the decimal point.

The command Readln helps you avoid format errors when the compiler is reading. Readln gets values from the input file, throws away anything up to and including the next carriage return on the input file, and moves down to the next line. This operation can be understood more easily by including a pointer, which points to the next unread character in the input file. At the beginning of the program, the pointer is positioned at the beginning of the file.

INPUT　　357.2
　　　　　∧
　　　　　21　19　32　29

　　　　　64　117

After performing an integer Read operation—as in the statement Read (Input, Num) —the pointer would point to the decimal point on the first line.

INPUT　　357.2
　　　　　　∧
　　　　　21　19　32　29

　　　　　64　117

To ensure that no error occurs, we could use Readln to move the pointer down to the next line.

INPUT　　357.2

　　　　　21　19　32　29
　　　　　∧
　　　　　64　117

This could be done in one of two equivalent ways:

```
Readln (Input, Number);
```

or

```
Read (Input, Number); Readln (Input);
```

After doing that, we could then execute the following statements without worry of error (assume a, b, c, d, and e are all integer variables):

```
Read (Input, a, b, c);
Readln (Input);
Read (Input, d , e);
```

Readln would ignore the fourth value on the second line. You will notice that blank lines and uneven spacing do not foil the Read operation, though spurious letters and punctuation in the input file will.

SELF
TEST

What would be the values of variables a through e after executing the three lines with the input file given above?

As it stands now, the program called Geometry is fine if we are using a batch-oriented system. Because the program is short and only requires one piece of input, however, it would be better to write an interactive program. The program as it is written would work in interactive mode, but it wouldn't be user friendly, because it wouldn't tell what it is doing or what type of data it expects. In order to do this, we would need to make one final modification.

```
PROGRAM Geometry (Input, Output);
(*************************************************************
 * Calculates certain derived values for a circle and       *
 * sphere where the value of the radius is read from the     *
 * terminal.                                                  *
 *************************************************************)
CONST    Pi = 3.1415926;
VAR      Radius : Real;                (* measured in inches *)
         Circumference, Area,          (* of the circle *)
         Volume, SurfaceArea : Real;   (* of the sphere *)
BEGIN
         Writeln (Output, 'Before I calculate some values',
                 ' for a circle and a sphere I need');
         Writeln (Output, 'to know just one thing: the',
                 ' value of the radius: ');
         Read (Input, Radius);
         Writeln (Output, 'Thanks for your cooperation');
         Writeln (Output);              (* being USER FRIENDLY *)
         Circumference := 2 * Pi * Radius;
         Area := Pi * Radius * Radius;
         Volume := 4 / 3 * Radius * Area;
         SurfaceArea := 4 * Pi * Radius * Radius;
         Writeln (Output, 'A circle of radius', Radius,
                 ' would have dimensions: ');
         Writeln (Output, '    Circumference = ',
                 Circumference);
         Writeln (Output, '    Area          = ', Area);
         Writeln (Output);
         Writeln (Output, 'A sphere of radius', Radius,
                 ' would have dimensions: ');
         Writeln (Output, '    Volume        = ', Volume);
         Writeln (Output, '    SurfaceArea   = ',
                 SurfaceArea);
END.
```

The program interaction would look like this:

INTERACTIVE SESSION

```
Before I calculate some values for a circle and a sphere I need
to know just one thing: the value of the radius:
3.5
Thanks for your cooperation

A circle of radius      3.500000E+00 would have dimensions:
    Circumference =     2.199115E+01
    Area          =     3.848451E+01

A sphere of radius      3.500000E+00 would have dimensions:
    Volume        =     1.795944E+02
    SurfaceArea   =     1.539380E+02
```

Standard Functions

Pascal provides standard functions, which are also called library functions, or built-in functions.

> **Standard functions:** Predefined functions that operate on a given argument to return a result dependent upon the argument and the definition of the function.

Table 3.3 lists many of the numerical standard functions that Pascal uses, including the argument type and the type of the value returned. It is not an exhaustive list—there are more to be learned. But they will be introduced at a time when they can be put to immediate use.

Standard functions are usually **unary functions**, functions that take a single variable or value as an argument and return another value which is a function of the first. The argument upon which these functions operate can be a value, a variable, or an expression, and it is given inside parentheses after the function name. The combination of function name and its argument is called the **function call**. For example:

```
x := Sqr (32);      (* x := 1024 *)
y := Sqrt (64);     (* y := 8.0  *)
```

With these standard functions, it is possible to write any form of exponentiation using a combination of Ln and Exp functions, including complex mathematical computations.

Table 3.3. Numerical Standard Functions

Sqr (x)	Argument can be real or integer, result will be the same type. Computes x^2.
Sqrt (x)	Argument can be any nonnegative number, result will be real. Computes $\sqrt{x}$.
Abs (x)	Argument can be real or integer, result will be the same type. Returns $-x$ if $x < 0$, otherwise returns x.
Sin (x)	Argument can be real or integer, result will be real. Calculates the sine of x, which is in radians.
Cos (x)	Argument can be real or integer, result will be real. Calculates the cosine of x, which is in radians.
Arctan (x)	Argument can be real or integer, result will be real (in radians). Computes the principal value of the arctangent of x.
Exp (x)	Argument can be real or integer, result will be real. Computes e^x.
Ln (x)	Argument can be any positive number, result is real. Computes $\log_e x$.
Trunc (x)	Argument must be real, result will be integer. Trunc (2.9) = 2; Trunc (-2.9) = -2. (Truncates towards zero.)
Round (x)	Argument must be real, result will be integer. Round (0.5) = 1; Round (-0.5) = -1.

$$x^{2/3} = \text{Exp (Ln (x)} * 2/3))$$
$$2^{16} = \text{Exp (Ln (2)} * 16)$$
$$\text{in general, } \log_n (x^y) = y \log_n (x)$$

Furthermore, all the trigonometric functions can be derived from the standard functions Sin (x), Cos (x), Arctan (x).

A common mistake is to use standard functions as though they were statements. Remember that a function call produces a single value; a function call cannot stand alone in a program in the way that a statement can. For example:

```
BEGIN
        X := 25;
        Sqrt (X);       (* This is an error *)
        Writeln (Output, X);
END.
```

This would be the same as trying to execute the following statement:

```
BEGIN
        X := 25;
        5.0;                (* This is just as much an error *)
        Writeln (Output, X);
END.
```

The number is written properly, but it isn't syntactically equivalent to a statement, which is the only element that can stand on its own between a BEGIN and its END. If we really wanted a program to calculate the square root of 25, we would write:

```
PROGRAM Sqrt25 (Output);  (* This is pretty silly *)
BEGIN
        Writeln (Sqrt (25));
END.                          (* That was pretty silly *)
```

The Writeln gives the appropriate context to the value calculated by calling the Sqrt function.

Each function has associated with it the type of value it will return. Most of the functions we have seen so far return real values. Several that don't are the **transfer functions**, so called because they transfer values from real to integer.

```
Num1 := Round (9.5);  (* Num1 is assigned to 10 *)
Num2 := Round (9.2);  (* Num2 is assigned to 9  *)
Num3 := Trunc (9.9);  (* Num3 is assigned to 9  *)
```

Trunc is short for *truncate*, which is what happens to its argument—the part behind the decimal point is thrown away. Round does what you expect; it rounds up if the decimal is greater than or equal to .5, otherwise, it truncates. If the argument is negative and its fractional part is .5, it will be rounded away from zero: Round (−4.5) = −5.

Programming Example 3.1

Assignment: Given the three dimensions of a box, calculate its volume, surface area, and the ratio of volume to surface area. Which has a higher ratio, a perfect cube or a long tie box? If you were going to make storage boxes as inexpensively as possible, what shape would they be?

Solution: First we should conceptualize the problem. Figure 3.3 shows a typical box. The box has length, width, and height. The problem solution can be broken down into the following outline:

> Box Calculations:
> > read dimensions
> > calculate volume
> > calculate surface area
> > calculate ratio
> > print values

Let's begin by defining the dimensions. We will assume that we will be reading the dimensions from a terminal. In this case, we will need to tell the user what to type.

```
(* Ask user for dimensions and read from terminal *)
Writeln (Output, 'Type the length of the box.');
Readln (Input, Length);
Writeln (Output, 'Type the width of the box.');
Readln (Input, Width);
Writeln (Output, 'Type the height of the box.');
Readln (Input, Height);
```

The next part to tackle is to calculate the volume. The volume of the box is the product of the three dimensions, or *lwh*.

```
(* Calculate the volume of the box *)
Volume := Length * Width * Height;
```

The surface area is the sum of the areas of the six faces of the box. There are three pairs of faces that have the same dimensions, so the total surface area is $2lw + 2lh + 2wh$.

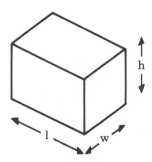

Figure 3.3: A Typical Box

```
(* Calculate the surface area of the box *)
SurfaceArea := 2 * Length * Width +
               2 * Length * Height +
               2 * Width  * Height;
```

This is one way to express the surface area, but not the only way or the best way. Notice that six multiplications and two additions are being performed here. A slightly faster way would be to factor out the 2's.

```
(* Calculate the surface area of the box *)
SurfaceArea := 2 * (Length * Width +
                    Length * Height +
                    Width  * Height);
```

An even faster way would be:

```
SurfaceArea := 2 * (Length * (Width + Height)
                  + Width * Height);
```

Here only three multiplication operations are carried out. In this short program, efficiency is not a huge concern, but if these calculations were being done thousands of times, it would be important to choose the most efficient method. In this case, choose the method that is easiest to read.

We need to calculate the ratio before printing the results. We can do this in either of two ways:

1. We can calculate the value first and then print it:

```
        Ratio := Volume / SurfaceArea;
        Writeln (Output, 'The box has a volume of ', Volume);
        Writeln (Output, ' and a surface area of ',
                         SurfaceArea);
        Writeln (Output, 'The ratio volume/surface area ',
                         'is ', Ratio);
```

2. We can save one memory location and calculate the ratio as we are printing it:

```
        Writeln (Output, 'The box has a volume of ', Volume);
        Writeln (Output, ' and a surface area of ',
                         SurfaceArea);
        Writeln (Output, 'The ratio volume/surface area ',
                         'is ', Volume/SurfaceArea);
```

One possible version of the entire program follows, with two sample executions and the results.

```
PROGRAM BoxDimensions (Input, Output);
(* This program gets the length, width and height of a      *)
(* box and calculates its volume and surface area.          *)
VAR      Length, Width, Height,            (* input values *)
         SurfaceArea, Volume : Integer; (* calculated vals *)
         Ratio : Real;                  (* Volume / SurfaceArea *)
BEGIN
         (* Tell the user what the program does.             *)
         Writeln (Output, 'This program calculates the',
                          ' volume, surface area, and the');
         Writeln (Output, 'ratio between them for a box.');
         (* Ask user for dimensions and read from terminal *)
         Writeln (Output, 'Type the length of the box.');
         Readln (Input, Length);
         Writeln (Output, 'Type the width of the box.');
         Readln (Input, Width);
         Writeln (Output, 'Type the height of the box.');
         Readln (Input, Height);
         (* Calculate the volume of the box *)
         Volume := Length * Width * Height;
         (* Calculate the surface area of the box *)
         SurfaceArea := 2 * Length * Width +
                        2 * Length * Height +
                        2 * Width * Height;
         Writeln (Output, 'The box has a volume of ', Volume);
         Writeln (Output, ' and a surface area of ',
                          SurfaceArea);
         Writeln (Output, 'The ratio volume/surface area ',
                          'is ', Volume/SurfaceArea);
END.
```

INTERACTIVE SESSION

```
This program calculates the volume, surface area, and the ratio
between them for a box.
Type the length of the box.
10
Type the width of the box.
3
Type the height of the box.
1
The box has a volume of          30
and a surface area of            86
The ratio volume/surface area is     3.488372E-01

This program calculates the volume, surface area, and the ratio
between them for a box.
Type the length of the box.
3
```

```
Type the width of the box.
3
Type the height of the box.
3
The box has a volume of              27
and a surface area of          54
The ratio volume/surface area is      5.000000E-01
```

From the sample results just calculated, it is clear that a cube has a much higher ratio of volume to surface area. A cube is, therefore, a more economical box in terms of storage area because, when boxes are made, the material is measured by surface area, not by the volume of the resulting box.

Programming Example 3.2

Assignment: Write a program that asks for an amount that a customer at a cash register owes, the amount of the bill being given to pay for it, and the amount of change in bills and coins.

Solution: In order to write this program, we will need to use pseudocode.

Here is a first try:

```
Make Change:
      read amount owed
      read amount tendered
      calculate amount to be returned
      break down by bills:
            twenties
            fives
            ones
      break down the change:
            quarters
            dimes
            nickles
            pennies
      report the amount returned
      report the quantity of each bill and coin
```

The first job is to read the values to be entered. In order to read them, variables will need to be declared.

```
PROGRAM MakeChange (Input, Output);
(*************************************************************
*   This program will ask for the amount owed and the       *
*   amount given and will report to the user the amount of   *
*   change to be returned and the numbers of bills and       *
*   coins given.                                             *
*************************************************************)
VAR     AmtOwed,                  (* Input from terminal *)
        AmtTendered : Real;  (* Input from terminal *)
BEGIN
        Writeln (Output, 'Type the amount you owe.');
        Readln (Input, AmtOwed);
        Writeln (Output, 'Type the amount you are giving.');
        Readln (Input, AmtTendered);
```

At this point we need to calculate the amount to be returned in dollars and cents.

```
        AmtReturned := AmtTendered - AmtOwed;
        Dollars := Trunc (AmtReturned);
        Cents := (AmtReturned - Dollars)*100;
```

This equation for Cents yields a real number, but we want both Dollars and Cents to be integers. We will use the transfer function Round.

```
        Cents := Round ((AmtReturned - Dollars)*100);
```

Using Dollars, Cents, and AmtTendered means that we will have to add them into the variable declaration part of the program.

```
        AmtReturned : Real; (* calculated from inputs *)
        Dollars, Cents : Integer; (* parts of AmtReturned *)
```

Now we are ready to calculate the breakdown of bills. In general, the number of bills given is the result of integer division of the amount left and the denomination of the bill.

```
        Twenties := Dollars DIV 20;
        Dollars := Dollars MOD 20     (* amount left *)
        Fives := Dollars DIV 5;
        Ones := Dollars MOD 5;        (* amount left *)
```

All these variables must be declared as integer variables.

The next task is to calculate all the coin amounts:

```
        Quarters := Cents DIV 25;
        Cents := Cents MOD 25;
        Dimes := Cents DIV 10;
        Cents := Cents MOD 10;
        Nickles := Cents DIV 5;
        Pennies := Cents MOD 5;
```

Finally, we must write the results. The entire program, including all the variable declarations and this last section, follows.

```
PROGRAM MakeChange (Input, Output);
(*************************************************************
*  This program will ask for the amount owed and the        *
*  amount given and will report to the user the amount of    *
*  change to be returned and the numbers of bills and        *
*  coins given.                                              *
*************************************************************)
VAR     AmtOwed,                (* Input from terminal *)
        AmtTendered : Real; (* Input from terminal *)
        AmtReturned : Real;     (* calculated from inputs *)
        Dollars, Cents : Integer; (* parts of AmtReturned *)
        Twenties, Fives, Ones,     (* quantities of bills  *)
        Quarters, Dimes, Nickles,
        Pennies : Integer;        (* quantities of coins  *)
BEGIN
        (* tell the user what the program does          *)
        Writeln (Output, 'This program makes change for a',
                        ' purchase at a store.');
        (* get the input values from the terminal *)
        Writeln (Output, 'Type the amount you owe.');
        Readln (Input, AmtOwed);
        Writeln (Output, 'Type the amount you are giving.');
        Readln (Input, AmtTendered);

        (* calculate the amount of change needed *)
        AmtReturned := AmtTendered - AmtOwed;

        (* break change into amounts of dollars and coins *)
        Dollars := Trunc (AmtReturned);
        Cents := Round ((AmtReturned - Dollars)*100);

        (* calculate the change in bills *)
        Twenties := Dollars DIV 20;
        Dollars := Dollars MOD 20;     (* amount left *)
        Fives := Dollars DIV 5;
        Ones := Dollars MOD 5;         (* amount left *)

        (* calculate the change in coins *)
        Quarters := Cents DIV 25;
        Cents := Cents MOD 25;
        Dimes := Cents DIV 10;
        Cents := Cents MOD 10;
        Nickles := Cents DIV 5;
        Pennies := Cents MOD 5;
```

```
                   (* write the results as neatly as possible *)
                   Writeln (Output, 'I owe you ', AmtReturned);
                   Writeln (Output, 'Here are', Twenties,' twenties,');
                   Writeln (Output, '        ', Fives, ' fives and');
                   Writeln (Output, '        ', Ones, ' ones.');
                   Writeln (Output, 'Also,    ', Quarters,' quarters,');
                   Writeln (Output, '        ', Dimes, ' dimes,');
                   Writeln (Output, '        ', Nickles, ' nickles,');
                   Writeln (Output, 'and      ', Pennies, ' pennies.');
                   Writeln (Output, 'Thank you!');
            END.
```

Here is a sample execution of this program. If you want to know how to improve the look of the output, read about field widths in Chapter 5.

INTERACTIVE SESSION

```
This program makes change for a purchase at a store.
Type the amount you owe.
13.11
Type the amount you are giving.
50
I owe you      3.689000E+01
Here are              1 twenties,
                      3 fives and
                      1 ones.
Also,                 3 quarters,
                      1 dimes,
                      0 nickles,
and                   4 pennies.
Thank you!
```

Common Errors and Debugging

1. **Naming variables with reserved words.** The reserved words VAR and TYPE are particularly susceptible to this error.

2. **Naming variables with Pascal-understood identifiers.** The following declarations are legal, but should be avoided!

```
VAR  Integer : Integer;
     Char : Char;
```

These declarations redefine the identifiers `Integer` and `Char` as variables; they are no longer understood as type identifiers. If the next line reads:

```
I, J : Integer;
```

an error will occur. The same type of error can happen if you name a variable `Writeln` or `Read`. Pascal will let you do it, but you'll be sorry you did.

3. **Type conflicts.** It is an error to try to store a real number in an integer variable.

```
Num := Limit * 2 * Pi / Max;   (* ERROR *)
```

One solution is simply to declare `Num` as a real variable. But if you want `Num` to be an integer, or if it must be an integer to be used correctly elsewhere, then use one of the transfer functions, `Trunc` or `Round`.

```
Num := Round (Limit * 2 * Pi / Max);
```

Note that it is not an error to do the reverse, to store an integer variable's value as a real variable.

```
Num := 10;
RealNum := Num;
RealNum := 15;
Writeln (Output, Num, RealNum);
```

The output for the previous lines of code would be:

```
10   1.500000E+01
```

Also note that using a single real value in an expression makes the result of the expression real, unless a transfer function is used.

```
Num := 2 * 3 + 2.0 * 4 + 5;
(* this is an ERROR, because 19.0 is real *)
```

4. **The only multiplication operator in Pascal is the ∗ sign.** All of the following are illegal expressions:

```
2N                   (* 2*N               *)
2 (N + 1)            (* 2*(N + 1)         *)
(3 + N) (2N - 1)     (* (3+N)*(2*N-1)     *)
3×6                  (* 3*6               *)
```

5. **Omitting commas in a `Writeln` statement.** In a `Writeln` statement where multiple expressions and strings are being written, each item must be separated by a comma.

```
Writeln (Output, 'A circle of radius ' Radius ' has');
          (* commas are needed here   ^ and   ^ *)
```

6. **Using a standard function as a statement.** Standard functions should only be used on the right side of an assignment statement or in a Write statement.

7. **Initializing a variable instead of declaring it.** Constants are given values when they are declared, but variables are not.

8. **Creating chain assignments.** It is illegal in Pascal to use the statement:

```
A := B := C := 0;
```

Hints for BASIC Programmers

Variable assignments in Pascal are much like they are in BASIC. The BASIC form of the assignment statement uses the keyword LET to indicate that it is not a statement of mathematical equality but an assignment. LET plays the same role as : = in Pascal.

With the addition of Read statements and variables, we can really expand the comparison between Pascal and BASIC. Let's take a look at a common introductory program, which calculates the amount of interest earned on a given amount of money at a given rate of interest.

```
10 REM CALCULATE INTEREST
20 REM A = AMOUNT; R = RATE OF INTEREST
30 REM I = CALCULATED AMOUNT OF INTEREST EARNED
40 REM N = NEW AMOUNT AFTER INTEREST ADDED
50 INPUT A,R
60 LET I = R*A
70 LET N = A+I
80 PRINT A, I, N
90 END

PROGRAM CalculateInterest (Input, Output);
(* This program calculates the interest on an amount of    *)
(* money. This asks for the original amount and the annual *)
(* interest rate. This program is meant to run BATCH.      *)
VAR      Amount,      (* before interest is added          *)
         Interest,    (* amount earned during period       *)
         Rate : Real; (* interest rate for one period      *)
BEGIN
         Readln (Input, Amount, Rate);
         Interest := Rate * Amount;
         Writeln (Output, 'You earned $', Interest, '.');
         Writeln (Output, 'Your final balance is now',
                     Amount + Interest,'.');
END.
```

You can see quickly one significant difference between the two programs: the Pascal program is wordier and looks more like English. The variable names are much longer, the comments are more like English sentences and fragments than abbreviations, and variable declarations take up space. At this point, it may seem like an awful lot of work to yield something that is fairly simple. But let's make a different comparison:

```
LET I = R*A
```

```
Interest := Rate * Amount;
```

Which of these two lines is easier to read and understand? Certainly the significance of the BASIC line would be impossible to interpret without the entire program as context. The Pascal statement makes sense even out of context. Think about having to read a 2,000-line program. Which types of statements would you rather look at in a program that long?

This example highlights one superiority of Pascal over BASIC—its self-documenting ability. Even without comments or remarks, Pascal is usually much easier to read and follow than BASIC.

If we look at the output both programs would generate, we see another difference between Pascal and BASIC. The BASIC program output looks like this:

OUTPUT
```
?1000, .085
   1000    85    1085
```

The Pascal program generated the following output:

OUTPUT
```
You earned $  8.500000E+01.
Your final balance is now  1.085000E+03.
```

Soon we will learn how to print numbers neatly.

SUMMARY

A **variable** is given a **type** by the **variable declaration**. However, variable declarations don't give variables values—the **assignment** statement is used to give values to variables. Values can be in the form of simple numerical constants or can be complex numerical expressions in which standard rules of arithmetic **precedence** govern how an expression is to be evaluated.

A `Write` statement operates like a `Writeln` statement, except that a carriage return is not printed at the end of the line. The `Write` statement can be used when writing several quantities on the same line.

Pascal **constants** should be used whenever a quantity is going to be used repeatedly in a program but will never change its value, as in the case of the constant `Pi` discussed in the geometry example. A constant must be declared before it is used; the declaration gives both the value and the type.

Often values for variables will not be calculated but will be given by the user or by an input file. Read and Readln statements operate on input files in much the same way that Write and Writeln statements operate on output files.

Pascal provides **standard functions** to allow more complex algebraic expressions, like those including trigonometric functions or exponentiation. A **function call** contains the function name and the argument and is syntactically equivalent to a value or an expression. The **transfer functions** are especially useful in converting values into integers, either by truncation (Trunc) or by rounding (Round). These functions can help you to avoid type conflict errors.

New Terms

variable	assignment	unary function
variable name	type compatibility error	function call
variable declaration	binary infix operator	transfer function
type	precedence	Write
real	constant	Read
integer	input file	Readln
machine representation	standard function	

EXERCISES

1. Write variable declarations with appropriate identifier names and types for each of the following quantities:
    a. the number of years a person has been alive
    b. the value of a person's height
    c. the amount of calories in a soft drink
    d. your grade point average
    e. your weight in kilograms
    f. your weight in ounces
    g. the ratio of daily food intake to body weight for a bird

2. For each of the following expressions, give the resulting values and the corresponding types. For example:

    3*5 + 2.0*4   23.0   real value

    a. 2 * 2 + 2 * 2 + 2 * 2 + 2
    b. 2 * (2 + 2 * (2 + 2 *(2 +2)))
    c. 2*7 / 2*7
    d. 806 MOD 8/3
    e. 133 DIV 11 DIV 11
    f. 99/4+6

g. 99 DIV 4 + 6
h. 99 DIV (4+6)
i. 99 MOD (4+6)
j. -99 DIV 4
k. -99 MOD 4
l. -1E10 / 1E-10

3. Find the syntax errors in the following variable declarations:

```
PROGRAM Test1 (Input, Output);
VAR      a, b, c,
         : Integer;
VAR      X, Y, Z : Real;
```

4. Find the syntax errors in the following variable declarations:

```
PROGRAM Test2 (Input, Output);
VAR      Temp : Boolean;
         Ch : Char;
         1, 2 : Integer;
         Real : X, Y, Z;
         'Hello' : Char;
```

5. What output does the following program produce?

```
PROGRAM Bidit (Output);
VAR      a, b, c : Integer;
BEGIN
         a := 1; b := 2; c:= b*a; Writeln (a,b);
         a := c*b; b := b*a; Writeln (c,a,b);
         c := 2*a + b; b := b; Writeln (c,b,a);
         c := c DIV a; b := a DIV c; a := a DIV 8;
         Writeln (c,b,a);
END.
```

6. Below is a program that executes with the given input file. Where does execution break down, if anywhere?

```
PROGRAM ThisIsFun (Input, Output);
VAR      Regular, Premium, Unleaded : Integer;
         Coke, DrPepper, Tab : Real;
BEGIN
         Readln (Coke, Regular);
         Readln (DrPepper); Read (Premium);
         Readln (Tab); Read (Unleaded);
         Writeln (Coke + DrPepper + Tab);
         Writeln (Regular, Premium, Unleaded);
END.
```

Here is the input file:

INPUT   29.5
          64.245 A69
          22.0 24
          22.69 89
          74.5

7. Write a Pascal statement that is equivalent to the statement below using only `Trunc`. Assume `Ball` is an integer and `Egg` is a real variable.

   `Ball := Round (Egg);`

8. Is `Writeln` a reserved word? What would happen if you declared `Write` or `Read` as a variable indentifier? Is it an error to have a variable named `Sqrt` or `Round`?

9. Declare constants that could be used to convert measurements
   a. from feet to inches
   b. from inches to feet
   c. from miles to feet
   d. from kilometers to meters
   e. from miles per hour to kilometers per hour

10. Write a program that prints the first six factorials to the output file, one per line. (Remember that 1 factorial = 1! = 1, 2! = 2 × 1, 3! = 3 × 2 × 1 = 6, 4! = 4 × 3! = 24, etc.)

11. Write a program to produce a box of stars that consists of four stars by four stars. The output should look like this:

    ```
    ****
    ****
    ****
    ****
    ```

    Now change it to produce a 5 × 5 box of stars. How easy would it be to make a box that consists of 100 × 100 stars?

12. Write a program that will take as input the speed in miles per hour of a vehicle and will write exactly how many seconds it should take to travel one mile. An example of the type of output would be: 60 mph = 60 seconds/mile.

13. Write a program to calculate the perimeter and area of a triangle when given the lengths of its sides. The perimeter is the sum of the lengths. The area can be represented as:

    $$A = \sqrt{s(s-a)(s-b)(s-c)}$$

    where $s = 1/2$ of the perimeter and a, b, and c are the three lengths.

EXTENDING THE LANGUAGE: PROCEDURES

The Procedure Call

Pascal uses sequential statement execution. In a single program run, the first statement in the main program is executed, then the second, then the next, until the program control comes to the final END. Large tasks can be extremely tedious and complicated to complete unless the task is broken down into subtasks. Imagine reading a book without chapter or section breaks—it might be hard to follow the flow. Subtasks do for a programmer what chapters do for someone who is writing or reading a book; subtasks aid in the organization and flow of the material. This chapter will show how to arrange your program in convenient subtasks.

The following example shows another useful function of the subtask. How would you write a program, using only the statements we have already learned, to produce the following output?

```
***
***
***

***

***
***
***
```

The output suggests the use of the `Writeln` statement.

```
PROGRAM MakePattern (Output);
BEGIN
        Writeln (Output, '***');
        Writeln (Output, '***');
        Writeln (Output, '***');
        Writeln (Output);
        Writeln (Output, '***');
        Writeln (Output);
        Writeln (Output, '***');
        Writeln (Output, '***');
        Writeln (Output, '***');
END.
```

This solution is logical, but not very satisfying. It is too tedious. The first thing any computer programmer would notice is that there are repeated sequences of statements that could be combined into logical units. If we had a single statement in Pascal that would make a line or make a box of stars, then we could think about the problem in the following way:

```
PROGRAM MakePattern (Output);
BEGIN
        MakeBox;                (* Make a 3x3 box of stars *)
        Writeln (Output);       (* Make a blank line       *)
        MakeLine;               (* Make a line of stars    *)
        Writeln (Output);       (* Make a blank line       *)
        MakeBox;                (* Make a 3x3 box of stars *)
END.
```

Then the entire program could be written by executing these statements. As you would expect, Pascal doesn't have MakeBox and MakeLine as built-in statements, but you can define the terms in any way you want. A **procedure** consists of programming commands identified by a single name that work together to perform a specific subtask in the main program. Only the identifying name appears in the main program; the name cues the individual commands. In the example above, MakeBox and MakeLine represent procedures and show the proper way to call a procedure in a main program.

Procedure call: The statement that invokes a procedure or tells the computer to execute a procedure.

A procedure call directs the program control to execute a subtask stored in some other location in the program and return to the next line of the main program.

What is the second reason for declaring procedures? Once declared, procedures can be executed repeatedly simply by calling them.

The procedure is the first of a set of Pascal features called **control structures.**

> **Control structure:** A statement that alters in some way the normal sequence of executed statements in a Pascal program.

Control structures create the logic of the program, the statements that control what the program does and in what order. The sequence of executed statements is also called the **flow of control** of a program. (See Figure 4.1.)

> **Flow of control:** The order in which each line or part of a program is executed. Normally, flow of control is sequential.

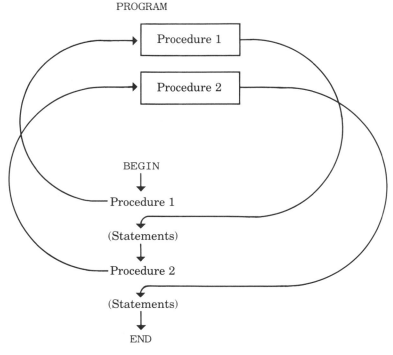

Figure 4.1: Flow of Control

SELF
TEST In terms of the flow of control of a program, what is the difference between a procedure call and an assignment statement?

The Procedure Declaration

The procedure call directs the program control to the location in the program where the procedure is defined. As in the case of variables, before procedures are used they must be declared. Procedure declarations are listed after the variable declaration part of the program, before the main program. For example, the previous problem might be solved using the following program:

```
PROGRAM MakePattern (Output);
     (* Makes 2 3x3 boxes separated by line of stars  *)
PROCEDURE MakeLine;    (* makes a 3-star line          *)
BEGIN
        Writeln (Output, '***');
END;    (* MakeLine *)

PROCEDURE MakeBox;     (* makes a 3x3 box of stars     *)
BEGIN
        Writeln (Output, '***');
        Writeln (Output, '***');
        Writeln (Output, '***');
END;    (* MakeBox *)

BEGIN   (* Main program *)
        MakeBox;
        Writeln (Output);
        MakeLine;
        Writeln (Output);
        MakeBox;
END.    (* Main program *)
```

The preceding program can be improved when we realize that procedures can call other procedures if they have been previously declared. We can use MakeLine in MakeBox, for example.

```
PROGRAM NewMakeBoxes (Output);
(***************************************************************
* This program makes a pattern of boxes and lines and         *
* prints them on the output file.                             *
***************************************************************)
PROCEDURE MakeLine; (* makes a 3-star line *)
BEGIN
        Writeln (Output, '***')
END;
```

```
PROCEDURE MakeBox;    (* makes a 3-line box *)
BEGIN
        MakeLine;
        MakeLine;
        MakeLine
END;

BEGIN    (* Main Program *)
        MakeBox;
        Writeln (Output);
        MakeBox;
        Writeln (Output);
        MakeBox
END.     (* Main Program *)
```

The syntax of a procedure declaration is much like a program declaration, as you can see in Figure 4.2.

As we have seen in examples above, procedures do not require other declarations. But you can declare constants, variables, and other procedures inside the procedure block, if necessary. The procedure block has the same structure as a program block and supports the same declarations. All the declarations inside a procedure must be complete before program execution. The following is a legal procedure declaration in Pascal:

```
PROCEDURE LargeE;
(* This procedure makes a large E composed of individual 'E's. *)
    CONST    Image  = 'E';
(*  VAR     would go here *)
    PROCEDURE MakeLineE; (* Makes a line of 5 Images *)
    BEGIN
            Writeln (Output, Image, Image, Image,
                                  Image, Image);
    END;
BEGIN
        MakeLineE;
        Writeln (Output, Image);
        MakeLineE;
        Writeln (Output, Image);
        MakeLineE;
END;
```

Figure 4.2: PROCEDURE Syntax

```
PROCEDURE <identifier>;
    <declaration part>;
    <compound statement>;    (* BEGIN -- END block *)
```

The procedure declaration is similar to a variable or a constant declaration; it assigns meaning to the identifier, or the procedure name. The procedure declaration must occur before the procedure call, because if the compiler comes across an identifier it doesn't recognize, it doesn't wait until the end of the compilation process to determine the meaning of the identifier. It complains immediately, and the user is made painfully aware of the problem. The procedure call can occur anywhere in the program, including in other procedures, as long as the procedure declaration comes first.

SELF TEST What is the difference between a procedure identifier and a variable identifier? What are the differences between the syntax of a procedure declaration and the syntax of a program?

Programming Example 4.1

Assignment: Write a program that tests the user's extrasensory perception (ESP). A common test for ESP asks one person to concentrate on an object, then asks a subject to tell what the object is by picking up mental signals from the first person.

Your program should be able to print out several different patterns: a star, a cross, a square, parallel lines, and a circle. It will print them in a fixed order that the subject will not know. Identify different patterns as individual procedures. You can easily specify a different order for further testing of advanced individuals.

Solution: Let's outline the main part of the program using pseudocode.

```
ESP Tester
     Introduction
     Give choices
     Cross
     Give choices
     Lines
     Give choices
     Square
     Give choices
     Circle
     Give choices
     Square
     ...
     Conclusion
```

This could go on as long as we would like. Now let's look at what might go in each procedure. The introduction and the procedure that gives the choices are fairly easy.

```
PROCEDURE Introduction;
(* This procedure introduces the user to the ESPTester.   *)
BEGIN
        Writeln (Output, 'Welcome to the ESPTester! This',
                 ' program tests your sixth sense.');
        Writeln (Output, 'I will concentrate on a design,',
                 ' and your job will be to try to');
        Writeln (Output, 'sense which design I am thinking',
                 ' about. You will type your guess');
        Writeln (Output, 'and then I will type the image.');
END;
```

```
PROCEDURE GiveChoices;
(* This procedure prints the image choices to the output. *)
BEGIN
        Writeln (Output, 'Concentrate! I am thinking about',
                         ' an object. Your choices are:');
        Writeln (Output, 'Star          Parallel Lines');
        Writeln (Output, 'Square        Circle');
        Writeln (Output, 'Cross');
END;
```

Each of the image procedures should give the user a chance to type a guess before the image is printed. The procedures would look like this:

```
PROCEDURE Cross;
(*  This procedure prints a Cross to the terminal *)
BEGIN
        Writeln (Output, 'What is your guess?');
        Readln (Input);   (* wait until user answers *)
        Writeln (Output, '   ***   ');
        Writeln (Output, '   ***   ');
        Writeln (Output, '*********');
        Writeln (Output, '*********');
        Writeln (Output, '   ***   ');
        Writeln (Output, '   ***   ');
END;
```

```
PROCEDURE Square;
(* This procedure prints a Square to the terminal *)
BEGIN
        Writeln (Output, 'What is your guess?');
        Readln (Input);  (* wait until user answers *)
        Writeln (Output, '********');
        Writeln (Output, '********');
        Writeln (Output, '********');
        Writeln (Output, '********');
        Writeln (Output, '********');
        Writeln (Output, '********');
END;
```

A better way to organize the material in these procedures would be to put all the preliminary messages, including the prompt for a guess and the Readln statement, into the GiveChoices procedure, and to call that procedure inside each image procedure.

```
PROCEDURE GiveChoices;
(* This procedure prints the image choices to the output. *)
BEGIN
        Writeln (Output, 'Concentrate! I am thinking about',
                         ' an object. Your choices are:');
        Writeln (Output, 'Star          Parallel Lines');
        Writeln (Output, 'Square        Circle');
        Writeln (Output, 'Cross');
        Writeln (Output, 'What is your guess?');
        Readln (Input);  (* wait until user answers *)
END;
```

```
PROCEDURE Cross;
(*  This procedure prints a Cross to the terminal *)
BEGIN
        GiveChoices;
        Writeln (Output, '   ***   ');
        Writeln (Output, '   ***   ');
        Writeln (Output, '*********');
        Writeln (Output, '*********');
        Writeln (Output, '   ***   ');
        Writeln (Output, '   ***   ');
END;
```

```
PROCEDURE Square;
(* This procedure prints a Square to the terminal *)
BEGIN
        GiveChoices;
        Writeln (Output, '********');
        Writeln (Output, '********');
        Writeln (Output, '********');
        Writeln (Output, '********');
        Writeln (Output, '********');
        Writeln (Output, '********');
END;
```

In this way, then, the main block part of the program can be short and simple.

```
BEGIN
        Introduction;
        Cross;
        Lines;
        Star;
        Lines;
        Square;
        Cross;
        Circle;
        Circle;
        Square;
        Lines;
        Conclusion;
END.
```

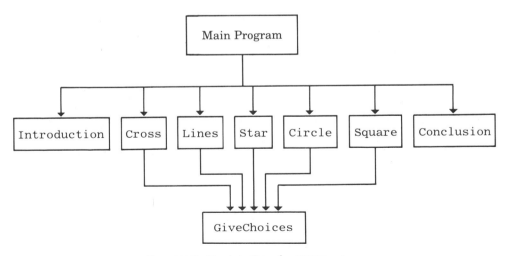

Figure 4.3: Module Tree for ESPTester

To illustrate how the different procedures fit together to solve the problem, examine Figure 4.3, which shows the module tree for this program. A **module tree** demonstrates graphically how the procedures and the main program are related and how some procedures are dependent on other procedures. Procedure GiveChoices, for example, is used in each of the procedures that draws a shape.

To complete the program, let's write procedure Conclusion.

```
PROCEDURE Conclusion;
(* This procedure tells the user his percentage correct.  *)
CONST   NumImages = 10;        (* images the user saw      *)
VAR     NumCorrect : Integer; (* of user's answers        *)
BEGIN
        Writeln (Output, 'I forgot to count, but I hope');
                 ' you remembered. How many did');
        Writeln (Output, 'you answer correctly?');
        Readln (Input, NumCorrect);
        Writeln (Output, 'You answered correctly ',
                NumCorrect * 100 DIV NumImages, '%.');
        Writeln (Output, 'Come back again for further');
                 ' ESP testing, or bring a friend.');
END;
```

The following is a sample execution of the ESPTester program, illustrating all its features.

INTERACTIVE SESSION

```
Welcome to the ESPTester! This program tests your sixth sense.
I will concentrate on a design, and your job will be to try to
sense which design I am thinking about. You will type your guess
and then I will type the image.
Concentrate! I am thinking about an object. Your choices are:
Star            Parallel Lines
Square          Circle
Cross
What is your guess?
Star
    ***
    ***
********
********
    ***
    ***
```

```
Concentrate! I am thinking about an object. Your choices are:
Star          Parallel Lines
Square        Circle
Cross
What is your guess?
```
Square
```
**********

**********

**********
Concentrate! I am thinking about an object. Your choices are:
Star          Parallel Lines
Square        Circle
Cross
What is your guess?
```
Square
```
      *
    ***
***********
   *******
  *********
**       **
Concentrate! I am thinking about an object. Your choices are:
Star          Parallel Lines
Square        Circle
Cross
What is your guess?
```
Star
```
**********

**********

**********
Concentrate! I am thinking about an object. Your choices are:
Star          Parallel Lines
Square        Circle
Cross
What is your guess?
```
Circle
```
********
********
********
********
********
********
Concentrate! I am thinking about an object. Your choices are:
Star          Parallel Lines
Square        Circle
Cross
```

What is your guess?
Parallel Lines
```
   ***
   ***
********
********
   ***
   ***
```
Concentrate! I am thinking about an object. Your choices are:
```
Star          Parallel Lines
Square        Circle
Cross
```
What is your guess?
Star
```
       **
    ********
  ************
 ***(Circle)***
  ************
    ********
       **
```
Concentrate! I am thinking about an object. Your choices are:
```
Star          Parallel Lines
Square        Circle
Cross
```
What is your guess?
Square
```
       **
    ********
  ************
 ***(Circle)***
  ************
    ********
       **
```
Concentrate! I am thinking about an object. Your choices are:
```
Star          Parallel Lines
Square        Circle
Cross
```
What is your guess?
Parallel Lines
```
*********

*********

*********
```
Concentrate! I am thinking about an object. Your choices are:
```
Star          Parallel Lines
Square        Circle
Cross
```

```
What is your guess?
Square
********
********
********
********
********
********
I forgot to count, but I hope you remembered. How many did
you answer correctly?
2
You answered correctly          20%.
Come back again for further ESP testing, or bring a friend.
```

SELF
TEST

How many times is each of the following procedures executed in a single run of ESPTester?

1. `Introduction`
2. `Square`
3. `Lines`
4. `GiveChoices`
5. `Conclusion`

Programming Example 4.2

Assignment: Write a program that produces a "personalized" letter for three people. The letters should have a personalized first line and closing and should be made up of paragraphs which are repeated in each letter. Use procedures to produce at least five different paragraphs as well as the three letters.

Solution: Let's look at the problem and break it down into parts. Suppose, for example, you plan to write letters to Mom, John (your best friend at home), and Natalie (your girl friend at home). This is just an example, so please don't regard this as a generalization about the gender or preference of the readership. It certainly wouldn't be appropriate to send the same letter to all three individuals, yet certain things could be said to any of them. Think how tedious it would be to type large portions of the letter three times, and using a photocopier is too gauche. With the computer we can save time, yet simulate personal letters.

Let's consider what you might have to say and to whom you might say it.

Mom's letter: Classes
Friends
Send money

John's letter:	Friends
	Parties and dating
	Classes
Natalie's letter:	Friends
	Classes
	Pledge of undying love

Now we begin to see our program shaping up. Or maybe you can't see it yet. We've written no Pascal code, but we have accomplished the program breakdown. We have established the subjects for our five paragraph procedures as well as a basic outline of our three letter procedures.

The next task is to name our biggest procedures and to write the main program. Remembering that we can't have spaces or apostrophes in identifier names, we squash the names from our outline to name our three procedures and add a comment for each that describes the purpose of the procedure.

```
PROCEDURE MomsLetter;
  (* Writes a letter to my mother on the output file *)

PROCEDURE JohnsLetter;
  (* Writes a letter to my good
    friend John on the output file *)

PROCEDURE NataliesLetter;
  (* Writes a letter to my hometown
    girl friend on the output file *)
```

The main program will then simply call each of these three procedures.

```
BEGIN (* Main Program *)
      MomsLetter;
      JohnsLetter;
      NataliesLetter
END.  (* Main Program *)
```

"Wait a minute!" you are saying to yourself, "We haven't even written these procedures, let alone the rest of the program. How can we write the main program now?" Good question. Actually, the sequence we have followed is common and extremely useful in programming. We are seeing another example of stepwise refinement or top-down programming. The top of the program is the main program (which, ironically enough, is at the bottom of the program in Pascal). The main program calls the big procedures, such as MomsLetter, which in turn call smaller, more detailed procedures, such as the one we will write to tell about classes. Trust me, we *will* end up with a finished and working program.

Let's tackle one of the letter procedures first. If we take the topics for paragraphs to be included in Mom's letter and make them procedure identifiers, we have essentially written our letter to Mom. All that is left is to write an opening and closing line.

```
PROCEDURE MomsLetter;
   (* Writes a letter to my mother on the output file *)
BEGIN
        Writeln (Output, 'Dear Mom,');
                                        (* gripping opening line *)
        Classes;
        Friends;
        SendMoney;
        Writeln (Output, '                        Love,');
        Writeln (Output);
        Writeln (Output, '                        Your son.')
END;                                (* nice personal touch *)
```

Now that wasn't very difficult. Of course, sooner or later we're going to have to actually write those paragraphs that make up the body of each of these letters. But all that takes is a little creative energy. The other two letter procedures are now easy to write as well.

```
PROCEDURE JohnsLetter;
   (* Writes a letter to my good
      friend John on the output file *)
BEGIN
        Writeln (Output, 'Hey John,');
        PartiesNDating;
        Friends;
        Classes;
        Writeln (Output, 'Gotta hit the sack ...');
                              (* the only way to end a letter *)
        Writeln (Output);     (* to an old HS friend *)
        Writeln (Output, '              Your bud')
END;

PROCEDURE NataliesLetter;
   (* Writes a letter to my hometown
      girl friend on the output file *)
BEGIN
        Writeln (Output, 'Dearest Natalie,');
        Friends;
        Classes;
        UndyingLove;
        Writeln (Output, '                    Love Always,');
        Writeln (Output);
        Writeln (Output)       (* don't end it-- leave space
                                  for a personal signature *)
END;
```

At this point, all that remains is to write the five procedures that contain the text of the paragraphs. It is easy to write the Pascal for these procedures, for they are merely a series of `Writeln` statements. The important thing to learn from this example is the sequence of steps leading to the solution. The correct sequence was not to begin with `Writeln` statements. The solution was found by breaking the problem down into successively smaller chunks until we were left with procedures that were easy to write. *In general, the more time you spend thinking about a problem before writing any Pascal code, the better the solution will be.*

I'll let you finish `MakeThreeLetters` from here, after I give a sample procedure.

```
PROGRAM MakeThreeLetters (Output);
(*************************************************************
* This program uses procedures and Writeln statements to    *
* produce three different letters. Each letter body is      *
* composed of three procedure calls from 5 different        *
* paragraph procedures.                                     *
*************************************************************)
PROCEDURE Classes;
(* Describes how well classes are going, and how much I love
   my computer science class.                              *)
BEGIN
    Write (Output, '    Classes are going well-- better');
    Writeln (Output, ' than I had hoped. I am really');
    Write (Output, 'enjoying my computer programming');
    Writeln (Output, ' class-- the instructor is very');
    Write (Output, 'interesting and the assignments are');
    Writeln (Output, ' fun and challenging. I''m also');
    Write (Output, 'getting plenty of typing practice');
    Writeln (Output, ' (as you can see). Of course, ');
    Write (Output, 'studying all the time');
    Writeln (Output, ' takes its toll elsewhere, but as');
    Write (Output, 'the motto goes around here, ');
    Writeln (Output, ' ''Work, Study, Get Rich''.')
END;

PROCEDURE Friends;
(* Describes life in the dorm, my roommate, etc. *)
BEGIN
        . . .
END;

PROCEDURE SendMoney;
(* Asks Mom for money and explains why, after only two weeks
   of the quarter, I already need more money to survive. *)
BEGIN
        . . .
END;
```

```
PROCEDURE PartyNDating;
(* Tells John how I really do more than just study, and how
   the dating scene is so depressing.                        *)
BEGIN
        . . .
END;

PROCEDURE UndyingLove;
(* Tells the girl of my dreams how she is the only one
   for me                                                     *)
BEGIN
        . . .
END;

PROCEDURE MomsLetter;
   (* Writes a letter to my mother on the output file *)
BEGIN
        Writeln (Output, 'Dear Mom,');
        Classes;
        Friends;
        SendMoney;
        Writeln (Output, '                         Love,');
        Writeln (Output);
        Writeln (Output, '                         Your son.')
END;

PROCEDURE JohnsLetter;
   (* Writes a letter to my good
      friend John on the output file *)
BEGIN
        Writeln (Output, 'Hey John,');
        PartiesNDating;
        Friends;
        Classes;
        Writeln (Output, 'Gotta hit the sack ...');
        Writeln (Output);
        Writeln (Output, '                    Your bud')
END;

PROCEDURE NataliesLetter;
   (* Writes a letter to my hometown
      girl friend on the output file *)
BEGIN
        Writeln (Output, 'Dearest Natalie,');
        Friends;
        Classes;
        UndyingLove;
        Writeln (Output, '                    Love Always,');
        Writeln (Output);
        Writeln (Output)
END;
```

```
BEGIN  (* Main Program *)
       MomsLetter;
       JohnsLetter;
       NataliesLetter
END.   (* Main Program *)
```

Figure 4.4 shows the module tree for this program.

Global and Local Variables

A Pascal procedure has a structure similar to that of a Pascal program, as we mentioned in the last section. Each has a declaration part followed by a statement part.

```
PROGRAM Example                      PROCEDURE Example;
        (Input, Output);  (* This procedure shows     *)
(* This program shows      *)  (* the similarity between   *)
(* the similarity between  *)  (* programs and procedures. *)
(* programs and procedures.*)
CONST   Min = 0;                     CONST    Max = 100.0;
VAR     X, Y, Z : Integer;           VAR      A, B, C : Real;
PROCEDURE Number1;                   PROCEDURE Num1;
. . .                                . . .

BEGIN     (* Main Program *)   BEGIN     (* Example *)
. . .                          . . .
END.      (* Main Program *)   END;      (* Example *)
```

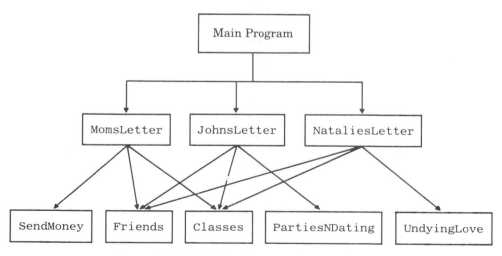

Figure 4.4: Module Tree for MakeThreeLetters

As a matter of fact, everything that can be declared in a program can be declared in a procedure. The element that differentiates a program declaration from a procedure declaration is the reserved word before the identifier. The part they have in common is called a block.

Block: A unit of Pascal code consisting of a declaration part (which may be empty) followed by the executable statements surrounded by a BEGIN-END pair.

A **block** consists of the declaration part followed by the statement part of the declaration. (See Figure 4.5.)

Figure 4.5: Block Syntax

```
<declaration part>;
<BEGIN-END  pair>
```

The block of the PROGRAM declaration consists of all of the constant, variable, and procedure identifiers declared in the main program, plus the executable statements of the main program. When an identifier is declared in the main program block, it is said to be a **global identifier.** A global identifier can be a variable, a constant, or a procedure. But when a variable is declared inside a procedure, it is called a **local variable.** Global identifiers can be used throughout the program, both in the main program statements as well as in each procedure. A local identifier, on the other hand, can only be used in the procedure in which it is defined. A local identifier is part of the procedure's local **environment,** which includes all local constant, variable, and procedure declarations. When a procedure finishes executing, its environment (all local variables) disappears from memory.

If you declare a global variable that will also be used inside a single procedure, include a comment about the meaning and usage of the global variable. This is especially important if the value of the global variable changes inside a procedure. In the next section we will see why changing the value of a global variable inside a procedure is not a good idea.

The program ESPTester used local declarations in Conclusion.

```
PROCEDURE Conclusion;
(* This procedure tells the user the percentage correct.   *)
CONST    NumImages = 10;        (* images the user saw      *)
VAR      NumCorrect : Integer;  (* of user's answers        *)
BEGIN
         Writeln (Output, 'I forgot to count, but I hope',
                  ' you remembered. How many did');
         Writeln (Output, 'you answer correctly?');
         Readln (Input, NumCorrect);
         Writeln (Output, 'You answered correctly ',
                  NumCorrect * 100 DIV NumImages, '%. ');
         Writeln (Output, 'Come back again for further',
                  ' ESP testing, or bring a friend. ');
END;
```

There are two local identifier declarations in this procedure, the constant NumImages and the integer variable NumCorrect. These were declared locally because they are used only in this procedure and nowhere else in the program. However, they could have been declared globally, at the top of the program, and the program would have executed anyway. In Chapter 6, the difference between local and global variables will be discussed more fully. For now, it is enough to remember that it is better to declare identifiers, especially variables, locally whenever possible.

SELF
TEST

1. What is the difference between a procedure call and a procedure declaration? Which cannot occur in the executable statements part of a program? Which can occur inside another procedure?
2. What is the difference between a local and a global variable? How can you distinguish between them in a program?

Common Errors and Debugging

1. **Calling a procedure before it has been defined.** Because we use the top-down approach of algorithmic refinement, it is tempting to declare the larger procedures first. The Pascal compiler, on the other hand, must see a procedure declaration before that identifier can be used in a procedure call. This is in contrast to BASIC, which allows or requires subroutines to be declared at the end of the main program and in any order. A Pascal program will look upside down to someone who is familiar with BASIC.

2. **Attempting to use a local variable outside the procedure in which it is defined.** This will result in the error statement, "identifier not declared." If the

same variable is needed in other procedures or in the main program, declare it globally.

3. **Writing code before you have written the algorithm.** This is a temptation for everyone, but it doesn't pay off. *In general, the more time you spend thinking about a problem before writing any Pascal code, the better the solution will be.* It is easy to revise an algorithm; it is much more difficult to debug malformed code.

Hints for BASIC Programmers

As we introduced the concept of a control structure in this chapter, you probably made the connection to BASIC control structures, most notably FOR-NEXT and GO TO. In both languages, a control structure alters the normal sequence of statement execution.

In Chapter 2, we learned that different sections of a Pascal program are referenced by name, not by line number. By now you should be able to see the implications. Each block of code in a Pascal program is grouped logically and bundled under one procedure name. Instead of transferring program control through extensive usage of GO TO or GOSUB statements, Pascal transfers program control with procedure calls.

A subroutine is the closest BASIC equivalent of a Pascal procedure. However, even if you have some background in BASIC, you may never have seen subroutines before. That is not unusual because subroutines are usually taught as an advanced control structure. If you have never seen a subroutine before, don't panic. You may, however, want to skip the remainder of this section.

One confusing feature of BASIC is that you can use any block of code, in any context, as a subroutine simply by placing a RETURN at the end of it. For example, suppose you want to call a subroutine from within another subroutine. Here is an entirely valid possibility:

```
190 LET I = 0
200 GOSUB 210
210 GOSUB 220
220 GOSUB 230
230 GOSUB 240
240 LET I = I + 1
250 RETURN
```

It is almost impossible to simulate this section of BASIC code correctly to determine the value of I after the execution of this fragment. (The final value of I is 16.)

Examine the flow of control in this segment:

```
200 GOSUB 400
210 (next statements) ...
400 REM BEGIN FIRST SUBROUTINE
    . . .
450 GOSUB 480
460 (next statements) ...
480 REM BEGIN SECOND SUBROUTINE
    . . .
498 RETURN
499 REM ENDS BOTH SUBROUTINES
```

The flow of control might still be a little difficult to follow. On the other hand, procedures in Pascal must be declared before they are used, and their definitions are separate from the context in which they are used. The logic is more apparent from the program design.

```
PROCEDURE Second;
BEGIN
        . . .
END;

PROCEDURE First;
BEGIN
        . . .
        Second;
        . . .
END;

BEGIN     (* Main Program *)
        . . .
        First;
        . . .
END.      (* Main Program *)
```

One final reminder for BASIC programmers: Pascal programs declare procedures at the top—not the bottom—in reverse of the order of the typical BASIC program. Don't let the fact that Pascal reads small procedure declarations first make you write the procedures in that order, however. The top-down method of design requires that you write your Pascal programs from the bottom up in terms of the final appearance of the page. You will begin with the main program and end with the little procedures that handle one small task. (See Figure 4.6.)

Algorithm   Pascal Program

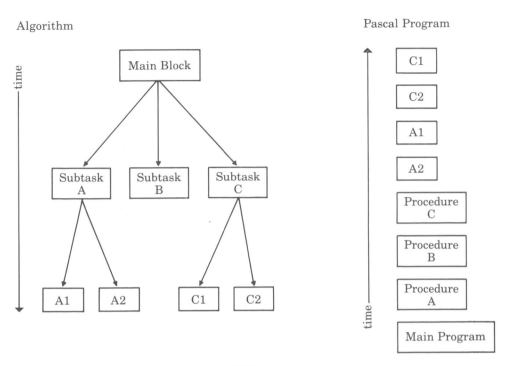

Figure 4.6: Top-Down Design: Writing Programs From the Bottom Up

SUMMARY

The Pascal **procedure** is one of the most fundamental **control structures** and is the building block of any long program. The procedure declaration is structured as a program is structured, with declarations preceding the BEGIN-END block. A procedure is invoked by the **procedure call,** which directs the program control to the first statement of the procedure. After a procedure is executed, the **flow of control** returns to the line following the call.

Variables that are declared in the the main program **block** are called **global** variables, while variables that are declared in a procedure are called **local** variables. Local variables can only be used in the block in which they are defined. If a variable is declared only in a procedure, then an attempt to access the value of that variable in the main program or anywhere outside its own procedure will cause an error. In this case, a global variable would be necessary. It is best to declare global variables only when local variables will not handle the problem.

New Terms

procedure	module tree	environment
procedure call	block	PROCEDURE
control structure	global identifier	
flow of control	local variable	

EXERCISES

1. What are two reasons for writing procedures?

2. The syntax of the following procedure is correct. What *is* wrong with it?

```
PROCEDURE WriteSqrt;
VAR     Num : Real;
BEGIN
        Write (Output, 'Type in a real number.');
        Readln (Input, Num);
        Writeln (Output, 'The square of ',
                    'your number is', Sqr (Num));
END;
```

3. What would this program print?

```
PROGRAM Test (Input, Output);
VAR     Greg, Bill, Buck : Integer;
PROCEDURE GetValues;
BEGIN
        Read (Input, Greg);
        Readln (Input, Bill, Buck);
END;
PROCEDURE CalcNPrintBill;
VAR     MK : Integer;
BEGIN
        MK := Bill * Buck;
        Read (Input, Greg);
        Writeln (Output, Greg, Bill, Buck, MK);
        Writeln (Output,  'Greg''s bill was for ',  Bill,
                        'nights at the Seattle Hilton, ');
        Writeln (Output,  'at $', Buck, ' per night, or ',
                        'a total of $', MK, '.');
END;
```

```
BEGIN
        GetValues;
        CalcNPrintBill;
        GetValues;
        CalcNPrintBill;
END.
```

Use the following input file.

INPUT
```
       195 3
   38    72
197    72 5
   41.50      17
33     51.2
```

4. Examine the following program. Where should the variables be declared? Of course, they
    could all be declared globally. Can any be declared locally? Which? Rewrite the program,
    adding comments as well as variable declarations.

```
PROGRAM Conversions (Input, Output);
CONST    InchesPerFoot = 12;
         FeetPerYard = 3;
         FeetPerMile = 5280;
PROCEDURE FeetToInches;
BEGIN
        Inches := Feet * InchesPerFoot;
        Writeln (Output, Feet, ' feet is',
                        Inches, ' inches.');
END;
PROCEDURE MilesToYards;
BEGIN
        Yards := Miles * FeetPerMile / FeetPerYard;
        Writeln (Output, Miles, ' miles is',
                        Yards, ' yards.');
END;
PROCEDURE FeetToMiles;
BEGIN
        Miles := Feet / FeetPerMile;
        Writeln (Output, Feet, ' feet is',
                        Miles, ' miles.');
END;
BEGIN
        Readln (Input, Feet);
        FeetToInches;
        FeetToMiles;
        MilesToYards;
END.
```

5. Write procedures to print your name in vertical block letters. Write one procedure for each letter, plus a procedure to space between words. For example, my program might produce the following output:

OUTPUT
```
RRRR
R   R
R   R
RRR
R   R
R   R

IIIII
  I
  I
  I
  I
IIIII

  CCC
C     C
C
C
C     C
  CCC

H     H
H     H
HHHHH
HHHHH
H     H
H     H
```

Why is it easier to produce vertical lettering than horizontal lettering?

6. Write a program like ESPTester that checks the user's ESP. Instead of printing clumsy shapes, print block digits 0 through 9 in an order determined by you, the programmer. The encouragement given to the subject is an important element in this kind of test. Make sure your program is very friendly and warm. Have the user report the score, then calculate the percentage of correct answers.

7. Write your own version of MakeThreeLetters to three people you really know, telling them, among other things, about your recent study of the art and science of computer programming.

8. Write a program to print all twelve verses of "The Twelve Days of Christmas." Your program can be a very long program, with 90 Writeln statements, or much shorter, with 12 procedures and only 24 Writeln statements.

9. Write a program that calculates a baseball player's slugging average. You will need to read from an input file or from the terminal the player's at bats (AB) and the number of singles (S), doubles (D), triples (T), and home runs (HR). His slugging average (AV) is:

$$AV = \frac{(S + 2D + 3T + 4HR)}{AB}$$

PROGRAMMING WITH STYLE

When we think of a computer language, we think of the need to communicate with a computer. However, computer programs are also meant to be read by human beings. Coworkers, spouses, and instructors will, at times, want to look at the programs we have written in order to understand, modify, evaluate, or simply use them. Features of a program that make it more readable are lumped together under a broad heading called **style**. In programming, there are two basic categories of style: format and documentation.

In general, format deals with how the program looks on a page.

> **Format:** The visual cues a program gives to the reader about its structure and logic.

Is the program easy to read? Are the different parts of the program distinguishable from one another? Documentation gives a reader clues as to the purpose and effect of the code and how it fits into the program as a whole.

> **Documentation:** Any part of the program code that improves the readability, modifiability, or usefulness of a program, including comments and well-chosen identifier names as well as specifications and descriptions of the algorithm external to the program.

Chapter 1 said that writing a computer program is like writing an essay. Essays and computer programs are not like physics problems, with the answers being either right or wrong. Programs are evaluated for style as well as correctness. Since others will be using or evaluating your programs after you finish with them (especially if they are grading them), you have a pragmatic reason for creating comprehensible formats and thorough documentation.

The second pragmatic reason, and a more important one, is that you will need to be able to read and understand your programs after you write them, assuming that you aren't simply writing them for the sheer joy of it. (Although that is certainly part of it, I'm sure.) Good programming style makes programs easier to debug, easier to read, and easier to modify. It is amazing how quickly you can forget why you did what you did, or what a certain part of your program was supposed to do. Documenting your program as you write it will safeguard against "antique" code that cannot be modified because it is impossible to understand. This future-oriented approach to programming doesn't always seem expedient, but it pays off in the long run.

Aesthetics constitutes the third reason to program with style. You want to have not only a working program but an elegant one—simple, efficient, yet beautiful. An efficient program that produces excellent results but is difficult to read is like eating a fancy French meal at a fast food restaurant—it's not quite as satisfying without the proper environment.

Program Style

The following program is legal and executable in Pascal:

```
program thisisugly (output); var
Why, who, where, when, what, how : integer;begin readln (
Who, what, when, where); readln (when, why,
how); writeln (Who+what+
Where, How+when+why)



                            end.
```

This is legal because, as you should remember, carriage returns and tabs are equivalent to spaces for the Pascal compiler. The computer can read this as easily as it can read a more conventionally formatted program. If programs were read only by computers, this coding would be fine. However, people also need to read your program. Several stylistic techniques should be employed in your programming in order to facilitate reading, understanding, debugging, and modifying your program by others.

Indentation and Blank Lines

The most basic of formatting tools—carriage returns, blank lines, and tabs— are missing from the previous example. White space isn't necessary, but it helps the reader make quick inferences about the structure of the program. As we write more sophisticated programs, visual cues about program structure and organization will become extremely important. The amount of space used to indent is an aesthetic design decision, but allow enough space so that the nesting and different program levels are readily apparent. Tabs of only one or two spaces aren't big enough. The examples in this book consistently use tabs of eight spaces unless the level of nesting renders that amount of space too large. Using an eight-space indentation makes the blocks in a program really stand out and greatly increases readability. Blank lines between procedures and loops distinguish logical program chunks. Review the previous program, then check the modified version that follows. What an improvement with less than a minute of editing!

```
program thisisugly (output);
var     Why,  who,where,when,what,how :  integer;
begin
        readln (Who,what,when,where);
        readln (when,why,  how);
        writeln (Who+what+Where,  How+when+why)
end.
```

You may develop your own style for indentation and the use of blank lines, but here are some guidelines.

Indentation Guidelines
1. Include a blank line between procedures and between the last procedure and the main block.
2. Indent all statements between any BEGIN and its corresponding END at least four spaces.
3. Indent the identifiers in VAR and CONST declarations.

Capitalization

You may have already noticed that, with the exception of the previous example, I consistently capitalize all the letters in reserved words and the first letter of distinct words within identifiers. I do this to differentiate between reserved words and identifiers in the program. Other books use boldface for reserved words and italics for identifiers, or some other scheme. In general, however, most students don't have the option of using italics and boldface. Hence, capitalization is one useful way to differentiate types of building blocks in a Pascal program. Any consistent scheme of capitalization is acceptable, except consistently capitalizing everything (unless you use a terminal that doesn't have lowercase letters) or consistently not using capital letters at all; these schemes fail to take advantage of having the use of both. Some Pascal dialects, especially those available for smaller machines, do not allow lowercase letters or will differentiate between lowercase and capital letters. In these cases, find another means of distinguishing words. Once we add capitalization to the style of the example, it begins to look pretty good.

```
PROGRAM ThisIsUgly (Output);
VAR     Why,  Who,Where,When,What,How :  Integer;
BEGIN

        Readln (Who,What,When,Where);
        Readln (When,Why, How);
        Writeln (Who+What+Where, How+When+Why)
END.
```

Identifiers

If you have programmed in BASIC, you probably have come to rely on a lot of variable names like X, Y, Z, I, J, and K. (Some extended versions of BASIC allow the use of more than one character or one letter and one digit.) In Pascal, identifiers can be as long as you wish. Therefore, identifier names should convey some meaning.

Hard-and-Fast Rule #1
Always use meaningful (mnemonic) identifier names.

The ability to use mnemonic identifiers is a self-documenting feature of Pascal. Mnemonic identifiers allow the code to be more transparent (understandable) to the reader of the program and help reduce the number of comments that are necessary. Although it takes more time to type longer variable names, variables like Row and Col are better than i and j because they convey meaning. Of course, the same rule applies to constant and procedure identifiers as well. A procedure named X needs a long comment to explain what it does and a reminder comment every time it is called.

As you begin to think about the advantages of longer variable names, you needn't go overboard. Pascal only differentiates a certain number of letters in identifier names, and that number is implementation dependent. Remember that most compilers will distinguish only eight or ten letters. Make sure the distinguishing part of a long name appears near the beginning of the identifier.

Constants

Constant declarations are not a necessary feature of Pascal. Why not just use the values in the text instead of declaring a constant? Well, as Chapter 3 showed, constants sometimes make a program much easier to read. Their presence in a Pascal program, like the presence of other elements discussed in this chapter, is not an issue of correctness but a matter of style. For example, suppose that a financial analysis program performs many complex calculations based on the current value of the prime interest rate. When the prime rate changes, say from 10.5 percent to 11.0 percent, the program needs to be updated. If the programmer must search through the entire program for 10.5 or 0.105 in order to replace it with 11.0 or 0.11, mistakes could easily be made that might cost the financial institution lots of money. However, if a single constant were declared, in this case PrimeRate = 10.5, a single change in the constant declaration would change the value everywhere the constant was used.

Perhaps one rule to follow would be that every number occurring in the text of the code other than -1, 0, 1, or 2 should be declared as a constant.

Hard-and-Fast Rule #2
Almost every number occurring in the text of the code
other than -1, 0, 1, or 2 should be declared as a constant.

This makes sense when you realize that values other than the cited numbers are usually arbitrary limitations, constraints, or target values that could change. Also, if you get in the habit of declaring constants, you will soon learn when this rule doesn't need to be followed.

One reason we are so diligent about declaring constants is illustrated above; we can affect the value of a constant in the definition rather than having to find every occurrence of the value in the program. A second reason to declare constants is that a single value, in the middle of an expression or other part of the code, might not convey obvious significance. The number 11.0 might not be significant to the reader of the program, but the identifier PrimeRate has meaning.

Comments

The comment is definitely the most important documentation feature of Pascal. It serves a much more vital role in the writing and debugging of a program than it receives credit for. The comment, because it can go anywhere in your Pascal program, is versatile and can appear beside tricky code as well as before or after it. Your tendency, as a new Pascal programmer enchanted with all the amazing features of the language, will probably be to spend all of your time writing the code, and neglect comments until the program works perfectly. At that time you will probably intersperse cursory comments throughout the text. That habit would probably last as long as you were writing programs for a grade, after which time you would probably stop writing comments entirely. This methodology does not take full advantage of comments. Let me say that more strongly in a positive statement: *Write comments before and during the writing of the program.*

It is in this way that comments can be a programming tool. If a procedure or program needs to be written, the comment can help you clarify exactly what you want it to do. If you cannot write the procedure or program comment, chances are that the program code will be difficult to write as well. It is amazing that people actually try to write a procedure before they know what it is supposed to do. Having to express that purpose in a comment helps you to gain an understanding of the task and the way you intend to go about it.

Therefore, consistent and clear commenting can be useful to you in writing a program and in debugging it. It can also make the code more readable, as do all the stylistic considerations. Consistent commenting does not mean commenting every line of code, but if you decide to comment every declaration in the program you will be a long way towards the goal.

Hard-and-Fast Rule #3
Comment almost every declaration.

Commenting every declaration means:

1. Including a comment about the program. Include the name of the author of the program, the program's use, any input files that are needed, the type of output produced, and a brief summary of the algorithm.
2. Describing the use of constants and variables. This description could simply be an elaboration on the identifier name. Some local variables, whose usages are obvious, may not need a comment. However, all global variables in the program should be commented.
3. Including comments that explain global variables used inside a procedure. This is very important because it can be difficult to read a procedure that uses global variables, even if they are commented consistently.
4. Explaining the purpose of each procedure and describing inputs, outputs, the algorithm, and the procedures it calls and those that call it.

Comments don't have to be long to be helpful, but if they are too short they are almost useless. They should be written in English and not as abbreviations. Nor should comments mimic the Pascal.

```
PROCEDURE Ridiculous;
(* declare a procedure called Ridiculous *)
VAR I, J, K : Integer; (* I, J, K are integer variables *)
BEGIN
        Readln (Input, I,J,K) (* get the values of I, J, K
                                    from the input file *)
        Writeln (Output, I+J+K); (* write the sum of I, J,
                                    and K to the output file *)
END;    (* Ridiculous *)
```

These comments are useless; anyone who knows Pascal learns nothing new. Comments should summarize broader algorithms and answer the questions "How?" and "Why?"

Procedures

The bulk of the work of Pascal programs is done in procedures, not in the main program. Ideally, the main program will be an easily readable list of procedure calls, which will invoke the procedures. The following is the main block of a program. Notice how easy to read it is. Without any other documentation or introduction and without seeing the bodies of the procedures called, it is readily apparent what the program is supposed to do and how the different parts of the program fit together to complete the task.

```
BEGIN   (************ Main Program ************)
        Readln (Input, NumStudents);
        ClassTot := 0;
        FOR EachStudent := 1 TO NumStudents DO BEGIN
                ReadNWriteNum;
                ReadNSumScores;
                CalcNPrintAve;
        END;
        PrintClassAve;
END.    (************ Main Program ************)
```

There are seven distinct statements in this main program. There are also seven numbers in a phone number. Contrary to what you may now be thinking, the preceding facts are not entirely unrelated. It has been said that 7 ± 2 numbers or items is all that a normal brain can remember in short-term memory. Once, at a conference of computer scientists, the participants were asked to estimate how many lines of code they could write and still guarantee that they had not made any mistakes. The average turned out to be seven. As experienced programmers, they knew how unpredictable errors can appear in fragments of code that are longer than just a few lines.

In general, it is easier to debug and to understand programs when they are broken down into short procedures. Obviously, *short* is subjective, but I usually understand *short* to mean fewer than 15 lines.

> **Short procedures:** Procedures with fewer than 15 lines. Short procedures tend to be easier to understand and debug than long procedures.

Make sure that all of your procedures and main programs have fewer than 15 lines, or fall into only two or three groups of code that are each 7 ± 2 lines long. My own preference is to write procedures of 7 ± 2 lines.

> **Hard-and-Fast Rule #4**
> Make sure that all of your procedures and main programs have fewer than 15 lines.

As we progress and learn more complicated control structures in Pascal, the value of short procedures will become more evident.

When writing a procedure on paper, get in the habit of writing the first line, then the comment. After you know you can write the comment, declare any local variables and leave at least two lines of space for unforeseen variables. At this point, add the BEGIN and the body of the procedure. As you need other variables in the procedure body, decide whether they can be declared as local variables or if they need to be declared globally. When you use a variable for the first time, go back and make sure you have declared and commented it. If you continue in this way, your program will be properly commented at each stage. This will make it easier for you to figure out what is wrong when it doesn't work, and it will certainly be easier for someone else to help you—your comments may highlight the difference between what you intend to do with a block of code and what is actually being done.

Semicolons Before ENDs

We learned earlier that semicolons before ENDs are unnecessary. However, as you have been programming, you will have no doubt come across the error of forgetting to put a semicolon at the end of a statement that needs one. If you think about whether or not the syntax of Pascal requires a semicolon, you should realize that an extra semicolon is always permissible, even if the statement occurs immediately before an END. If you get into the habit of putting a semicolon at the end of every statement, you may get into trouble later on when the syntax forbids it. But by that time, you will be experienced enough to remember when you need a semicolon and when you don't.

A semicolon before END also makes it easier to modify a program or procedure. Suppose you wanted to add a line between the last line and the END in the following program.

```
PROGRAM ThisIsUgly (Output);
VAR     Why,Who,Where,When,What,How : Integer;
BEGIN
        Readln (Who,What,When,Where);
        Readln (When,Why,How);
        Writeln (Who+What+Where, How+When+Why)
END.
```

You would need to alter the previous line by adding a semicolon before adding the line. This is easier with some editors than with others, but the semicolon could easily be forgotten. However, if you get into the habit of putting semicolons before ENDs, then you will never have this problem.

Output Style

You are undoubtedly interested in output, and in good-looking output at that. Here, finally, is what you need to know to make output look sharp.

Field Widths

If you've seen the output of your own programs, you've seen that Pascal allows more spaces than are necessary when printing integers and always prints real numbers in exponential notation, an ugly format that is difficult to read. You are probably dissatisfied with the way Pascal prints numbers. So far, you have only seen the results of the default format for output, which is neither appropriate nor aesthetic in most cases. A **default** is a format or value that a computer uses in the absence of instructions to the contrary. In order to override the default format, one uses field widths.

A **field width** is a value given in a Write or Writeln statement that specifies the minimum amount of space to allocate to a given value. To change the field width of integers and other types of variables (characters and booleans), a single value is given. To change the field width of reals, a second value can be specified that expresses the desired number of digits behind (to the right of) the decimal point. Some examples:

```
a := 5;  b := 10;
Writeln (Output, 15:3, ' is the sum of', a:2, ' and', b:3,'.');
Pi := 3.1415926;
Writeln (Pi, ' = ', Pi:10:7);
Writeln (Output, 'Truncate text':5,'*':b, '!':b-a,'*');
```

These Write statements produce the following:

OUTPUT
```
15 is the sum of 5 and 10.
   3.141593E+00 =   3.1415930
Trunc         *     ! *
```

Field widths are defined with a colon followed by a value or expression. Field width definitions follow the variable or value to be written. If the value is a character string, and the field width, n, is smaller than the length of the string, only the first n characters will be printed.

If you don't know how large the number is going to be but want it to be printed in the smallest possible space, give it a field width of 1. Defining field width as "1" ensures that an element whose length could vary always fits neatly into an English phrase.

```
Writeln (Output, 'The cost is $', Cost:1:2)
                 (* prints the cost in dollars and cents *)
```

OUTPUT
```
The cost is $ 27.92
```

Notice that a leading blank is always produced when writing real numbers. This is not the case for integers.

The ability to specify in one statement the format for several different Write statements would be convenient. If the format needed to be changed, changing a single statement is all that would be necessary. Unfortunately, Pascal requires that each Write or Writeln contain any nondefault formatting in the statement itself, so this convenience is not possible. In order to change the format of the output, each statement must be changed. If you use a variable or constant to specify the common field width, however, you could alter the field width between runs of the program or at different points within the run. For example:

```
CONST    FieldSize = 4;
VAR      Number, Sum : Integer;
BEGIN
         . . .
         Writeln (Output, Number : FieldSize);
         Writeln (Output, Sum : FieldSize);
         . . .
```

Note again that if the value will not fit in the space given, Pascal will give the value exactly the amount of space needed to be printed.

> **Hard-and-Fast Rule #5**
> Specify field widths when writing numerical values to an output file.

This hard-and-fast rule makes sense. If you don't specify a field width when writing a number, the default value will be used, and the output is certain to look worse or at least no better than if you specified an appropriate field width value.

Files and Input/Output Procedures

The standard input/output (I/O) procedures—Read, Readln, Write, and Writeln—are wonderfully flexible in the number and type of arguments that they can accommodate. The **arguments** are the values, variables, and expressions in parentheses after the name of the procedure. We have been taking advantage of the fact that Read and Readln know how to read both integers and reals, and that Write and Writeln don't write numbers the way they are stored in the computer, but in a format readable by humans. We have not, however, taken advantage of the fact that Read knows to read from the input file and that Write knows to write on the output file. For example, when dealing with only one input file and one output file, as all of our programs have so far, the following statements are legal:

```
Readln (Num);
Read (Ans, a, b, c);
Writeln;
Write ('The number is ', Num:1, ' and');
Writeln (' the sum is ', a+b+c:1, '.');
Writeln ( 'The answer is ', Ans);
```

I mention this because it is standard practice to write programs in this shorthand form. However, I will continue using the longer and more explicit form of the standard I/O procedures, because later we will deal with more than one input file or more than one output file. File specifications will no longer be optional, but necessary. At that point, I want to have encouraged good programming habits so that you won't make common mistakes with multiple files. I suggest that you continue to use the following format for your Read and Write operations:

```
Readln (Input, Num);
Read (Input, Ans, a, b, c);
Writeln (Output);
Write (Output, 'The number is ', Num:1, ' and');
Writeln (Output, ' the sum is ', a+b+c:1, '.');
Writeln (Output, 'The answer is ', Ans);
```

The specification of Input for a Read or Readln operation is the default; you do not have to specify it. However, getting into the habit of mentioning it when it is not necessary will cost little but save much hassle at future points when trying to use more than one file. The same is true for Output and Write or Writeln.

A question to think about: What would happen if either of the following lines were found in a program?

```
Writeln (Input, 'This won''t work.');
Readln (Output, Ans);
```

The answer: Pascal knows that the identifier Input means an input file that is only open for reading. If you try to write to an input file, you will get a run-time error; the error will get past the compiler. The same is true of Output, which Pascal knows is a file only open for writing. There are ways of writing output on files that were input files and of reading files that were output files earlier in the execution of the program. We will learn about them later.

User Friendliness

As computers have become more accessible, the software market has grown rapidly. An important characteristic of any program is the degree to which it is user friendly. A **user-friendly program** describes what it is doing, tells what information it needs from the user, and prints results in a meaningful and flexible way. If a prospective user must spend several hours reading the program code before it is clear how to use the program, then the program is not user friendly.

It is imperative that interactive programs be written in such a way that the user is never guessing about what to do. When input is needed, the user should be prompted with a Write statement. Even when you are writing a program, it is easy to forget what you are supposed to enter at what times. After you have programmed awhile, you will learn how to help the user. You should always anticipate that users will need help or will not enter data or commands correctly. We will see specific programming techniques that will be useful in improving the interaction between the computer and the user. At this point, these guidelines should be helpful in making your interactive programs as friendly as possible:

Interactive Program Guidelines
1. Always announce your intentions to the user. Tell the user what the program is supposed to do.
2. Always prompt the user to enter data when it is needed. Never have a Read statement without a Write statement immediately preceding it.
3. When printing results, always tell what the numbers are. Include units, if appropriate. Never write a program that produces only a list of numbers.

Common Errors and Debugging

1. **Writing programs that are virtually impossible for humans to read.** Use the concepts of style discussed in this chapter to improve program readability.

2. **Constructing sloppy procedures.** Check your procedures for statements or subtasks that are extraneous. Write procedure comments before writing code to make sure you understand what the procedure is supposed to do. In general, the more time spent thinking before writing code, the better that code will be.

3. **Writing programs that are impossible to debug.** Usually this results from long, twisted procedures that attempt large, ill-defined tasks. Good program breakdown and top-down design result in shorter, easy-to-read procedures that are crucial to debugging.

4. **Writing programs that are user hostile or user neutral.** The program was made for humans, not humans for the program. Be as helpful and as open as possible about what the program is doing and what information it needs from the user to do it.

Hints for BASIC Programmers

Much of the guidance given in this chapter on format and documentation may be unfamiliar to you, even if you have done a lot of programming in BASIC. The issue of style is a relatively new concept in programming, and many BASIC textbooks predate the recent trend toward style as a design priority. If your experience has led you to develop good style habits, great! Pascal will reinforce them and help you to write beautiful and clear programs. If this is not the case, you will probably need to unlearn several things.

One of the biggest psychological obstacles to overcome in the transition from BASIC to Pascal is the notion that subroutines are only useful when the same code executes in several different places in the program. A BASIC program will often contain a very long main program—by far the majority of the lines of code—with the few small but important subroutines falling at the end. This is not the way you should write programs.

If you don't develop the ability to break down a task into constituent subtasks, you won't be able to derive the full benefits of Pascal, and you may find yourself wanting to go back to BASIC. That is a tragedy you want to prevent.

SUMMARY

Style consists of **format,** the visual cues that a program gives to the reader about its structure, and **documentation,** the textual cues that a program gives the reader. This chapter introduced a number of hard-and-fast rules and other guidelines that will be emphasized throughout the rest of the book.

1. Include a blank line between procedures and between the last procedure and the main block.

2. Indent all statements between any BEGIN and its corresponding END at least four spaces.

3. Indent the identifiers in VAR and CONST declarations.

4. Capitalize all the letters in reserved words and the first letters of distinct words within identifiers.

5. Always use meaningful (mnemonic) identifier names.

6. Almost every number occurring in the text of the code other than -1, 0, 1, or 2 should be declared as a constant.

7. Comment almost every declaration.

8. Make sure that all of your procedures and main programs have fewer than 15 lines.

9. Write the procedure comment after writing the procedure heading but before writing the procedure block. If you can write the comment, then you understand the procedure well enough to write the code.

10. Put a semicolon at the end of every statement, even before an END.

11. Specify field widths when writing numerical values to an output file.

12. Include the input and output file specifications in the I/O procedures, even when it is not necessary.

13. Always announce your intentions to the user of an interactive program. Tell the user what the program is supposed to do.

14. Always prompt the user for data in an interactive program. Never have a Read statement without a Write statement immediately preceding it.

15. When printing the results of your program, always tell what the numbers are. Include units, if appropriate. Never write a program that produces only a list of numbers.

New Terms

style	default	user-friendly program
format	field width	7 ± 2
documentation	argument	

EXERCISES

1. Here is a long program. What does it do? Even though you can't understand all the Pascal code, it is easy to read. What do you think you should read first? Then what? What are some of the aspects of this program that make it easy to understand?

```pascal
PROGRAM Alphabetize (Input, Output);
CONST    LineLen = 60;
         MaxLines = 120;
TYPE     Word = PACKED ARRAY [1..LineLen] OF Char;
         ArrayLines = ARRAY [1..MaxLines] OF Word;

VAR      ArrayOfStudents : ArrayLines;
         NumStuds : Integer;

FUNCTION Cap (Ch:Char) : Char;
BEGIN
         IF ((CH>='a') AND (ch <='z'))
            THEN Cap:= Chr(Ord(Ch)+Ord('A')-Ord('a'))
            ELSE Cap := Ch;
END;

PROCEDURE ReadFirstWord (VAR W : Word;
                         VAR Cntr : Integer);
VAR      Ch : Char;
BEGIN
         Cntr := 0;
         REPEAT  Read (Input, Ch);
                 Cntr := Cntr + 1;
                 W [Cntr] := Cap (Ch);
         UNTIL  (Ch=' ');
END;

PROCEDURE ReadRestOfLine (VAR W : Word;
                          VAR Cntr : Integer);
BEGIN
         WHILE NOT Eoln (Input) DO BEGIN
                 Cntr := Cntr + 1;
                 Read (Input, W[Cntr]);
         END;
         Readln (Input);
END;

FUNCTION OutOfOrder (W2, W1:Word) : Boolean;
BEGIN
         OutOfOrder := (W2 < W1);
END;
```

```
PROCEDURE Swap (VAR W1, W2 : Word);
VAR     Temp : Word;
BEGIN
        Temp := W1;
        W1 := W2;
        W2 := Temp;
END;


PROCEDURE ReadFile (VAR A : ArrayLines;
                    VAR Cntr : Integer);
VAR     Cntr2 : Integer;
BEGIN
        Cntr := 0;
        WHILE NOT Eof (Input) DO BEGIN
                Cntr := Cntr + 1;
                ReadFirstWord (A[Cntr], Cntr2);
                ReadRestOfLine (A[Cntr], Cntr2);
        END;
END;


PROCEDURE SortArray (VAR A : ArrayLines;
                     Num : Integer);
VAR     I, J : Integer;
BEGIN
        FOR J := Num DOWNTO 2 DO BEGIN
            FOR I := 2 TO J DO BEGIN
                IF (OutOfOrder (A[I], A[I-1]))
                    THEN Swap (A[I],A[I-1]);
            END;
        END;
END;


PROCEDURE WriteOneLine (VAR W : Word);
VAR     Cntr : Integer;
BEGIN
        FOR Cntr := 1 TO LineLen DO
                Write (Output, W[Cntr]);
        Writeln (Output,',-');
END;


PROCEDURE WriteArray (VAR A : ArrayLines;
                      Num : Integer);
VAR     J : Integer;
BEGIN
        FOR J := 1 TO Num DO BEGIN
                Write (Output,'! ');
                WriteOneLine (A[J]);
        END;
END;
```

```
BEGIN
        ReadFile (ArrayOfStudents, NumStuds);
        SortArray (ArrayOfStudents, NumStuds);
        WriteArray (ArrayOfStudents, NumStuds);
END.
```

2. Here is another long program. What does it do? Can you tell? How is the program different from the first? If you had to evaluate both, which would you rather use? Why?

```
Program Alphabetize (input, output);
TYPE Word = Packed Array [1..60] of Char;
VAR A : Array [1..120] of Word;
Cntr1, Cntr2, I, J : Integer;
Ch : char;
Function Cap (ch:char) :char;
Begin
IF ((CH>='a') AND (ch <='z'))
Then cap:=Chr(Ord(ch)+Ord('A')-Ord('a'))
Else Cap := ch;
End;
Function OutOfOrder (W2,W1:Word) : Boolean;
Begin
OutOfOrder := (W2<W1);
End;
Procedure Swap (VAR W1,W2 : Word);
VAR Temp : Word;
Begin
Temp := W1;
W1 := W2;
W2 := Temp;
End;
Begin
Cntr1 := 0;
WHILE Not EOF (input) DO Begin
Cntr2 := 0; Cntr1 := Cntr1 + 1;
REPEAT  Read (input, Ch);
Cntr2 := cntr2 + 1;
A[cntr1, cntr2] := Cap (Ch);
UNTIL   (Ch=' ');
While Not EOLN (input) Do Begin
Cntr2 := Cntr2 + 1;
Read (input, A[cntr1,cntr2]);
End;
Readln (input);
End;
FOR J := Cntr1 DOWNTO 2 DO Begin
FOR I := 2 TO J DO Begin
IF (OutOfOrder (A[I], A[I-1])) THEN
        Swap (A[I],A[I-1]);
End;
```

```
End;
FOR J := 1 TO Cntr1 DO BEgin
Write (output,'! ');
FOR I := 1 TO 60 Do Write (output,A[J,I]);
Writeln (output,',-');
End;
End.
```

3. Here is a third program, which you should be able to understand. Revamp the style, changing the indentation, capitalization, and identifier names. Add comments and constants where appropriate. Look at the output, and try to clean it up by specifying field widths. Make the program interactive and user friendly. Make it chatty and cheerful.

```
program example (input, output); var a,b,c,
d,e,f : real; begin read (input, a, b, c);
read (input,d); e := a + b + c + d;
f := e/4; writeln (output, e); writeln
(output, f)end.
```

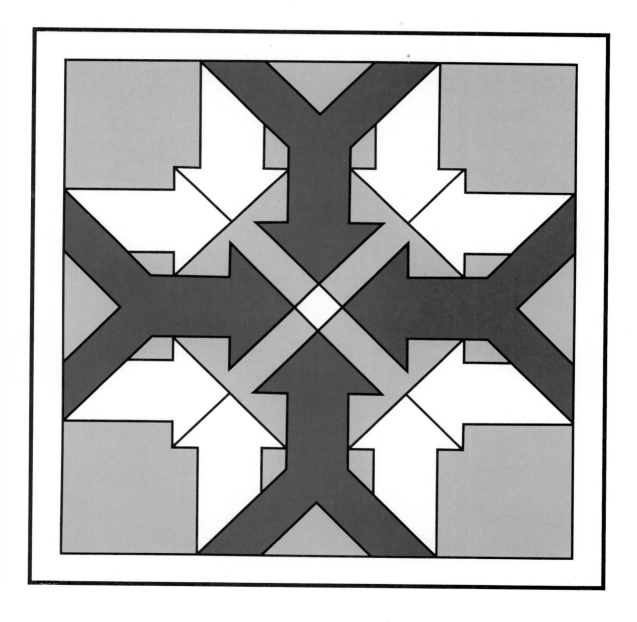

PROCEDURES, PARAMETERS, AND FUNCTIONS

We have discussed the distinction between local variables and global variables but haven't seen how they can be used together. Let's take a look at the relationship between global and local variables in an example. Suppose we want a program that calculates a car's miles per gallon (mpg) and the cost of gasoline to run the car. The program will read the price of gas, the number of gallons of the last fill-up, and the number of miles traveled between fill-ups, then calculate the results. We begin with the following rough outline in pseudocode.

    GasFigures:
        Read the values—price, gallons, miles driven
        Calculate values—mpg, $/mile
        Print the calculated values

This can be specified a little more explicitly by examining what the first two tasks entail.

    Read the values:
        Ask for the price/gallon of the last fill
        Read price
        Ask for the number of gallons
        Read gallons
        Ask for the number of miles
        Read miles

    Calculate the values
        mpg = miles/gallons
        $/mile = price/mpg

At this point, we are ready to write the program. Each task mentioned in the first algorithmic breakdown becomes a procedure.

```
PROGRAM GasFigures (Input, Output);
(**************************************************************
*  This program calculates the miles per gallon (MPG) and   *
*  cost per mile of a car when given the price/gallon,       *
*  the amount of the most recent fill-up, and the number     *
*  of miles driven on the tank since the previous fill.      *
**************************************************************)
VAR     PricePerGallon,   (* of gasoline at the last fill *)
        Gals,            (* gallons of gas during last fill-up *)
        Miles,           (* driven between last two fills   *)
        MilesPerGallon,  (* calculated from input           *)
        BucksPerMile     (* calculated from input           *)
            : Real;

PROCEDURE ReadValues;
(* This procedure reads the values from the terminal       *)
(* input for the variables Price, Gals, and Miles in       *)
(* order to make the calculations.                         *)
BEGIN
        Writeln (Output,  'This program calculates MPG and',
                          'the cost/mile for your car.');
        Writeln (Output,  'What was the price of gasoline',
                          ' at the last fill?(in $)');
        Readln (Input, PricePerGallon);
        Writeln (Output,  'How many gallons did it take ',
                          'to fill the tank?');
        Readln (Input, Gals);
        Writeln (Output,  'How many miles had been driven',
                          ' since the previous fill-up?');
        Readln (Input, Miles);
END;

PROCEDURE CalculateValues;
(* This procedure takes the global values read and         *)
(* calculates the MPG and the cost per mile to drive the   *)
(* car.                                                    *)
BEGIN
        MilesPerGallon := Miles/Gals;
        BucksPerMile := PricePerGallon/MilesPerGallon;
END;

PROCEDURE WriteValues;
(* This procedure writes the calculated values  of         *)
(* MilesPerGallon and BucksPerMile to the output file.     *)
BEGIN
        Writeln (Output,  'The car gets', MilesPerGallon:1:1,
                          ' miles per gallon.');
        Writeln (Output,  'Gas for this car costs $',
                          BucksPerMile:1:2, ' per mile.');
END;
```

```
BEGIN    (* Main Program *)
         ReadValues;
         CalculateValues;
         WriteValues;
END.     (* Main Program *)
```

Notice that all the variables declared in this program are global variables. We use global variables because each variable is used in more than one procedure, and we haven't yet seen how to use information in more than one procedure without declaring a global variable. This deficiency leads to a poorly designed program because the main program doesn't give a clear reflection of what is actually happening. All the references to the global variables are hidden in the procedures, and the manipulations of the variables aren't visible in the main program. Suppose, for example, the main program looked like this:

```
BEGIN    (* Main Program *)
         ReadValues (Price, Gallons, Miles);
         CalculateValues (Price, Gallons, Miles,
                          BucksPerMile, MilesPerGallon);
         WriteValues (BucksPerMile, MilesPerGallon);
END.     (* Main Program *)
```

This is a new version of the main program, with each procedure's variables included in parentheses after the procedure name. A main program written this way is much clearer to the person reading this program. The reader can see what each procedure does and what variables each procedure uses. This version looks something like the syntax of a function call that Chapter 3 discussed. Yet these are procedures, not functions. This version of the main program demonstrates the syntax of procedure calls when procedures have parameters. We will now define parameters and see how they are declared and used.

Value Parameters

To introduce the idea of a parameter, let's examine the shortest and simplest of the procedures in the GasFigures program, PROCEDURE WriteValues. If we include parameters according to the example in the last main program, this is what the result might look like:

```
PROCEDURE WriteValues (BPM, MPG : Real);
(* This procedure writes the calculated values  of        *)
(* MPG and BPM (BucksPerMile) to the output file.         *)
BEGIN
         Writeln (Output, 'The car gets', MPG:1:1,
                          ' miles per gallon.');
         Writeln (Output, 'Gas for this car costs $',
                          BPM:1:2, ' per mile.');
END;
```

In the original version, the variables used inside this procedure were the global variables used throughout the program, and their declarations were placed at the top of the program. In this version, the variable names are not the same as those of the global variables, and their declarations occur inside the procedure, in what is called the formal parameter list.

> **Formal parameter:** A variable that is declared and used inside a procedure whose value is associated with another variable outside the procedure.

> **Formal parameter list:** The list of the variables used as formal parameters inside a procedure and their types.

The formal parameter list operates in the same way a local variable declaration section operates. It declares any variables that are needed for local usage. The variables declared in the formal parameter list are available for local usage only; they are part of the environment of the procedure. When the procedure is finished, all the variables in its local environment disappear.

The formal parameter list always follows the declaration of a procedure name and precedes the semicolon that ends the procedure heading. The syntax of a formal parameter list is like that of a variable declaration section surrounded by parentheses; commas separate variables of the same type, and semicolons separate variables of different types. Each variable in a formal parameter list must be given a type. Here are some examples of legal procedure headings with formal parameter lists:

```
PROCEDURE WriteValues (BPM, MPG : Real);

PROCEDURE Family (Dick, Jane : Real; Dave, Wayne : Integer;
                  Cheryl, Dan : Real);
. . .
PROCEDURE Friends (Al, Steve, Brian, Jordan, Mark : Integer;
                   Jennie, Shannon, Lisa, Heidi : Real);
```

In PROCEDURE WriteValues, there are two formal parameters, BPM and MPG, both of type Real. As mentioned, a formal parameter list operates like a local variable declaration section, in that it allocates memory space to the variables mentioned. But it does more than simply allocate memory locations; it also initializes their contents. To see how this takes place, look at the combination of procedure declaration and procedure call.

```
PROCEDURE WriteValues (BPM, MPG : Real);
BEGIN
. . .
END;

BEGIN    (* Main Program *)
         . . .
         WriteValues (BucksPerMile, MilesPerGallon);
END.     (* Main Program *)
```

At the point in the program where the PROCEDURE WriteValues is called, BucksPerMile and MilesPerGallon have been calculated. Suppose their calculated values were 0.20 and 28.5 respectively. In this case, when WriteValues is executed, the variables in the procedure call will be referenced, and their values will be given to the formal parameters. This means that BPM, listed first, will be given the value of the first argument, BucksPerMile, or 0.20. Likewise, MPG will be given the value of MilesPerGallon, 28.5. Therefore, when the values of BPM and MPG are printed by the procedure, the correct values are sent to the output file.

In order to use a procedure, it is necessary to have two things: the procedure declaration and the procedure call. In the same way, in order to use parameters it is necessary to have both a formal parameter list in the procedure declaration and an actual parameter list in the procedure call.

Actual parameter list: The list of variables or expressions that is to be evaluated and given to the procedure being called.

Actual parameter: A variable that occurs in the parameter list in a procedure call.

The formal parameter list and the actual parameter list for a given procedure always have the same number of parameters. If they do not, then a syntax error results. The correspondence between formal parameters and actual parameters is not by name, but by position in the list; that is, the first formal parameter is always assigned the value of the first actual parameter, the second with the second, and so on. Therefore, the types of corresponding formal and actual parameters must be identical, or a syntax error due to type incompatibility results.

Parameters are like mathematical arguments in a function: the Sqrt function produces different results depending on the value of its argument. In the same way, procedures using parameters produce different results depending on the value of the parameters. Furthermore, an actual parameter list can give an expression that will be evaluated and assign the result to the formal parameter. For example, suppose we wrote the GasFigures program differently:

```
BEGIN     (* Main Program *)
          ReadValues (Price, Gallons, Miles);
          WriteValues (Miles/Gals, Price/(Miles/Gals));
END.      (* Main Program *)
```

Not only does this cut one entire procedure from the program, it eliminates the need for two variables. However, because the calculation of the values isn't explicitly named, this presentation obscures the fact that there are really three things going on in this program. Furthermore, the significance of the two expressions Miles/Gals and Price/(Miles/Gals) is not clear. Giving them variable names uses two more memory locations but makes the program easier to read.

What we have seen so far are examples of value parameters. **Value parameters** specify exactly that: values. Value parameters can also be called input parameters, because, in the same way a program gets values from an input file, a procedure gets values from value parameters. Actually, you have seen value parameters before; the standard procedures Write and Writeln use value parameters as arguments to specify what they should write to the output file.

The actual parameter, the parameter outside the procedure, can be a variable, constant, or expression. The actual parameter determines the value of the formal parameter, the parameter inside the procedure. The formal parameter interacts with the local variables but differs from local variables in that its value is defined by processes outside the procedure. Local variables are defined inside the procedure.

SELF TEST

Given the following procedure headings and procedure calls, identify which syntaxes are correct and which are illegal and tell why.

```
VAR      A, B, Z : Real; X, Y, C : Integer;
PROCEDURE First (Old, New : Real);
. . .
PROCEDURE Second (New : Integer; Old1, Old2 : Real);
. . .
```

1. First (A, B, C)
2. Second (X, B, Z)
3. First (X, Z)
4. First (A, B)

5. Second (C, B, A)
6. Second (C, A, A)
7. Second (B, Z)

Variable Parameters

In order to write PROCEDURE ReadValues for the GasFigures program, we need to know about variable (VAR) parameters. Let's examine another simple example. Suppose we wanted to write a procedure called Average that takes two numbers and returns a third that is the average of the first two. Suppose the following was in the main program:

```
BEGIN
        Readln (Input, X, Y);
        Average (X, Y, Z);
        Writeln (Output, 'The average of ', X,
                        ' and ', Y, ' is ', Z);
        . . .
END.
```

The procedure seems simple.

```
PROCEDURE Average (Num1, Num2, Ave : Real);
BEGIN
        Ave := (Num1 + Num2) / 2.0;
END:
```

What is wrong with this procedure? Let's look at what happens when it is executed. Suppose X represents the value 16.0, and Y, 22.0. The procedure environment is:

```
PROCEDURE Average (Num1, Num2, Ave : Real);      Num1   | 16.0 |
BEGIN                                            Num2   | 22.0 |
        Ave := (Num1 + Num2)/2.0;                Ave    |      |
END;
```

After the procedure statement has been executed, and before program control returns to the main program, the environment is:

```
Num1        | 16.0 |
Num2        | 22.0 |
Ave         | 19.0 |
```

But now what happens? The procedure is exited, the local values vanish, and all the work the computer did to calculate the average of two numbers is wasted. At no time did the global variable Z change.

This is because we were working exclusively with value parameters, or input parameters. Ave shouldn't be an input parameter, it should be an output parameter. It receives its value inside the procedure and needs to be sent out. This is a job for variable parameters.

A variable parameter is declared in the parameter list with the word VAR in front of it.

> **Variable parameter:** A formal parameter that is associated with the memory location of the actual parameter. Any changes to the formal parameter inside the procedure result in corresponding changes to the actual parameter.

If the value of the variable parameter changes inside the procedure, the value of the actual parameter is changed as well. We use variable parameters to ensure that the value we calculate inside a procedure will be sent out of it to the environment in which the procedure was called.

```
PROCEDURE Average (Num1, Num2 : Real; VAR Ave : Real);
BEGIN
        Ave := (Num1 + Num2)/2.0;
END;
```

Now when the environment of the procedure is set up, it looks different than before:

```
PROGRAM  IllustrateVarParams (Input, Output);
VAR X, Y, Z : Real;                                         X   │  16.0  │
                                                            Y   │  22.0  │
                                                            Z   │        │◄──┐
PROCEDURE Average (Num1, Num2 : Real; VAR Ave : Real);          
BEGIN                                                       Num1 │  16.0 │
        Ave := (Num1 + Num2) / 2.0;                         Num2 │  22.0 │
END;                                                        Ave ●─────────┘

BEGIN (* Main Program *)
        X := 16.0; Y := 22.0;
        Average (X, Y, Z);
        Writeln (Output, 'The average of ', X,
                        ' and ', Y, ' is ', Z);
END.
```

Notice that no box is set up for Ave inside the procedure. The effect is as if a pointer were attached at one end to the formal parameter name Ave and attached at the other end to the actual parameter that corresponds to it. When the statement is executed, the value calculated to be stored into Ave, 19.0, goes to the location to which Ave is pointing—Z. So Z and Ave are linked. Now, after the procedure statement is executed, the following global environment exists:

```
        X   │  16.0  │
        Y   │  22.0  │
        Z   │  19.0  │
```

When the procedure is exited, the formal parameter memory locations Num1 and Num2 are released, and the formal parameter Ave removes the pointer. The value calculated for Ave, which was stored in Z, is intact. Variable parameters aren't new—you've seen them before. Like Write and Writeln, which use value parameters for their arguments, Read and Readln use variable parameters for their arguments, because the variables that are sent in to Read and Readln will be assigned new values.

SELF TEST

Given PROCEDURE Average, as defined above, predict what the following code will do.

```
VAR     A, B, C, D : Real;
BEGIN
        A := 13.0;  B := 29.0;
        Average (A, B, C);
        Average (A, C, D);
        Average (C, D, A);
        Average (A, B, B);
        Writeln (Output, A:1:1,  B:1:1,  C:1:1,  D:1:1);
        Average (A * 3, 20 - B, C);
        Average (A, C, C);
        Average (A, C, B);
        Average (C, B, A);
        Average (A, B, D);
        Writeln (Output, A:1:1,  B:1:1,  C:1:1,  D:1:1);
END.
```

Variables and Parameters

In Chapter 4, we talked about global and local variables. We described the syntactical difference between the two types of declarations. Now, with all of the additional and potentially confusing rules about parameters, it might be tempting to wonder why we don't simply always use global variables. Why do we declare local variables? Why should we use parameters?

Local Versus Global

Declaring variables locally keeps the information "close"; the variable declaration is inside the procedure in which it is used. It is somewhat like organizing a house. It would not be wrong to put all of the kitchen utensils, the gardening tools, and the carpentry tools together in one box in the basement, but it wouldn't make a great deal of sense. It would be better to put all of the kitchen things in the kitchen, the gardening things in the tool shed, and the carpentry tools on the bench. It makes sense to place things close to where they are actually used.

It is best to keep variable definitions in the procedure where they are used so you can refer to them easily.

In contrast, some tools, such as a vacuum cleaner, must be in a place easily accessible to all parts of the house. Any variable that is needed in the main program *must* be declared globally.

The precepts of style presented in Chapter 5 also support this type of reasoning and suggest another hard-and-fast rule.

Hard-and-Fast Rule #6
Only variables used in the main program should be declared globally.

Parameters Versus Global Variables

Only variables used in the main program should be global. That statement implies that there is a reverse requirement for nonlocal variables that are not used in the main program. How should two procedures communicate? Parameters, of course. This leads to another rule.

Hard-and-Fast Rule #7
All variables that cannot be local in a single procedure should be passed into procedures by means of variable or value parameters.

Let me justify that last rule. If a variable gets its initial value in a procedure and is no longer needed by the time the procedure is finished, then it can be declared locally inside that procedure. That is how local variables have been used throughout this book. However, if a procedure either calculates a value needed elsewhere, or uses a value calculated elsewhere, then communication must occur. The choice is not *whether* to communicate between procedures or between parts of the program, but *how* to do so. The communication can occur implicitly, through the use of global variables, or explicitly, by using parameters. Explicit communication is preferred because it helps the reader of the program know what is going on behind the scenes. Nothing is hidden. No procedure changes the values of global variables without the knowledge of the reader.

To highlight the difference between explicit and implicit communication, let's look at both versions of the main block of program GasFigures, with and without parameters.

```
BEGIN     (* Main Program *)
          ReadValues;
          CalculateValues;
          WriteValues;
END.      (* Main Program *)

BEGIN     (* Main Program *)
          ReadValues (Price, Gals, Miles);
          CalculateValues (Price, Gals, Miles,
                           BucksPerMile, MilesPerGallon);
          WriteValues (BucksPerMile, MilesPerGallon);
END.      (* Main Program *)
```

With the parameters in the procedures, the same amount of communication is going on between the different procedures. However, the communication is explicit—one can tell by looking at the main program how the different procedures depend on each other and on the global data. It makes the main program easier to read and to follow.

Furthermore, observe the difference parameterization makes on one of the procedures. First, the unparameterized version:

```
PROCEDURE CalculateValues;
(* This procedure takes the global values read and          *
 * calculates the MPG and the cost per mile to drive the    *
 * car.                                                      *)
BEGIN
        MilesPerGallon := Miles/Gals;
        BucksPerMile := Price/MilesPerGallon;
END;
```

Compare this version, which uses parameters.

```
PROCEDURE CalculateValues (Price, Gals, Miles : Real;
                           VAR BPM, MPG : Real);
(* This procedure takes the global values read and          *
 * calculates the MPG and the cost per mile (BPM)           *
 * to drive the car.                                        *)
BEGIN
        MPG := Miles/Gals;
        BPM := Price/MPG;
END;
```

The parameterized version is easier to read on two accounts:

1. Each procedure is easier to read because all of the variables in a procedure will either be local variables or parameters. In either case, the type declaration will be inside the procedure and available for reference.
2. The main program or procedure calls located in other procedures will be

more transparent; the extent and nature of communication that occurs between the environment (the calling procedure or the main program) and the called procedure will be explicit at the procedure call.

There is another stylistic argument for using parameters. If you have a procedure like Average (see page 127) or a procedure called Swap, which swaps the values stored in two variables, you may want to execute these procedures with more than one set of variables. If you rely on global variables, then the procedure isn't general, and can only be used for one set of variables.

These stylistic concerns are also referred to as modularity and portability, and are common criteria for good program code.

Modularity: The degree to which the procedure is modular, or complete on its own with no outside (global) references.

Portability: The degree to which a procedure is **portable,** able to be moved into another environment (another program or defining procedure) without affecting its ability to perform its given task.

When programs look like a plate of pasta (spaghetti programs), then they are not modular. BASIC programs are often virtually impossible to break down into clean, distinct parts or modules. (See Figure 6.1.) If a procedure is dependent on a number of global variables, then when it is moved into another program, it is not likely that an environment with the needed global variables will exist. Therefore, the goal is to make each procedure as modular and portable as is *reasonably* possible.

Figure 6.1: It Is Easier to Organize Blocks Than Spaghetti

Variable Versus Value Parameters

Now that we understand that variables should be as local as possible, and that procedures should be fully parameterized (and have at least an idea what that means), we still are left with the task of deciding which should be value parameters and which should be variable parameters. An easy rule applies: *if the variable changes value inside a procedure, and the changed value is needed after the end of the procedure, use a variable parameter.* In most other cases, then, the parameter can be a value parameter. (A huge data structure presents an exception. We will discuss this case in another chapter.)

Variable parameters are also called **reference parameters,** or **passed-by-reference parameters,** because any reference to the formal parameter inside the procedure is also a reference to the actual parameter. For example, when PROCEDURE Average is executed, a reference to Ave inside the procedure is equivalent to a reference to the global variable Z:

```
PROCEDURE Average (Num1, Num2 : Real; VAR Ave : Real);
BEGIN
        Ave := (Num1 + Num2) / 2.0;

END;
BEGIN     (* Main Program *)
        Readln (Input, X, Y);
        Average (X, Y, Z);
        . . .
END.
```

This is not the case with Num1 and Num2. When the reference is made to Num1 and Num2, the values are obtained from the local storage boxes set up inside PROCEDURE Average. All value parameters such as Num1 and Num2 are passed-by-value parameters. The values are passed in from X and Y. But if Num1 and Num2 were changed, X and Y would remain unaffected.

```
PROCEDURE Average (Num1, Num2 : Real; VAR Ave : Real);
BEGIN
        Ave := (Num1 + Num2) / 2.0;
        Num1 := 2 * Num1;       (* this doesn't affect the *)
                                (* values of X and Y       *)
        Num2 := Num2 / 2.0;
END;
```

It seems then, from the discussion, that a variable parameter can do everything a value parameter can do, and more. If that is true, then why bother with value parameters at all? Why not make every parameter a variable parameter?

First of all, it is simply not true that a variable parameter can do everything a value parameter can do. In fact, the difference between value parameters and variable parameters results in the fact that, while it is possible to send an expression in to a value parameter, a single variable must be passed to a variable parameter.

```
Average (X, Y, (X + Y) / 2);   (* this produces an error *)
Average (X + Y, X - Y, Z)      (* while this does not *)
```

This makes sense when you realize that a formal reference parameter needs to have one storage location to refer to. An expression has no storage location, only a value.

The main reason, however, that we try to distinguish between value and variable parameters is again one of style (an issue that never dies). When you look at a program header, you should be able to tell immediately if the program uses both an input and an output file. In the same way, when you are trying to understand a procedure, both how it works and how it fits in to the entire program, you want to be able to look at it and quickly identify the input parameters and the output parameters. If all of the parameters were variable parameters, then a distinction could only be made by the context of the procedure and the calling environment. The code would be much more difficult to read and debug.

Blocks, Scope, and Activations

Examine the following program and count as many syntax errors as you can find.

```
PROGRAM Names (Output);
CONST    Names = 3;
VAR      Tom : Real;
         Dick : Integer;

PROCEDURE Harry;
CONST    Tom = 44;
VAR      Names : Integer;
         Harry : Real;

PROCEDURE Dick;
CONST    Dick = 1.414;
VAR      Tom, Harry : Integer;
         Names : Real;

BEGIN
      (* Point A *)
END;

BEGIN
      (* Point B *)
END;

BEGIN
      (* Point C *)
END.
```

Were you able to find all of the errors? Depending on how you counted, you may have come up with as many as nine errors, all declaring an identifier that has already been declared. Actually, this is a working program, with no syntactical errors. (Yes, I know, it was a trick question.)

The program can most clearly be understood if we point out the block at each level of the program. A program block is a global declaration part and a main program BEGIN-END block.

```
CONST    Names = 3;
VAR      Tom : Real;
         Dick : Integer;
PROCEDURE Harry;
. . .
BEGIN
         (* Point C *)
END.
```

Notice that procedure Dick is declared *within* the procedure Harry. Within the global block, each identifier (Names, Tom, Dick, Harry) is only declared once, and only has one meaning. At the time that any statements in Point C are executed, Names is a constant with the value of 3, Tom is a real variable, Dick is a integer variable, Harry is a procedure, and the *procedure* Dick is unknown.

Now let's look at the block for PROCEDURE Harry:

```
CONST    Tom = 44;
VAR      Names : Integer;
         Harry : Real;

PROCEDURE Dick;
. . .
BEGIN
         (* Point B *)
END;
```

Again, inside the block for PROCEDURE Harry, each of the four identifiers is only given one meaning, and there are no errors. An error would be detected if the following occurred.

```
VAR      Tom : Integer;
PROCEDURE Tom;
```

This is an error because within the same block the identifier Tom would be given two different meanings.

We say a global identifier has global scope, which means it normally is understood in the entire program. When an identifier is used outside its scope, the compiler will complain about an undeclared identifier.

> **Scope:** The range of statements within a program in which an identifier is given meaning by the compiler.

The scope of the constant Names ($=3$) is the entire program, including points A, B, and C. However, because Names is given other meanings inside procedures Harry and Dick, we say that the activation of the constant Names is only in the main block, at Point C.

> **Activation:** The range within a program where an identifier is understood as a specific class and type.

The activation of an identifier is the entire block in which it is declared, plus all the subblocks (which are in procedures in the block), unless in one of the subblocks the identifer is redefined (as in the case above). So while the scope of the constant Tom ($=44$) is the blocks including points A and B, the activation of the constant Tom is only the block including Point B. Figure 6.2 shows the way this program could be broken down into nested blocks.

SELF TEST

In order to drive this point home, consider these questions about the previous example:

1. At Point C, what does the identifier Dick represent?
2. At Point B, what does the identifier Dick represent?
3. At Point A, what does the identifier Dick represent?
4. What is the scope of the real variable Harry?
5. What is the activation of the real variable Harry?

Finally, let me emphasize that it is definitely not a good idea to have several different variables, with distinct meanings and uses, share the same name, as in the example above. This example illustrates the difference between scope and activation, but is not illustrative of superlative style. Distinct variable names keep things clear. This is true even between actual and formal parameters. Perhaps a good rule is that when you write a procedure that is generic (like Average, which might use many different variables), then you should use generic formal parameters, and when the procedure is specific to one usage (like ReadValues), you should use the same names for the formal parameters and the actual parameters.

PROGRAM Names (Output);

```
CONST     Names = 3;
VAR       . . .

PROCEDURE Harry;

    CONST     Tom = 44;
    VAR       . . .

    PROCEDURE Dick;

        CONST     Dick = 3.14159;
        VAR       . . .

        BEGIN
            (* Point A *)
        END;

    BEGIN
        (* Point B *)
    END;

BEGIN
    (* Point C *)
END.
```

Figure 6.2: Scope and Blocks

Programming Example 6.1

Assignment: Write a program to do angle conversions from degrees, minutes, and seconds to decimal degrees and finally to radians. Your program should take as input three values (degrees, minutes, and seconds) and should produce the equivalents as output. (Recall that there are 60 seconds in one minute, and 60 minutes in one degree of arc. There are 2π ($\pi = 3.14159$) radians in 360 degrees.)

Solution: First we need to break up the problem into the obvious and largest tasks.

Convert Angles:
    DMSToDecimalDegrees—convert from degrees, minutes,
        and seconds to decimal degrees
    DegreesToRadians—convert from degrees to radians

Let's take a closer look at DMSToDecimalDegrees first. This can be further broken down as

DMSToDecimalDegrees:
     read the values Degrees, Minutes, Seconds
     convert degrees to decimal
     convert minutes to decimal, add to total
     convert seconds to decimal, add to total
     write the total

The procedure is starting to take shape, and we can begin writing the actual code.

```
PROCEDURE DMSToDecimalDegrees;
(* This procedure reads from the input file the values of *)
(* an angle measured in degrees, minutes, and seconds and *)
(* writes out the angle's value in decimal degrees.       *)
CONST    MinsPerDegree = 60;
         SecsPerDegree = 3600;
VAR      Degrees, Minutes, Seconds : Integer;
         DecDegrees : Real;
BEGIN
         Writeln (Output, 'Input values for degrees, ',
                           'minutes, and seconds.');
         Readln (Input, Degrees, Minutes, Seconds);
         DecDegrees := Degrees;
         DecDegrees := DecDegrees + Minutes / MinsPerDegree;
         DecDegrees := DecDegrees + Seconds / SecsPerDegree;

         Writeln (Output, DecDegrees: 1: 3,
                          ' is the value in degrees.');
END;
```

This is easy to understand, because each step in the process is explicitly delineated. The three lines could have been written more succinctly in one long calculation.

```
DecDegrees := Degrees + Minutes/MinsPerDegree
                      + Seconds/SecsPerDegree;
```

Once we have the value of degrees in decimal, we can convert to radians very simply.

```
PROCEDURE DegreesToRadians;
(* This procedure uses DecDegrees to calculate the      *)
(* value of the angle in radians.                       *)
CONST   Pi = 3.14159;
        PiRadians = 180;     (* 180 degrees = Pi radians *)
VAR     Radians : Real;
BEGIN
        Radians := Pi * DecDegrees / PiRadians;
        Writeln (Output, Radians:1:3,
                        ' is the value in radians.');

END;
```

If we didn't realize it before, we see now that DecDegrees must be a parameter to this procedure, and hence cannot be a local variable in the previous procedure. DecDegrees must be a parameter because the value is calculated in the first procedure and used in the second to calculate the value of radians. Since DecDegrees is calculated in the first procedure, it must be declared a variable parameter. In the second procedure, the value of DecDegrees is not changed, and so it should be declared a value parameter.

Notice that the constants and other variables were declared locally in the procedures in which they were used, keeping the number of global variables to a minimum. The final program follows.

```
PROGRAM ConvertAngles (Input, Output);
(************************************************************
* This program does angle conversions from degrees, minutes*
* and seconds to decimal degrees and finally to radians.   *
* The program asks the user for the three values and then  *
* prints the converted values.                             *
************************************************************)
VAR     DecDegrees : Real;  (* The value of the angle
                                converted to decimal        *)


PROCEDURE Introduction;
(* Tells the user what the program does.                 *)
BEGIN
        Writeln (Output, 'This program does angle',
                    ' conversions from degrees, minutes');
        Writeln (Output, 'and seconds to decimal degrees',
                    ' and finally to radians.');
END;
```

```
PROCEDURE DMSToDecimalDegrees (VAR DecDegrees : Real);
(* This procedure reads from the input file the values of *)
(* an angle measured in degrees, minutes, and seconds and *)
(* writes out the angle's value in decimal degrees.       *)
CONST    MinsPerDegree = 60;
         SecsPerDegree = 3600;
VAR      Degrees, Minutes, Seconds : Integer;
BEGIN
         Writeln (Output, 'Input values for degrees, ',
                          'minutes, and seconds.');
         Readln (Input, Degrees, Minutes, Seconds);
         DecDegrees := Degrees + Minutes/MinsPerDegree
                                 + Seconds/SecsPerDegree;
         Writeln (Output, DecDegrees:1:3,
                          ' is the value in degrees.');
END;


PROCEDURE DegreesToRadians (DecDegrees : Real);
(* This procedure uses DecDegrees to calculate the value *)
(* of the angle in radians.                              *)
CONST    Pi = 3.14159;
         PiRadians = 180;    (* 180 degrees = Pi radians *)
VAR      Radians : Real;
BEGIN
         Radians := Pi * DecDegrees / PiRadians;
         Writeln (Output, Radians:1:3,
                          ' is the value in radians.');
END;


BEGIN    (* Main program *)
         Introduction;
         DMSToDecimalDegrees (DecDegrees);
         DegreesToRadians (DecDegrees);
END.     (* Main program *)
```

The following are two sample interactive sessions for the previous program.

INTERACTIVE SESSION

```
This program does angle conversions from degrees, minutes
and seconds to decimal degrees and finally to radians.
Input values for degrees, minutes, and seconds.
35 43 59
 35.733 is the value in degrees.
 0.624 is the value in radians.
```

```
This program does angle conversions from degrees, minutes
and seconds to decimal degrees and finally to radians.
Input values for degrees, minutes, and seconds.
298 19 25
 298.324 is the value in degrees.
 5.207 is the value in radians.
```

Functions

We have already seen examples of standard Pascal functions, such as Sqrt, Trunc, and Exp. Each of these functions takes an argument or parameter and returns a result. Suppose we want to write a new function called Cube, which takes a value and returns its cube. Without user-defined functions, we could do this in a roundabout way by using a procedure with a variable parameter:

```
PROCEDURE Cube (Num : Integer; VAR Result : Integer);
(* This procedure takes a number, Num, and returns, *)
(* in Result, its Cube                              *)
BEGIN
        Result := Num * Num * Num;
END;
```

This is a little bit clumsy because of the syntactical difference between a procedure and a function. Suppose we want to write the square and the cube of a number.

```
        Read (Input, I);
        Cube (I, ItsCube);
        Writeln (Output, I:10, Sqr (I):10, ItsCube:10);
```

Because a call to Cube is a statement, it is not equivalent to a call to Sqr, which is syntactically equivalent to a value. If we could declare our own function called Cube, using it would be easier, and equivalent to using Sqr.

```
        Read (Input, I);
        Writeln (Output, I:10, Sqr (I):10, Cube (I):10);
```

In Pascal, a function is declared much like a procedure, as Figure 6.3 shows. The function declaration looks exactly like a procedure declaration except for

Figure 6.3: FUNCTION Syntax

```
FUNCTION <identifier> (<parameter list>): <type>;
<block>;
```

two features: (1) the reserved word, FUNCTION, which introduces it and (2) a function is given a type, like a variable, which expresses the type of the result that will be returned. For example:

```
FUNCTION Cube (Num : Integer) : Integer;
(* This function expects an integer argument and *)
(* returns its cube.                             *)
BEGIN
        Cube := Num * Num * Num;
END;
```

Notice that inside the function, Cube is treated like a variable and an assignment can be made to it. It should not be used on the right side of an equation inside the function, or the compiler will interpret it as another function call and complain about an incorrect number of arguments.

Declaring Cube as a function allows the user to use the calculated value without having to allocate a memory cell in which to store the value, as is the case when printing. Another situation in which to use a function is when the value calculated is only used in another expression to calculate a value that is stored.

Functions can be declared as any of the types that we know how to use. For example, here is a real-valued function:

```
FUNCTION CubeRt (X : Real) : Real;
(* This function expects a real parameter and returns *)
(* its cube root.                                     *)
BEGIN
        CubeRt := Exp (Ln (X) / 3);
END;
```

Character Variables

We have only alluded to the fact that other types of variables exist besides real and integer. Pascal is useful for more than number crunching, however, and other types of variables allow the programmer to store other types of data.

The next variable type we will look at and use is the character type Char. If a variable is declared to be of type Char, the programmer expects it to have a letter, digit, punctuation mark, symbol, or a space as value. A character variable is exactly one letter long; it can never hold all of the letters in a word, for example. Declaring, reading, writing, and assigning character variables is like working with any other type.

```
VAR      Ch, Answer : Char;
BEGIN
         Write (Output, 'Do you like me?');
         Read (Input, Ans);
         Ch := '*';
         Write (Output, Ch, Ans);
         . . .
```

Suppose we wanted to write a function to change a lowercase letter into a capital letter. Before we can do this, we must learn about two more standard functions in Pascal.

1. Ord (Ch) returns the code number of a character from the character set.
2. Chr (Num) returns the character in the character set for the given code number.

These functions are the inverse of each other. That is:

```
Chr (Ord (Ch)) = Ch
Ord (Chr (Num)) = Num
```

Therefore, even though we can't add letters, we can convert characters by adding numbers to their ordinals and then converting. For example:

```
Chr (Ord ('A') + 1) = 'B'
Chr (Ord ('a') + 25) = 'z'
```

The difference between 'a' and 'A' is the same as the difference between 'b' and 'B', and so on all the way through the alphabet. With these two functions in our repertoire, we should be able to write the function Capitalize:

```
FUNCTION Capitalize (Ch : Char) : Char;
(* This function expects a small letter as an argument *)
(* and returns its capital. It will not work properly  *)
(* if the character given it is not a small letter.     *)
BEGIN
        Capitalize := Chr (Ord (Ch)+ Ord ('A')- Ord ('a'));
END;
```

Programming Example 6.2

Assignment: Write a function called RoundTo which takes a real value and a specified number of digits behind the decimal, and returns a real value rounded correctly. Read a number from a file, round it to zero, one, and two digits, and print out the results.

Solution: This program should be fairly short. The whole problem can be broken down simply as:

> Read the number
> Round number to zero digits, print
> Round number to one digit, print
> Round number to two digits, print

Except for the fact that we need to write the desired function, the program is simple.

```
BEGIN
        Read (Input, Number);
        Writeln (Output, 'The number read was ', Number);
        Write (Output, RoundTo (Number, 0):10:3);
        Write (Output, RoundTo (Number, 1):10:3);
        Write (Output, RoundTo (Number, 2):10:3);
        Writeln (Output);
END.
```

This is a good way to use a function. Notice that we didn't have to use a variable location to store each rounded value; we simply printed it and continued.

Now that we have called the function RoundTo, let's give the function declaration. This will require a little thought.

How do we round numbers? If we use Round, we will always round them to the nearest integer. That will not give us the answer we want, in most cases. How can we round to tenths? We can use the Round function to round to any place we desire by using some simple arithmetic transformations. For example:

```
Round (Number*10) / 10.0
```

will produce Number rounded to the tenths place. Likewise,

```
Round (Number*100) / 100.0
```

produces Number rounded to two digits behind the decimal. In general,

$$\text{Round (Number} * 10^n)/10^n$$

will produce a number that is rounded to n digits behind the decimal.

Therefore, we can write the function outline by using the previous observations:

> RoundTo:
> Find divisor: Exp (n*ln 10)
> Return Round (Number*Divisor)/Divisor

This can be written in Pascal as:

```
FUNCTION RoundTo (Number : Real; Digits : Integer) : Real;
VAR       Divisor : Real;
BEGIN
          Divisor := Exp (Digits * Ln (10.0));
          RoundTo := Round (Number*Divisor)/Divisor;
END;
```

The entire program and sample output follow.

```
PROGRAM TestRound (Input, Output);
(************************************************************)
(* This program is used to test the RoundTo function by    *)
(* reading a number and rounding it to zero, one and two   *)
(* digits. This program is batch oriented.                 *)
(************************************************************)
VAR       Number : Real;   (* the number read, to be rounded *)


FUNCTION RoundTo (Number : Real; Digits : Integer) : Real;
(* This function rounds a real number to the number of     *)
(* digits behind the decimal that is specified. It uses    *)
(* the Round function, multiplying and then dividing by    *)
(* the appropriate power of 10.                            *)
VAR       Divisor : Real;   (* the appropriate power of 10   *)
BEGIN
          Divisor := Exp (Digits * Ln (10.0));
          RoundTo := Round (Number*Divisor)/Divisor;
END;


BEGIN     (* Main program *)
          Read (Input, Number);
          Writeln (Output, 'The number read was ', Number);
          Write (Output, RoundTo (Number, 0):10:3);
          Write (Output, RoundTo (Number, 1):10:3);
          Write (Output, RoundTo (Number, 2):10:3);
          Writeln (Output);
END.      (* Main program *)
```

```
OUTPUT  The number read was    1.234568E+02
          123.000    123.500    123.460
```

Common Errors and Debugging

Errors in the syntax and execution of parameters are among the most common in programming. It is important to learn this material well.

1. **Declaring a parameter type that doesn't agree with declaration.** Detecting type incompatibility requires careful cross-checking between the formal parameter list in the procedure declaration and the actual parameter list in the procedure call. Also take care not to leave out one of the parameters in either place. If you do, you will get a message such as "number of parameters does not agree with declaration."

2. **Using a value parameter when the variable changes inside the procedure.** Sometimes a variable is initialized or calculated in a procedure, but the reserved word VAR is left off the parameter declaration. Remember to check your parameters, because this error is difficult to detect (the compiler can't) and your results will be incorrect. If your program seems to read data and makes some calculations, but the results are always zeros, then it is likely that somewhere there is a value parameter which should be a variable parameter.

3. **Trying to access a declared variable when it is not activated.** This error occurs when the variable is out of its scope or when it is hidden by a more local declaration. Using parameters consistently usually prevents the former, and using distinct variable names will probably protect you from the latter.

4. **Declaring a function without a type.** If you don't want to return a value, then specify PROCEDURE rather than FUNCTION.

5. **Using a function name as a variable on the right-hand side of an assignment.** For example:

```
FUNCTION RoundTo (Number : Real; Digits : Integer) : Real;
VAR     Divisor : Real;   (* the appropriate power of 10   *)
BEGIN
        Divisor := Exp (Digits * Ln (10.0));
        RoundTo := Round (Number*Divisor);
        RoundTo := RoundTo/Divisor;
END;
```

When the function name appears on the left, it is an assignment. However, when it appears on the right, it looks like a function call to the compiler. The error message you will probably receive is that there are an incorrect number of actual parameters (zero) in your function call; the function needs two. If you ever want to do something like this, use a temporary variable, and then make one assignment at the end of the function definition.

```
FUNCTION RoundTo (Number : Real; Digits : Integer) : Real;
VAR      Divisor : Real;  (* the appropriate power of 10    *)
         TmpRoundTo : Real;   (* temporary value of the fn *)
BEGIN
         Divisor := Exp (Digits * Ln (10.0));
         TmpRoundTo := Round (Number*Divisor);
         RoundTo := TmpRoundTo/Divisor;
END;
```

6. **Not assigning a value to a function name inside the body of the function.** The function should contain an assignment that gives to the function name the value that has been calculated.

7. **Calling a function as if it were a procedure.** A function cannot stand alone as a statement. Often, a function will be used in an assignment or a Write statement.

8. **Producing a function that creates side effects.** A function is supposed to make one calculation and return one result. If any of the parameters of the function change—and hence must be declared formally as variable parameters—the function is really acting like a procedure and should be declared as a procedure. Functions should rarely do anything to change the global data structure.

Hints for BASIC Programmers

You probably never had to deal with local variables and parameters in BASIC, and they could easily be the stumbling block to bigger and better programs in Pascal. It is difficult to get out of the comfortable habit of using a global variable any time you need one and without having to declare it. But those times are over.

When you write a procedure for a program, think about it the way you think about any program: What input does it need to do its job? What output or results do I want it to produce? The answers to these questions are the parameters you need for the procedure, both the input or value parameters, as well as the output or variable parameters. The discipline of consistent parameterization helps organize a program and may help to organize your thoughts as you write the program. In general, what a good pseudocode outline does for the logic of a program, consistent parameterization does for the variables.

If you are thinking that Pascal is nothing like BASIC and are just about ready to give up, wait until the next chapter. You will be off to a good start with the next feature of Pascal, the FOR loop.

SUMMARY

Parameters allow communication between procedures and ensure that variable declarations will be as local as possible. Every variable in a procedure should be either a local variable or a parameter from another procedure or from the main program. Only variables that are actually used in the main program need to be declared as global variables. Programming in this way leads to **modular** and **portable** programs which are much easier to read and debug.

Variable parameters or **passed-by-reference** parameters, should only be used when the variable receives an updated value in the procedure it is sent to, and the new value is used later. Otherwise, the variable should be declared as a **value parameter.**

The **scope** of an identifier is the range of statements within a program in which it is given meaning by the compiler. The scope is usually the block in which the identifier is defined. The scope of a global variable is the entire program. The **activation** of an identifier is the same as the scope of the identifier, unless the identifier is given another definition at a lower level of the block structure. In this case, the activation of the original definition of the identifier is the block in which it is defined and any subblock in which the identifier is not given a second declaration.

Pascal user-defined functions are like the standard Pascal functions, in that they return a single value as a result and are the syntactic equivalents of values or expressions. A FUNCTION declaration looks like a procedure declaration, except that the type of the function is given after the parameter list and a colon, in much the same way that a variable is given a type. Functions are useful when we don't want to use an entire statement to calculate a given value.

New Terms

formal parameter	variable parameter	scope
formal parameter list	modularity	activation
actual parameter list	modules	FUNCTION
actual parameter	portability	VAR
value parameter	reference parameter	CHAR

EXERCISES

1. Using PROCEDURE Average on page 127, evaluate the output of the following section of code.

```
a := 10.0; b := 20.0;
Average (a, b/a, c);
Writeln (a:10:2, b:10:2, c:10:2);
Average (c, a, b);
Writeln (a:10:2, b:10:2, c:10:2);
Average (c*a, b*b, a);
Writeln (a:10:2, b:10:2, c:10:2);
```

```
Average (a, b, b);
Writeln (a: 10: 2, b: 10: 2, c: 10: 2);
```

2. For each of the following procedures, determine whether the parameters should be variable or value parameters.

(a) PROCEDURE CalcMean
      SumScores
      NumScores
      Mean
	(c) PROCEDURE CheckData
	      AmountOf Input
	      SumData
	      MaxValue
	      DataOK

(b) PROCEDURE DetermineLargest
      A
      B
      C
      Largest
	(d) PROCEDURE WriteResults
	      AmountOf Input
	      SumData
	      MaxValue
	      DataOK

3. Given the following main program, write the procedures that are called. The program should ask the user for a three-digit number, reverse the digits of the number, then print out the reversed number.

```
BEGIN    (* Main Program *)
         GetNumber;
         ReverseNumber;
         PrintNumber;
END.     (* Main Program *)
```

Don't forget to make some variable and parameter declarations as you realize the types and quantity you will need.

4. Write a program to solve the same task as above, but with a different program breakdown. Define the procedures called in the following program.

```
BEGIN    (* Main Program *)
         GetDigits;
         PrintReversedDigits;
END.     (* Main Program *)
```

Hint: In either case, you will need to isolate the digits, although the number will be read as one integer.

5. Write a procedure to convert angles from radians to decimal degrees to degrees, minutes, and seconds. This is the converse of Programming Example 6.1.

6. Write a function that takes the x, y, and z coordinates of a point in three-dimensional space and returns the distance from the origin.

7. Write a function that takes an integer between 1 and 26 and returns the letter of the alphabet that falls at that position.

8. Write a function that asks for the user's age and calculates the first year that the user will be able to or was able to vote in a presidential election. Comment any assumptions you need to make.

9. Write a function called Encoder, which, when given an A, will return a Z. It should always return the letter of the alphabet on the other side of the halfway point—B becomes Y, C becomes X, and so forth.

10. Write functions that convert values
    a. from feet to inches
    b. from inches to feet
    c. from miles to feet
    d. from kilometers to meters
    e. miles per hour to kilometers per hour
    f. from apples to oranges

11. Write a function that returns the area of a triangle when given the lengths of the three sides. (See Exercise 11, Chapter 3.)

12. Write a procedure to calculate the area and the perimeter of the triangle.

13. Write a function that calculates a baseball player's slugging average. (See Exercise 9, Chapter 4.)

14. The geometric mean of two numbers is defined as the square root of their product. Write a function that returns the geometric mean of any two nonnegative numbers.

DEFINITE REPETITION

Repetition

We have already seen how we might write a procedure to produce a box of four stars by four stars on the output file.

```
PROCEDURE MakeBox;
(* Makes a 4x4 box of stars using MakeLine, which *)
(* makes a line of 4 stars                        *)
BEGIN
        MakeLine;
        MakeLine;
        MakeLine;
        MakeLine;
END;
```

As you may have already realized, modifying this procedure could become tedious. Suppose we wanted a 5×5 box instead. We could add a star to the character string inside of MakeLine, and add one more call to MakeLine in MakeBox. That's not too hard, but if I asked you to produce two 100×100 boxes in this way, you would revolt. There must be a better way!

The better way is called repetition, and it is fundamental to all computer programming. In Pascal, we use a FOR loop to repeat statements. But before we try to write a program that will produce a 100×100 box of stars, let's look at a simpler example of a FOR loop.

```
FOR Row := 1 TO 4 DO
        Writeln (Output, '****');
```

This statement directs the computer to print four lines of four stars to the output file. The FOR loop is the second control structure that you have seen in Pascal. (The first was PROCEDURE.)

The FOR loop in Pascal is controlled by a variable that takes values over a range and quits after the desired number of repetitions. When you want to repeat some action a specific number of times, the FOR loop should be used. The specific syntax of the FOR loop is shown in Figure 7.1. The identifier in a FOR loop is called the **control variable** or **index variable,** and it can be of any scalar variable type.

> **Scalar variable:** Any variable that has values that can be counted and listed. Given one value of a scalar variable, it is always possible to calculate the next value in the sequence.

Integers and characters are legal scalar variables. Real numbers aren't scalar variables; it wouldn't make sense to do a FOR loop from 0.0 to 1.5, for example,

```
FOR X := 0.0 TO 1.5 DO        (* this is illegal *)
        Writeln (Output, Sqrt (X));
```

because it is impossible to list all of the values between those two numbers; they can't be ordered and counted. (Though the quantity of numbers on the real number line between 0 and 1.5 is infinite, Pascal can only represent a large but finite set of them. Most versions of Pascal are accurate up to seven significant digits; less than 10^7 distinguishable numbers are accessible between 0.0 and 1.5. The distinguishable numbers are not evenly spaced and certainly not countable by any normal means.) For example, it is easy to write out the alphabet to the output file, assuming Letter is a Char variable.

```
FOR Letter := 'A' TO 'Z' DO Write (Output, Letter);
```

Note, as an aside, that this procedure does not work on some IBM machines, because the entire alphabet in the IBM character set (EBCDIC) is not ordered consecutively. The following loop would work on an IBM machine.

```
FOR Letter := 'A' TO 'F' DO Write (Output, Letter);
```

Figure 7.1: FOR Syntax

```
FOR <identifier> := <Expression> TO <Expression> DO
    <Statement>
```

The first expression in a FOR loop is referred to as the **initial value.** The second expression in a FOR loop is the **final value.** The initial value and the final value can be anything that evaluates to a value of the appropriate type. Constants such as 1, 0, 100 are legal, as are declared constants and variables, such as Row, Size, NumStars. More complicated expressions are also legal.

```
FOR Row := -Size TO Size DO ...
FOR Col := 1 TO Abs (Trunc (Sin (Row/Size*Pi) *Size)) DO ...
```

Expressions with real values are not legal as initial or final values of FOR loops.

The statement of a FOR loop is, as it implies, one statement. The FOR loop only has control over the next statement in the program flow. The statement can be anything, including another FOR loop or a procedure call.

SELF TEST

Write a procedure to calculate and print the value of X^n, where X is a real variable and n is a nonnegative integer.

Compound Statements

As the syntax diagram expressed, the FOR loop only has control over one statement. It can only repeat execution of the next complete statement in the program. At times, however, we want to repeat more than one statement in a FOR loop. This requires the use of a compound statement. A legal **compound statement** is used syntactically as a single statement and is constructed with the BEGIN-END pair of delimiters. Compound statements can be nested inside each other.

```
PROGRAM CompoundStmts (Output);
BEGIN
    BEGIN
        Writeln (Output, 'This is a ');
        Writeln (Output, 'compound statement.')
    END;
    BEGIN
        Writeln (Output, 'This is another one');
        Writeln (Output, 'like the first.')
    END;
    BEGIN
        BEGIN
            Writeln (Output, 'Compound statements can be nested');
            Writeln (Output, 'like this one, or even empty');
            Writeln (Output, 'like the next one.')
        END
    END;
    BEGIN
    END
END.
```

The main program of the preceding example can be said to comprise one compound statement with four statements in it, and each of those statements comprises a compound statement with zero to two statements. The third compound statement has one—not three—statements in it. The statement also happens to be a compound statement with three statements in it. Between each compound statement there is a semicolon, and before the final END, after the last compound statement, no semicolon is needed. The same rules apply within each of the compound statements; no semicolon occurs before the end of the compound statement. The program structure is completely analogous to the following list:

$$((1,2),(3,4),((5,6,7)),()).$$

Each BEGIN is translated into a left parenthesis, each simple statement to the corresponding number, each semicolon into a comma, and each END into a right parenthesis. Notice how the left and right parentheses balance.

If, therefore, you want more than one statement under the control of the FOR loop, you can use a compound statement. The BEGIN-END block separates all of the statements to be repeated, as in the following example, which averages an input file of numbers. Assume that the first number in the file is the number of values to be averaged.

```
PROGRAM AverageNumbers (Input, Output);
(* This procedure reads a list of numbers from an input  *)
(* file and sums and averages them. The first number in  *)
(* the input file is the amount of numbers which are to   *)
(* be averaged.                                           *)
VAR     HowMany,        (* How many numbers, read from input *)
        Num,                    (* each number read *)
        Total,                  (* the total of all numbers  *)
        Cntr : Integer;         (* FOR loop counter *)
        Average : Real;         (* calculated and reported   *)
BEGIN
        Total := 0;
        Read (Input, HowMany);
        FOR Cntr := 1 TO HowMany DO BEGIN
                Read (Input, Num);
                Total := Total + Num;
        END;
        Average := Total / HowMany;
        Writeln (Output, 'The average of ', HowMany:1,
                        ' numbers was ', Average:1:2);
END.
```

Using a clear, consistent indentation scheme really makes this procedure easy to read. It is clear that the FOR loop controls two statements, a Read operation and an assignment. The END matches the FOR loop BEGIN.

This program illustrates a common and often confusing use of the FOR loop, that of calculating a running total. Notice the statements inside the FOR loop:

```
Read (Input, Num);
Total := Total + Num;
```

Every number read from the file (except HowMany) will be added to Total immediately after it is read. Total was first initialized to zero. Pascal doesn't assume that a previously unused variable has a value of zero—the value could be anything. A value must be set or **initialized** before the operation begins. Inside the FOR loop, Total contains the current sum of the numbers that have been read. Notice that only one variable, Num, is needed to read each value, because once it is added to Total, the value is no longer needed, and a new value is read.

How Does It Work?

The syntax and the examples above suggest a clue and a general rule about the workings of the FOR loop. First, however, there are some peculiarities in Pascal's version of definite looping that are worth discussing in greater detail.

The first question people who have programmed before ask is: "How can I specify an increment in Pascal?" The increment is a BASIC element that allows programmers to construct a loop in which, each time through the loop, the control variable changes by some value other than 1. They want to be able to use a statement like:

```
FOR i := 2 TO 10 STEP 2 DO ... (* illegal attempt to count
                                   by twos from 2 to 10  *)
```

Pascal cannot execute this task because the language specifies that the index variable will be increased to the next ordinal value in the type of the variable. If an index has the value 10, the next time through the loop it will be 11—with one exception. To learn about the exception, read on.

The step aspect of a FOR loop isn't essential to the programmer (as converted Pascal programmers soon find out), because the same effect can be simulated through the use of other variables in the FOR loop.

```
FOR Row := 1 TO Size Div 2 DO BEGIN
        Length := 2 * Row; Width := Row * 3 - 2;
        Writeln (Length:3, Width:3, Length * Width:6);
END;
```

Stepping by 2, Length receives all the values it would if it were in a FOR loop from 2 to Size. Likewise, Width is in a simulated loop from 1 to (Size Div 2) * 3 - 2, stepping each time by 3.

Another way to get around this limitation is by using a redundant feature of Pascal, the DOWNTO modification of the FOR loop. The DOWNTO version of the FOR loop is the exception I spoke of. Instead of increasing to the next ordinal value, the ordinal value of the control variable decreases by 1.

```
FOR Countdown := 10 DOWNTO 0 DO
        Writeln (Output,'T-minus ',Countdown:1,' seconds.');
Writeln (Output, 'We have lift-off!');
```

OUTPUT
```
T-minus 10 seconds.
T-minus 9 seconds.
T-minus 8 seconds.
T-minus 7 seconds.
T-minus 6 seconds.
T-minus 5 seconds.
T-minus 4 seconds.
T-minus 3 seconds.
T-minus 2 seconds.
T-minus 1 seconds.
T-minus 0 seconds.
We have lift-off!
```

What do you think Pascal does with the following piece of code?

```
FOR Scores := 100 TO 0 DO Writeln (Scores);
```

There is no syntactical error. To understand what happens, we need to realize how the FOR loop works. The variable is initialized to the initial value and then a test is performed. If the variable has a value less than or equal to the final value, then the loop statement (or compound statement) is executed. At the end of the loop statement, the loop variable increases to the next value, the test is repeated, and the loop is entered if the test condition is again satisfied. Therefore, in the example above, *the test is false at the outset and the loop statement is never executed.* For a DOWNTO loop, the loop's statement is executed if the control variable is greater than or equal to the final value. What will happen with the following piece of code?

```
FOR j := 2 TO 2 DO Write (Output, 'Senseless');
```

The loop variable j will be initialized to a value equal to 2. Since $(2 <= 2)$ is true, the Write statement will be executed. Then j will increase to a value of 3. The statement $(j <= 2)$ is no longer true, so the loop will terminate. The Write statement will be executed only once.

The following example shows another way the experienced programmer tries to simulate the step feature.

```
FOR Odds := 1 TO 100 DO BEGIN
        Writeln (Output, Odds);
        Odds := Odds + 1;
END;
```

This seems as if it would print all odd numbers between 1 and 100. However, Pascal will not accept this because changing or even threatening the value of a FOR loop index is forbidden. Compilers are supposed to find the following conditions, which are said to threaten to change the value of a FOR loop index variable:

1. an assignment to the index (as above),
2. passing the index as a variable parameter,
3. an attempt to give the index a new value through Read or Readln,
4. the use of the index as another FOR loop index inside the first; for example,

```
FOR I := 1 TO 10 DO
        FOR I := 10 DOWNTO 1 DO ...
```

Another way to run into problems is by trying to use a FOR loop control variable after the execution of the loop. After the loop terminates, the value of the control variable is undefined until another assignment is made. Therefore, the following code will produce an error.

```
FOR Cntr   := 0 TO 9 DO
        Write (Output, Cntr );
Writeln (Output, Cntr );    (* this is an error *)
```

However, a FOR loop control variable may be used again or reinitialized.

```
FOR Cntr   := 0 TO 9 DO
        Write (Output, Cntr);
FOR Cntr   := 10 DOWNTO 0 DO
        Write (Output, Cntr);
Cntr   := 24;
```

Once inside a FOR loop, it is impossible to alter the limits of the loop. The values are only calculated once.

```
FOR Cntr := 1 TO Row DO
        Row := Row - 1;
```

The final value of Row is 0, not *Row*/2.

Finally, Standard Pascal requires that all FOR loop indices be local variables in the procedure in which the FOR loop is used. In other words, if a procedure contains the following code:

```
FOR Row := 1 TO 10 DO Write (Output, '*');
```

then Row must be a local variable inside that procedure. Only if a FOR loop is contained in the main program would it be legitimate for the FOR loop index to be a global variable. In this case, defining the FOR loop index as a global variable is mandatory. This rule is not enforced by all compilers, yet some will enforce it. Since it is a characteristic of Standard Pascal, you should be aware of it.

It is common to use constant values as limits of FOR loops. Remember to define constants so that the values of the FOR loop limits have meaningful names that are easy to change if the requirements of the program change. Recall Hard-and-Fast Rule #2: Almost every number occurring in the text of the code other than $-1, 0, 1,$ or 2 should be declared as a constant.

SELF
TEST

How well do you understand the FOR loop?

1. Write a FOR loop that writes the square roots of the first 10 positive integers. How many times is a test performed in the execution of this loop?
2. What would be the result of the following loop?

```
Num := 2; Total := 0;
FOR Num := 1 TO Num + 1 DO
    Total := (Total + 1) * Num;
Write (Output, Total);
```

Nested Repetition

We often want to repeat a series of repeated actions. When we repeat a series of repeated actions, we are using **nested repetition.** Again, using our example of a square, we could execute the following section of code to produce a box of stars on the output file.

```
FOR Row := 1 TO Max DO BEGIN
        FOR Col := 1 TO Max DO
                Write (Output, Image);
        Writeln (Output);
END;
```

This is an example of a **nested loop**, or a loop that appears within another loop. Notice that the Write (Output, Image) statement is executed Max × Max times, while the Writeln (Output) statement is only executed Max times. Perhaps an easier way to see what is happening is to look at the following code:

```
FOR Row := 1 TO Max DO BEGIN
    Write (Output, Row : 2, ':');
    FOR Col := 1 To Max DO
        Write (Output, Col : 2);
    Writeln (Output);
END;
```

Assume that Max = 6.

OUTPUT
```
1:  1 2 3 4 5 6
2:  1 2 3 4 5 6
3:  1 2 3 4 5 6
4:  1 2 3 4 5 6
5:  1 2 3 4 5 6
6:  1 2 3 4 5 6
```

The flow of control for this nested loop structure is like that of a train going around two circular tracks, one inside of another. (See Figure 7.2.) Each loop has a switching house on it, and a little man is sitting at the switch counting the number of times the train makes it past him. The train must enter the inner

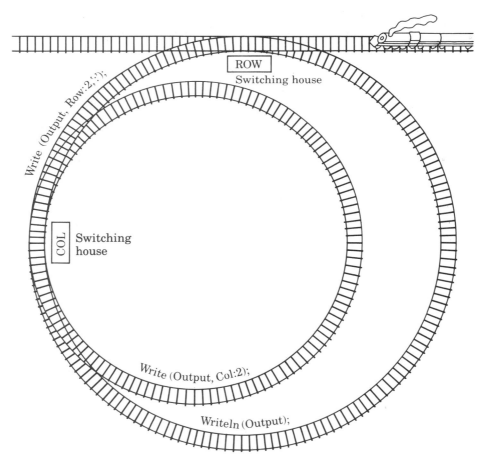

Figure 7.2: Flow of Control for Nested Loops

loop a specified number of times and leave it a specified number of times before it can leave the pair of circles entirely. The specified number of circles is analogous to Max in the program above. When the number of circles reaches Max, then each man allows the train to leave his loop.

Take a look at the following code.

```
FOR i := 1 TO Max DO
        FOR j := 1 TO Max DO
                Write (Output, Image);
        Writeln (Output);
```

What does it do? Think about it a moment before reading on. This example yields a single line with Max × Max images on it, because Writeln is not under the control of either FOR loop and is only executed once. This example shows another way to get into trouble.

```
FOR i := 1 TO Max DO BEGIN
        FOR j := 1 TO Max DO BEGIN
                Write (Output, Image);
        Writeln (Output);
        END;
END;
```

This example yields a series of Max × Max lines in the output file, each with a single image on it. In this case, Writeln is under the control of the inner FOR loop.

Notice that neither example will produce the desired result. These examples emphasize the fact that indentation doesn't matter to the compiler. It takes its cues from the reserved words and syntax structure of the loops, even when the indentation scheme seems to controvert them. These examples also emphasize the importance of correct indentation for understanding a program. Recall the indentation guidelines:

1. Include a blank line between procedures and between the last procedure and the main block.
2. Indent all statements between any BEGIN and its corresponding END at least four spaces.
3. Indent the variables in a variable declaration.

To return to the example that began our discussion of FOR loops: If we want to produce two boxes, each of 100 stars by 100 stars, the program would be:

```
PROGRAM MakeLargeBoxes (Output);
        (*Makes two large squares of images*)

CONST   Size = 100;
        Image = '*';
```

```
PROCEDURE MakeLine;
        (* makes a line of Size images *)
VAR     Col : Integer;
BEGIN
        FOR Col := 1 TO Size DO Write (Output, Image);
        Writeln (Output);
END;    (* Makeline *)

PROCEDURE MakeBox;
        (* makes a box which is Size by Size Images *)
VAR Row : Integer;
BEGIN
        FOR Row := 1 TO Size DO MakeLine;
        Writeln (Output);       (* blank line to separate *)
                                (* adjacent boxes *)
END;    (* MakeBox *)

BEGIN
        MakeBox;        (* -or- FOR NumBoxes := 1 TO 2 DO *)
        MakeBox;        (*                  MakeBox;         *)
END.
```

SELF
TEST
We saw how to make two vertical boxes. Now alter the last program to make two 6 × 6 boxes next to each other on the page. Remember to leave at least one space to separate the boxes.

Iteration

Suppose we want to write out the first twenty perfect squares. You might suggest the following outline.

> Number = 1
> Repeat twenty times:
>   Write the number and then its square
>   Increment number

We can use the FOR loop to get the desired number of repetitions and the FOR loop index variable to make the statement vary from line to line of output.

```
FOR Number := 1 TO 20 DO
        Writeln ('The square of ', Number:2, ' is ',
                Number*Number:3);
```

This is not strict repetition, because each line is slightly different from the others. This is an example of iteration. **Iteration** occurs when the variable of the FOR loop is actually used in the statement(s) under its control. For the next example, recall the MakeBox procedure from the last section. Now our job will be to make a right triangle rather than a box.

OUTPUT
```
*
**
***
****
*****
```

Break down this program into logical chunks. (Hint: Break down the output into logical chunks, and see if a pattern emerges.) Since we know that output is produced a line at a time, that could be how we should break it down.

Repeat 5 times:
Make one row

This algorithm suggests a simple FOR loop.

```
FOR Row := 1 TO Size DO (* Size is a global constant = 5 *)
        MakeRow;
```

If MakeRow will put the correct number of stars on a line, then we have ourselves a working program. How many stars per row do we need? The number of stars per row is a function of the row that we are looking at: Number of Stars = Row.

```
FOR Row := 1 TO Size DO BEGIN
        FOR Col := 1 TO Row DO Write (Output, '*');
                (* this inner loop would be the *)
                (* body of Procedure MakeRow *)
        Writeln (Output);
END;
```

The limit for the inner FOR loop is set as the value of the index of the outer FOR loop. The inner FOR loop is executed five times, each time with a different value as its upper limit.

SELF
TEST

Write a FOR loop that produces a right triangle standing on its point.
```
*****
****
***
**
*
```

Programming Example 7.1

Assignment: Having access to definite repetition affords us the opportunity to deal with more interesting problems. Suppose we want to write a program that reads student ID numbers and homework scores for each student, then writes out the numbers, the scores, and an average of the scores to an output file.

INPUT
```
3
178297359 98 94 95 96 99 95
183345545 74 85 88 59 72 90
182329781 66 84 57 92 60 77
```

The first line indicates the number of students for whom the data is recorded.

Solution: How should we program this?

> **Read the Number of Students**
> **Repeat NumberOfStudents Times:**
> > **Read and write Student Number**
> > **Read and sum the scores**
> > **Calculate and print the Average**
> **Print the Class Average**

Often the input file provides a clue to program breakdown. Look for patterns and elements that are different. In general, different parts of your program will handle different parts of the input file. Now we can translate the pseudocode into Pascal.

```
Readln (Input, NumStudents);
FOR EachStudent := 1 TO NumStudents DO BEGIN
        ReadNWriteNum ( );
        ReadNSumScores ( );
        CalcNPrintAve ( );
END;
PrintClassAverage ( );
```

Again we use the top-down method. We have dealt with the biggest problem, that of reading the input file and producing the correct output file, by breaking it down into subproblems, such as reading and writing one number, or summing scores on a line. The empty pairs of parentheses after each procedure name hold the place of a parameter list. As we write each procedure, the need for parameters will become apparent. The code above will work if each procedure works. We can verify that each procedure works by writing each one correctly. ReadNWriteNum is easy to write and needs no parameters. The only needed variable can be a local variable, since it will be used nowhere else in the program.

```
PROCEDURE ReadNWriteNum;
  (* Writes the StudentNum on the line after
     reading it from Input *)
VAR      StudentNum : Integer;
BEGIN
        Read (Input, StudentNum);
        Write (Output, StudentNum);
END;
```

The next procedure will require a little thought. In order to calculate a running sum, the variable we use for the total, SumScores, must be initialized to zero.

```
PROCEDURE ReadNSumScores (VAR SumScores : Integer);
     (* Reads NumScores scores from the Input file, writes *)
     (* them to an output file, and calculates the total,  *)
     (* which is returned as SumScores.                    *)
     (* Global CONST NumScores = 6                         *)
VAR      Score,      (* The value read on the input line   *)
         ScoreNum    (* The loop index                     *)
         : Integer; (* SumScores is a global variable      *)
BEGIN
        SumScores := 0; (* initialize the running sum      *)
        FOR ScoreNum := 1 TO NumScores DO BEGIN
                Read (Input, Score);
                Write (Output, Score:6);
                SumScores := SumScores + Score;
        END;
END;
```

Without the FOR loop, the last procedure would have been tedious, because it would have required six variables to hold the six scores. If the number of scores were changed, radical changes would need to be made. SumScores cannot be a local variable in this procedure, because its value is used in the next procedure to find the average of the scores. Therefore, it must be a global variable, and by the rules we've been using, a parameter. It is a variable parameter because its value is calculated inside the procedure and used after the procedure executes.

The last two procedures are fairly straightforward as well.

```
PROGRAM AverageScores (Input, Output);
(* This program reads NumStudents lines of ID numbers   *)
(*   and scores from an input file and sums the scores    *)
(*   and writes the ID Num, the scores, and the average   *)
(*   to the output file for each student.                 *)
CONST    NumScores = 6;   (* Six scores per student        *)
VAR      EachStudent,     (* loop counter in Main Program *)
         NumStudents,     (* The amount of input in file  *)
         SumScores        (* The individual's total       *)
             : Integer;
         ClassTot         (* The summed total for all of  *)
            : Real;       (* the students in the class    *)


PROCEDURE ReadNWriteNum;
(* Writes the student number on the line after reading  *)
(*  it from the Input file                              *)
VAR     StudentNum : Integer;
BEGIN
        Read (Input, StudentNum);
        Write (Output, StudentNum);
END;


PROCEDURE ReadNSumScores (VAR SumScores : Integer);
    (* Reads NumScores scores from the Input file, writes *)
    (* them to an output file, and calculates the total,  *)
    (* which is returned as SumScores.                    *)
    (* Global CONST NumScores = 6                         *)
VAR     Score,       (* The value read on the input line   *)
        ScoreNum     (* The loop index                     *)
        : Integer;   (* SumScores is a global variable     *)
BEGIN
        SumScores := 0; (* initialize the running sum     *)
        FOR ScoreNum := 1 TO NumScores DO BEGIN
                Read (Input, Score);
                Write (Output, Score:6);
                SumScores := SumScores + Score;
        END;
        Readln (Input); (* finished with the input line *)
END;


PROCEDURE CalcNPrintAve (SumScores : Integer;
                         VAR ClassTot : Real);
(* Calculates each student's average from the SumScores *)
(* and keeps track of the running class total.          *)
VAR     Average : Real;
```

```
BEGIN
        Average : = SumScores/NumScores;
        Writeln (Output, Average: 8: 2);
        ClassTot : = ClassTot + Average;
END;

PROCEDURE PrintClassAve (ClassTot : Real);
(* Calculates and prints average ClassTot for the class  *)
BEGIN
        Writeln (Output);
        Writeln (Output, 'The class average was',
                ClassTot/NumStudents: 8: 2);
END;

BEGIN    (************ Main Program ************)
        Readln (Input, NumStudents);
        ClassTot : = 0;
        FOR EachStudent : = 1 TO NumStudents DO BEGIN
                ReadNWriteNum;
                ReadNSumScores (SumScores);
                CalcNPrintAve (SumScores, ClassTot);
        END;
        PrintClassAve (ClassTot);
END.     (************ Main Program ************)
```

OUTPUT

178297359	98	94	95	96	99	95	96.17
183345545	74	85	88	59	72	90	78.00
182329781	66	84	57	92	60	77	72.67

The class average was   82.28

More on Character Variables

After programming with numbers for so long, it is often easy to forget that Pascal can handle nonnumeric data like characters that make up names.

Suppose that in the AverageScores program, instead of reading a student number from the input file, the input file were formatted so that the first 16 characters on each line contained the name of each student, padded on the end by spaces. The first score would begin in column 17 on each line. We can write a new procedure, to be inserted into the former program, to read the name and record it, rather than the ten digits, on the output file. To summarize:

PROCEDURE ReadNWriteName:
    Repeat 16 times:
        Read a character from the input file
        Write it on the output file

This translates into a nice, straightforward procedure.

```
PROCEDURE ReadNWriteName;
(* Reads the name, writes it to the output file *)
CONST    NumChars = 16; (* max number of chars in name *)
VAR      Cntr : Integer;
         Ch : Char; (* holds each character as it is read *)
BEGIN
         FOR Cntr := 1 TO NumChars DO BEGIN
                 Read (Input, Ch);
                 Write (Output, Ch);
         END;
END;
```

Because we wrote the last program so well, we can alter it easily by changing ReadNWriteNum to ReadNWriteName in the main program. Now also might be a good time to add a short procedure to produce the heading for the output table.

```
PROCEDURE Heading;
(* Produces table and column headings for the output *)
VAR      Cntr : Integer;
BEGIN
         Writeln (Output, 'Scores and averages',
                         ' for the class.');
         Writeln (Output);
         Write (Output, 'Name',' ':12);
         FOR Cntr := 1 TO NumScores DO
                 Write (Output, Cntr:6);
         Writeln (Output, ' Average');
END;
```

The advantage of a heading that uses a FOR loop to produce the headings is that if the constant NumScores is increased or decreased, the correct heading will still result. The new version of output follows.

OUTPUT Scores and Averages for the Class

Name	1	2	3	4	5	6	Average
Superman	40	40	40	40	40	40	40.00
Lazy Boy	22	19	28	20	14	6	18.17
Mort Snerd	35	39	34	30	36	27	33.50

The class average was 30.56

Programming Example 7.2

Assignment: Write a program that uses FOR loops and produces an hourglass figure of stars on the output file. The figure should look like this:

```
OUTPUT   **********
          ********
           ******
            ****
             **

             **
            ****
           ******
          ********
         **********
```

Solution: We know we could use a sequence of Write statements to solve this, but the assignment specifies the use of FOR loops. We must think of another way. We want to break the problem into simpler and simpler parts, until the solution seems obvious.

You could break this program into the top half and the bottom half. For example, if we wrote the following main program:

```
PROGRAM HourGlass;
(* Produces an hourglass figure to the output file *)

BEGIN
        TopHalf;     (* produces a down-pointing triangle *)
        Writeln (Output);
        BottomHalf; (* produces an up-pointing triangle *)
END;
```

we would know that it would work, given that TopHalf and BottomHalf do what they are supposed to do.

Break down the problem line by line, since output must be written that way. We could outline TopHalf as follows:

PROCEDURE TopHalf:
    Repeat for the number of Rows
        Produce one row
        Writeln

To translate to Pascal:

```
PROCEDURE TopHalf;
(* produces the top half of an hourglass figure *)
VAR    Row : Integer;
BEGIN
       FOR Row := 1 TO Width DIV 2 DO BEGIN
           OneRow;
           Writeln (Output);
       END;
END;
```

Why `Width DIV 2`? What is `Width`? `Width` is going to be a global constant. A quick inspection of the figure will reveal that the number of rows is dependent on the number of stars on the first line of the figure, or `Width`. Therefore, `Width` will be defined to have the value 10, and the `TopHalf` procedure will produce five rows.

Now all we need to do is write PROCEDURE `OneRow`, and the problem will be solved. `TopHalf` will do what it is supposed to do if `OneRow` works. But `OneRow` isn't simple—its effect is different depending on what row is being written. Let's examine the relationship between the number of stars and spaces on a row and the row number.

Row	*Spaces*	*Stars*
1	0	10
2	1	8
3	2	6
4	3	4
5	4	2

From this table, can we deduce a pattern? Is there an algebraic way to express the number of spaces or stars on a given row as a function of the row number? The number of spaces seems easy.

```
Number of spaces := Row - 1
```

The number of stars is only slightly more complicated.

```
Number of stars := 12 - 2*Row
```

Now we might see how PROCEDURE `OneRow` might come together.

PROCEDURE OneRow:
        Repeat (Row − 1) times: Write a space
        Repeat (12 − 2∗Row) times : Write a star

If we put (12 - 2*Row) in terms of the global constant Width, and use the variable Row in our procedure, we can write the Pascal version of OneRow.

```
PROCEDURE OneRow;
(* This procedure produces one row of spaces and stars *)
VAR       Spaces, Stars : Integer;
BEGIN
        FOR Spaces : = 1 TO Row-1 DO Write (Output,' ');
        FOR Stars : = 1 TO Width + 2 - 2 * Row DO
                Write (Output, '*');
END;
```

Where does the variable Row get its value? From PROCEDURE TopHalf. But since the value of Row needs to be used outside of TopHalf, in PROCEDURE OneRow, Row needs to be declared as a value parameter so it can be accessed in PROCEDURE OneRow.

```
PROGRAM HourGlass (Output);
(************************************************************)
(* This program produces an hourglass figure of stars     *)
(* with blank spaces in the background.                    *)
(************************************************************)
CONST   Width = 10;  (* Width across the top of the figure *)

PROCEDURE OneRow (Row : Integer);
(* This procedure produces one row of spaces and stars     *)
VAR       Spaces, Stars : Integer;
BEGIN
        FOR Spaces : = 1 TO Row-1 DO Write (Output,' ');
        FOR Stars : = 1 TO Width-2*(Row-1) DO
                Write (Output, '*');
END;

PROCEDURE TopHalf;
(* produces the top half of an hourglass figure            *)
VAR     Row : Integer; (* value of the current row         *)
BEGIN
        FOR Row : = 1 TO Width DIV 2 DO BEGIN
            OneRow (Row);
            Writeln (Output);
        END;
END;
```

What about BottomHalf? We could write another procedure like OneRow that would put the correct number of spaces and stars on each line, or we could notice that `TopHalf` turned upside down is `BottomHalf`. How do we turn a procedure, which is essentially just a single FOR loop, upside down? Simply, with a DOWNTO.

```
PROCEDURE BottomHalf;
(* produces the bottom half of an hourglass figure        *)
VAR     Row : Integer; (* value of the current row        *)
BEGIN
        FOR Row := Width DIV 2 DOWNTO 1 DO BEGIN
                OneRow (Row);
                Writeln (Output);
        END;
END;
```

If we number the lines in the reverse order when we use `OneLine`, the lines will come out as we expect, shortest to longest instead of vice versa. The complete program solution follows.

```
PROGRAM HourGlass (Output);
(*********************************************************)
(* This program produces one hourglass figure on the    *)
(* output file. The size of the figure is completely     *)
(* determined by the CONST Width. This program uses FOR  *)
(* loops.                                                *)
(*********************************************************)
CONST   Width = 10;     (* Width across top of figure    *)
        Image = '*';    (* declared to be able to vary    *)
                        (*   the image which makes figure *)

PROCEDURE OneRow (Row : Integer);
(* makes one row of spaces and stars                     *)
VAR     Spaces, Stars : Integer; (* FOR loop indices      *)
BEGIN
        FOR Spaces := 1 TO Row-1 DO Write (Output, ' ');
        FOR Stars := 1 TO Width-2*(Row-1) DO
                Write (Output, Image);
END;

PROCEDURE TopHalf;
(* produces the top half of an hourglass figure          *)
VAR     Row : Integer; (* value of the current row        *)
BEGIN
        FOR Row := 1 TO Width DIV 2 DO BEGIN
                OneRow (Row);
                Writeln (Output);
        END;
END;
```

```
PROCEDURE BottomHalf;
(* produces the bottom half of an hourglass figure        *)
VAR     Row : Integer; (* value of the current row          *)
BEGIN
        FOR Row := Width DIV 2 DOWNTO 1 DO BEGIN
                OneRow (Row);
                Writeln (Output);
        END;
END;

BEGIN    (* Main Program *)
        TopHalf;
        Writeln (Output);
        BottomHalf;
END.     (* Main Program *)
```

OUTPUT
```
* * * * * * * * *
 * * * * * * * *
  * * * * * *
   * * * *
    * *

    * *
   * * * *
  * * * * * *
 * * * * * * * *
* * * * * * * * *
```

There is no reason why the rows must be numbered 1 through 5, or 5 down to 1. The FOR loop limits can be anything, even negative. Suppose we numbered the rows from −5 to 5, then took the absolute value of the row number to calculate how many stars and spaces.

Row	Stars	Spaces
−5	10	0
−4	8	1
−3	6	2
⋮		
0	0	5
1	2	4
⋮		
5	10	0

If we figure out the FOR loop limits for Spaces (which writes

(Width DIV 2) - Abs (Row)

spaces) and for Stars (which writes

2 * Abs (Row)

stars), then we can consolidate TopHalf and BottomHalf.

```
PROCEDURE HourGlass;
(* Makes both the top and bottom halves of the hourglass  *)
VAR      Row, TempRow : Integer;
BEGIN
        FOR TempRow := -Width DIV 2 TO Width DIV 2 DO BEGIN
                Row := Abs (TempRow);
                OneRow (Row);
        END;
END;
```

Since this procedure combines the two different FOR loops, there is no need for two different procedures. Verify for yourself that it doesn't produce any stars on the lines that are supposed to remain blank (when Row equals 0).

Programming Example 7.3

Assignment: A common and simple method of calculating depreciation schedules for business investments is called the sum-of-the-years'-digits method. The method yields an easily calculated schedule of depreciation so that any amount can be totally depreciated in any specified number of years. Write a program that reads an amount and a number of years and calculates a depreciation schedule over the full term.

Example: If $10,000 is to be depreciated over three years, then the sum of the years' digits is $1 + 2 + 3 = 6$. The depreciation schedule can be calculated as:

$$\text{Amount in } n\text{th year} = \frac{\text{Total Amount} \times (3 - n + 1)\,\text{years}}{\text{sum of years' digits}}$$

This table summarizes the results.

n	*Amount Depreciated*
1	$5,000
2	$3,333
3	$1,667
Total	$10,000

Solution: Break the problem down into the largest constituent parts.

> Depreciation Schedule:
> > Read the values
> > Calculate sum of the years' digits
> > Calculate and print schedule

Figuring that reading the values will be easy enough to do, let's look at the procedure that calculates the sum of the years' digits.

> SumYearsDigits:
> > Initialize Sum to zero
> > Loop over the years:
> > > Sum : = Sum + Digit

In this algorithm, we can see that Years can be a value parameter into the procedure—its value is used but not changed. However, the Sum is calculated, and must be a variable parameter.

To translate the algorithm into Pascal:

```
PROCEDURE SumYearsDigits (Years : Integer;
                          VAR Sum : Integer);
(* This procedure uses the variable Years to sum the      *)
(* values of the digits between 1 and Years, and returns  *)
(* the value in the parameter Sum.                        *)
VAR     Digit : Integer;      (* FOR loop control variable *)
BEGIN
        Sum : = 0;
        FOR Digit : = 1 TO Years DO
                Sum : = Sum + Digit;
END;
```

It is already clear that Years and Sum will have to be declared globally, since they will both be used outside of this procedure. However, Digit is a local variable, since it is only used inside this procedure. FOR loop control variables must be declared locally.

More pseudocode breaks down the calculation and printing of the values.

CalcNPrintSchedule:
    print headings, Amount, Years
    loop over each year:
        print year and amount depreciated, using Sum
    print total amount depreciated

The three global variables used in this procedure are Amount, Years, and Sum. These values were either read or previously calculated, so they should be value parameters into this procedure.

```
PROCEDURE CalcNPrintSchedule (Amount, Years, Sum : Integer);
(* This procedure calculates the depreciation schedule   *)
(* for a business investment of Amount to be depreciated  *)
(* over Years years. Sum is the sum of the years' digits. *)
VAR     ThisYear : Integer;   (* FOR loop control variable *)
        Total,                (* total depreciated, = amount *)
        DepAmt : Real;   (* one year's depreciation amount *)
BEGIN
        Total : = 0.0;
        Writeln (Output, 'The total amount to be deprec',
              'iated over ',Years:1, ' years is ', Amount:1);
        Writeln (Output);
        Writeln (Output, 'Year':10, 'Depreciation':20);
        Writeln (Output, '----':10, '------------':20);
        FOR ThisYear : = 1 TO Years DO BEGIN
                DepAmt : = Amount * (Years-ThisYear+1)/Sum;
                Writeln (Output, ThisYear:10, DepAmt:20:2);
                Total : = Total + DepAmt;
        END;
        Writeln (Output, 'Total':10, Total:20:2);
END;
```

The main program is short and easy to read.

```
PROGRAM DeprecSchedule (Input, Output);
(**************************************************************
* This program calculates depreciation schedules for       *
* investments using the sum-of-the-years'-digits method.    *
* The program asks the user for an Amount to be depreciated*
* and the number of Years in which to depreciate the        *
* investment. It then produces the payment schedule for     *
* the user. This program was written by Rich Lamb.          *
**************************************************************)
VAR     Years, (* the number of years over which to dep.  *)
        Sum,                 (* sum of the years' digits     *)
        Amount : Integer; (* original amount to dep.        *)
    . . .
```

```
BEGIN    (* Main Program *)
         Readln (Input, Amount, Years);
         SumYearsDigits (Years, Sum);
         CalcNPrintSchedule (Amount, Years, Sum);
END.     (* Main Program *)
```

A sample output file follows, using the input values of 125,000 and 11.

OUTPUT   The total amount to be depreciated over 11 years is 125000

Year	Depreciation
----	------------
1	20833.33
2	18939.39
3	17045.45
4	15151.52
5	13257.58
6	11363.64
7	9469.70
8	7575.76
9	5681.82
10	3787.88
11	1893.94
Total	125000.00

If you add the column of amounts, you will find that it doesn't quite add up correctly; they total 125,000.01. Why not exactly 125,000? The computer has only a limited amount of storage space available to each real number and can usually hold only about seven digits accurately. When 125,000.01 is rounded to seven digits, it becomes 125,000.0. A bank might worry about the **round-off error,** but you shouldn't be too concerned with it, at least not at your current level of programming.

Programming Example 7.4

Assignment: Calculate a grading curve for a set of chemistry midterm examination scores. The curve will be determined from the mean (*M*) and standard deviation (*S*) of the scores. The grades will be awarded as follows:

Score	*Grade*
$> M + 2.0 \times S$	A+
$> M + 1.5 \times S$	A
$> M + 1.0 \times S$	A−
$> M + 0.7 \times S$	B+
$> M + 0.3 \times S$	B
$> M$	B−
$> M - 0.3 \times S$	C+
$> M - 0.7 \times S$	C
$> M - 1.0 \times S$	C−
$> M - 1.3 \times S$	D+
$> M - 1.7 \times S$	D
$> M - 2.0 \times S$	D−
$< M - 2.0 \times S$	F

The mean will be calculated by adding the scores and dividing the sum by the number of scores. The standard deviation will be calculated from the following formulas:

$$\text{standard deviation} = \sqrt{\frac{1}{N} \sum_{i=1}^{N} (\text{Score}_i - M)^2}$$

$$= \sqrt{\frac{1}{N} (\sum_{i=1}^{N} \text{Score}_i^2) - M^2}$$

The input file will contain the scores, one score per line. The first line on the input file will contain the amount of input in the file. Add the values and their squares, calculate the mean and standard deviation, then print a table of the results.

Solution: The problem has some involved calculations, but at least the breakdown of the main program is straightforward.

    Grading Curve:
        Read Amount of input
        Calculate mean
        Calculate standard deviation
        Print curve

The steps that calculate the mean and the standard deviation can't be too far apart. We want to read the scores only once, therefore, we want to do all we need to do with each score before we go on to the next one. Perhaps this algorithm shows a better way.

> Grading Curve:
> > Read the data:
> > > Read Amount of input
> > > Sum values and the squares
> > Calculate the mean
> > Calculate the standard deviation
> > Print the grading curve

Let's now take a closer look at ReadTheData.

> Read Amount of Input
> Loop Amount of input times:
> > Read a value
> > Sum values
> > Sum the values squared

This pseudocode converts almost line by line into Pascal.

```
PROCEDURE ReadTheData;
(* This procedure reads the values and keeps track of the *)
(* running sum and the sum of the squares of the values.  *)
BEGIN
        Sum : = 0;
        SumSqu : = 0;
        Read (Input, AmountOfInput);
        FOR Cntr : = 1 TO AmountOfInput DO BEGIN
                Read (Input, Num);
                Sum : = Sum + Num;
                SumSqu : = SumSqu + Num * Num;
        END;
END;
```

This procedure isn't finished, because no variables have been declared. Obviously, some of the information from ReadTheData will be needed by other procedures. The variable Cntr must be local. Num might as well be local, because we won't need to know the specific numbers outside of this procedure. The others will probably be needed later, so we'll declare them as variable parameters.

```
PROCEDURE ReadTheData (VAR AmountOf Input, Sum,
                                 SumSqu : Integer);
(* This procedure reads the values and keeps track of the *)
(* running sum and the sum of the squares of the values.  *)
VAR     Cntr,               (* FOR loop counter *)
        Num : Integer;      (* the score read from the file *)
```

The next two procedures are mathematically complicated, but not difficult in terms of programming.

```
PROCEDURE CalcMean;
(* This procedure calculates the mean of the scores, given *)
(* the sum of the scores and the amount of input.          *)
BEGIN
        Mean := Sum/AmountOf Input;
END;


PROCEDURE CalcStdDev ;
(* This procedure calculates the standard deviation of the *
* scores, when given the calculated value of the mean and  *
* the sum of the squares of the values and amount of input*)
BEGIN
        StdDev := Sqrt (SumSqu/AmountOf Input - Mean*Mean);
END;
```

But we see that these two procedures aren't finished; they both lack variable or parameter declarations. All the variables that don't change their values can be sent in as value parameters. Mean in CalcMean and StdDev in CalcStdDev are assigned values. After making these distinctions, we can finish these procedures.

```
PROCEDURE CalcMean (Sum, AmountOf Input : Integer;
                                VAR Mean : Real);
(* This procedure calculates the mean of the scores, given *)
(* the sum of the scores and the amount of input.          *)
BEGIN
        Mean := Sum/AmountOf Input;
END;

PROCEDURE CalcStdDev (SumSqu, AmountOf Input : Integer;
                         Mean : Real; VAR StdDev : Real);
(* This procedure calculates the standard deviation of the *)
(* scores, when given the calculated value of the mean and *)
(* the sum of the squares of the values and amount of      *)
(* input.                                                  *)
BEGIN
        StdDev := Sqrt (SumSqu/AmountOf Input - Mean*Mean );
END;
```

The final procedure is simply a series of Writeln statements, using Mean and StdDev as value parameters. Here is the whole program, including global variable declarations.

```
PROGRAM GradingCurve (Input, Output);
(***********************************************************)
(* This program takes an input file of test scores for a  *)
(* class and calculates the mean and standard deviation of*)
(* the scores. It then calculates and prints a grading    *)
(* curve for the class based on the standard deviation and*)
(* the mean. The first number in the file is the number of*)
(* scores to be read.                                     *)
(***********************************************************)


VAR     AmountOfInput,     (* number of scores in the file *)
        Sum,               (* sum of the scores            *)
        SumSqu : Integer; (* sum of the squares of scores *)
        Mean,              (* mean (average) value of scores *)
        StdDev : Real;    (* Standard deviation of scores  *)


PROCEDURE ReadTheData (VAR AmountOfInput, Sum,
                           SumSqu : Integer);
(* This procedure reads the values and keeps track of the *)
(* running sum and the sum of the squares of the values.  *)
VAR     Cntr,              (* FOR loop counter             *)
        Num : Integer;    (* the score read from the file *)
BEGIN
        Sum := 0;
        SumSqu := 0;
        Read (Input, AmountOfInput);
        FOR Cntr := 1 TO AmountOfInput DO BEGIN
                Read (Input, Num);
                Sum := Sum + Num;
                SumSqu := SumSqu + Num * Num;
        END;
END;


PROCEDURE CalcMean (Sum, AmountOfInput : Integer;
                        VAR Mean : Real);
(* This procedure calculates the mean of the scores, given*)
(* the sum of the scores and the amount of input.         *)
BEGIN
        Mean := Sum/AmountOfInput;
END;
```

```
          PROCEDURE CalcStdDev (SumSqu, AmountOfInput : Integer;
                                  Mean : Real; VAR StdDev : Real);
     (* This procedure calculates the standard deviation of the*)
     (* scores, when given the calculated value of the mean and*)
     (* the sum of the squares of the values and amount of     *)
     (* input.                                                 *)
     BEGIN
          StdDev := Sqrt (SumSqu/AmountOfInput - Mean*Mean );
     END;


     PROCEDURE PrintCurve (Mean, StdDev : Real);
     (* This procedure prints out the grading curve, which is *)
     (* solely dependent on the values of the mean and        *)
     (* standard deviation of the set of scores.              *)
     BEGIN
          Writeln (Output, 'Grading Curve for',
                            ' Chemistry Midterm Exam');
          Writeln (Output);
          Writeln (Output, 'If your score was > than':30,
                            ' your grade was:');
          Writeln (Output, Mean + 1.7*StdDev:30:1, 'A+':8);
          Writeln (Output, Mean + 1.3*StdDev:30:1, 'A':7);
          Writeln (Output, Mean + 1*StdDev:30:1, 'A-':8);
          Writeln (Output, Mean + 0.7*StdDev:30:1, 'B+':8);
          Writeln (Output, Mean + 0.3*StdDev:30:1, 'B':7);
          Writeln (Output, Mean :30:1, 'B-':8);
          Writeln (Output, Mean - 0.3*StdDev:30:1, 'C+':8);
          Writeln (Output, Mean - 0.7*StdDev:30:1, 'C':7);
          Writeln (Output, Mean - 1*StdDev:30:1, 'C-':8);
          Writeln (Output, Mean - 1.3*StdDev:30:1, 'D+':8);
          Writeln (Output, Mean - 1.7*StdDev:30:1, 'D':7);
          Writeln (Output, Mean - 2.0*StdDev:30:1, 'D-':8);
          Writeln (Output, 0.0:30:1, 'F':7);
          Writeln (Output);
          Writeln (Output, 'Class Mean:', Mean:1:1,
                    ' Class Standard Deviation:', StdDev:1:1);
     END;


     BEGIN    (* Main Program *)
          ReadTheData (AmountOfInput, Sum, SumSqu);
          CalcMean (Sum, AmountOfInput, Mean);
          CalcStdDev (SumSqu, AmountOfInput, Mean, StdDev);
          PrintCurve (Mean, StdDev);
     END.     (* Main Program *)


OUTPUT  Grading Curve for Chemistry Midterm Exam
```

```
If your score was > than your grade was:
                    101.4        A+
                     95.3        A
                     90.7        A-
                     86.1        B+
                     80.0        B
                     75.4        B-
                     70.8        C+
                     64.7        C
                     60.2        C-
                     55.6        D+
                     49.5        D
                     44.9        D-
                      0.0        F
```

Class Mean: 75.4 Class Standard Deviation: 15.3

Common Errors and Debugging

A common technique used to debug programs is called **tracing execution,** or **hand simulation.** When a program is not working the way you think it should, it is almost never the computer's fault. Something is wrong with the way the code is written. However, sometimes it is difficult to determine what is wrong because the code is complicated. In order to find what may be a fairly small error, it is often necessary to simulate the part of the computer and trace the execution of the program by hand.

It is usually about the time that FOR loops appear on the scene that hand simulation becomes necessary. The necessary tools are a piece of paper, a pencil, some time, and a lot of patience. Consider the following program, which is supposed to produce a pleasing pattern of repeated hourglasses across and down the page. The desired result is a diamond checkerboard. However, the program doesn't work.

```
PROGRAM HourGlasses (Input, Output);
(* This program extends the hourglass figure by repeating *)
(* it across the page and down the page.                  *)

CONST   Image = '*';
        Width = 10;
VAR     NumReps,          (* the FOR loop counter *)
        Reps : Integer;   (* the number given by the user  *)
```

```
        PROCEDURE OneRow (Row : Integer);
        (* makes one row of spaces and stars                  *)
        VAR      Spaces, Stars : Integer;
        BEGIN
                 FOR Spaces := 1 TO (Width DIV 2) - Row DO
                         Write (Output, ' ');
                 FOR Stars := 1 TO 2 * Row DO
                         Write (Output, Image);
                 Writeln (Output);
        END;



        PROCEDURE HourGlass (Reps : Integer);
        (* Makes both the top and bottom halves of the hourglass *)
        VAR     Row,                   (* absolute value of counter   *)
                TempRow,               (* FOR loop counter            *)
                NumReps : Integer;(* Num of repetitions across   *)
        BEGIN
                 FOR TempRow := -Width DIV 2 TO Width DIV 2 DO BEGIN
                         Row := Abs (TempRow);
                         FOR NumReps := 1 TO Reps DO
                                 OneRow (Row);
                 END;
        END;



        BEGIN
                 Write (Output, 'Type the number of repetitions:');
                 Readln (Input, Reps);
                 FOR NumReps := 1 TO Reps DO HourGlass (Reps);
        END.
```

The output is much too long to include in total, but here is a portion.

OUTPUT   Type the number of repetitions: 3
```
*********
*********
*********
 *******
 *******
 *******
  ******
  ******
  . . .
```

Let's compare the output with what we were hoping for.

```
OUTPUT   *****************************
         *******   *******   *******
          ******    ******    ******
           ****      ****      ****
            **        **        **

            **        **        **
           ****      ****      ****
         . . .
```

The erroneous output seems to be giving the right amount of stars, but they are on too many lines. The placement of the Writeln statement in the program is probably in error.

There are several ways we could attempt to fix the problem, having tentatively decided what it is. We could start by moving the Writeln statement, executing the program repeatedly until it works, or we could try to figure out exactly where we want the Writeln. Look at OneRow.

```
PROCEDURE OneRow (Row : Integer);
(* makes one row of spaces and stars                *)
VAR      Spaces, Stars : Integer;
BEGIN
        FOR Spaces := 1 TO (Width DIV 2) - Row DO
                Write (Output, ' ');
        FOR Stars := 1 TO 2 * Row DO
                Write (Output, Image);
        Writeln (Output);
END;
```

Upon the first entry into OneRow, Row has the value 5 because TempRow began with the value −5, and Row is the absolute value of TempRow. A hand simulation will help us trace the execution of this procedure. Draw a box that holds the value of Row, which is currently 5. Beside the box, write *Output* and reproduce the output that the loop would produce. Do the same for each loop. How many spaces does the first loop print? None. How many stars does the second loop print? Ten. That is correct! What happens next? Writeln produces a carriage return on the output line. Incorrect! The simulation shows us that we want to wait until more OneRows have been executed before the Writeln is executed. After taking the Writeln statement out of OneRow, let's look at PROCEDURE HourGlass.

```
PROCEDURE HourGlass (Reps : Integer);
(* Makes both the top and bottom halves of the hourglass  *)
VAR     Row,                   (* absolute value of counter    *)
        TempRow,               (* FOR loop counter             *)
        NumReps : Integer; (* Num of repetitions across    *)
```

```
BEGIN
        FOR TempRow := -Width DIV 2 TO Width DIV 2 DO BEGIN
                Row := Abs (TempRow);
                FOR NumReps := 1 TO Reps DO
                        OneRow (Row);
        END;
END;
```

At the beginning of this loop, TempRow receives the value −5. When the loop completes its execution, it will have the value 5. The compound statement will be repeated eleven times. This is also the number of rows that one complete hourglass figure should contain. Therefore, the misplaced Writeln statement should be placed inside the loop, after the NumReps FOR loop.

```
FOR TempRow := -Width DIV 2 TO Width DIV 2 DO BEGIN
        Row := Abs (TempRow);
        FOR NumReps := 1 TO Reps DO
                OneRow (Row);
        Writeln (Output);
END;
```

Now that we fixed that problem, we can execute the program again to see if it works. This time, the output we get looks interesting, but—again—is not what we wanted.

OUTPUT
```
******************************
 ******** ******** ********
  ******   ******   ******
   ****     ****     ****
    **       **       **
 . . .
```

The problem can be discovered by looking at the second row in the desired figure.

```
 ******** ******** ********
```

In order to create this line, the procedure OneRow must be executed three times with the value of Row at 4. What is the pattern that needs to be repeated three times? Currently, procedure OneRow produces a single space followed by eight stars. If we think of the repeated pattern for this row as a single space followed by eight stars followed by another single space, then this pattern, when repeated three times, will produce the desired line.

```
 ********  ********  ********
```

Here is the rewrite that produces the desired line.

```
PROCEDURE OneRow (Row : Integer);
(* makes one row of spaces and stars *)
VAR      Spaces, Stars : Integer;
BEGIN
        FOR Spaces := 1 TO (Width DIV 2) - Row DO
                Write (Output, ' ');
        FOR Stars := 1 TO 2 * Row DO
                Write (Output, Image);
        FOR Spaces := 1 TO (Width DIV 2) - Row DO
                Write (Output, ' ');
END;
```

Will this work for all the rows? Verify it for yourself by performing a hand simulation with paper and pencil. When Row is 5, no spaces are written at all, which is correct. When Row is 3, two spaces will be written at the beginning and at the end of each repetition of OneRow. The pattern will always stay centered, and each call to OneRow will always produce Width characters, either stars or spaces. Add up the FOR loop limits and prove that to yourself.

It is not usually necessary to trace the entire run of a program to find the mistake. Usually, if you can prove to yourself that part of the code actually works, you can concentrate on looking for the part that doesn't. But it is good to understand enough about the FOR loop, for example, so that you can verify for yourself whether it works or not.

There are a lot of common errors associated with FOR loops. Here are some that were mentioned already along with some others.

1. **Not using a compound statement when needed in a FOR loop.** The FOR loop only controls one statement. Sometimes the indentation scheme can be misleading.

```
FOR Counter := 1 TO AmountOfInput DO
        Read (Input, Num);
        Sum := Sum + Num;
            (* this statement is only executed once*)
Write (Output, Sum);
```

Instead of reading and summing all the values in an input file, this loop will only repeat the Read operation, reading through the input file but not summing the values.

2. **Putting a semicolon after the DO:**

```
FOR Counter := 1 TO AmountOfInput DO;
BEGIN
        Read (Input, Num);
        Sum := Sum + Num;
END;
```

This looks better than the previous example, because the BEGIN-END is included. Yet this is still incorrect, in fact, worse. The semicolon after the DO is not a syntax error, and is difficult to detect. Since a semicolon separates statements, the compiler interprets this FOR loop as a command to repeat the empty statement the number of times represented by AmountOfInput. When the loop is finished, exactly one number is read and summed.

One way to avoid this error is always to put the BEGIN on the same line and after the DO. You will never be tempted to put a semicolon between DO and BEGIN on the same line, as you might if DO ended the line.

```
FOR Counter := 1 TO AmountOfInput DO BEGIN
        Read (Input, Num);
        Sum := Sum + Num;
END;
```

3. **Attempting to change the value of the FOR loop index.** Changing the value of the FOR loop index is illegal. This chapter shows ways to get around it.

4. **Using a global variable as a FOR loop control variable inside a procedure.** The only time a FOR loop control variable can be global is when the FOR loop occurs in the main program.

5. **Attempting to access the value of the control variable of a FOR loop after termination of the loop.** The value is undefined until reinitialized. It is not an error to reuse a FOR loop variable in a separate FOR loop, because the variable is reinitialized.

6. **Accumulating round-off errors in computations.** It is beyond the scope of this book to describe how to avoid or minimize round-off errors. However, you should be able to recognize when round-off errors occur and understand why they occur. When you are working with large real numbers, the computer usually cannot maintain the accuracy of any more than about seven digits. Therefore, in dollar amounts over $100,000, the computer will usually not present the cents accurately.

Hints for BASIC Programmers

As we discuss the concept of looping in Pascal, you should master the concepts more quickly because of your BASIC background. The FOR loop in Pascal is one of the features with the strongest analogue in BASIC, the FOR-NEXT loop. To highlight their similar structure, let's take a look at two programs, each designed to calculate factorials of numbers given as input by the user. Both are interactive programs.

```
60   PRINT "ENTER TOTAL NUMBER DESIRED"
70   INPUT T
80   FOR C=1 TO T
```

```
90   PRINT "ENTER NUMBER TO CALCULATE FACTORIAL"
100  INPUT N
110  LET F = 1
120  FOR S = 1 TO N
130  LET F = F*S
140  NEXT S
150  PRINT N,F
160  NEXT C
200  END
```

```
PROGRAM Factorials (Input, Output);
VAR     AmtOfInput,
        Num, Fact,
        Cntr1, Cntr2 : Integer;
BEGIN
        Writeln (Output, 'Enter the total number of ',
                'factorials desired.');
        Read (Input, AmtOfInput);
        FOR Cntr1 := 1 TO AmtOfInput DO BEGIN
                Writeln (Output, 'Enter a number.');
                Read (Input, Num);
                Fact := 1;
                FOR Cntr2 := 1 TO Num DO
                        Fact := Fact * Cntr2;
                Writeln (Output, Num:2, Fact:12);
        END;
END.
```

Even with very little in the way of documentation, it is easy to see how the Pascal program works, but it would take several lines of comment to make the BASIC program as readable.

What this demonstrates is the similarity between Pascal and BASIC in the looping structures. The FOR-NEXT loop, when combined with the IF and GO TO statements, is a very flexible control structure that can provide a wide range of looping mechanisms. Pascal has several different looping mechanisms, of which the FOR loop is the first. The GO TO construction of BASIC is taboo in Pascal, and you will be warned again when the temptation to use GO TO might be great.

Because of the syntax of the FOR loop, Pascal does not need a reserved word analogous to NEXT. In Pascal, the compound statement allows the FOR loop to control several statements, and it is more versatile than NEXT, as you will learn. The NEXT statement is also limited because it must indicate which FOR loop it terminates—NEXT S, for example. Pascal prevents ambiguity because an END is automatically matched up with the most recent unmatched BEGIN.

When you learned to program in BASIC, you may not have learned to indent, but you can see now how indentation highlights the logic of the Pascal program. Each block of indented code is subordinated to the sheltering control structure.

SUMMARY

The FOR loop is a Pascal control structure that allows definite repetition of a single statement or a **compound statement.** The FOR loop duration is determined by the **initial values** and **final values** given to the control variable. In a normal FOR loop, the loop terminates when the value of the control variable exceeds the final value. When the DOWNTO version of the FOR loop is used, the loop terminates when the value of the control variable is lower than the final value.

FOR loops are nested when one FOR loop controls another within it. This structure can be used to repeat a series of repeated actions. The control variable of a FOR loop can be used in the body of the FOR loop in a process called **iteration.**

New Terms

control variable	initialize	tracing execution
scalar variable	nested repetition	FOR loops
initial value	nested loop	TO
final value	iteration	DOWNTO
compound statement	round-off error	

EXERCISES

1. Exactly what does the following procedure produce on the output file?

```
PROCEDURE X;
VAR      Num, F, S : Integer;
BEGIN
         F := 1; S := 0;
         FOR Num := 1 TO 10 DO BEGIN
                 F := F * Num;
                 S := S + Num;
                 Writeln (Output, F:Num, S:Num);
         END;
END;
```

   Give the variables meaningful names and comment the procedure.

2. Write a program to write out a 20 × 20 multiplication table. Use field widths to keep the table on an 80-character screen.

3. Write a procedure that will write out values in base 3 from 0000 to 2222. (Hint: first solve the problem for 0 to 2, then for 00 to 22, and so forth.)

4. Write a program that only prints one half of the multiplication table.

1	2	3	4	5	6	7	8	9	10
2	4	6	8	10	12	14	16	18	20
3		9	12	15	18	21	24	27	30
4			16	20	24	28	32	36	40
5				25					
6					etc.				

5. Take the problem discussed in Programming Example 7.2 on page 169, and instead of making hourglass figures, use the Sin and the Round or Trunc functions to make circles, ellipses, or some sort of round figures. Begin by writing a program that will produce one figure, then repeat it across and down the page.

6. Write a program that will use an input file containing the following information to produce a pattern of stars and spaces that spells something or outlines an interesting figure.

```
<number of lines of input, not including the first>
<# of pairs on line> <#> <#> <#> <#> ...
<# of pairs on line> <#> <#> <#> <#> ...
<# of pairs on line> <#> <#> <#> <#> ...
...
```

The first number in the file is the number of lines of input. Each of the remaining lines has one number signifying the number of pairs of numbers on the line. After that, the numbers themselves follow, all separated by spaces. The first number specifies how many spaces, and the second specifies how many stars to write on the lines of output. A new line on the input file means a new line on the output file. For example, the line:

```
3 0 5 10 5 10 5
```

would result in the following being sent to the output file.

```
*****          *****          *****
```

Here is a sample input file. It should be obvious when the program works, because the output will be recognizable.

INPUT
```
5
9 0 8 2 8 3 6 3 3 3 2 2 8 3 6 3 7 3 6
13 0 2 11 2 5 2 4 2 2 4 2 2 2 2 8 2 4 2 2 2 4 2 2 2 3 2
12 0 8 5 2 5 8 2 2 1 2 1 2 2 6 4 2 4 2 2 7 3 2 4 2
13 6 2 5 2 5 2 4 2 2 2 2 4 2 2 8 2 4 2 2 2 2 2 4 2 3 2
11 0 8 5 2 5 2 4 2 2 2 3 3 2 2 9 6 3 2 4 2 2 6
```

7. Write a program to produce a pyramid of blocks, with the width of the block being declared a constant, and the height being half of the width.

```
                         ******
                         ******
                         ******
                  ******************
                 ******************
                ******************
          ******************************
         ******************************
        ******************************
   **********************************************
  **********************************************
 **********************************************
```

Here, for example, width = 6 and the height of each brick is three lines.

8. The infinite series

$$\sum_{k=0}^{\infty} \frac{1}{k!}$$

converges to e. Write a program to calculate and print the first ten partial sums of this series.

9. Write a program to calculate the first 15 triangle numbers, where the nth triangle number is $1 + 2 + 3 + \ldots + n$. The output should look like this:

OUTPUT
```
 1 = 1
 3 = 1 + 2
 6 = 1 + 2 + 3
10 = 1 + 2 + 3 + 4
. . .
```

Try to get the last line of output on one screen line (80 characters maximum).

10. Write a program to calculate interest on a time deposit. Input the starting amount (A), the yearly interest rate (i), the number of times per year the interest is compounded (n), and the term in years of the bond. Recall that

$$M = M + \frac{iM}{n}$$

for each period the bond is held.

11. Write a procedure that determines both roots of the quadratic equation. Assume that both roots are real. The procedure should take as input a, b, and c and return $x1$ and $x2$.

12. Write a procedure to compute the value of π by calculating the area of one quarter of a circle with a radius of 2 inches. $(A = \pi r^2 = 4\pi$, therefore $\pi = 1/4A$.) Use the trapezoid approximation scheme.

$$A = \sum_{i=1}^{100} dA$$

$$dA = dx \cdot \left(\frac{Y_1 + Y_2}{2}\right)$$

$$Y_1 = \sqrt{R^2 - X^2}$$

$$Y_2 = \sqrt{R^2 - (X + dX)^2}$$

$$X_i = R - idx$$

$$dX = \frac{R}{100}$$

Hint: Declare a function that takes two arguments, the radius and the x coordinate, and returns the Y value, and use that to find Y_1 and Y_2. Try to make your procedure clear and efficient, since the calculations will be done many times.

13. The harmonic series

$$\frac{1}{1} + \frac{1}{2} + \frac{1}{3} + \frac{1}{4} + \frac{1}{5} + \cdots$$

diverges, in that it will grow infinitely large given an infinite number of terms. To show how quickly the sum grows, sum the first 10, 100, and 1,000 terms, and print the results.

14. The harmonic series diverges, while the alternating harmonic series converges. Estimate the value of the sum of the alternating series by summing the first 10, 100, and 1,000 terms and printing the results.

$$\frac{1}{e} = \frac{1}{2} - \frac{1}{3} + \frac{1}{4} - \frac{1}{5} + \cdots + \frac{1}{100}$$

15. In the Fibonacci sequence, 1, 1, 2, 3, 5, 8, . . . , any term is calculated as the sum of the previous two terms, where the first two terms are both 1. Print out the first 20 Fibonacci numbers.

16. Easter Sunday is always the first Sunday after the first full moon after the vernal equinox. This date is determined by the motions of the earth and moon and so can be defined mathematically. To calculate the date in a given year:

$$A = Year \text{ MOD } 19$$
$$B = Year \text{ MOD } 4$$
$$C = Year \text{ MOD } 7$$
$$D = (19A + 24) \text{ MOD } 30$$
$$E = (2B + 4C + 6D + 5) \text{ MOD } 7$$

The date for Easter Sunday is March $(22 + D + E)$. If the quantity in parentheses is higher than 31, then the date is in April. Write a program that prints the dates of Easter Sunday from 1985 to the year 2000.

17. You have been asked to process some of the information for the census in your town. Write a program that will read an input file with data organized by household. The first number on the file will contain the number of households for which data was obtained. Using one line per household, the data for each household will be:

```
<# of females eligible to vote><# of males eligible to vote>
<# of girls><# of boys>
```

Make a report that details the total population and its breakdown by sex and the total population of eligible voters and its breakdown by sex.

CONDITIONAL EXECUTION

Suppose we have an input file of numbers and want to test each number to determine if it is a perfect square. The required program seems simple enough, but it cannot be written using only the statements in Pascal that we already have discussed. In fact, up to this point we can only write programs that do the same things to different sets of data. But we cannot write a program that carries out different actions depending on the data it receives. This capability is called conditional execution.

> **Conditional execution:** The selection of one action among two or more actions based on the existence of certain conditions.

IF-THEN-ELSE

In order to implement conditional execution, we use the IF statement. The syntax of the IF statement is shown in Figure 8.1. The ELSE clause can be left off if it is not needed. ELSE will be executed only if the test fails. If the test is true, the THEN statement is executed. With both statements, a procedure call or a compound statement is syntactically equivalent to the single statement, so the branches can be as long as desired. (See Figure 8.2.)

Figure 8.1: The IF Statement

```
IF < test >
        THEN < statement >
        ELSE < statement >;
```

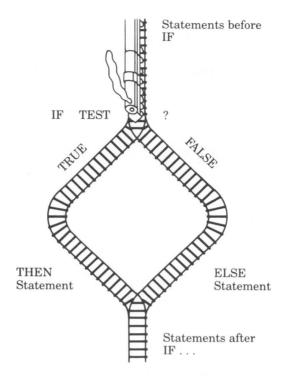

Statements before
IF

IF   TEST   ?

TRUE   FALSE

THEN   ELSE
Statement   Statement

Statements after
IF . . .

Figure 8.2: How the IF Works

For example, to determine if a number is a perfect square in the problem above, we could write the following code.

```
Read (Input, Num);
SquareRoot := Round (Sqrt (Num));
IF (Num = SquareRoot * SquareRoot)
        THEN Writeln (Output, Num:1, ' is the square of ',
                            SquareRoot:1)
        ELSE Writeln (Output, Num:1, ' is not a perfect ',
                            'square. ');
```

The test is (Num = SquareRoot * SquareRoot). Notice that this expression is not an assignment, and it doesn't use the assignment operator, :=. Instead, it is a boolean test, and it is either true, if Num really is equal to

```
SquareRoot * SquareRoot,
```

or false otherwise.

> **Boolean expression:** An expression that evaluates to one of the two boolean values, true and false.

There are six relational operators with which boolean tests can be made, and Table 8.1 lists the Pascal versions. One very important feature of the IF-THEN-ELSE statement is that there is no semicolon between the THEN statement and the ELSE. If a semicolon is placed after the THEN statement, the compiler thinks that the IF-THEN statement is complete and that there is no optional ELSE clause. When it comes across the ELSE, it doesn't understand why it is there and complains to the programmer.

```
Readln (Input, Num);
IF (Num >= 0)
        THEN Writeln (Output, Num, Sqrt (Num));
                    (* this semicolon produces an error *)
        ELSE Writeln (Output, Num, ' has no real',
                            ' square root.');
```

This error is sometimes difficult to catch, especially when a compound statement is used. Suppose, for example, we have a game program that pits the user against the computer. A procedure evaluates the final scores, determines who is the winner, and keeps track of the user's win-loss record.

```
PROCEDURE ReportWinner (UserScore, CompScore : Integer;
                VAR UserWins, UserLosses : Integer);
(* This procedure reports the outcome of the game to the   *)
(* user at the terminal, and keeps track of the user's      *)
(* Win-Loss record.                                          *)
BEGIN
        IF (UserScore > CompScore)
            THEN BEGIN
                Writeln (Output, 'You won!');
                UserWins := UserWins + 1;
            END (* it is tempting to want to put a ';' here *)
            ELSE BEGIN
                Writeln (Output, 'I won!');
                UserLosses := UserLosses + 1;
            END;
END;
```

One way to write your IF-THEN-ELSE statements so you aren't tempted to misplace semicolons is to put the BEGIN at the end of the first line and the END at the beginning of the ELSE line.

Table 8.1. Relational Operators

Operator	Meaning
=	Equal to
>	Greater than
<	Less than
>=	Greater than or equal to
<=	Less than or equal to
<>	Not equal to

```
PROCEDURE ReportWinner (UserScore, CompScore : Integer;
                  VAR UserWins, UserLosses : Integer);
(* This procedure reports the outcome of the game to the  *)
(* user at the terminal, and keeps track of the user's    *)
(* Win-Loss record.                                        *)
BEGIN
        IF (UserScore > CompScore) THEN BEGIN
                Writeln (Output, 'You won! ');
                UserWins := UserWins + 1;
        END ELSE BEGIN
                Writeln (Output, 'I won! ');
                UserLosses := UserLosses + 1;
        END;
END;
```

With the END ELSE BEGIN all on one line, the Pascal compiler won't complain about your style, and neither will anyone who is working with your program—as long as you are consistent. The procedure also looks better; it is more compact and the structure of the IF statement is clearer than in the first method.

There is a potential problem when using IF statements with real numbers. Because of the limitations inherent in computer calculations, most real numbers cannot be expressed precisely within the computer. The actual value calculated as the square root of 25 may be slightly more or less than exactly 5.0000000. . . . In this case, it is virtually impossible to check if two real numbers are equal in the way that it is possible with integers.

```
IF (Sqrt (X) = Y)    (* this probably won't work *)
        THEN Writeln (Output, X, ' is the square of', Y);
```

To compare two real numbers, we must add a little mathematical sophistication. Perhaps we say that we will be satisfied if the difference between the numbers is less than 10^{-4}. If that is true, then we can use the following test.

```
CONST    Epsilon = 1E-4;
. . .

        IF (Abs (Sqrt (X) - Y) < Epsilon)
            THEN Writeln (Output, X, ' is the square of', Y);
```

SELF
TEST
Write a procedure that asks the user's sex and height and predicts the value of the user's weight. Use any prediction scheme you like, but differentiate between males and females. It doesn't need to be accurate.

Nesting

It is also possible to nest IF statements to combine them for more complicated conditional executions. For example, in PROCEDURE ReportWinner if UserScore equals CompScore, then the procedure declares that the computer won. That may reflect the computer's preference, but, in order to be fair, a tie should really be reported. Let's restructure the procedure.

```
PROCEDURE ReportWinner (UserScore, CompScore : Integer;
                        VAR UserWins, UserLosses, Ties : Integer);
(* This procedure reports the outcome of the game to the   *)
(* user at the terminal, and keeps track of the user's     *)
(* Win-Loss-Tie record.                                     *)
BEGIN
        IF (UserScore > CompScore) THEN BEGIN
                Writeln (Output, 'You won!');
                UserWins := UserWins + 1;
        END ELSE IF (UserScore < CompScore) THEN BEGIN
                Writeln (Output, 'I won!');
                UserLosses := UserLosses + 1;
        END ELSE BEGIN    (* UserScore = CompScore *)
                Writeln (Output, 'We tied...');
                Ties := Ties + 1;
        END;
END;
```

Perhaps another way to write this to make the nested structure even more obvious is to use compound statements even where they are not necessary. One style rule you could implement is to always use compound statements for the THEN and ELSE clauses of IF-THEN-ELSE statements. If the program needs restructuring and statements are added throughout the IF statement, no additional BEGIN-END pairs will be needed nor will any be forgotten—they are already included. For example:

```
PROCEDURE ReportWinner (UserScore, CompScore : Integer;
                 VAR UserWins, UserLosses, Ties : Integer);
(* This procedure reports the outcome of the game to the    *)
(* user at the terminal, and keeps track of the user's      *)
(* Win-Loss-Tie record.                                      *)
BEGIN
        IF (UserScore > CompScore) THEN BEGIN
                Writeln (Output, 'You won!');
                UserWins := UserWins + 1;
        END ELSE BEGIN
                IF (UserScore < CompScore) THEN BEGIN
                        Writeln (Output, 'I won!');
                        UserLosses := UserLosses + 1;
                END ELSE BEGIN   (* UserScore = CompScore  *)
                        Writeln (Output, 'We tied...');
                        Ties := Ties + 1;
                END;
        END;
END;
```

Nesting is useful and often necessary when a decision has several different possible outcomes or when there are several different contingencies that would result in the same outcome. One problem emerges when nesting IF statements that does not apply to nesting compound statements or FOR loops. In a nested IF statement, it is not always obvious to which IF statement a given ELSE clause belongs. For example, consider the case of a movie ticket salesperson making a decision about whether or not to admit a person to the movie. The information needed to make the decision is:

1. the rating of the movie, G, PG, R, or X;
2. the age of the customer;
3. whether or not the customer is accompanied by a parent.

The rules the ticket salesperson must abide by are the following:

1. Anyone may purchase a ticket for a G or PG movie.
2. Persons 17 or older may purchase a ticket to any movie.
3. Those under 17 will be admitted to R-rated movies only with a parent, and never to X-rated movies.

A simple Pascal function takes these values as input and returns either 'Y' or 'N', for *yes* or *no*.

```
FUNCTION MoviePatrol (Rating, Parent : Char;
                      Age : Integer) : Char;

(* This function takes the values of the movie's rating,  *)
(* (where G, P, R and X are the only values of the rating)*)
(* the age of the person trying to buy a ticket, and      *)
(* whether or not the person is accompanied by a parent,  *)
(* and returns a 'Y' (Yes) value if the person should be  *)
(* allowed to buy a ticket.                               *)

BEGIN



    IF (Age >= 17)
        THEN MoviePatrol := 'Y'
        ELSE IF (Rating = 'X')
            THEN MoviePatrol := 'N'
            ELSE IF (Rating = 'R')
                THEN IF (Parent = 'Y')
                    THEN MoviePatrol := 'Y'
                    ELSE MoviePatrol := 'N'
                ELSE MoviePatrol := 'Y';
END;
```

Notice that the final two lines in the procedure are ELSE clauses. From the indentation and the intent of the procedure, it is easy to see how they match up to the IF statements that precede them. The first of the two ELSE clauses belongs to IF (Parent = 'Y'), the nearest IF statement to that ELSE clause. The last ELSE in the block matches up with the IF (Rating = 'R'), and it specifies the action to be taken if the movie is neither X-rated nor R-rated, in which case the function always returns 'Y'. Notice, too, that there is only one semicolon in the entire block of code, at the end of the final ELSE clause. If a semicolon occurred anywhere else in the procedure, then an error would result. For example:

```
BEGIN

        IF  (Age  >=  17)
            THEN MoviePatrol  : =  'Y'
            ELSE  IF  (Rating  =  'X')
                THEN  MoviePatrol  : =  'N'
                ELSE  IF  (Rating  =  'R')
                    THEN  IF  (Parent  =  'Y')
(* error on this line *)  THEN  MoviePatrol  : =  'Y';
                            ELSE  MoviePatrol  : =  'N'
                        ELSE  MoviePatrol  : =  'Y';
END;
```

In this case, the semicolon ends the IF (Parent = 'Y') statement, and the ELSE is left dangling.

Dangling ELSE: The ELSE clause left over after an IF statement has been prematurely terminated by a semicolon.

The compiler will not understand what to do with the ELSE, and an error will result.

The problem of the mismatched ELSE statement can be better seen by restructuring the previous procedure.

```
BEGIN     (* incorrect *)
        MoviePatrol  : =  'N'
        IF  (Age  >=  17)
            THEN  MoviePatrol  : =  'Y'
            ELSE  IF  (Rating  =  'R')
                THEN  IF  (Parent  =  'Y')
                    THEN  MoviePatrol  : =  'Y'
                ELSE  IF  (Rating  <>  'X')
                    THEN  MoviePatrol  : =  'Y';
END;  (* incorrect *)
```

The logic and the indentation scheme would indicate that this block is the same as the previous block. However, the indentation scheme has no influence over the Pascal compiler. It understands the code by reading reserved words and semicolons. This block of code allows kids to enter the theater *only if the movie is R-rated*. Obviously, this subtle error can cause serious problems in large programs and is difficult to detect. A correct version of this structure would require the use of a compound statement to indicate to the computer that the last IF statement is supposed to end before the final ELSE clause.

```
BEGIN    (* Correct *)
        MoviePatrol := 'N'
        IF (Age >= 17)
            THEN MoviePatrol := 'Y'
            ELSE IF (Rating = 'R')
                THEN IF (Parent = 'Y') THEN BEGIN
                    MoviePatrol := 'Y';
                END ELSE IF (Rating <>'X')
                    THEN MoviePatrol := 'Y';
END;     (* Correct *)
```

This procedure could be combined with the following main program, which is used to collect the data needed to make a decision.

```
BEGIN    (* Main Program *)
        Writeln (Output, 'What is the movie''s rating?');
        Readln (Input, Rating);
        Writeln (Output, 'How old is the purchaser?');
        Readln (Input, Age);
        IF (Age < XLimit) THEN BEGIN (* XLimit = 17 *)
            Writeln (Output, 'Is the purchaser accompanied',
                             ' by a parent? (Y or N)');
            Readln (Input, Parent);
        END;
        IF (MoviePatrol (Rating, Parent, Age) = 'Y')
            THEN Writeln (Output, 'Admission granted')
            ELSE Writeln (Output, 'Admission denied');
END.     (* Main Program *)
```

Here are a couple of sample interactions that use the previous program.

INTERACTIVE SESSION

```
What is the movie's rating?
R
How old is the purchaser?
16
```

```
Is the purchaser accompanied by a parent? (Y or N)
N
Admission denied

What is the movie's rating?
G
How old is the purchaser?
25
Admission granted
```

With the addition of IF statements, it is often easy to write blocks of code that are long and complicated. Remember Hard-and-Fast Rule #4: Make sure that all of your procedures and main programs have fewer than 15 lines.

SELF
TEST

Write program fragments that:

1. ask for the user's age and print out whether or not she or he is old enough to attend school, drive, vote, or drink alchoholic beverages.
2. ask for three numbers from the terminal and print out the largest of the three.
3. ask the user to type the current date, and verify that it is a legal date.

Assertions (Optional)

Examine MoviePatrol again. If you were to look at it for the first time, what would you have to do to verify for yourself that it does what it is designed to do? You would need to go through a logical reasoning process to determine that MoviePatrol would only be assigned the value of 'Y' if (1) the patron is 17 or older, or (2) the movie is G or PG, or (3) the movie is R-rated, the patron is 16 or younger, and the patron is accompanied by a parent. As in many cases where any of several sets of conditions may be met, ensuring the existence of one set of conditions can be tricky. One way we can formalize this process is through the use of assertions. An **assertion** is a statement, occurring in the form of a comment, which the programmer believes to be true in all cases at the point where the assertion occurs. For example, suppose that the previous definition of MoviePatrol were commented as follows:

```
FUNCTION MoviePatrol (Rating, Parent : Char;
                      Age : Integer) : Char;
```

```
(* This function takes the parameters and returns 'Y' if  *)
(* the patron should be allowed to buy a ticket to the    *)
(* movie. The conditions which must exist for the patron  *)
(* to be allowed to buy a ticket are                      *)
(* 1) the patron is 17 or older, OR                       *)
(* 2) the movie is rated G or PG, OR                      *)
(* 3) the  movie is rated R, the patron is 16 or younger, *)
(*     and the patron is accompanied by his or her parent. *)
BEGIN
                    (* Assume valid input:               *)
                    (* Parent = 'Y' or 'N', Age >= 0     *)
                    (* Rating = 'G', 'P', 'R', or 'X'    *)
        MoviePatrol := 'N';
        IF (Age >= 17)
            THEN                      (* condition 1 satisfied *)
                MoviePatrol := 'Y'
            ELSE IF (Rating = 'R')
                THEN                  (* Patron < 17, Rating = R *)
                    IF (Parent = 'Y') THEN BEGIN
                                  (* condition 3 satisfied *)
                        MoviePatrol := 'Y';
                END ELSE              (* Rating <> 'R'          *)
                    IF (Rating <> 'X') THEN
                                  (* Rating = G or PG       *)
                                  (* condition 2 satisfied *)
                        MoviePatrol := 'Y';
END; (* MoviePatrol = 'N' °°unless condition 1, 2, or 3 was *)
     (* satisfied                                            *)
```

This seems like a tedious process for such a simple function. However, it illustrates the precision of assertions and the power they have in proving that a piece of code works or in helping you to find the logical flaw. As I wrote the assertions, I realized that, in order to satisfy condition (2) after the test (Rating <> 'X'), I needed to assume that the only values of Rating were 'G', 'P', 'R', and 'X'. I could not assume, simply because the rating was not 'R' or 'X', that it must necessarily be 'G' or 'P'. This insight might cause me to return to the calling environment of this function to verify that the rating given will always be one of those four choices. Otherwise, errors could be introduced into the operation of this function.

In the commented version of this function, there were two different types of assertions. The three lines of comments after the BEGIN statement tell the reader what type of input the function is expecting and are called precondition assertions. **Precondition assertions** indicate the conditions that must be true for the code to work properly in all cases. The code does nothing to ensure that the preconditions are in fact true; it is merely assumed that they are. The second type of assertions, **postcondition assertions,** indicate what the programmer thinks will always be true on the basis of the logic of the code itself. When the comment reports that the first condition has been satisfied, the logic of the boolean test indicates that, at this point in the flow of control of the program, the requirements of the first condition—that the user be 17 or older—are fully met.

You aren't likely to begin to comment your code in the manner described above; it would be too wordy. However, it is good to think in terms of assertions, and to comment procedures using the ideas, if not the words, discussed above. A procedure comment should contain assumptions you are making about the data coming into the procedure and assumptions about the input file being used. The comment should also indicate what is being produced, the postconditions that will be true when the procedure is finished.

Boolean Operators and Expressions

Certain operations may require multiple tests before they can be or should be executed by the program. Tests can be combined by the use of nested IF statements, as we saw in the last section. However, that can sometimes become rather awkward.

```
IF  (a>b)
    THEN IF  (b>c)
        THEN IF  (c>d)
            THEN Writeln (a,' is the greatest.');
```

The coding above shows a legal use of IF statements, but not necessarily the best use. Tests can also be combined into boolean expressions such as:

```
IF  (a>b)  AND  (b>c)  AND  (c>d)
        THEN Writeln (a, ' is the greatest.');
```

AND, OR, and NOT are the three **boolean operators** that Pascal understands. AND and OR are binary infix operators and are similar to arithmetic operators. They take boolean expressions and evaluate them using boolean arithmetic. When two tests are joined by an AND, both tests must be true for the result to be true. If either test is false, then the result of the expression is false.

```
(x>=6)  AND  (x<=10)
```

is true if and only if x is in the range between 6 and 10, inclusive. When two tests are joined by an OR, both tests must be false for the result to be false. If either (or both) of the tests is true, then the result will be true.

```
(x>0)  OR  (x<0)
```

will be true in all cases except if x is 0. On the other hand,

```
(x>0)  AND  (x<0)
```

will never be true, because for no value of x would both conditions be satisfied.

The third boolean operator, NOT, is a unary prefix operator. A **unary prefix operator** affects only one expression or value. Unlike AND and OR, NOT changes the truth value of the expression that follows it. Hence, NOT is a **prefix operator** because the value follows the operator. (**Infix operators** are found between the first and second arguments.) If an expression is true, then a NOT makes the expression false.

$$\text{NOT } (X > 0) = (X <= 0)$$
$$\text{NOT } (X = 0) = (X <> 0)$$
$$\text{NOT } ((Ch = 'Y') \text{ OR } (Ch = 'y')) = ((Ch<>'Y') \text{ AND } (Ch<>'y'))$$

Although they are not functions, AND, OR, and NOT are like boolean functions that require either one or two boolean values as their arguments, but they are written in either infix or prefix notation. Pascal functions require **postfix notation,** with parameters in parentheses after the function name.

As with arithmetic operators, rules of precedence govern boolean and relational operators. Parentheses help to avoid confusion at all times, and expressions inside parentheses are always evaluated first. The complete order of precedence is found in Table 8.2.

One unexpected error could occur because of the order of precedence. If you write the following statement, you will get an error complaint from the compiler.

```
IF Rating = 'R' AND Age < 17 AND Parent = 'Y' THEN
      MoviePatrol := 'Y';
```

The error occurs because AND is of greater precedence than any of the relational operators, so the compiler attempts to understand the test as:

```
IF Rating = ('R' AND Age) < (17 AND Parent) = 'Y' THEN
      MoviePatrol := 'Y';
```

The problem here is that neither 'R' nor Age are boolean-valued expressions or variables. The compiler complains because AND is only defined using boolean expressions. This can be remedied simply by the use of parentheses.

```
IF (Rating = 'R') AND (Age < 17) AND (Parent = 'Y') THEN
      MoviePatrol := 'Y';
```

Table 8.2: Order of Precedence of Operators

NOT, - (negation)
*, /, DIV, MOD, AND
+, -, OR
=, <>, <, >, <=, >=, IN

The moral of the story is that it is better to use more sets of parentheses than you might think are absolutely necessary. If you aren't sure about the rules of precedence, you can enforce your own with the consistent use of parentheses.

We now know enough to improve upon some of the things we've already done. When we wrote FUNCTION Capitalize on page 142, we assumed that it would receive a small letter and return a capital. Suppose, however, that we want to capitalize all MaxChar characters in a name, some of which may be spaces, periods, and other punctuation, and some of which may already be capitalized. Let's rewrite the function so that it only capitalizes the letter if it is lowercase:

```
FUNCTION Cap (Ch : Char) : Char;
(* capitalizes small letters but leaves any other
   characters unchanged. *)
BEGIN
        IF (Ch >= 'a') AND (Ch <= 'z')
                THEN Cap := Chr (Ord (Ch) + Ord ('A')
                               - Ord ('a'))
                ELSE Cap := Ch;
END;


PROCEDURE ReadNWriteName;
(* Reads MaxChar characters and writes them out in
   all capital letters.                          *)
VAR    I : Integer;
       Ch : Char;
BEGIN
       FOR I := 1 TO MaxChars DO BEGIN
               Read (Input, Ch);
               Write (Output, Cap (Ch));
       END;
END;
```

One often surprising fact about boolean expressions is that all of the tests are evaluated, even if the result is determined from the first expression. For example, in the case of a test of the form:

```
IF <expression 1> OR <expression 2>
    THEN ...
```

the truth of the entire test is assured if <expression 1> evaluates as true. However, the second expression will be evaluated anyway. The same is true even if the first expression of an AND test is false. The falsity of the entire test is certain, but the second test will be performed anyway. This can cause problems when writing code like the following:

```
IF (X > 0) AND (Y / X < 1)
        THEN ...
```

In this case, when X equals 0, the first test evaluates as false, but the second test is evaluated anyway. Trying to divide Y by zero causes an arithmetic overflow error that terminates execution of the program. In order to avoid this, it would be necessary to nest the two tests in two IF statements.

```
IF  (X  >  0)  THEN
        IF  (Y  /  X  <  1)  THEN  . . .
```

SELF
TEST

Evaluate the following boolean expressions, given that A equals 12 and B equals 6.

1. (NOT (A > 10) OR (B < A DIV 2))
2. (A > B) AND (B * A = A * A DIV 2)
   AND (B < A - B)
3. (A > 0) AND (A < 0)
4. (A > 0) OR (A < 0)
5. (A > B) AND (B > 0) AND
   ((A < B) OR (B < 0) OR (A > B))

Boolean Variables and Constants

It was mentioned early in the book that there are four kinds of simple variable types in Pascal: integer, real, char, and boolean. So far we haven't seen examples of boolean variables or their use. We can store the boolean constants TRUE and FALSE in variables that we can use later in a boolean test. For example:

```
VAR     Safe,
        ReadyToQuit : Boolean;
BEGIN
        Safe  : =  TRUE;
        ReadyToQuit  : =  FALSE;
   . . .
```

Boolean variables are also convenient for clarifying the meaning of tests and for storing the results of boolean tests. Look again at the MoviePatrol segment on page 202. Rather than declaring Parent as a character variable that takes on the values 'Y' for "yes, the child is with a parent," and 'N', for "no, the child is not with a parent," why not declare Parent as a boolean variable that takes on the values true and false, respectively?

```
VAR       Ans : Char;
          Parent : Boolean;
BEGIN
 . . .

          Writeln (Output, 'Is the purchaser accompanied',
                          ' by a parent?(Y or N)');
          Readln (Input, Ans);
          Parent := (Ans = 'Y') OR (Ans = 'y');
```

To present another example, suppose that we wanted to analyze a number to determine whether it is prime, perfect, or neither. A prime number is one whose only exact divisors are 1 and itself. For example, 2, 3, 5, 7, 11, 13, and 17 are prime. A perfect number, on the other hand, is one whose exact divisors, excepting itself, sum to equal the number. For example, 6 has three exact divisors, not including itself: 1, 2, and 3. And, $6 = 1 + 2 + 3$. Likewise, $28 = 1 + 2 + 4 + 7 + 14$.

We'll say our analysis will take a number as an input parameter and will determine whether it is in the correct range (>1). If so, the procedure will check to see if it is prime or perfect. If it is neither, we will label it *boring*. Before we write an outline of what we want to do, we should observe a couple of facts:

1. When we find one divisor, we have found two (unless the divisor is the square root of the number). For example, once we know that 4 divides evenly into 28, we also know that $28 \div 4$, or 7, divides evenly. Therefore, we only need to check divisors up to the square root of the number.
2. If we find just one even divisor, then we know the number cannot be prime. If there is a divisor, we will find it by the time we check the square root of the number.

An outline incorporating these facts looks like this:

```
PROCEDURE AnalyzeNumber:
     IF Number is valid (>1)
          THEN loop for all possible divisors:
               IF it is an even divisor
                    THEN number isn't prime, add both
                                        divisors to total
          IF divisor total = Number
               THEN it is perfect
```

This outline can be encoded into Pascal.

```
PROCEDURE AnalyzeNumber (Num : Integer);
(* Takes a number and, if >1, checks to see whether it is *)
(* prime, perfect, or neither and reports the result to   *)
(* the output file.                                       *)
VAR     IsPrime : Boolean;
              (* IsPrime is true until even divisor found *)
        PossFact,         (* candidate for being a factor  *)
        Limit,            (* the trunced value of the sqrt *)
        Sum : Integer;    (* sum of exact divisors         *)
BEGIN
    IF (Num<=1) THEN BEGIN
        Writeln (Output, Num, ' is not in correct range')
    END ELSE BEGIN
        Limit := Round (Sqrt (Num));
        IsPrime := TRUE;
        Sum := 1;        (* 1 divides everything, so add it *)
        FOR PossFact := 2 TO Limit DO BEGIN
            IF (Num Mod PossFact = 0) THEN BEGIN
                IsPrime := FALSE;
                Sum := Sum + PossFact + Num DIV PossFact;
            END;
        END;
        IF (Sum = Num)
            THEN Writeln (Num, ' is a perfect number.')
            ELSE IF IsPrime
                THEN Writeln (Num, ' is a prime number.')
                ELSE Writeln (Num, ' is a boring number.');
    END;
END;
```

The only problem with this procedure is that it will always count the square roots of perfect squares twice in the sum of the divisors. To ensure that this doesn't happen, let's modify the fragment inside the FOR loop.

```
IF (Num Mod PossFact = 0) THEN BEGIN
    IsPrime := FALSE;
    IF (PossFact = NUM DIV PossFact)
        THEN Sum := Sum + PossFact
        ELSE Sum := Sum + PossFact
                  + Num DIV PossFact;
END;
```

This procedure would be clumsy without the use of a boolean variable. You could, for example, count the number of divisors found, and if the count were zero at the end, then the number would be prime. However, that is clumsy because no one is really interested in how many divisors are found, only whether divisors exist. Another way to write the procedure is to set an integer variable as 0 at the beginning and as 1 if the test is satisfied. This procedure simulates a boolean variable, using the two values 0 and 1 like TRUE and FALSE. But again, this is clumsy. It is not clear why 0 should mean one thing and 1 another. Rather, the simple test at the bottom of the procedure we wrote is clear and elegant.

```
IF IsPrime THEN Writeln ...
```

Notice that it doesn't need to read

```
IF (IsPrime = TRUE) THEN ...
```

This would be redundant. It would be like using the test

```
IF (X>0) = TRUE THEN ...
```

Since IsPrime is already a boolean-valued variable, it can be used as the syntactical equivalent of a boolean test.

Don't forget to initialize boolean variables to the default value, which in the previous case was TRUE, before they are used in a loop. This is analogous to initializing integer variables to zero before they are used to compute a sum.

The following is sample output for the previous procedure, using an input file with integers in it.

OUTPUT
```
 25 is a boring number.
 27 is a boring number.
 28 is a perfect number.
 29 is a prime number.
 30 is a boring number.
495 is a boring number.
496 is a perfect number.
  1 is not in correct range
  3 is a prime number.
  5 is a prime number.
  6 is a perfect number.
  0 is not in correct range
```

Another use of boolean variables is in making the same test in several parts of the program. Suppose the condition for solution were a complex expression, such as:

```
(X>0) AND (X<=MaxNum) AND ((Y>X) OR (Z>X)) AND (Y<>Z)
```

If we need the result of this test several times, but only want to calculate it once (to save time and to make the program easier to read), then we can assign it to a variable.

```
Solvable := (X>0) AND (X<=MaxNum) AND ((Y>X)
            OR (Z > X)) AND (Y<>Z);
...
```

```
IF Solvable THEN ...
...
IF Solvable THEN ...
```

Boolean constants can also change the results of the program from execution to execution. For example, the use of a global boolean constant called Debugging can be of enormous help by giving status messages at critical points in the execution of the program.

```
CONST   Debugging = TRUE; (* set to false when the program
                               is finally working *)
...
IF Debugging THEN PrintVariables (   );
...
IF Debugging THEN PrintVariables (   );
```

Once the program is running correctly, the status messages may be sloppy and unnecessary and can be removed simply by turning off the debugging switch, which sets Debugging to False.

Boolean Functions

Boolean functions are often the most useful types of functions, because they can be used in place of a boolean test. For example, suppose we wrote a program that plays a game with the user. After explaining the rules, we want to give the user the chance to stop playing. So we'll write a function called WantsToPlay, which returns True if the user indeed does want to play. We could then use the function in the following context.

```
BEGIN   (* Main Program *)
        GiveInstructions;
        IF WantsToPlay THEN PlayGame;
END.    (* Main Program *)
```

The function itself is fairly simple.

```
FUNCTION WantsToPlay : Boolean;
(* This function asks the user if she or he wants to play *)
(* the game just described. Returns True if she          *)
(* or he does want to play.                               *)
VAR     Ans : Char; (* the user's one-character response  *)
BEGIN
        Writeln (Output, 'Do you want to play this game?',
                      ' (Y or N) ==>');
        Readln (Input, Ans);
        WantsToPlay := (Ans = 'Y') OR (Ans = 'y');
END;
```

One thing to notice about this little function is the final line. It is equivalent semantically to the following piece of code.

```
IF (Ans = 'Y') OR (Ans = 'y')
    THEN WantsToPlay : = TRUE
    ELSE WantsToPlay : = FALSE;
```

The first version used is shorter, although not quite as transparent. It sometimes isn't obvious that you can assign the value of a complicated boolean expression to a boolean variable without using an IF statement, but it is an elegant way to store a conditional value.

At this point, it is instructive to take another look at the MoviePatrol function discussed earlier. A simpler way to code the function would be to use the fact that Parent is a boolean variable in assigning the value to the function in the case where the movie is R-rated.

```
FUNCTION MoviePatrol (Rating : Char; Parent : Boolean;
                      Age : Integer) : Boolean;
(* This function takes the values of the movie's rating,    *)
(* (where G, P, R and X are the only values of the rating)  *)
(* the age of the person trying to buy a ticket, and        *)
(* whether or not the person is accompanied by a parent,    *)
(* and returns a TRUE value if the person should be         *)
(* allowed to buy a ticket.                                 *)
BEGIN
     IF (Age >= 17)
         THEN MoviePatrol : = TRUE
         ELSE IF (Rating = 'X')
             THEN MoviePatrol : = FALSE
             ELSE IF (Rating = 'R')
                 THEN MoviePatrol : = Parent
                 ELSE MoviePatrol : = TRUE;
END;
```

However, we could combine all we know about boolean operators and produce one long test.

```
BEGIN
     MoviePatrol : = (((Rating = 'X') OR (Rating = 'R'))
                     AND (Age >= 17)) OR
                     ((Rating = 'R') AND (Age < 17)
                     AND Parent) OR
                     (Rating = 'P') OR (Rating = 'G');
END;
```

While this is relatively short and requires only one statement, this type of expression is neither easy to read nor easy to debug. In general, it is probably better to get into the habit of using a powerful combination of boolean operators and nested IF tests. This will result in efficient yet readable code.

SELF
TEST

Write boolean-valued functions for each of the following tasks:

1. Take an age and return a boolean value indicating whether or not the person is old enough to vote.
2. Take three ordered numbers as parameters and indicate whether or not they were given in descending order.
3. Take three parameters for day, month, and a year in this century, and indicate whether or not the date given is valid.

Efficiency and Style

Study PROGRAM AverageScores that begins on page 166. We now know how to make it a little more useful. Suppose the teacher who uses this program would like it to assign grades on the following 0 to 40-point scale.

Value	Grade
Ave $>=38$	A+
$38 >$Ave $>=36$	A
$36 >$Ave $>=34$	A-
$34 >$Ave $>=31$	B+
$31 >$Ave $>=28$	B
$28 >$Ave $>=25$	B-
$25 >$Ave $>=20$	C
$20 >$Average	F

This grading scale plus our newly acquired knowledge of conditional execution might suggest one solution to the problem of assigning grades.

```
Procedure DetermineGrade (Ave : Real);
(* This procedure determines and writes the grade for the *)
(* student with the given average                          *)
BEGIN
    Write (Output, ' ':6); (* add space on the output line *)
    IF (Ave>=38) THEN Writeln (Output, 'A+');
    IF (Ave<38) AND (Ave>=36) THEN Writeln (Output, 'A');
    IF (Ave<36) AND (Ave>=34) THEN Writeln (Output, 'A-');
    IF (Ave<34) AND (Ave>=31) THEN Writeln (Output, 'B+');
    IF (Ave<31) AND (Ave>=28) THEN Writeln (Output, 'B');
    IF (Ave<28) AND (Ave>=25) THEN Writeln (Output, 'B-');
    IF (Ave<25) AND (Ave>=20) THEN Writeln (Output, 'C');
    IF (Ave<20) THEN Writeln (Output, 'F');
END;
```

What is wrong with this approach? The procedure would compile and execute correctly, it looks good, and is easy to read. What could be the problem? The problem, as you have probably recognized, is one of efficiency. The procedure does at least twice as many tests as it needs to do in order to do its job. There are two reasons why it is inefficient:

1. Suppose the average is greater than 38 and passes the first test. The procedure could quit at this point—it writes out the grade and could stop. But, because of the way it is written, it continues checking all of the other possibilities, only to find (not surprisingly) that none of them work.
2. Suppose the average is less than 38. It fails the first test, so goes on to the second, which, in essence, repeats the first test backwards. Instead of checking (Ave>=38) it is now checking (Ave<38). If the procedure had been structured so that a failure on the first test assumed passing the second test, fewer tests would need to be performed.

Both of these problems can be addressed with the IF-THEN-ELSE statement. In cases where a number of mutually exclusive options are available dependent upon certain conditions, the ELSE clause is the easiest and most efficient way of ensuring the choice of only one option. The restructured procedure might look like this.

```
PROCEDURE DetermineGrade (Ave : Real);
(* This procedure determines and writes the grade for the *)
(* student with the given average                          *)
BEGIN
    Write (Output, ' ':6); (* add space on the output line *)
    IF (Ave>=38) THEN Writeln (Output, 'A+')
      ELSE IF (Ave>=36) THEN Writeln (Output, 'A')
        ELSE IF (Ave>=34) THEN Writeln (Output, 'A-')
          ELSE IF (Ave>=31) THEN Writeln (Output, 'B+')
            ELSE IF (Ave>=28) THEN Writeln (Output, 'B')
              ELSE IF (Ave>=25) THEN Writeln (Output, 'B-')
                ELSE IF (Ave>=20) THEN Writeln (Output, 'C')
                  ELSE Writeln (Output, 'F');
END;
```

Notice that this entire procedure needs only two semicolons—after the first line of the procedure and after the first line of the statement part. The entire structure of seven IF statements is one of the two statements in the procedure, and if a semicolon ended any of the lines except the last, ELSE would be misplaced, and an error would occur. With all of the nested IF statements, it is tempting to slip a semicolon in there. Be careful!

Another issue, that of style, comes up when several IF statements are nested in this way. Proper indentation (which, according to the indentation scheme I have been following, I did not accomplish), sometimes makes the program code look awkward. Perhaps a better way to write the previous procedure would be to indent only the first ELSE, then run them straight down the page to signify that they are all part of the same statement.

```
PROCEDURE DetermineGrade (Ave : Real);
(* This procedure determines and writes the grade for the *)
(* student with the given average                         *)
BEGIN
    Write (Output, ' ':6); (* add space on the output line *)
    IF (Ave>=38) THEN Writeln (Output, 'A+')
        ELSE IF (Ave>=36) THEN Writeln (Output, 'A')
        ELSE IF (Ave>=34) THEN Writeln (Output, 'A-')
        ELSE IF (Ave>=31) THEN Writeln (Output, 'B+')
        ELSE IF (Ave>=28) THEN Writeln (Output, 'B')
        ELSE IF (Ave>=25) THEN Writeln (Output, 'B-')
        ELSE IF (Ave>=20) THEN Writeln (Output, 'C')
        ELSE Writeln (Output, 'F');
END;
```

Random Numbers and Decision Making

Occasionally we want the computer to take an action or return a result that is *seemingly* random—different at different times under the same circumstances. We can get the computer to simulate random (though not irrational) behavior by the generation of "random" numbers.

> **"Random" number:** A number generated by a seemingly unordered and unpredictable algorithm. More appropriately named *pseudorandom* numbers.

In general, a sequence of numbers is an ordered list of numbers that shows relationship. Consider the following sequences.

$$1, 2, 3, 4, 5, \ldots$$
$$1, 3, 5, 7, 9, \ldots$$
$$1, 4, 9, 16, 25, \ldots$$
$$1, 1, 2, 3, 5, 8, \ldots$$

Each of the numbers in these sequences is related to the others in some way. (The last sequence is the Fibonacci sequence, where any number is the sum of the two previous numbers.) But consider the following sequence.

$$10, 3, 81, 29, 4, \ldots$$

Although this isn't an entirely random sequence (because I thought it up and I find it virtually impossible to simulate total randomness), the relationship between these numbers is fairly obscure. If we had a method of generating "random" numbers by the computer, then we could program the computer to do things in a "random" fashion. This would, in certain cases, be helpful and interesting, and in most cases surprise the user of our programs.

In certain Pascal implementations, there is a function called Random that returns a random number between 0 and 1. It returns a different random number every time, and there is seemingly no relationship between successive calls of the function. The function takes an argument, called the Seed, which can be a global variable that is used only in the function Random. Seed should be initialized to some "random" value before the function is used. This is often done by asking the user to supply a value at the terminal. That value is read and used as the initial value of Seed. After that, every call to the function Random will change the value of Seed. (If your Pascal implementation doesn't have this function, see Programming Example 8.1 for a definition of a similiar function you can use, as well as an illustration of its use.)

So how do we use Random to make decisions or to generate numbers? Let's write a procedure called Dice that simulates two random rolls of a die by naming two numbers between 1 and 6. We could then use this procedure in a program that plays craps, Monopoly, or backgammon.

The problem in writing this little procedure is that the number that Random returns is between 0 and 1 (including 0, but always less than 1). How do we generate numbers between 1 and 6?

Suppose that we start with the random number and multiply it by 6.

```
Num := Random (Seed) * 6;
```

Now we know that Num will be between 0 and 6, because we have multiplied the original range by 6. But Num is a real number, and our result should be an integer. Let's convert Num to an integer:

```
Num := Round (Random (Seed) * 6);
```

However, there is still something wrong with this. Figure 8.3 shows the range we began with and how the rounding takes place.

Figure 8.3: The Range of Num

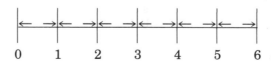

For each of the whole numbers 1, 2, 3, 4, and 5, there is a unit range of values that are rounded to the number. (Values between 1.5 and 2.5 are rounded to 2, and so forth.) Yet only one-half of a unit range of values rounds to 0 and 6.

If we take a different approach, using Trunc, we can see how this will work.

```
Num : = Trunc (Random (Seed) * 6) + 1;
```

This will ensure that all the values will fall between 1 and 6, with an equal likelihood of landing on any particular value.

SELF
TEST

Can you think of an alternative way to use Round and still produce the desired distribution in Random?

Now we are ready to write PROCEDURE Dice.

```
PROCEDURE Dice (VAR D1, D2 : Integer);
(* This procedure uses the function Random to generate     *)
(* two values between 1 and 6.                             *)
BEGIN
        D1 : = Trunc (Random (Seed) * 6) + 1;
        D2 : = Trunc (Random (Seed) * 6) + 1;
END;
```

This procedure leads us to a more general form of Random, which will take low and high values of a generated number and will return random numbers evenly distributed over the range from Low to High.

```
FUNCTION RandNum (Low, High : Integer) : Integer;
(* Returns a random number between Low and High, inclusive*)
BEGIN
        RandNum : = Trunc (Random (Seed) * (High - Low + 1))
                    + Low;
END;
```

Programming Example 8.1

Assignment: Use the random number generator RandNum to generate data for a math tutoring program. The math tutor will generate arithmetic problems for the user at the terminal and ask the user for the answers. The user will type responses that the computer will evaluate as either correct or incorrect. If the user types an incorrect response, the computer will ask if the user wants a hint and will give a hint that the response was either too high or too low. Then the computer will ask for a second response. If the user is still incorrect, the computer will give the correct answer and go on. The computer will keep track of and report the number of first-time-correct responses.

INTERACTIVE SESSION

```
Welcome to Math Tutor!
How many problems do you want to attempt?==>
6
Type any number to get started.
99132
39 + 9
48
Very good!
47 + 17
54
Incorrect. Do you want a hint?
Y or N==>
y
Your guess was too low. Try again.
47 + 17
64
That's better.
56 - 25
31
Very good!
64 - 33
41
Incorrect. Do you want a hint?
Y or N==>
n
64 - 33
21
You are just guessing. The correct answer is 31
1577 / 83
19
Very good!
81 * 50
4050
Very good!
You scored 66.67%. Keep practicing!
```

Solution: This program will be considerably longer than the others we have done, because the level of complexity is greater. However, the program shouldn't be any more difficult to write, especially if we break it down suitably.

Math Tutor:
      Introduction
      Get number of problems
      Loop for the number of problems
            Generate one problem
            Print the problem
            Get the user's answer
            Calculate the computer answer
            Evaluate the answer
      Report the user's percentage and evaluation

The main program should be easy to write, even though some of the procedures it calls will be rather complicated. We'll also leave out some of the parameters for now.

```
BEGIN    (* Main program *)
         Introduction (NumProblems);
         FOR WhichProb := 1 TO NumProblems DO BEGIN
                GenerateOneProblem (    );
                PrintTheProblem (    );
                GetUsersAnswer (User    );
                CalcAns (CompAns    );
                EvaluateAnswer (CompAns, User    );
         END;
         ReportScore (NumProblems, TotalCorrect);
END.     (* Main Program *)
```

We'll assume you can envision the simple procedure Introduction, which introduces the math tutor and finds out how many problems the user wants to work. Introduction also gets an initial Seed value for Random. Let's take a look at GenerateOneProblem, first in pseudocode.

GenerateOneProblem:
      Generate 2 random numbers (between 1 and 100)
      Pick an operator: +, −, *, or /

We can see how we'll use the random number generator. We will store the operator as a character variable, and the one we will use will depend on the random number we generate using RandNum.

```
PROCEDURE GenerateOneProblem (VAR Num1, Num2 : Integer;
                                  VAR Operator : Char);
(* This procedure generates two random numbers between     *)
(* 1 and 100 for use in an arithmetic problem. The operator *)
(* (+, -, * or /) will be determined by the random number  *)
(* generator as well.                                        *)
CONST  MaxOperand = 100;   (* max number given in this prob  *)
       NumOperators = 4;   (* choose a random num, 1 to 4   *)
VAR    OpNum : Integer;    (* The random number chosen      *)

BEGIN
      Num1 : = RandNum (1, MaxOperand);
      Num2 : = RandNum (1, MaxOperand);
      OpNum : = RandNum (1, NumOperators);
      IF (OpNum = 1) THEN Operator : = '+'
          ELSE IF (OpNum = 2) THEN Operator : = '-'
          ELSE IF (OpNum = 3) THEN Operator : = '*'
          ELSE IF (OpNum = 4) THEN Operator : = '/';
END;
```

Procedures `PrintTheProblem` and `GetUsersAnswer` are short and straightforward (just a `Writeln` and `Readln`, respectively). Let's define `CalcAns`, which looks similar to `GenerateOneProblem`.

```
PROCEDURE CalcAns (Num1, Num2 : Integer; Op : Char;
                        VAR CompAns : Integer);
(* This procedure is given an arithmetic problem (+, -,  *)
(* * or /) and calculates the correct answer. Notice it  *)
(* uses Num2 as the solution to a division problem. This *)
(* is because the problem will be given as (Num1*Num2) / *)
(* Num1.                                                  *)
BEGIN
      IF (Op = '+') THEN CompAns : = Num1 + Num2
          ELSE IF (Op = '-') THEN CalcAns : = Num1 - Num2
          ELSE IF (Op = '*') THEN CompAns : = Num1 * Num2
          ELSE IF (Op = '/') THEN CompAns : = Num2;
END;
```

We have written `CalcAns` as a procedure with one variable parameter and several value parameters. Any time you write a procedure with one variable parameter, it would often be better programmed as a function. We will convert `CalcAns` to a function definition.

```
FUNCTION CalcAns (Num1,Num2 : Integer;Op : Char) : Integer;
(* This procedure is given an arithmetic problem (+, -,     *)
(* * or /) and calculates the correct answer. Notice it    *)
(* returns Num2 as the answer of a division problem,        *)
(* because of the way the problem is generated.             *)
BEGIN
        IF (Op = '+') THEN CalcAns := Num1 + Num2
            ELSE IF (Op = '-') THEN CalcAns := Num1 - Num2
            ELSE IF (Op = '*') THEN CalcAns := Num1 * Num2
            ELSE IF (Op = '/') THEN CalcAns := Num2;
    END;
```

Notice that the answer calculated for a division problem is simply the second number generated. This is because of the way a division problem will be specified. The first random number calculated will be multiplied by the second to get the first number given in the problem (the numerator). The first random number will be given as the number to divide into the product given. The answer in this case is simply the second random number generated.

The big challenge is to write EvaluateAnswer. A lot is involved in this process, especially when the user types an incorrect answer. Let's break the procedure into more detailed pseudocode.

Evaluate Answer:
      IF answer is correct THEN
          increment score
          Write "Very Good!"
      ELSE
          Ask if user wants a hint
          if yes then give a hint
          get second guess
          evaluate second guess

The Pascal here isn't obvious, so let's define a couple more procedures used in EvaluateAnswer.

```
PROCEDURE EvaluateAnswer (ComputerAns, User : Integer;
                     Op : Char; Num1, Num2 : Integer;
                     VAR Score : Integer);
(* This procedure takes the computer's answer and compares*)
(* it with the user's. If the user is incorrect, the user *)
(* is prompted for another try, after possibly receiving  *)
(* a hint. The user's correct total is summed.            *)
VAR     Ans : Char; (* The user's response to Y/N question*)
```

```
BEGIN
        IF (ComputerAns = User) THEN BEGIN
                Score := Score + 1;
                Writeln (Output, 'Very good!');
        END ELSE BEGIN
                Writeln (Output, 'Incorrect. Do you want',
                                   ' a hint?');
                Writeln (Output, 'Y or N==>');
                Readln (Input, Ans);
                IF (Ans = 'Y') OR (Ans = 'y')
                        THEN GiveHint (User, ComputerAns);
                PrintTheProblem (Num1, Num2, Op);
                GetUsersAnswer (User);
                EvaluateSecondGuess (User, ComputerAns);
        END;
END;
```

We have made use of two new procedures, GiveHint and Evaluate-
SecondGuess. Both are short and relatively easy.

```
PROCEDURE GiveHint (User, CompAns : Integer);
(* This procedure tells whether the user's guess was too   *)
(* high or too low.                                         *)
BEGIN
        IF (User > CompAns)
                THEN Writeln (Output, 'Your guess was too',
                                      ' high. Try again.')
                ELSE Writeln (Output, 'Your guess was too',
                                      ' low. Try again.');
END;
```

```
PROCEDURE EvaluateSecondGuess (User, CompAns : Integer);
(* This procedure tells the user whether or not the        *)
(* second guess was correct.                               *)
BEGIN
        IF (User = CompAns)
                THEN Writeln (Output, 'That''s better.')
                ELSE Writeln (Output, 'You are just ',
                        'guessing. The correct answer is ',
                        CompAns:1);
END;
```

The whole program, with parameters and variable declarations in place,
follows.

```
PROGRAM MathTutor (Input, Output);
(************************************************************)
(* This program uses a random number generator to generate*)
(* random arithmetic problems. The user will be asked to  *)
(* type the correct answer and will be evaluated by the    *)
(* program. The program will allow the user to try a       *)
(* second time if an incorrect response is given. The      *)
(* program will tally the number correct and will give the*)
(* user a final evaluation and percentage.                 *)
(************************************************************)

VAR     Num1, Num2, (* the two operands of the arith prob *)
        TotalCorrect,   (* the total number correct        *)
        NumProblems,        (* the number of problems given *)
        WhichProb,              (* the FOR loop index       *)
        ComputerAns,            (* the correct answer       *)
        User : Integer; (* the user's answer to the prob    *)
        Op : Char;              (* the operator character   *)
        Seed : Integer; (* for the random number generator  *)

PROCEDURE Introduction (VAR NumProblems : Integer);
(* This procedure introduces the user to MathTutor and     *)
(* asks for the number of practice problems desired.        *)
(* Also initializes the global variable Seed.               *)
BEGIN
        Writeln (Output, 'Welcome to Math Tutor!');
        Writeln (Output, 'How many problems do you',
                        ' want to attempt?==>');
        Readln (Input, NumProblems);
        Writeln (Output, 'Type any number to get started.');
        Readln (Input, Seed);
END;

PROCEDURE PrintTheProblem (N1, N2 : Integer; Op : Char);
(* This procedure prints the problem to the terminal.      *)
(* If the problem is a division problem, then an evenly     *)
(* dividing problem is given.                               *)
BEGIN
        IF (Op <> '/')
                THEN Writeln (Output, N1:1, Op:2, ' ', N2:1)
                ELSE Writeln (Output, N1*N2:1, Op:2, ' ', N1:1);
END;

PROCEDURE GetUsersAnswer (VAR UserAns : Integer);
(* This procedure reads the user's answer to the problem   *)
BEGIN
        Readln (Input, UserAns);
END;
```

```
FUNCTION Rand (VAR Seed : Integer) : Real;
(* This function generates a random real number between 0 *)
(* and 1. Seed changes each time Rand is executed.        *)
CONST    Modulus = 32769;
         Multiplier = 10924;
         Increment = 11830;
BEGIN
         Seed := (Multiplier * Seed + Increment) MOD Modulus;
         Rand := Seed / Modulus;
END;


FUNCTION RandNum (Low, High : Integer) : Integer;
BEGIN
         RandNum := Trunc (Rand (Seed)*(High-Low+1)) + Low;
END;


PROCEDURE GenerateOneProblem (VAR Num1, Num2 : Integer;
                                VAR Operator : Char);
(* This procedure generates two random numbers between 1   *)
(* and 100 for use in an arithmetic problem. The operator  *)
(* (+, -, * or /) will be determined by the random number  *)
(* generator as well.                                      *)
CONST  MaxOperand = 100;  (* max number given in this prob *)
       NumOperators = 4;  (* choose a random num, 1 to 4   *)
VAR    OpNum : Integer;   (* indicates operator chosen     *)

BEGIN
       Num1 := RandNum (1, MaxOperand);
       Num2 := RandNum (1, MaxOperand);
       OpNum := RandNum (1, NumOperators);
       IF (OpNum = 1) THEN Operator := '+'
          ELSE IF (OpNum = 2) THEN Operator := '-'
          ELSE IF (OpNum = 3) THEN Operator := '*'
          ELSE IF (OpNum = 4) THEN Operator := '/';
END;


FUNCTION CalcAns (Num1,Num2 : Integer;Op : Char) : Integer;
(* This procedure is given an arithmetic problem (+, -,   *)
(* * or /) and calculates the correct answer. Notice it   *)
(* returns Num2 as the answer of a division problem,      *)
(* because of the way the problem is generated.           *)
BEGIN
       IF (Op = '+') THEN CalcAns := Num1 + Num2
          ELSE IF (Op = '-') THEN CalcAns := Num1 - Num2
          ELSE IF (Op = '*') THEN CalcAns := Num1 * Num2
          ELSE IF (Op = '/') THEN CalcAns := Num2;
END;
```

```
PROCEDURE GiveHint (User, CompAns : Integer);
(* This procedure tells whether the user's guess was too  *)
(* high or too low.                                        *)
BEGIN
        IF (User > CompAns)
                THEN Writeln (Output, 'Your guess was too',
                                      ' high. Try again.')
                ELSE Writeln (Output, 'Your guess was too',
                                      ' low. Try again.');
END;




PROCEDURE EvaluateSecondGuess (User, CompAns : Integer);
(* This procedure tells the user whether or not his       *)
(* second guess was correct.                              *)
BEGIN
        IF (User = CompAns)
                THEN Writeln (Output, 'That''s better.')
                ELSE Writeln (Output, 'You are just ',
                              'guessing. The correct answer is ',
                              CompAns:1);
END;




PROCEDURE EvaluateAnswer (ComputerAns, User : Integer;
                    Op : Char; Num1, Num2 : Integer;
                    VAR Score : Integer);
(* This procedure takes the computer's answer and compares*)
(* it with the user's. If the user is incorrect, the user *)
(* is prompted for another try, after possibly receiving  *)
(* a hint. The user's correct total is summed.            *)
VAR     Ans : Char; (* The user's response to Y/N question*)
BEGIN
        IF (ComputerAns = User) THEN BEGIN
                Score := Score + 1;
                Writeln (Output, 'Very good!');
        END ELSE BEGIN
                Writeln (Output, 'Incorrect. Do you want',
                                 ' a hint?');
                Writeln (Output, 'Y or N==>');
                Readln (Input, Ans);
                IF (Ans = 'Y') OR (Ans = 'y')
                        THEN GiveHint (User, ComputerAns);
                PrintTheProblem (Num1, Num2, Op);
                GetUsersAnswer (User);
                EvaluateSecondGuess (User, ComputerAns);
        END;
END;
```

```
PROCEDURE ReportScore (NumProbs, NumCor : Integer);
(* This procedure calculates and prints the percentage    *)
(* correct and comments on the user's performance.        *)
VAR       Percentage : Real;
BEGIN
          Percentage := NumCor / NumProbs;
          Write (Output, 'You scored', Percentage*100: 1: 2,
                  '%. ');
          IF (Percentage < 0.5)
              THEN Writeln (Output, 'You need help!')
              ELSE IF (Percentage < 0.75)
                  THEN Writeln (Output, 'Keep practicing!')
                  ELSE IF (Percentage < 0.90)
                      THEN Writeln (Output, 'Pretty good!')
                      ELSE Writeln (Output, 'Great!');
END;

BEGIN    (* Main program *)
         Introduction (NumProblems);
         FOR WhichProb := 1 TO NumProblems DO BEGIN
                 GenerateOneProblem (Num1, Num2, Op);
                 PrintTheProblem (Num1, Num2, Op);
                 GetUsersAnswer (User);
                 EvaluateAnswer (CalcAns (Num1, Num2, Op),
                     User, Op, Num1, Num2, TotalCorrect);
         END;
         ReportScore (NumProblems, TotalCorrect);
END.
```

The module tree for this program is given in Figure 8.4.

One final note should probably be given concerning FUNCTION Rand. This function uses a variable parameter, changing the value of Seed as a side effect of the function call. This is what ensures that a different "random" number is given by the function every time. Furthermore, this variable is a global variable and occurs in no other parameter lists because Seed is a variable that is only used in Rand and really should be transparent. Once it has been initialized in the introduction procedure, the programmer doesn't need to worry about the value of Seed, nor is it ever necessary to access its value.

Common Errors and Debugging

Declaring a global boolean constant called Debugging, and using it extensively, can help you debug your program. Often, when a program is not working, it produces no output or interaction of any kind to inform you of the nature or

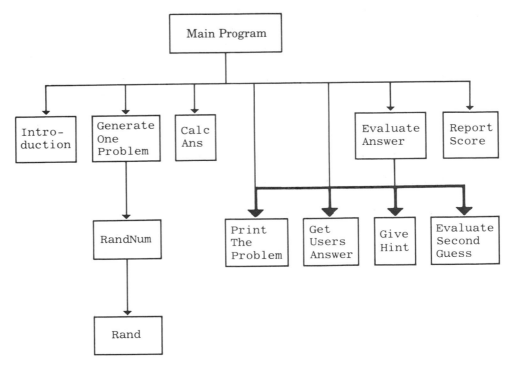

Figure 8.4: Module Tree for MathTutor

extent of the problem. The use of a debugging constant allows the program, while still in development, to send helpful messages to the output file or terminal. The messages may give you a clue as to what is working correctly and where the problem might be found. Sometimes even a simple message that tells that a certain procedure has been entered or exited can be helpful.

```
PROCEDURE WhatsIt;
BEGIN
        IF Debugging THEN Writeln (Output,
                                'Procedure WhatsIt entered. ');
        . . .
        IF Debugging THEN Writeln (Output,
                                'Procedure WhatsIt exited. ');
END;
```

Often, however, the problem isn't locating the bug, but trying to figure out why the bug exists. Often bugs are caused because the result we expect from a boolean test is not what we get. Therefore, the computer doesn't carry out the statements we want it to. A procedure like PrintVariables mentioned on page 214 could print the values of all the variables being used, and help you figure out if anything has a value that you don't expect. You might discover an uninitialized variable, for example, or some variable whose value is not current that is changing the value of a boolean test.

As with the FOR loop, the IF statement brings to Pascal its own characteristic errors.

1. **Putting a semicolon between the THEN clause and ELSE.** An easy way to avoid this is by getting into the habit of using the compound statement with the IF statement.

```
IF <test> THEN BEGIN
        <statements>
    END ELSE BEGIN
        <statements>
END;
```

In this way, you will never be tempted to put a semicolon after the END and before the ELSE.

2. **Using boolean operators in improperly formed tests.** This can be avoided with consistent use of parentheses.

```
IF Rating = 'R' AND Age < 17 AND Parent
  (* this causes an error *)
```

becomes

```
IF (Rating = 'R') AND (Age < 17) AND Parent
```

3. **Testing boolean variables incorrectly.** Although this isn't a syntax error, it is gauche to use the following boolean tests:

```
IF (Done = FALSE) THEN BEGIN ...
IF (Debugging = TRUE) THEN PrintValues (   );
```

Instead, you should make use of the fact that you are working with boolean functions, variables, or constants, which readily allow such easy-to-read lines of code as:

```
IF NOT Done THEN BEGIN ...
IF Debugging THEN PrintValues (   );
```

4. **Ignoring round-off error.** In a boolean test of equality between two reals, quantities that are algebraically equal may not test as equals because of the round-off error involved in storing the values in the machine. Subtracting the numbers and comparing the absolute value of the result to some epsilon (a very small number, usually about 10^{-4}) usually achieves satisfactory results. To express the process in code, do not use

```
IF (Value = Sqrt (Num)) THEN ...
```

Qualify the expression to compensate for round-off error in this manner.

```
IF (Abs (Value - Sqrt (Num)) < Epsilon) THEN ...
```

5. **Performing illegal arithmetic calculations.** Remember, even if the boolean test is determined from the first expression, all expressions are evaluated. Here is an example:

```
IF (X>=0) AND (Sqrt (X) < 1.0) THEN ...
```

If X is less than 0, then a call to Sqrt will produce an error. Most compilers will evaluate both expressions even if the condition (X>=0) is not met. The compiler continues to test even when the final result is inevitably false. This can be avoided by a double IF statement.

```
IF (X>=0) THEN BEGIN
        IF (Sqrt (X) < 1.0) THEN ...
```

This particular case can also be avoided by algebraically altering the tests to achieve the same effect.

```
IF (X>=0) AND (X<1.0) THEN ...
   (* if both are true, then the Sqrt (X) is < 1.0 *)
```

Hints for BASIC Programmers

One problem with Pascal IF statements for a BASIC programmer lies in the fact that BASIC IF statements do more than simple conditional execution. IF statements in BASIC are used to implement conditional loop structures (discussed in the next chapter) as well as to implement a case selection structure (mentioned in Chapter 11). Probably the most fundamental use of an IF in BASIC, however, is still as a decision-making control structure, a role shared by the Pascal IF. Let's look at a sample of BASIC using this classical structure.

The program we will look at calculates tuition for a state university. Suppose that the tuition is a function of the number of units for which the student is enrolled and whether or not the student is a resident of the state. If the student is a resident taking no more than 12 units, then the tuition bill for the semester is $1,000. If the student takes more than 12 units, tuition is an additional $80 for each unit above 12. If the student is a nonresident of the state, the tuition bill is $2,500 plus $175 for each excess unit.

```
100 REM TUITION CALCULATION PROGRAM
110 REM I = STUDENT ID NUMBER
120 REM U = NUMBER OF UNITS ENROLLED
130 REM S = INSTATE (1 FOR YES, 0 FOR NO)
```

```
140 REM T = TUITION
200 INPUT I, U, S
210 IF S=1 THEN 270
220 IF U>12 THEN 250
230 T = 2500
240 GO TO 310
250 T = 2500+175*(U-12)
260 GO TO 310
270 IF U>12 THEN 320
280 T = 1000
290 GO TO 310
300 T = 1000+80*(U-12)
310 PRINT I, T
320 GO TO 100
330 END
```

This segment of code could be translated into Pascal fairly easily.

```
PROGRAM Tuition (Input, Output);
(* This program calculates tuition for students at a state *)
(* university, based on their unit load and whether or     *)
(* not they are residents of the state.                    *)
(* This was written as a batch program.                    *)
CONST   WhichState = 13;       (* just for example         *)
VAR     StudentNum,
        Units,
        StateNum,              (* between 1 and 50          *)
        Tuition : Integer;
        InState : Boolean;
BEGIN
        Readln (Input, StudentNum, Units, StateNum);
        InState := (StateNum = WhichState);
        IF InState THEN BEGIN
            IF (Units < 12)
                THEN Tuition := 1000
                ELSE Tuition := 1000 + (Units - 12) * 80;
        END ELSE BEGIN
            IF (Units < 12)
                THEN Tuition := 2500
                ELSE Tuition := 2500 + (Units - 12) * 175;
        END;
END.
```

The only drawback with Pascal in this case is that it is necessary to do more typing, because the identifier names are longer. The advantages should be obvious. The indentation scheme makes the organization of the code a lot easier to handle. Furthermore, it is very easy to alter the code or to add lines without throwing off a line numbering system.

The new structured BASIC has borrowed the ELSE clause from Pascal to strengthen the capabilities of its IF statement. Instead of specifying a simple statement, the THEN and ELSE clauses of an IF statement can be as long as is desired. In this case, a final delimiter is needed. The delimiter is different in different extensions of BASIC, but it is often called IFEND. IFEND gives the BASIC programmer more power and flexibility, and allows BASIC users to emulate Pascal design and style. However, Pascal specifies that THEN and ELSE clauses (including a compound statement) are single statements. Therefore, in Pascal there is no need for a delimiter that functions as IFEND. This makes the structure of the Pascal IF statement analogous to that of the FOR loop and other structures we'll see later.

A result of this Pascal feature is the fact that you are not allowed to put a semicolon after the THEN statement and before the ELSE. In this case, the semicolon acts as a BASIC IFEND and makes the Pascal compiler think you have terminated the IF statement.

SUMMARY

Conditional execution, through the IF statement, allows the computer to select one action among two or more alternatives based on the result of a boolean test. Boolean tests are most often constructed with the relational operators. The IF statement, like the FOR statement in Pascal, controls only one statement in each of its THEN and ELSE clauses. However, as with the FOR statement, the compound statement can be used as the syntactical equivalent of a single statement.

IF statements can be nested to allow the computer to make more complicated decisions. When nesting IF statements, it is easy to lose track of which ELSE clause goes with which IF statement. Misplaced semicolons can add to the confusion and cause errors in syntax. The **dangling ELSE** clause is caused by a premature termination of the IF statement by a semicolon after the THEN statement.

AND, OR, and NOT are the three **boolean operators**; they are used to construct more complicated boolean expressions. Because of the rules of precedence, it is easy to cause syntax errors when using boolean operators unless all expressions joined by boolean operators are in parentheses.

Boolean variables store the value of a complicated test that will be used several times in a program or make the significance of a test more clear to the reader. A boolean constant, such as Debugging, can receive a value that changes between executions of a program. Boolean functions are among the most useful types of functions because their values can be used directly in boolean tests.

Game programs or the need for different results every time a program is executed often require the generation of a **random number.** Some implementations of Pascal have a built-in random number generator, which is usually a function that returns a real value between zero and one. From this, we can produce random numbers between any two numbers.

New Terms

conditional execution	postcondition assertion	IF-THEN-ELSE
boolean expression	boolean operator	AND
boolean value	unary prefix operator	OR
relational operator	prefix operator	nested IF statement
dangling ELSE	infix operator	NOT
assertion	postfix notation	
precondition assertion	random number	

EXERCISES

1. What does the following program produce?

```
PROGRAM What (Output);
CONST Base = 2;
VAR i, j, k : integer;
BEGIN
    FOR i := 0 TO Base DO BEGIN
        FOR j := 0 TO Base DO BEGIN
            FOR k := 0 TO Base DO
                IF (i=0)
                    THEN IF (j=0)
                        THEN Write (Output, k:5)
                        ELSE Write (Output, j:4, k:1)
                ELSE Write (Output, i:3, j:1, k:1);
            Writeln (Output);
        END;
        Writeln (Output);
    END;
END.
```

2. In plane geometry, the sum of any two sides of a triangle must be greater than the third side. Write a boolean function that contains three arguments. Each argument proposes the length of a side. The function should tell whether the cited sides could constitute a real triangle on a plane.

3. Write a function, Greatest, that takes two integer values and returns the value that is greater. Write a two-line main program that reads four values from the input file and writes the largest value to the output file. Use multiple calls to Greatest inside of the Writeln statement.

4. Leap years happen every four years (as we all know). And they don't happen if the year is a multiple of 100 unless the year is also a multiple of 400. For example, the year 1900 was not a leap year, but the year 2000 will be a leap year. Write a boolean function that takes one argument, the year, and returns TRUE if the year is a leap year.

5. Write a program to calculate payroll checks. The input file will indicate the number of employees and each successive line will read:

```
<name><soc. security num><hours><pay/hr>
```

The employee name will be 20 characters long, padded with spaces. The Social Security number will be read as one integer, and the hours worked and the pay/hour will be real numbers. Compute the gross pay on the following scale:

Time	Calculated Pay
0–40 hours	Straight time
40–50 hours	1.5 × hourly rate
over 50 hours	2.0 × hourly rate

After gross pay is calculated, make deductions for federal income tax at the following rate:

Less than $400	10%
Over $400	10% of first $400, 15% of amount over

Also deduct 6.5 percent for Social Security tax and 2 percent for state tax. Write a report for each employee, something on the order of:

```
John Doe               999999999
    Hours worked:    46.5    Hourly Wage:  $10.00
    Gross Pay:      497.50
    Federal Tax:     54.13
    Soc. Security:   32.34
    State Tax:        9.95
    -------------------
    Net Pay:        401.08

Jane Smith ...
```

6. Gymnastics scores are calculated by averaging scores from six judges, after throwing out the lowest and highest scores. Write a procedure that reads six scores from a line of input, throws out the lowest and highest values, averages the remaining integers, and prints the average.

7. Write a program that uses an input file to produce phone bills. The input file will begin with the number of customers to process, followed by data for each customer. Organize the data as follows:

```
<customer's phone number><number of calls made>
<base cost per month>
<long dist. number called><charge/min><time><minutes>
<long dist. number called><charge/min><time><minutes>
<long dist. number called><charge/min><time><minutes>
. . .
<next customer's data>
. . .
```

The phone numbers will be a sequence of seven or ten digits without dashes or parentheses. The charge/minute is the normal rate, which is discounted depending on the time of day. Code the daytime rate as (1), the evening rate as (2), and the nighttime rate as (3). The evening rate is calculated by multiplying the charge/min by 0.70, or 70 percent. The nighttime rate is only 40 percent of the regular rate. Your program should produce a monthly bill for each customer in the input file that shows the regular usage cost and itemizes total long distance costs. Use blank lines to separate data for different customers.

8. Write a boolean function, RealClose, that takes two real values and a real epsilon called Epsilon, and returns TRUE if the values are within Epsilon of each other.

9. The MathTutor's Rand function shown on page 227 uses the MOD function to generate pseudorandom numbers. This function can be generalized for any values of Modulus, Multiplier, and Increment. The general formula for this is

$$X_{n+1} = (\text{Multiplier} * X_n + \text{Increment}) \text{ MOD Modulus}$$

where the Modulus is greater than 0, and the Multiplier, Increment, and X_0, the starting value, are all less than Modulus. The best sequences are found when Modulus, Increment, and Multiplier are all relatively prime, meaning they share no common factors. Develop your own random number generator using Modulus, Multiplier, and Increment. All values should be less than 100.

10. Have you ever wanted to see if a coin toss or a die roll were truly random? If you have spent time flipping hundreds of coins, then here is an exercise you'll like. Write a program using Rand to simulate 500 coin tosses. Count how many turn up heads and how many turn up tails. Report the results. If they aren't divided exactly evenly, state why.

11. The amount of tax you pay is determined by your income and your filing status: single, head of household, married filing jointly, or married filing separately. The tax rate goes up by about 1 percent every $1,000, but this varies between categories. Design an algorithm to calculate a person's estimated tax given the income and category. Use the following figures to write a program to estimate the tax you will pay next year. Assume that the rate increases by 1 percent every bracket.

Filing Status	Bracket Size	Beginning Rate
Single	$1,000	11% over $2,300
Head of Household	$1,100	11% over $2,300
Married, Jointly	$1,500	11% over $3,400
Married, Separate	$ 900	11% over $1,700

If the income is high enough, the maximum tax rate is 50 percent. (This is reached after 40 brackets.)

12. Write a program to roll a pair of dice 100 times. Keep track of how many twos, threes, and so forth up to twelves are rolled. Print out the results. What type of distribution did you get? What did you expect?

13. Often, reporting results numerically makes the meaning of those results difficult to interpret. An alternative format would report results graphically, allowing the eye to see dramatic differences quickly. Write a program that reads an input file of numbers, writes them out one per line, then makes a horizontal bar of stars whose length is proportional to the size of the number. The first number in the file will indicate how many numbers there are, and the second will indicate the size of the largest number. Make the bar for the largest number extend almost all the way across the screen.

14. Combine the parts of the previous two programs to write a program that rolls a die 500 times and then reports its results graphically.

15. Write a program that reads 500 characters from a file and counts the number of spaces, periods, commas, and capital letters. Print the total number of each element as well as percentages of the total number of characters read.

16. The Fibonacci sequence, 1, 1, 2, 3, 5, 8 . . . is defined so that any term is the sum of the two previous terms. The ratio between any two adjacent terms, a_n/a_{n-1}, approaches what is known as the golden ratio, ψ.

$$\psi = \frac{\sqrt{5} + 1}{2}$$

The golden ratio is "golden" in that $1 + 1/\psi = \psi$. Write a program to print the first 20 approximations of the golden ratio from the Fibonacci sequence. Print the results in tabular form, and print both the ratio and its reciprocal. For example:

n	A(n)	A(n)/A(n-1)	A(n-1)/A(n)
1	1		
2	1	1.0000	1.0000
3	2	2.0000	0.5000
4	3	1.5000	0.6667
5	5	1.6667	0.6000
6	8	1.6000	0.6250

17. Write a much-needed improvement for the ESPTester program described in Programming Example 4.1. Your program should generate a random order of shapes and should ask the user to type in the name (or number) of the shape before it is printed. Keep track of the number of shapes the user guessed correctly, and give an opinion of the user's ESP ability.

CONDITIONAL REPETITION

Often, we will want to repeat something an indefinite number of times. It is not always easy or even possible to determine how many pieces of input there will be in an input file, for example. Or, suppose we wanted a program to count the occurrences of E in an input file of text. We want to read every character in the file, but in order to use a FOR loop, we would have to know how many characters there were.

One way to get around this is to have a flag variable. Suppose we want to sum and average all the numbers in a file, and we know there will be less than 10,000 of them, but at least one. Furthermore, we know that the last number, and only the last number, is zero. We can then write the following clumsy piece of code.

```
Read (Input, Num);  Sum := 0;
Nums Found := 0;
FOR Cntr := 1 TO 10000 DO
        IF (Num<>0) THEN BEGIN
                NumsFound := NumsFound + 1;
                Sum := Sum + Num;
                Read (Input, Num);
        END;
Writeln (Output, 'The Sum of ',NumsFound:1,
                 ' numbers is ',Sum:1);
Writeln (Output, 'Their average is ',Sum / NumsFound:1:2);
```

There are several problems with this. First of all, suppose there are more than 10,000 numbers in the input file. Then the procedure doesn't do its job. Suppose there are less than 100. The computer wastes a lot of time looping without doing anything. Secondly, the structure doesn't really suggest what is actually happening. It would be ideal if the program stopped looping altogether when NUM equaled 0. (BASIC programmers will recognize how to do this—use a GO TO. In structured Pascal, however, we don't use GO TOs. Pascal does have a GOTO statement, but, apart from slightly snobbish references such as this one, we will mention it only in the Appendix.) Pascal features an easier and more elegant method.

The WHILE Loop

The WHILE loop is essentially a combination of a FOR loop that yields repetition and an IF-THEN statement that yields conditionality, hence the term *conditional repetition*. You've had enough experience with syntax diagrams; I'll show you the solution to the previous problem with a WHILE loop, and you try to come up with the syntax.

```
Read (Input, Num); Sum := 0;
NumsFound := 0;
WHILE (Num<>0) DO BEGIN
        NumsFound := NumsFound + 1;
        Sum := Sum + Num;
        Read (Input, Num);
END;
Writeln (Output, 'The sum of ',NumsFound:1,
                 ' numbers is ',Sum:1);
Writeln (Output, 'Their average is ',Sum/NumsFound:1:2);
```

After examining this example carefully, if you guessed that

```
WHILE < test > DO
        < statement >;
```

then you were correct. The test is just like any boolean test—it can be a boolean variable or function. (It should never be a boolean constant! Why not?) The statement can, of course, be a compound statement or a procedure call.

The WHILE statement introduces another real jump in power for the programmer. Recall the function that asks if the user wants to play the game. Instead of merely letting the user play it once, the computer can allow the user to play as many times as she or he likes.

```
. . .
FUNCTION WantsToPlay : Boolean;
. . .
BEGIN    (* Main Program *)
        GiveInstructions;
        InitializeGame ( < parameters > )
        WHILE WantsToPlay DO PlayGame ( < parameters > );
        SignOff;
END.     (* Main Program *)
```

The WHILE loop executes the statement under its control until the test becomes false. Therefore, the statement under the control of the WHILE loop must perform some action that allows the test to eventually become false. If the test begins with a true condition, and if the condition never becomes false or is never changed by the statement, then the loop is said to be infinite, and the executing program is said to be in an infinite loop.

Infinite loop: A piece of program code that loops on a condition that will never change or allow the loop to terminate.

For example:

```
Read (Input, Ch);
WHILE (Ch<>' ') DO
        Write (Output, Ch);
WHILE (X<0) DO
        X := X - 1;
```

The statement under the control of the first WHILE loop will never change the value of Ch. If Ch is initially something other than a space, then it will remain so, and the character will be printed forever. In the second loop, subtracting 1 from the variable X will not do anything to change the fact that X < 0. X will never become nonnegative if it begins with a negative value; therefore, the loop will execute until an error overflow occurs—when X receives a value below -MaxInt. It is also for this reason that I said never to use a boolean constant in the WHILE loop test; it will result in an infinite loop.

SELF
TEST
Write a procedure that sums odd numbers beginning with 1, until the sum is greater than 1985. Print the number of odds summed, their sum, and the square root of the number summed.

Eoln and Eof

Often, it is necessary to deal with files of unknown lengths with no flag value at the end. Inserting a flag value into the file may be inconvenient. Or it may be necessary to deal with input files with incomplete data at points, so it is not possible to read the expected number of scores on a line, for example. Eoln (Input) is a boolean-valued function that is true when the input file has been read up to but not including an end-of-line marker. (The carriage return-line feed (CRLF), although usually considered two characters by the computer, is viewed as a single character by the Pascal processor, so it will trigger a true response from the Eoln function.) Eof (Input) is a boolean-valued function that is true when the entire file, including the final Eoln marker, has been read.

Normally, an input file will look like a long sequence of characters. The computer doesn't really think of it as a two-dimensional matrix of characters, but as a one-dimensional string. Interspersed throughout the string are end-of-line markers, which are read like a single character. The end-of-file marker is located after the final end-of-line marker in the file. For example:

```
16      33  29  \/  11  82     17  4  \/  96  62  \/  ■
```

A sample input file follows. There are three lines of numbers on this file, each terminated by an end-of-line marker, represented by a \/. Following the last end-of-line marker is an end-of-file marker, represented by a ■. Initially, before any Read statement has been executed, the input file pointer (↑) points to the beginning of the file.

```
16      33  29  \/  11  82     17  4  \/  96  62  \/  ■
↑
```

After reading three integer values, the pointer has now moved over to the end of the first line of input.

```
16      33  29  \/  11  82     17  4  \/  96  62  \/  ■
                ↑
```

It is at this point that the standard boolean function Eoln is true. At any previous point, the condition of Eoln was false. After one more Read statement is executed, the pointer has moved past the first end-of-line marker onto the second line, and the Eoln condition is false once again.

```
16      33  29  \/  11  82     17  4  \/  96  62  \/  ■
                   ↑
```

If, however, a Readln statement were executed, then the input file pointer would move up to *and past* the end-of-line marker of the second line, and Eoln would still be false.

```
  16      33 29 ∨ 11 82    17 4 ∨ 96 62 ∨ ■
                                ↑
```

Immediately after a Readln statement, the only way that Eoln could be true is if the current line on the input file is blank. Finally, once all the values in the input file have been read, and a Readln statement is executed, then the condition Eof becomes true.

```
  16      33 29 ∨ 11 82    17 4 ∨ 96 62 ∨ ■
                                            ↑
```

Suppose we wanted to write a small procedure that would average the numbers on each line in a file of numbers and print the average before going on to the next line. Since we don't know how many values are on a given line or how many lines any given input file may have, we'll use two indefinite loops.

OneLine:
    Initialize sum and counter
    While not done with line do:
        Read a number
        Increment counter
        Add the number to the sum
    Print results

WholeFile:
    While not done with file do OneLine

In Pascal:

```
PROCEDURE OneLine (VAR Sum, HowMany : Integer);
(* sums the values on a single line in the input file,   *)
(* prints their average, also keeps track of running sum *)
(* and HowMany numbers are read to calculate an average  *)
(* for the whole file                                    *)
(* This procedure assumes that there are no trailing     *)
(* blanks on the end of data lines.                      *)
VAR     LineHowMany, LineSum,      (* values for this line *)
        Num : Integer;             (* current number read  *)
```

```
BEGIN
        LineHowMany := 0; LineSum := 0;
        WHILE NOT Eoln (Input) DO BEGIN
               Read (Input, Num);
               LineHowMany := LineHowMany + 1;
               LineSum := LineSum + Num;
        END;
        Writeln (Output, 'Average of ',LineHowMany:1,
                      ' numbers is ', LineSum/LineHowMany:1:2);
        Readln (Input);    (* throws away carriage return *)
        Sum := Sum + LineSum;
        HowMany := HowMany + LineHowMany;
END;
```

Because of the way the WHILE loop is constructed, this procedure assumes that there are no blanks after the last integer on the line and that the CLRF immediately follows the last integer. In this case, as soon as all of the values have been read from a line, Eoln becomes true, and this WHILE loop terminates. In most cases, the Eoln marker may be true after the last item of input on the line. If the input has been typed in from the keyboard, the person entering the data may have accidentally typed an extra space before typing the carriage return. In this case, the WHILE loop would not terminate correctly, and data from more than one line would be read as if it were all on the same line. When you make assumptions about the format of the data, be sure to document them.

On some machines, the input line may be padded with blanks, in which case Eoln may not work as expected. In these cases, you can eliminate leading blanks with the procedure SkipSpaces, which is discussed in Chapter 16. This procedure would ensure that the compiler reached Eoln before trying to read a value beyond the end of the line.

In order to complete our averaging-and-summing assignment, we write the main program, which calls the previous procedure.

```
PROGRAM WholeFile;
(******************************************************)
(* Sums values on each line of the file, using OneLine    *)
(* prints average for each line, then computes the average*)
(* for the whole file.                                    *)
(******************************************************)
VAR     Sum, HowMany : Integer;

BEGIN   (* Main Program *)
        Sum := 0;
        HowMany := 0;
        WHILE NOT Eof (Input) DO OneLine (Sum, HowMany);
        Writeln (Output);
        Writeln (Output, 'Total average of ',HowMany:1,
                 ' numbers is ', Sum/HowMany:1:2);
END.    (* Main Program *)
```

Note that if the input file pointer is sitting on the end-of-line marker immediately preceding the end-of-file marker, then the Eof is still false. That is one reason why it is important to execute a Readln in the OneLine procedure; after the completion of that procedure for the last line in the input file, the Eof test will be true. The following are the input and output files that were used to test this program.

INPUT
```
12 14 15 16 18
22 24 25 26 20 27
30 34 35 37 39
41 44 42 46 49 48 42 49 43
50 52 55 58 54 58 56
61 63
```

OUTPUT
```
Average of 5 numbers is   15.00
Average of 6 numbers is   24.00
Average of 5 numbers is   35.00
Average of 9 numbers is   44.89
Average of 7 numbers is   54.71
Average of 2 numbers is   62.00
Total average of 34 numbers is 38.38
```

The nested WHILE loop structure is hidden, because the two loops are in different procedures. It can be seen a little more clearly when we try to use FUNCTION Cap to capitalize all of the letters in a file.

```
PROGRAM CapitalizeFile (Input, Output);
VAR     Ch : Char;

FUNCTION Cap (Ch : Char) : Char;
BEGIN
        IF (Ch>='a') AND (Ch<='z')
                THEN Cap := Chr (Ord (Ch) + Ord('A')
                                - Ord ('a'))
                ELSE Cap := Ch;
END;

BEGIN   (* Main Program *)
        WHILE NOT Eof (Input) DO BEGIN
                WHILE NOT Eoln (Input) DO BEGIN
                        Read (Input, Ch);
                        Write (Output, Cap (Ch));
                END;
                Writeln (Output);
                Readln (Input);
        END;
END.    (* Main Program *)
```

Write a program that encodes an input file by translating every occurrence of A to B, B to C, C to D, and so forth. Translate lowercase letters in the same way.

Invariant Assertions (Optional)

As you begin to write programs with more complex loops, it is going to be more difficult to understand the code that you have written. You will need to comment more than procedure and variable declarations—you have probably already started commenting parts of the code that are confusing.

One technique for commenting loops is the use of invariant assertions. An assertion is a comment statement that the programmer believes to be true. An **invariant assertion** is a statement about a loop whose validity does not change as the loop progresses. For example, suppose I want to calculate the value of n^2 by adding up the first n odd numbers. (This is always true: $1 = 1$, $4 = 1 + 3$, $9 = 1 + 3 + 5$, $16 = 1 + 3 + 5 + 7$, and so forth.) This loop is rather simple to write.

```
Square := 0; Cntr := 0;
WHILE (Cntr < N) DO BEGIN
        Cntr := Cntr + 1;
        Odd := Cntr * 2 - 1;
        Square := Square + Odd;
END;
```

Assume that N has been given a value previously, and that all variables are properly declared. If you had come across this fragment of code without the above introduction, would it be obvious to you what it is trying to accomplish, or that it works correctly?

Well, we can add some comments that explain what it is trying to do and why we think it works. The most basic thing we know is that if Square is going to have the right value, it must be equal to the sum of the first N odd integers. Is there any way we can demonstrate with comments that Square actually receives that value? We can use invariant assertions.

```
Square := 0; Cntr := 0;
        (* The value of Square is the sum of the   *)
        (* first Cntr (=0) odd numbers.            *)
WHILE (Cntr < N) DO BEGIN
        (* The value of Cntr will be increased      *)
        (* until it equals the value of N.          *)
        (* 0 <= Cntr < N                            *)
    Cntr := Cntr + 1;
        (* 1 <= Cntr <= N                           *)
    Odd := Cntr * 2 - 1;
        (* Odd has the value of the Cntr-th odd     *)
        (* number                                   *)
```

```
        Square : = Square + Odd;
            (* 1 <= Cntr <= N and Square is the sum of *)
            (* the first Cntr odd numbers              *)
    END;
            (* Cntr = N and Square is the sum of the   *)
            (* first N odd numbers                      *)
```

Each assertion in the loop is true during every repetition of the loop. It is not true that each assertion is true at any point in the loop, however. For example, the last assertion inside the loop, that Square is the sum of the first Cntr odd numbers, is not true after Cntr is increased and before the final statement in the loop. However, after each execution of the loop, we do know that the final assertion is true. Therefore, once the loop completes execution, the postcondition assertion that Cntr = N implies that Square is the sum of the first N odd integers, which proves that the loop works correctly.

When actually writing programs, it is never necessary to go into this much detail in commenting your code. However, it is good to be familiar with these concepts and to try to include informal invariant assertions into your commenting style.

Programming Example 9.1

Assignment: One high-powered technique for encryption (coding secret messages) involves converting a message into numbers and performing sophisticated mathematical manipulations with large prime numbers. Write a program that will find the two highest prime numbers that are less than the square root of MaxInt, the standard constant representing the highest representable integer on your implementation. Print out the prime numbers and their product, which should be slightly less than MaxInt. Print out your system's value of MaxInt for comparison.

Solution: This program should not be too difficult to write. But we will want to develop an especially efficient algorithm to determine whether or not a number is prime, because we will work with extremely large numbers that will take some time to test. The basic algorithm will begin at the square root of MaxInt and count down until we come across one and then another prime number. We can then write the results of the search and the multiplication to the output file. In pseudocode, this is simply:

> Initialize the candidate
> Find the first prime
> Find the second prime
> Write the results

Suppose we begin with the variable Candidate and initialize it to the highest value we want to check. We can send it to a procedure GetPrime, which decreases Candidate until a prime is found. Then we can write the main program and parameterize the procedure calls.

```
BEGIN    (* Main Program *)
         Initialize (Candidate);
         GetPrime (Candidate, First);
         GetPrime (Candidate, Second);
         WriteResults (First, Second);
END.     (* Main Program *)
```

The initialization procedure is not trivial, because we must think about what initial value we desire Candidate to have. We want it to be less than or equal to the square root of MaxInt, but we also want it to be odd. There is no sense in checking any even numbers to see if they are prime. The only even number which is prime is 2, and we will be a long way from 2. Therefore, the initialization procedure would be the following.

```
PROCEDURE Initialize (VAR Cand : Integer);
(* This procedure initializes Cand to be the highest odd  *)
(* number less than the Sqrt of MaxInt.                   *)
BEGIN
         Cand := Round (Sqrt (MaxInt));
         IF (Cand MOD 2 = 0)
                  THEN Cand := Cand - 1;
END;
```

The next task is to write the outline for the procedure GetPrime. At first glance, it looks like this could be a function instead of a procedure, because it seems like only one parameter needs to be a variable. However, we soon realize that Candidate also should be a variable parameter, because it will be decreased each time the procedure is called; consecutive calls to the procedure will yield different results. The algorithm used is simple.

GetPrime:
Loop until Candidate is prime:
Subtract 2 from Candidate

We can call a boolean function, PrimeCheck, which takes a single integer argument and returns true if it is prime. Using this, the Pascal version of this procedure is as simple as the pseudocode.

```
PROCEDURE GetPrime (VAR Cand, PrimeNum : Integer);
(* This procedure uses the function PrimeCheck to check    *)
(* each odd number <= the original Cand, and it stops      *)
(* when a prime number is found.                           *)
BEGIN
        WHILE NOT PrimeCheck (Cand) DO
                Cand : = Cand - 2;
        PrimeNum : = Cand;
END;
```

Obviously, PrimeCheck will do most of the work. As we noted before, if a number is not divisible by any number less than its square root, then it is a prime number, and no other divisors can be found. Therefore, first we need to calculate the limit beyond which we needn't search for divisors. After that, we simply divide all possible divisors until we find a division or until we reach the limit. The algorithm for PrimeCheck is:

PrimeCheck:
    Limit is square root of Candidate
    Loop until an exact divisor found or
            the limit is passed:
        Increment factor
    PrimeCheck is TRUE if no divisor found

Because we have decided to deal only with odd candidates, we will begin searching for divisors at Factor : = 3. Furthermore, we only have to try odd divisors, because even numbers can't divide an odd number. Therefore, when we increase Factor by increments, we should increase it by 2.

```
FUNCTION PrimeCheck (Cand : Integer) : Boolean;
(* This function checks an odd integer to determine if it *)
(* is a prime number. No even factors are examined.       *)
VAR    Factor, Limit : Integer;
BEGIN
        Limit : = Round (Sqrt (Cand));
        Factor : = 3;
        WHILE (Factor < Limit) AND (Cand MOD Factor <> 0) DO
                Factor : = Factor + 2;
        PrimeCheck : = (Cand MOD Factor <> 0);
END;
```

The final procedure, WriteResults, is simple. However, upon running this version of the program, we find that the program calculated the same value for each of the prime numbers. Can you spot the error in the program as it now stands?

The problem was that Candidate, when it returns from GetPrime after the first call, has the same value as First, which is a prime number. When GetPrime is called again, the first Candidate checked happens to be prime, since Candidate hasn't changed. In order to prevent getting the same prime number as the result for each call to GetPrime, subtract 2 from the value of Candidate before recalling the procedure.

```
BEGIN     (* Main Program *)
          Initialize (Candidate);
          GetPrime (Candidate, First);
          Candidate := Candidate - 2;
          GetPrime (Candidate, Second);
          WriteResults (First, Second);
END.      (* Main Program *)
```

The entire program and a copy of the output file follow. Notice that there is no input file for this program. The module tree for this program is found in Figure 9.1.

```
PROGRAM LargePrimes (Output);
(************************************************************)
(* This program calculates a large composite number which *)
(* is the product of two large primes. The algorithm used *)
(* is that the two largest primes less than the Sqrt of   *)
(* MaxInt are found, and their product is given as the    *)
(* answer. This output could be used to determine an      *)
(* encrypting scheme.                                     *)
(************************************************************)
VAR     Candidate,             (* current number being tested *)
        First, Second : Integer; (* highest primes found   *)
```

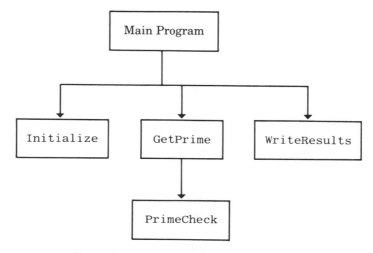

Figure 9.1: Module Tree for LargePrimes

```
PROCEDURE Initialize (VAR Cand : Integer);
(* This procedure initializes Cand to be the highest odd  *)
(* number less than the Sqrt of MaxInt.                    *)
BEGIN
        Cand := Round (Sqrt (MaxInt));
        IF (Cand MOD 2 = 0)
                THEN Cand := Cand - 1;
END;


FUNCTION PrimeCheck (Cand : Integer) : Boolean;
(* This function checks an odd integer to determine if it *)
(* is a prime number. No even factors are examined.       *)
VAR     Factor, Limit : Integer;
BEGIN
        Limit := Round (Sqrt (Cand));
        Factor := 3;
        WHILE (Factor < Limit) AND (Cand MOD Factor <> 0) DO
                Factor := Factor + 2;
        PrimeCheck := (Cand MOD Factor <> 0);
END;


PROCEDURE GetPrime (VAR Cand, PrimeNum : Integer);
(* This procedure uses the function PrimeCheck to check    *)
(* each odd number <= the original Cand, and it stops      *)
(* when a prime number is found.                           *)
BEGIN
        WHILE NOT PrimeCheck (Cand) DO
                Cand := Cand - 2;
        PrimeNum := Cand;
END;


PROCEDURE WriteResults (First, Sec : Integer);
(* This procedure writes out the values of the two prime  *)
(* numbers and also writes their product.                 *)
BEGIN
        Writeln (Output, 'The two primes found are: ',
                        First:1, Sec:10);
        Writeln (Output, 'Their product is ',First*Sec:1);
        Writeln (Output, 'The value of MaxInt is ',
                        MaxInt:1);
END;


BEGIN   (* Main Program *)
        Initialize (Candidate);
        GetPrime (Candidate, First);
        Candidate := Candidate - 2;
        GetPrime (Candidate, Second);
        WriteResults (First, Second);
END.    (* Main Program *)
```

OUTPUT   The two primes found are: 185363   185359
         Their product is 34358700317
         The value of MaxInt is 34359738367

Programming Example 9.2

Assignment: Write a program that reads an input file consisting of data from the census of a small town. The input file is in the following format: each line represents the data for one household. The line contains the ages of each member in the household, followed immediately by an M or an F for their sex. If the person is 18 or older, an R or an N will follow the sex to indicate whether or not the person is a registered voter. If the person is less than 18, no such designation will be given. For example, one line might read: 39MR 37FR 16F 15F 13M. The program should count the number eligible to vote in the next election, the number of unregistered inhabitants who are 18 or over, and the number of minors in the town. It should also break these numbers down by sex, report the average age of the population, count how many households are in the town, and calculate the average number of people per household.

Solution: This program's complexity lies mainly in keeping all of the different variables straight. We will need variables to count all of the different categories of people in the census: male and female registered voters, male and female unregistered adults, and male and female children. We will also need a running sum of all the ages of people, SAge, in order to calculate an average age. Finally, we will need a variable to hold the number of households that have been read (equal to the number of lines of data in the file).

The algorithm used to produce our report is a familiar one: We initialize variables, loop until Eof, and then report the findings.

        Census Counter:
              Initialize variables
              Loop until End of File:
                    increment number of households
                    read one household
              Report totals

This outline delays for a moment the question of what it looks like to actually read and process the data for one person—we'll deal with that after we have written the main program. Since we know most of the global variables, we can go ahead and write the main program, calling procedures with the parameters we know they will need.

```
BEGIN      (* Main Program *)
           Initialize (MRegVoters, FRegVoters, SAge,
                       MUnreg, FUnreg, MKids, FKids, NumHHlds);
           WHILE NOT Eof (Input) DO BEGIN
                   NumHHlds := NumHHlds + 1;
                   ReadOneHouseHold (MRegVoters, FRegVoters,
                       SAge, MUnreg, FUnreg, MKids, FKids);
           END;
           Report (MRegVoters, FRegVoters, SAge, MUnreg,
                   FUnreg, MKids, FKids, NumHHlds);
END.       (* Main Program *)
```

PROCEDURE `Initialize` is simple—it merely sets all of the variables we send into it to a value of zero. Let's think about `ReadOneHousehold`. We want it to read all of the individuals on one line, then to get rid of the `Eoln` marker to prepare for the next line. This procedure ensures that, when the entire file is read, the main program will find the `Eof` marker and terminate properly. A simple way to write this algorithm would be:

Read One Household:
    Loop until Eoln:
        Read one person
    Throw away Eoln marker

To translate to Pascal:

```
PROCEDURE ReadOneHouseHold (VAR MRegVoters, FRegVoters,
                SAge, MUnreg, FUnreg, MKids, FKids : Integer);
(* This procedure counts the values of the different    *)
(* categories for one household. The procedure reads the *)
(* data until the Eoln and then flushes the Eoln marker.  *)
BEGIN
        WHILE NOT Eoln (Input) DO
                ReadOnePerson (MRegVoters, FRegVoters, SAge,
                        MUnreg, FUnreg, MKids, FKids);
        Readln (Input);
END;
```

Now we cannot easily break the problem down any further. We must look at what is involved in counting a single individual's statistics.

Read One Person:
        Read age, sex
        Add age to sum of ages
        IF (age > = voting age)
                THEN read registered
                        classify adult: Female registered,
                                        Male registered,
                                        Female unregistered,
                                        Male unregistered
                ELSE classify children: Boy or Girl

Because of the complexity of the decisions, this algorithm produces an unusually long procedure. It is about as long a procedure as we normally would want to write.

```
PROCEDURE ReadOnePerson (VAR MRegVoters, FRegVoters, SAge,
                    MUnreg, FUnreg, MKids, FKids : Integer);
(* This procedure categorizes one person in a household    *)
(* and increments the appropriate values.                  *)
CONST   VotingAge = 18;
VAR     Sex, Reg : Char;
        Age : Integer;
BEGIN
        Read (Input, Age);
        SAge : = SAge + Age;
        Read (Input, Sex);
        IF (Age >= VotingAge) THEN BEGIN
            Read (Input, Reg);
            IF (Sex = 'F')
                THEN IF (Reg = 'R')
                        THEN FRegVoters : = FRegVoters + 1
                        ELSE FUnreg : = FUnreg + 1
                ELSE IF (Reg = 'R')
                        THEN MRegVoters : = MRegVoters + 1
                        ELSE FUnreg : = FUnreg + 1;
        END ELSE BEGIN    (* dealing with kids only *)
            IF (Sex = 'F')
                THEN FKids : = FKids + 1
                ELSE MKids : = MKids + 1;
        END;
END;
```

The concept of the final procedure, Report, is simple, but it is probably the most difficult procedure in the program to write. That is because, when writing output procedures, little details usually take a lot of time to get exactly right. It is a long procedure (the final version is 21 lines), but it doesn't make any sense to break it up in any way. In general, once your programs begin to produce the correct output, it will be difficult to set them aside until they produce beautiful output as well.

The final program follows.

```
PROGRAM CensusCount (Input, Output);
(* This program reads an input file consisting of data    *)
(* for the census of a small town. The input file is in   *)
(* the following format: each line represents the data    *)
(* for one household. The line contains the ages of each   *)
(* member in the household, followed immediately by an M  *)
(* or an F for their sex. If the person is 18 or older,   *)
(* an R or an N will follow the sex to indicate whether   *)
(* the person is a registered voter or not. If the person *)
(* is less than 18, no such designation will be given.    *)
(* For example, one line might read:                      *)
(*        39MR 37FR 16F 15F 13M                           *)
(* The program counts the number eligible to vote in      *)
(* the next election, the number of unregistered persons  *)
(* who are 18 or over, and the number of                  *)
(* minors in the town and breaks these numbers down by    *)
(* sex. The program also counts how many households are   *)
(* in the town and calculates the average number of       *)
(* people per household.                                   *)
VAR     MRegVoters,          (* Male registered voters    *)
        FRegVoters,          (* Female registered voters *)
        SAge,                (* Sum of the ages           *)
        MUnreg, FUnreg,      (* M, F unregistered voters *)
        MKids, FKids : Integer;(* M, F kids               *)
        NumHHlds : Integer;  (* Number of households      *)


PROCEDURE Initialize (VAR MRegVoters, FRegVoters,SAge,
          MUnreg, FUnreg, MKids, FKids, NumHHlds : Integer);
BEGIN
          MRegVoters := 0; FRegVoters := 0;
          SAge := 0;
          MUnreg := 0; FUnreg := 0;
          MKids := 0; FKids := 0;
          NumHHlds := 0;
END;


PROCEDURE ReadOnePerson (VAR MRegVoters, FRegVoters,SAge,
                    MUnreg, FUnreg, MKids, FKids : Integer);
(* This procedure categorizes one person in a household   *)
(* and increments the appropriate values.                 *)
CONST   VotingAge = 18;
VAR     Sex, Reg : Char;
        Age : Integer;
```

```
BEGIN
        Read (Input, Age);
        SAge := SAge + Age;
        Read (Input, Sex);
        IF (Age >= VotingAge) THEN BEGIN
            Read (Input, Reg);
            IF (Sex = 'F')
                THEN IF (Reg = 'R')
                    THEN FRegVoters := FRegVoters + 1
                    ELSE FUnreg := FUnreg + 1
                ELSE IF (Reg = 'R')
                    THEN MRegVoters := MRegVoters + 1
                    ELSE FUnreg := FUnreg + 1;
        END ELSE BEGIN    (* dealing with kids only *)
            IF (Sex = 'F')
                THEN FKids := FKids + 1
                ELSE MKids := MKids + 1;
        END;
END;


PROCEDURE ReadOneHouseHold (VAR MRegVoters, FRegVoters,
                SAge, MUnreg, FUnreg, MKids, FKids : Integer);
(* This procedure counts the values of the different    *)
(* categories for one household. The procedure reads the *)
(* data until the Eoln and then flushes the Eoln marker. *)
BEGIN
        WHILE NOT Eoln (Input) DO
                ReadOnePerson (MRegVoters, FRegVoters, SAge,
                    MUnreg, FUnreg, MKids, FKids);
        Readln (Input);
END;


PROCEDURE Report (MRegVoters, FRegVoters, SAge, MUnreg,
                FUnreg, MKids, FKids, NumHHlds : Integer);
(* This procedure reports the results of the census.     *)
VAR     Total, MTotal, FTotal,
        RegTot, UnregTot, KidTot : Integer;
BEGIN
        MTotal := MRegVoters + MUnreg + MKids;
        FTotal := FRegVoters + FUnreg + FKids;
        Total := MTotal + FTotal;
        RegTot := MRegVoters + FRegVoters;
        UnregTot := MUnreg + FUnreg;
        KidTot := MKids + FKids;
        Writeln (Output, ' ':25, 'Census Report');
        Writeln (Output);
        Writeln (Output, ' ':10, '   Voters     ',
                'Other Adults    Children      Total');
```

```
                Writeln (Output, ' ':10, '   M      F      M       ',
                                 'F      M      F      M       F');
                Writeln (Output, ' ':10, MRegVoters: 3, FRegVoters: 6,
                                 MUnreg: 7, FUnreg: 6,
                                 MKids: 7, FKids: 6,
                                 MTotal: 7, FTotal: 6);
                Write (Output, '% total:  ');
                Writeln (Output, MRegVoters/Total*100: 4: 1,
                                 FRegVoters/Total*100: 6: 1,
                                 MUnreg/Total*100: 7: 1,
                                 FUnreg/Total*100: 6: 1,
                                 MKids/Total*100: 7: 1,
                                 FKids/Total*100: 6: 1,
                                 MTotal/Total*100: 7: 1,
                                 FTotal/Total*100: 6: 1);
                Write (Output, '% class:  ');
                Writeln (Output, MRegVoters/RegTot*100: 4: 1,
                                 FRegVoters/RegTot*100: 6: 1,
                                 MUnreg/UnregTot*100: 7: 1,
                                 FUnreg/UnregTot*100: 6: 1,
                                 MKids/KidTot*100: 7: 1,
                                 FKids/KidTot*100: 6: 1);
                Write (Output, '% total:  ');
                Writeln (Output, RegTot/Total*100: 7: 1,
                                 UnregTot/Total*100: 13: 1,
                                 KidTot/Total*100: 13: 1);
                Writeln (Output);
                Writeln (Output, 'The average age was ',
                                 SAge/Total: 1: 1);
                Writeln (Output, NumHHlds: 1, ' households were',
                                 ' counted.');
                Writeln (Output, 'The average number of people',
                                 ' per household was ', Total/NumHHlds: 1: 1);
        END;


BEGIN    (* Main Program *)
         Initialize (MRegVoters, FRegVoters, SAge,
                     MUnreg, FUnreg, MKids, FKids, NumHHlds);
         WHILE NOT Eof (Input) DO BEGIN
                 NumHHlds := NumHHlds + 1;
                 ReadOneHouseHold (MRegVoters, FRegVoters,
                     SAge, MUnreg, FUnreg, MKids, FKids);
         END;
         Report (MRegVoters, FRegVoters, SAge, MUnreg,
                 FUnreg, MKids, FKids, NumHHlds);
END.     (* Main Program *)
```

The module tree for the previous program is shown in Figure 9.2. The output file it generates looks like this:

OUTPUT

Census Report

	Voters		Other Adults		Children		Total	
	M	F	M	F	M	F	M	F
	21	23	8	11	14	13	43	47
% total:	23.3	25.6	8.9	12.2	15.6	14.4	47.8	52.2
% class:	47.7	52.3	42.1	57.9	51.9	48.1		
% total:	48.9		21.1		30.0			

The average age was 27.7
28 households were counted.
The average number of people per household was 3.2

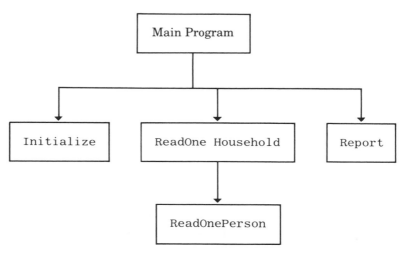

Figure 9.2: Module Tree for CensusCount

The REPEAT Loop

The WHILE loop is sufficient to perform any type of indefinite looping desired. However, for certain looping and testing combinations, it is awkward to use the WHILE loop. It is in these cases that the REPEAT loop may be useful.

The easiest way to think of a REPEAT loop, which is another indefinite loop construct in Pascal, is that it is an upside down WHILE loop. The test is at the bottom of the loop rather than the top.

```
WHILE NOT Eof (Input) DO        REPEAT OneLine (Sum, HowMany);
    OneLine (Sum, HowMany)      UNTIL  Eof (Input);

WHILE (X>0) DO                  REPEAT X := X - 1;
    X := X - 1;                 UNTIL  (X<=0);
```

There are several important differences between the two loops. First of all, because the WHILE test is at the top of the loop, the test is evaluated *before* entrance into the loop. This means that the WHILE loop won't be entered accidentally. However, sometimes the WHILE loop code is inconvenient or even clumsy, because the test needs to be "primed":

```
PROCEDURE ReadNWriteWord;
VAR Ch : Char;
BEGIN
        Read (Input, Ch); (* prime the pump *)
        WHILE (Ch <> ' ') DO BEGIN
                Write (Output,Ch);
                Read (Input, Ch);
        END;
END;
```

The REPEAT loop is entered the first time, before the test is evaluated. But this has its disadvantages as well.

```
PROCEDURE ReadNWriteWord;
VAR Ch : Char;
BEGIN
        REPEAT Read (Input, Ch);
                Write (Output,Ch);
        UNTIL (Ch = ' ');
END;
```

The problem here is that the extra space gets printed, which may or may not be the desired result.

The second difference between WHILE and REPEAT is that the REPEAT loop terminates when the test becomes true as the syntax implies: "Repeat *until* the test is true" as opposed to "*while* the test is true repeat." When the WHILE loop test becomes false the loop terminates. Therefore, you need to be careful when translating code from WHILE to REPEAT to make sure you invert the test.

```
WHILE NOT Eof DO ...                REPEAT ... UNTIL Eof
WHILE (x < 0) DO ...                REPEAT ... UNTIL (x >= 0)
```

A final difference between the two constructs: A REPEAT loop does not require a compound statement. The UNTIL signals the end of the sequence of statements under the control of the loop. Therefore, more than one statement can occur between the REPEAT and the UNTIL without the need of a BEGIN-END pair.

SELF
TEST

Using REPEAT loops, rewrite PROGRAM CapitalizeFile on page 246. What must be assumed about the input file for this version to work correctly?

Comparative Advantages: FOR, WHILE, REPEAT

With three different looping constructs available, the choice of the correct one for a given task might seem almost arbitrary. However, each has its advantages, and they should be drawn upon whenever possible.

The FOR loop should be used when a numerical counter is needed and when the exact number of repetitions is known and is expressible as a constant or an expression involving other variables in the program. Here, for comparison, are a FOR loop and a WHILE loop doing the same thing.

```
FOR Cntr := 1 to 20 DO          Cntr := 0;
    Writeln (Output, Cntr);     WHILE (i < 20) DO BEGIN
                                    Cntr := Cntr + 1;
                                    Writeln (Output, Cntr);
                                END;
```

Because we need to set up a counter, provision must be made to initialize the counter to zero and to increase it by increments in the loop. This is done automatically by the FOR loop. The WHILE loop counter, on the other hand, must be initialized before entrance into the loop, and an extra statement must be added to increment the counter. The result is to make the code less transparent to the reader of the program, because it isn't as obvious that the loop repeats only 20 times.

On the other hand, there are obviously times when a WHILE loop or REPEAT loop can do what a FOR loop cannot. Sometimes a FOR loop seems to work until we take into account anomalies in the input file. For example, in the AverageScores program that begins on page 166, we expected six values on every line. What would have happened if there had only been five scores on one line? The computer would have tried to read the sixth, but it wouldn't have found another score on the line, so it would have gone to the next line. There it would have found the first letter in the next student's name, and an error would have resulted, because it expected a digit. To correct for this possibility, we could have used a WHILE loop.

```
SumScores := 0;
WHILE NOT Eoln (Input) DO BEGIN (* sum scores on line *)

        Read (Input, Score);
        SumScores := SumScores + Score;
END;
```

At this point, we are vulnerable to another possibility. If we have declared a constant NumScores, which is the the number of scores that each student has, suppose there are more than NumScores values on one particular line. We only want to read NumScores scores, but with the above code, we'll keep reading. An extra blank at the end of the line on the input file is another possibility that is sometimes hard to anticipate.

```
    35   37 29   16   21   35  \/
                             ↑
```

If this were the case, then after six scores had been read, the conditions of Eoln would not be met, and an attempt would be made to read another score. After finding no other scores on the current line, the compiler would look at the next line. Instead of finding a digit, the compiler would see the first character in the next student's name. This would cause a Read operation error.

A way to try to prevent this is to have two escapes from the loop, one at Eoln and one after NumScores values have been read.

```
SumScores := 0; NumValuesRead := 0;
WHILE NOT Eoln (Input) AND
        (NumValuesRead<NumScores) DO BEGIN
      Read (Input, Score);
      NumValuesRead := NumValuesRead + 1;
      SumScores := SumScores + Score;
END;
```

Even this improvement is not foolproof. What would happen in the unlikely event that there are *fewer* than NumScores values on a line and also trailing blanks after the last value? In this case it would probably be best either to reorganize your data file or to look in more depth at the nature of file handling, which is discussed in detail in Chapter 15.

The advantage of the WHILE loop over the REPEAT loop in this case lies in the possibility of encountering a line with no scores on it. The REPEAT loop would barrel ahead, thinking that at least one score would be on the line, and get itself into trouble. The WHILE loop is more cautious, testing the water before diving in.

However, often the caution of a WHILE loop is more clumsy than useful. For example, in a game program, it makes more sense to wait and ask if the user wants to play again after the game has been played once. Instead of writing the code with a WHILE loop, a REPEAT could be used.

```
GiveInstructions;              GiveInstructions;
WHILE WantsToPlay DO           REPEAT PlayGame (   );
      PlayGame (   );          UNTIL  WantsToQuit;
```

If a boolean variable is used as the test, and if its conditions must be met before entrance into a WHILE loop, then a REPEAT loop is usually better.

Programming Example 9.3

Assignment: Write a program to simulate a guessing game that the user plays with the computer. The computer generates a random number between 1 and 1,000. The user picks a number in the same range. Then the computer and the user alternate guesses until both have guessed the other's number. After each guess, the player whose number is being guessed gives a hint that the number is either too high or too low or says that it is correct. Your program should count the number of turns each takes and report the winner for each round. The computer should allow the user to play the game repeatedly until the user wants to quit.

Solution: Several procedures and functions that we have already studied will come in handy in this program. It is always convenient to use or modify existing code, if it is well written and portable. We will, therefore, transport the RandNum function and Rand from the last chapter into our program, since we will need to generate random numbers. We will also be able to use a variation on ReportScore, discussed in the previous chapter, and the boolean function WantsToQuit, which we developed earlier in this chapter. With that much well-outlined—if not totally correct—code, let's try to write a pseudocode version of the main program.

> Guessing Game:
>> Initialize the random Seed
>> Loop until the user wants to quit:
>>> Initialize game variables
>>> Get random computer number
>>> Loop until both guessed correct:
>>>> User guesses
>>>> Computer guesses
>>> Report the score of the game

To design the main program, we will need to know something about the necessary variables. We will obviously need to store the value of the computer's secret number, CompNum, as well as the number of turns each player has taken. We will also keep track of the progress of each player with a pair of boolean variables, UserDone and CompDone. Each of these conditions are met when one player has guessed the other's number. Finally, the computer will need to keep track of the current boundaries of the user's number. At the beginning, the Low and High values will be 1 and 1,000. But as the computer makes guesses, those values converge until the computer is able to guess the user's number. (In all probability, the user will be using the same algorithm.) Here is a reasonable guess at the structure of the main program:

```
BEGIN    (* Main Program *)
         InitRand (Seed);
         REPEAT  Initialize (High, Low, UserTurns, CompTurns,
                             UserDone, CompDone);
                 CompNum := RandNum (Low, High);
                 REPEAT  UserGuess (CompNum, UserTurns,
                                    UserDone);
                         MakeGuess (High, Low, CompTurns,
                                    CompDone);
                 UNTIL UserDone AND CompDone;
                 ReportScore (UserTurns, CompTurns);
         UNTIL WantsToQuit;
END.      (* Main Program *)
```

Because the initial values of these variables are fairly important to the correct operation of the procedures, here is the Initialize procedure.

```
PROCEDURE Initialize (VAR Hi, Lo, User, Comp : Integer;
                      VAR UserDone, CompDone : Boolean);
(* This procedure sets or resets the values of Hi and Lo  *)
(* for the start of a new game.                           *)
CONST   High = 1000; Low = 1;            (* Game Parameters *)
BEGIN
        Hi := High; Lo := Low;
        User := 0; Comp := 0;
        UserDone := FALSE; CompDone := FALSE;
END;
```

Procedure UserGuess will ask the user for a guess, then compare the guess to the computer's secret number. The procedure will either write out a hint or will report that the user guessed correctly. If the latter, then the boolean variable UserDone will be satisfied and reflect the fact that the user is done guessing. With this verbal description of the algorithm, the Pascal is quickly written.

```
PROCEDURE UserGuess (CompNum : Integer;
                     VAR UserTurns : Integer;
                     VAR UserDone : Boolean);
(* This procedure allows the user to try to guess the     *)
(* computer's number, and gives the user a hint if the    *)
(* guess is not correct. If it is, then UserDone is set    *)
(* to TRUE.                                                *)
VAR     Guess : Integer;
```

```
BEGIN
        IF NOT UserDone THEN BEGIN
            Writeln (Output, 'What is your guess?');
            Readln (Input, Guess);
            IF (CompNum < Guess)
                THEN Writeln (Output, 'Too high!')
                ELSE IF (CompNum > Guess)
                    THEN Writeln (Output, 'Too low!')
                    ELSE Writeln (Output, 'Correct!');
            UserDone := (CompNum = Guess);
            UserTurns := UserTurns + 1;
        END;
END;
```

The algorithm for MakeGuess will be a mirror image of UserGuess, in that the guess will be calculated and written—not read—and the hint will be read—not calculated and written. In order to do this, we must design an algorithm to determine the guess. The method we will use is called a binary search, where the number we are looking for is initially in some range from Low to High. The guess made will be the midpoint of the range. If the guess is too high, then High is changed to be one less than the value of the guess. Likewise, if the guess is too low, then the value of Low is given as the guess plus one. The procedure, using this algorithm, is given below.

```
PROCEDURE MakeGuess (VAR Hi, Lo, CompTurns : Integer;
                    VAR CompDone : Boolean);
(* This procedure makes a guess at the user's secret word.*)
(* The strategy is to do a binary search.                 *)
VAR    Guess : Integer;        (* Computer's guess         *)
       Response : Char;        (* High, Low, or Correct    *)
BEGIN
        IF NOT CompDone THEN BEGIN
            Guess := (High + Low) DIV 2;
            Writeln (Output, 'My guess is ', Guess:1,'. ',
                'Type C (correct), L (Low), or H (High).');
            Readln (Input, Response);
            IF (Response = 'L')
                THEN Low := Guess + 1
                ELSE IF (Response = 'H')
                    THEN High := Guess - 1
                    ELSE CompDone := TRUE;
            CompTurns := CompTurns + 1;
        END;
END;
```

Notice that in both of the procedures MakeGuess and UserGuess, if the condition of CompDone or UserDone (respectively) is satisfied, then the procedure will do nothing, not even increase the value of the number of turns taken. This allows the main program loop to continue alternating execution of the two loops until both players are finished.

In addition to the random-number-generating procedures, the remaining procedures are `ReportScore` and `WantsToQuit`, and we need to modify them slightly.

Given the above algorithm, the guesses will progress something like this: 500, 250, 125, 63, 94, 78, 86, 90, 92, 93. A clever user could figure out that a number like 91 or 93 will be chosen last, but a number like 63 or 94 will be chosen early on in the game. In order to foil those who might figure this out, let's use the random number generator to generate a random number for the computer's guess of the user's number. The guess will be in the vicinity of the midpoint of the range, but not always exactly the midpoint. We will calculate the midpoint and then add to it a random number that is centered around zero.

```
CONST   OffSet = 0.025;          (* the degree of randomness *)
. . .
BEGIN
. . .
        Range := Round ((High - Low) * OffSet);
        Guess := (High + Low) DIV 2 +
                  RandNum (-Range, Range);
```

The `Range` is about 2.5 percent of the difference between `High` and `Low`, and the guess is assigned the midpoint of the interval, plus some random number between -Range and +Range. This is a nice technique for calculating a random number that is centered around a certain value. The final version of the program with these changes follows:

```
PROGRAM NumGuess (Input, Output);
(***********************************************************)
(* This program simulates a number guessing game between  *)
(* the computer and the student. Both the user and the    *)
(* computer choose a number between 1 and 1000, and they  *)
(* each try to guess the other's number. The computer     *)
(* uses a slightly randomized binary search. The computer *)
(* reports the outcome of the game and allows the user to  *)
(* play again.                                            *)
VAR     CompNum,          (* The computer's secret number *)
        Low, High : Integer; (* changing range of user's  *)
                          (* secret number.               *)
        UserDone,         (* TRUE when the number is       *)
        CompDone : Boolean; (* guessed.                    *)
        UserTurns,        (* how many guesses taken to     *)
        CompTurns : Integer; (* guess the number.          *)
        Seed : Integer;   (* begins the random number      *)
                          (* sequence.                     *)
```

```
PROCEDURE InitRand (VAR Seed : Integer);
(* This procedure asks the user for an initial seed value *)
BEGIN
        Writeln (Output, 'Type any 5 digit number to',
                         ' begin:');
        Readln (Input, Seed);
END;


FUNCTION Rand (VAR Seed : Integer) : Real;
(* This function generates a random real number between 0 *)
(* and 1. Seed changes each time Rand is executed.        *)
CONST   Modulus = 32769;
        Multiplier = 10924;
        Increment = 11830;
BEGIN
        Seed := (Multiplier * Seed + Increment) MOD Modulus;
        Rand := Seed / Modulus;
END;


FUNCTION RandNum (Low, High : Integer) : Integer;
(* Returns a random number between Low and High, inclusive*)
BEGIN
        RandNum := Trunc (Rand (Seed) * (High - Low + 1))
                   + Low;
END;


PROCEDURE Initialize (VAR Hi, Lo, User, Comp : Integer;
                      VAR UserDone, CompDone : Boolean);
(* This procedure sets or resets the values of Hi and Lo  *)
(* for the start of a new game.                           *)

CONST   High = 1000; Low = 1;            (* Game Parameters *)
BEGIN
        Hi := High; Lo := Low;
        User := 0; Comp := 0;
        UserDone := FALSE; CompDone := FALSE;
END;


PROCEDURE UserGuess (CompNum : Integer;
                     VAR UserTurns : Integer;
                     VAR UserDone : Boolean);
(* This procedure allows the user to try to guess the     *)
(* computer's number, and gives the user a hint if the    *)
(* guess is not correct. If it is, then UserDone is set    *)
(* to TRUE.                                               *)
VAR     Guess : Integer;
```

```
BEGIN
        IF NOT UserDone THEN BEGIN
            Writeln (Output, 'What is your guess?');
            Readln (Input, Guess);
            IF (CompNum < Guess)
                THEN Writeln (Output, 'Too high!')
                ELSE IF (CompNum > Guess)
                    THEN Writeln (Output, 'Too low!')
                    ELSE Writeln (Output, 'Correct!');
            UserDone := (CompNum = Guess);
            UserTurns := UserTurns + 1;
        END;
END;


PROCEDURE MakeGuess (VAR Hi, Lo, CompTurns : Integer;
                     VAR CompDone : Boolean);
(* This procedure makes a guess at the user's secret word.*)
(* The strategy is to do a binary search, with a little  *)
(* randomness thrown in to try to better the results of  *)
(* the game.                                             *)
CONST   OffSet = 0.025;         (* the degree of randomness *)
VAR     Guess : Integer;        (* Computer's guess          *)
        Range : Integer;        (* used to determine size of*)
                                (* randomness in guess       *)
        Response : Char;        (* High, Low, or Correct     *)
BEGIN
        IF NOT CompDone THEN BEGIN
            Range := Round ((High - Low) * OffSet);
            Guess := (High + Low) DIV 2 +
                    RandNum (-Range, Range);
            Writeln (Output, 'My guess is ', Guess:1,'. ',
                'Type C (correct), L (Low), or H (High).');
            Readln (Input, Response);
            IF (Response = 'L')
                THEN Low := Guess + 1
                ELSE IF (Response = 'H')
                    THEN High := Guess - 1
                    ELSE CompDone := TRUE;
            CompTurns := CompTurns + 1;
        END;
END;


PROCEDURE ReportScore (User, Comp : Integer);
BEGIN
        Writeln (Output, 'I took ', Comp:1, ' turns, and ',
                    'you took ', User:1, ' turns.');
        IF (User < Comp)
            THEN Writeln (Output, 'You won!')
            ELSE IF (User > Comp)
```

```
                        THEN Writeln (Output, 'I won!')
                        ELSE Writeln (Output, 'We tied...');
END;


FUNCTION WantsToQuit : Boolean;
VAR     Response : Char;
BEGIN
        Writeln (Output, 'Do you want to play again?');
        Readln (Input, Response);
        WantsToQuit := (Response = 'N') OR (Response = 'n');
END;


BEGIN   (* Main Program *)
        InitRand (Seed);
        REPEAT  Initialize (High, Low, UserTurns, CompTurns,
                            UserDone, CompDone);
                CompNum := RandNum (Low, High);
                REPEAT  UserGuess (CompNum, UserTurns,
                                   UserDone);
                        MakeGuess (High, Low, CompTurns,
                                   CompDone);
                UNTIL UserDone AND CompDone;
                ReportScore (UserTurns, CompTurns);
        UNTIL WantsToQuit;
END.    (* Main Program *)
```

The module tree for this program is shown in Figure 9.3.

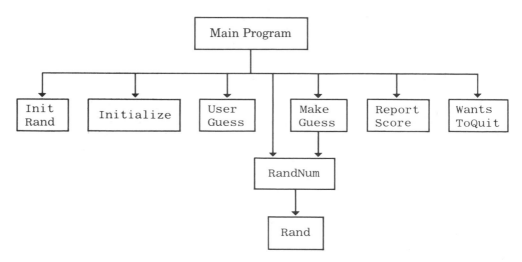

Figure 9.3: Module Tree for NumGuess

A sample run of the previous program is long, but it illustrates the advantages of randomizing the computer's guess. It also makes the game a great deal more interesting to play!

INTERACTIVE SESSION

```
Type any 5 digit number to begin:
29044
What is your guess?
500
Too low!
My guess is 506. Type C (correct), L (Low), or H (High).
L
What is your guess?
750
Too high!
My guess is 765. Type C (correct), L (Low), or H (High).
L
What is your guess?
625
Too high!
My guess is 885. Type C (correct), L (Low), or H (High).
L
What is your guess?
562
Too low!
My guess is 944. Type C (correct), L (Low), or H (High).
H
What is your guess?
593
Too high!
My guess is 913. Type C (correct), L (Low), or H (High).
L
What is your guess?
578
Too low!
My guess is 929. Type C (correct), L (Low), or H (High).
H
What is your guess?
586
Too high!
My guess is 921. Type C (correct), L (Low), or H (High).
L
What is your guess?
582
Too high!
```

```
My guess is 925. Type C (correct), L (Low), or H (High).
L
What is your guess?
580
Too low!
My guess is 927. Type C (correct), L (Low), or H (High).
C
What is your guess?
581
Correct!
I took 9 turns, and you took 10 turns.
I won!
Do you want to play again?
N
```

Common Errors and Debugging

Up to this point, we have usually made an assumption that the input file would be structured correctly and contain the appropriate data needed to solve the problem and that the user of interactive programs would be totally cooperative. Well, as we all know, real life is not always like that. In fact, users of computer programs commonly type incorrect data or inappropriate responses to questions. If we aren't prepared, these responses can cause problems in our programs, ranging from slight problems affecting the format of the output to run-time errors that shut down operation.

A program that doesn't break when it receives bad data is called **robust**. Like other programming virtues, such as modularity and portability, robustness is a quality we want in our programs. Robustness is usually something added to a program after it is at least partially running because that is when all the possible breakdowns are discovered.

When you are writing a program, spend some time brainstorming all the possible things that could go wrong in the input file or with the user that might affect the proper execution of your program. Some things, like finding a letter in the input file when you are expecting to read an integer, cannot be corrected at this time. However, suppose you ask a question expecting a yes or no (Y or N) answer. What does your program do if the user types M? Does it interpret that as an N? In this case, you can use your new knowledge of conditional repetition to continue to ask the question until a Y or N has been given.

```
FUNCTION WantsToPlay : Boolean;
VAR     Ans : Char;
BEGIN
        Write (Output, 'Do you want to play again?');
        REPEAT  Writeln (Output, 'Type Y or N) ==>');
                Readln (Input, Ans);
        UNTIL (Ans = 'Y') OR (Ans = 'y') OR
              (Ans = 'N') OR (Ans = 'n');
        WantsToPlay := (Ans = 'Y') OR (Ans = 'y');
END;
```

Checking data as it comes from the user is always wise, because you have to assume that the user is going to make mistakes. As I emphasized before, programs are made for human beings—not the other way around.

The common errors associated with the material in this chapter are the following:

1. **Writing infinite loops.** These can be caused in a number of ways:
   a. **Including a semicolon after the DO in a WHILE loop.** This is one of the most difficult infinite loops to detect because the computer is doing nothing, but doing it an infinite number of times. In other words, no arithmetic overflow error will occur, as it does when 1 is added to or subtracted an infinite number of times. It is also difficult to spot on your program listing; it is necessary to be looking for it:

   ```
   WHILE NOT Eoln(Input) DO;
       ReadOneLine (      );
   ```

   b. **Omitting a needed BEGIN.** This also may cause an infinite loop, though it is more easily detected. For example, the following loop can be spotted easily by examining the output as it is sent to the terminal—the same value will be written repeatedly.

   ```
   Read (Input, Num);
   WHILE (Num <> FlagValue) DO
       Writeln (Output, Num);
       Read (Input, Num);
   ```

   c. **Not changing the value of the test inside the loop.** This often can be avoided or found by carefully cross-checking variables throughout the program.

   ```
   REPEAT
       X:= X + 1;
       Writeln (Output, X, Sqrt(X):10:4);
   UNTIL Num >= 100;
   ```

2. **Not performing the test at the correct point.** Consider the following code, which is supposed to process a file of student data.

```
WHILE (StudentNum<>0) DO BEGIN
       Read (Input, StudentNum);
       ProcessStudentsData (StudentNum, ... );
END;
```

The flag value, marking the end of the file, is when StudentNum is 0. However, after the flag value is read, a final attempt will be made to process that student's data, but there won't be any data in the input file. Prevent this by carefully writing code such as:

```
Read (Input, StudentNum);
WHILE (StudentNum<>0) DO BEGIN
       ProcessStudentsData (StudentNum, ... );
       Read (Input, StudentNum);
END;
```

In this case, you can put the Read statement after all processing. Note too that the loop must be primed by an initial Read statement before the loop is entered.

3. **Not throwing away the Eoln marker when reading until Eof.** Eof is *not* satisfied when the input file pointer is pointing at the last Eoln marker. A Readln should occur after every loop such as

```
WHILE NOT Eoln (Input) DO BEGIN
       . . .
END;
```

This will ensure that the Eof marker will be encountered properly.

Hints for BASIC Programmers

There is no single way to effect conditional repetition in most BASIC implementations. Rather, there are a lot of different ways to perform the combination of a loop structure and conditional program control. The crude combination of a FOR loop and an IF statement suggested at the beginning of the chapter as a solution is in fact one of the common ways this type of control structure is programmed in BASIC. For example, here is a BASIC program that totals and averages an unknown number of test scores and stops when the test score is less than 0, the lowest legal score.

```
100 REM - TEST SCORE CALCULATIONS
110 REM S = SCORE
120 REM T = TOTAL
130 REM N = NUMBER OF SCORES
140 REM A = AVERAGE
```

```
200 LET T = 0
210 FOR I = 1 TO 1000
220    INPUT S
230    IF S<0 THEN 260
240    LET T = T+S
250 NEXT I
260 LET N = I-1
270 LET A = T/N
280 PRINT N, T, A
290 END
```

This program assumes that there will be less than 1,000 scores, which for most college classes is a safe assumption. However, the fact remains that the program will not execute its given task if there are more than 1,000 numbers in the input file. In general, no solution requiring conditional repetition will be satisfactory when the control structure is built from a definite repetition FOR loop. The Pascal version looks like this:

```
BEGIN
        Total := 0; NumScores := 0;
        WHILE NOT Eof (Input) DO BEGIN
                NumScores := NumScores + 1;
                Read (Input, Score);
                Total := Total + Score;
        END;
        Writeln (Output, NumScores, Total, Total/NumScores);
END.
```

Perhaps a more general and more powerful form of the WHILE loop in BASIC is created by using both the GO TO and the IF statements. For the previous task, the code in BASIC might look something like this:

```
 90 T = 0
100 N = 0
110 READ S
120 IF S<0 THEN 170
130    LET N = N+1
140    LET T = T+N
150    READ N
160    GO TO 120
170 LET A = T/N
180 PRINT N, T, A
190 END
```

A REPEAT loop structure can also be imitated in BASIC by putting the IF test at the end of the loop. For example, suppose we wanted to calculate how long it will take to double the money in a bank account at a certain yearly interest rate.

```
100  REM  A  =  AMOUNT
110  REM  R  =  RATE  OF  INTEREST
120  REM  Y  =  YEARS
190  INPUT  R
200  LET  A  =  100
210  LET  Y  =  0
220     LET  A  =  A+A*R
230     LET  Y  =  Y  +  1
240     IF  A<200  THEN  220
250  PRINT  R,  Y,  A
260  END
```

This loop structure could be implemented in Pascal as:

```
BEGIN
        Readln  (Input,  Rate);
        Amount  : = 100;  Years  : = 0;
        REPEAT  Years  : = Years + 1;
                Amount  : = Amount + Amount * Rate;
        UNTIL  (Amount >= 200.0);
        Writeln  (Output, Rate, Years, Amount);
END.
```

The WHILE loop also has its parallel in structured BASIC. The use of the WHILE loop in Pascal is essentially the same as in BASIC, except for the fact that there is sometimes a WEND statement in BASIC, which operates as the IFEND does—it ends the WHILE loop. Again, because of the specifications of the syntax in Pascal, no WEND statement is necessary.

SUMMARY

Conditional repetition means that a block of code is repeated an unpredetermined number of times. Conditional repetition is implemented in Pascal by means of the WHILE and REPEAT loops. Without either of these control structures, it would be possible to simulate their effect by using a crude combination of the FOR loop and the IF statement. The resulting code is always inefficient and unclear to the reader of the program. The WHILE and REPEAT loops dramatically increase the power of the programmer.

The WHILE loop has a boolean test at the top of the loop, and the conditions of the test must be satisfied for the controlled statement or statements to be executed. The REPEAT loop has its test at the bottom of the loop, and the statements will continue to be executed until the test is satisfied. The statements in a REPEAT loop will always be executed at least once, before the first test is made.

The standard boolean functions Eoln and Eof are very useful in reading an input file when the exact format is unknown. By using the WHILE loop in conjunction with Eoln or Eof, it is possible to read data from a line or an entire file and avoid getting a read error or mishandling the input.

With three possible looping control structures in Pascal, it is important to be able to distinguish when the different types should be used. A FOR loop should be used when a numerical counter is needed and when the exact number of repetitions needed is known. When the exact number is not known, then a WHILE or REPEAT loop will be needed. When there is a possibility that the loop does not need to repeat, then the WHILE loop, with its test at the top, should be used. When variables need to be initialized before the test occurs, it is often better to use a REPEAT loop than a WHILE loop. If conditional loops are not carefuly constructed, infinite loops that are difficult to find may result.

New Terms

infinite loop	WHILE	REPEAT
invariant assertion	Eoln	
robust	Eof	

EXERCISES

1. What does the following code produce on the output file?

```
Cntr := 1; Max := 5;
WHILE (Cntr < Max) DO BEGIN
    SmallCntr := 0;
    WHILE (SmallCntr < Cntr) DO BEGIN
        REPEAT  SmallCntr := SmallCntr + 1;
        UNTIL (SmallCntr >= Max - Cntr);
        Writeln (Output, SmallCntr);
    END;
    Cntr := Cntr + 1;
END;
```

2. Identify the problem(s) in each of the following indefinite loops. How would you correct each?

```
a. Read (Input, X);
   WHILE (X>0.0) DO BEGIN
           Y := Sqrt (X);
           Writeln (Output, X:10:5, Y:10:7);
   END;
```

```
b. X := 0.0;
   REPEAT  Writeln (Output, X:5:1, Sqrt (X):8:5);
           X := X + 0.2;
   UNTIL (X=1.0);
```

c. Read (Input, Ch);
```
   WHILE (Ch<>' ') DO
           Write (Output, Ch);
           Read (Input, Ch);
```

d. WHILE (Num>=0) DO BEGIN
```
           Read (Input, Num);
           Write (Output, Num:5:1, Sqrt (Num):8:5);
   END;
```

3. Rewrite each of the following loops to produce an efficient and elegant structure.

a. Cntr := 1;
```
   WHILE (Cntr <= MaxCnt) DO BEGIN
       IF IsPrime (Cntr) THEN BEGIN
           Writeln (Output, Cntr:1, ' is a prime number.');
           PrimeCnt := PrimeCnt + 1;
           Sum := Sum + Cntr;
       END ELSE BEGIN
           Writeln (Output, Cntr:1, ' is a composite number.');
           NonPrimeCnt := NonPrimeCnt + 1;
           Sum := Sum + Cntr;
       END;
   END;
```

b. IF Eoln (Input) THEN BEGIN
```
           Readln (Input);
           Writeln (Output);
   END ELSE BEGIN
           REPEAT   Read (Input, Ch);
                   Write (Output, Cap (Ch));
           UNTIL Eoln (Input);
           Readln (Input);
           Writeln (Output);
   END;
```

c. Read (Input, Num); Quantity := 0;
```
   FOR Cntr := 1 TO 100 DO BEGIN
           IF (Num > 0.0) THEN BEGIN
                   Percent := Percent + Num * 100;
                   Read (Input, Num);
                   Quantity := Quantity + 1;
           END;
   END;
```

d. Writeln (Output, 'What is the answer to this question?');
```
   GetUsersAnswer (UsersAnswer);
   WHILE NOT ValidResponse (UsersAnswer) DO BEGIN
           Writeln (Output, 'What is the answer to this ',
                           'question?');
           GetUsersAnswer (UsersResponse);
   END;
```

4. A new game has been developed at Monte Carlo. Cards are dealt face up to the player until a red card appears. The player is paid 2^n, where n is the number of black cards in the player's hand. How much should the house charge its customers to play this game? Write a program to simulate playing this game 100 times. Write it assuming an infinitely large deck, that is, that the chance of dealing a red card remains 1 out of 2. Print out the average payoff over the 100 games. Use RandNum, the random-number-generating procedure introduced on page 220.

5. Rewrite the solution to the previous exercise to reflect the fact that the deck has only 26 black cards and 26 red cards—that the chance of continuing to get a black card decreases as black cards are dealt. How does the average payoff compare to that calculated previously?

6. Write a procedure that accepts a number as a parameter and prints its prime factorization to the output file. If the number is prime, it should merely write prime and return the value True for a boolean flag parameter. Use this procedure to read a file of numbers, write their factorizations, and count how many primes occurred. Sample output:

OUTPUT
```
  15 = 3 * 5
1024 = 2 * 2 * 2 * 2 * 2 * 2 * 2 * 2 * 2 * 2
  31 = 31 (prime)
  17 = 17 (prime)
1728 = 2 * 2 * 2 * 2 * 2 * 2 * 3 * 3 * 3
```

7. The greatest common divisor (GCD) of a pair of numbers is the largest number that evenly divides both of them. The easiest method of calculating it is to repeatedly subtract the smaller number from the larger, replacing the larger with the difference, until the two remaining numbers are equal. For example:

25 and 65	
$a = 25$	$b = 65$
	$b = 65 - 25 = 40$
	$b = 40 - 25 = 15$
$a = 25 - 15 = 10$	
	$b = 15 - 10 = 5$
$a = 10 - 5 = 5$	
$a = b = 5$, GCD $= 5$	

Write a function that takes two arguments, A and B, and returns the GCD.

8. The least common multiple (LCM) of a pair of numbers is the lowest integer that is evenly divisible by both of the numbers. It is related to the GCD in the following way:

$$LCM(a,b) = \frac{a \times b}{GDC(a,b)}$$

Write a function that takes two arguments and uses the GCD function written in Exercise 7 and returns the LCM of the two numbers.

9. Write a program that determines the smallest value that can be distinguished from zero (epsilon) on your Pascal implementation.

10. Write a program that calculates the geometric mean of a file of numbers. The geometric mean of n numbers is defined as:

$$e^{\frac{(\ln(x_1) + \ln(x_2) + \dots + \ln(x_n))}{n}}$$

11. A drunkard lives across the street from a bar. He is presently in the middle of the street and must get out of the street in five minutes, or he will be picked up by the cops. The street is ten paces wide, and he takes one step about every ten seconds, but the direction he will head, toward the bar or toward home, is random. Write a program to simulate twenty journeys of the drunken man. Report the number of times he ended up at home, the number of times he ended up at the bar, and the number of times he spent the night in jail. Also, report the average amount of time it took him to get out of the street when he was able to make it.

INPUT AND OUTPUT

Discussing input and output at this point in the book may seem rather ridiculous because you have been creating input and producing output since the beginning of the book. You have now reached the point, however, where you need to learn new ways to work with input and output. Before moving ahead, let's review.

So far, we have used the standard input and output procedures.

```
Read (Input, <variable-list>)
Readln (Input, <variable-list>)
Write (Output, <expression-list>)
Writeln (Output, <expression-list>)
```

We differentiate between <variable-list> and <expression-list> because we can only do a Read operation on variables, but we can write out the values of variables, constants, expressions, functions, and character strings (string constants).

Field widths can be given to any type of value in a Write statement, even character strings. When a field width is larger than the value to be written needs, the value is right-justified, meaning that the extra spaces in the field appear as blanks before the number, and the last digit falls in the rightmost space. When a given field width is too small, the value will be printed in the minimum number of spaces, yet the whole value will be printed. This is true unless the value is a character string, in which case it will be truncated to fit the specified field width.

Eoln and Eof are two standard boolean functions that take one parameter, the input file name, and are satisfied if the file pointer is at the end of the line or the file, respectively. They are used to read a file of unspecified format without losing the information about where the ends of lines go. For example, when reading numbers, the Read operation will skip right over the end of one line when looking for a value. If we only want to read a number if there is still one left on the current line, we can write:

```
IF NOT Eoln (Input)
        THEN Read (Input, Num);
```

In general, we use a nested WHILE loop structure to process a whole file of information we need to look at.

```
WHILE NOT Eof (Input) DO BEGIN
        WHILE NOT Eoln (Input) DO
                DoOneChunk (      );
        Readln (Input);
END;
```

All along in this text, we have seen examples of the superiority of Pascal over BASIC. However, as you have perhaps realized, BASIC is easier to use when it comes to reading and writing character strings. In order to read a character string, BASIC requires a single READ statement. In Pascal, as we have seen, it is necessary to read a single character at a time. Also, we do not know how to store a character string for later use. Be patient with Pascal, because the advantages we'll soon learn about will far outweigh the inadequacy of Pascal in this area.

Multiple Input and Output Files

In all the examples and exercises so far, we have seen programs that either generate their own data to work with, read data from an input file, or read from the terminal. Suppose you want to write a program that reads from an input file *and* reads from a terminal. Both would be considered input files; how would you distinguish between them to the computer?

Suppose, for example, that we wanted to modify the problem of Programming Example 8.1 so that, instead of generating random arithmetic problems, we read them from an input file. Everything else about the problem would be the same, but we would change PROCEDURE GenerateOneProblem to ReadOneProblem. Instead of needing just one file called Input, we'll use two files, called TermIn and InFile. TermIn designates input from the terminal; InFile designates input from a file. The program requires several changes before these identifiers will be understood.

```
PROGRAM  MathTutor (TermIn, InFile, Output);

VAR      TermIn,
         InFile:  Text;
```

The first line is somewhat familiar—all the files used must be declared in the program header. Notice that Input is not in there at all; there is nothing sacred about that file name. However, the variable declaration section looks a little strange. It seems as if TermIn and InFile are being declared as variables!

Well, they are, as file variables of type Text. **File variables** are variables, and they are also files. (Remarkable!)

We can think of the program header as the parameter list for the program. All of the files listed are the variable parameters needed for input to or output from the program. We have always used Input and Output as the names of our program parameters, but there is no reason why this should always be so. Input in Pascal is an identifier.

One doesn't need to declare Input and Output as variables of type Text because Pascal already knows about them—they are standard identifiers. If we want to change the output file name to OutFile, then we have to declare it as a variable of type Text as well, since we know there is nothing sacred about output file names either.

```
PROGRAM MathTutor (TermIn, InFile, OutFile);

VAR       TermIn,
          InFile,
          OutFile  : Text;
. . .
BEGIN
          (* Main Program *)
          Reset (TermIn);
          Reset (InFile);
          Rewrite (OutFile);
          . . .
END.
```

The next thing that must be done to MathTutor when using a file other than Input or Output is that the file must be opened for reading or writing, respectively. Each input file must be reset using Reset, a standard Pascal procedure. The only parameter is the name of the file to be reset. The Reset procedure opens the file for reading and places the file pointer at the head of the file so that the first value to be read is the first value on the first line of the file. In all of the programs we have seen so far, the input file is only reset once, and it is done automatically. However, it is possible to reset an input file and read from it more than once, simply by executing repeated calls to Reset. However, for most of the programs you will write, it should be only necessary to read input files once, and it is considered bad programming practice to reset input files more than once unless the problem specification demands it.

Each output file must be "rewritten" using the standard procedure Rewrite. This procedure is entirely analogous to the Reset procedure; it opens the file for writing and places the file pointer to the top of the file named, so that the next character or value printed will be printed at the beginning of the top line in the file.

These two procedures must be executed before anything is read or written to any of these files, so it is usually best to execute them as the first elements in a main program. You usually want to reset or rewrite files only once, so don't put the statements inside of a procedure that may be executed several times. Furthermore, once a file has been Reset, it is illegal to attempt to Write on it. Likewise, an error will occur if an attempt is made to Read from a file open only for writing.

Finally, every time a reference to the input or output file occurs, specify the name you gave it. For example, in the MathTutor program:

```
PROCEDURE ReadOneProblem (VAR Num1, Num2 : Integer;
                              VAR Op : Char);
BEGIN
        Readln (InFile, Num1, Op, Num2);
END;

PROCEDURE WriteProblem (Num1, Num2 : Integer; Op : Char);
BEGIN
        Write (OutFile, Num1:1, Op:2, ' ', Num2:1, '=');
END;

PROCEDURE GetUserAnswer (VAR User : Integer);
BEGIN
        Readln (TermIn, User);
END;
```

This rule also applies to Eoln and Eof. Both functions take arguments, such as:

```
IF Eoln (TermIn) THEN ...

WHILE NOT Eof (InFile) DO ...
```

There are therefore four places where program elements must change in order to introduce multiple input or output files:

1. The program header

   ```
   PROGRAM MathTutor (TermIn, InFile, OutFile);
   ```

2. The variable declaration section

   ```
   VAR     TermIn,
           InFile,
           OutFile : Text;
   ```

3. The main program

```
BEGIN
        Reset (TermIn);
        Reset (InFile);
        Rewrite (OutFile);
        . . .
```

4. The parameters

```
Readln (TermIn, Ans);
Read (InFile, Num1, Op, Num2);
Write (OutFile, Num 1:1, Op:2, ' ', Num2:1, '=');
Writeln (OutFile);
IF Eoln (TermIn) THEN ...
WHILE NOT Eof (InFile) DO ...
```

It is easy to forget to make each change, especially in the last category. If you execute your program with a Read (Input, Ans) statement, the compiler probably won't notice, but you will have an uninitialized file error. And if Input was accidentally left in the program header, it might go looking in some stray file for an Answer, when Answer was sitting on the screen unread and ignored.

SELF TEST

Two distinct messages were encoded by merging the characters from each of two files into one file. The odd-numbered characters give the first message; the even-numbered characters give the second message. Write a procedure to decode the message by printing it into two output files. Assume the messages are the same length.

Programming Example 10.1

Assignment: Write a short program that takes an input file of text and makes a copy to an output file and also prints the file on a screen. The program should print the text in blocks of 20 lines, and then wait for the user to type a C to continue. If the user types any other character, printing to the screen should stop, although the copy to the output file should continue. (See Figure 10.1.)

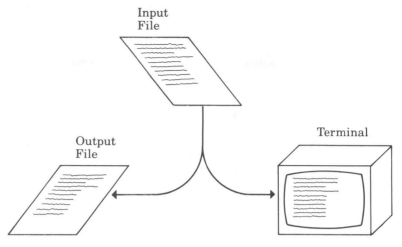

Figure 10.1: Print in Blocks

Solution: This program combines reading from an input file and from the terminal. It will be an interactive program by definition. It also will be a simple program with just a couple of tricky parts. The main algorithm will look like this:

```
PrintInBlocks:
     OpenFiles
     WHILE NOT at the End of the InFile DO
          Initialize counter := 0
          Loop until screen is full or EOF
               DoOneLine
               Increment counter
          IF NOT Eof (InFile) THEN
               Prompt for a 'C' to continue
          IF Character was not a 'C' THEN
               Turn off printing to screen
```

We might as well use the input file names we used in the last section, when we rewrote `MathTutor`.

```
PROGRAM PrintInBlocks (TermIn, InFile,
                          OutFile, TermOut) ;
(************************************************************)
(* This program takes an input file of text and makes a    *)
(* copy to an output file, but also prints the file,       *)
(* exactly as it looks, on the terminal screen. The program*)
(* prints the text in blocks of 20 lines and then waits for*)
(* the user to type a carriage return before continuing.   *)
(* If the user types any other character before typing a   *)
(* carriage return, the screen printing is terminated, and *)
(* the copy to the output file is completed.               *)
(************************************************************)
VAR     TermIn, TermOut,           (* terminal I/O files   *)
        InFile, OutFile : Text;    (* input file and copy  *)
        LineCounter : Integer;     (* used to print only 20*)
                                   (* at one time.         *)
        PrintToScreen : Boolean;   (* TRUE unless user      *)
                                   (* turns it off.         *)
        Ch : Char;                 (* user's response       *)

BEGIN      (* Main Program *)
        OpenFiles (TermIn, InFile, TermOut, OutFile);
        PrintToScreen := TRUE;
        WHILE NOT Eof (InFile) DO BEGIN
            LineCounter := 0;
            REPEAT
                DoOneLine (PrintToScreen);
                LineCounter := LineCounter + 1;
            UNTIL (LineCounter = 20) OR Eof (InFile);
            IF NOT Eof (InFile) AND PrintToScreen THEN BEGIN
                Write (TermOut, 'Type C <CR> to continue,');
                Write (TermOut, ' any character to quit.');
                Readln (TermIn, Ch);
                PrintToScreen := (Ch = 'C') OR (Ch = 'c');
            END;
        END;
END.
```

Notice that the main program calls a procedure, OpenFiles, and specifies four parameters. There is no reason why input or output files, which are variables, shouldn't be included as parameters in Read or Write procedures. However, whenever a file is sent as a parameter, it must be declared a variable parameter in the formal parameter list, because it will be changed either by reading from it or writing to it. Sending a file variable as a value parameter usually produces a run-time error. Because we will usually work only with procedures that are written for a specific input file, it is often misleading to put the file variables in the parameter list. Later in the book, however, you will write several different procedures and functions that are used on several different input or output files. In these cases, it is wise to fully parameterize the procedures and include file variables as variable parameters in the formal parameter lists.

```
PROCEDURE OpenFiles (VAR TermIn, InF, TermOut, OutF : Text);
(* This procedure opens the text files for reading and    *)
(* writing.                                                *)
BEGIN
        Reset (TermIn);
        Reset (InF);
        Rewrite (TermOut);
        Rewrite (OutF);
END;
```

Let's look at DoOneLine.

```
PROCEDURE DoOneLine (PrintToScreen : Boolean);
(* Processes one line of the InFile and copies it on    *)
(*  one line of the OutFile. If PrintToScreen is True,   *)
(*  then it will do so.                                  *)
VAR    Ch : Char;
BEGIN
        WHILE NOT Eoln (InFile) DO BEGIN
                Read (InFile, Ch);
                Write (OutFile, Ch);
                If PrintToScreen THEN Write (TermOut, Ch);
        END;
        Readln (InFile);
        Writeln (OutFile);
        IF PrintToScreen THEN Writeln (TermOut);
End;
```

We must remember to Readln at the end of the procedure, or the next time the procedure is called, the input file pointer will be sitting on Eoln and the WHILE loop will never be entered. An infinite loop will result.

Programming Example 10.2

Assignment: Write a program that takes two input files, a form letter and a list of addresses. The program should print as many copies of the form letter as there are addresses, with one letter to each name in the file. The letter input file will contain a \ every time a line from the address file is to be inserted into the output. The address file will contain addresses; each address will have one line for each \ in the letter file. There will be a blank line to separate addresses on the list. (See Figure 10.2.)

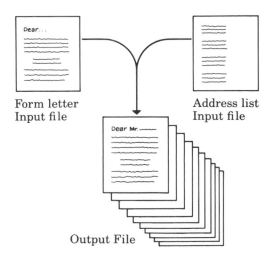

Figure 10.2: Form Letters

Solution: Neither of the input files should be the terminal. Therefore, the program can be batch-oriented, using two input files and no terminal interaction.

The algorithm we will use is:

Form Letters:
       Loop while there are addresses remaining:
           Make one letter to next address
           End the page

This simple algorithm is converted easily into Pascal. Remember, the input file `List`, holding the addresses, must be `Reset` before we can do an `Eof` test on the file.

```
BEGIN    (*Main Program *)
         Reset (List);
         WHILE NOT Eof (List) DO BEGIN
                 MakeOneLetter;
                 Page (Output);
         END;
END.     (* Main Program *)
```

You may notice the use of the standard identifier `Page`. `Page` is a Pascal procedure that begins a new page on the output file. `Page` is a standard procedure, like `Write` and `Writeln`, but unlike the previous two procedures, it never takes more than one parameter, the file name.

PROCEDURE `MakeOneLetter` is not difficult either, once we understand the format of the form letter. The form letter will be comprised mainly of characters, which we will want to print to the output file. However, whenever the computer finds a \ in the letter file, then control should switch to a procedure that reads one line from the address file. Then control switches back to reading from the letter file. We will assume that the letter file does not end with a \. We must also remember that this procedure calls Reset on Letter every time it is called. This is because we are going to repeatedly read and copy the letter into the output file until we have gone all the way through the address list.

```
PROCEDURE MakeOneLetter;
(* This procedure alternates between reading from the      *)
(* Letter file and reading from the List file, until the   *)
(* end of the Letter file is encountered.                  *)
BEGIN
        Reset (Letter);
        CopyLetterTilStop;
        WHILE NOT Eof (Letter) DO BEGIN
                CopyListTilEoln;
                CopyLetterTilStop;
        END;
        Readln (List);   (* Throw away blank lines between *)
END;                     (* addresses                      *)
```

Now all we must do is write the two procedures mentioned in MakeOne-Letter. CopyLetterTilStop is slightly difficult. We must not lose track of any Eoln markers without doing a Writeln to the output file to ensure that the lines match and are not too long. We want each letter to look exactly like the form letter, with the names inserted correctly.

```
PROCEDURE CopyLetterTilStop;
(* This procedure copies the text from the Letter file to *)
(* the output file until it runs across the StopChar or   *)
(* the Eof. The stop character directs reading to come    *)
(* from the address list input file.                      *)
CONST   StopChar = '\';   (* not likely to occur in letter *)
VAR     Ch : Char;
BEGIN
        REPEAT  IF Eoln (Letter) THEN BEGIN
                        Readln (Letter);
                        Writeln (Output);
                END ELSE BEGIN
                        Read (Letter, Ch);
                        IF (Ch <> StopChar)
                                THEN Write (Output, Ch);
                END;
        UNTIL (Ch = StopChar) OR Eof (Letter);
END;
```

This procedure could have been structured in other ways that used a WHILE loop or different tests (like Eoln) in the UNTIL part, but all the structures are about the same in terms of efficiency. This structure is easy to read. Notice that it can handle multiple blank lines. It will do this because it will not attempt to read any character from Letter if the pointer is at the end of the line. As long as Eoln is TRUE, the loop simply does a Readln on the input file and a Writeln to the output file.

The other copy procedure is very easy. It copies characters from one file to another until it reaches Eoln.

```
PROCEDURE CopyListTilEoln;
(* This procedure copies one line of text from the address*)
(* list file to the output file, producing 'personalized' *)
(* form letters.                                           *)
VAR     Ch : Char;
BEGIN
        WHILE NOT Eoln (List) DO BEGIN
            Read (List, Ch);
            Write (Output, Ch);
        END;
        Readln (List);
END;
```

The final program follows.

```
PROGRAM FormLetter (Letter, List, Output);
(************************************************************)
(* This program takes two input files, a form letter and  *)
(* an address list, and sends addresses a version of the  *)
(* form letter for each individual on the address list.    *)
(* The form letter file is formatted to specify where any *)
(* fields from the address list file should go.            *)
(************************************************************)


VAR     Letter, List : Text;      (*input files needed      *)


PROCEDURE CopyLetterTilStop;
(* This procedure copies the text from the Letter file to *)
(* the output file until it runs across the StopChar or    *)
(* the Eof. The stop character directs reading to come     *)
(* from the address list input file.                       *)
CONST   Stop Char = '\'; (* not likely to occur in letter *)
VAR     Ch : Char;
```

```
BEGIN
        REPEAT  IF Eoln (Letter) THEN BEGIN
                     Readln (Letter);
                     Writeln (Output);
                END ELSE BEGIN
                     Read (Letter, Ch);
                     IF (Ch <> StopChar)
                          THEN Write (Output, Ch);
                END;
        UNTIL (Ch = StopChar) OR Eof (Letter);
END;


PROCEDURE CopyListTilEoln;
(* This procedure copies one line of text from the address*)
(* list file to the output file, producing 'personalized' *)
(* form letters.                                           *)
VAR     Ch : Char;
BEGIN
        WHILE NOT Eoln (List) DO BEGIN
            Read (List, Ch);
            Write (Output, Ch);
        END;
        Readln (List);
END;


PROCEDURE MakeOneLetter;
(* This procedure alternates between reading from the     *)
(* Letter file and reading from the List file, until the  *)
(* end of the Letter file is encountered.                 *)
BEGIN
        Reset (Letter);
        CopyLetterTilStop;
        WHILE NOT Eof (Letter) DO BEGIN
                CopyListTilEoln;
                CopyLetterTilStop;
        END;
        Readln (List);   (* Throw away blank line between *)
END;                     (* addresses                     *)

BEGIN   (* Main Program *)
        Reset (List);
        WHILE NOT Eof (List) DO BEGIN
                MakeOneLetter;
                Page (Output);
        END;
END.    (* Main Program *)
```

Here are parts of a sample letter input file and a sample address list input file.

```
                                        March 1, 1985
    \
    \
    \


Dear \,

      If you find it as hard to make time for necessary
shopping as I do, you'll appreciate our direct-by-mail
shopping service. As a Small Oil Credit Cardholder, you
. . .
```

Here is the address list, in the proper format.

```
Liz Argetsinger
2200 Oakwood Dr.
Lexington, KY 40502
Ms. Argetsinger
Ms. Argetsinger

Nate Bacon
P.O. Box 3831
San Francisco, CA 94105
Mr. Bacon
Mr. Bacon

David and Elisa Bosley
P.O. Box 10264
Stanford, CA 94305
Mr. and Mrs. Bosley
Mr. and Mrs. Bosley

Rachel Brown
2306 Ferndale
Ames, IA 50010
Ms. Brown
Ms. Brown
```

And finally, the form letter, the masterpiece of the "individual touch":

March 1, 1985

OUTPUT   Liz Argetsinger
2200 Oakwood Dr.
Lexington, KY 40502

Dear Ms. Argetsinger,
     If you find it as hard to make time for necessary
shopping as I do, you'll appreciate our direct-by-mail
shopping service. As a Small Oil Credit Cardholder, you
are entitled to a 15-day Free home examination of our
top-quality products at attractive prices. Yes, you
don't even have to leave your home!

          TAKE ADVANTAGE OF OUR CONVENIENT PAYMENT PLAN
Ms. Argetsinger, as a long-standing Credit Cardholder in
good standing, you have the option of paying convenient
monthly installments via your Small Oil account, as
outlined in each of the enclosed brochures.

                    ORDER NOW!
Right now-- why not look over the super values featured
in the enclosed brochures. Then, simply check the appropriate boxes on the enclosed order form. Do it now, so
that you don't miss out on these fine values!

                         Sincerely

                         C. Gregory Read
                         Consumer Services

Common Errors and Debugging

1. **Forgetting to initialize files.**
   a. If you forget to Reset or Rewrite input or output files other than Input or Output, you will get an error the first time you attempt to access one of the files.
   b. If you forget to specify Readln (InFile, ...), then you will probably get a similar error. It is best not to use Input as a file name when you have more than one input file, because it is more difficult to spot initializing errors. As a default, the compiler reads from Input, and if Input is lying around, errors

will result which may be difficult to detect. The same applies to using Output as a file name.

2. **Encountering system-dependent quirks.** File handling is one aspect of Pascal programming that is very system dependent. This is often true of programming languages because external file handling is part of the operating system as well as part of the data structure or of the software.

    a. The files listed in the program header are assigned to actual files in memory, to the terminal, or to the printer in a variety of different ways, depending on the system used. Some systems will allow you to omit files from the program header, then receive actual file names through the Reset or Rewrite procedures. For example, suppose the letter file on the disk was named 'Form.Let'. Some systems would allow you to type Reset (Letter, 'Form.Let'). Some systems specify that the file name must be equivalent to the file variable name and a certain specified three-letter extension, with a period in the middle. This is obviously something you will need to check out at your implementation.

    b. The first character of the line on IBM output files is often interpreted as a carriage control character. In this case, all of the Write or Writeln statements used in a program should print at least one extra space at the beginning of each line, before the results are printed. Otherwise, the data that is printed will lose its first character, and the character could do unexpected things to the printer carriage, like making it double space or overprint.

3. **Specifying illegal file operations.** It is illegal to try to write to a file open to reading, or to read from a file open to writing. Suppose for example, that you accidentally have the following in the main program.

    ```
    Reset (OutFile);       (* These lines are *)
    Rewrite (InFile);      (* NOT errors *)
    ```

    You will get errors if you try to execute

    ```
    Readln (InFile);       (* These lines are *)
    Writeln (OutFile);     (* then errors     *)
    ```

    because Pascal doesn't have an intrinsic understanding of which identifiers are output file identifiers and which identifiers are input file identifiers (except, of course, Input and Output, and even those can be overriden, as we'll see later).

4. **Specifying illegal file parameters.** It is illegal to send a file that specified the formal parameter as a value parameter into a procedure. Whenever you are using a file parameter, the formal parameter should be declared as a variable parameter.

Hints for BASIC Programmers

Much of BASIC is written for terminal interaction, where the input is supplied by the user when the prompt asks for it. However, in many structured or extended versions of BASIC, there is a command that is somewhat analogous to the Pascal Reset:

100 OPEN "DATA" FOR INPUT AS FILE 1

After the file is open as file 1, it is possible to read from that file (and not the terminal) by using the special form of the INPUT command.

110 INPUT #1, A, B, C

In the same way, extended versions of BASIC allow the programmer to open files for writing in a way that is entirely analogous to the Pascal Rewrite procedure.

200 OPEN "RESULTS" FOR OUTPUT AS FILE 3

The PRINT # command works in the same way.

210 PRINT #3, A, B, C

Pascal, like BASIC, only works with sequential-access files. **Sequential access** means that the values are read from the top of the file down to the bottom, in sequence. The alternative would be **random access,** a storage capacity that is not available for files.

With BASIC, it is necessary to close any open files before termination of the execution.

150 CLOSE 1, 3, 5

This statement closes files 1, 3, and 5, which were opened during the execution. Pascal, on the other hand, does not require the programmer to close the files opened during the execution of a program. Some versions of Pascal have a Close procedure, but in general all open files are closed when the execution is terminated. The only disadvantage to this is that if the program crashes during execution, then all of the data written to open files will be lost. If the files were closed by an intelligent program that perceived a crash coming, then the results would be saved.

SUMMARY

Multiple input and output files are commonly needed when a program requires input from the user and also reads an input file of data or produces a permanent output file. It is possible to write programs that read from and write to many input and output files.

However, since the default in Pascal is to have one file, Input, for reading, and one file, Output, for writing, it is necessary to specify that this is not the case in the following ways:

1. including multi-file specifications in the program header
2. including multi-file specifications in the variable declaration section
3. when initializing the input or output files, using Reset or Rewrite
4. when using the standard I/O procedures and Readln, Read, Writeln, Write, Eof, Eoln, and Page

If you don't declare the file variables as global (or perhaps local, in some cases), then you will get the error "identifier not declared." If you fail to specify which file you are attempting to read from or write to, then the error "unopened file" will probably occur. This error will also result from forgetting to initialize the file with Reset or Rewrite.

New Terms

file variable	Reset	Rewrite
sequential access	Text	
random access	Page	

EXERCISES

1. Write the results of the following I/O statements. Note any errors in syntax.
   a. a := 10; b := 3;
   b. Write (Output, a:b);
   c. Writeln (Output, b:a);
   d. Writeln (Output, 'a *', b, '=' a*b:1);
   e. Readln (Input, a:2, b);
   f. Writeln (Output, 'This is a test':3);
   g. Readln (Input, 'a');

2. Each of the following programs claims to copy an input file to an output file. What does each really do?

   a. PROGRAM CopyFile (In, Out);
      VAR   Ch : Char;
             In, Out : Text;

```
      BEGIN
              Reset (In); Rewrite (Out);
              WHILE NOT Eof (In) DO BEGIN
                      WHILE NOT Eoln (In) DO BEGIN
                              Read (In, Ch);
                              Write (Out, Ch):
                      END;
                      Readln (In);
              END;
      END.
```

b.
```
   PROGRAM CopyFile (In, Out);
      VAR     Ch : Char;
              In, Out : Text;
      BEGIN
              Reset (In); Rewrite (Out);
              WHILE NOT Eof DO BEGIN
                      WHILE NOT Eoln DO BEGIN
                              Read (In, Ch);
                              Write (Out, Ch);
                      END;
                      Readln (In);
                      Writeln (Out);
              END;
      END.
```

c.
```
   PROGRAM CopyFile (In, Out);
      VAR     Ch : Char;
              In, Out : Text;
      BEGIN
              Reset (In); Rewrite (Out);
              WHILE NOT Eof (In) DO BEGIN
                      WHILE NOT Eoln (In) DO BEGIN
                              Read (In, Ch);
                              Write (Out, Ch);
                      END;
                      Writeln (Out);
              END;
      END.
```

d.
```
   PROGRAM CopyFile (In, Out);
      VAR     Ch : Char;
              In, Out : Text;
```

```
        BEGIN
                Reset (In); Rewrite (Out);
                WHILE NOT Eof (In) DO BEGIN
                        WHILE NOT Eoln (In) DO BEGIN
                                Read (In, Ch);
                                Write (Out, Ch);
                        END;
                        Readln;
                        Writeln;
                END:
        END.
```

3. Computer interviews. Write a program that reads questions (one per line) from an input file, writes them to the user's terminal, then reads the answers (character by character) and writes them with the questions to the output file. Read the questions until the end of the input file.

4. Write a procedure, SafeIntRead, that reads from the input file characters and converts them to integers. It should accept an optional + or − and any digits 0 through 9. The failure to find one digit should satisfy the conditions of an error flag. Otherwise, the procedure should terminate by reading a space or other nondigit or by an overflow, which should also turn on the error flag. Assume that reading more than ten digits will cause an overflow.

5. A familiar parlor game begins with a story like this:

    ```
    One day, <someone's name> and <someone else's name>
    were <an -ing word>, when, <an adverb>, out of the
    nearby <a noun>, came a <an adjective> <a noun>.
    "<exclamation>," they exclaimed, and they <adverb>
    ran to the <a place>.
    ```

    The leader asks the group to supply the elements in brackets, without reading the story. Then the leader reads the story, including the responses, and people laugh and enjoy the silly story they have created.

    Write a program that uses the story above as an input file, asks the user at the terminal for the responses, and writes out the final story with the responses. Hint: You will need four files. Think about the program breakdown in terms of which files are being used when.

6. Write a program that reads three input files of text that contain the material typed in one minute by three different people interviewing for the job of clerk/typist. Assume the rest of their qualifications are identical. Therefore, the one who typed the most text with the fewest errors should get the job. Each typed from the same copy, which is correctly given in a fourth input file. Count the number of characters each applicant typed and the number of errors each made. To calculate each applicant's score, subtract from the number of characters 5 times the number of errors made. Your output should print the results and report which of the three applicants should get the job.

7. Write a program that helps the user decode an input file. The input file has been encoded by a shift algorithm—each character is shifted to another in a consistent fashion. For

example, if A is encoded by the letter D, then B is encoded by the value E, C by F, and so forth. First assume the encoded text is shifted forward one character. In your decoding program, begin by shifting backward one character and printing three lines of the input file to the terminal. Allow the user to either accept or reject the translation. If the translation is accepted, then reset the input file and print the complete translation to the output file. If the translation is rejected, then retranslate defining the shift value as 2. Continue retranslating until the message is accepted by the user, or until all possible shifts have been attempted.

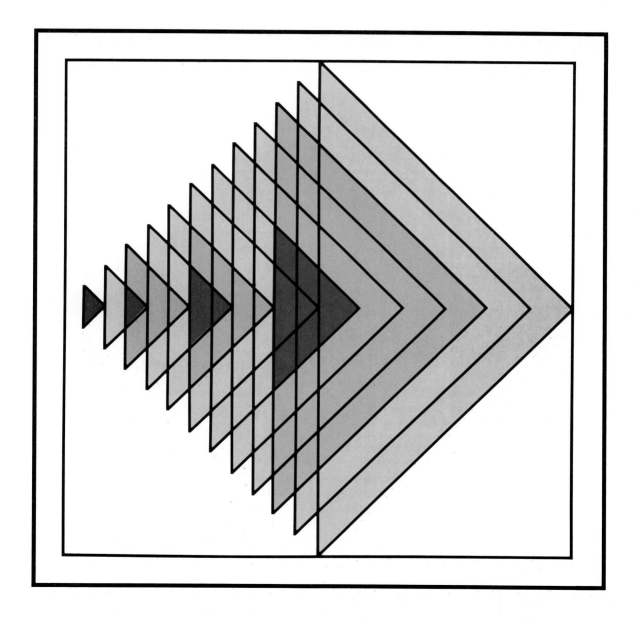

CONDITIONAL EXECUTION: CASE

As the chapter title suggests, the IF statement is not the only control structure in Pascal that allows conditional execution. The IF statement is ideal when we want to decide between two alternatives. However, as we have seen, the IF statement alone can produce awkward and unwieldy code when we need to decide between a host of options. Although we could get by without it, the CASE statement brings refreshing clarity into our decision-making code. You soon will wonder how you managed for ten chapters without it.

The CASE Statement

Suppose we wanted to write a function that would take numerical representations of a month and year in this century as input parameters and return the number of days in the month.

```
FUNCTION DaysInMonth (Month, Year : Integer) : Integer);
(* This procedure takes the value of the month and year    *)
(* and returns the number of days in that month, assuming  *)
(* that the year is in this century. (Year is in the form  *)
(* of 83 for 1983.)                                        *)
```

We know already one way we could write this function. We could use a nested IF statement with several tests connected by OR conjunctions.

```
BEGIN
     IF (Month = 2)
          THEN IF (Year MOD 4 = 0)
                    THEN Days := 29
                    ELSE Days := 28
          ELSE IF (Month = 4) OR (Month = 6) OR
                    (Month = 9) OR (Month = 11)
```

```
                        THEN Days : = 30
                        ELSE Days : = 31;
            DaysInMonth : = Days;
END;
```

This is a little bit awkward, and in Pascal there is an easier way to do this. If we use the CASE statement, we can rewrite the previous code.

```
BEGIN
        CASE Month OF
            2 : IF (Year MOD 4 = 0)
                        THEN Days : = 29
                        ELSE Days : = 28;
            4, 6, 9, 11 :       Days : = 30;
            1, 3, 5, 7, 8, 10, 12 : Days : = 31;
        END;
        DaysInMonth : = Days;
END;
```

The example illustrates the syntax of the CASE statement, which is formally summarized in Figure 11.1.

The idea of case selection as an important control structure in computer programming languages is a fairly recent idea and was first implemented with the CASE statement in Pascal. CASE is not a necessary feature of Pascal; it doesn't add to the power a programmer has to carry out the task required. Essentially, CASE enhances convenience and style.

The CASE statement is one example of Pascal syntax that calls for an END without a BEGIN. The END is necessary to indicate to Pascal when the list of values is complete. If another BEGIN were inserted after OF, for example, an error would occur, because a constant value is expected next. Again, as usual, the statements can be compound statements or procedure calls. The value list can either be a single value or a list of values separated by commas. No variables or expressions can occur inside the value list, and there is no way to abbreviate a whole sequence of values. Each value must be listed separately. The expression

Figure 11.1: CASE Statement Syntax

```
CASE <expression> OF
    <value-list> : <statement>;
    <value-list> : <statement>;
    <value-list> : <statement>;
      . . .
END;
```

is usually a single variable name, but can also be an expression that results in one of the values. The expression and the values must be of the same type, and neither can be real. The same property of reals prevents the programmer from using a real-valued variable in a FOR loop; real variables don't have enumerable or listable values.

We can now use the CASE statement to advance the ever-popular AverageScores program a little further. The status of the main program is currently:

```
BEGIN     (* Main Program *)
          Readln (Input, NumStudents);
          ClassTot := 0;
          Headings;
          FOR EachStudent := 1 TO NumStudents DO BEGIN
                  ReadNWriteName;
                  ReadNSumScores (Total);
                  CalcNWriteAve (Total, Ave, ClassTot);
                  CalcNWriteGrade (Ave);
          END;
          CalcClassAve (ClassTot, NumStudents);
END.      (* Main Program *)
```

In PROCEDURE ReadNSumScores, we have assumed that each score is weighted the same in the overall grade determination. This, however, is a little unrealistic. For example, though the assignments may all have a maximum score of 40 points, it is very likely that the last ones were considerably more difficult than the first. Someone who failed to do very well on the first but who aced the last few should get more credit than someone who found the first one easy but struggled on the last few. Suppose we want to weight the scores by the following percentages:

Score Number	Percent of Final Grade
1, 2	10%
3	15%
4, 5	20%
6	25%

Because the weighting depends on the case or the value of the score number, it seems like a perfect opportunity to use a CASE statement. PROCEDURE ReadNSumScores is a little different now.

```
PROCEDURE ReadNSumScores (VAR Total : Real);
(* This procedure reads until Eoln or until NumScores    *)
(* values have been read, and adds up each weighted score,*)
(* using the following weights: scores 1&2, 10%; score 3, *)
(* 15%; scores 4&5, 20%; score 6, 25%.                    *)
VAR    NumVals : Integer;
BEGIN
```

```
        NumVals := 0;
        Total := 0.0;
        WHILE NOT Eoln (Input) AND
                        (NumVals < NumScores) DO BEGIN
                NumVals := NumVals + 1;
                Read (Input, Score);
                Total := Total + WeightVal (Score, NumVals);
        END;
        Readln (Input);
END;
```

The WeightVal function is a simple CASE statement.

```
FUNCTION WeightVal (Score, ValNum : Integer) : Real;
(* weights the value of the score and returns weighted    *)
(* value.                                                  *)
BEGIN
        CASE ValNum OF
            1,2 : WeightVal := Score * 0.10;
              3 : WeightVal := Score * 0.15;
            4,5 : WeightVal := Score * 0.20;
              6 : WeightVal := Score * 0.25;
        END;
END;
```

SELF
TEST
Write a procedure that reads from input a value between 1 and 7 and writes one of the seven colors in the rainbow to the output file. Red = 1, Orange = 2, Yellow = 3, Green = 4, Blue = 5, Indigo = 6, Violet = 7. Write your procedure so that no error would occur if invalid data are given.

Programming Example 11.1

Assignment: Write a program that asks the user's birthday and prints out the day of the week on which that date occurred. Assume that all birthdays are in this century and are given numerically as Month, Day, Year, where Year is two digits. Calculate the day by counting the number of days that elapsed between Tuesday, January 1, 1901, and the birthday given.

Solution: The problem can be broken down into three tasks.

Calculate Weekday:
    Get Birthday—Month, Day, Year
    Calculate the total number of days since 1/1/01
    Calculate and print the day of the week

This can be converted into three simple procedure calls with parameters for Month, Day, and Year, and the total number of days that have elapsed.

```
BEGIN     (* Main Program *)
          GetBirthday (Day, Month, Year);
          Total := CalcNumDays (Day, Month, Year);
          WriteDay (Total MOD 7);
END.      (* Main Program *)
```

The task of getting the values involves only Read and Write statements. Let's work on adding up the number of days between January 1, 1901 and the given date. This we should be able to do in four steps.

CalcNumDays:
    Add the days in current month
    Add the days in all previous months this year
    Add the days in all previous years
    Add the leap year days not counted

In order to get the days right, let's suppose someone typed 1 8 01. In this case, the number of days would be exactly 7—one week. Therefore, the number of days equals the date in the month minus 1.

In order to do the months, we need to sum up the days in all of the previous months before the current one. FUNCTION DaysInMonth (see page 304) will give us the number of days in any month we specify.

Therefore, we can make an attempt at the procedure CalcNumDays.

```
FUNCTION CalcNumDays (Day, Month, Year : Integer) : Integer;
(* This function calculates the total number of days      *)
(* which have occurred since Tuesday, January 1, 1901.    *)
VAR     MonthCntr, Total : Integer;
BEGIN
        Total := Day - 1;
        FOR MonthCntr := 1 TO Month - 1 DO
            Total := Total + DaysInMonth (MonthCntr, Year);
        Total := Total + 365 * (Year - 1);
        Total := Total + (Year - 1) DIV 4;   (* leap days  *)
        CalcNumDays := Total;
END;
```

Probably the most certain way of finding these equations for the years and the leap days is simply by trial and error, using simple dates, like 1-1-02, 1-1-04, and 1-1-05.

The other two procedures are relatively straightforward. Here is the entire program:

```pascal
PROGRAM DayOfBirth (Input, Output);
(************************************************************)
(* This program asks for the user's birthday and returns   *)
(* the day of week it occurred, with a little rhyme about  *)
(* the particular day.                                      *)
(************************************************************)

VAR     Day, Month, Year,                (* Date of birth *)
        Total: Integer;      (* number of days this century *)

PROCEDURE GetBirthday (VAR Day, Month, Year : Integer);
(* This procedure asks for the user's birthday, which is   *)
(* typed and read in the form of three integers, in the    *)
(* usual form: Month Day Year. The year is given in two    *)
(* decimals and is assumed to be in the current century.   *)
BEGIN
        Writeln (Output, 'Please type your birthday as ',
                         'shown in the example.');
        Writeln (Output, 'Month Day Year (19__) :   5 16 60',
                         ' for example.');
        Readln (Input, Month, Day, Year);
END;


FUNCTION DaysInMonth (Month, Year : Integer) : Integer;
(* This function takes the month and the year and returns  *)
(* the number of days in that month, assuming that the     *)
(* year is in this century.                                *)
BEGIN
        CASE Month OF
            2 : IF (Year MOD 4 = 0)
                    THEN DaysinMonth := 29
                    ELSE DaysinMonth := 28;
            4, 6, 9, 11 :              DaysinMonth := 30;
            1, 3, 5, 7, 8, 10, 12 : DaysinMonth := 31;
          END;
END;


FUNCTION CalcNumDays (Day, Month, Year : Integer) : Integer;
(* This function calculates the total number of days       *)
(* that have occurred since Tuesday, January 1, 1901.      *)
VAR     MonthCntr, Total : Integer;
BEGIN
        Total := Day - 1;
        FOR MonthCntr := 1 TO Month - 1 DO
            Total := Total + DaysInMonth (MonthCntr, Year);
```

```
                    Total := Total + 365 * (Year - 1);
                    Total := Total + (Year - 1) DIV 4;  (* leap days  *)
                    CalcNumDays := Total;
      END;


      PROCEDURE WriteDay (Day : Integer);
      (* This procedure prints out the correct line of the      *)
      (* birthday poem for the given Day. Legal values are 0-6. *)
      (* 0 means Tuesday since Jan. 1, 1901 was a Tuesday.       *)
      BEGIN
              CASE Day OF
                  6 : Writeln (Output, 'Monday''s child is fair',
                                       ' of face.');
                  0 : Writeln (Output, 'Tuesday''s child is full',
                                       ' of grace.');
                  1 : Writeln (Output, 'Wednesday''s child is ',
                                       'full of woe.');
                  2 : Writeln (Output, 'Thursday''s child has ',
                                       'far to go.');
                  3 : Writeln (Output, 'Friday''s child is ',
                                       'loving and giving.');
                  4 : Writeln (Output, 'Saturday''s child works',
                                       'hard for his living.');
                  5 : BEGIN
                      Writeln (Output, 'The child that is born ',
                                       'on the sabbath day,');
                      Writeln (Output, 'is bonny and blyth, and',
                                       'good and gay.');
                      END;
              END;
      END;


      BEGIN    (* Main Program *)
              GetBirthday (Day, Month, Year);
              Total := CalcNumDays (Day, Month, Year);
              WriteDay (Total MOD 7);
      END.     (* Main Program *)
```

See Figure 11.2 for a module tree of this program.

INTERACTIVE SESSION

```
Please type your birthday as shown in the example.
Month Day Year (19__) :  5 16 60 for example.
3 6 62
Tuesday's child is full of grace.
```

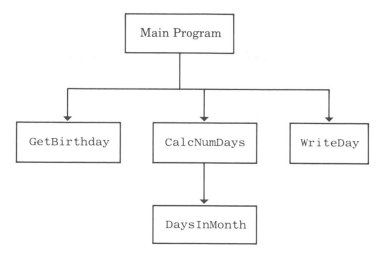

Figure 11.2: Module Tree for `DayOfBirth`

When to Use CASE or IF

Although the IF statement was invented long before Pascal, and although Pascal was the first language to use the CASE statement, the IF statement has not been superseded by the CASE statement. The IF statement can be used to join conditions and to evaluate boolean expressions in a way totally impractical for the CASE statement. For example, it is easy to combine all the following tests into one IF statement.

```
IF (NOT Eoln (Input) AND (I<Max)) OR OnNextLine (LineCt)
        THEN ReadIt (      )
        ELSE DumpIt (      );
```

The only easy way to do this with a CASE statement would be:

```
CASE (NOT Eoln (Input) AND (I<Max))
                    OR OnNextLine (LineCt) OF
        TRUE : ReadIt (      );
        FALSE : DumpIt (      );
END;
```

This, however legal, is a bad use of a CASE statement. CASE statements generally imply that several cases are being listed, and should not be used when a more straightforward approach would warrant the use of an IF-THEN-ELSE statement.

Use a CASE statement whenever there is a set of different options dependent on the value of a single variable. This was the case with `DaysInMonth` and `WeightVal`. Another example is an interactive program with a lot of commands that the user can type to make the computer execute different actions. Often, the commands will be mnemonic characters that help the user remember the many available options. For example, below is a possible control procedure for a program that handles an extensive scoring and grading program. (We will look at programs like this more carefully in Chapter 17.)

```
GetCommand (Com) ;
CASE Com OF
          'A' : AddNewScores  (           ) ;
          'E' : EditScores (           ) ;
          'C' : ChangeScore  (          ) ;
          'N' : NewName (            ) ;
          'S' : SumScores  (           ) ;
          'D' : DropStudent (            ) ;
          'T' : TypeSection (            ) ;
          'H' : Help;
          'Q' : (*Do nothing-- Quit *) ;
          'W' : WriteOnFile (            ) ;
    END;
```

SELF
TEST

For each of the program structures described below, decide whether to use a CASE or an IF statement.

1. a procedure that calculates a separate total for the number of periods, commas, spaces, semicolons, and colons in an input file
2. a procedure that counts the total number of capital and small letters in an input file
3. a procedure that assigns grades to scores on a five-point quiz
4. a procedure that assesses speeding fines based on the excess speed of the vehicle and the number of previous violations of the defendant

Increasing the Power of CASE

Some versions of Pascal (such as Pascal 8000, for example) allow you to use subrange notation in a value list.

```
CASE Score OF       (* nonstandard usage *)
      90..100 :  Grade : = 'A';
      80..89  :  Grade : = 'B';
      70..79  :  Grade : = 'C';
      60..69  :  Grade : = 'D';
       0..59  :  Grade : = 'F';
  END;
```

This is, however, nonstandard, and you should not get in the habit of relying on features like this. On the other hand, it seems like this would be a desirable instance to use a CASE statement. We could write it, in Standard Pascal, like this:

```
CASE Score OF
    90, 91, 92, 93, 94, 95, 96, 97, 98, 99, 100 :
                                        Grade : = 'A';
    80, 81, 82, 83, 84, 85, 86, 87, 88, 89 : Grade : = 'B';
    70, 71, 72, 73, 74, 75, 76, 77, 78, 79 : Grade : = 'C';
    60, 61, 62, 63, 64, 65, 66, 67, 68, 69 : Grade : = 'D';
     0,  1,  2, ...                        : Grade : = 'F';
END;
```

This is long and tedious. It would be ideal to find a shorthand way to express this like the first example, which was as standard as the second version. One way to do this is by scaling. **Scaling** allows us to represent a series of values with labels that are easier to handle. Suppose we scale down the variable we are using by dividing it by 10. We find we can write a much simpler CASE statement.

```
CASE (Score DIV 10) OF
    9, 10 : Grade : = 'A';
    8     : Grade : = 'B';
    7     : Grade : = 'C';
    6     : Grade : = 'D';
    0, 1, 2, 3, 4, 5 : Grade : = 'F';
END;
```

The result of this CASE statement is the same as those of the previous two, but it is easier to read and it is written in Standard Pascal. Often, when dealing with numeric variables, the CASE statement can be made more powerful and elegant through some simple algebraic manipulation.

Perhaps more common extensions to Pascal are the OTHERS, ELSE, and OTHERWISE clauses which can be placed at the end of a CASE statement. For example, suppose for some reason, that Score was negative. With the previous CASE statement, a negative value is not taken into account, and an error results. Many versions of Pascal will not report this execution error, but it *is* an error if the calculated case is not in any of the value lists. To avoid this error, we could use an OTHERS clause.

```
CASE (Score DIV 10) OF
    9, 10 : Grade : = 'A';
    8     : Grade : = 'B';
    7     : Grade : = 'C';
    6     : Grade : = 'D';
    0, 1, 2, 3, 4, 5 : Grade : = 'F';
    OTHERS : Writeln (Output, 'Error, improper Score: ',
                      Score: 1);
END;
```

The OTHERS clause, with the error message, will only be executed if the value of Score DIV 10 is not between 0 and 10 inclusive.

The OTHERS clause works well when reading commands from the terminal. For example, if the procedure GetCommand on page 312 returned a command, Com, which was not equal to one of the legal commands, then an OTHERS clause could have written out an error message and told the user to type a valid command.

```
GetCommand (Com);
CASE Com OF
   . . .
   OTHERS : BEGIN
               Writeln (Output, 'That is not a',
                                ' legal command.');
               Help;
            END;
END;
```

Again, since OTHERS is nonstandard, you will need to see if it is available on your compiler, and you will need to evaluate whether or not you want to use nonstandard Pascal. It isn't necessary, and it is always possible to write CASE statements so that they will never encounter bad data (usually by preceding the CASE statement with an IF statement).

```
IF (Score <= 100) AND (Score >= 0) THEN BEGIN
   CASE (Score DIV 10) OF
      9, 10 : Grade := 'A';
      8     : Grade := 'B';
      7     : Grade := 'C';
      6     : Grade := 'D';
      0, 1, 2, 3, 4, 5 : Grade := 'F';
   END;
END ELSE Writeln (Output, 'Error: invalid Score:',Score:1);
```

Programming Example 11.2

Assignment: The simple children's game Rock, Paper, Scissors is easily simulated by the computer. Write a program that allows the user to play this game against the computer. It should prompt the user for a value, either R, P, or S. The computer should generate its own value using a random number generator, then print the result. The computer should continue playing until the user wants to quit. The computer should then conclude by printing out the percentage score and an evaluation of the user's performance.

Solution: In this program, we'll use CASE statements rather than IF statements. The breakdown of the main program looks like this:

Rock, Paper, Scissors:
        Repeat playing one game
        Until the user wants to quit
        Report the user's final score

Let's break down the first procedure, PlayOneGame.

PlayOneGame:
        Get computer's choice
        Get user's choice
        Compare the two choices:
                Rock crushes scissors
                Scissors cut paper
                Paper wraps rock
        Update Wins, Losses, Ties

It is apparent from the pseudocode that we will need at least three main program variables: Wins, Losses, and Ties, which will be updated in PlayOneGame and used to calculate the final score. This means we'll need to initialize Wins, Losses, and Ties.

```
PROCEDURE Initialize (VAR Wins, Losses, Ties : Integer);
(* This procedure initializes the variables used to keep   *)
(* track of the performance of the user.                   *)
BEGIN
        Wins : = 0;
        Losses : = 0;
        Ties : = 0;
END;


BEGIN    (* Main Program *)
        Initialize (Wins, Losses, Ties);
        REPEAT PlayOneGame (Wins, Losses, Ties);
        UNTIL WantsToQuit;
        ReportScore (Wins, Losses, Ties);
END.     (* Main Program *)
```

Before we write PlayOneGame, let's study WantsToQuit.

```
FUNCTION WantsToQuit : Boolean;
(* This function asks the user if she or he wants to quit *)
(* playing and returns TRUE if the answer is 'Y'(es).     *)
VAR     Ans : Char;
BEGIN
        Writeln (Output, 'Do you want to quit?');
        Readln (Input, Ans);
        WantsToQuit : = (Ans='Y') OR (Ans='y');
END;
```

The comparison between the two choices in `PlayOneGame` is going to be a long CASE statement with nested CASE statements in it. Let's look at the Pascal.

```
PROCEDURE PlayOneGame (VAR Wins, Losses, Ties : Integer);
(* This procedure allows the user to play one game of Rock *
 * Scissors Paper. The computer and the user each choose   *
 * and then the outcome is determined and printed. The     *
 * scores are updated.                                    *)
VAR      UserChoice,             (* either 'R', 'S', or 'P' *)
         ComputerChoice : Char;  (* randomly chosen         *)
BEGIN
        GetComputerChoice (ComputerChoice);
        Writeln (Output, 'What is your choice?  (R,S,P)');
        Readln (Input, UserChoice);
        CASE ComputerChoice OF
            'R' : CASE UserChoice OF
                'R' : BEGIN
                         Ties := Ties + 1;
                         Writeln (Output, 'Rock ties Rock');
                      END;
                'P' : BEGIN
                         Wins := Wins + 1;
                         Writeln (Output, 'Paper wraps Rock');
                      END;
                'S' : BEGIN
                         Losses := Losses + 1;
                         Writeln (Output, 'Rock crushes',
                                          ' scissors');
                      END;
            'S' : CASE UserChoice OF ...
```

This is a long and gnarly procedure. Is there any way we can shorten the CASE statement? There are a few tricks we can use. For example, we can determine whether the outcome is a win, loss, or tie before we enter the CASE statement, which will shorten the whole nested CASE structure by a factor of 4.

```
PROCEDURE PlayOneGame (VAR Wins, Losses, Ties : Integer);
(* This procedure allows the user to play one game of Rock *
 * Scissors Paper. The computer and the user each choose   *
 * and then the outcome is determined and printed. The     *
 * scores are updated.                                    *)
VAR      UserChoice,             (* either 'R', 'S', or 'P' *)
         CompChoice : Char;      (* randomly chosen         *)
BEGIN
        GetComputerChoice (CompChoice);
        Writeln (Output, 'What is your choice?  (R,S,P)');
        Readln (Input, UserChoice);
        IF (CompChoice=UserChoice) THEN Ties := Ties + 1
```

```
        ELSE IF ((CompChoice='R') AND (UserChoice='S'))
            OR ((CompChoice='P') AND (UserChoice='R'))
            OR ((CompChoice='S') AND (UserChoice='P'))
            THEN Losses := Losses + 1
            ELSE Wins := Wins + 1;
    CASE CompChoice OF
        'R' : CASE UserChoice OF
            'R' : Write (Output, 'Rock ties Rock');
            'P' : Write (Output, 'Paper wraps Rock');
            'S' : Write (Output,'Rock crushes Scissors');
            END;
        'P' : CASE UserChoice OF
            'R' : Write (Output, 'Paper wraps Rock');
            'P' : Write (Output, 'Paper ties paper');
            'S' : Write (Output, 'Scissors cut paper');
            END;
        'S' : CASE UserChoice OF
            'R' : Write (Output,'Rock crushes Scissors');
            'P' : Write (Output, 'Scissors cut paper');
            'S' : Write (Output, 'Scissors tie',
                                    ' Scissors');
            END;
    END;
END;
```

Even though this way to write the procedure is a little more inefficient (it makes the same test twice), it is more compact and easy to read. It is a matter of style which is preferable to you, as both are valid and have reasons to commend them.

Using the procedure GetProblem from Chapter 8 as our model, let's briefly look at GetComputerChoice.

```
PROCEDURE GetComputerChoice (VAR CompChoice : Char);
(* This procedure generates a random number between 1 and *)
(* 3 and determines the choice (R,P or S) of the computer. *)
BEGIN
    CASE RandNum (1, 3) OF
        1 : CompChoice := 'R';
        2 : CompChoice := 'P';
        3 : CompChoice := 'S';
    END;
END;
```

Finally, PROCEDURE ReportScore just takes a little creativity.

```
PROCEDURE ReportScore (Wins, Losses, Ties : Integer);
(* This procedure reports the user's win-loss-tie record  *)
(* and evaluates the user's performance.                  *)
VAR    Total : Integer; (* sum of Wins, Losses, and Ties *)
       Percent : Integer; (* between 0 and 100            *)
```

```
BEGIN
        Total := Wins + Losses; (* don't count ties *)
        Percent := Round (Wins * 100/Total);
        Writeln (Output, 'Your record was ', Wins:1,'-',
                        Losses:1, '-', Ties:1,'.');
        Writeln (Output, 'That is ', Percent:1, '%');
        CASE Percent DIV 10 OF
            0, 1 : Writeln (Output, 'Hang it up!');
            2    : Writeln (Output, 'Keep practicing!');
            3    : Writeln (Output, 'Not rotten...');
            4, 5 : Writeln (Output, 'Just average.');
            6    : Writeln (Output, 'Not half bad.');
            7, 8 : Writeln (Output, 'You must have ESP!');
            9, 10: Writeln (Output, 'You must be cheating!');
        END;
END;
```

INTERACTIVE SESSION

```
Type any integer to begin
843219
What is your choice? (R,S,P)
R
Rock ties Rock    Do you want to quit?
n
What is your choice? (R,S,P)
R
Rock crushes Scissors    Do you want to quit?
n
What is your choice? (R,S,P)
P
Scissors cut paper    Do you want to quit?
N
What is your choice? (R,S,P)
S
Rock crushes Scissors    Do you want to quit?
N
What is your choice? (R,S,P)
R
Rock crushes Scissors    Do you want to quit?
N
What is your choice? (R,S,P)
R
Rock crushes Scissors    Do you want to quit?
Y
Your record was 3-2-1.
That is 60%
Not half bad.
```

Common Errors and Debugging

1. **Creating illegal CASE syntax.** It is tempting to either insert a BEGIN after the first line of a CASE statement or to forget the END that terminates it. Remember that a CASE statement is one of the two instances in Pascal where syntax calls for an END without a BEGIN.

2. **Doing a CASE on a real-valued expression.** If a real-valued variable or expression is being examined, the best way to deal with it is probably by using an IF statement or a set of nested IF statements. Another possiblity would be to truncate or round the numbers, then deal with it as an integer CASE.

3. **Not having the value in the set of value lists.** If the value of the expression is not found in any of the lists, it is an error. This can be anticipated with the use of OTHERS or ELSE, both of which are nonstandard extensions to Pascal. An IF statement could also be used to prevent any errors.

```
IF (Score < 0) OR (Score > 100)
        THEN Writeln (Output, 'Improper Datum: ',
                              Score: 1)
        ELSE CASE (Score DIV 10) OF
                9, 10 : Grade := 'A';
                8      : Grade := 'B';
                7      : Grade := 'C';
                6      : Grade := 'D';
                0,1,2,3,4,5 : Grade := 'F';
        END;
```

Hints for BASIC Programmers

The CASE statement, like the conditional loop structures, is not a part of any standard BASIC, although it can be implemented very crudely through a set of nested IF statements. In general, the CASE statement adds to programming languages the flexibility and convenience that selecting one of many alternatives should have. For example, because of the expandability of the CASE statement, new alternatives and corresponding actions can be added easily. This is not possible in ordinary BASIC, where nested IF statements would be used and GO TOs would proliferate. In BASIC, expanding the case selection section of code either requires major restructuring or produces a program full of spaghetti code.

The CASE statement's parallel in structured BASIC is the ON-GO TO statement. The ON-GO TO in BASIC is not nearly as flexible as the CASE statement for several reasons:

1. Each value of the ON-GO TO must be an integer (no character cases are allowed) and the values must begin at 1 and be consecutively arranged.
2. With the ON-GO TO, a line must be given for every alternative case, so there can be no abbreviation when multiple values are to cause the same action to occur.

For example, compare the CASE statement in DaysInMonth in Pascal with its corresponding structure in BASIC.

```
BEGIN
        CASE Month OF
            2 :  IF  (Year MOD 4 = 0)
                            THEN Days : = 29
                            ELSE Days : = 28;
            4, 6, 9, 11 :         Days : = 30;
            1, 3, 5, 7, 8, 10, 12 : Days : = 31;
        END;
        DaysInMonth : = Days;
END;
```

```
 95 IF M>6 THEN 110
100 ON M GO TO 210, 220, 210, 230, 210, 230
105 GO TO 240
110 ON M-6 GO TO 210, 210, 230, 210, 230, 210
210 LET D=31
215 GO TO 240
220 IF INT(Y/4)=Y/4 THEN LET D=29 ELSE LET D=28
225 GO TO 240
230 LET D=30
```

The problem with the BASIC version is that it is not obvious what is happening, as is so often the case with BASIC. The Pascal version is more readable. The most difficult aspect of the BASIC version is that it is not apparent which cases are related, because each separate value needs a line number destination. The ability to group cases with a common action is important in Pascal.

SUMMARY

The CASE statement can combine the selection power of several nested IF statements into a single statement which is usually read and modified more easily. The CASE statement is best suited for use whenever there is a set of different options from which to select an action based on the value of a single variable or expression. The CASE statement cannot be used with real-valued expressions and should not be used with boolean expressions. (The IF statement is well suited for both of these uses.)

The CASE statement can be made more elegant and powerful through the use of **scaling** and through the use of nonstandard but common extensions to the language such as OTHERS, ELSE or OTHERWISE clauses. These clauses appear at the end of a CASE statement to execute a statement when the calculated value of the expression is not given in any of the value lists. In Standard Pascal, this can be simulated through the combination of an IF statement and the CASE statement.

New Terms

scaling
CASE

EXERCISES

1. Write a program to convert a digitized image to a file of characters that prints on a line printer. The image is stored as rows of digits between 0 and 7, where 7 is very dark and 0 is white.

Digit	Character
0	' '
1	' . '
2	' ; '
3	' + '
4	' = '
5	' % '
6	' # '
7	' @ '

The image is stored as 60 lines with 80 digits on each line. Hint: Read the digits as characters.

2. Write a program that asks for the user's birthdate and the current date, and calculates the user's age in days, then in years to two decimals.

3. Write a program that reads an input file of student names and grades and calculates each student's grade point average (GPA). The input file will be organized as follows:

```
<name><units><grade><units><grade>...
<name><units><grade><units><grade>...
...
```

Read the lines until Eof. The name will be exactly 20 characters long, padded by blanks if necessary. The <units> will be an integer, followed by a space, which will be followed by the <grade>. The grade will be either A, B, C, D, F. If the student's average is below 2.0, report that she or he is in danger of probation. If the GPA is below 1.5, report that the student is on probation. If the GPA is above 3.5, put the student on the dean's list. Output should be the name, the GPA, and any warnings or honors for each name in the input file.

4. Write a CASE statement which, given a value in the real variable Duration, prints out the value as the correct number of units of time. If Duration is between 10^{-15} and 10^{-12}, the value is printed out in femtoseconds. If Duration is greater than 10^{-12} but less than 10^{-9}, the time is printed in picoseconds, and so on. Use the following conversions.

Unit	Seconds
Femtosecond	10^{-15}
Picosecond	10^{-12}
Nanosecond	10^{-9}
Microsecond	10^{-6}
Millisecond	10^{-3}

5. Write a program that will print a calendar for any month in the current century. Ask the user for the month (represented by the numbers 1 through 12) and the year (0 through 99).

6. Rewrite the MathTutor program that begins on page 226 using CASE statements rather than IF statements when appropriate. Make it so that it will continue giving problems until the user wants to quit.

7. Write a program that accepts as input a string of digits and writes them out one at a time in big block figures.

8. Write a program that prints regular geometric figures. Ask the user to type L (line), T (triangle), S (square), P (pentagon), H (hexagon), or O (octagon). Print out the corresponding figure, then reprompt the user. Continue until the user types Q to quit. (This program could ask the user to type a digit expressing the number of sides in the desired figure rather than use the letter code.)

9. Write a program that prints Simplified Integrated Modular Prose. Write three procedures that receive a random number and print part of a subject–verb–direct object sentence. Each procedure should choose from a list of about ten different phrases that serve the same function in a sentence. For example, the subject procedure may choose from a list of the following alternatives:
   a. experimental studies of sphere-packing models
   b. the arrangement of the ribosomal-protein genes on the *E. coli* chromosome
   c. the coordinated synthesis of systematic organizational proposals
   d. the ecogenetic differentiation of rice
   Your program should generate a paragraph of meaningless but intelligent-sounding sentences. In order to give your output more coherence, find a technical article on a subject that interests you and take all the subject, verb, and direct object phrases from the article. To produce even more complex sentences, add a fourth procedure that adds subordinate phrases that begin with *although* or *since*.

EXTENDING THE LANGUAGE: TYPES

When we learned about procedures in Chapter 4, we extended our programming power significantly. Procedure declarations teach Pascal new words and give them meaning as executable actions. This is a common idea in programming languages—that of setting apart a piece of code to be executed as a unit and invoked at any time in the main program or other procedures. We have also seen how to extend the language by declaring variable and constant identifiers. We now push beyond constants, variables, and procedures to extend our power once again. In this chapter, we will examine a new kind of declaration: the declaration of types.

Enumerated Type Declarations

When all computer data were in numbers, expression in a computer language was pretty awkward. Even after regular programming languages like FORTRAN and BASIC came along, people were still used to programming with numbers, which they used to signify different responses such as yes or no, black or red, and so forth. For example:

INTERACTIVE SESSION

```
Computer: Play again? (1 = yes, 0 = no)
    User: 0
Computer: Good-bye.
```

Now, with the use of character variables, the interaction can be a little more conversational.

INTERACTIVE SESSION

```
Computer: Would you like to play again? (Yes or No)
    User: No, I don't think so.
Computer: Thank you for playing. So long...
```

The use of boolean variables means that it isn't necessary to do the same thing for tests.

```
IF (Prime=1) THEN Writeln (Number, ' is a prime number.')
             ELSE Writeln (Number, ' is not a prime number.');
(* can now be replaced with: *)
IF Prime THEN Writeln (Number, ' is a prime number.')
         ELSE Writeln (Number, ' is not a prime number.');
```

Suppose we want to declare a variable that takes on different values depending on the day of the week in question. We could say that the variable has integer values from 1 to 7, where 1 is Sunday and 7 is Saturday. But why should 1 be Sunday? How do we keep track of the fact that 6 is Friday, 4 is Wednesday, and so forth? Or perhaps we could use letters, S for Sunday, M for Monday, and so forth. But what about when one letter is not enough to differentiate, as with Saturday and Sunday, Tuesday and Thursday? Is there a better way? Yes. (You could have guessed.) It is actually easier than you might think.

```
PROGRAM TypeExample (Input, Output);
(* This merely gives an example of an enumerated type     *)
(* declaration.                                            *)
CONST   Max = 16;
TYPE    Day = (Sunday, Monday, Tuesday, Wednesday,
                  Thursday, Friday, Saturday);
VAR     Yesterday, Today, Tomorrow : Day;
...
```

There are several things to notice about a type declaration.

1. It fits after the CONST declarations and before the variable declarations in any declaration section. In most cases, types are only declared globally. (Why this is will be explained later.)
2. The identifier that is the name of the new type is followed by an equal sign, as with CONST declarations, and not a colon, as with variables.
3. All the values that the type can assume are **enumerated** (listed); hence the name **enumerated type**. The values can be any legal identifier (not numbers or character strings). The values are enclosed in parentheses.

The thing to realize is that the computer is not too bright about type declarations. For example, the computer wouldn't be the one to complain (although others might) if I declared Day differently.

```
Day = (Sunday, Tuesday, Thursday, Monday, Friday,
        Saturday, Wednesday);
```

It wouldn't even know any better if I declared

```
Day = (Sunday, Bleenday, Thirsty, Monday, Fryday,
        Saturday, Weddingday);
```

It doesn't know which identifiers make up legal days; that is why it takes a type statement to tell it. Once we see how easy it is to declare types, we can really go crazy.

```
TYPE    Colors = (Red, Orange, Yellow, Green, Blue,
                    Indigo, Violet);
        Seasons = (Fall, Winter, Spring, Summer);
        Elements = (Earth, Water, Air, Fire);
        AlivePresidents = (Nixon, Ford, Carter, Reagan);
        Pods = (Brachiopod, Arthropod, Cephalopod,
                Gastropod, Pelecypod);
        PokerHand = (Junk, AceHigh, OnePair, TwoPair,
                    ThreeOfAKind, Straight, FullHouse,
                    Flush, FourOfAKind, StraightFlush,
                    RoyalFlush)
```

This is great, yet there are several things to watch out for. No value can occur in more than one list of values for a type declaration. For example:

```
TYPE    Colors = (Red, Orange, Yellow, Green, Blue,
                    Indigo, Violet);
        Fruit = (Apple, Orange, Banana, Lemon, Grape, Pear);
```

The second line would give an error, because Orange is already declared as a legal color value. Likewise, it is illegal to list character values, character strings, or numbers (integer or real) in a type declaration, because they are not legal identifier names and already have types associated with them. Value identifiers for enumerated types cannot be declared as variables in the same program block. (Actually, they can in certain cases, but never should be, because trouble will result.)

SELF
TEST

Write enumerated type declarations for each of the following type identifiers:

1. HairColor
2. Sex
3. MaritalStatus
4. HouseholdRodents

Use of Enumerated Types

Well, now that we know all there is to know about enumerated type declarations, how do we use them? Essentially, we use them as we use any type; we create a variable of that type and do things with it. What is wrong with the following program?

```
PROGRAM SomethingIsWrong (Output);
TYPE    Day = (Sunday, Monday, Tuesday, Wednesday,
                Thursday, Friday, Saturday);
BEGIN
        Day := Tuesday;
        IF (Day = Tuesday)
            THEN Writeln (Output,'This must be Belgium.')
            ELSE Writeln (Output,'I am lost.');

END.
```

One thing it is easy to forget when we begin using enumerated types is the difference between a type and a variable of that type. The above program doesn't declare any variables, yet it tries to use Day as if it were one. It would be the same as trying to do this:

```
PROGRAM ThisIsWrongToo (Input, Output);
BEGIN
        Readln (Integer, Char);
        Writeln (Char, Integer);
END.
```

We know that Integer and Char as well as Boolean and Real are type identifiers; they don't represent spaces in memory where values can be stored. The same is true for our own enumerated type declarations. Remember this: *declaring a type does not allocate memory space; a variable of that type must also be declared.* We will need to remind ourselves of this again and again in the next several chapters.

However, once we begin declaring variables, we can use enumerated types in virtually every way we can use char, integer, real, and boolean variables, through assignments, tests, FOR loops, CASE statements, as parameters, or as the results of functions. The only thing we can do with the simple types that we cannot do with enumerated, user-defined types is read them from and write them to files with the simple Read, Readln, Write, and Writeln procedures. (This only applies to files of type Text. In Chapter 16, we learn how to read them from and write them to files of different types.) We can, however, write our own procedures to get around this limitation. Furthermore, there are certain things that we won't usually want to do with variables of enumerated types, as we'll see later in this chapter.

For example, assuming the TYPE declarations above, we can do the following:

```
Lambda := 750; (* wavelength in nanometers *)
FOR Color := Red TO Violet DO BEGIN
        Lambda := Lambda - 50;
        CASE Color OF
                Red : Write (Output, 'Red   ');
             Orange : Write (Output, 'Orange');
             Yellow : Write (Output, 'Yellow');
              Green : Write (Output, 'Green ');
               Blue : Write (Output, 'Blue  ');
             Indigo : Write (Output, 'Indigo');
             Violet : Write (Output, 'Violet');
        END;
        Writeln (Output,': Wavelength = ', Lambda:1,
                    ' hv = ', C/Lambda:1:2);
END;
IF (Today = Monday)
        THEN ItsMyBirthDay (LetsCelebrate)
        ELSE WhoCares (IDont);
IF (Today = Monday) AND (Color = Blue)
        THEN ItsABlueMonday (LikeUsual)
        ELSE LetsParty;
```

It is easy to see how enumerated types can be used to make the program code read a lot more like real English. It helps those who must read the program, because they may not be aware that 1 means red or that F means Fall.

Did the use of the FOR loop throw you? How does the computer know what to do with

```
FOR Color := Red TO Violet DO BEGIN
```

Look at the type declaration: Red is listed first, Violet last. Pascal automatically sets up an ordering of enumerated types, and gives each value an ordinal number. Recall the Ord function: Ord ('A') returns the code number for which 'A' is the character. In the same way, then

```
FOR Color := Red TO Violet DO
        Writeln (Output, Ord (Color));
```

would write the ordinal values of the seven different colors. What is Ord (Red)? Pascal always sets up its ordinal type values beginning with 0, so Ord (Red) equals 0, and Ord (Violet) equals 6. When we used Ord last, we were working with characters. When dealing with characters, the inverse function of Ord is Chr, such that

```
Chr (Ord (Ch)) = Ch
```

and

```
Ord (Chr (Num)) = Num
```

However, there is no such built-in function for dealing with enumerated types. There is a simple way to get around this, but first we need to look at a couple more built-in functions that come in handy with enumerated types.

```
TYPE     Day = (Sunday, Monday, Tuesday, Wednesday,
                  Thursday, Friday, Saturday);
VAR      Today, Tomorrow, Yesterday : Day;
BEGIN
         Today : = Tuesday;
         Tomorrow : = Succ (Today);   (* the successor fn *)
         Yesterday : = Pred (Today); (* the predecessor fn *)
         . . .
END.
```

Succ, the **successor function,** takes any ordinal type and returns the next value. It is an error if there is no next value, so Succ (Saturday) would be an error. Pred, correspondingly, is the **predecessor function,** and returns the value that immediately precedes the value given it. Pred (Sunday) gives an error. One result of this is that it is not usually safe to use a WHILE construct to loop through all of the values of an enumerated type. For example:

```
Day : = Sunday;
WHILE (Day <= Saturday) DO BEGIN
        PrintSchedule (Day);
        Day : = Succ (Day);
END;
```

This procedure will result in an error when Day has the value of Saturday and then the Succ function is applied to Day. It is equivalent to the problem you could get if you were trying to count up to MaxInt with integers.

```
Cntr : = 1;
WHILE (Cntr <= MaxInt) DO BEGIN
        Writeln (Output, Cntr);
        Cntr : = Cntr + 1;
END;
```

Of course, you would never write this code, but that is what the previous WHILE loop is like.

In order to work around this problem, it almost always works to use a loop that ends before the last value is dealt with, and then to deal with the last value separately, outside the loop.

```
Day := Sunday;
REPEAT  PrintSchedule (Day);
        Day := Succ (Day);
UNTIL (Day = Saturday);
PrintSchedule (Day);
```

Pred, Succ, and Ord are defined for all ordinal types (integer, char, boolean, and enumerated types). Here are some examples of how expressions involving these would be evaluated:

```
Pred (10) = 9              Succ (FALSE) = TRUE
Pred ('C') = 'B'           Ord (FALSE) = 0
Pred (TRUE) = FALSE        Ord (-10) = -10
Succ (2) = 3               Ord (Succ ('A')) = Ord ('A') + 1
Succ ('3') = '4'
```

Now we know enough to write an inverse function to correspond with the Ord function. The one we will write will return the day of the week given an integer as a parameter. We will call it Dro, since it is the inverse of Ord.

```
PROGRAM VerifyDate (Input, Output);
(* This program knows that the day is Tuesday. It asks the*)
(* user to see if he or she knows, and then evaluates the *)
(* answer.                                                *)

TYPE    Day = (Sunday, Monday, Tuesday, Wednesday,
                 Thursday, Friday, Saturday);
VAR     Today : Day;
        Date : Integer;

FUNCTION Dro (Num : Integer) : Day;
VAR     Temp : Day; Cntr : Integer;
BEGIN
        Temp := Sunday;    (* initialize to 'zero' *)
        FOR Cntr := 1 TO Num DO (* begin at 1 because *)
                           (* the Ord of Sunday is zero  *)
             Temp := Succ (Temp);
        Dro := Temp;
END;

BEGIN   (* Main Program *)
        Today := Tuesday;
        Writeln (Output, 'What day do you think today ',
                         'is (0-6)?');
        Readln (Input, Date);
        IF (Date >= 0) AND (Date <= Ord (Saturday))
```

```
            THEN IF (Today = Dro (Date))
                THEN Writeln (Output, 'You''re right!')
                ELSE Writeln (Output, 'Wrong!')
            ELSE Writeln (Output, 'Illegal input');
END.    (* Main Program *)
```

A procedure similar to Dro must be written for every enumerated type declared; no one procedure can be written that is general enough to work for all types. However, each procedure is structured in exactly the same way, so it is not too difficult to produce the different procedures when needed.

Because enumerated types have the property of being ordered, we can also write the following FOR loops:

```
FOR Color := Violet DOWNTO Red DO ...
FOR Today := Friday DOWNTO Monday DO ...
```

Also, relational operators in boolean tests work as you would expect them to work.

```
(Sunday < Monday)
(Tuesday < Friday)
(Violet > Green)
```

Of course, comparison of variables of different types is illegal, because it is like comparing apples and oranges—they can't be compared.

```
TYPE    Apples = (RedDelicious, YellowDelicious,
                    Washington, Green);
        Oranges = (California, Florida, Navel);
VAR     OneFruit : Apples;
        AnotherFruit : Oranges;
BEGIN
        . . .
        IF (OneFruit <= AnotherFruit)   (* Error here *)
                THEN ...
```

SELF
TEST

Write the following functions using the enumerated types declared in this section.

1. A function called DayBefore that takes a day of the week and returns the day before. It should work for each day.
2. A function like Dro for colors instead of days of the week.
3. A function that asks the name of the user's favorite pod (Brachiopod, Arthropod, and so forth) and returns the correct value of the enumerated type. After you write this function, try to imagine a time when you would possibly need to use it.

Subrange Types

What does it mean when we make the following variable declarations?

```
VAR     Score : Integer;
        Letter : Char;
        WeekDay : Day;
```

We are saying that any integer is a legal value of the variable Score, that any character is a legal value for the variable Letter, and that any Day (Sunday through Saturday) is a legal value for the variable Weekday. Is this really what we want to say? Actually, when we have declared these variables or others like them in the past, we have known that only certain values would be appropriate, but that hasn't affected our declaration. Now we can see how to specify the values we intend a variable to assume.

```
CONST   ScoreMax = 100;
TYPE    Day = (Sunday, Monday, Tuesday, Wednesday,
               Thursday, Friday, Saturday);
        Weekdays = Monday .. Friday;
        ScoreRange = 0 .. ScoreMax;
        LetterType = 'A' .. 'Z';
VAR     Score : ScoreRange;
        Letter : LetterType;
        WeekDay : WeekDays;
```

What we have done is declared **subrange types**. A **subrange** is a defined subset of a declared type. Every subrange type must have a **host type,** or the base type from which the subrange is taken. Any ordinal type, including enumerated or user-defined ordinal types, can have subranges. No subrange of type Real can be declared. Figure 12.1 shows the relationship between a subrange type and its host type.

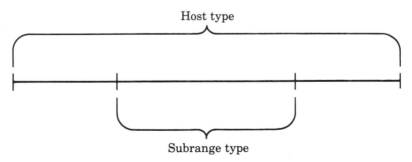

Figure 12.1: Relationship Between Host and Subrange Types

The symbols used to declare a subrange type are the two dots (. .), or ellipses, which separate the lower bound of the subrange from the upper bound. Even if there are only one or two values in the subrange, these ellipses must be used.

```
TYPE    One = 1 .. 1;     (* a variable of this type is
                             essentially a constant, but must
                             still be initialized, unlike a
                             constant  *)
        ZeroOrOne = 0 .. 1; (* a boolean-like variable *)
```

Furthermore, all of the values of a subrange must be contiguous, and the lower bound must be less than or equal to the upper bound. Illegal type declarations would include:

```
TYPE    GPARange = 0.0 .. 4.0; (* no real subranges *)
        WeekEnd = Sunday, Saturday; (* not contiguous *)
        Grades = 'A'..'D', 'F';    (* not contiguous *)
        EvenNums = 0, 2, 4, 6, 8;  (* not contiguous *)
        Countdown = 10 .. 0;  (* lower bound (10) greater
                                 than upper bound (0) *)
```

Subrange types enhance program readability. Subranges, like meaningful variable names, are self-documenting features of a program. You, the programmer, gain no new power, but type and variable declarations become more straightforward and the declaration gives more information. For example, when ScoreRange is declared, we realize that all the scores reported must be between 0 and the maximum score.

A negative effect of using subrange types is that any improper data will crash the program unless the most stringent measures are taken to prevent it. This is both a blessing and a curse. It is useful because it helps you find places where your program might otherwise accept meaningless and error-introducing data. It is also a hassle because protective measures must be encoded to ensure that no program crashes occur. The following procedure, which reads voter ages from an input file with voter statistics on it, is an example. It returns the value of the voter's age if it is legal and returns Legal as a boolean flag.

```
PROGRAM AnalyzeVoterStats (Input, Output);

CONST   LegalVotingAge = 18;
        MaxAge = 120;   (* not to disenfranchise those older
                           than 120, but let's be serious... *)
TYPE    LegalRange = LegalVotingAge .. MaxAge;
VAR     . . .
```

```
PROCEDURE ReadVoterAge (VAR Age : LegalRange;
                          VAR Legal : Boolean);
VAR     Temp : Integer;
BEGIN
        Read (Input, Temp);
        Legal := (Temp<=MaxAge) AND (Temp>=LegalVotingAge);
        IF Legal THEN Age := Temp;
END;

PROCEDURE ReadVoter (Age : LegalRange; ...);
VAR     Legal : Boolean;
        BEGIN
        ReadVoterAge (Age, Legal);
        IF NOT Legal
                THEN Readln (Input)
                ELSE BEGIN ...
END;
```

In this chapter, we have been talking about defining new types and then declaring variables of the new type. The step of defining a type can be bypassed by simply declaring the variable.

```
VAR     Color : (Red, Orange, Yellow, Green, Blue,
                  Indigo, Violet);
        Score : 0..100;
```

There are several problems with this, however. First of all, all parameters must be declared with a one-word type identifier. No subranges are allowed in formal parameter lists. For example:

```
FUNCTION CalculateTax (TaxableIncome : 0..100000;
                        TaxBracket : 0..50) : 0..50000;
                          (* Illegal *)
```

This would not be a legal function declaration because 0..100000 is not a legal type identifier. However, if the appropriate subrange type declarations were made ahead of time, then the following would work.

```
FUNCTION CalculateTax (TaxableIncome : IncomeRange;
                        TaxBracket : Percentage) : TaxRange;
```

Therefore, except for variables defined locally that never pass to other procedures, it is probably better to declare all types before declaring any variables. It is also for this reason that almost all of a program's type declarations should be global. Hence, constant declarations, which are often used in type declarations, should also usually be global.

SELF
TEST

Declare subrange types for men's or women's clothing sizes, whichever you know more about. Write a procedure that prompts a user of the appropriate sex for values of all the sizes needed to prepare an outfit for a wedding.

Programming Example 12.1

Assignment: Write a function, `CalculateTax`, that takes two parameters, `TaxableIncome` and `Status`, and returns the amount of tax in dollars owed to the government. Status can be one of these values: `Single`, `Head`, `MarriedJoint`, or `MarriedSep`. Determine the amount of tax by using the following table.

Filing Status	Bracket Size	Beginning Rate
Single	$1,000	11% over $2,300
Head of Household	$1,100	11% over $2,300
Married, Jointly	$1,500	11% over $3,400
Married, Separate	$ 900	11% over $1,700

For every variable, specify the range in which the values will fall in the type declaration.

Solution: This calls for some global type declarations.

```
TYPE    StatusType = (Single, Head, MarriedJoint,
                      MarriedSep);
        IncomeRange = 0..100000; (* we won't worry about *)
                                 (* anything higher.     *)
        TaxRange = 0..50000; (* no more than half taxed  *)
```

The amount of tax owed will be calculated from income according to the progression of brackets for an individual, and the category the taxpayer is in. For example, if a single person makes $4,300, then the number of filled tax brackets is two, the $2,300 to 3,299 bracket, and the $3,300 to 4,299 bracket. The amount of tax owed would simply be the amount of tax on the first bracket added to the amount of tax on the second bracket: $0.11 \times 1,000 + 0.12 \times 1,000 = \$230$. Our job is to break down the calculations necessary to generalize this solution, and then to write an algorithm.

Calculate Tax:
    Determine Bracket size and beginning value based
        on Status value
    Calculate number of brackets
    Calculate tax for each bracket and sum the tax
        on all the brackets
    Return the value of the tax.

The pseudocode is fairly general; we'll need to specify what each part is supposed to do a little more clearly.

First of all, let's look at the process that determines the bracket size.

```
(* to determine BracketSize, look at the filing status *)
CASE Status OF
    Single : BEGIN
               BracketSize : = 1000;
               BeginningValue : = 2300;
          END;
    Head : BEGIN
               BracketSize : = 1100;
               BeginningValue : = 2300;
          END;
    MarriedJoint : BEGIN
               BracketSize : = 1500;
               BeginningValue : = 3400;
          END;
    MarriedSep : BEGIN
               BracketSize : = 900;
               BeginningValue : = 1700;
          END;
END;
```

To calculate the number of brackets, we subtract the value below which income is not taxed from the income, then divide income by the bracket size.

```
NumBrackets : = (TaxableIncome-BeginningValue)
               DIV BracketSize;
```

Let's check this calculation. For a single person with taxable income of $25,000, the number of brackets should be

```
(25000-2300) DIV 1000 = 22700 DIV 1000 = 22
```

This is really the number of filled brackets. We'll handle the final amount, the leftover $700 which isn't included in this calculation, separately.

Calculating the tax is a simple loop through all of the brackets.

Set tax rate to 11%
Initialize tax to zero
Loop over all filled brackets:
      tax := tax + rate*BracketSize
      increment tax rate
Deal with the final, unfilled bracket

This can be converted easily into Pascal code.

```
TaxRate := 0.11;
Tax := 0;
FOR WhichBracket := 1 TO NumBrackets DO BEGIN
        Tax := Tax + TaxRate*BracketSize;
        TaxRate := TaxRate+0.01;
END;
Tax := Tax + TaxRate * ((TaxableIncome-BeginningValue)
                    MOD BracketSize);
                (* this line adds the leftover amount *)
```

This works except when the income is really high, because the maximum tax rate is 50 percent. A minor correction to this algorithm leaves us with this final form of the function CalculateTax:

```
CONST   MaxBrackets = 40;
TYPE    StatusType = (Single, Head, MarriedJoint,
                    MarriedSep);
        IncomeRange = 0..100000;  (* no worry about anything
                                        higher. **)
        TaxRange = 0..50000;  (* no more than half taxed  *)
        BracketRange = 0..2000;

VAR     Status : StatusType;
        Income : IncomeRange;
        Ans : Char;

FUNCTION CalculateTax (Status : StatusType;
                        TaxableIncome : IncomeRange):
                        TaxRange;
(* This function takes the filing status of the user and  *)
(* the amount of his or her taxable income and returns    *)
(* the amount of tax the user will need to pay next year. *)
VAR     BracketSize : BracketRange;
        BeginningValue : TaxRange;
        Tax : Integer; (* dummy variable, hold the value  *)
                    (* that is returned by the function  *)
```

```
        TaxRate : Integer; (* begins at 11% and goes up    *)
        NumBrackets,
        WhichBracket : Integer;
BEGIN
    (* to determine BracketSize, look at the filing status *)
        CASE Status OF
            Single : BEGIN
                BracketSize : = 1000;
                BeginningValue : = 2300;
            END;
            Head : BEGIN
                BracketSize : = 1100;
                BeginningValue : = 2300;
            END;
            MarriedJoint : BEGIN
                BracketSize : = 1500;
                BeginningValue : = 3400;
            END;
            MarriedSep : BEGIN
                BracketSize : = 900;
                BeginningValue : = 1700;
            END;
        END;
        NumBrackets : = (TaxableIncome-BeginningValue)
                    DIV BracketSize;
        TaxRate : = 11;
        Tax : = 0;
        FOR WhichBracket : = 1 TO NumBrackets DO BEGIN
                Tax : = Tax + TaxRate * BracketSize;
                TaxRate : = TaxRate + 1;
        END;
        Tax : = Tax + TaxRate*((TaxableIncome-BeginningValue)
                    MOD BracketSize);
                (* this line adds the leftover amount *)
        CalculateTax : = Tax DIV 100; (* eliminate %age *)
END;
```

Here are examples of the previous function used in a running program.

INTERACTIVE SESSION

```
Type your taxable income
4300
Type your status :S, H, M, J
S
Your tax is 230
```

```
Type your taxable income
25000
Type your status :S, H, M, J
H
Your tax is 4727


Type your taxable income
50000
Type your status :S, H, M, J
H
Your tax is 15352
```

Debugging and Types

Even though subrange types are more work than simply using Integer, Char, or any other base types for variables, they pay off in debugging. If an invalid value enters the data when you are using subrange types, then the program crashes because the value is out of the subrange. Having the program crash may seem like a bad thing to you, but it is a lot better than either spending days trying to find the bug or spending millions of dollars doing something the wrong way because you never noticed the bug. When programs produce results with profound repercussions in business, government, economics, and so forth, techniques that highlight slightly invalid data may make the difference between a fixed bug and an expensive, serious error.

To protect your program from crashing because of a subrange type variable, you will need to take the precautions that, ideally, you should be taking anyway. For example, suppose you have a variable, Day, which can assume values between 1 and 31. If the variable is read from the input file or the terminal, an illegal value could be entered accidentally. To protect the variable, a two-step read process is necessary.

```
CONST    DayMax = 31;
TYPE     DayType = 1..DayMax;
VAR      Day : DayType;
         SafeDay : Integer;
...

         Readln (Input, SafeDay);
         IF (SafeDay >=1) AND (SafeDay <= DayMax)
              THEN Day := SafeDay
              ELSE Error (SafeDay);
```

SELF TEST Take the procedure about clothing sizes that you wrote for the SELF TEST on page 335 and make it robust by preventing read errors.

Types and Data Abstraction

An important feature in Pascal is the ability to define a data type and to define some operations of that type. Once the operations are defined, then the programmer can forget about the specifics of the data type, and simply use the procedures and functions that manipulate it. This is called data abstraction.

> **Data abstraction:** The ability to remove from the usage of a data type any specific knowledge about how it is stored or manipulated.

For example, if we can define a type called Hour, which takes values from zero to 23, then we can define different operations on variables of type Hour.

```
TYPE    Hour = 0..23;

FUNCTION Future (TimeNow : Hour; Later : Integer) : Hour;
(* This function calculates a time in the future, given   *)
(* the current time and the number of hours later.        *)
CONST   MaxHours = 24;
VAR     Temp : Integer;
BEGIN
        Temp := (TimeNow + Later) MOD MaxHours;
        Future := Temp;
END;
```

In this way, we can define many different operations that will act on a variable of type Hour, like ReadHour and WriteHour procedures, an analogous Past function, or an HourDiff function, which would calculate the difference between two given hours.

Once we have defined these terms, we could use them in a larger program, such as a program that builds a weekly work schedule for a manufacturing plant.

Common Errors and Debugging

1. **Declaring illegal values.** A legal enumerated type value is any identifier that hasn't been declared already. Numbers and characters are *not* legal type values, since they aren't legal identifiers and already belong to a type. Character strings are also illegal as type values.

2. **Using a type as a variable.** Remember, *declaring a type does not allocate memory space*; only a variable declaration will do that. A naming convention that helps is ending every type identifier with Type.

```
TYPE     ColorType = (Red, Orange, Yellow, Green,
                        Blue, Indigo, Violet);
         DayType = (Sunday, Monday, Tuesday,
                    Wednesday, Thursday, Friday,
                    Saturday);
VAR      Color : ColorType;
         Day : DayType;
```

It becomes less tempting to use the type identifier as a variable because of the built-in reminder that it is only a type.

3. **Coding multiple occurrences of TYPE in one block.** As with CONST and VAR, TYPE should only occur once in each declaration part or in procedures.

4. **Declaring a value that is out of subrange.** When using a variable whose value is out of the subrange, it is often easy to go out of the subrange. For example, if the declaration looks like this:

```
VAR      Counter : 1..100;
```

and the variable is initialized to zero:

```
Counter := 0;
```

then an error will occur. The same error will occur if Counter is increased past 100. Be careful to consider all possible values when making subrange declarations, and be sure to account for boundary errors (like 0 and 101) when using subrange variables.

5. **Attempting to read or write the values of enumerated types.** It seems tempting, but it is an error to send an enumerated type variable to the standard procedures Read, Readln, Write, or Writeln. In general, a CASE statement in a separate procedure is the best way to deal with this.

```
PROCEDURE WriteColor (Color : ColorType);
BEGIN
        CASE Color OF
            Red    : Writeln (Output, 'Red   ');
            Orange : Writeln (Output, 'Orange');
            Yellow : Writeln (Output, 'Yellow');
            Green  : Writeln (Output, 'Green ');
            Blue   : Writeln (Output, 'Blue  ');
            Indigo : Writeln (Output, 'Indigo');
            Violet : Writeln (Output, 'Violet');
        END;
END;
```

Hints for BASIC Programmers

Since there is really no parallel between BASIC and Pascal in the area of types, what needs to be emphasized is that types should be used. You are probably getting used to the idea of using boolean variables to store information of a binary nature; the same thing is true when using variables that assume a small range of values. Declaring types utilizes the same documentation advantages as (1) using identifier names that are longer than one letter, (2) using CONSTs, (3) using procedures to break down the control structure, (4) using boolean functions instead of long boolean expressions, and (5) using all the other more explicit forms of documentation, such as commenting and parameterization.

SUMMARY

The ability to define new types of data in Pascal does for data handling what the ability to define procedures does for control structures—it allows the programmer to extend the language of Pascal and make it more like a human language. The most important feature of the type declarations we examined in this chapter is that they make programs simpler to read and understand. **Enumerated types** are declared by listing all the possible values a variable of the given type can assume. The values are listed in order, and the computer can compare different values for ranking and inequality. A variable of an enumerated type can be increased or decreased by increments by using Succ or Pred functions respectively. The Ord function is defined for all enumerated types, and returns the ordinal rank of the value of the argument.

      Subrange types can be declared over any enumerated **host type**, such as integer, boolean, character, or any enumerated type. Subranges are useful as documentation, for they indicate a variable's expected values to the reader. They are also useful in detecting data errors, because the computer program will crash if an attempt is made to store a value that is outside the subrange of the variable. This is advantageous, because a program that crashes is more desirable than one that produces erroneous results that go undetected. Subrange and enumerated types allow the programmer to separate the structural details of a data type from its use. This capacity is called **data abstraction**.

New Terms

enumerated	subrange type	Pred
enumerated type	host type	Succ
successor function	data abstraction	Chr
predecessor function	TYPE	
subrange	Ord	

EXERCISES

1. Write type declarations appropriate for the following uses:
    a. months of the year
    b. summer months (subrange of previous type)
    c. some men's names
    d. some women's names
    e. small letters
    f. legal test scores
    g. keys on a piano
    h. VHF TV channels
    i. UHF TV channels
    j. years in the current century
    k. days in any month
    l. Western states
    m. hair color
    n. months of a pregnancy

    Which of these are enumerated types? Which are subrange types?

2. Which of the following type declarations will produce a syntax error? Assume they all occur in the same type declaration section of a program.

    ```
    a. TodayType = (Tuesday);
    b. Untrue = (TRUE, FALSE);
    c. Truth = Boolean;
    d. Falsity = FALSE..FALSE;
    e. Exclamations = (Wow, Yow, Ow, Ouch);
    f. Bow = Wow..Ow;
    g. Small = 0.0 .. 1.0;
    h. Large = 100 .. 1000;
    i. Backwards = 10 .. -10;
    j. ROYGBIV = (R, O, Y, G, B, I, V);
    k. Colors = R..V;
    l. ColorType = ROYGBIV;
    m. SmallType = Real;
    n. Blue = 'B', 'I', 'V';
    o. BogusType = Falsity;
    ```

3. Declare two types, Number and Digit, whose values are, respectively, the integers 0 through 9 and the characters 0 through 9.

4. Write a function that will convert a digit to its corresponding number. The digit "1", for example, would convert to the integer value 1.

5. Write a function that will convert a number to its corresponding Digit.

6. Write more functions and procedures that build on the TYPE Hour declaration on page 340. Write functions Past and HourDiff, as well as procedures ReadHour and WriteHour. Write any other hour manipulation procedures you think might be useful.

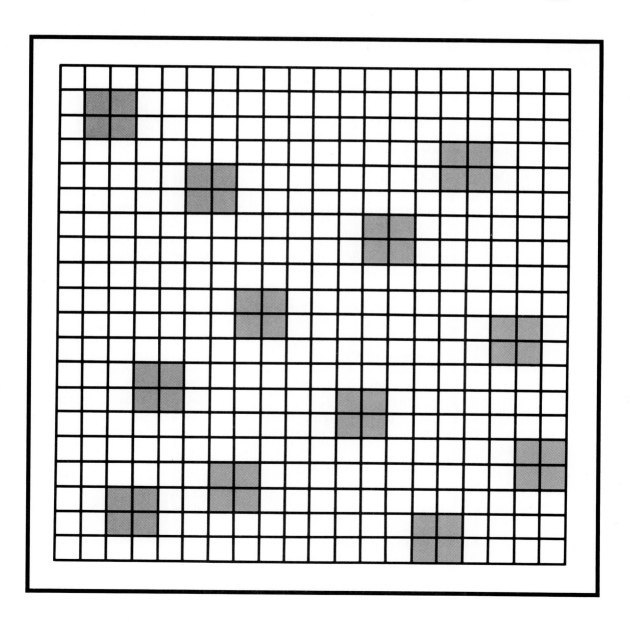

STORING DATA: ARRAYS

In Chapter 4 you learned that a control structure is a statement that alters in some way the normal sequence of executed statements in a Pascal program. You now know how to use all the different types of control structures defined in Pascal: the procedure, the FOR loop, the IF and CASE statements, and the WHILE and REPEAT loops. Most of the power of the computer programs you have written up to this point has issued from the use of these control structures to process a relatively small amount of data. Most of the programs you have written have not used many variables—probably all used less than 100.

However, much of the power of modern computers lies in their ability to store large quantities of data and to retrieve and process this data exceedingly quickly. In order to do this, programs use large data structures to organize the data that they need to store in order to perform the task given to them.

> **Data structure:** A system of organizing data for ease of storage, processing, and retrieval.

Some data structures are more effective at storing data than others, and specific data structures are designed to handle specific applications. The next four chapters discuss the major data structures used in Pascal and their differences and advantages. Chapter 17 then focuses on how control structures and data structures work together to solve large problems.

Introducing Arrays

In the grading program that we have written and rewritten, we read in each student's name and scores, wrote them out, and calculated average and grade. Suppose, however, I want to sort the students—either alphabetically by last name or by average—and print out a sorted list. If I want to keep track of a student's name for later reference, then I need a structure that stores large amounts of information. I could declare 600 or 700 variables, each of type Char, in order to store the names of 30 students, but I'd probably run out of meaningful variable names, and keeping track of all of them would be impossible. When mathematicians consider many variables, they structure data in this fashion:

$$a_1, a_2, a_3, \ldots, a_n$$
$$b_1, b_2, b_3, \ldots, b_n$$

or

$$a_{1,\,1}, a_{1,\,2}, a_{1,\,3}, \ldots, a_{1,\,n}$$
$$a_{2,\,1}, a_{2,\,2}, a_{2,\,3}, \ldots, a_{2,\,n}$$
$$a_{3,\,1}, a_{3,\,2}, a_{3,\,3}, \ldots, a_{3,\,n}$$
$$\ldots$$
$$a_{n,\,1}, a_{n,\,2}, a_{n,\,3}, \ldots, a_{n,\,n}$$

In this way, mathematicians create large numbers of variables without repeated runs through the Latin and Greek alphabets. This system also makes the relatedness between different groups of variables explicit. The important idea is that different values are stored in distinct variables that differ by number, not by name. All n variables in the sequence

$$a_1, a_2, \ldots, a_n$$

have the same name, a. The number, or the subscript, is what differentiates them and makes them distinct.

We know of examples of this type of structure in areas of life not primarily mathematical. For example, my address when I was a student was P.O. Box 10106. The location of my box was indicated by the number, which told the postal service employee where to put letters that were addressed to me. Out of all the rows of boxes at the post office, mine could be easily found by using my number in the context of the sequence of box numbers. (See Figure 13.1.) In the same way, people at apartment complexes essentially live in a huge storage structure where individual "memory locations" (apartments) are differentiated by numbers.

Sequential storage locations in memory that bear a common name and are differentiated by numbers or subscripts are called an **array.** There is a great advantage to being able to work with arrays, and the programmer's computing power is increased tremendously as arrays are introduced. We'll soon see exactly how this happens.

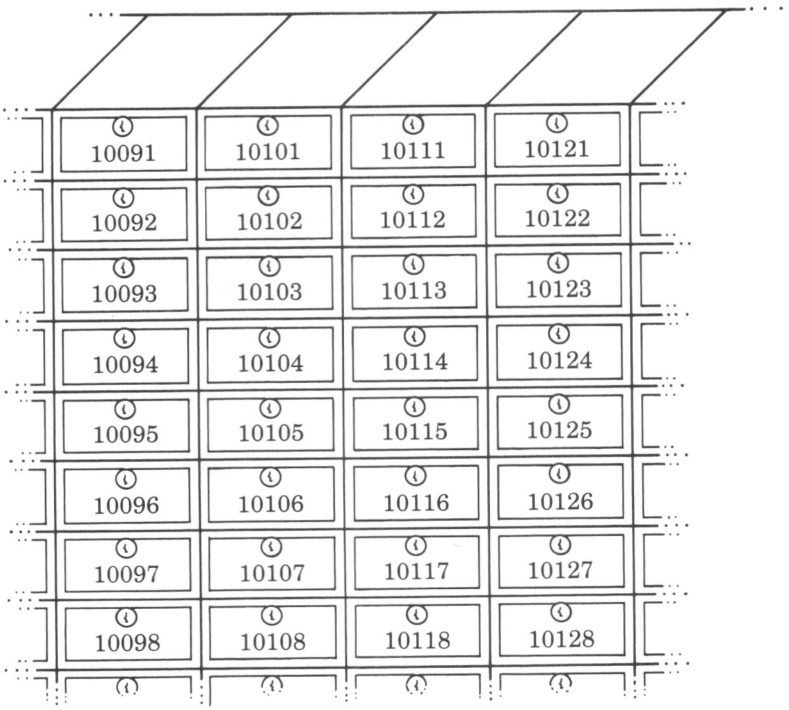

Figure 13.1: Post Office Boxes as an Array

Array Declarations

Arrays are the first in the set of structured types in Pascal; others are records, sets, files, and pointers.

> **Structured type:** Any type composed of more than one element or one memory location.

Examples give the best introduction to the syntax of arrays.

```
PROGRAM SomeArrayDeclarations (Output);
CONST    MaxChars = 16;
         MaxScores = 6;

TYPE     Word = ARRAY [1..MaxChars] OF Char;
         Scores = ARRAY [1..MaxScores] OF Integer;
```

```
VAR     StudName : Word;
        StudScores : Scores;
```

The words ARRAY and OF are reserved words, and the rest of the declaration defines what type of array is being declared. The arrays declared here are illustrated in Figure 13.2.

When an array is declared, the computer needs to know three pieces of information: (1) what type of data will be stored in the locations, (2) how many memory locations will be needed, and (3) what they will be called. The first piece of information is derived from the base type or component type of the array declaration.

> **Base type or Component type:** The type of the individual components that make up an array.

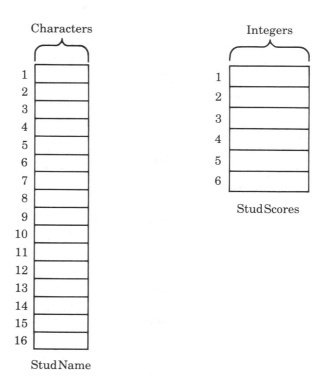

Figure 13.2: Array Variables

The base type of Word is Char, and the base type of Scores is Integer. That means that a variable of type Word is made up of boxes that store characters, and nothing else. Scores specifies integer-size boxes.

The second and third pieces of information concern the number and labeling of the boxes. Arrays are said to be indexed, or subscripted.

> **Index or Subscript:** The value of the label of a specific component in an array.

An array index in Pascal is specified by a bracketed expression or value after the array name. Parentheses are not used to do this in Pascal, so the array variable does not look like a procedure call with parameters. The index type is usually inferred from the subrange type that specifies the number and labels of the boxes.

> **Index type:** The type of the values that specify the index of an array component.

For example:

```
Word = ARRAY [1..MaxChars] OF Char;
```

The index type is Integer, and the labels or indices may fall in the range of 1 to the value of MaxChars. Notice here that the index type is Integer and the base type is Char. There is no need for the two to be the same. As we'll see, arrays can be indexed by any ordinal type. Figure 13.3 shows the syntax of an array declaration.

Another way to declare index types is to declare the subrange as a subrange type and then to use the subrange type in the array declaration.

```
CONST    MaxChars = 16;
TYPE     WordRange = 1..MaxChars;
         Word = ARRAY [WordRange] OF Char;
```

Figure 13.3: Array Declaration Syntax

```
TYPE    <identifier> = ARRAY [<simple type>]
                            OF <component type>;
```

Enumerated types and even simple ordinal types can also be used as the index type or base type of an array.

```
TYPE    Colors = (Red, Orange, Yellow, Green,
                          Blue, Indigo, Violet);
        Word = ARRAY [1..16] OF Char;
        Rainbow = ARRAY [1..7] OF Colors;
        Wavelengths = ARRAY [Colors] OF Real;
        Lies = ARRAY [Boolean] OF Char;
        Keyboard = Array [Char] OF Char;
        Questions = ARRAY [1..Max] OF Boolean;
```

To perform a job involving encryption, for example, suppose we needed (1) an array to store a file of text, (2) an array to count the frequency of occurrences of letters in a file, and (3) an array to store a replacement code. We can construct an array to suit each of these needs.

```
CONST   MaxCharsInFile = 1000;
TYPE    Letters = 'A'..'Z';
        TextArray = ARRAY [1..MaxCharsInFile] OF Char;
            (* index  type = Integer; base type = Char   *)
        FreqArray = ARRAY [Letters] OF Integer;
            (* index type = Letters; base type = Integer *)
        CodingArray = ARRAY [Letters] OF Letters;
            (* index type = base type = Letters          *)
```

These array types are illustrated in Figure 13.4.

SELF TEST Define an array to count the number of accidents occurring on any given day of the week for use in a program that compares the number of accidents on different days and shows statistically on which days most accidents occur.

Use of Arrays: Reading and Initializing

Arrays can be used in the same way other variables can be used. Their elements can be read, initialized, assigned, or written. However, entire arrays cannot normally be the arguments of Read or Write statements, cannot be the expression of a CASE statement or involved in boolean tests, and cannot be the results of functions. Following are several different examples of how arrays can be read or initialized as individual elements or loops through the entire arrays.

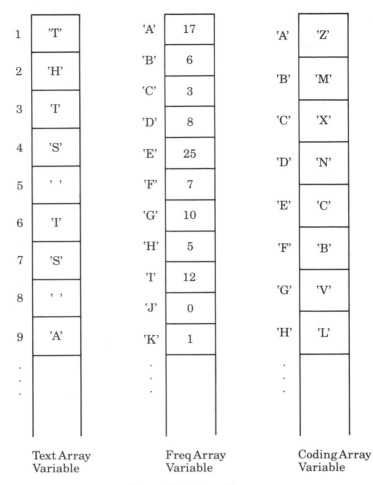

Figure 13.4: Array Types

```
VAR  TA : TextArray;              (* see above for definitions *)
     FA, FA1 : FreqArray:
     CA : CodedArray;
BEGIN                 (* this is just a series of different ways
                                             to use arrays *)
        Read (Input, TA[i]); (* read an individual element *)
        FOR i := 2 TO 100 DO  (* read the next 99 elements*)
              Read (Input, TA[i]); (* of the text array *)
        i := 101;
        (* now finish reading the text array until the    *)
        (* Eof, writing out each character as it is read   *)
        WHILE NOT Eof (Input) DO BEGIN
```

```
            i := i + 1;
            Read (Input, TA[i]);
            Write (Output, TA[i]);
    END;
    ...
    FA ['A'] := 0;              (* initialize one element  *)
    FOR Ch := 'A' TO 'Z' DO
            FA[Ch] := 0;    (* initialize freqs to 0    *)
    FA1 := FA; (* set whole arrays equal to each other*)
```

The preceding was not an example of superlative style, but it does demonstrate different legal usages of arrays in reading and initialization. Each of the following statements produces an error.

```
Read (TA);    (* an entire array cannot be read at once    *)
Writeln (TA); (* an entire array cannot be written at once *)
FA := 0;      (* FA is not an integer                       *)
FA := FA + 1; (* addition must go on element by element.    *)
FUNCTION InitArray (FA : FreqArray) : FreqArray;
           (* Function result must be an unstructured type *)
CASE TA OF            (* array cannot be a CASE expression *)
IF (FA=0) THEN        (* array not a simple type           *)
WHILE (TA<>TA1) DO ... (* array not a simple type          *)
```

If the components that constitute an array are simple types (char, boolean, integer, real), the array can be read and written, but entire arrays cannot be read or written at once. There is no easy way in Pascal to initialize the entire array; you must initialize an array element by element.

Use of Arrays: Sequential Searching

Often, when working with an array, it is necessary to search through the array for a certain value or a certain range of values. The easiest way to do this is to begin at the top of the array and examine each element until all the desired elements are found or until the end of the array is reached.

For example, suppose we have an input file of numbers, one per line, and are asked to print out all the values that are greater than the average. This problem requires the use of an array because all of the numbers must be read in order to determine the average before any of them can be printed. Here is a simple outline of the solution.

> Print high numbers:
> > Read numbers into array and calculate their sum
> > Calculate average
> > Prints all numbers greater than the average

The first and second parts of this algorithm should be easy to program; the third part is simply an IF statement inside a FOR loop that tests every value in the array.

```
PROGRAM PrintHighNumbers (Input, Output);
(* This program prints out all the values in an input   *)
(* file that are larger than the average of all the     *)
(* numbers in the file.                                  *)

CONST   MaxNums = 100;
TYPE    NumArray = ARRAY [1..MaxNums] OF Integer;
VAR     Nums : NumArray;
        Cntr, HowMany, Sum, Ave: Integer;

BEGIN
        HowMany := 0;    (* read the numbers into the file *)
        WHILE (HowMany < MaxNums) AND
                        NOT Eof (Input) DO BEGIN
            HowMany := HowMany + 1;
            Readln (Input, Nums [HowMany]);
            Sum := Sum + Nums [HowMany];
        END;

        Ave := Trunc (Sum / HowMany); (* calculate ave    *)

        FOR Cntr := 1 TO HowMany DO       (* search & print *)
            IF (Ave < Nums [Cntr])   (* high values    *)
                        THEN Writeln (Output, Nums [Cntr]);
END.
```

Notice that the program uses two different counters. The first counter, HowMany, is used in the WHILE loop until the end of the file is encountered. Then HowMany contains the number of values in the array. In order to use this number, we used a second variable, Cntr, in a FOR loop that used HowMany as its upper limit. The use of a variable to contain the number of values stored in an array is an important programming technique.

SELF TEST
Write a boolean function that takes an array of type ScoreArray and an integer value and returns TRUE if the value is found in the array and FALSE if the value is not in the array.

Use of Arrays: Procedure ReadWord

A procedure that reads a word from a file and stores it in an array of characters provides a good example of array use. This procedure, appropriately enough, is called ReadWord, a procedure that reads one word from a file. Before specifying the exact definition of one word, we can write the procedure declaration line and include the parameter list.

```
PROCEDURE ReadWord (VAR W : Word);
```

This assumes that the following declarations have been made at the beginning of the program:

```
CONST    MaxChar = 16;           (* for example *)
TYPE     Word = ARRAY [1..MaxChar] OF Char;
```

To define one word, we need to know what the procedure is being used for. A procedure that reads words into a dictionary might use an input file that has one word on each line of the file. A procedure that counts the number of words in a file might expect many words on a line with each word separated by a space or a punctuation mark. A procedure that reads a file of names and records might specify that a comma separates words. Each of these applications would require a slightly different ReadWord procedure. Of those mentioned, here is the easiest to write. Each word is separated by an Eoln marker.

```
PROCEDURE ReadWord (VAR W : Word);
(* This procedure reads a word until the end of line or    *)
(* until the array is full.                                *)
VAR     Cntr : Integer;
BEGIN
        Cntr := 0;
        WHILE (Cntr < MaxChar) AND NOT Eoln (Input) DO BEGIN
                Cntr := Cntr + 1;
                Read (Input, W[Cntr]);
        END;
END;
```

A second version, which might be used when reading in a formatted input file in a record-keeping program, stops reading the word when a comma is encountered. Notice that the comma is *not* stored in the array.

```
PROCEDURE ReadWord (VAR W : Word);
(* This procedure reads a word until a comma is found or   *)
(* until the array is full.                                *)
CONST    StopChar = ',';    (* The char that ends the word *)
VAR     Cntr : Integer;
        Ch : Char;
BEGIN
        Cntr := 0;
        Read (Input, Ch);
        WHILE (Cntr < MaxChar) AND (Ch <> StopChar) DO BEGIN
                Cntr := Cntr + 1;
                W[Cntr] := Ch;
                Read (Input, Ch);
        END;
END;
```

SELF
TEST

Write a procedure that reads an input file of dates of accidents and increases the value of the counter array that you declared in the SELF TEST on page 351. The input file contains an unspecified number of lines, each of the form

```
Monday, December 24, 1984, 12:44PM
```

Hint: You are only interested in the day of week.

Use of Arrays: Array Indexing

Indexing arrays over a noninteger set of values is an important concept in Pascal that greatly increases the readability and practicality of arrays. For example, recall FUNCTION Capitalize, which capitalizes a letter if it is small and, otherwise, leaves it unchanged.Without character indices, you would have to use the following algorithm to count the number of times a letter occurred.

```
WHILE NOT Eof (Input) DO BEGIN (* difficult freq. count *)
        Read (Input, Ch);
        Ch := Capitalize (Ch);    (* capitalize the character *)
        IF (Ch >= 'A') AND (Ch <= 'Z') THEN BEGIN
                Index := Ord (Ch) - Ord('A') + 1;
                FA[Index] := FA[Index] + 1;
        END;
END;
```

The calculation of the index could be bypassed completely if the character were used as the index of the array.

```
TYPE    FreqArray = ARRAY ['A'..'Z'] OF Integer;

FUNCTION IsALetter (Ch : Char) : Boolean;
BEGIN
        IsALetter := (Ch >= 'A') AND (Ch <= 'Z');
END;
PROCEDURE CountLetters (VAR FA : FreqArray);
(* easy frequency count, using the characters themselves to
   index the array. *)
VAR Ch : Char;
BEGIN
        WHILE NOT Eof (Input) DO BEGIN
                Read (Input, Ch);
                Ch := Capitalize (Ch);
                IF IsALetter (Ch)
                        THEN FA[Ch] := FA[Ch] + 1;
        END;
END;
```

Note that FUNCTION IsALetter would be more complex if we were working with EBCDIC character codes, which are used on some IBM computers. In this case,

```
FUNCTION IsALetter (Ch : Char) : Boolean;
(* For use with EBCDIC character codes. A-I are conti-    *)
(* guous, J-R are contiguous, and S-Z are contiguous.     *)
BEGIN
        IsALetter := ((Ch >= 'A') AND (Ch <= 'I'))
                 OR ((Ch >= 'J') AND (Ch <= 'R'))
                 OR ((Ch >= 'S') AND (Ch <= 'Z'));
END;
```

Suppose we wanted to read a file that contained the 26 letters of the alphabet in a mixed-up order. The order in which they enter the program establishes a new code. The first letter will translate A, the second, B, and so on. We could use another type declaration, CodedArray, to declare a variable to store this array.

```
TYPE    Letters = 'A'..'Z';
        CodedArray = ARRAY [Letters] OF Letters;

PROCEDURE ReadCode (VAR CA : CodedArray);
VAR     Index : Char;
BEGIN
        FOR Index := 'A' TO 'Z' DO
                Read (Input, CA[Index]);
END;
```

This array could then be used to encode a file of English text. The procedure to encode an English text file using FUNCTION IsALetter would be:

```
PROCEDURE Encode (VAR CA : CodedArray);
(* Translates a file of English text into code using the
   CodedArray that was read in earlier.  *)
VAR     Ch : Char;
BEGIN
        WHILE NOT Eof (Input) DO
            IF Eoln (Input) THEN BEGIN
                Writeln (Output);
                Readln (Input);
            END ELSE BEGIN
                Read (Input, Ch);
                Ch := Capitalize (Ch);
                IF IsALetter (Ch)
                    THEN Write (Output, CA[Ch])
                    ELSE Write (Output, Ch);
            END;
END;
```

Use of Arrays: Bubble Sort

Suppose we want to write a procedure to take the number of times specific letters occur in a file, sort the resulting data according to frequency, then return and print the result. One way to sort an array is to compare adjacent elements repeatedly, swapping them if they are out of order, until the array has been sorted. For example, study the left column in the following one-dimensional array of numbers and assume we want to arrange the array in ascending order. If we were to go through the array, swapping the adjacent elements that were out of order, then the array would be transformed as follows:

Original	Pass 1	Pass 2	Pass 3	Pass 4	Pass 5	Pass 6	Pass 7	Pass 8
16	8	8	8	2	2	2	2	0
8	14	14	2	8	8	8	0	2
14	16	2	14	14	14	0	8	8
39	2	16	16	16	0	14	14	14
2	39	39	18	0	16	16	16	16
91	44	18	0	18	18	18	18	18
44	18	0	39	39	39	39	39	39
18	0	44	44	44	44	44	44	44
0	91	91	91	91	91	91	91	91

Suppose we call each set of swaps a pass through the array. We could have probably sorted this list in our heads in about as much time as it takes us to write it out. But the computer can't process information in the same way we can. Even though the computer must perform many operations, comparisons, and swaps, it is pretty fast. Undoubtedly, the computer would beat anyone if we gave it a list of 100 elements to sort.

This sorting method is guaranteed to sort a list of n items in n - 1 passes if not less. One way to encode this sort might be:

```
FOR Pass := 1 TO n-1 DO          (* n - 1 passes *)
        FOR Pair := 1 to n-1 DO   (* n - 1 adjacent pairs
                                       to be compared *)
            IF A[Pair] > A[Pair + 1]
                THEN Swap (A[Pair],A[Pair + 1]);
```

This will work if we say that the procedure Swap actually swaps the values of the two array elements. However, we can make this procedure a little faster if we notice some things about how the sort actually works. Notice the last few elements in each column. The largest value in the array, 91, is at the bottom of the array after one pass. After two passes, the last two elements, 44 and 91, are intact. After three passes, 39, 44, and 91 are in place. In each successive pass, the largest number remaining in the stack has sunk to the bottom, while the "lighter" numbers are bubbling to the top; hence the name bubble sort. Therefore, there really is no reason to continue to compare numbers all the way down to the bottom of the array, because they are already sorted. A **bubble sort** is a sort whose passes become shorter and shorter because it drops sorted elements from each successive pass. A new way to encode this might be:

```
FOR Pass := 1 TO n-1 DO
    FOR Pair := 1 TO n - Pass DO   (* not n-1, but n-Pass *)
        IF A[Pair] > A[Pair + 1]
            THEN Swap (A[Pair],A[Pair + 1]);
```

Why do we only go up to n - Pass? What would happen if we tried to compare A[n] with A[n+1]? If n is the maximum index of the array declaration, then the array index would be out of bounds. If n is simply the number of filled elements in the array, then we might just get an array element we don't want into the list like another zero or an uninitialized array element.

The following code could serve as the procedures to sort an array.

```
PROCEDURE Swap (VAR One, Two : Integer);
(* Swaps the values stored in One and Two *)
VAR Temp : Integer;
BEGIN
        Temp := One;
        One := Two;
        Two := Temp;
END;


PROCEDURE BubbleSort (VAR A : ArrayType;
                      NumElements : Integer);
(* Sorts array A with NumElements in it. Calls PROCEDURE *)
(* Swap.                                                 *)
VAR     Pass, Pair : Integer;
BEGIN
        FOR Pass := NumElements-1 DOWNTO 1 DO
            FOR Pair := 1 to Pass DO
                IF A[Pair] > A[Pair+1]
                    THEN Swap (A[Pair],A[Pair+1]);
END;
```

Notice that we passed adjacent array elements into the swap procedure, but the formal parameter names were One and Two. That is less complicated than passing the whole array into the procedure and makes more sense. The parameter to BubbleSort is of type ArrayType. This is any defined type that is being used and not a standard type identifier.

SELF
TEST

For each of the following versions of the bubble-sorting algorithm, state whether or not the code works. If it doesn't, specify the change that would make it work. Assume all called procedures or functions are properly defined.

```
1. FOR I := NumElements DOWNTO 2 DO
       FOR J := 1 TO I DO
           IF (NumArray [I] > NumArray [I-1])
               THEN Swap (NumArray [I], NumArray [I-1]);
2. FOR I := NumElements DOWNTO 2 DO
       FOR J := 1 TO I DO
           IF (NumArray [J] > NumArray [J-1])
               THEN Swap (NumArray [I], NumArray [I-1]);
3. FOR I := 1 TO NumElements - 1 DO
       FOR J := NumElements - 1 DOWNTO I DO
           IF (NumArray [J] > NumArray [J-1])
               THEN Swap (NumArray [J], NumArray [J-1]);
4. FOR I := 1 TO NumElements - 1 DO
       FOR J := NumElements - 1 DOWNTO I DO
           IF OutOfOrder (NumArray [J], NumArray [I])
               THEN Swap (NumArray [J], NumArray [I]);
```

Use of Arrays: Binary Search

Often, when working with a large array, it is necessary to search the array quickly for specific values. For example, the phone company has assigned credit card numbers to its customers to bill long-distance phone calls. When a customer dials a call, the computer must verify that the calling card number is a valid number. We can write a program to do the same thing by implementing a search algorithm.

First of all, we must define the data structure that we will use. In order to simplify the problem slightly, we will assume that the credit card numbers are integers less than MaxInt, and, therefore, can be stored as integers in an array. We will further simplify the problem by assuming that there will be no more than 1,000 numbers in the array of valid credit card numbers. Therefore, the array type declaration would be:

```
CONST    MaxNums = 1000;
TYPE     CardNumArray = ARRAY [1..MaxNums] OF Integer;
```

The algorithm we could use to verify a number's validity might be:

Read array from input file
Read number from terminal
Loop through the entire array:

If number is equal to array element,
then it is valid
If number not found, then number is invalid
Write results to terminal

This program could be used by an operator at a terminal to verify card numbers as they are given by customers. In this case, we might want to rewrite the algorithm to allow the testing of multiple numbers.

Read array from input file
While not finished loop:
Read number from terminal
Loop through the entire array:
If number is equal to array element,
then it is valid
If number not found, then number is invalid
Write results to terminal

This program is fairly straightforward.

```
CONST    MaxNums = 1000;
TYPE     CardNumArray = ARRAY [1..MaxNums] OF Integer;
VAR      Cards : CardNumArray; (* holds the card numbers   *)
         HowMany : Integer;     (* how many numbers read    *)
         Number : Integer; (* The number to be searched for *)
         Found : Boolean; (* indicates the result of search *)

         CardNumFile, (* input file where card numbers are *)
         Terminal : Text; (* where the numbers to be        *)
                          (* verified are read from         *)

BEGIN    (* Main Program *)
         ReadCardNumArray (Cards, HowMany);
         REPEAT
             Writeln (Output, 'Enter number to verify.');
             Readln (Terminal, Number);
             Search (Cards, HowMany, Number, Found);
             IF Found
                 THEN Writeln (Output, 'Card is valid.')
                 ELSE Writeln (Output, 'Card is invalid.');
         UNTIL Finished;
END.     (* Main Program *)
```

Writing the procedure ReadCardNumArray is fairly easy.

```
PROCEDURE ReadCardNumArray (VAR Cards : CardNumArray;
                                VAR HowMany : Integer);
(* This procedure reads the input file containing the     *)
(* card numbers and stores them in the array. It returns  *)
(* the value of HowMany, the amount of numbers stored.    *)
(* The input file is called CardNumFile, with one number  *)
(* per line of input.                                     *)

BEGIN
        Reset (CardNumFile);
        HowMany := 0;
        WHILE NOT Eof (CardNumFile) AND
                (HowMany < MaxNums) DO BEGIN
              HowMany := HowMany + 1;
              Readln (CardNumFile, Cards [HowMany]);
        END;
END;
```

In the main program, Finished is used as a boolean variable, but it is a simple boolean function which asks the user if she or he is finished.

```
FUNCTION Finished : Boolean;
(* Returns TRUE if the user is finished              *)
VAR     Ans : Char;
BEGIN
        Writeln (Output, 'Are you finished? (Y or N)');
        Readln (Terminal, Ans);
        Finished := (Ans = 'Y') OR (Ans = 'y');
END;
```

The only difficult procedure is Search. Let's look at the expanded algorithmic description.

> Search:
>> Found gets false
>> While not found, loop through entire array:
>>> If number equals element,
>>>> then found gets true

This can be put into Pascal as:

```
PROCEDURE Search (VAR Cards : CardNumArray;
                      HowMany, Number : Integer;
                      VAR Found : Boolean);
(* This procedure searches the Card array to find the    *)
(* given Number. If it is not in the array, then Found is *)
(* returned FALSE, otherwise, Found is returned TRUE.     *)
VAR     Cntr : Integer;
BEGIN
```

```
        Cntr  : = 0;
        Found  : = FALSE;
        WHILE  (Cntr  <  HowMany)  AND  NOT  Found  DO  BEGIN
                Cntr  : =  Cntr  +  1;
                Found  : =  (Number  =  Cards [Cntr]);
        END;
END;
```

The only problem with this sequential search is that, for a very large array of numbers, it takes a long time to run through the entire data structure looking for a match. If the number is found quickly, it doesn't take too long. But if the number is at the bottom of the array, or if it isn't in the array at all, the procedure could use a lot of computer time. If the telephone company is verifying thousands of numbers per minute, it would certainly want a faster algorithm than this one.

This job calls for the use of another kind of search called a binary search. If the array is sorted by number, either increasing or decreasing, then a binary search can significantly decrease the amount of time it takes to find any given number in the array. Instead of comparing the first element, and then the second, and so forth, the **binary search** compares the middle element in the array to the number being sought. If it is equal to the number, then it is finished. If it is higher than the number, the search moves to the side of the array containing the lower numbers, splits that remainder in half, and again checks the middle element. If the middle element of the array is lower than the desired number, it moves to the side of the array containing the higher numbers and splits that remainder in half. In each pass, the binary search splits the remaining numbers in half. Therefore, with 1,000 elements in an array, only ten numbers need to be checked before we know whether the number is in the array, because 2^{10} is greater than 1,000. See Figure 13.5 for an illustration of how this works.

The pseudocode for a binary search is:

```
Binary Search:
        Initialize Top and Bottom
        While not Found and Top<>Bottom, loop:
                Compare midpoint element to number
                If not found then
                        If number too low,
                                Then move bottom to midpoint − 1
                                Else move top to midpoint + 1
```

This algorithm will work, except in the case where Top becomes equal to Bottom. In this case, the element located at the index Top may or may not be equal to the number in question. In order to take this possibility into account, we should design an exclusive check for it.

Binary Search:
    Initialize Top and Bottom
    While not Found and Top<>Bottom, loop:
        Compare midpoint element to number
        If not found then
            If number too low,
                Then move bottom to midpoint − 1
                Else move top to midpoint + 1
        If not found then compare current top element to
            number

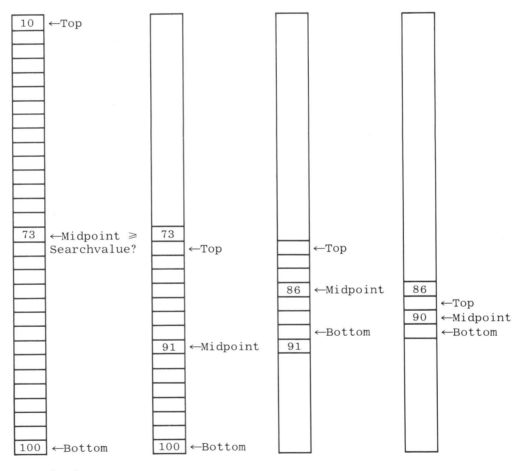

Searchvalue = 90

Figure 13.5: Binary Search Algorithm

The Pascal procedure that implements this algorithm is:

```
PROCEDURE Search (VAR Cards : CardNumArray;
                       HowMany, Number : Integer;
                       VAR Found : Boolean);
(* This procedure uses a binary search to search the Card *)
(* array to find the given Number. If it is not in the    *)
(* array, then Found is returned FALSE, otherwise, Found   *)
(* is returned TRUE.                                       *)
VAR     Top, Bottom, Which : Integer;
BEGIN
        Top := 1;
        Bottom := HowMany;
        Found := FALSE;
        WHILE NOT Found AND (Top < Bottom) DO BEGIN
            Which := (Top + Bottom) DIV 2;
                      (* take the midpoint of the section *)
            Found := (Number = Cards[Which]);
            IF NOT Found THEN (* make the section smaller *)
                IF (Number < Cards[Which])
                    THEN Bottom := Which - 1 (* half size *)
                    ELSE Top := Which + 1;
        END;
        Found := Found OR (Number = Cards[Top]);
END;
```

This algorithm is a good example of how considerations of efficiency often take over when writing programs of this size. With the addition of arrays to your repertoire of Pascal capabilities, it is much easier to write very large programs that make many computations. It is at this point that efficient algorithms—rather than simple algorithms—become especially important. The sequential search algorithm, for example, is certainly less complex than the binary search algorithm, but it is less efficient. The final version of the program follows.

```
PROGRAM SearchCardNums (Terminal, CardNumFile, Output);
(**************************************************************)
(* This program searches through an array of valid credit *)
(* card numbers for a given number to determine if it is   *)
(* valid or invalid. If the number is not found in the     *)
(* array, it is determined to be invalid. A binary search  *)
(* algorithm is used.                                      *)
(**************************************************************)
CONST   MaxNums = 1000;
TYPE    CardNumArray = ARRAY [1..MaxNums] OF Integer;
VAR     Cards : CardNumArray; (* holds the card numbers   *)
        HowMany : Integer;       (* how many numbers read    *)
        Number : Integer; (* The number to be searched for *)
        Found : Boolean; (* indicates the result of search *)
```

```
                CardNumFile, (* input file where card numbers are *)
                Terminal : Text; (* where the numbers to be        *)
                                 (* verified are read from         *)


FUNCTION Finished : Boolean;
(* Returns TRUE if the user is finished                   *)
VAR     Ans : Char;
BEGIN
        Writeln (Output, 'Are you finished? (Y or N)');
        Readln (Terminal, Ans);
        Finished := (Ans = 'Y') OR (Ans = 'y');
END;


PROCEDURE ReadCardNumArray (VAR Cards : CardNumArray;
                            VAR HowMany : Integer);
(* This procedure reads the input file containing the    *)
(* card numbers and stores them in the array. It returns *)
(* the value of HowMany, the amount of numbers stored.   *)
(* The input file is called CardNumFile.                 *)

BEGIN
        Reset (CardNumFile);
        HowMany := 0;
        WHILE NOT Eof (CardNumFile) AND
               (HowMany < MaxNums) DO BEGIN
            HowMany := HowMany + 1;
            Read (CardNumFile, Cards [HowMany]);
        END;
END;


PROCEDURE Search (VAR Cards : CardNumArray;
                  HowMany, Number : Integer;
                  VAR Found : Boolean);
(* This procedure uses a binary search to search the Card *)
(* array to find the given Number. If it is not in the    *)
(* array, then Found is returned FALSE, otherwise, Found  *)
(* is returned TRUE.                                      *)
VAR     Top, Bottom, Which : Integer;
BEGIN
        Top := 1;
        Bottom := HowMany;
        Found := FALSE;
        WHILE NOT Found AND (Top < Bottom) DO BEGIN
            Which := (Top + Bottom) DIV 2;
            Found := (Number = Cards[Which]);
            IF NOT Found THEN
                IF (Number < Cards[Which])
                    THEN Bottom := Which - 1
                    ELSE Top := Which + 1;
```

```
            END;
            Found := Found OR (Number = Cards[Top]);
   END;

   BEGIN    (* Main Program *)
            ReadCardNumArray (Cards, HowMany);
            Reset (Terminal);
            REPEAT
                Writeln (Output, 'Enter number to validate.');
                Readln (Terminal, Number);
                Search (Cards, HowMany, Number, Found);
                IF Found
                    THEN Writeln (Output, 'Card is valid.')
                    ELSE Writeln (Output, 'Card is invalid.');
            UNTIL Finished;
   END.     (* Main Program *)
```

A sample interactive session follows. The input file contained all of the odd numbers less than 1,000.

INTERACTIVE SESSION

```
Enter number to validate.
721
Card is valid.
Are you finished? (Y or N)
n
Enter number to validate.
28
Card is invalid.
Are you finished? (Y or N)
n
Enter number to validate.
433
Card is valid.
Are you finished? (Y or N)
n
Enter number to validate.
2
Card is invalid.
Are you finished? (Y or N)
n
Enter number to validate.
1035
Card is invalid.
Are you finished? (Y or N)
y
```

SELF
TEST

Examine the following binary search procedure and indicate whether or not the procedure works correctly and the conditions under which it might work correctly.

```
Top := 1; Bottom := HowMany; Found := FALSE;
WHILE NOT Found AND (Top < Bottom) DO BEGIN
    Midpoint := (Top + Bottom) DIV 2;
    Found := (Number = NumArray [Midpoint]);
    IF NOT Found THEN
        IF (Number > NumArray [Midpoint])
            THEN Bottom := Midpoint - 1
            ELSE Bottom := Midpoint + 1;
END;
Found := Found OR (Number = NumArray [Midpoint]);
```

Packed Arrays

One disadvantage of arrays of characters is that they cannot be treated in the same way character strings can be treated. They must be examined, read, and written letter by letter. The situation is similar to using one spiral notebook for each of five classes. You may get tired of carrying around all five notebooks all day, or of not having the notebook you need at certain times. Perhaps you then decide to use one three-ring binder with lots of paper and separators that indicate different classes. All of your notes fit into one binder, so you always have everything you need. This switch is like the switch from a regular array to a packed array. A **packed array** stores the most information into the least amount of space. Like the binder, that means that a quantity of data to be treated as a unit can be carried around more easily. However, the cost for retrieving information out of the array will go up. In the case of your binder, it is now harder to find a certain page of the notes for a particular class. Likewise, when using a packed array, it is more time-consuming for the computer to find any particular element in the array.

The best type of array to pack is an array of characters, because it can then be dealt with as a character string. The standard procedures Write and Writeln will work with packed arrays of characters as parameters. For example, the following code, with the given declarations, illustrates the use of packed arrays.

```
PROGRAM TestPackedArrays (Input, Output);
(* This program simply illustrates the use of Packed    *)
(* Arrays of characters.                                *)
CONST   MaxChars = 6;
TYPE    Word = PACKED ARRAY [1..MaxChars] OF Char;
VAR     W1, W2 : Word;
```

```
PROCEDURE ReadWord (VAR W : Word);
(* This procedure reads a word until the end of line or   *)
(* until the array is full.                               *)
VAR     Cntr : Integer;
BEGIN
        Cntr := 0;
        WHILE (Cntr < MaxChar) AND NOT Eoln (Input) DO BEGIN
                Cntr := Cntr + 1;
                Read (Input, W[Cntr]);
        END;
END;

BEGIN
        ReadWord (W1);
        ReadWord (W2);
        IF (W1 = 'Hello ')
                THEN Writeln (Output, 'Hi ', W2)
                ELSE IF (W1 = 'HELLO ')
                        THEN Writeln (Output,'HI ', W2)
                        ELSE Writeln (Output, W1, W2);
END.
```

It is legal to make comparisons between W1 and 'Hello ', but W1 must be declared to have the same number of characters in it (6) as the character string to which it is being compared. Otherwise, a type conflict error occurs. It would be handy if packed array variables could be used in CASE statements, but structured types cannot be the subjects of a CASE statement, so the following is illegal.

```
CASE W1 OF           (* illegal CASE statement *)
   'Eat   ' : Writeln (Output, 'I am hungry.');
   'Drink ' : Writeln (Output, 'I am thirsty.');
   'Sleep ' : Writeln (Output, 'I think I''ll',
                        ' take a short nap.');
END;
```

Packed arrays of characters can, however, be compared for inequality.

```
IF (W1 < W2)
        THEN Write (Output, W1, W2)
        ELSE Write (Output, W2, W1);
```

The ordering is by character code for the characters, so a<b, A<B, and usually A<a. If the capitalization of the letters is consistent—either all lowercase or all uppercase or uppercase for only first letters, for example—then an alphabetical sort could easily be constructed. (See Figure 13.6 for a comparison of packed and regular arrays.)

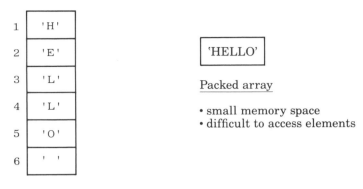

Regular array

• large memory space
• easy to access elements

Figure 13.6: Comparison of Packed and Ordinary Arrays

A handy tool to use when reading in packed arrays of characters from an input file is a constant called Blank, which allows the programmer to initialize a word to all blanks.

```
CONST    MaxChars = 10;
         Blank = '          '; (* 10 spaces *)
TYPE     Word = PACKED ARRAY [1..MaxChars] OF Char;

PROCEDURE ReadWord (VAR W : Word);
(* This procedure reads a word until the end of line or     *)
(* until the array is full.                                 *)
VAR      Cntr : Integer;
BEGIN
         W := Blank;     (* initialize entire word to blanks *)
         Cntr := 0;
         WHILE (Cntr < MaxChar) AND NOT Eoln (Input) DO BEGIN
                Cntr := Cntr + 1;
                Read (Input, W[Cntr]);
         END;
END;
```

This is a good use of a packed array constant: without it, the job of initializing the array would require more work:

```
FOR Cntr := 1 TO MaxChar DO W[Cntr] := ' ';
```

If any particular array will be manipulated and individual elements swapped or repeatedly accessed, then it should not (and, in many versions of Pascal, cannot) be declared as a packed array. For example, the Swap procedure would not accept elements of a packed array as actual parameters; it is an error in Pascal to send components of packed structures into procedures as variable parameters. The following coding could circumvent the restriction.

```
PROCEDURE Swap (VAR A : ArrayType; Index : Integer);
VAR       Temp : Integer;
BEGIN
          Temp := A[Index]
          A[Index] := A[Index+1]
          A[Index+1] := Temp;
END;
```

However, this is not a very well-styled procedure, because it is sent the entire array as a parameter, when it needs only two elements of the array to complete its task. It is best not to use packed arrays if the array needs to be sorted.

SELF
TEST
Write a version of ReadWord that reads letters or digits until the compiler encounters a nonalphanumeric character or Eoln.

Programming Example 13.1

Assignment: A histogram is often used to illustrate the distribution of scores for the purpose of assigning grades. A histogram can show the degree to which scores are curved or grouped.

> **Histogram:** A graphical representation of the relative frequencies of values or the ranges of values in a data set.

Write a program that produces a histogram of a set of test scores. Assume that no more than 100 scores (integers) are in the input file. Determine the high and low value and count the frequencies of the scores falling into each of ten ranges between the low and the high value. Print the histogram values in some aesthetically pleasing format that allows easy interpretation of the data. Figure 13.7 shows one interpretation of the data.

Solution: This is going to be somewhat like the letter-frequency algorithm, where each letter read became the index to an array of integers, and the value in the corresponding box increased by 1. However, in this case, the index will be a little more difficult to obtain, and will be calculated from each score read from the input file to the array.

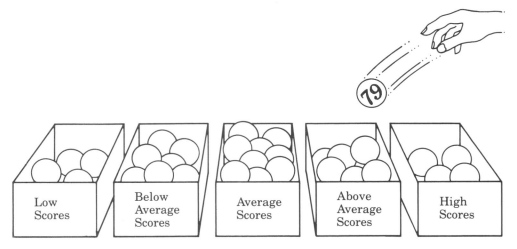

Figure 13.7: Bins for a Score Histogram

First of all, let's write a pseudocode algorithm of the solution.

Print a histogram:
        Read the scores from the input file
        Determine the high and the low values
        Determine the bin sizes from the high and low values
        Initialize the histogram
        Loop through the array:
                Increment the appropriate bins
        Print out the histogram

Therefore, a first guess at the main program looks something like this.

```
BEGIN    (* Main Program *)
        ReadScores (Scores, HowMany);
        FindExtremes (Scores, Low, High);
        InitBins (Hist);
        IncrementBins (Scores, Hist, HowMany, Low, High);
        PrintHist (Hist);
END.     (* Main Program *)
```

However, when we think a little more about ReadScores, it becomes clear that it makes sense to determine the extremes, Low and High, while reading the scores into the array. In this way the compiler passes through the array fewer times, which is more efficient. PROCEDURE ReadScores is written handily.

```
PROCEDURE ReadScores (VAR Scores : ScoreArray;
                           VAR HowMany, Low, High : Integer);
(* This procedure reads the scores from the input file    *)
(* into an array. It keeps track of the number of scores  *)
(* entered, as well as the Low and High values stored.     *)
BEGIN
        HowMany := 0;
        Low := 100; High := 0;
        WHILE NOT Eof (Input) AND (HowMany < Max) DO BEGIN
            HowMany := HowMany + 1;
            Read (Input, Scores[HowMany]);
            IF (Low > Scores[HowMany])
                THEN Low := Scores[HowMany]
                ELSE IF (High < Scores[HowMany])
                    THEN High := Scores[HowMany];
        END;
END;
```

Notice that Low and High are both initialized to values that cannot possibly remain the low or high values in the set of scores. You should realize why this is necessary. If a default value were allowed for Low, then the low value for a set of scores might always remain zero.

The InitBins procedure is simple to write, but increasing the correct bins by increments is a little more difficult. The pseudocode algorithm for IncrementBins is:

> Increment bins:
> > Loop over all the scores:
> > > Calculate index from low and high values
> > > Increment appropriate bin

Without getting too mathematical, this becomes a simple procedure.

```
PROCEDURE IncrementBins (VAR Scores : ScoreArray;
                             VAR Hist : HistArray;
                             HowMany, Low, High : Integer);
(* This procedure goes through the Scores array and for    *)
(* each element in the array increments the appropriate    *)
(* bin, using the function WhichBin to determine the       *)
(* correct index.                                          *)
VAR     Index,                  (* Calculated by WhichBin  *)
        Cntr : Integer;         (* FOR loop index          *)
BEGIN
        FOR Cntr := 1 TO HowMany DO BEGIN
            Index := WhichBin (Scores[Cntr], Low, High);
            Hist[Index] := Hist[Index] + 1;
        END;
END;
```

Notice that a function was used, WhichBin. This is where the appropriate bin index is calculated for each score. The value of the index depends on the score, the low and the high values. This function is written by considering certain cases. When a score is given that equals Low, the result should be 1, the first box. Likewise, when a score is given that equals High, the result should be NumBins, the maximum bin index.

```
FUNCTION WhichBin (Score, Low, High : Integer) : Integer;
(* This function calculates the index of the appropriate  *)
(* Histogram bin to be incremented, given the values of    *)
(* the Low and High scores and the current Score.          *)
VAR     Range : Integer;
BEGIN
        Range := High - Low + 1;
        WhichBin := (Score - Low) * NumBins DIV Range + 1;
END;
```

The final job is to print the histogram. We will do this by printing one star on a horizontal line for each score that fell into each bin. For this, we will need a nested FOR loop structure. But we want to make sure that we print out the values of the limits for each bin. That makes the results much more readable and meaningful. The algorithm would be:

Print histogram:
      Write number of scores
      Calculate bin size used
      Set low bin limit
      Loop over number of bins
            Write low bin limit
            Recalculate bin limit (high value)
            Write high bin limit
            Loop over value of bin:
                  Write one asterisk
            Write a carriage return

To produce this algorithm, we took advantage of the fact that once a lower bin limit was printed, the next bin's lower limit would always be one more than the previous bin's upper limit. This algorithm converts into Pascal very nicely.

```
PROCEDURE PrintHist (VAR Hist : HistArray;
                    HowMany, Low, High : Integer );
(* This procedure prints the values of the histogram bins *)
(* in horizontal bars of asterisks.                        *)
VAR     Bin, Cntr : Integer;    (* FOR Loop indices        *)
        BinSize : Real;
        BinLimit : Integer;     (* Low score value in Bin  *)
```

```
BEGIN
        Writeln (Output, HowMany:1, ' scores:');
        Writeln (Output);
        BinSize := (High - Low) / NumBins;
        BinLimit := Low;
        FOR Bin := 1 TO NumBins DO BEGIN
                Write (Output, BinLimit:3, ' -- ');
                BinLimit := Low + Trunc (Bin*BinSize);
                Write (Output, BinLimit:3, '    ');
                BinLimit := BinLimit + 1;
                FOR Cntr := 1 TO Hist[Bin] DO
                        Write (Output, '*');
                Writeln (Output);
        END;
END;
```

The module tree for this program is given in Figure 13.8.
The following are sample input and output files for this program.

INPUT
```
44  48  42  52  56  57  70  79  74  68  65  64  63  62
60  46  55  57  60  56  62  63  64  65  64  63
69  70  74  73  75  69  68  67  63  67  68  71  81  73  74
49  53  65  66  69  70  57  58  73
73  48  49  50  51  52  53  67  63  67  68  71
81  73  74  49  53  65  66  69  70  57  58  73
54  53  56  57  58  59  59  59    60  61  61  61  62  60  61
```

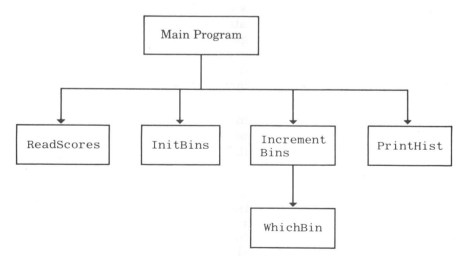

Figure 13.8: Module Tree for Histogram

OUTPUT   89 scores:

```
42 -- 45   **
46 -- 49   ******
50 -- 53   ********
54 -- 57   **********
58 -- 61   **************
62 -- 65   ***************
66 -- 69   **************
70 -- 73   ************
74 -- 77   *****
78 -- 81   ***
```

Programming Example 13.2

Assignment: Some current astrophysics research is done with simple computer programs that try to detect order in seemingly random events in the sky. The data for these programs are very precise measurements of the time intervals when certain high-energy (gamma-ray) radiation came from a particular segment of the sky. It is postulated that some of these gamma rays are emitted by pulsating neutron stars, which are very small, compact stars with a lot of mass and energy. The time data can be analyzed to determine if the emissions are regular. For example, if gamma rays are measured every second, then it is possible that a pulsating star is emitting them in a one-second cycle. The more regular the occurrences of the gamma rays, the more likely it is that they are not simply random events, unrelated to each other.

Next we will write a simple program to analyze gamma-ray time data to determine if there is any statistically improbable regularity. We will use a technique called folding. You will read the time data into an array of real numbers. Begin with a given period, which is the length of time between two pulses of the star that may be generating these gamma rays. Put the numbers into different bins in a histogram, according to the **phase** of each event. The phase is the fractional part of the time divided by the period. For example, if the period is one second ($P=1$), and the event happened at time 12.52, the phase is 0.52, or about half a period. If there are five bins in the histogram, then this event would be placed in the third bin, which covers phases from 0.40 to 0.60. This kind of algorithm is called a **folding algorithm** because the data are "folded" around different possible periods to determine whether or not the data are periodic.

After calculating the phases of each event and constructing a histogram, use the function below to calculate the chi-square value for each histogram. A **chi-square value** indicates the degree to which it is statistically unlikely to have a distribution of random events fill the bins in that way. A high chi-square value indicates a high chance that the distribution represents periodic and not random data. To state the chi-square value mathematically,

$$\text{Mean} = \frac{\text{NumEvents}}{\text{NumBins}}$$

$$\chi^2 = \sum_{i=1}^{\text{NumBins}} \frac{(H_i - \text{Mean})^2}{\text{Mean}}$$

You will print the values of a period and the histogram it generated if the chi-square value is higher than a minimum value, say 20.0.

```
FUNCTION ChiSqu (H : HistArray; Mean : Real;
                 NumBins : Integer) : Real;
(* Calculates the value of the Chi Square test for the    *)
(* given histogram                                        *)
VAR    Chi : Real;                 (* temporary value     *)
       Bin : Integer;              (* FOR loop counter    *)
BEGIN
       Chi := 0.0;
       FOR Bin := 1 TO NumBins DO BEGIN
              Chi := Chi + Sqr (H[Bin]-Mean)/Mean;
       END;
       ChiSqu := Chi;
END;
```

You will do the described operations in a loop, each time increasing the value of the period in the following manner.

```
Period := Period + Period*Period/(TimeSpan*NumBins*2);
```

This will ensure that the period is increased slowly enough to find the period of the pulsating star if the data contains one. Execute the loop enough times to find a period with a high value from the chi-square test. The data given at the end of this section is actual data from a gamma-ray telescope in Arizona.

Solution: In order to outline a solution, let's think about the major subtasks that need to be performed.

Data Folding:
    Read Data: Events, initial period
    Make a table heading
    Loop over the number of trials:
        Initialize the histogram
        Calculate phases and fill bins
        Calculate Chi Square value for filled histogram
        If Chi Square value > Cutoff
            Then report the period and the histogram
        Calculate the next period to check

As we look at our outline and take into account the calculation for the new period, we see that we are going to need a lot of variables that we can read from the input file. The type declarations for the array of events (real numbers) and the histogram array (integers) are pretty straightforward; we end up with the following global data structures.

```
CONST     MaxEvents = 50;
          MaxBins = 10;
TYPE      EventArray = ARRAY [1..MaxEvents] OF Real;
          HistArray = ARRAY [1..MaxBins] OF Integer;

VAR       Hist : HistArray;      (* Histogram of event phases *)
          Events : EventArray;   (* Array of event times       *)

          Chi,      (* Calculated Chi Squ. value for histogram *)
          ChiCut,         (* Chi square cutoff, lowest value *)
          Period : Real;  (* current period being tested      *)

          NumTrials,      (* number of periods to test        *)
          WhichTrial,     (* FOR loop counter in Trial loop    *)
          NumEvents,      (* number of events read into array*)
          NumBins,    (* number of bins desired in Histogram *)
          TimeSpan : Integer; (* approximate time difference*)
                          (* between first and last event *)
```

With the global variables that we know we will need, combined with the outline of the tasks that the program will need to perform, we can write the fully parameterized main program now.

```
BEGIN     (* Main Program *)
          ReadData (Period, ChiCut, NumTrials, NumBins,
                    NumEvents, TimeSpan, Events);
          Heading (NumTrials, NumEvents, NumBins, TimeSpan,
                    Period, ChiCut);
          FOR WhichTrial := 1 TO NumTrials DO BEGIN
                    InitHist (Hist);
                    FillBins (Hist, Events, Period, NumEvents,
                            NumBins);
                    Chi := ChiSqu (Hist, NumEvents/NumBins,
                            NumBins);
                    IF (ChiCut<Chi) THEN BEGIN
                            Report (Hist, Period, Chi, NumBins,
                                    WhichTrial);
                    END;
                    Period := Period + Period*Period/
                                    (TimeSpan*NumBins*2);
          END;
END.      (* Main Program *)
```

By now we are pretty good at reading input into arrays. PROCEDURE ReadData is straightforward.

```
PROCEDURE  ReadData  (VAR Period, ChiCut : Real;
                      VAR NumTrials, NumBins, NumEvents,
                          TimeSpan : Integer;
                      VAR Events : EventArray);
(* This procedure reads all the data from an input file   *)
(* that is organized in the order in which the parameters *)
(* are found.                                             *)
VAR     Cntr : Integer;                  (* FOR loop counter *)
BEGIN
        Readln (Input, Period, ChiCut);
        Readln (Input, NumTrials, NumBins, NumEvents,
                   TimeSpan);
        FOR Cntr := 1 TO NumEvents DO BEGIN
               Read (Input, Events[Cntr]);
        END;
END;
```

We could have written the program so that TimeSpan was calculated from the data, rather than read from the input file. We also could have used a WHILE loop instead of a FOR loop, eliminating the need to read the number of events in the file NumEvents.

```
Readln (Input, Period, ChiCut);
Readln (Input, NumTrials, NumBins);
NumEvents := 0;
WHILE NOT Eof (Input) AND
              (NumEvents<MaxEvents) DO BEGIN
              NumEvents := NumEvents + 1;
              Read (Input, Events[NumEvents]);
END;
TimeSpan := Events [NumEvents] - Events [1];
```

A simple FOR loop initializes the bins in the histogram to zero. We'll look at how to construct the heading after we know what we want to put in our report. Let's write an outline for the procedure that fills the bins according to the phases of each event.

Fill Bins:
    Loop over all the events:
        Calculate the phase of each event
        Calculate the corresponding Bin index
        Increment the appropriate Bin

Remember that the phase is the fractional remainder of the time of the event divided by the period being tested. The fractional remainder can be obtained by calculating the entire value of the division, then subtracting the truncated or integer part of it. The rest of the procedure is easy.

```
PROCEDURE FillBins (VAR H : HistArray;
                    VAR Events : EventArray; Period : Real;
                    NumEvents, NumBins : Integer);
(* This procedure loops through the array of events and    *)
(* calculates the phase of each event and then increments  *)
(* the corresponding bin in the histogram.                 *)
VAR     Phase : Real;
        Bin, Cntr : Integer;
BEGIN
        FOR Cntr := 1 TO NumEvents DO BEGIN
                Phase := Events[Cntr]/Period;
                Phase := Phase - Trunc (Phase);
                                        (* take fraction *)
                Bin := Trunc (Phase*NumBins) + 1;
                H[Bin] := H[Bin] + 1;
        END;
END;
```

The next job is to calculate the chi-square value of the histogram. The function, which is mathematically interesting but not difficult, was given in the assignment, and the function call was given in the the main program. The chi-square value of the calculated histogram is then compared with the chi-square value used as the cutoff. Obviously, if we are testing hundreds or thousands of different periods, we don't want to see the results for each period tested, only those with relatively high chi-square tests, which indicate a higher possibility of a regular pulse.

Now we must write the procedure that writes out the data if the computer has found something significant. We need to know the Period, the chi-square value, and we would like to see the histogram values. It would also be good to know the current value of the trial counter, so we can see if we should extend the search by testing more values.

```
PROCEDURE Report (H : HistArray; Period, Chi : Real;
                  NumBins, WhichTrial : Integer);
(* This procedure reports the finding of a successful  *)
(* trial. (A success means that, for the Histogram,    *)
(* (Chi>ChiCut).)                                      *)
VAR     Bin : Integer;
        BinFW : Integer;         (* The field width of   *)
                                 (* each Bin printed     *)
BEGIN
        Write (Output, WhichTrial:4, Period:14:8,
                Chi:8:3, ' ':4);
```

```
        BinFW := 30 DIV NumBins;
        FOR Bin := 1 TO NumBins DO BEGIN
                Write (Output, H[Bin]:BinFW);
        END;
        Writeln (Output);
END;
```

Notice how we used the variable BinFW to format the histogram. In this way, when the value of NumBins changes, the report format will change without going over the 80-column edge of the terminal or of many printers. We want the output to look clean and to be easy to read.

At this point, we know enough to write the simple heading procedure, which is structured identically to the Report procedure and labels the columns in the table.

Figure 13.9 shows a module tree for the entire program, which follows.

```
PROGRAM Fold (Input, Output);

(* This program uses a histogram to perform a data-folding    *)
(* algorithm on periodic time data to determine the period. The *)
(* input is the time data and the output is the list of        *)
(* all calculated periods that are statistically unlikely.     *)

CONST   MaxEvents = 50;
        MaxBins = 10;

TYPE    EventArray = ARRAY [1..MaxEvents] OF Real;
        HistArray = ARRAY [1..MaxBins] OF Integer;
```

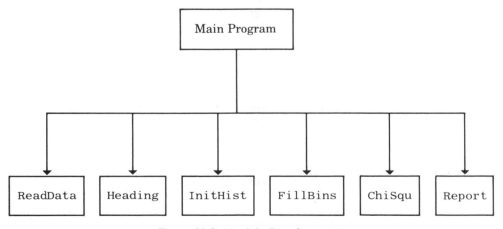

Figure 13.9: Module Tree for Fold

```
VAR     Hist : HistArray;      (* Histogram of event phases *)
        Events : EventArray;   (* Array of event times      *)

        Chi,    (* Calculated Chi Squ. value for histogram *)
        ChiCut,         (* Chi square cutoff, lowest value *)
        Period : Real;  (* current period being tested     *)

        NumTrials,       (* number of periods to test       *)
        WhichTrial,      (* FOR loop counter in Trial loop  *)
        NumEvents,       (* number of events read into array*)
        NumBins,    (* number of bins desired in Histogram *)
        TimeSpan : Integer; (* approximate time difference*)
                            (* between first and last event *)

PROCEDURE InitHist (VAR H : HistArray);
(* This procedure initializes the Histogram array before  *)
(* each trial is made.                                     *)
VAR     Bin : Integer;
BEGIN
        FOR Bin := 1 TO MaxBins DO H [Bin] := 0;
END;


FUNCTION ChiSqu (H : HistArray; Mean : Real;
                 NumBins : Integer) : Real;
(* Calculates the value of the Chi Square test for the    *)
(* given histogram                                        *)
VAR     Chi : Real;                 (* temporary value    *)
        Bin : Integer;              (* FOR loop counter   *)
BEGIN
        Chi := 0.0;
        FOR Bin := 1 TO NumBins DO BEGIN
                Chi := Chi + Sqr (H[Bin]-Mean)/Mean;
        END;
        ChiSqu := Chi;
END;
PROCEDURE FillBins (VAR H : HistArray;
                    VAR Events : EventArray; Period : Real;
                    NumEvents, NumBins : Integer);
(* This procedure loops through the array of events and   *)
(* calculates the phase of each event and then increments *)
(* the corresponding bin in the histogram.                *)
VAR     Phase : Real;
        Bin, Cntr : Integer;
BEGIN
        FOR Cntr := 1 TO NumEvents DO BEGIN
                Phase := Events[Cntr]/Period;
                Phase := Phase - Trunc (Phase);
                                        (* take fraction *)
                Bin := Trunc (Phase*NumBins) + 1;
                HBin := H[Bin] + 1;
```

```
          END;
END;


PROCEDURE ReadData (VAR Period, ChiCut : Real;
                    VAR NumTrials, NumBins, NumEvents,
                        TimeSpan : Integer;
                    VAR Events : EventArray);
(* This procedure reads all the data from an input file  *)
(* that is organized in the order in which the parameters *)
(* are found.                                             *)
VAR    Cntr : Integer;               (* FOR loop counter *)
BEGIN
        Readln (Input, Period, ChiCut);
        Readln (Input, NumTrials, NumBins, NumEvents,
                     TimeSpan);
        FOR Cntr := 1 TO NumEvents DO BEGIN
               Read (Input, Events[Cntr]);
        END;
END;


PROCEDURE Report (H : HistArray; Period, Chi : Real;
                  NumBins, WhichTrial : Integer);
(* This procedure reports the finding of a successful   *)
(* trial. (A success means that, for the Histogram,     *)
(* (Chi>ChiCut).)                                       *)
VAR    Bin : Integer;
       BinFW : Integer;          (* The field width of  *)
                                 (* each Bin printed    *)
BEGIN
        Write (Output, WhichTrial:4, Period:14:8,
                    Chi:8:3, ' ':4);
        BinFW := 30 DIV NumBins;
        FOR Bin := 1 TO NumBins DO BEGIN
               Write (Output, H[Bin]:BinFW);
        END;
        Writeln (Output);
END;


PROCEDURE Heading (NumTrials, NumEvents, NumBins,
                   TimeSpan : Integer; Period, ChiCut : Real);
(* Prints a heading for the output                      *)
VAR    Bin : Integer;
       BinFW : Integer;
BEGIN
        Writeln (Output,
                    'Results of Data Folding Algorithm':48);
        Writeln (Output);
        Writeln (Output, NumEvents:1, ' Events, ',
                     NumTrials:1, ' Trials, ');
```

```
                Writeln (Output, 'Time span: ',TimeSpan:1);
                Writeln (Output);
                Writeln (Output, 'Chi square cutoff: ',ChiCut:6:3);
                Writeln (Output);
                BinFW := 30 DIV NumBins;
                Write (Output, 'Trial      Period   Chi Squ.      ');
                FOR Bin := 1 TO NumBins DO BEGIN
                        Write (Output, Bin:BinFW);
                END;
                Writeln (Output);
        END;

        BEGIN    (* Main Program *)
                ReadData (Period, ChiCut, NumTrials, NumBins,
                        NumEvents, TimeSpan, Events);
                Heading (NumTrials, NumEvents, NumBins, TimeSpan,
                        Period, ChiCut);
                FOR WhichTrial := 1 TO NumTrials DO BEGIN
                        InitHist (Hist);
                        FillBins (Hist, Events, Period, NumEvents,
                                NumBins);
                        Chi := ChiSqu (Hist, NumEvents/NumBins,
                                NumBins);
                        IF (ChiCut<Chi) THEN BEGIN
                                Report (Hist, Period, Chi, NumBins,
                                        WhichTrial);
                        END;
                        Period := Period + Period*Period/
                                (TimeSpan*NumBins*2);
                END;
        END.     (* Main Program *)
```

The following input file contains actual gamma-ray telescope data taken in 1982.

```
INPUT   0.0128  20.0    (* Initial Period, Chi-square cutoff *)
        2000 5 25 90    (* NumTrials, NumBins, NumEvents, TimeSpan *)
         2.72921   9.75296  11.36342  11.86855  14.95873  16.88632
        19.93177  21.73425  22.61797  26.25215  27.09547  29.22746
        34.10667  37.81957  42.45462  44.52988  47.32703  48.47780
        56.70759  57.63541  58.64226  62.54921  64.12362  68.42799
        86.34249
```

Here is the output generated by the previous input file. The data indicates that a pulsating star could have emitted the gamma rays with a period of about 12.98148 milliseconds. When this program was first executed, about 10^5 periods were tried, ranging from 1 millisecond to 90 seconds. With the histogram for 12.98148 milliseconds and a chi-square value of 49.2, the probability of the distribution occurring randomly is about one in a billion. Since only 10^5 periods were examined, the result is still fairly significant.

OUTPUT   Results of Data Folding Algorithm

25 Events, 2000 Trials,
Time span: 90

Chi square cutoff: 20.000

Trial	Period	Chi Squ.	1	2	3	4	5
981	0.01298092	23.600	1	8	13	0	3
982	0.01298111	22.000	0	12	9	1	3
983	0.01298130	25.600	0	14	7	2	2
984	0.01298148	49.200	1	19	1	2	2
985	0.01298167	43.200	2	18	2	3	0
986	0.01298186	32.000	4	16	2	3	0
1427	0.01306497	20.400	3	2	14	3	3
1501	0.01307902	21.200	3	1	4	14	3

Common Errors and Debugging

1. **Confusing the types.** It is easy to get the base type and the index type of an array confused. When working with an array, keep its type declaration in mind so that you don't try to add 1 to an array element of type character, or try to use a character variable to index an array whose indices are integers.

2. **Generating an array index that is out of bounds.** This is probably the most common run-time error with arrays. For example, suppose we wrote a function to check two arrays to see if they are equal.

```
Function ArrayEqual (A1, A2 : ArrayType) : Boolean;
(* This function produces an error *)
VAR    I : Integer;

BEGIN
        I := 1;
        WHILE (A1[I] = A2[I]) AND (I <=MaxChars) DO
                I := I + 1;
        ArrayEqual := (I > MaxChars);
END;
```

This seems like it would work. If I becomes greater than MaxChars, that means every location in both arrays was checked and the arrays were equal. However, when I becomes greater than MaxChars, which is guaranteed to happen if the arrays are equal, the reference to A1[I] will give an error, because the array index, I, is out of bounds—no longer between 1 and MaxChars.

A second attempt to write this function might yield:

```
FUNCTION ArrayEqual (A1, A2 : ArrayType) : Boolean;
(* This function also produces an error *)
VAR      I : Integer;
BEGIN
        I : = 0;
        WHILE  (A1[I]  =  A2[I]) AND  (I  <  MaxChars) DO
               I : = I + 1;
        ArrayEqual : = (A1[I]  <>  A2[I]);
END;
```

This function produces an error every time because I begins at zero, and so A1[I] is undefined; I is of bounds. We must write a function like this in this manner:

```
FUNCTION ArrayEqual (A1, A2 : ArrayType) : Boolean;
(*this function correctly compares two arrays and  *
* returns TRUE if they are equal                   *)
BEGIN
        I : = 0;
        REPEAT I : = I + 1;
        UNTIL (A1[I]  <>  A2[I]) OR I = MaxChars;
        ArrayEqual : = (A1[I]  =  A2[I]);
END;
```

This error may also be generated where reading or calculating values of the indices. For example, if we simply wrote

```
Read (Input, Ch);
Freq [Ch] : = Freq [Ch] + 1;
```

in an array that counted the number of specific letters in a file, we would get an array index error when a space or punctuation mark was read. We must safeguard against this. Or suppose we had the following code.

```
i : = 0;
WHILE NOT Eof (Input) DO BEGIN
        I : = I + 1;
        Read (Input, Scores[I]);
END;
```

If there are more scores in the input file (an eventuality we must consider), then we'll get an array index error. This can be prevented by a second test in the WHILE loop.

```
I := 0;
WHILE NOT Eof (Input) AND
          (I < MaxScores) DO BEGIN
        I := I + 1;
        Read (Input, Scores[I]);
END;
```

3. **Losing end-of-line markers.** When reading a text file into an array of char-
    acters, the end-of-line markers are stored as blanks. This shouldn't cause a prob-
    lem, unless an attempt is made later to write the array to an output file. If this
    is done, the information about where the end of a line should occur is lost. One
    way to retain this information is through the use of an artificial end-of-line
    marker, usually a character that one doesn't expect to find in the text of the
    input file, such as the backslash character, \. The following algorithms could
    be used to read and write such an array.

```
(* Read an input file character by character, and *)
(* store the Eoln marker as a '\'.                 *)
Cntr := 0;
WHILE NOT Eof (Input) AND (Cntr < MaxChars) DO BEGIN
        Cntr := Cntr + 1;
        IF Eoln (Input) THEN BEGIN
                Readln (Input);
                TextArray[Cntr] := '\';
                        (* Store Eoln character *)
        END ELSE Read (Input, TextArray[Cntr]);
END;

(* Write out a text array, ending the output line when *)
(* the Eoln marker, a '\' is encountered               *)
FOR Cntr := 1 TO Length DO
        IF (TextArray[Cntr] = '\')
                THEN Writeln (Output)
                ELSE Write (Output, TextArray[Cntr]);
```

Hints for BASIC Programmers

Initially this chapter may have been reassuring to BASIC programmers because
arrays in Pascal look much like they do in BASIC. To highlight the similarities
before pointing out a few differences, let's look at the example of a bubble-sorting
algorithm in each language.

```
 50   DIM A(100)
100   REM - SORT A 100-ELEMENT ARRAY FROM LOWEST TO HIGHEST
110   FOR K = 100 TO 2 STEP -1
120     FOR I = 2 TO K
130       IF A(I-1) <= A(I) THEN 170
140         LET T = A(I)
150         LET A(I) = A(I-1)
160         LET A(I-1) = T
170     NEXT I
180   NEXT K


        FOR Pass := NumElements DOWNTO 2 DO
            FOR Pair := 2 TO Pass DO
                IF A[Pair-1] > A[Pair]
                    THEN Swap (A[Pair-1], A[Pair]);
```

The Pascal code is obviously a little cleaner and easier to read, both because of the self-documenting nature of the longer identifier names and because it is unnecessary to use a line number to change the program control. However, when BASIC is indented, it is easy to see the structural similarity between the two pieces of code. The same can be said for other common array manipulations; initializing, reading, searching, and sorting arrays in Pascal are very similar to the same operations in BASIC.

One big difference between Pascal and BASIC in their implementations of arrays is the flexibility Pascal has in indexing arrays. BASIC arrays are usually indexed as either 0 or 1 up to the maximum index, given in the DIM statement. However, sometimes it is more convenient to index the array differently, either by starting at a different low value or by indexing an array with characters, subrange, or user-defined types. To repeat one example in this chapter:

```
TYPE    FreqArray = ARRAY ['A'..'Z'] OF Integer;
```

Other examples are:

```
CONST   MinStudNum = 1900;
        MaxStudNum = 2100;

TYPE    Currency = (One, Five, Ten, Twenty, Fifty, Hundred);
        Bills = ARRAY [Currency] OF Integer;
        Scores = (Prob1, Prob2, MidTerm, Prob3, Final);
        Grades = ARRAY [Prob1..Final] OF Integer;
        Class = ARRAY [MinStudNum..MaxStudNum] OF Real;
```

A second difference between Pascal and BASIC is that Pascal arrays can contain data of almost any type. In BASIC, character strings and integer arrays are treated differently; in Pascal, they are declared, read, sorted, and written almost identically. This allows more flexible and useful arrays, as does the flexibility in indexing. This also allows for multidimensional arrays and other large data structures that we will examine in the next chapters.

SUMMARY

We introduce the idea of a **data structure** with the Pascal array. Arrays allow the creation of vast quantities of organized data storage with single declarations, and also allow for the facile manipulation of such data. Arrays are composed of sequential memory locations which are indexed, or referred to, by a variable or value of the **index type**. The sequential memory locations hold values of the **base type** of the array. The index type can be any scalar type, including integers, characters, and enumerated types. The base type can be any type, including reals.

Arrays can be used to read and store entire words or files of characters. Often it will be necessary to search for a particular value or set of values in an array. This can be done using a sequential search. When the values in the array are sorted, we use a **binary search.** It is possible, using a **bubble sort** or other sorting algorithms, to sort an array. The bubble sort is not the fastest sort algorithm, but it is easy to implement and works well on relatively small arrays.

Packed arrays are more efficient in terms of storage space than are regular arrays, although they are less efficient when accessing individual elements. When using arrays of characters as words, it is often convenient to think of a word as a single entity, and accessing individual elements is not necessary. In this case, it is probably more efficient and easier to use packed arrays.

__ New Terms __

data structure	index type	folding
array	bubble sort	chi-square value
structured type	binary search	ARRAY
base type	packed array	OF
index	histogram	PACKED

EXERCISES

1. Declare an array that will take as indices all the possible sums of a roll of two dice, and then use this array to write a program that simulates 500 or 1,000 dice rolls and counts how many times each sum appears. Print out the actual count and the percentage of the total number of rolls in tabular form. Calculate the theoretical values. Do your answers agree?

2. Write a program that prints out Pascal's Triangle, a triangle named for Blaise Pascal that looks like this:

```
                1
             1     1
          1     2     1
       1     3     3     1
    1     4     6     4     1
 1     5    10    10     5     1
```

If you want, you can print it against the left margin, but do it evenly. The numbers are generated by the rule that each number, other than the 1's on the edges, is the sum of the two numbers on the line above it, to the left and right.

```
                1

            1  +  1
               =
        1  +  2  +  1
           =     =
     1     3     3     1
```

Generate 20 rows and print them out. Print the sum of the values in each row off to the right side. What is the relationship of the row number to the sum of the values in the row?

3. Revise the Pascal's Triangle program of the previous problem to store, not the numbers themselves, but only a boolean value based on whether the number is even or odd. Remember, begin with one odd, and follow these rules:

odd + odd = even
even + even = even
even + odd = odd

Now print out a pattern of stars and spaces, based on whether the number is odd (print a star) or even (print a space). Do this for 80 rows, a full screen's width. Do you see how ordered Pascal's Triangle is?

4. A palindrome is a word, number, or sentence whose characters are the same when reversed. For example:

Madam, I'm Adam.
Eve.

are both palindromes (the first palindromic conversation). Note that spaces, punctuation, and capitalization are ignored. The following are also palindromes.

747
A man, a plan, a canal: Panama!
(A comment on Teddy Roosevelt)
Able was I ere I saw Elba.
(A comment made by Napoleon on his death bed)

Write a program that reads in a line of input and determines whether or not it is a palindrome.

5. Write a program that adds two integers. Each integer may have as many as 100 digits. The program should read the integers into arrays, character by character, and the addition should be done column by column.

6. Write a procedure, `Insert`, which takes four parameters: a sorted array of numbers, an integer indicating how many numbers are in the array, a value to be inserted into the sorted array at the correct location, and a boolean error flag. The procedure should return the array with the value inserted so that the array is still sorted. If the array is full, then the boolean error flag should be set to TRUE and the array should return unchanged.

7. Write a procedure, `Delete`, which takes the same four parameters as the procedure described above, except that the value is to be deleted from the sorted array. If the value is not found, then the boolean error flag should be set to TRUE. When the value is deleted, make sure that all the values following the deleted value's index move up one slot in the array.

8. Write a boolean function, `InOrder`, which takes two parameters, an array of some simple type and a boolean flag value `LowToHigh`. Define `LowToHigh` as TRUE when the array is supposed to be sorted from the lowest value to the highest value and FALSE when it is the other way around. `InOrder` should return TRUE if the array has been correctly sorted.

9. Write a procedure, `Compress`, which takes a sorted array and the number of elements in the array and eliminates duplicate values and zero-valued elements and compresses the array into the number of memory locations filled.

10. Write a procedure, `UnsortedCompress`, which takes an unsorted array and the number of elements in the array and eliminates duplicate values or zero-valued elements. Because the array is unsorted, you will need to write an efficient algorithm to ensure that every element will be compared to every other element.

11. Write a program that reads an input file and keeps track of which characters were found in the input file. Include all characters discovered only once. Keep track of spaces, punctuation, and digits as well as upper- and lowercase characters. Print out a sorted list of the characters found in the file. Hint: Keep the array sorted at all times and insert new characters into the list at the appropriate points.

12. Write a program that reads a list of numbers and writes out the sorted list, along with the index of each number in the original list. For example, if the input file were 10 86 22 56 31 8 the output would look like this:

Number	Index
86	2
56	4
31	5
22	3
10	1
8	6

13. Write a program that reads an input file with an unspecified number of lines in the format:

`<First Name><space><Middle Initial><Last Name>`

The output of the program should look like this:

```
Lamb, Richard C.
Peatman, William E.
Bosley, Elisa P.
   . . .
```

14. When an electron (matter) collides with a positron (antimatter), both particles are annihilated. Simulate random particle interactions in a mythical one-dimensional space. Declare an array 80 characters long, and space five electrons (–) and five positrons (+) evenly along the line. Allow them to move one cell to the left or the right, determining the direction of the motion of each with the Random function. When like particles collide, they bounce off each other, and when opposite particles collide, they are annihilated. Print out the history of the interactions of the particles as a series of lines of characters. Continue a fixed amount of time, or until all the particles have been annihilated. Increase the number of particles and reexecute. What is the effect if all the electrons begin on one side of the line and all the positrons on the other, rather than being alternately placed?

15. In our discussion of data abstraction, we used the procedure Future to calculate a future hour, given the current hour and a time difference (see page 340). Use the concept of data abstraction and this procedure to build a program that helps a manager develop a work schedule for each employee.

16. Declare an enumerated type called Times with values of Day, Month, and Year. Declare an array type, DateType, which holds all the needed values for a date in it. Write procedures to read and write variables of DateType, as well as procedures that add or subtract an integer number of days to variables of DateType.

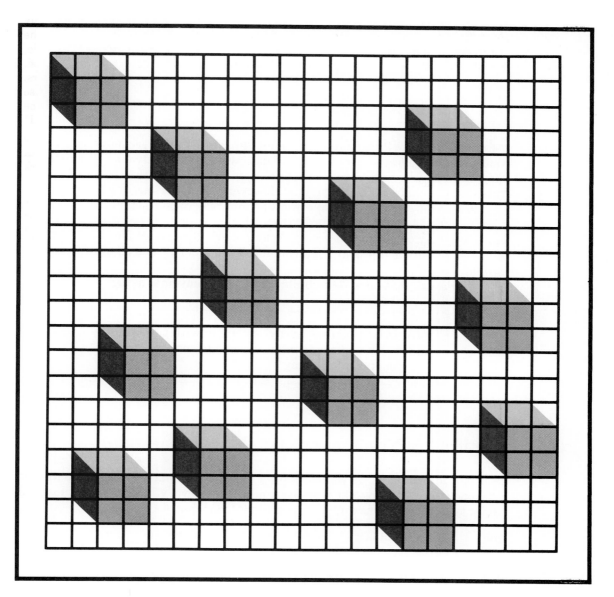

MULTIDIMENSIONAL ARRAYS

After using arrays for a while, it becomes almost natural to see how any program that uses or generates fair amounts of data would effectively use the array data structure. Words, test scores, frequencies, or histograms are all common structures that could be stored in arrays. However, a need for larger data structures will arise soon. If we can store a word as an array of characters, why not store a dictionary as an array of words? We can store a set of test scores, but can we store an array of sets of test scores? What about a tic-tac-toe board? Or a three-dimensional tic-tac-toe board? The number of dimensions and possibilities would be endless.

In Pascal, it is possible to build up multidimensional arrays.

> **Multidimensional array:** An array with two or more index types where both are needed to specify a single component in the array.

Declaring Multidimensional Arrays

Suppose, for example, we want to store an entire dictionary in the computer for reference as a spelling checker. We could forget everything we have learned about type declarations and declare a global variable.

```
VAR     Dict : ARRAY [1..MaxWords, 1..MaxChars] OF Char;
```

But that is not usually the way we think of a dictionary. We usually picture a dictionary as a list of words, and not as a two-dimensional array of characters.

```
TYPE     Word = PACKED ARRAY [1..MaxChar] OF Char;
         Dictionary = ARRAY [1..MaxWords] OF Word;
VAR      Dict : Dictionary;
```

If we build up our two-dimensional array as an array of Word, then it is easy to see how to work with them.

```
ReadWord (Dict[i]);        (* read the ith word *)
IF (Dict[10][1] = 'A')     (* IF the 1st letter of the 10th *)
         THEN ...          (* word is 'A', THEN...   *)
```

In this case, we can think of the Dict as a single array whose components are of type Word. The fact that Dict is a two-dimensional array of characters is not important. In parts of the code where individual characters would need to be accessed, the single word, and not the entire array of words, would be used. For example, let's write the declaration for a procedure to read one word into the Dict.

```
PROCEDURE ReadWord (VAR W : Word);
(* This procedure reads a word until the end of line or    *)
(* until the array is full.                                *)
VAR      Cntr : Integer;
BEGIN
         Cntr := 0;
         WHILE (Cntr < MaxChar) AND NOT Eoln (Input) DO BEGIN
                 Cntr := Cntr + 1;
                 Read (Input, W[Cntr]);
         END;
END;
```

This procedure is nothing more than the familiar ReadWord. The entire array does not appear in this procedure. It is simply concerned with reading a single word into memory.

Now, let's write a procedure to read the dictionary from an input file.

```
PROCEDURE ReadDict (VAR Dict : Dictionary;
                    VAR NumWords : Integer);
BEGIN
         NumWords := 0;
         WHILE NOT Eof (Input) AND
                 (NumWords<MaxWords) DO BEGIN
                 NumWords := NumWords + 1;
                 ReadWord (Dict[NumWords]);
         END;
END;
```

Notice that, in this procedure, each word is dealt with as a unit. Notice also that this procedure will work no matter what the input file looks like. You must design PROCEDURE ReadWord with an awareness of the structure of the input file, but

PROCEDURE ReadDict is independent of the structure of the input file. That is an important design strategy—write the big procedures like ReadDict before the small ones like ReadWord, and let the small ones worry about details like the format of the input file. Of course, multidimensional arrays can be declared of any types and size. The following might be the beginnings of some type declarations for a game of three-dimensional tic-tac-toe.

```
CONST    MaxSquares = 4;
TYPE     Line = 1..MaxSquares;
         Square = (Empty, Red, Blue);
         Plane = Array[Line,Line] of Square;
         Qubic = Array[Line] of Plane;

VAR      Board : Qubic;
```

There are actually several different legal ways to declare multidimensional arrays. If we wanted a shorter way to declare Qubic we could have said:

```
Qubic = ARRAY [Line] OF ARRAY[ Line] OF
                        ARRAY [Line] OF Square;
```

Notice that this *does* conform to the syntax of arrays given previously:

```
<identifier> = ARRAY [<simple type>] OF <component type>;
```

The component type of Qubic is itself an array, whose component type is itself an array, whose component type is Square. There are several even shorter ways this could be expressed, all equivalent to this:

```
Qubic = ARRAY [Line, Line] OF ARRAY [Line] OF Square;
Qubic = ARRAY [Line] OF ARRAY [Line, Line] OF Square;
Qubic = ARRAY [Line, Line, Line] OF Square;
```

If these are valid, then why use the formulation we looked at originally?

```
Plane = ARRAY [Line, Line] OF Square;
Qubic = ARRAY [Line] OF Plane;
```

The reason I broke this down, and the reason the Dictionary type declaration was broken down into Word, an array of Char, and Dictionary, an array of Word, is that it is possible in this way to pass only part of the entire array as parameters. Suppose, for example, I had a procedure that would check one plane for any three-in-a-rows. If I have declared Plane, then I can use it as a parameter.

```
PROCEDURE CheckPlane (P : Plane; ...);
BEGIN
 .
 .
 .
END
```

The procedure call might look like this:

```
CheckPlane (Board[1]);
```

which sends the first plane into the procedure to be checked. If Plane were not declared as a separate type, then the only valid parameter to send would be the entire board. In the same way, if Word had not been declared before Dictionary, it would be impossible to write a procedure, like ReadWord or WriteWord, without sending the whole dictionary in as a parameter.

Accessing Multidimensional Arrays

As there are several different ways to declare multidimensional arrays, there are several different ways to obtain access to their individual elements.

```
Read (Input, x, y, z);
Board [x, y, z] := Red;
```

or

```
Board [x, y] [z] := Red;
```

or

```
Board [x] [y, z] := Red;
```

or

```
Board [x] [y] [z] := Red;
```

```
ReadWord(Dict[i]);
IF (Dict[i,1] = 'A') THEN ...
```

or

```
IF (Dict[x] [1] = 'A') THEN ...
```

For example, suppose we want to read a matrix of numbers into the following two-dimensional array.

```
TYPE    Matrix = ARRAY [1..NumRows, 1..NumCols] OF Integer;
VAR     Mat : Matrix;
```

This could be done in several ways, depending on how the input file was organized. If each value is on a different line, then the following code will do the job.

```
FOR Row := 1 TO NumRows DO
        FOR Col := 1 TO NumCols DO
                Readln (Input, Mat[Row, Col]);
```

However, if the input file looks like the matrix it is supposed to represent, with one row's data on a single line, then the previous code will not work. For example, if NumRows equals 3 and NumCols equals 6, the data might look like this.

```
10 16 22 19 25 23
13 18 15 22 19 30
14 28 16 12 17 25
```

The following code includes the needed changes.

```
FOR Row := 1 TO NumRows DO BEGIN
        FOR Col := 1 TO NumCols DO
                Read (Input, Mat[Row, Col]);
        Readln (Input);
END;
```

SELF
TEST
Write a procedure that inverts the values in a square matrix. The value of every element $A_{i,j}$ is placed in array location $A_{j,i}$.

Programming Example 14.1

Assignment: Write a program that reads in a line of NumScores scores for each of NumStudents students in a class. For each student, calculate the average of the scores, assuming even weighting. For each of the scores, calculate the average score of the class. Print a table, numbering each student and each score. Assume NumScores <= 8 for the purpose of formatting the heading. Print each student's average and each score's average. Instead of printing the scores, print a + if the score is above the average for that set of scores, and print a - if it is not. For example:

OUTPUT

Student Number	1	2	3	4	5	6	Average
1	+	+	−	+	+	+	92.00
2	+	−	+	+	−	−	76.17
3	−	+	−	−	−	−	61.83
. . .							
Class Averages	82.5	78.4	73.0	81.2	87.0	71.5	75.51

Notice that you will want to calculate the class average, which is the average of all the student averages.

Solution: This should be a pretty easy extension of the previous discussion about reading two-dimensional arrays. First of all, let's write an outline for the main program:

> Pluses and Minuses:
>> Read the data
>> Calculate student averages
>> Calculate averages for each set of scores
>> Print table

The first procedure will be essentially what we saw in the previous discussion. For now, let's use the following TYPE declarations.

```
CONST    NumScores = 6;
         NumStudents = 25;

TYPE     StudentScores = ARRAY [1..NumScores] OF Real;
         ClassScores = ARRAY [1..NumStudents] OF StudentScores;
```

The first procedure, therefore, is simply:

```
PROCEDURE ReadData (VAR Class : ClassScores);
(* This procedure reads the class scores from the input   *)
(* file. The information is stored as rows of scores, one *)
(* row for each student in the class. Each row contains   *)
(* NumScores scores.                                      *)
VAR      Row, Col : Integer;
BEGIN
         FOR Row := 1 TO NumStudents DO BEGIN
                FOR Col := 1 TO NumScores DO
                        Read (Input, Class [Row, Col]);
                Readln (Input);
         END;
END;
```

The next step is to average each student's scores. Notice that we will need to store the average because we want to print out all of the averages when we print the table. We could declare another array for the averages, or we could include the averages in the array we already have. One way of doing this is by adding one more element in the array declaration, the zeroth element, which we can use to store the averages.

```
TYPE      StudentScores = ARRAY [0..NumScores] OF Real;
          ClassScores = ARRAY [0..NumStudents] OF StudentScores;
```

We could now write a procedure to calculate the student averages and to store them in the zeroth element of each line of the array.

```
PROCEDURE StudentAves (VAR Class : ClassScores);
(* This procedure calculates each student's average and   *)
(* stores the average in the zeroth element of the        *)
(* student's row of scores.                                *)
VAR      Row, Col : Integer;
BEGIN
        FOR Row := 1 TO NumStudents DO BEGIN
             Class [Row, 0] := 0.0;    (* Initialize *)
             FOR Col := 1 TO NumScores DO
                  Class [Row, 0] := Class [Row, 0] +
                                       Class [Row, Col];
             Class [Row, 0] := Class [Row, 0] / NumScores;
        END;
END;
```

This procedure is short and the logic is separate from the ReadData procedure. However, it could be argued, on the grounds of efficiency, that we should combine the two procedures into one that functions as the two. We would only have to go through the array once, not twice, to read and to average the scores. The dual-purpose procedure is as follows.

```
PROCEDURE ReadNCalc (VAR Class : ClassScores);
(* This procedure serves both to read the data from the   *)
(* input file and to calculate each student's average.    *)
VAR      Row, Col : Integer;
BEGIN
        FOR Row := 1 TO NumStudents DO BEGIN
             Class [Row, 0] := 0.0;      (* Initialize *)
             FOR Col := 1 TO NumScores DO BEGIN
                  Read (Input, Class [Row, Col]);
                  Class [Row, 0] := Class [Row, 0] +
                                       Class [Row, Col];
             END;
             Class [Row, 0] := Class [Row, 0] / NumScores;
        END;
END;
```

This procedure is more efficient because it reduces the amount of work the computer must do, and it is certainly an acceptable way to program. However, for the sake of clarity, we will continue to write the program with the original outline, using two procedures instead of the single procedure to read and average the scores.

The next problem is to calculate the averages for each of the sets of scores. This problem is very similar to the problem of calculating each student's average. In fact, it is identical except that the orientation toward rows is replaced with an orientation toward columns.

```
PROCEDURE ScoreAves (VAR Class : ClassScores);
(* This procedure calculates the average for each set of  *)
(* scores and stores the average in the zeroth element of *)
(* each column of scores. The class average of the student*)
(* averages is found in the position Class [0, 0].        *)
VAR     Row, Col : Integer;
BEGIN
        FOR Col := 0 TO NumScores DO BEGIN
            Class [0, Col] := 0.0;    (* Initialize *)
            FOR Row := 1 TO NumStudents DO
                Class [0, Col] := Class [0, Col] +
                                  Class [Row, Col];
            Class [0, Col] := Class [0, Col] / NumStudents;
        END;
END;
```

The final task is to write out the table. This may take a little more thought, so let's take a closer pseudocode look at the task.

> Print Table:
>   Print Heading
>   Loop over NumStudents:
>   Print student number
>   Loop over NumScores:
>   IF Score > Average
>   THEN Print +
>   ELSE Print −
>   Print student's average
>   Print score averages, class average

This procedure can now be written easily in Pascal.

```
PROCEDURE PrintTable (VAR Class : ClassScores);
(* This procedure prints the table by rows, printing the  *)
(* average of each row at the end and the average of each  *)
(* column at the bottom. Instead of printing the values,   *)
(* a plus or a minus is printed, depending on whether or   *)
(* not the value is higher than the calculated average     *)
(* for each set of scores.                                 *)
VAR     Row, Col : Integer;
```

```
BEGIN
      Heading;
      FOR Row := 1 TO NumStudents DO BEGIN
          Write (Output, Row:8);
          FOR Col := 1 TO NumScores DO
              IF (Class [Row, Col] > Class [0, Col])
                  THEN Write (Output, '     +')
                  ELSE Write (Output, '     -');
          Writeln (Output, Class [Row, 0]:7:2);
      END;
      Write (Output, 'Class Averages ');
      FOR Col := 1 TO NumScores DO
          Write (Output, Class [0, Col]:5:1);
      Writeln (Output, Class [0,0]:7:2);
END;
```

The entire program and a sample of the output follow.

```
PROGRAM PlusNMinus (Input, Output);
(*****************************************************)
(* This program reads class test scores from an input *)
(* file and calculates each student's average score and *)
(* also the average score for each set of scores. The *)
(* data are summarized in a table that contains a plus or *)
(* a minus for each student for each score recorded. A *)
(* plus is given when the student's score is higher than *)
(* the average for the set of scores, and otherwise a *)
(* minus is recorded. The student's average, as well as *)
(* the average for each set of scores, and the class *)
(* average, is recorded as well. *)
(*****************************************************)


CONST   NumScores = 6;
        NumStudents = 25;

TYPE    StudentScores = ARRAY [0..NumScores] OF Real;
        ClassScores = ARRAY [0..NumStudents]
                           OF StudentScores;

VAR     Class : ClassScores;

PROCEDURE ReadData (VAR Class : ClassScores);
(* This procedure reads the class scores from the input *)
(* file. The information is stored as rows of scores, one *)
(* row for each student in the class. Each row contains *)
(* NumScores scores. *)
VAR     Row, Col : Integer;
```

```
BEGIN
        FOR Row := 1 TO NumStudents DO BEGIN
                FOR Col := 1 TO NumScores DO
                        Read (Input, Class [Row, Col]);
                Readln (Input);
        END;
END;


PROCEDURE StudentAves (VAR Class : ClassScores);
(* This procedure calculates each student's average and     *)
(* stores the average in the zeroth element of the          *)
(* student's row of scores.                                 *)
VAR     Row, Col : Integer;
BEGIN
        FOR Row := 1 TO NumStudents DO BEGIN
            Class [Row, 0] := 0.0;    (* Initialize *)
            FOR Col := 1 TO NumScores DO
                Class [Row, 0] := Class [Row, 0] +
                                    Class [Row, Col];
            Class [Row, 0] := Class [Row, 0] / NumScores;
        END;
END;


PROCEDURE ScoreAves (VAR Class : ClassScores);
(* This procedure calculates the average for each set of  *)
(* scores and stores the average in the zeroth element of *)
(* each column of scores. The class average of the student*)
(* averages is found in the position Class [0, 0].        *)
VAR     Row, Col : Integer;
BEGIN
        FOR Col := 0 TO NumScores DO BEGIN
            Class [0, Col] := 0.0;    (* Initialize *)
            FOR Row := 1 TO NumStudents DO
                Class [0, Col] := Class [0, Col] +
                                    Class [Row, Col];
            Class [0, Col] := Class [0, Col] / NumStudents;
        END;
END;


PROCEDURE Heading;
(* This procedure is used by PrintTable to print the       *)
(* heading with the correct number of columns, properly    *)
(* labeled.                                                *)
VAR     Col : Integer;
BEGIN
        Write (Output, 'Student Number');
        FOR Col := 1 TO NumScores DO Write (Output, Col:5);
        Writeln (Output, '  Average');
END;
```

```
PROCEDURE PrintTable (VAR Class : ClassScores);
(* This procedure prints the table by rows, printing the   *)
(* average of each row at the end and the average of each   *)
(* column at the bottom. Instead of printing the values,    *)
(* a plus or a minus is printed, depending on whether or     *)
(* not the value is higher than the calculated average       *)
(* for each set of scores.                                   *)
VAR      Row, Col : Integer;
BEGIN
        Heading;
        FOR Row := 1 TO NumStudents DO BEGIN
            Write (Output, Row:10, '    ');
            FOR Col := 1 TO NumScores DO
                IF (Class [Row, Col] > Class [0, Col])
                    THEN Write (Output, '    +')
                    ELSE Write (Output, '    -');
            Writeln (Output, Class [Row, 0]:8:2);
        END;
        Write (Output, 'Class Averages ');
        FOR Col := 1 TO NumScores DO
            Write (Output, Class [0, Col]:5:1);
        Writeln (Output, Class [0,0]:7:2);
END;


BEGIN    (* Main Program *)
        ReadData (Class);
        StudentAves (Class);
        ScoreAves (Class);
        PrintTable (Class);
END.     (* Main Program *)
```

INPUT
```
10 12 14 15 16 18
12 13 14 15 16 17
11 13 15 17 19 16
10 10 10 20 20 20
10 20 10 20 10 20
```

OUTPUT

Student Number	1	2	3	4	5	6	Average
1	-	-	+	-	-	-	14.17
2	+	-	+	-	-	-	14.50
3	+	-	+	-	+	-	15.17
4	-	-	-	+	+	+	15.00
5	-	+	-	+	-	+	15.00
Class Averages	10.6	13.6	12.6	17.4	16.2	18.2	14.77

Figure 14.1 shows the module tree for PROGRAM PlusNMinus.

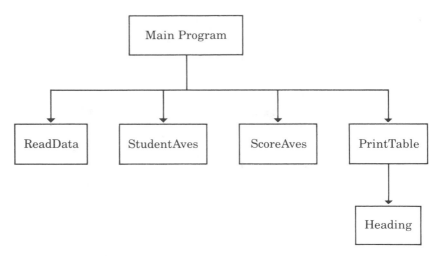

Figure 14.1: Module Tree for `PlusNMinus`

Programming Example 14.2

Assignment: Write a program that writes, in large letters, a message given by the user at the terminal. The program should first read an input file that contains large versions of each letter in the alphabet. Each letter should consist of seven columns by five rows and lie on its side. The input file also contains a blank line between letters.

Solution: This is obviously a job for a multidimensional array. Let's look at the data structure before we design the algorithm. The alphabet will be comprised of 26 LetterTypes, one for each character. Therefore, the main data structure can be declared as follows.

```
TYPE    Alphabet = ARRAY ['A' .. 'Z'] OF LetterType;
```

The data structure to hold an image for each letter is a two-dimensional array of characters. Each character spans seven columns by five rows.

```
CONST   Width = 5;
        Length = 7;

TYPE    LetterType = ARRAY [1..Width, 1..Length] OF Char;
        Alphabet = ARRAY ['A'..'Z'] OF LetterType;
```

Therefore, although we'll probably never have to think about it this way, we are dealing with a three-dimensional array of characters in this problem.

A very rough outline of the solution can be sketched easily from the statement of the problem.

Big Letters:
>   Reset input file
>   Read alphabet from input file
>   Read message from the terminal
>   Write message with big letters

Using just a few variables, we translate the algorithm to Pascal.

```
BEGIN    (* Main Program *)
        Reset (InFile);
        ReadAlphabet (Letters);
        ReadMessage (Message, NumChars);
        WriteMessage (Message, NumChars, Letters);
END.     (* Main Program *)
```

The variable `Message` is a simple one-dimensional array of characters indexed by integers.

Let's take a look at the `ReadAlphabet` procedure. We can break this down simply by calling a procedure that reads one letter.

```
PROCEDURE ReadAlphabet (VAR Letters : Alphabet);
(* This procedure reads the entire InFile of Letter       *)
(* images stored as rectangles of characters.             *)
VAR     Ch : Char;
BEGIN
        FOR Ch := 'A' TO 'Z' DO
                ReadLetter (Letters [Ch]);
END;
```

We are assuming as we write these procedures that the input file does indeed have the proper data for all 26 letters. If this is true, then the procedure that reads a letter is also fairly straightforward, although it involves two nested FOR loops.

```
PROCEDURE ReadLetter (VAR Let : LetterType);
(* This procedure reads one letter from the InFile. The   *)
(* letter is stored as a rectangle of characters.         *)
VAR     Row, Col : Integer;
```

```
BEGIN
        FOR Row := 1 TO Width DO BEGIN
            FOR Col := 1 TO Length DO
                Read (InFile, Let [Row, Col]);
            Readln (InFile);
        END;
        Readln (InFile);
END;
```

Notice that, since ReadLetter is located inside a FOR loop from 'A' TO 'Z', the inner Read statement is actually inside three nested FOR loops, and it executes a total of $5 \times 7 \times 26$, or 910 times.

The procedure that reads the message is fairly simple to write. Let's take a look at the procedure that writes the message. For each letter in the message, we want to print the pattern of the corresponding letter.

```
PROCEDURE WriteMessage (Message : MessageType;
                NumChars : Integer; VAR Letters : Alphabet);
(* This procedure writes out the message to the output    *)
(* file.                                                  *)
VAR     Cntr : Integer;
BEGIN
        FOR Cntr := 1 TO NumChars DO
                WriteLet (Letters [Message [Cntr]]);
END;
```

Suppose, however, that we try to use the message character as the index to the Letters array. If a character occurs in the message that is not an uppercase letter (a space perhaps), then the error message "array index out of bounds" will appear. Perhaps we can avoid the error with some defensive programming.

```
PROCEDURE WriteMessage (Message : MessageType;
                NumChars : Integer; VAR Letters : Alphabet);
(* This procedure writes out the message to the output    *)
(* file.                                                  *)
VAR     Cntr, Lines : Integer;
        Ch : Char;
BEGIN
        FOR Cntr := 1 TO NumChars DO BEGIN
            Ch := Message [Cntr];
            IF IsALetter (Ch)
                THEN WriteLet (Letters [Cap (Ch)])
                ELSE FOR Lines := 0 TO Length DO
                        Writeln (Output);
        END;
END;
```

This version doesn't handle bad input in the most graceful manner possible—it merely prints a space instead of printing a character or typing out an error message. However, in most cases that is probably acceptable, since the most likely violation to the nonletter rule is a space anyway.

The major procedure left to write is WriteLet, which is analogous to ReadLetter.

```
PROCEDURE WriteLet (Let : LetterType);
(* This procedure writes one letter to the output file.   *)
VAR    Row, Col : Integer;
BEGIN
       FOR Row := 1 TO Width DO BEGIN
           FOR Col := 1 TO Length DO
               Write (Output, Let [Row, Col]);
           Writeln (Output);
       END;
       Writeln (Output);
END;
```

See Figure 14.2 for a module tree of BigLetters. Sample output is given below.

INTERACTIVE SESSION

Type the message you want to have printed out==>**Happy Birthday**

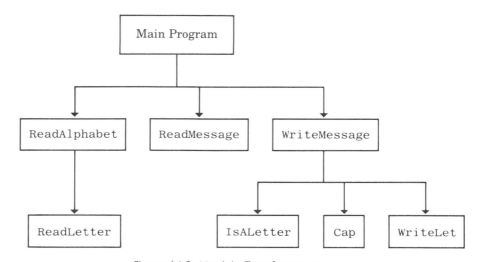

Figure 14.2: Module Tree for Bigletters

OUTPUT
```
*******
      *
      *
      *
*******

 ******
      *  *
      *  *
      *  *
 ******

*******
      *  *
      *  *
      *  *
      **

*******
      *  *
      *  *
      *  *
      **

         *
       *
***
       *
         *


*******
*    *  *
*    *  *
*    *  *
 **  **

*       *
*       *
*******
*       *
*       *

*******
      *  *
    **  *
  *  *  *
*    **
```

```
        *
        *
* * * * * *
        *
        *

  * * * * * *
     *
     *
     *
  * * * * * *

  * * * * * *
  *         *
  *         *
  *         *
   * * * * *

  * * * * * *
       *   *
       *   *
       *   *
  * * * * * *

          *
       *
  * * *
       *
          *
```

Common Errors and Debugging

1. **Accessing individual elements improperly.** It is easy when working with
    multidimensional arrays to confuse the indices, which will usually result in the
    error message "array index out of bounds." For example, consider a short pro-
    cedure to read in a file of characters.

```
CONST   RowMax = 24;
        ColMax = 80;
TYPE    LineArray = ARRAY [1..ColMax] OF Char;
        TextArray = ARRAY [1..RowMax] OF LineArray;
```

```
PROCEDURE ReadText (VAR TA : TextArray);
VAR     Row, Col : Integer;
BEGIN
        Row := 0;
        WHILE NOT Eof (Input) AND
                        (Row < RowMax) DO BEGIN
                Row := Row + 1; Col := 0;
                WHILE NOT Eoln (Input) AND
                        (Col < ColMax) DO BEGIN
                        Col := Col + 1;
                        Read (Input, TA [Col, Row]);
                END;
                Readln (Input);
        END;
END;
```

This procedure has all the earmarks of being protected against array index errors—the provision in the WHILE loop tests for lines that are too long or text with too many lines. However, the fact that Row and Col are switched in accessing individual array elements means that an error will occur when the value of Col exceeds the value of RowMax. It is very likely that somewhere in the input file a line with more than 24 characters will show up and a run-time error will occur.

2. **Producing memory size errors.** It is easy to get carried away with the power of multidimensional arrays and to declare an array that your system cannot handle because of its size. For example, the previous array was declared to be an array of 24 lines of 80 characters. That is not a huge amount of space, but suppose we had declared RowMax as 240. For many systems, this array with nearly 20,000 memory locations would be more than the capacity available to the user. In many cases, packing some component of the structure will keep it within memory size. For example, if each line in the data structure used above were declared to be a PACKED array of characters, the amount of storage space required to contain a line of text would be significantly smaller; therefore, more rows of data could be stored.

Hints for BASIC Programmers

A crucial difference between Pascal and BASIC is that Pascal allows multidimensional arrays. This is not simply because Pascal is larger or allows more data to be stored. In fact, a two-dimensional array structure could be simulated in BASIC, although in a very clumsy fashion.

```
10    DIM A(50), B(50), C(50), D(50), E(50), S(50)
90    REM - READ MATRIX VALUES AND CALCULATE THE SUMS OF ROWS
100   FOR K = 1 TO 50
110     INPUT A(K), B(K), C(K), D(K), E(K)
120     LET S(K) = A(K) + B(K) + C(K) + D(K) + E(K)
130   NEXT K
```

The problem with this coding is not that there isn't enough storage space. The problem is that it would be very difficult to increase the column dimension of the "two-dimensional array." If, for example, a sixth element, F(K), were needed in each row, then lines 10, 110, and 120 would need to be changed. If 20 rather than five elements were to be stored for each row of data, the very simple program would be very tedious to write. The Pascal version, of course, is much simpler.

```
TYPE    Matrix = ARRAY [1..RowMax, 1..ColMax] OF Integer;
VAR     Mat : Matrix;
. . .

        FOR Row := 1 TO RowMax DO BEGIN
                FOR Col := 1 TO ColMax DO
                        Read (Input, Mat [Row, Col]);
                Readln (Input);
        END;
```

The main difference between Pascal and BASIC is in the way data structures are treated. With the addition of TYPE declarations in Pascal, any new type declaration can specify a single component of a more complex type or data structure. What this means is that two-dimensional arrays of characters can be thought of as one-dimensional arrays of words or lines or names.

```
TYPE    Word = PACKED ARRAY [1..WordLen] OF Char;
        Name = PACKED ARRAY [1..NameLen] OF Char;
        Line = PACKED ARRAY [1..LineLen] OF Char;
        Dictionary = ARRAY [1..DictLen] OF Word;
        NameList = ARRAY [1..NameLisLen] OF Name;
        TextArray = ARRAY [1..TextLen] OF Line;
```

This more closely reflects how humans tend to group and organize data. No one thinks of a dictionary as a two-dimensional array, but people are more likely to think of it as a list of words. Because of Pascal's ability to build data types from other defined types, the level of complexity of the data structure is determined only by the programmer's needs and the computer's available memory. The increased power, flexibility, and modifiability this feature gives Pascal over BASIC is incalculable.

SUMMARY

A **multidimensional array** is useful for working with many different applications, such as arrays of words, or multiple sets of numbers, or two- and three-dimensional game boards. Multidimensional arrays are declared in the same way as arrays with a single dimension—as an ARRAY indexed over a subrange of some base type, where the base type of this array is another, simpler array. In this way, a dictionary, for example, can be declared as an array of words.

Multidimensional arrays and arrays with one dimension are used in similar ways. An n-dimensional array requires n indices in order to specify a single element in the array. It is often necessary to use n nested FOR loops in order to store, process, and print the values in an n-dimensional array.

EXERCISES

1. Programming Example 7.4 on page 177 involved reading a set of scores and determining a grading curve by calculating the mean and standard deviation. Rewrite this program so that it will take as input a name and a score on each line of the file and produce as output the list of names and scores as well as assigning a letter grade to each score. This task will involve an array of names (each name an array of characters) as well as an array of scores.

2. Implement a bubble sort on a list of numbers. Modify this procedure to alphabetize a list of names. Is there any way to make the sort procedure so general that it will perform both tasks, depending on the parameters you give it?

3. Write a procedure that calculates a three-dimensional multiplication cube in which the value stored in any location is equal to the product of its three indices. Write out the values of a $10 \times 10 \times 10$ cube. Write a function that, given the three indices, returns the value stored in the array.

4. Write a program that counts the occurrences of all two-letter pairs in an input file. For example, in the word *Mississippi,* the following two-character combinations occur.

Mississippi	
MI	1 time
IS	2 times
SS	2 times
SI	2 times
IP	1 time
PP	1 time
PI	1 time

Spaces and punctuation continue to serve as separators. For example, assume that *n't* is not the same as *nt*. Because of the large number of combinations, only print out the most common occurrences, say those over 1 percent or 0.5 percent of the total number of pairs.

5. Write a program that reads a piece of text and stores each word it finds in an array of words. Then sort the array and print out the words in alphabetical order. Only print each different word once, but do print how many occurrences there were of each word in the file.

6. Write a program that encodes a message into Morse code and decodes a message from Morse code into English. The message should be located in the input file. Read the message in and from it; determine which type of operation needs to be performed. Write the result to the output file. Enter the Morse code using another input file. Assume the message will be less than 1,000 characters, that a space occurs between patterns, and that the message contains only letters.

   The following table shows the English-to-Morse code conversion.

A	. −	J	. − − −	S	. . .
B	− . . .	K	− . −	T	−
C	− . − .	L	. − . .	U	. . −
D	− . .	M	− −	V	. . . −
E	.	N	− .	W	. − −
F	. . − .	O	− − −	X	− . . −
G	− − .	P	. − − .	Y	− . − −
H	. . . .	Q	− − . −	Z	− − . .
I	. .	R	. − .		

7. A magic square of order *n* is an *n*-by-*n* matrix of numbers, where each row, column, or diagonal of numbers adds up to the same number. For example, the following is a magic square of order 3.

8	1	6
3	5	7
4	9	2

One rule for generating a magic square of order *n* when *n* is odd is to place the numbers in the square as follows: begin with the number 1 in the middle box along the top of the square. Each successive number will be placed in the cell up and to the right. When the move puts you off the top of the square, you go to the bottom row of the square and right one column. Likewise, when you move off the right edge of the square, you go up one row on the far left column. Whenever you come across a cell that is already filled, move straight down from the previously placed cell instead of moving up and to the right. If everything works correctly, all n^2 cells will be filled when the value n^2 is placed. The sum of the rows should be $(n^3 + n)/2$. Write a program that produces magic squares for any odd order less than 20. Print them out neatly and give the sum of any row.

8. A Latin square of order n contains the numbers 1 through n in each of its n^2 cells in such a way that no number is repeated in the same row or column. For example:

1	2	3	4
2	3	4	1
3	4	1	2
4	1	2	3

These squares can be used, for example, in round-robin tournaments to ensure that every team plays every other team once and only once. Write a boolean function that takes a two-dimensional array and checks to see if the array really is a valid Latin square.

9. Write a program that generates and prints a Latin square of any order less than 20.

10. Greco-Latin squares are simply Latin squares with the additional requirement that no number be repeated along either of the two diagonals, or any diagonal constructed as in the following illustration.

			4	
				5
1				
	2			
		3		

Greco-Latin squares of any odd order n are constructed as follows: Place the numbers 1 through n consecutively in the top row of the square. In the first cell of the second row, place the number 3. From there, count consecutively up to n and then begin again at 1. In the third row, place the number 5 in the first cell and count up. Always begin again at 1 after n is placed in a cell. For all the remaining rows, increment the starting cell by two, until the value is greater than n, at which point you begin with 2 and continue.

1	2	3	4	5
3	4	5	1	2
5	1	2	3	4
2	3	4	5	1
4	5	1	2	3

Remember that the smallest Greco-Latin square is of order 5. Write a program to produce Greco-Latin squares of any odd order n, where $5 <= n <= 20$.

11. A magic cube is a three-dimensional matrix of numbers, where each row, column, or diagonal sums to the same number. The smallest known magic cube is of order 7, and it can be thought of as the superposition of three Greco-Latin squares upon one another in seven ways. The Greco-Latin squares are made by the method described in the previous section. Here are the three squares, the first one completely filled in, while only the first column of the last two is given.

```
G-L Square 1          G-L Square 2          G-L Square 3

0 1 2 3 4 5 6         0 1 2 3 4 5 6         0 1 2 3 4 5 6
2 3 4 5 6 0 1         3                     4
4 5 6 0 1 2 3         6                     1
6 0 1 2 3 4 5         2                     5
1 2 3 4 5 6 0         5                     2
3 4 5 6 0 1 2         1                     6
5 6 0 1 2 3 4         4                     3
```

Each cell in the first plane of the magic cube is represented by the following formula.

```
Plane1 [Row, Col] := 7*7*GL1 [Row, Col] + 7*GL2 [Row, Col]
                        + GL3 [Row, Col]
```

In other words, the value of the top right corner is 666_{base7}, or 342. The values for all the other planes involve shifting the rows of the original Greco-Latin squares. A general formula for any nth plane of the magic cube is:

```
Plane-N [Row, Col] := 7*7*GL1 [Row + 2*(N-1), Col]
                       + 7*GL2 [Row + 3*(N-1), Col]
                       +    GL3 [Row + 4*(N-1), Col]
```

where it is understood that all of the additions are done using the MOD function, so that the final index value will be between 1 and 7.

Write a program that will generate and print a magic cube of order 7. You can either have the program read the three Greco-Latin squares from an input file, or you can have the program generate the squares before using them.

12. Exercise 11.9 on page 322 illustrated an example of Simplified Integrated Modular Prose (SIMP). Implement a SIMP program, but instead of using a CASE statement and Write statements, read the SIMP tables from an input file and store them in several arrays of lines, where each line is an array of characters. Generate random indices for the arrays, and print out a paragraph of SIMP.

13. Write a program that initializes a 10 by 10 grid with 10 randomly placed positrons and 10 randomly placed electrons (see Exercise 13.14). The particles move in a random direction—up, down, left, right, or diagonally in any direction. When a positron moves into a cell occupied by an electron or vice versa, the antimatter–matter collision annihilates both particles. Write a program to simulate the interaction over time. Vary the parameters and reexecute the program. Give the user the ability to allow more than one unit of time between printouts of the situation.

14.   A popular trivia game uses question cards that have six categories of questions on one side of the card and the answers on the back. Write a data structure for a trivia card, using an array of characters as the basic building block of the structure. Be sure to provide separate spaces for each question and answer. Think of several different categories of questions for each card. Write a procedure that reads questions and answers from an input file into your data structure.

15.   Use the procedure and data structures developed in the previous problem and write a program that allows several players to play a trivia game on a game board. Each square on the board is one of six colors. Each color represents one of the categories of questions that must be answered by the person landing on the square. Develop your own rules for winning the game.

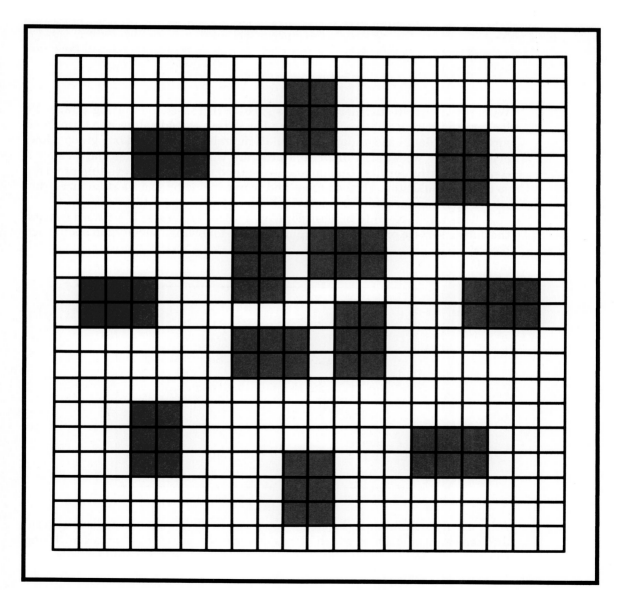

STORING DATA: RECORDS

With the ability to use arrays comes greatly increased computing power. No longer are we limited to working with a few variables and values at a time. Now, virtually no data base or data manipulation problem is beyond our grasp. However, suppose we wanted to write a program that would set up matches for a computer dating service. Or, suppose we wanted to expand our grading program so that we could store all the names and scores in one huge data structure, from which information could be retrieved or changed.

This might seem to be best done by a series of arrays. If we were writing the dating service program, we might want the following information about each person:

```
┌─────────────────────────────────────────────────┐
│                                                   │
│   Person                                          │
│                                                   │
│   Name _____ Sex:    M    F            │
│                                                   │
│   Age _____ Height _____ Weight _____          │
│                                                   │
│   Smoker:    Y    N                               │
│                                                   │
│   Interests                                       │
│                                                   │
│                                                   │
└─────────────────────────────────────────────────┘
```

A lot of information must be stored. One way to do it would be to have several different arrays, each of which stores one specific piece of information. Using the concepts we already know, this is essentially the way it would be done.

```
CONST     MaxPeople = 100;
          MaxChar =   30;
TYPE      SexType =   (Male, Female);
          Word =      PACKED ARRAY [1..MaxChar] OF Char;
          Answers =   PACKED ARRAY [1..MaxPeople] OF Boolean;
          NamesArr =  ARRAY [1..MaxPeople] OF Word;
          Numbers =   ARRAY [1..MaxPeople] OF Integer;
          Sexes =     ARRAY [1..MaxPeople] OF SexType;
VAR       Names : NamesArr;
          Ages,       (* in years *)
          Heights,    (* in inches *)
          Weights     (* in pounds *)
               :   Numbers;
          Smoker,     (* TRUE means Yes, FALSE means No *)
               :   Answers;
          Sex :       Sexes;
```

To keep things straight, the age of the first person in the Names array will be found in the first box in the Ages array, and that person's sex will be found in the first box of the Sex array, and so forth. (See Figure 15.1.) However, this could be *very* tedious to work with. For example, suppose our task was to sort such a structure alphabetically by last names. Recall PROCEDURE Swap from the last section. In this case, Swap might look like the following:

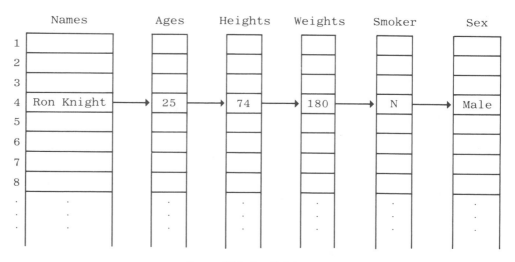

Figure 15.1: Parallel Arrays

```
PROCEDURE Swap  (VAR Name1, Name2 : Word;
                     VAR Age1, Age2, Height1, Height2,
                         Weight1, Weight2 :  Integer;
                     VAR Smoker1, Smoker2 : Boolean;
                     VAR Sex1, Sex2 : SexType);
VAR     TempName : Word;
        TempAge, TempHeight, TempWeight : Integer;
        TempSmoker : Boolean;
        TempSex : SexType;
BEGIN
        TempName : = Name1;
        Name1 : = Name2;
        Name2 : = TempName;
        TempAge : = Age1;
. . .
```

With all these parallel arrays, even a simple data manipulation becomes extremely tedious. Rather, what we'd really like is just one big array that can store all these values in some kind of logical order. We cannot do this with a multidimensional array because different component types need to be stored in different arrays (unless this were done using all integer arrays, where some complicated algorithm was used to encode and later decode the integers into meaningful Names, Sexes, and the rest).

As you have probably already deduced, there is an easier way to solve this problem. (This is also one place where people who have programmed in BASIC and who have remained loyal to the memory of their former programming language often trade in their loyalty and decide that Pascal really is a superior language.) But enough rhetoric; let's take a look at records.

Declarations

A Pascal record is like an array in that it is a structured type, built of components. The difference is that an array contains components, or boxes, that hold values that are all of the same type. A record can contain components of different types, including arrays. A record can join in one data structure boxes that hold integers, booleans, reals, user-defined enumerated types, characters, and even arrays of characters or other records. For example, here are two type declarations, the familiar Word, which is an array, and a new type called Person, which will hold all the information we want for the computer dating service program.

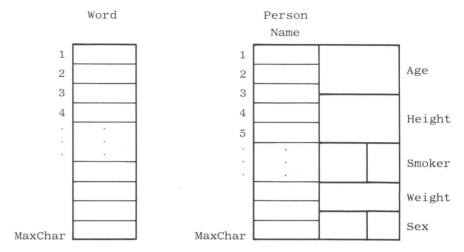

Figure 15.2: Record Structure in Memory

```
TYPE    SexType = (Male, Female);
        Word =     PACKED ARRAY OF [1..MaxChar] Char;
        Person =   RECORD
           Name : Word; (* Last name, First name *)
           Age,                    (* in years *)
           Height,                 (* in inches *)
           Weight : Integer;       (* in pounds *)
           Smoker : Boolean;       (* T = yes, F = no *)
           Sex :       SexType;
        END;
```

In memory, these data structures might look something like Figure 15.2.

As we have seen with arrays, records can be treated as entire units, or their components can be treated individually. An entire record holding one prospect's statistics can be passed through the program until a match is found. Both the entire record and its components are easily accessible. In this case the record operates like an index card containing several different types of values. (See Figure 15.3.)

There are a few specific things to notice about RECORD declarations. First, as with the CASE statement, there is no BEGIN, but RECORD declarations are terminated by END. Second, all the types must be declared before the record is declared. The parts of the record, called **fields,** are declared like variable declarations but are not variable declarations. Name, Age, Height, and so forth are all fields of the type Person. Again, what must be realized is that, in all the complexity of record type declarations, no variables are declared until a VAR declaration specifies a variable of the RECORD type.

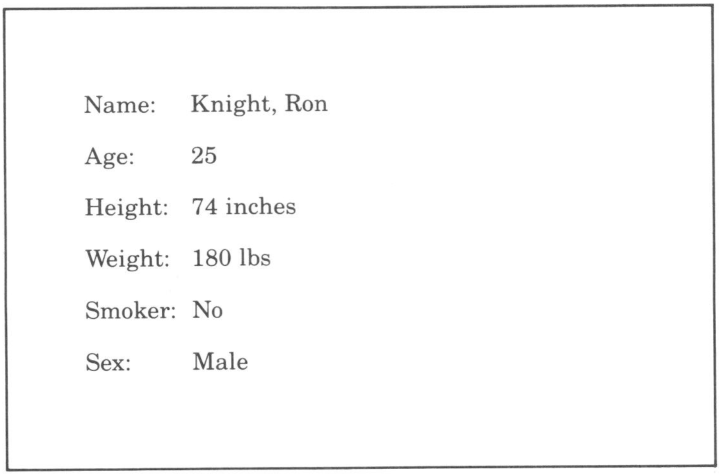

Figure 15.3: A Record Structure is Like an Index Card

```
VAR     P :   Person;
```

Now, with P declared, places for Name, Age, Height, and the rest are set aside in the computer's memory and can be accessed at any time.

Usage

How do we obtain access to individual components in the variable P, the Person we have set up? With arrays, individual components were indexed with subscripts. Correspondingly, individual components of records are named by their field name, and the variable name is separated from the field name by a period.

```
P.Age  : = 18;
Read (P.Height);
P.Smoker  : = FALSE;
ReadWord (P.Name);
```

All of these are legal statements in Pascal (assuming PROCEDURE ReadWord has been defined correctly). Incorrect attempts might include trying to use subscripts where they are not appropiate.

```
P[Age]  : = 18;        (* This is wrong since
                          this would imply that P
                          is an array and Age is a
                          legal value for the index
                          of that array.            *)
```

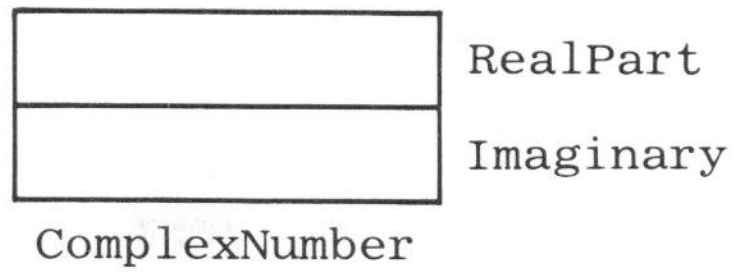

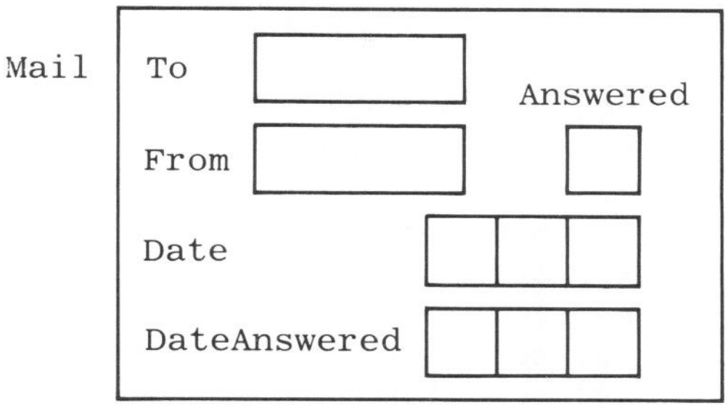

Figure 15.4: Record Types

```
Read (Input, P.1)     (* This is wrong since
                         a field name that is a legal
                         identifier and is declared
                         in the type declaration must
                         be given.                      *)
Read (Input, P);      (* This is probably wrong, since
                         it is an error to send any
                         structured type to the Read
                         procedures, except when reading
                         from or writing to a file of
                         records.                        *)
```

Records can be declared and used in many applications. Essentially, any type of information requiring several different types of storage is a good candidate for a record. (See Figure 15.4 for how these record types might be illustrated.)

```
TYPE    ComplexNumber = RECORD
            RealPart,
            Imaginary : Real;
        END;
        Times =     (Day, Month, Year);
        DateArr =   ARRAY[Times] OF Integer;
        Name =      PACKED ARRAY [1..MaxChar] OF Char;
        Mail =      RECORD
            To,
            From :          Name;
            Date :          DateArr;
            Answered :      Boolean;
            DateAnswered :  DateArr;
        END;
```

```
VAR      Yesterday, Today : DateArr;
         First, Last : Name;
         Letter : Mail;
```

Record variables can be set equal to one another, if the variables are of the same type.

```
VAR      X, Y, Z : ComplexNumber;
```

```
Read (X.RealPart);
Read (X.Imaginary);
Y := X;
Z.RealPart := X.RealPart * Y.Imaginary;
Z.Imaginary := -X.Imaginary * Y.RealPart;
WriteComplex (X);        (* takes a complex number *)
WriteComplex (Y);        (* and writes both parts  *)
WriteComplex (Z);        (* to the output file      *)
```

SELF TEST

Given the preceding set of TYPE and VAR declarations, examine the following variable uses and identify the syntactical errors. Not every line has an error.

```
1. Yesterday.Day := 1;
2. Read (Input, First[Cntr]);
3. Mail.To := First;
4. Today[1] := 1;
5. Today[Year] := 1984;
6. Letter.To := First;
7. Letter[Date] := Today;
```

Arrays of Records

It is almost always the case that declaring one variable of a record type isn't enough to solve the problem. In the example that motivated our discussion about records, we had 100 prospective dates for which data needed to be stored. Once we have the capability to declare a structure that contains the information about one person, the next step seems obvious: declare an array of those records, one component for each person. If a record can be likened to an index card, then an array of records is like a file of index cards. (See Figure 15.5.)

This is as easy as declaring an array of words, which we learned about in the last chapter. We build up arrays by building up their components until we create the data structure we desire.

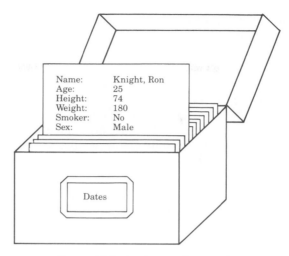

Figure 15.5: An Array of Records

```
CONST    MaxChar   = 20;
         MaxPeople = 100;
TYPE     Word   =    PACKED ARRAY [1..MaxChar] OF Char;
         SexType =   (Male, Female);
         Person =    RECORD
             Name :     Word;
             Age,
             Height,
             Weight :   Integer;
             Smoker :   Boolean;
             Sex : SexType;
         END;
         PoolArr = ARRAY [1..MaxPeople] OF Person;

VAR      Dates : PoolArr;
```

Notice that with only one variable declaration, we allocate a massive space in memory for the solution to the current problem.

Accessing individual components of arrays of records is no more difficult than what has been done before. It is important to remember the following rules, however:

Component access rules:
1. Arrays need [index]
2. Records need . field name

If we want to specify the second character of the name of the 55th person in the pool, we can say:

```
Dates[55].Name[2]
```

Dates is an array, so it takes index 55. Dates[55] is one element in the Dates array, hence, it is a Person, which is declared to be a record. Therefore Dates[55] takes a "dot field name," Dates[55].Name. This variable, Dates[55].Name, is declared by the record declaration to be of type Word, which is an array. Therefore, to specify the second letter, we use another subscript:

```
Dates[55].Name[2].
```

How can we obtain access to a record within a record? For example, suppose the following declarations were made.

```
TYPE    Word =         PACKED ARRAY [1..MaxChars] OF Char;
        Player =       RECORD
            Name :          Word;
            Height :        60..90;        (* in inches *)
            PtsPerGame,
            TotPoints,
            TotRebs,
            TotAssts,
            GamesPlayed :   Integer;
            Assists :       0..50;
            Starter :       Boolean;
            JerseyNum :     0..55;
            FieldPctg,
            FreeThrowPctg,
            FoulsPerGame :  Real;
        END;
        TeamStats = RECORD
            Wins,
            Losses,
            GamesPlayed :   0..100;
            TotalPts,
            TotalOpponentsPts,
            TotRebounds,
            TotOppRebounds,
            Fouls,
            OpponentsFouls : Integer;
            AveHeight :         Real;
        END;
        RosterArray = ARRAY [1..MaxPlayers] OF Player;
        Team =         RECORD
            Name :      Word;
            Stats :     TeamStats;
            Roster :    RosterArray;
        END;
```

```
        AllTeams  =        ARRAY [1..MaxTeams] OF Team;

VAR     NBA  :            AllTeams;
```

With declarations like this, it can be confusing to access individual components, but consistent applications of the component access rules will keep things clear. (See Figure 15.6 for a pictorial representation of the variable, NBA.)

1. NBA is an array of Teams,
2. NBA[1] is a Team (a record),
3. NBA[1].Stats is a TeamStats record,
4. NBA[1].Stats.Wins is an integer (a record within a record),
5. NBA[1].Roster is an array of Players (roster array),
6. NBA[1].Roster[1].Name is the name of the first player on the roster of the first team.

SELF TEST

Test your own ability to read the data structure given above. For each of the following variables, tell the type name of the variable, and whether the variable is a record or an array. If it is an array, give the base type.

1. NBA[1].Stats.Losses
2. NBA[1].Roster[1]
3. NBA[1].Name
4. NBA[1].Roster[1].JerseyNum
5. NBA[1].Roster[1].Name[1]

Using Large Data Structures

Declaring huge data structures like NBA is one thing; using them is another. Such structures are confusing and difficult to read—at least for the programmer, though not for the computer. There are several ways to simplify large data structures. The first is common to structured programming in general and the second is a specific control structure in Pascal.

Let's go back to our computer dating program. Suppose we have an input file with all the information stored for each person, one person per line. First we want to write a set of procedures that reads the data into the array of records we declared. Without even thinking about how the data is stored in the input file, we can write the following procedure.

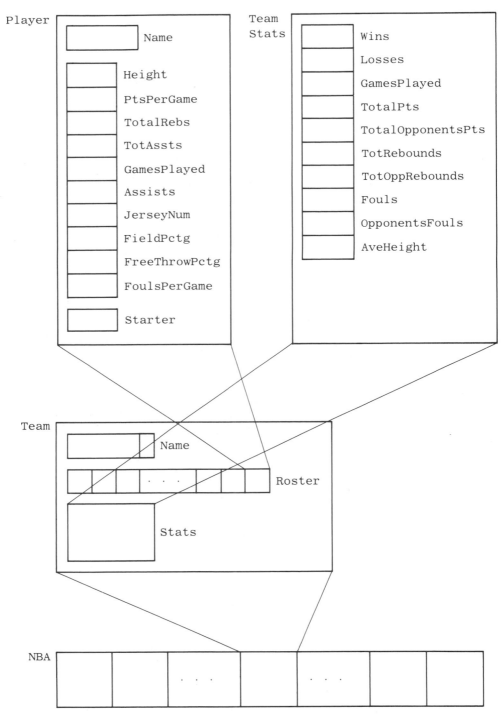

Figure 15.6: The Variable NBA

```
PROCEDURE ReadDates (VAR Dates : PoolArr;
                         VAR NumDates : Integer);
(* This procedure reads the entire pool of dates from the *)
(* input file, using ReadPerson.                          *)
BEGIN
    NumDates:= 0;
    WHILE (NumDates < MaxPeople) AND
            NOT Eof (Input) DO BEGIN
        NumDates := NumDates + 1;
        ReadPerson (Dates[NumDates]);
    END;
END;
```

Now all we need to do is write PROCEDURE ReadPerson, which reads all the information for one person in the file. Notice the parameter we pass into ReadPerson is not the whole array, but a single Person record.

PROCEDURE ReadPerson must know how the input file is formatted. For example, suppose input looks like this.

```
Ron Knight, M 25 74 180 N
```

The name is between 1 and MaxChar characters, and it is ended by a comma. Sex (designated M or F), age, height, weight and N or S (for nonsmoker or smoker) follow, separated by spaces. We can now write ReadPerson, worrying about the details of conversion a little bit later:

```
PROCEDURE ReadPerson (VAR  P : Person);
(* This procedure reads the data into the record   *)
(* structure for a single person.                  *)
BEGIN
    ReadWord (P.Name);
    ReadSex (P.Sex);
    Read (Input, P.Age, P.Height, P.Weight);
    ReadSmoker (P.Smoker);
END;
```

Because we are writing a procedure that reads in the values for a single person, we don't have to worry about subscripts to indicate for which person we are reading the name, sex, and other data. In Pascal and in other structured programming languages, procedural breakdown is the first means to simplify the use of large data structures.

Before writing the other procedures we have already used in the solution to ReadPerson, let's look at the second way to simplify the use of records in large data structures: the WITH statement. Using the WITH statement, we can rewrite ReadPerson to make it slightly easier.

```
PROCEDURE ReadPerson (VAR  P : Person);
(* This procedure reads the data into the record   *)
(* structure for a single person.                  *)
BEGIN
```

```
            WITH P DO BEGIN
                    ReadWord (Name);
                    ReadSex (Sex);
                    Read (Input, Age, Height, Weight);
                    ReadSmoker (Smoker);
            END;
    END;
```

The WITH statement works like an abbreviation; it only takes record variables, and expects either one statement or a compound statement. A procedure called inside the WITH statement doesn't have access to the same abbreviations inside its body. However, for each statement under the control of the WITH structure, all that is necessary to access a field of the record specified is to name the field itself, as in the example above. Outside the control of the WITH, the full variable name is needed.

```
BEGIN
    WITH P DO BEGIN
            ReadWord (Name);
            ReadSex (Sex);
            Read (Input, Age, Height);
    END;
    Read (Input, P.Weight);
    ReadSmoker (P.Smoker);
END;
```

WITH statements can be compounded for use with multiple record structures. If we use the TYPE declarations that created the NBA variable, we could write the following.

```
WITH NBA[i] DO BEGIN
    ReadWord (Name);
    WITH Stats DO BEGIN
            Read (input, Wins, Losses);
            GamesPlayed := Wins + Losses;
            Read (input, TotalPts, TotalOpponentsPts);
            Read (input, TotRebounds, TotOppRebounds);
            Read (input, Fouls, OpponentsFouls);
            Readln (input, AveHeight);
    END;
    ReadRoster (Roster);
END;
```

This is an example of nesting WITH statements. Another way to achieve the same effect would be to use one compound WITH statement.

```
WITH NBA[i], Stats DO BEGIN
    ReadWord (Name);
    Read (input, Wins, Losses);        (* from NBA[i].Stats *)
    . . .
END;
```

However, this construction is confusing and would probably be best avoided.

Now we can finish all of the procedures that read in the file of information for the computer dating program.

```
PROGRAM MatchMaker (Input, Output);
(********************************************************)
(* This program fragment reads data on a pool of        *)
(* prospective dates for a computer dating program.     *)
(********************************************************)
CONST   MaxChar  = 20;
        MaxPeople = 100;
TYPE    Word  =      PACKED ARRAY [1..MaxChar] OF Char;
        SexType =    (Male, Female);
        Person =     RECORD
            Name :     Word;
            Age,
            Height,
            Weight :   Integer;
            Smoker :   Boolean;
            Sex    :   SexType;
        END;
        PoolArr = ARRAY [1..MaxPeople] OF Person;

VAR     Dates : PoolArr;



PROCEDURE ReadWord (VAR W : Word);
(* This famous procedure reads a word from the input file. *)
(* The format expected is that the "word", which may be    *)
(* longer than one actual word, will be terminated by a    *)
(* StopChar, in this case a comma.                         *)
CONST   Stopchar = ',';
VAR     Cntr :       Integer;
        Ch :         Char;
BEGIN
        W := Blank;
        Cntr := 0;
        REPEAT
                Cntr := Cntr + 1;
                Read (Input, W[Cntr]);
        UNTIL (Cntr = MaxChar) OR (W[Cntr] = Stopchar);
        IF (W[Cntr] = Stopchar) THEN BEGIN
                W[Cntr] := ' ';
        END ELSE BEGIN           (* Throw away extra spaces *)
                REPEAT  Read (Ch);
                UNTIL (Ch = Stopchar) OR Eoln (Input);
        END;
END;
```

```
FUNCTION SkipSpaces : Char;
(* This fun little function returns the next nonspace   *)
(* character in the input file.                         *)
VAR     Ch : Char;
BEGIN
        REPEAT Read (Input, Ch);
        UNTIL (Ch <> ' ');
        SkipSpaces := Ch;
END;



PROCEDURE ReadSex (VAR S : SexType);
(* This procedure interprets an 'M' or an 'F' in the input*)
(* file and returns Male or Female as the sex of the    *)
(* person whose data is being read from the input file. *)
(* This procedure uses the character function SkipSpaces.*)
VAR     Ch : Char;
BEGIN
        Ch := SkipSpaces;
        IF (Ch = 'M')
                THEN Sex := Male
                ELSE Sex := Female;
END;



PROCEDURE ReadSmoker (VAR S : Boolean);
(* This procedure interprets an 'N' or an 'S' in the    *)
(* input file and returns TRUE or FALSE depending on    *)
(* whether the person is a smoker (S) or not (N).       *)
VAR     Ch : Char;
BEGIN
        Ch := SkipSpaces;
        S := (Ch = 'S');
END;



PROCEDURE ReadPerson (VAR P : Person);
(* This procedure reads the data into the record structure*)
(* for a single person.                                 *)
BEGIN
        WITH P DO BEGIN
                ReadWord (Name);
                ReadSex (Sex);
                Read (Input, Age, Height, Weight);
                ReadSmoker (Smoker);
        END;
END;
```

Sorting

Suppose we found that the input file we have to work with must be sorted alphabetically before it can be useful to us. We can use a bubble sort algorithm, or we can use a slightly faster algorithm called selection sort. In a **selection sort,** the computer looks through the array for the element that appears first alphabetically or numerically and places that element at the top of the array. Then the computer looks at the remaining array and does the same until the whole array is sorted. For example, if we were trying to get an increasing array of integers, a selection sort would produce the following partial solutions on its way to the final solution.

Original	Pass 1	Pass 2	Pass 3	Pass 4
18 (top)	6	6	6	6
96	96 (top)	18	18	18
25	25	25 (top)	18	20
117	117	117	20	20
31	31	31	117 (top)	25
6 (low)	18 (low)	96	31	31 (top, low)
20	20	20 (low)	96	96
			25 (low)	117

After five passes, this list happens to be sorted, even though the top hasn't quite made it to the bottom.

The procedure uses two FOR loops, a nested iteration. One pass through the array looks like this.

```
First := Top;
FOR ThisOne := Top TO Bottom DO
        IF (A[ThisOne] < A[First])
                THEN First := ThisOne;
Swap (A[Top], A[First]);
```

Each pass sees the value of the index Top move down one position in the array, until Top is finally one less than the Bottom, which is a constant value, the number of elements in the array.

```
FOR Top := 1 TO Bottom - 1 DO BEGIN
```

With the sorting we want to do, we only want to compare one field in the record, because we can't compare entire records for inequality, only for equality. We want to compare the names, which are declared as packed arrays of characters and can be compared directly.

Now we can put the whole procedure together.

```
PROCEDURE SelectionSort (VAR Dates : PoolArr;
                              Bottom : Integer);
(* This procedure uses the selection sort algorithm to     *)
(* sort an array of person records alphabetically by name. *)
VAR     Top, First, ThisOne : Integer;
BEGIN
        FOR Top := 1 TO Bottom - 1 DO BEGIN
            First := Top;
            FOR ThisOne := Top TO Bottom DO
                IF (Dates[ThisOne].Name < Dates[First].Name)
                    THEN First := ThisOne;
            Swap (Dates[Top], Dates[First]);
        END;
END;
```

Even though we are sorting according to names, we want the names to be attached to the rest of the data—that's the reason we used records in the first place. Therefore, whole records should be swapped.

```
PROCEDURE Swap (VAR Person1, Person2 : Person);
VAR Temp : Person;
BEGIN
        Temp := Person1;
        Person1 := Person2;
        Person2 := Temp;
END;
```

A selection sort is generally faster than a bubble sort. A selection sort makes slightly more comparisons but calls PROCEDURE Swap far fewer times— only once per number of passes (proportional to number of elements in the array) as opposed to several or many swaps per pass for a bubble sort.

SELF
TEST

Write selection sort and bubble sort algorithms to sort an array of numbers, keeping track of the number of comparisons and swaps each algorithm makes. Run both on the same large set of data and compare results.

Programming Example 15.1

Assignment: Write a program to run a computer dating service. The information stored for each client in the pool will be a great deal larger than what we have been working with in the examples in this chapter. Assume that people have filled out a questionnaire, and the data have been entered into an input file. The data are as follows.

```
<Name 1>,<Phone>,<Sex (M or F)> <Age>
<Height in inches><Weight in pounds>
<Answers to question #1>
<Answers to question #2>
<Answers to question #3>

<Name 2>,<Phone>,<Sex (M or F)> <Age>
<Height in inches><Weight in pounds>
<Answers to question #1>
<Answers to question #2>
<Answers to question #3>

<Name 3>...
```

The questions asked covered areas of interest and often had more than one possible answer for each individual. Therefore, the answers section contains numbers that correspond to the boxes that the individual checked. For example, if the data reads

```
2
3 5 9
2 7 8
4
. . .
```

then the person placed an X in box 2 of question 1; boxes 3, 5, and 9 of question 2; boxes 2, 7, and 8 of question 3; box 4 of question 4, and so forth.

The compatibility rating between two individuals can be calculated most simply as the number of boxes checked by both individuals. Assume no more than 30 questions and 20 responses per question.

The program should read the input file and store the data for each person in a record. The program should then ask the user to type in her or his name. If the program finds the name in the data structure, it should calculate a matching score for everyone in the input file, sort the data by scores, then print out the top five names and phone numbers along with their score. If the program doesn't find the person's name, it should print an error message and terminate execution.

Solution: This obviously calls for a complex data structure involving an array of records. Let's begin the data structure and see what we need.

```
Person = RECORD
        Name : Word;
        Phone : Word;
        Age,           (*in years*)
        Height,        (*in inches*)
        Weight : Integer;   (*in lbs*)
        Sex : SexType; (*Male or Female*)
        Answers : AnswerType;
END;
```

This looks like it should give us what we need to read in the data. But we also need to calculate a score for each person, a measure of that person's compatibility with the user. Therefore, we should add the `Score` to the declaration of `Person`.

`Word` and `SexType` are old standby definitions. The question remaining is how we should store the answers to the questions. We could simply read each answer into an array of answers to each question.

```
TYPE Answers = ARRAY [1..MaxAnswers] OF Integer;
     AllAnswers = ARRAY [1..MaxQuestions] OF Answers;
```

However, if we think down the line a little, it will be difficult to tell if a person's answers matched another person's because there is no guarantee that the responses would be in order (lowest to highest). Two different people may type in a different number of responses for the same question. The search algorithm would be time-consuming and inefficient.

An array of booleans would provide a better structure for each question. A value in position 12 that satisfies the boolean test means that 12 was one of the answers given to the question by the individual. This will make comparison between individuals very easy. The entire set of TYPE declarations is, therefore:

```
CONST    MaxAnswers = 30; MaxPeople = 200;
         MaxQuestions = 20;
         MaxChars = 20;
TYPE     SexType = (Male, Female);
         Word = PACKED ARRAY [1..MaxChars] OF Char;
         AnswersArr = PACKED ARRAY [1..MaxAnswers] OF Boolean;
         AllAnswers = ARRAY [1..MaxQuestions] OF AnswerArr;

         Person = RECORD
                    Name : Word;
                    Phone : Word;
                    Age,              (*in years*)
                    Height,           (*in inches*)
                    Weight : Integer;    (*in lbs*)
                    Sex : SexType; (*Male or Female*)
                    Answers : AnswerType;
                    Score : Integer;
END;
```

With the data structure well outlined, we can begin to work on the program outline. The task can be broken down into the following subtasks.

Match Maker:
  Read data for the pool of dates
  Read Subject's name
  Assign scores to each date in pool
  Sort the entire pool by score
  Print the best matches

The first task, to read the data from the input file, is very similar to the program segment we saw earlier. We will begin by recalling PROCEDURE ReadDates.

```
PROCEDURE ReadDates (VAR Dates : PoolArr;
                          VAR NumDates : Integer);
(* This procedure reads the entire pool of dates from the *)
(* input file, using ReadPerson.                          *)
BEGIN
    NumDates:= 0;
    WHILE (NumDates < MaxPeople) AND
            NOT Eof (Input) DO BEGIN
        NumDates := NumDates + 1;
        ReadPerson (Dates[NumDates]);
    END;
END;
```

Most of PROCEDURE ReadPerson is already written, except for the code that reads the answers to the questions. We will read all of the answers to one question in a procedure called ReadAnswers.

```
PROCEDURE ReadPerson (VAR P : Person);
(* This procedure reads all of the data for a single    *)
(* person from the input file.                          *)
VAR      Quest : Integer;       (* FOR loop counter over all *)
                                (* questions in input file.  *)
BEGIN
        ReadWord (P.Name);
        ReadWord (P.Phone);
        Read (Input, P.Age);
        Read (Input, P.Height);
        Read (Input, P.Weight);
        ReadSex (P.Sex); Readln (Input);
        FOR Quest := 1 TO MaxQuests DO
                ReadAnswers (P.Answers [Quest]);
        Readln (Input);
END;
```

ReadAnswers is not too difficult, but we must remember to initialize each of the boolean answers to FALSE before we begin reading the values. The only tricky part is to realize that the number being read is the *index* of the array element which receives a value of TRUE.

```
PROCEDURE ReadAnswers (VAR Ans : AnswersArr);
(* This procedure reads all of the answers and stores them*)
(* in an array of boolean values for one question for an  *)
(* individual in the array of people.                     *)
VAR      Cntr, Which : Integer;
```

```
BEGIN
        FOR Cntr := 1 TO MaxAnswers DO
                Ans [Cntr] := FALSE;
        WHILE NOT Eoln (Input) DO BEGIN
                Read (Input, Which);
                Ans [Which] := TRUE;
        END;
        Readln (Input);
END;
```

The job of getting the name of the person for whom the dates will be selected (the subject) is more than simply a job of reading the name from the input file. After reading the name, we will need to find the person's name in the array of records, so we can compare the subject's record with each record in the pool. The subtask can be outlined as follows.

> Get Subject's Record:
> Prompt terminal for name
> Read subject's name
> Binary search pool for subject's record

Prompting the user for the name is easy, a simple Writeln statement. The procedure ReadWord cannot be used in this case because we are reading from the terminal, and because we don't expect the user to have to type a comma (the StopChar) after typing the name. Instead, we will have to write another procedure, like ReadWord, which reads from the terminal until the Eoln has been reached. The binary search procedure that we used in the last chapter can be slightly modified for use in this context. We will assume that the input file is sorted alphabetically before we read it in. We will also have to add two more text files, TermIn and TermOut. We cannot use Input and Output to prompt for and to read the data, because they are already in use. Input is the pool data file and Output is the final report file.

Keeping these necessary changes in mind, the two procedures, Term-ReadWord and GetSubject, can be cannibalized with only slight modification from code that we have already written.

```
PROCEDURE TermReadWord (VAR W : Word);
(* This procedure reads a word from the terminal. The word*)
(* is terminated by the Eoln marker.                       *)
VAR     Cntr : Integer;
BEGIN
        Cntr := 0; W := Blank;
        WHILE (Cntr<MaxChars) AND NOT Eoln (TermIn) DO BEGIN
                Cntr := Cntr + 1;
                Read (TermIn, W[Cntr]);
        END;
        Readln (TermIn);
END;
```

```
PROCEDURE GetSubject (VAR Subject : Person;
                      VAR Pool : PoolType;
                      NumPeople : Integer;
                      VAR Failed : Boolean);
(* This procedure asks the user at the terminal for the    *)
(* name of the subject who is to be matched against all     *)
(* of the prospective dates in the memory of the computer.  *)
(* It then searches through the pool looking for the        *)
(* subject's record. If the record is found, it is returned *)
(* as Subject. If not, then Failed is returned TRUE.        *)
VAR     Name : Word;
        Top, Bottom,                 (* used in binary search *)
        Which : Integer;
BEGIN
        Writeln (TermOut, 'What is the name of the ',
                 'subject to be matched?');
        TermReadWord (Name);
        Top := 1; Bottom := NumPeople;
        Failed := TRUE;
        WHILE Failed AND (Top <= Bottom) DO BEGIN
            Which := (Top + Bottom) DIV 2;
            Failed := (Name<>Pool[Which].Name);
            IF Failed THEN BEGIN
                IF (Name<Pool[Which].Name)
                    THEN Bottom := Which - 1
                    ELSE Top := Which + 1;
            END ELSE Subject := Pool[Which]; (* found it! *)
        END;
        Failed := Failed AND (Name<>Pool[Which].Name);

END;
```

The next step in the solution is to assign scores to each person in the pool. We'll use a very simple method: one point will be given for each response that the subject and the prospective date have in common. The method will assign higher scores to people who respond as the subject did to each of the questions. We will write one procedure, AssignAllScores, which will call a second procedure Assign, for each person in the pool.

```
PROCEDURE AssignAllScores (VAR Subject : Person;
                           VAR Pool : PoolType;
                           NumPeople : Integer);
(* This procedure calls Assign for each prospective date *)
(* in the entire pool. The dates are all given scores in *)
(* comparison with the Subject being matched.            *)
VAR     Cntr : Integer;
BEGIN
        FOR Cntr := 1 TO NumPeople DO
                Assign (Subject, Pool [Cntr]);
END;
```

The procedure `Assign` simply loops through the entire data structure of answers and counts the number that both the subject and the prospective match answered positively. The pseudocode outline would be:

> Assign:
>> Initialize Score to zero
>> Loop over all questions:
>>> Loop over each answer to the question:
>>>> IF (Subject Answer = Date Answer = TRUE)
>>>> THEN increment score

Notice that we don't simply count the number of times the subject's answer equals the date's answer. If neither of them gave a certain response to a question, then both of the boolean values would be the same, although the value would be FALSE. We only want to count the number of positive responses the two gave in common. This outline converts into a simple Pascal procedure.

```
PROCEDURE Assign (VAR Subject, Date : Person);
(* This procedure assigns a score to the prospective date.*)
(* The score is calculated by adding one point for each    *)
(* answer that both the Subject and the Date answered       *)
(* affirmatively.                                           *)
VAR     Score,                    (* calculated for each date *)
        Quest, Ans : Integer; (* FOR loop counters           *)
BEGIN
        Score := 0;
        FOR Quest := 1 TO MaxQuests DO
            FOR Ans := 1 TO MaxAnswers DO
                IF Subject.Answers [Quest, Ans] AND
                     Date.Answers [Quest, Ans] THEN
                    Score := Score + 1;
        Date.Score := Score;
END;
```

The sort procedure can be essentially the same as that written earlier in the chapter for the selection sort algorithm. In order to print the top five matches, after the list has been sorted, we must compose a procedure to write out the vital statistics of one person in the pool, and use it for each person in the pool. PROCEDURE `PrintOneDate` will be used in `PrintTopDates`.

```
PROCEDURE PrintOneDate (Date : Person);
(* This procedure prints the vital stats for one date.    *)
BEGIN
        WITH Date DO BEGIN
            Writeln (Output, Name);
            Writeln (Output, Phone);
            Write (Output, 'Age:', Age:3, '  Height:',
                            Height:3, ' inches');
```

```
        IF Sex=Male
                THEN Write (Output, '  Sex: Male')
                ELSE Write (Output, '  Sex: Female');
        Writeln (Output, '  Score: ', Score:1);
        Writeln (Output);
      END;
  END;
```

Finally, we should take a look at the main program. The procedures as we have written or mentioned them would be organized in the following order:

```
BEGIN    (* Main Program *)
      Reset (TermIn); Rewrite (TermOut);
      ReadPool (Pool, NumPeople);
      GetSubject (Subject, Pool, NumPeople, Failed);
      AssignAllScores (Subject, Pool, NumPeople);
      SortByScores (Pool, NumPeople);
      PrintTopDates (Subject, Pool, NumPeople);
END.     (* Main Program *)
```

The problem with this is that if the attempt to get the subject's data failed (Failed = TRUE), then it will be meaningless to assign scores to all the records in the Pool. Therefore, we will not try to execute the other procedures if Failed comes back TRUE from GetSubject.

```
BEGIN    (* Main Program *)
      Reset (TermIn); Rewrite (TermOut);
      ReadPool (Pool, NumPeople);
      GetSubject (Subject, Pool, NumPeople, Failed);
      IF NOT Failed THEN BEGIN
              AssignAllScores (Subject, Pool, NumPeople);
              SortByScores (Pool, NumPeople);
              PrintTopDates (Subject, Pool, NumPeople);
      END ELSE BEGIN
              Writeln (TermOut, 'Sorry, but your record ',
                        'could not be found in our files.');
      END;
END.     (* Main Program *)
```

See if you can think of any limitations or problems the program might have as it is currently written.

The exchange between the computer and the user at the terminal looks something like this:

INTERACTIVE SESSION

```
Welcome to MatchMaker!

This service helps you to find one or many
interesting people who share your interests and your
```

desire to meet interesting people. Since you have already
answered the questions in our brochure, your name is
already in our data banks, as well as all of the
information we need to make scientific and accurate
matches.

What is your name?
Ron Knight
Thank you! Your matches are being written to the output file.

The output file that was generated highlights some of the problems with
the current program. Examine it and see if you can identify some of them.

OUTPUT   The following people have interests very much similar
to your own. They were the top 5 matches in our records.

Matches for Ron Knight

Ron Knight
 487-3189
Age: 25 Height: 74 inches Sex: Male Score: 133

Lola
 555-1212
Age: 19 Height: 67 inches Sex: Female Score: 125

Julie
 487-2300
Age: 22 Height: 68 inches Sex: Female Score: 113

Alex Van Riesen
 346-5728
Age: 22 Height: 75 inches Sex: Male Score: 103

Mary
 Dial M for Murder
Age: 68 Height: 60 inches Sex: Female Score: 102

Figure 15.7 shows a module tree for PROGRAM MatchMaker.
There are several algorithmic and stylistic problems with the solution to
the original task, as the program is currently written:

1. In all cases, the highest scoring record, the one that will head the list given
   as output, will be the subject's own record. Obviously, by the algorithm we
   have selected, the person most compatible with any individual in the pool
   is that person. This makes mathematical sense, but it doesn't make prac-

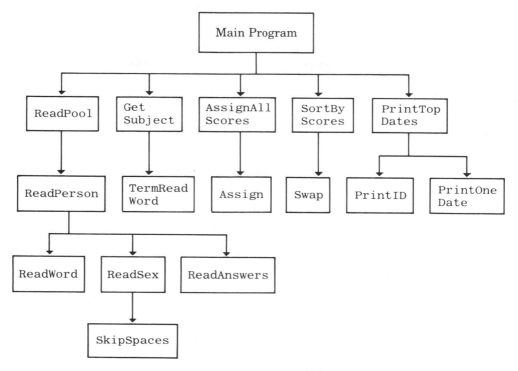

Figure 15.7: Module Tree for MatchMaker

tical sense. No one wants to find their own name at the top of a computer dating service they have paid for!

2. Furthermore, the algorithm doesn't take into account the sexual preferences of the subject and the dates. As it is written now, the sex of the prospective dates is not used in calculating their scores. A subject's match list will probably contain both males and females.

3. The other vital statistics are not taken into consideration in making matches. When the information is available, it should be used to find the best solution possible, if it isn't too costly to do so. Some subjects might have definite expectations on the appropriate age, height, and weight of their dates.

4. The subject is not allowed to emphasize the need for compatibility in certain areas and to deemphasize the need for compatibility in others. For example, religious background might be important to one subject; compatibility in that area might be more important than compatibility in music or TV shows.

After writing a long program like the one just written, it is good to be able to look at the program and list its limitations. If those limitations are too expensive to correct in terms of programmer or computer time, then it is probably best to leave the program as it is. However, sometimes the program can be improved with relatively small amounts of additional work. For example, the first two limitations to the `MatchMaker` program could be eliminated with only a small amount of additional effort. The third and fourth limitations would probably require a major restructuring of the data and a new `Assign` procedure.

Variant Record Structures

Occasionally, you may want to create a data structure that has more flexibility than either the array or the record as we have seen them up to this point. For example, suppose you want a data structure to hold all of the information needed to specify dimensions of a number of geometric shapes. You may want to set aside memory locations for the radius if the shape is a circle; the length of a side if it is a square; the length and width if it is a rectangle; the length, height, and acute angle if it is a parallelogram; and so forth. (See Figure 15.8.)

One way to do this, of course, would be to declare a huge record that could contain any and all necessary information.

```
TYPE    Shapes = (Circle, Triangle, Square, Rectangle,
                  Parallelogram, Trapezoid)
        TriangSides = ARRAY [1..3] OF Real;
        AngleArr = ARRAY [1..4] OF Real;        (* in radians *)
```

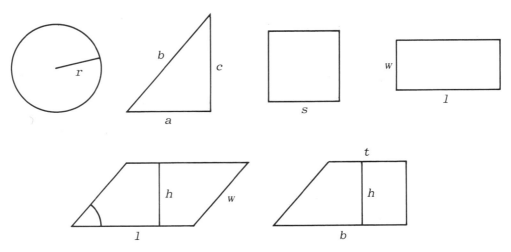

Figure 15.8: Geometric Shapes and Dimensions

```
ShapeRec = RECORD
    Which : Shapes;
    Area, Perimeter : Real;  (* for any shape          *)
    Angles : AngleArr;       (* for any shape          *)
    Radius : Real;           (* for a circle           *)
    Sides : TriangSides;     (* for a triangle         *)
    Side,                    (* for a square           *)
    Length, Width,           (* for a rectangle        *)
    Height, (* for a parallelogram or a trapezoid *)
    Base, Top : Real;        (* for a trapezoid        *)
END;
```

This is enough information to store any of these types of simple geometric figures. Using simple geometric equations, the areas, circumferences, or perimeters could be calculated from the available data. However, this means that, for any given shape, there will be several unused fields, because not all of the fields apply to any single shape. It would be great if we could find a custom-made record structure for each of the different shapes, yet have enough compatibility from one structure to another to handle them with the same procedures. Obviously, it wouldn't solve anything to declare six different record structures, one for each shape, because then we would need six different procedures to read them in, write them out, and so on.

What we want to do we can do with variant records. A **variant record** is a record structure that utilizes different fields depending on the value of one field called the tag field. A variant record allows the programmer to define a single structure that contains different kinds of information; the kind of information depends on how the record is used. The shape of the structure depends on one of the values inside the structure. For example:

```
TYPE    Shapes = (Circle, Triangle, Square, Rectangle,
                  Parallelogram, Trapezoid, Line, Point);
        TriSides = ARRAY [1..3] OF Real;
        AngleArr = ARRAY [1..4] OF Real;      (* in radians *)

        ShapeRec = RECORD
            Area, Perimeter : Real;  (* for any shape      *)
            Angles : AngleArr;       (* for any shape      *)
            CASE Which : Shapes OF   (* the TAG field      *)
                Circle : (Radius : Real);
                Triangle : (Sides : TriSides);
                Square : (Side : Real);
                Rectangle : (RLength, RWidth : Real);
                Parallelogram : (PHeight, PLength, PWidth
                                 : Real);
                Trapezoid : (Base, Top, Side1, Side2,
                             THeight : Real);
                Line : (LLength : Real);
                Point : ();
        END;
```

448 STORING DATA: RECORDS

In this example, the record called ShapeRec has three fixed fields: Area, Perimeter, and Angles. **Fixed fields** exist in the record in all cases. A variant record structure must also contain a tag field. The **tag field** is the field in a variant record variable that determines which variable fields will be included in the variable's structure. The tag field in this example is Which, and depending on the value of Which, the record utilizes anywhere from zero to five more fields. Which is a variable of type Shapes, therefore, the values in the CASE statement value lists are of that type. If, for example, the tag field has a value Rectangle, then the record carries two more fields, called the variable fields, RLength and RWidth. **Variable fields** are fields in a variant record structure whose existence depends on the value of the tag field. For example, if Which has the value Point, then there are no other fields in the record. In this case, to try to access RLength would produce an error.

Suppose we wanted a procedure to use the dimensions of any shape to calculate the shape's area. The previous record structure could be used in the following way.

```
PROCEDURE CalcArea (VAR NGon : ShapeRec);
(* This procedure calculates the area of any given Shape   *)
(* and returns the value of the area of the Shape.         *)
CONST   Pi = 3.141593;
VAR     S : Real;                     (* used in calculating area *)
BEGIN
        WITH NGon DO BEGIN
            CASE Which OF
                Circle : Area := Pi * Radius * Radius;
                Triangle : BEGIN
                            S := Perimeter / 2;
                            Area := Sqrt (Sqr (S - Sides[1]) +
                                          Sqr (S - Sides[2]) +
                                          Sqr (S - Sides[3]));
                    END;
                Square : Area := Side * Side;
                Rectangle : Area := RLength * RWidth;
                Parallelogram : Area := PLength * PHeight;
                Trapezoid : Area := (Base + Top) / 2.0 *
                                        THeight;
                Line, Point : Area := 0;
            END;
        END;
END;
```

One thing to notice is that a variant record declaration contains only one END delimiter. The CASE statement, used to implement the variant fields, does not have a corresponding END. The reserved word END concludes the record declaration. This means that there can only be one tag field and one CASE statement in a record declaration and that the variant part of the record must be declared after the fixed part of the record, if there is a fixed part. (A fixed part is not necessary.) The general form of the record declaration is found in Figure 15.9.

```
RECORD
     <fixed field list 1>;
     <fixed field list 2>;
     ...
     <fixed field list n>;
     CASE <tag field identifier> : <tag type identifier> OF
         <tag value list 1> : ( <variant field list 1> );
         <tag value list 2> : ( <variant field list 2> );
         ...
         <tag value list m> : ( <variant field list m> );
END;
```

Figure 15.9: Record Structure

Programming Example 15.2

Assignment: One simple method of implementing graphics programs is through the use of turtle graphics. The method is called **turtle graphics** because the commands are like those we would need to give a turtle with a pen attached to his stomach. If we want a straight line, we tell the turtle to crawl forward. If we want a square, we tell the turtle to go forward, turn left, go forward again, turn left, go forward, turn left, and go forward. We assume that, as the turtle goes over the page, he draws a line that marks where he has been and produces the desired image.

The assignment is to write a graphics program that uses simple turtle graphics. The program will control a turtle on a page that is the size of the terminal screen. The program user should be able to command the turtle to move and face in any direction, including diagonals. The program should also allow the user to raise the turtle's pen so that she or he can move the turtle without drawing. When the pen is down, an instruction to move should produce a line on the page. The user should also be able to control what character the turtle is writing with.

Also, include utility commands in your program; incorporate the commands erase, draw (which prints the page image on the screen or output file), home (which moves the turtle to the upper left-hand corner of the page), and center (which moves the turtle to the center of the page).

Solution: If we try to visualize the mechanism that our program is supposed to simulate, that of a turtle crawling across a page or easel, then we can quickly divide the needed information into information regarding the turtle (his position, direction, and the state of his pen) and information regarding the easel (what characters are stored in each position on the page).

The information regarding the turtle is:

1. two integer values indicating the turtle's position, his Row and Col on the page,
2. an integer value, Dir, that gives the turtle's direction as a numeral between 0 and 7 (see Figure 15.10),
3. a boolean value, PenDown, which indicates whether or not the pen is currently touching the page, and
4. a character value, PenChar, which defines the character that the turtle's pen produces.

Since the information we need about the turtle consists of several different types of values, a record structure seems necessary.

```
TYPE    TurtleRec = RECORD
            Row, Col,         (* Turtle's current position *)
            Dir : Integer;    (* direction facing, 0--7    *)
            PenDown : Boolean; (* TRUE when writing         *)
            PenChar : Char;   (* What is written by turtle *)
        END;
```

The easel, on the other hand, is made up of many rows with many characters on each row. The data structure of choice here is the two-dimensional array of characters.

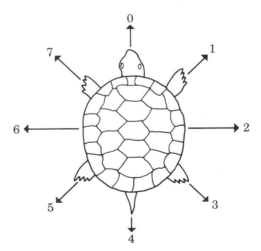

Figure 15.10: Turtle Directions

```
EaselArr = ARRAY [1..MaxRows, 1..MaxCols] OF Char;
```

The main program outline can be broken down into several small tasks and the main subtask of reading and executing the various commands that the program understands. The rough pseudocode is:

```
Turtle Draw:
        Introduction
        Initialize Turtle and Easel
        Loop:
               Get a command
               Execute command
        UNTIL Command is to quit
```

If we give procedure names to each of the necessary commands, then we can use a CASE statement to implement the control structure that reads and executes a legal command. If we assume that procedures that alter the turtle data take Turtle as a parameter, and that procedures that alter easel data take Easel, then we can write the main program this way:

```
BEGIN     (* Main Program *)
          Introduction;
          Init (Easel, Turtle);
          REPEAT   TurtleReport (Turtle);
                   GetCommand (Com);
                   CASE Com OF
                        'U' : PenUp (Turtle);
                        'D' : PenDown (Turtle);
                        'F' : Face (Turtle);
                        'M' : Move (Easel, Turtle);
                        'C' : Center (Turtle);
                        'H' : Home (Turtle);
                        'P' : NewPenChar (Turtle);
                        'E' : Erase (Easel);
                        'W' : Draw (Easel);
                        'Q' : Quit ;
                        '?' : Help;
                   END;
          UNTIL (Com = 'Q');
END.      (* Main Program *)
```

Fortunately, most of these procedures are small and relatively easy to write. For example, here are a couple of the easier ones.

```
PROCEDURE Center (VAR Turtle : TurtleRec);
(* This procedure moves the turtle to the center of the    *)
(* page. The turtle is made to face direction 0.           *)
```

```
BEGIN
        WITH Turtle DO BEGIN
                Row := MaxRows DIV 2;
                Col := MaxCols DIV 2;
                Dir := 0;
        END;
END;


PROCEDURE PenUp (VAR Turtle : TurtleRec);
(* This procedure disables the pen to prevent the turtle  *)
(* from marking while he moves.                           *)
BEGIN
        IF Turtle.PenDown
            THEN Turtle.PenDown := FALSE
            ELSE Writeln (TermOut, 'Pen was already up!');
END;
```

Predictably, procedures Home and PenDown will look very much like these two. Furthermore, once we write Erase, we can use Erase and Home to give us most of Init.

```
PROCEDURE Erase (VAR Easel : EaselArr);
(* This procedure erases the easel, setting it to all ' 's*)
VAR     Row, Col : Integer;
BEGIN
        FOR Row := 1 TO MaxRows DO
            FOR Col := 1 TO MaxCols DO
                Easel [Row, Col] := ' ';
END;


PROCEDURE Init (VAR Easel : EaselArr;
                VAR Turtle : TurtleRec);
(* This procedure initializes all the global data.      *)
BEGIN
        Erase (Easel);
        Home (Turtle);
        WITH Turtle DO BEGIN
                PenDown := FALSE;
                PenChar := ' ';
        END;
END;
```

Several of the commands will take arguments along with the command. For example, the command Face takes a direction that is represented by a number between 0 and 7. The procedure Face must read the direction from the terminal, verify that it is legal, and then change the turtle's direction.

```
PROCEDURE Face (VAR Turtle : TurtleRec);
(* This procedure makes the turtle face in a given     *)
(* direction.                                          *)
VAR      Dir : Integer;
BEGIN
        Read (TermIn, Dir);
        IF (Dir >= 0) AND (Dir <= 7)
            THEN Turtle.Dir := Dir
            ELSE Writeln (TermOut, 'Illegal direction: ',
                                   'must be 0--7.');
END;
```

Another comand that takes an argument is P, which is executed by PROCEDURE NewPenChar. Immediately, this procedure seems to be simple.

```
PROCEDURE NewPenChar (VAR Turtle : TurtleRec);
(* This procedure allows the user to change the character *)
(* the turtle uses as his pen mark as he moves over the   *)
(* page. This procedure does not change PenDown.          *)
BEGIN
        Read (TermIn, Turtle.PenChar);
END;
```

However, the problem here is that the user may type a space after the command character and before the character that is to be the new PenChar. Therefore, in order to allow the user to type any number of spaces before typing the PenChar, we will revive our old standby procedure, SkipSpaces. However, just to be different, we will make it a Char function and return the first nonspace character as its value. We will also call it TermSkipSpaces, because it reads from the terminal input file. Now we have a new definition of NewPenChar.

```
FUNCTION TermSkipSpaces : Char;
(* This function returns the first nonspace character on *)
(* the terminal input line.                              *)
VAR      Ch : Char;
BEGIN
        REPEAT Read (TermIn, Ch);
        UNTIL (Ch <> ' ');
        TermSkipSpaces := Ch;
END;
```

```
PROCEDURE NewPenChar (VAR Turtle : TurtleRec);
(* This procedure allows the user to change the character *)
(* the turtle uses as his pen mark as he moves over the   *)
(* page. This procedure does not change PenDown.          *)
BEGIN
        Turtle.PenChar := TermSkipSpaces;
END;
```

PROCEDURE Draw is much like Erase. Therefore, the only difficult command procedure is Move. Notice that Move is the only command procedure to make use of both Turtle and Easel. All the other commands only act on one or the other of the main data structures. Move also takes an argument. The easiest way to break down this task is to think of moving *n* spaces as moving one space *n* times.

```
PROCEDURE Move (VAR Easel : EaselArr;
                VAR Turtle : TurtleRec);
(* This procedure handles the entire move operation by     *)
(* calling MoveOneSpace for each move that it is supposed *)
(* to make. It reads the argument from the terminal and   *)
(* calls MoveOneSpace the correct number of times.        *)
VAR     NumSpaces, Spaces : Integer;
BEGIN
        Read (TermIn, NumSpaces);
        FOR Spaces := 1 TO NumSpaces DO
                MoveOneSpace (Easel, Turtle);
END;
```

Moving in one direction is like moving in any other direction except that the changes to Row and Col are different. Suppose we had a procedure called Change, which takes four parameters, Turtle, Easel, the change in Row, and the change in Col. Sometimes, depending on the direction the turtle is facing, there would be no change to one of the two coordinates. Once we have established an algorithm for Change, then MoveOneSpace can be written easily.

```
PROCEDURE MoveOneSpace (VAR Easel : EaselArr;
                        VAR Turtle : TurtleRec);
(* This procedure moves the turtle forward one space, the *)
(* direction entirely determined by Turtle.Dir.           *)
BEGIN
        CASE Turtle.Dir OF
            0 : Change (-1, 0, Turtle, Easel);
            1 : Change (-1, 1, Turtle, Easel);
            2 : Change (0, 1, Turtle, Easel);
            3 : Change (1, 1, Turtle, Easel);
            4 : Change (1, 0, Turtle, Easel);
            5 : Change (1, 1, Turtle, Easel);
            6 : Change (0, -1, Turtle, Easel);
            7 : Change (-1, -1, Turtle, Easel);
        END;
END;
```

The procedure Change makes the needed changes in the Row and Col values of the turtle record. It also draws with the PenChar if the pen is actually down (PenDown = TRUE).

```
PROCEDURE Change (RowDiff, ColDiff : Integer;
                    VAR Turtle : TurtleRec;
                    VAR Easel : EaselArr);
(* This procedure makes the position change in the turtle*)
(* and also changes the easel if the Pen is down. This is*)
(* called by MoveOneSpace.                               *)
BEGIN
        WITH Turtle DO BEGIN
                Row := Row + RowDiff;
                Col := Col + ColDiff;
                IF PenDown THEN
                        Easel [Row, Col] := PenChar;
        END;
END;
```

The only problem with this could come when the turtle attempts to move off the end of the page. If Row equals 1, and the turtle attempts to move in direction 6 (to the left), then the new value of Row is 0. A simple procedure will protect against column or row values that are too high or too low.

```
PROCEDURE CheckWrap (VAR Pos : Integer; Max : Integer);
(* This procedure checks the boundary conditions and makes*)
(* the turtle's position wrap around if he goes off the   *)
(* end of the page in any direction.                      *)
BEGIN
        IF (Pos = 0)
                THEN Pos := Max
                ELSE IF (Pos > Max)
                        THEN Pos := Pos - Max;
END;


PROCEDURE Change (RowDiff, ColDiff : Integer;
            VAR Turtle : TurtleRec; VAR Easel : EaselArr);
(* This procedure makes the position change in the turtle *)
(* and also changes the easel if the Pen is down. This is *)
(* called by MoveOneSpace.                                *)
BEGIN
        WITH Turtle DO BEGIN
                Row := Row + RowDiff;
                CheckWrap (Row, MaxRows);
                Col := Col + ColDiff;
                CheckWrap (Col, MaxCols);
                IF PenDown THEN
                        Easel [Row, Col] := PenChar;
        END;
END;
```

The only substantive procedure remaining is the one to get the command from the terminal. This is fairly straightforward, although we want to make sure that the procedure verifies that the command is legal. If it is not a legal command, the procedure should issue a help message and reprompt the user until a valid command has been given.

> Get Command:
> > Prompt user for a command
> > Read command
> > Loop while not a valid command:
> > > Give error message
> > > Tell legal commands
> > > Prompt user for a command
> > > Read command

Instead of simply reading the command from the terminal, we will put the function TermSkipSpaces to use, since it is already written and working. This will ensure that no extra spaces or blank lines from the terminal will produce errors in reading the commands.

```
PROCEDURE GetCommand (VAR Com : Char; LegalComs : ComSet);
(* This procedure prompts the user and reads the command  *)
(* from the Terminal. If the command is not a legal        *)
(* command, then the procedure reprompts after giving the *)
(* user Help.                                              *)

    PROCEDURE PromptNRead (VAR Com : Char);
    BEGIN
            Writeln (TermOut, 'What is your command?');
            Com := TermSkipSpaces;
    END;

BEGIN    (* GetCommand *)
        PromptNRead (Com);
        WHILE NOT ((Com='U') OR (Com='D') OR (Com='F')
                   (Com='C') OR (Com='H') OR (Com='P')
                   (Com='E') OR (Com='W') OR (Com='M')
                   (Com='Q') OR (Com='?'))
            DO BEGIN
                Writeln (TermOut, 'That is an illegal ',
                                  'command');
                Help;
                PromptNRead (Com);
        END;
END;    (* GetCommand *)
```

The Quit procedure is an interesting one. Quit makes sure that the user doesn't terminate the session accidentally. Therefore, we will ask the user to verify the command to quit. We will also warn the user if the current drawing has not been printed by keeping around a boolean variable, SafeToQuit, which is satisfied unless a Move command has been executed since the last Write command or since the beginning of the execution.

```
PROCEDURE Quit (SafeToQuit : Boolean; VAR Com : Char);
(* This procedure verifies that the user really does want *)
(* to quit. Changes the value of Com if the Quit is       *)
(* aborted.                                                *)
VAR     Ans : Char;
BEGIN
        Writeln (TermOut, 'Are you sure you want to quit?');
        IF NOT SafeToQuit
            THEN Writeln (TermOut, 'Your current picture',
                                   ' has not been drawn.');
        Ans := TermSkipSpaces;
        IF (Ans<>'Y') AND (Ans<>'y') THEN Com := ' ';
END;
```

We are certainly getting a lot of mileage out of TermSkipSpaces.

Figure 15.11 shows the module tree. The final program follows.

```
PROGRAM TurtleDraw (TermIn, TermOut, Output);
(**************************************************************)
(* This program produces simple pictures using a turtle    *)
(* graphics package of commands. The user controls the     *)
(* movement of a "turtle" that moves around an "easel,"    *)
(* which is a two-dimensional array of characters. The     *)
(* turtle has a pen on his stomach, and when the pen is    *)
(* down, then the turtle marks on the easel as he moves.   *)
(* The user may use several different commands, all of     *)
(* which are described in the Help procedure.              *)
(**************************************************************)
CONST   MaxRows = 24;
        MaxCols = 60;

TYPE    TurtleRec = RECORD
                Row, Col,        (* Turtle's current position *)
                Dir : Integer;   (* direction facing, 0--7    *)
                PenDown : Boolean; (* TRUE when writing       *)
                PenChar : Char;  (* What is written by turtle *)
            END;

        EaselArr = ARRAY [1..MaxRows, 1..MaxCols] OF Char;

VAR     Turtle : TurtleRec; (* The data on turtle position*)
        Easel : EaselArr;   (* the Page - 2-dim char array*)
        Com : Char;         (* most recent legal command  *)
        SafeToQuit : Boolean; (* TRUE when no changes to   *)
                              (* the easel have been made  *)
        TermIn, TermOut : Text; (* Terminal I/O files      *)
```

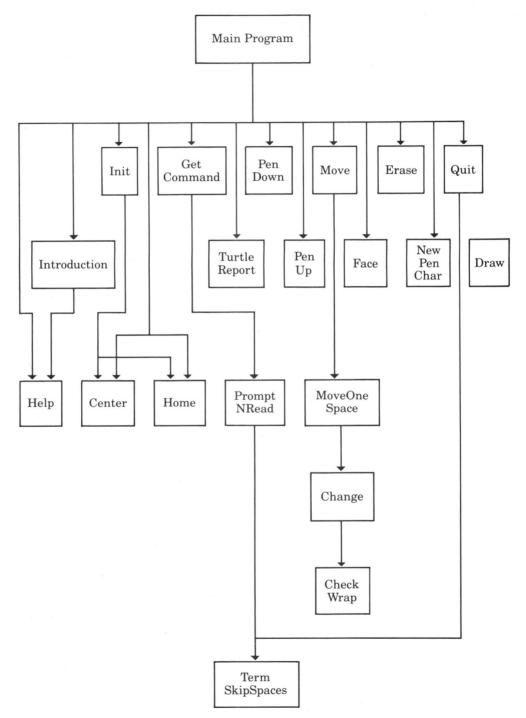

Figure 15.11: Module Tree for TurtleDraw

```
PROCEDURE Erase (VAR Easel : EaselArr);
(* This procedure erases the easel, setting it to all ' 's*)
VAR     Row, Col : Integer;
BEGIN
        FOR Row := 1 TO MaxRows DO
            FOR Col := 1 TO MaxCols DO
                Easel [Row, Col] := ' ';
END;


PROCEDURE TurtleReport (Turtle : TurtleRec);
(* This procedure merely reports current values for turtle*)
BEGIN
        WITH Turtle DO BEGIN
                Write (TermOut, 'Turtle position: ',
                        '[',Row:1,',',Col:1,']   ');
                Write (TermOut, 'Facing: ', Dir:1,'  ');
                Write (TermOut, 'PenChar = ''',
                        PenChar,'''');
                IF PenDown
                    THEN Writeln (TermOut, '  Pen is down')
                    ELSE Writeln (TermOut, '  Pen is up');
            END;
END;


PROCEDURE Home (VAR Turtle : TurtleRec);
(* This procedure moves the turtle to Home, where his     *)
(* position is (1,1) and he is facing direction 2.        *)
BEGIN
        WITH Turtle DO BEGIN
                Row := 1;
                Col := 1;
                Dir := 2;
            END;
END;


PROCEDURE Center (VAR Turtle : TurtleRec);
(* This procedure moves the turtle to the center of the   *)
(* page. The turtle is made to face direction 0.          *)
BEGIN
        WITH Turtle DO BEGIN
                Row := MaxRows DIV 2;
                Col := MaxCols DIV 2;
                Dir := 0;
            END;
END;


PROCEDURE Init (VAR Easel : EaselArr;
                VAR Turtle : TurtleRec);
(* This procedure initializes all the global data.        *)
```

```
BEGIN
        Erase (Easel);
        Home (Turtle);
        WITH Turtle DO BEGIN
                PenDown := FALSE;
                PenChar := ' ';
        END;
END;


PROCEDURE PenUp (VAR Turtle : TurtleRec);
(* This procedure disables the pen to prevent the turtle  *)
(* from marking while he moves.                           *)
BEGIN
        IF Turtle.PenDown
            THEN Turtle.PenDown := FALSE
            ELSE Writeln (TermOut, 'Pen was already up!');
END;


PROCEDURE PenDown (VAR Turtle : TurtleRec);
(* This procedure enables the pen to allow the turtle to  *)
(* mark the easel while he moves.                         *)
BEGIN
        IF Turtle.PenDown
            THEN Writeln (TermOut, 'Pen was already down!')
            ELSE Turtle.PenDown := TRUE;
END;


PROCEDURE Face (VAR Turtle : TurtleRec);
(* This procedure makes the turtle face in given direction*)
VAR     Dir : Integer;
BEGIN
        Read (TermIn, Dir);
        IF (Dir >= 0) AND (Dir <= 7)
            THEN Turtle.Dir := Dir
            ELSE Writeln (TermOut, 'Illegal direction: ',
                                    'must be 0--7.');
END;


FUNCTION TermSkipSpaces : Char;
(* This function returns the first nonspace character on  *)
(* the terminal input line.                               *)
VAR     Ch : Char;
BEGIN
        REPEAT Read (TermIn, Ch);
        UNTIL (Ch <> ' ');
        TermSkipSpaces := Ch;
END;
```

```
PROCEDURE NewPenChar (VAR Turtle : TurtleRec);
(* This procedure allows the user to change the character *)
(* the turtle uses as his pen mark as he moves over the   *)
(* page. This procedure does not change PenDown.          *)
BEGIN
        Turtle.PenChar := TermSkipSpaces;
END;


PROCEDURE Draw (VAR Easel : EaselArr);
(* This procedure draws the easel on the output file.    *)
VAR     Row, Col : Integer;
BEGIN
        FOR Row := 1 TO MaxRows DO BEGIN
                FOR Col := 1 TO MaxCols DO
                        Write (Output, Easel [Row, Col]);
                Writeln (Output);
        END;
END;


PROCEDURE CheckWrap (VAR Pos : Integer; Max : Integer);
(* This procedure checks the boundary conditions and makes*)
(* the turtle's position wrap around if he goes off the   *)
(* end of the page in any direction.                      *)
BEGIN
        IF (Pos = 0)
                THEN Pos := Max
                ELSE IF (Pos > Max)
                        THEN Pos := Pos - Max;
END;


PROCEDURE Change (RowDiff, ColDiff : Integer;
                VAR Turtle : TurtleRec; VAR Easel : EaselArr);
(* This procedure makes the position change in the turtle *)
(* and also changes the easel if the Pen is down. This is *)
(* called by MoveOneSpace.                                *)
BEGIN
        WITH Turtle DO BEGIN
                Row := Row + RowDiff;
                CheckWrap (Row, MaxRows);
                Col := Col + ColDiff;
                CheckWrap (Col, MaxCols);
                IF PenDown THEN
                        Easel [Row, Col] := PenChar;
        END;
END;


PROCEDURE MoveOneSpace (VAR Easel : EaselArr;
                        VAR Turtle : TurtleRec);
(* This procedure moves the turtle forward one space, the *)
(* direction entirely determined by Turtle.Dir.           *)
```

```
BEGIN
        CASE Turtle.Dir OF
              0 : Change (-1,  0, Turtle, Easel);
              1 : Change (-1,  1, Turtle, Easel);
              2 : Change ( 0,  1, Turtle, Easel);
              3 : Change ( 1,  1, Turtle, Easel);
              4 : Change ( 1,  0, Turtle, Easel);
              5 : Change ( 1,  1, Turtle, Easel);
              6 : Change ( 0, -1, Turtle, Easel);
              7 : Change (-1, -1, Turtle, Easel);
        END;
END;


PROCEDURE Move (VAR Easel : EaselArr;
                VAR Turtle : TurtleRec);
(* This procedure handles the entire move operation by     *)
(* calling MoveOneSpace for each move that it is supposed   *)
(* to make. It reads the argument from the terminal and     *)
(* calls MoveOneSpace the correct number of times.          *)
VAR     NumSpaces, Spaces : Integer;
BEGIN
        Read (TermIn, NumSpaces);
        FOR Spaces := 1 TO NumSpaces DO
               MoveOneSpace (Easel, Turtle);
END;


PROCEDURE Quit (SafeToQuit : Boolean; VAR Com : Char);
(* This procedure verifies that the user really does want *)
(* to quit. Changes the value of Com if Quit is aborted.  *)
VAR     Ans : Char;
BEGIN
        Writeln (TermOut, 'Are you sure you want to quit?');
        IF NOT SafeToQuit
            THEN Writeln (TermOut, 'Your current picture',
                                   ' has not been drawn.');
        Ans := TermSkipSpaces;
        IF (Ans<>'Y') AND (Ans<>'y') THEN Com := ' ';
END;


PROCEDURE Help;
(* This procedure writes out the list of valid commands.  *)
BEGIN
        Writeln (TermOut, 'The list of valid commands:');
        Writeln (TermOut, 'U : pen Up -- disables marking');
        Writeln (TermOut, 'D : pen Down -- enables marking');
        Writeln (TermOut, 'F <#> : Face -- turns turtle:');
        Writeln (TermOut, '                      701');
```

```
          Writeln (TermOut, '                 6T2');
          Writeln (TermOut, '                 543');
          Writeln (TermOut, 'M <#> : Moves # times forward');
          Writeln (TermOut, 'C : Center -- moves turtle to',
                            ' the middle of the page');
          Writeln (TermOut, 'H : Home --moves turtle to top',
                            ' left of the page');
          Writeln (TermOut, 'P <ch> : new PenChar -- deter',
                            'mines char turtle writes with');
          Writeln (TermOut, 'E : Erase -- erases the easel');
          Writeln (TermOut, 'W : Write -- writes easel');
          Writeln (TermOut, 'Q : Quit -- quits program');
          Writeln (TermOut, '? : Help -- writes this message');
END;


PROCEDURE Introduction;
(* This procedure introduces the program to the user.      *)
BEGIN
          Writeln (TermOut, 'This program produces simple',
                            ' pictures using a turtle');
          Writeln (TermOut, 'graphics package of commands.',
                            ' The user controls the');
          Writeln (TermOut, 'movement of a "turtle" that',
                            ' moves around an "easel,"');
          Writeln (TermOut, 'which is a two-dimensional',
                            ' array of characters. The');
          Writeln (TermOut, 'turtle has a pen on his sto',
                            'mach, and when the pen is');
          Writeln (TermOut, 'down, then the turtle marks',
                            ' on the easel as he moves.');
          Writeln (TermOut, 'The user may use several differ',
                            'ent commands, as follows:');
          Help;
END;


PROCEDURE PromptNRead (VAR Com : Char);
(* Prompts user for a command and reads the character      *)
BEGIN
          Writeln (TermOut, 'What is your command?');
          Com := TermSkipSpaces;
END;


PROCEDURE GetCommand (VAR Com : Char; LegalComs : ComSet);
(* This procedure prompts the user and reads the command  *)
(* from the Terminal. If the command is not a legal       *)
(* command, then the procedure reprompts after giving the *)
(* user Help.                                             *)
```

```
BEGIN    (* GetCommand *)
        PromptNRead (Com);
        WHILE NOT ((Com='U') OR (Com='D') OR (Com='F')
                   (Com='C') OR (Com='H') OR (Com='P')
                   (Com='E') OR (Com='W') OR (Com='M')
                   (Com='Q') OR (Com='?'))
            THEN BEGIN
                Writeln (TermOut, 'That is an illegal ',
                                  'command');
                Help;
                PromptNRead (Com);
            END;
END;     (* GetCommand *)


BEGIN    (* Main Program *)
        Reset (TermIn); Rewrite (TermOut);
        Introduction;
        Init (Easel, Turtle, LegalComs);
        REPEAT  TurtleReport (Turtle);
                GetCommand (Com, LegalComs);
                CASE Com OF
                    'U' : PenUp (Turtle);
                    'D' : PenDown (Turtle);
                    'F' : Face (Turtle);
                    'M' : Move (Easel, Turtle);
                    'C' : Center (Turtle);
                    'H' : Home (Turtle);
                    'P' : NewPenChar (Turtle);
                    'E' : Erase (Easel);
                    'W' : Draw (Easel);
                    'Q' : Quit (SafeToQuit, Com);
                    '?' : Help;
                END;
                SafeToQuit := (SafeToQuit AND
                              (Com<>'M')) OR (Com = 'W');
        UNTIL (Com = 'Q');
END.     (* Main Program *)
```

INTERACTIVE SESSION

This program produces simple pictures using a turtle
graphics package of commands. The user controls the
movement of a "turtle" that moves around an "easel,"
which is a two-dimensional array of characters. The
turtle has a pen on his stomach, and when the pen is
down, then the turtle marks on the easel as he moves.

The user may use several different commands, as follows:
The list of valid commands:
```
   U : pen Up -- disables marking
   D : pen Down -- enables marking
   F <#> : Face -- turns turtle:
                    701
                    6T2
                    543
   M <#> : Moves # times forward
   C : Center -- moves turtle to the middle of the page
   H : Home --moves turtle to top left of the page
   P <ch> : new PenChar -- determines char turtle writes with
   E : Erase -- erases the easel
   W : Write -- writes easel
   Q : Quit -- quits program
   ? : Help -- writes this message
```
Turtle position: [1,1] Facing: 2 PenChar = ' ' Pen is up
What is your command?
D
Turtle position: [1,1] Facing: 2 PenChar = ' ' Pen is down
What is your command?
P+
Turtle position: [1,1] Facing: 2 PenChar = '+' Pen is down
What is your command?
M75
Turtle position: [1,16] Facing: 2 PenChar = '+' Pen is down
What is your command?
C
Turtle position: [12,30] Facing: 0 PenChar = '+' Pen is down
What is your command?
M24
Turtle position: [12,30] Facing: 0 PenChar = '+' Pen is down
What is your command?
F3
Turtle position: [12,30] Facing: 3 PenChar = '+' Pen is down
What is your command?
P∗
Turtle position: [12,30] Facing: 3 PenChar = '*' Pen is down
What is your command?
M1000
Turtle position: [4,10] Facing: 3 PenChar = '*' Pen is down
What is your command?
C
Turtle position: [12,30] Facing: 0 PenChar = '*' Pen is down
What is your command?
M1
Turtle position: [11,30] Facing: 0 PenChar = '*' Pen is down
What is your command?
F2

```
Turtle position: [11,30]   Facing: 2  PenChar = '*'  Pen is down
What is your command?
M60
Turtle position: [11,30]   Facing: 2  PenChar = '*'  Pen is down
What is your command?
Q
Are you sure you want to quit?
Your current picture has not been drawn.
N
Turtle position: [11,30]   Facing: 2  PenChar = '*'  Pen is down
What is your command?
W
Turtle position: [11,30]   Facing: 2  PenChar = '*'  Pen is down
What is your command?
Q
Are you sure you want to quit?
Y
```

Figure 15.12 shows the output of this program.

Figure 15.12

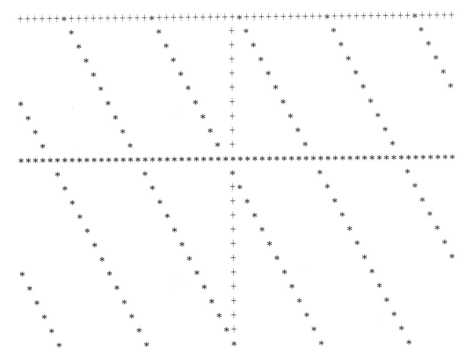

Common Errors and Debugging

1. **Declaring a record without an END delimiter.** Remember, a record statement, like a CASE statement, requires an END even though it does not contain a BEGIN.

2. **Declaring a record with more than one END delimiter.** The record declaration becomes doubly confusing when using a variant record structure, because only one END statement is needed, while the code seems to require two—one to end the CASE statement, and one to terminate the record definition. Just remember: no single record structure can have two tag fields or two sets of variant fields.

3. **Violating the component access rules for structured types.** Remember: Arrays need [index] and records need . field name.
   A good way to remember which structured types are arrays and which are records is to include Rec or Arr in the type name, PersonRec or StudentArr, for example. When data structures grow larger, it becomes more difficult to keep each type in mind, and it becomes easier to make mistakes. Give yourself as much help as possible by using helpful variable names.

4. **Working with more than two levels of a structured variable at a time.**

```
WHILE NOT Eoln (Input) DO BEGIN
    Cntr := Cntr + 1;
    Read (Input, Class.Students[Which].Name[Cntr]);
END;
```

The preceding code doesn't necessarily cause a syntax or execution error, but it makes errors much more likely and more difficult to spot. Always break down large record and array structures by using parameterized procedures and a WITH statement.

```
        WITH Student DO BEGIN
            ReadWord (Name);
            . . .
        END;
    . . .
        FOR Which := 1 TO Class.NumStudents DO
            ReadStudent (Class.Students[Which]);
```

5. **Allowing the array index out of bounds.** This is a familiar error, but now there is another way to get around it. With the help of the record structure, you can give every array a second field, called Length or Len or whatever. In this way, you will always know exactly how many elements are in use. The maximum value for this number should be the constant that is the highest index in the array.

```
FOR Which := 1 TO Class.NumStudents DO
    ReadStudent (Class.Students[Which]);
```

6. **Attempting to access an empty array element.** This problem can be dealt with in exactly the same way as the previous problem—by creating a record structure that includes a field that tells the length of the nonempty array.

Hints for BASIC Programmers

By this point in the course, you can no longer be called BASIC programmers since you know how to do as much or more in Pascal than you ever could do in BASIC. You also know almost all the most useful features of Pascal. If, after reading this chapter and working with records and arrays of records, you are not convinced that Pascal has anything to offer the BASIC programmer, you probably never will be convinced. However, if you find that programming with arrays of records allows you to do things you couldn't even imagine doing in BASIC, then you will probably never return to BASIC (except for occasional quick programs, perhaps).

Most of the similarity between Pascal and BASIC comes in the treatment of control structures, like the FOR loop, the IF statement, and the procedure. Pascal diverges widely from BASIC in the area of structured data types, like the array and the record, and a few others you have yet to learn about. If you begin to see your programming style slipping and falling back to your BASIC tendencies, then go back and reread some of the earlier Hints for BASIC Programmers sections. From now on, the material is new for everyone, and there aren't a lot of hints that BASIC programmers need that new programmers don't also need.

SUMMARY

The record is the second example we have seen in Pascal of a structured type. The record allows the programmer to combine components, called **fields**, in a much more flexible manner. Any amount and kind of data can be grouped into a single record. Individual fields in a record are accessed by the variable name followed by a period and the field name.

An array of records is the most common data structure using records. This structure is exceedingly powerful in its ability to organize and manipulate large amounts of various types of related data in efficient and elegant algorithms. It is necessary to break down large data structures into smaller parts through the use of procedures that handle only part of the whole. In this way, the code that handles these data structures doesn't become long and difficult to read. The WITH statement also helps to make code-processing record structures more readable.

The **selection sort** algorithm is slightly more complicated but is usually faster than the bubble sort algorithm. In general, the selection sort makes about the same number of comparisons, but calls the swapping procedure far fewer times than the bubble sort.

Variant records can be declared when the information needed in a certain record depends on one of the values in the record. A variant record structure has certain **fixed fields** and a **tag field,** which determines the rest of the structure. A variant record structure also contains **variable fields** for each of the values of the tag field.

New Terms

field	fixed field	turtle graphics
selection sort	tag field	RECORD
variant record	variable field	WITH

EXERCISES

1. Using array and record structures, write appropriate TYPE declarations for each of the following uses.
   a. a playing card
   b. a poker hand of five playing cards
   c. a deck of cards
   d. listing of a company from *Fortune* 500's list
   e. the entire *Fortune* 500 list
   f. a phone book entry
   g. an entire phone book
   h. a card catalogue entry in a library book
   i. the entire card catalogue
   j. an entry of a restaurant in a restaurant guide

2. Using your declaration for a deck of cards, write a procedure to initialize each rank and suit in the deck. Hint: If you declared type declarations correctly, this procedure should consist of two simple FOR loops.

3. Use the random number generator given on page 227 and the initialized deck of cards from the preceding problem to write a procedure that shuffles the deck of cards. Shuffling can involve swapping each card with a random card in the array.

4. Modify a selection sort and a bubble sort to calculate and print the number of comparisons and the number of swaps each one does on a random array of twenty integers. Which one performed fewer total operations (swaps + comparisons + increments and tests of the FOR loop counters)? Which do you think was faster?

5. Write a program that reads a file of information on the freshman class at a university and produces roommate matches. You will need to develop your own criteria for what makes a good match, and you will also need to add several fields in the standard record Person, like a boolean field called Matched which can be initialized to FALSE and set to TRUE if a match has been made. Go through the array and match people if a match is possible. If no match is possible, leave the person unmatched and move on to the next

person. At the end, report roommate pairs or the fact that the person is still unmatched. For example, your code might contain:

```
IF (P1.Smoker = P2.Smoker) AND
   (P1.Sex = P2.Sex) AND
        THEN Domatch (P1,P2);
```

You may want to take height and age into account. Who wants a roommate who is 14 inches taller?

6. Write a program that uses the procedures to initialize and shuffle cards that you wrote in problems 2 and 3 to play a game of blackjack. The computer can be dealer and banker.

Blackjack is played by dealing each player two cards, only one face up. Each card has a value equal to the number on it and face cards have a value of 10. The ace has a value of 1 or 11. The point of the game is to have a total point value of 21 in your hand, or as close as possible to 21 without going over. Going over is called busting. A point score of 2 beats a bust. After the two cards are dealt, the player can choose to take another card, a *hit*, or to stop, *stay*. If the player says "Hit," the dealer gives the player another card. The player's turn stops when she or he either busts or decides to stay. The dealer then reveals the face-down card, or *hole card*. The dealer must continue taking cards until the point score is 17 or greater, at which time the dealer must stop. The winner is the person whose point score is closest to but not more than 21. If there is a tie, the bet is returned; otherwise, the winner takes the loser's bet. Your program should ask for the player's bet and then deal. It should give the player an initial bankroll of $1,000, not allow a bet that is more than the player has, and does not allow the player to play without money.

7. Write a program that does complex arithmetic. A complex number is one that has real and imaginary parts. Complex operations are calculated as follows.

$$(X_1 + Y_1 i) + (X_2 + Y_2 i) = (X_1 + X_2) + i(Y_1 + Y_2)$$
$$(X_1 + Y_1 i) - (X_2 + Y_2 i) = (X_1 - X_2) + i(Y_1 - Y_2)$$
$$(X_1 + Y_1 i) \times (X_2 + Y_2 i) = (X_1 \times X_2 - Y_1 \times Y_2) + (X_1 \times Y_2 - Y_1 \times X_2)i$$

Assume that the input will be read as:

$$+ \ X_1 \ Y_1 \ X_2 \ Y_2$$
$$\times \ X_1 \ Y_1 \ X_2 \ Y_2$$

The operation will be first on the line, followed by four real numbers. Print out the equation for each line in the input file and then the result.

8. Using procedures developed in Exercises 2 and 3, write a procedure called BridgeDeal, which deals four hands of thirteen cards each into an array structure. Send each of these hands into a function called BridgeHandCount, which returns the point value of the hand. Points are determined as follows.

Each ace	= 4 points		
King	= 3 points	Doubleton (only 2 of a suit)	= 1 point
Queen	= 2 points	Singleton (only 1 of a suit)	= 2 points
Jack	= 1 point	Void (none of a suit)	= 3 points

9. If you know how to bid in bridge, use the procedures written in Exercise 8 to write a procedure that determines a good opening bid for a certain hand.

10. Improve MatchMaker by making the following changes (ranked easiest to most difficult):
    a. Alter the algorithm so that the subject's own name never appears on her or his own list of dates.
    b. Modify the algorithm, and perhaps the data structure, to take the sex of each person in the pool into account. If you make any assumptions about the preferences of the subject and the dates, make those explicit in the documentation. If you allow flexibility on the part of the subject, you will probably need to alter the data structure slightly.
    c. Use age, height, and weight in calculating matches. Be sure to document the assumptions you make about the subject's preferences.
    d. Allow the subject to emphasize the need for compatibility in certain areas and to deemphasize the need for compatibility in others. This will require a fairly substantial change to both the algorithm and the data structure.

11. Write a data structure to hold all sorts of information about students at a large university. Each record structure should contain the name, student ID number, and class of each student plus all of the courses the student has ever taken, the academic year in which the course was taken, the number of units it was taken for, and the grade received.

12. Write a program that reads data from an input file for the data structure described above. Calculate each student's GPA and make an honor roll listing those with a GPA $>= 3.5$. The national honor society, Phi Beta Kappa, usually elects the top 2 percent of the junior class and the top 5 percent of the senior class into membership. Write procedures to recommend the appropriate students for election.

13. Nancy, a very popular person on campus, is having a hard time organizing her life. She has many friends, acquaintances, and contacts from different contexts—classes, parties, past or present dorms, friends of friends, friends of acquaintances, acquaintances of friends. Each of these people has various attributes that may be important to Nancy in the future, because she is planning to go into business management where who she knows may become very important. Write a program that allows Nancy to organize her black book so that she can retrieve, for example, a list of possible dates for the weekend or study partners for specific classes. Her program should be able to tell her, for example, who to go to for help on a research paper in any field or to whom she should send Christmas cards.

14. George the grocer is having a hard time knowing what items are in stock and when to reorder. Write a program that stores the item name, brand name, quantity in stock, wholesale and retail prices, and wholesaler or distributor name for each item in his store. George isn't very good with computers, so you'll need to write a program that is very user friendly. The program should produce George's current inventory in a pleasing format. The program should also be able to sort the inventory by comparing any of the fields alphabetically or numerically. Write a procedure that allows George to update the inventory numbers easily without retyping or reentering the entire file.

15. Write a program that helps the user decide on a restaurant. The input file should be a list of restaurants that includes the phone number and address, a one-word description of the type of food (the options could be standardized: Mexican, Chinese, Hamburgers, Deli, and so forth), a one-word description of the price range (SkyHigh, Expensive, Moderate, Cheap), the date the user last ate there, and a rating of 1 to 5. The program should give the user a list of restaurants based on the preferences the user has that

particular evening. The program should then update the record of the restaurant selected by changing the date of the most recent visit. The new data base should be printed on an output file.

16. Write a program that serves as a library's card catalogue file. Each card should have spaces for all the relevant information for a book. Your program should allow the user to search for and see listings for all the books under a certain subject or by a certain author. The program should also allow library staff (who know the secret password) to add or delete books from the card catalogue.

17. Write a program that helps a directory-assistance operator. The program should allow ready access to all records that match a certain last name and should also contain the address and city of each person in the data base as well as each person's phone number.

18. One version of solitaire is played without even dealing any cards. The shuffled deck is examined in order, and cards are removed according to the following rules:
    a. A pair of cards is removed if there are exactly two cards between them in a shuffled deck and if they are the same suit.
    b. Four cards in a row are removed if the rank of the first card matches the rank of the fourth card.

    The point of the game is to try to completely eliminate all the cards from the deck. Obviously, this has much to do with how the cards are arranged. Write a program that simulates the play of the game. Use the card-handling procedures written in problems 2 and 3. Think of some interesting way to produce output for the execution of the program. Evaluate the final number of remaining cards.

19. Another way to play solitaire is to deal the 52 shuffled cards into 13 piles, 12 of them arranged like the numbers on the face of a clock and the 13th pile in the center of the circle. The first card in the center pile is turned over. It is placed at the bottom of the pile which is equal to its rank, face up. That is, if the card is a 7, then it is placed under the 7 o'clock pile and the top card of that pile is turned up and placed under its corresponding pile. Jacks are put under the 11 o'clock pile, queens under the 12 o'clock pile, and kings under the pile in the center. Play continues until the four kings turn up, or until all the rest of the piles show cards that are face up. The player is considered to have won if the kings' pile remains unfinished until the end. Write a program that will simulate this game of solitaire.

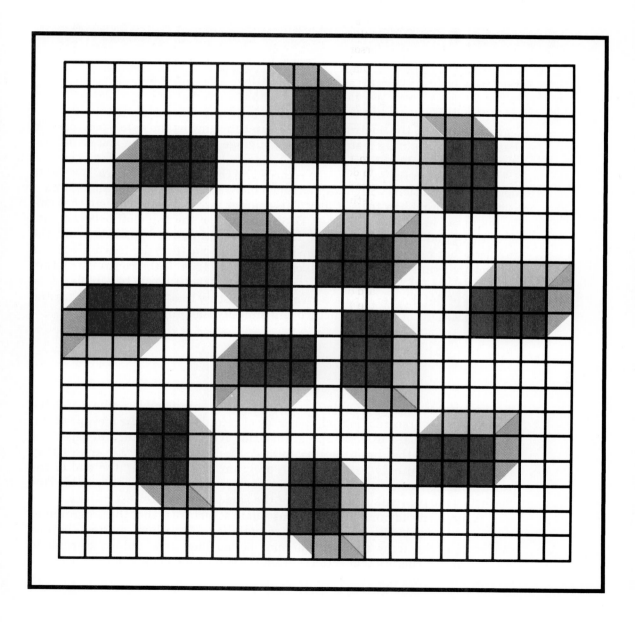

MORE DATA STRUCTURES: FILES AND SETS

At this point, you should be able to write any program you want to write. You have learned all the control structures and the important data structures in Pascal. The remaining features of the language are extras, and you could program happily without them.

However, these features, like records and the CASE statement, allow you to do certain operations with data in a much more straightforward manner, and it is worth learning how to use them. This chapter introduces the concept that will be discussed in detail in Chapter 17, the concept of the trade-off between data structures and control structures. In general, the more information about the problem that we store in a well-constructed data structure, the less difficult the control structure is to write. The converse is also true. If the control structure does all the work of a program, then its data structure can be simpler. One objective of the chapters on data structure is to show that thorough analysis and "decomposition" of a data structure will simplify the program solution.

Files

It seems impossible for any data structure to be more flexible and expandable than an array of records. Indeed, the array of records is one of the most powerful data structures used in Pascal programs. However, there are certain aspects of arrays of records that limit their usefulness. First, because they are arrays, they store information only as long as the program is running. At the end of the execution, the locations in memory no longer retain the values they held. This characteristic prevents repeated use of the same data in later executions.

A second disadvantage of arrays as a data structure is that the programmer must know their length at the time of compilation. If the data set grows beyond the limits of the array, the program must be modified. It would be desirable to create a data structure that could contain the same kind of data but did not have the limitations of size and impermanence.

The data structure that solves these problems is the file. Actually, you have been using this data structure all along in the form of input and output files. Using an input file, you have been able to bring data into your program for manipulation and calculations. Likewise, using an output file, you have been able to record your results in memory for later use.

Text Files Reconsidered

Input and Output are two standard files of type Text. A text file is a file of characters in which Eoln and Eof are defined at each point in the file. We have thought of a text file as looking like this:

```
24  82  10  ∨

This is a text file∨

10  27  39  ∨

102.1FM∨

x∨
■
```

The ∨ is the Eoln marker and the ■ is the Eof marker. This is a fine way to think about a file, although it really looks more like this:

```
24  82  10  ∨This is a text file∨10  27  39  ∨  102.1FM∨x∨■
```

The end-of-line markers and end-of-file markers exist in the file like any other characters and are only used by the line printer or the terminal to indicate formatting when the file is displayed.

After a text file has been reset, or at the beginning of a program, the first character in the file is in a window called the **file buffer variable,** which contains the next character to be read. The file buffer variable is accessed by the file identifier followed by the symbol ∧. Therefore, if we want the variable Ch to have the value of the next character on the line, we could say:

```
Ch := Input^;
```

Notice that this is like a Read statement, except that it doesn't change the file buffer at all. A Read statement makes the assignment and then moves the file buffer to the next character in the file.

SELF
TEST

Suppose we wanted to read an integer from a file unless the next character is an A, in which case we want to throw away the line. How would you write a code fragment for this?

Two Procedures: Get and Put

We just saw that it is possible to simulate the action of a Read statement with the use of the file buffer variable. We can completely simulate both Read and Write by using the standard procedures Get and Put. Get takes one parameter, the input file variable being used, and moves the file buffer over one character. The file must be an input file for Get to work. The Read operation, for characters, can be completely simulated by:

```
Read (Input, Ch);          Ch := Input^;
                           Get (Input);
```

Put does for output files what Get does for input files—it moves the buffer over one space. A Write operation can be performed by:

```
Write (Output, Ch);        Output^ := ch;
                           Put (Output);
```

Get and Put are not always the best choices; in most cases, Read and Write will get the job done better, especially when working with numbers, which is difficult if you are using Get and Put.

But Get and Put obviously have their place. An example of a good use of the file buffer variable and Get is in a procedure called SkipSpaces, which is supposed to go along the input file and stop at the first nonspace character. This is done automatically when reading numbers, but can often be useful when reading text or character commands from the terminal.

```
PROCEDURE SkipSpaces;
(* This procedure skips all spaces on the input line and  *)
(* returns with the cursor on top of the next nonspace    *)
(* character in the file.                                 *)
BEGIN
        WHILE (Input^ = ' ') DO Get (Input);
END;
```

SELF
TEST

Given the following input file, what will be the result of the following piece of code?

INPUT   This is nice.

```
SkipSpaces; Read (Input, Ch);
SkipSpaces; Read (Input, Ch);
SkipSpaces; Write (Output, Ch);
```

File Parameters

SkipSpaces would be a good procedure to use in a number of different programs or on several different files in the same program. As we have learned, procedures for reading or manipulating files that aren't specialized should be parameterized. We can declare InFile to be a parameter into the procedure SkipSpaces.

```
PROCEDURE SkipSpaces (VAR InFile : Text);
(* This procedure skips all spaces on the input line and  *)
(* returns with the cursor on top of the next nonspace    *)
(* character in the file.                                  *)
BEGIN
        WHILE (InFile^ = ' ') DO Get (InFile);
END;
```

This can be used with all the different input files that the program may be using, including Input and TerminalIn.

Another input procedure that is good to parameterize is the familiar

```
PROCEDURE ReadWord (VAR W : Word; VAR InFile : Text);
```

Note that file parameters must *always* be declared as variable parameters, because it is impossible to read the file or write it without changing the file. It is an error to try to send a file as a value parameter.

SELF TEST

Write a version of ReadWord that will read a word from any input file until Eoln. Write a version of WriteWord that will write the word to any output file.

Files of Other Types

Files do not only have to be of type Text; they can be of any simple or structured data type, except one that contains files in it. In other words, we can declare files of integers, real numbers, boolean values, arrays, or even records.

```
TYPE    Word = ARRAY [1..Max] OF Char;
        SexType = (Male, Female);
        NumFile = FILE OF Integer;
        DictFile = FILE OF Word;
        PERSON = Record
                    Name : Word;
                    Age, Height, Weight : Integer;
                    Sex : SexType;
        END;

        PersonFile = FILE OF Person;
```

```
VAR       NFile : NumFile;
          Dictionary : DictFile;
          Class : PersonFile;
```

The advantage of having files of structured types is that reading and writing them is very easy. For example, if you have a huge, complicated record structure for each of several thousand people represented in Class, all that is necessary is a simple Read statement for each record.

```
Cntr := 0;
WHILE NOT Eof (Class) DO BEGIN
        Cntr := Cntr + 1;
        Read (Class, People [Cntr]);
END;
```

If the data were stored as a file of text, the read procedure would be much more complicated, as the examples we saw in the last chapter.

The problems with this data structure result from the fact that a file of records—or anything other than characters—does not look like a file of characters. First, a record file cannot be created by a person typing in names in an editor. A program must be written to take input from a text file or from the terminal and store it in a record structure. Once the data is stored in the record structure, the program can reread, delete, or alter the information. When it is printed out to a record file, it cannot normally be read by humans, but another program can work with the same data structure and read the file for use or manipulation.

A second problem arises when we want to change the structure of the records after we have created them. If we desire to add a field or two to the existing record, we must write a program to read in the original data, move the fields over to a second record that has the extended structure, then write out the record. For example:

```
Reset (OldFile);
Rewrite (NewFile);
WHILE NOT Eof (OldFile) DO BEGIN
        Read (OldFile, OldRecord);
        NewRecord.Name := OldRecord.Name;
        NewRecord.Age := OldRecord.Age;
        NewRecord.Sex := OldRecord.Sex;
        Get Address (OldRecord, Address);
        NewRecord.Address := Address;
        Write (NewFile, NewRecord);
END;
```

Using a structured file could result in having to make awkward changes like this. If you are writing a program with a huge data structure that will be executed many times, however, you may want to consider using a structured file type anyway because of the time you will save in the Read and Write operations.

Remember, Readln, Writeln, and Eoln are defined only on text files. A moment's thought will reveal the reason—only text files are structured in lines of data.

Programming Example 16.1

Assignment: Write a program for a department store that merges two sorted files of customer records. Produce a third file, which is the sorted composition of the two. Assume that each file is a file of Person records with a Name field, and that you will perform an alphabetical sort on Name. The two files will be Previous and New and the output file will be called Updated. The program should be able to handle files of any length.

Solution: Perhaps the first step in the solution would be to represent graphically what is going to happen. Two sorted files are going to be merged by comparing the Name field of the top record in one file with that of the top record of the other. The resulting file should be alphabetized as in Figure 16.1.
An attempt at a merge-sorting algorithm for this would be:

Initialize files
Get one record from each file
Loop:
      Write the alphabetically higher record to output
      Replace with another record from corresponding
          input file
Until end of either input file
Write remaining records from nonempty input file to output

This can be written as a main program in Pascal as follows:

```
BEGIN    (* Main Program *)
         InitFiles (Previous, New, Updated);
         Read (Previous, PrevPerson);
         Read (New, NewPerson);
         MergeBoth (Previous, New, Updated,
                    PrevPerson, NewPerson);
         IF Eof (Previous)
                 THEN EmptyFile (New)
                 ELSE EmptyFile (Previous);
END.     (* Main Program *)
```

The only part of this program with tricky logic is in MergeBoth. But it is much simpler to sort two records than to sort an array of records.

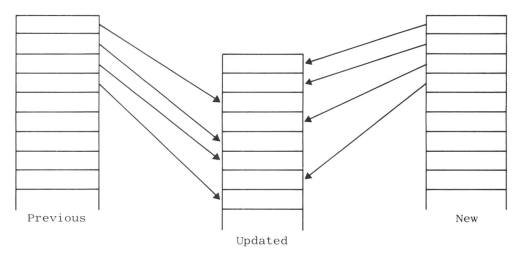

Figure 16.1: Merge Sort

```
PROCEDURE MergeBoth (VAR Prev, New, Up : PersonFile;
                     VAR PrevPers, NewPers : Person);
(* This procedure merges and sorts two sorted files of   *)
(* Person records.                                        *)
BEGIN
        REPEAT  IF (PrevPers.Name > NewPers.Name) THEN BEGIN
                        Write (Up, PrevPers);
                        Read (Prev, PrevPers);
                END ELSE BEGIN
                        Write (Up, NewPers);
                        Read (New, NewPers);
                END;
        UNTIL Eof (Prev) OR Eof (New);
        IF Eof (Prev)
                THEN Write (Up, NewPers)
                ELSE Write (Up, PrevPers);
END;
```

This program would work fine, but it would be even simpler and would involve fewer variables if we worked directly with the file buffer variables. The final program, using buffer variables, is:

```
PROGRAM MergeSort (Previous, New, Updated);
(* This program merges and sorts two sorted files of      *)
(* person records. The files can be any length.           *)
CONST   Max = 16;
```

```
TYPE    Word = PACKED ARRAY [1..Max] OF Char;
        Person = RECORD
           Name : Word;
           . . .
        END;

        PersonFile =  FILE OF Person;

VAR     Previous, New,           (* input files        *)
        Updated : PersonFile;    (* resulting file      *)

PROCEDURE InitFiles (VAR Prev, New, Up : PersonFile);
BEGIN
        Reset (Prev);
        Reset (New);
        Rewrite (Up);
END;

PROCEDURE MergeBoth (VAR Prev, New, Up : PersonFile);
(* This procedure merges and sorts two sorted files of   *)
(* Person records.                                       *)
BEGIN
        REPEAT  IF (Prev^.Name > New^.Name) THEN BEGIN
                     Write (Up, Prev^);
                     Get (Prev);
                END ELSE BEGIN
                     Write (Up, New^);
                     Get (New);
                END;
        UNTIL Eof (Prev) OR Eof (New);
END;

PROCEDURE CopyFile (VAR Source, Dest : PersonFile);
(* This procedure copies all of the remaining records    *)
(* from the Source file to the Dest file.                *)
BEGIN
        WHILE NOT Eof (Source) DO BEGIN
             Write (Dest, Source^);
             Get (Source);
        END;
END;

BEGIN   (* Main Program *)
        InitFiles (Previous, New, Updated);
        MergeBoth (Previous, New, Updated);
        IF Eof (Previous)
             THEN CopyFile (New, Updated)
             ELSE CopyFile (Previous, Updated);
END.    (* Main Program *)
```

Sets

In Programming Example 15.1 we presented a computer dating program in which we used a boolean array over the number of possible responses to a particular question. Suppose we consider the set of all responses that a person typed for a particular question. Answers to question 1 would be:

{1, 7, 14, 18, 25}

This would be represented, according to the data structure we used, as:

TFFFFFTFFFFFFTFFFTFFFFFFFTFFFFF

Obviously, the set notation above is easier to work with than a long array of Ts and Fs. Pascal is the only language that has, as a data type, a SET that allows easy manipulation of a collection of boolean values. Membership in the set satisfies the boolean test, and exclusion does not. The idea of a set in mathematics provides a good introduction to a Pascal SET.

Set: An unordered collection of **elements** or members.

In Pascal, we can declare sets of any simple type, including subrange and enumerated types. You can probably predict by now that you aren't allowed to use a set of real numbers.

Sets are easy to declare. Here are some examples.

```
TYPE    Responses = SET OF 0..30;
        Colors = (Red, Orange, Yellow, Blue,
                  Green, Indigo, Violet);
        ColorSet = SET OF Colors;
        LetterSet = SET OF 'A'..'Z';
        NumSet = SET OF 0..9;
        DigSet = SET OF '0'..'9';

VAR     Digits : DigSet;
        Numbers : NumSet;
        Col : ColorSet;
        Vowels, Consonants, All : LetterSet;
```

As always, declaring a TYPE does not create any variables. Furthermore, *declaring variables of set types does nothing to initialize the set.* An initialization is needed.

```
        Vowels := ['A', 'E', 'I', 'O', 'U'];
        Numbers := [0..9];
```

```
Digits := ['0'..'8','9'];
Consonants := ['A'..'Z'] - Vowels;
```

Notice the use of the minus sign in the initialization of Consonants. Actually, several arithmetic operators are defined on set variables with special set operations.

+	Union	the **union** of two sets contains all the elements in either or both of the sets.
*	Intersection	the **intersection** of two sets contains only the elements occurring in both sets.
-	Set difference	the **set difference** between two sets contains all the elements in the first set that are *not* in the second set.

Suppose we want to add 'Y' to the set of Vowels and delete it from the set of Consonants. We can do this by making 'Y' a set and using the set operations.

```
Vowels := Vowels + ['Y'];
Consonants := Consonants - ['Y'];
```

Notice we must first make 'Y' a set by enclosing it in brackets. The + operation is defined for integers, reals, and sets. It is not defined for characters. Likewise, if we wanted to subtract 0 from the set of numbers, we would use

```
Numbers := Numbers - [0];        (*correct*)
```

If we were to try

```
Numbers := Numbers - 0;          (*incorrect*)
```

we would get a type conflict error, because an integer cannot be subtracted from a set.

Sets can be compared with each other for equality or inequality. All six of the relational operators (=, >, <, >=, <=, <>) are defined on sets. In addition, there is a seventh relational operator defined on sets that determines membership in a set, IN.

```
IF Ch IN Digits THEN...
```

The IN operator is an infix operator and requires two operands. The second should be a set and the first should be of the same type as the elements of the set. The result of the test is true if the first operand is an element of the second operand, a set.

```
('A' IN Vowels) is true
('Z' IN Vowels) is false
('Z' IN (Vowels + Consonants)) is true
```

We can use the input file buffer in conjunction to safely read a number that may contain commas, dashes, or letters. Suppose we want to write a function that will return the next number in the input file that we give it, stopping only when it hits a space or a period. In other words:

10,921	would return	10921
505-232-4783	would return	5052324783
B27A63.ABC	would return	2763

The test we are going to employ will make use of the set of Digits, because that is what we are looking for.

```
IF (InFile^ IN Digits)
       THEN...
       ELSE...
```

The entire function follows.

```
FUNCTION FindNumber (VAR InFile : Text) : Integer;
(* This function returns the next number in a file, only   *)
(* stopping when it hits a period or a space. Any non-      *)
(* digits are ignored.                                       *)
(* One of the few times when a VAR parameter into a         *)
(* function is acceptable.                                   *)
VAR     Num : Integer; Dig : Char;
BEGIN
        SkipSpaces (InFile); Num := 0;
        REPEAT IF (InFile^ IN DIGITS)
              THEN BEGIN
                        Read (InFile, Dig);
                        Num := Num*10 + Ord(Dig) - Ord('0');
              END ELSE IF NOT (InFile^ IN [' ','.'])
                        THEN Get (Input);
        UNTIL (InFile^ IN [' ','.']);
        FindNumber := Num;
END;
```

SELF
TEST

Suppose a set type has three possible elements, 0, 1, and 2.

1. How many distinct set values exist for this set type? List them.
2. How many distinct set values exist for a set of n elements?

Programming Example 16.2

Assignment: Write a program that takes a prose input file and prints it out as blank verse poetry. Assume that a new line begins after every piece of punctuation that terminates a phrase or sentence: a period, comma, colon, semicolon, dash, exclamation mark, or question mark. Don't worry about quotation marks. Remember to capitalize the first word of each line. Print the poem out to an output file.

Solution: The program is pretty simple, but it may require a few revisions to make the output look good. For a first attempt, let's try a pseudocode version of the main program.

> Initialize Punctuation
> Repeat for the entire file:
> > Read a character
> > Write a character
> > If character was a punctuation mark, then end the line

If this is all it is, it is simple enough.

```
Punctuation := ['.', ',', ';', ':', '!', '?'];
WHILE NOT Eof (InFile) DO BEGIN
        Read (InFile, Ch);
        Write (OutFile, Ch);
        IF (Ch IN Punctuation) THEN Writeln (OutFile);
END;
```

However, this isn't going to capitalize the beginning of each phrase correctly. In order to do that, we can add a boolean flag that tells us when we need to capitalize the next letter printed.

```
Punctuation := ['.', ',', ';', ':', '!', '?'];
MakeCap := TRUE;
WHILE NOT Eof (InFile) DO BEGIN
        Read (InFile, Ch);
        IF MakeCap THEN BEGIN
                Write (OutFile, Cap (Ch));
                MakeCap := FALSE;
        END ELSE Write (OutFile, Ch);
        IF (Ch IN Punctuation) THEN BEGIN
                Writeln (OutFile);
                MakeCap := TRUE;
        END;
END;
```

Yet there is still a problem. Usually, the character after a punctuation mark is a space. Sometimes two or more spaces follow. The version above will capitalize a space, an operation that has no effect. By the time the compiler finds a character that we want to capitalize, MakeCap is no longer true. To fix this we use our handy SkipSpaces procedure.

```
IF (Ch IN Punctuation) THEN BEGIN
        Writeln (OutFile);
        MakeCap := TRUE;
        SkipSpaces (Input);
END;
```

But this improvement does not go far enough, because we end up with lines that go beyond the edge of the screen or the paper. We want to format the output so it looks like real poetry. Let's restructure the main program so it deals with a single word at a time, and then checks to see if a new line must be made.

```
BEGIN    (* Main Program *)
        Punctuation := ['.', ',', ';', ':', '!', '?'];
        MakeCap := TRUE; Cntr := 0;
        WHILE NOT Eof (Input) DO BEGIN
            SkipSpaces (Input);
            CopyNextWord (Ch, Cntr, Punctuation);
            IF (Ch IN Punctuation) THEN BEGIN
                Writeln (Output);
                MakeCap := TRUE; Cntr := 0;
            END ELSE IF (Cntr>Margin) THEN BEGIN
                Writeln (Output); Cntr := 0;
            END;
        END;
END.    (* Main Program *)
```

As you can see from the context, CopyNextWord starts after any spaces have been skipped, and prints characters until either the next space or the next punctuation mark is encountered. The character returned as a variable parameter is the last character printed. Cntr is also increased every time a character is printed, and therefore represents the current column position on the output line. Notice that Cntr is reinitialized every time a Writeln statement is executed.

Another improvement can be made. When a line of poetry is longer than the margin allows, the remaining part of the line is put on the next line and indented. Let's implement a simple indentation in such a case, rather than printing continuation lines at the left margin.

```
CONST   Margin = 65;
        Indent = 4;
  . . .
        IF (Ch IN Punctuation) THEN BEGIN
            Writeln (Output);
```

```
          MakeCap := TRUE; Cntr := 0;
     END ELSE IF (Cntr>Margin) THEN BEGIN
          Writeln (Output);
          Write (Output, ' ':Indent);
          Cntr := Indent;
     END;
```

Finally, when we execute what we have written, we notice one slight problem: the program doesn't execute without a read error. We have not properly disposed of the Eoln marker. After skipping all the spaces, we should check to make sure that we have not hit the end of the line. If we have, then we should execute a Readln and continue. The final version of the main program is seen in the following complete program.

```
PROGRAM BlankVerse (Input, Output);
(*************************************************************)
(* This program reads as input a text file and converts    *)
(* it very stupidly to "blank verse." Every sentence or     *)
(* phrase begins a new line, and lines longer than the      *)
(* margin are broken at a word and indented to finish.      *)
(* This program demonstrates the use of sets.               *)
(*************************************************************)

CONST    Margin = 50;
         Indent = 4;
TYPE     CharSet = SET OF Char;

VAR      Ch : Char;        (* the most recent character read *)
         Cntr : Integer; (* counts the current column pos. *)
         MakeCap : Boolean; (* TRUE when next letter is to *)
                            (* be capitalized.             *)
         Punctuation : CharSet; (* signals end of lines*)

PROCEDURE SkipSpaces (VAR InFile : Text);
(* This procedure skips all spaces on the input line and   *)
(* returns with the cursor on top of the next nonspace      *)
(* character in the file.                                    *)
BEGIN
        WHILE (InFile^ = ' ') OR (Ord (InFile^) = 9)
            DO Get (InFile);
END;

FUNCTION Cap (Ch : Char) : Char;
(* returns the capitalized version of a letter             *)
BEGIN
        IF (Ch >= 'a') AND (Ch <= 'z')
            THEN Cap := Chr (Ord(Ch) + Ord('A') - Ord('a'))
            ELSE Cap := Ch;
END;
```

```
          PROCEDURE CopyNextWord (VAR Ch : Char; VAR Cntr : Integer;
                                  Punct : CharSet);
          (* Copies the input file to the output file until a space *)
          (* or a punctuation mark is encountered.                   *)

          BEGIN
                  REPEAT
                      Read (Input, Ch);
                      IF MakeCap THEN BEGIN
                          Write (Output, Cap(Ch));
                          MakeCap := FALSE;
                      END ELSE Write (Output, Ch);
                      Cntr := Cntr + 1;
                  UNTIL (Ch IN Punct) OR (Ch = ' ');
          END;

          BEGIN     (* Main Program *)
                  Punctuation := ['.', ',', ';', ':', '!', '?'];
                  MakeCap := TRUE; Cntr := 0;
                  WHILE NOT Eof (Input) DO BEGIN
                      SkipSpaces (Input);
                      IF NOT Eoln (Input) THEN BEGIN
                          CopyNextWord (Ch, Cntr, Punctuation);
                          IF (Ch IN Punctuation) THEN BEGIN
                              Writeln (Output);
                              MakeCap := TRUE; Cntr := 0;
                          END ELSE IF (Cntr>Margin) THEN BEGIN
                              Writeln (Output);
                              Write (Output, ' ':Indent);
                              Cntr := Indent;
                          END;
                      END ELSE Readln (Input);
                  END;
          END.      (* Main Program *)
```

Using the first paragraph of Chapter 5 as the input file, the previous program produced the following output.

OUTPUT
```
When we think of a computer language we think of the
     need to communicate with a computer.
However,
Computer programs are also meant to be read by human
     beings.
Coworkers,
Spouses,
And instructors will,
At times,
Want to look at the programs we have written in order
     to understand,
```

```
Modify,
Evaluate,
Or simply to use them.
Features of a program that make it more readable are
     lumped together under a broad heading called style.
In programming,
There are two basic categories of style:
Format and documentation.
```

Programming Example 16.3

Assignment: Write a program that reads a line of input and writes out all the characters that appear on that line of text.

Solution: The program solution can be broken down into two main parts.

> Characters on a Line:
>> Read the line, making the set of characters
>> Write out the set of characters

According to this simple outline, there needs to be only one global variable, a set of characters. Given that, we can write our first attempt at the main program of the solution.

```
TYPE    LetSet = SET OF Char;

VAR     WhichLetters : LetSet; (* The letters found      *)
. . .
BEGIN   (* Main Program *)
        MakeSet (WhichLetters);
        WriteSet (WhichLetters);
END.    (* Main Program *)
```

Let's look at what is involved in MakeSet. Essentially, like a lot of the reading procedures we've written before, we will be looping until the end of the line of input.

> Make Set:
>> Initialize set of found chars to the null set
>> Loop until Eoln:
>>> Read a character
>>> If it is a letter
>>>> Then add it to the set

Since we are using sets, we might as well use a set of all the letters to determine if the character read is a valid letter, and not a space, digit, or punctuation mark. This converts pretty easily into Pascal.

```
PROCEDURE MakeSet (VAR Which : LetSet);
(* This procedure makes the set of letters that occurs   *)
(* in the input line.                                     *)
VAR     Ch : Char;
        All : SET OF Char;
BEGIN
        All := ['A'..'Z','a'..'z'];
        Which := [];            (* initialize to null set *)
        WHILE NOT Eoln (Input) DO BEGIN
            Read (Input, Ch);
            IF (Ch IN All)
                THEN Which := Which + [Cap(Ch)];
        END;
END;
```

This procedure uses the familiar function Cap, which prevents a letter being added to the set as both a capital and a small letter. The set will be made up entirely of capital letters.

The remaining procedure is a model for a very useful type of procedure in Pascal. Because Pascal doesn't allow a variable of a set type to be written to a text file, it is always necessary to loop through the base type of the set from the lowest value to the highest, printing out each value that is a member of the set. This general algorithm will print out the values of any set. In the case of a character set, the pseudocode is:

> Write Set:
>> Loop Ch from 'A' to 'Z' while set is not empty:
>>> IF Ch in the set then
>>>> Remove Ch from the set
>>>> Write Ch on output file

Implementing a FOR loop on a character variable is no more difficult than doing the same with an integer variable. However, when we are using an indefinite loop structure, such as a WHILE loop, it is necessary to come up with a statement equivalent to

```
Cntr := Cntr + 1;
```

Well, recall the standard function Succ, which takes any ordinal type value and returns the successor of that value. We can use that to increment our character counter from 'A' to 'B' and eventually to 'Z'.

```
PROCEDURE WriteSet (LS : LetSet);
(* This procedure writes all the letters that are in the  *)
```

```
(* given set to the output file, one at a time.            *)
VAR     Ch : Char;
BEGIN
        Ch := 'A';
        WHILE (Ch <= 'Z') AND (LS <> []) DO BEGIN
            IF (Ch IN LS) THEN BEGIN
                LS := LS - [Ch];
                Write (Output, Ch);
            END;
            Ch := Succ (Ch);
        END;
        Writeln (Output);
END;
```

Notice how the set difference operator (–) deletes elements from a set, but that the element must be made into a set before attempting to do this. Again, the statement

```
LS := LS - Ch;
```

would have been an error, because the variable Ch is not a set variable. This is an easy error to make.

The program, as it is written now, will work fine, but the output is not as nice as it could be. Specifically, when a lot of letters are found on the input line, it is difficult to spot which ones are missing. In order to make the data easier to interpret, let's alter the main program a little bit.

```
BEGIN   (* Main Program *)
        MakeSet (WhichLetters, AllLetters);
        Write (Output, 'Letters IN line:    ');
        WriteSet (WhichLetters);
        Write (Output, 'Letters NOT in line: ');
        WriteSet (AllLetters - WhichLetters);
END.    (* Main Program *)
```

Notice that the top line of the output file contains all the letters that were found in the input line, and the bottom line contains those that were not found in the input line. WriteSet has been spruced up slightly, to further aid in making a distinction. The complete program follows.

```
PROGRAM LettersOnALine (Input, Output);
(*************************************************************)
(* This program determines which letters occurred in an     *)
(* input line and writes out both the set of letters found  *)
(* as well as the set of those not found on the input       *)
(* line.                                                     *)
(*************************************************************)
TYPE    LetSet = SET OF Char;
```

```pascal
VAR     WhichLetters : LetSet; (* The letters found      *)
        AllLetters : LetSet; (* 'A'..'Z', 'a'..'z'        *)

FUNCTION Cap (Ch : Char) : Char;
(* returns the capitalized version of a letter, so that   *)
(* both small and capital versions of the same letter are *)
(* put into the set of letters.                           *)
BEGIN
        IF (Ch >= 'a') AND (Ch <= 'z')
            THEN Cap := Chr (Ord(Ch) + Ord('A') - Ord('a'))
            ELSE Cap := Ch;
END;

PROCEDURE WriteSet (LS : LetSet);
(* This procedure writes all the letters that are in the  *)
(* given set to the output file, one at a time.           *)
VAR     Ch : Char;
BEGIN
        Ch := 'A';
        WHILE (Ch <= 'Z') AND (LS <> []) DO BEGIN
            IF (Ch IN LS) THEN BEGIN
                LS := LS - [Ch];
                Write (Output, Ch);
            END ELSE Write (Output, ' ');
            Ch := Succ (Ch);
        END;
        Writeln (Output);
END;

PROCEDURE MakeSet (VAR Which, All : LetSet);
(* This procedure makes the set of letters that occurs    *)
(* in the input line.                                     *)
VAR     Ch : Char;
BEGIN
        All := ['A'..'Z','a'..'z'];
        Which := [];
        WHILE NOT Eoln (Input) DO BEGIN
            Read (Input, Ch);
            IF (Ch IN All)
                THEN Which := Which + [Cap(Ch)];
        END;
END;

BEGIN   (* Main Program *)
        MakeSet (WhichLetters, AllLetters);
        Write (Output, 'Letters IN line:     ');
        WriteSet (WhichLetters);
        Write (Output, 'Letters NOT in line: ');
        WriteSet (AllLetters - WhichLetters);
END.    (* Main Program *)
```

With the following as input:

```
Alas, poor Yorick, I knew him well.
```

the program produced this output:

```
Letters IN line:    A C E  HI KLMNOP RS    W Y
Letters NOT in line: B D FG  J         Q    TUV X Z
```

Note that this program is more like a program fragment that might be used in another program that acts on entire input files. This program could also be modified very easily to handle files rather than lines of data.

Common Errors and Debugging

1. **Attempting to declare a set whose base type is too large.** Most versions of Pascal do not allow a set to have a base type with a large number of values in it. A set is usually limited to something like 72 or 144 members; therefore, the base type cannot have more values in it than this limit. Specifically, the following declarations are often not allowed:

```
Primes : SET OF Integer;
Letters : SET OF Char;
```

Deal with this limitation by declaring the base types of sets to be limited and appropriately defined subrange types.

```
Primes : SET OF 1..MaxNum;
Letters : SET OF 'a'..'z';
```

2. **Attempting to add elements to sets.** Remember, the set operators + (union), ∗ (intersection), and − (difference) can only be used with set variables of the same type. It is illegal to try to use any of these operators between a set and an element of that set. In order to make a single element into a set, simply put the brackets around the constant value or the variable name.

```
Vowels := Vowels + ['Y'];
Which := Which + [Ch];
```

The only operator for use with set elements is the IN operator. In this case, the first operand *must* be an element of the base type of the set, and the second operand *must* be a set.

3. **Attempting to read or write a set variable.** It is necessary to read or write sets element by element, assuming the elements are standard types that can be read or written, like integers or characters. The algorithm in Programming Example 16.2 shows how to write all of the values of a set.

SUMMARY

Although it is possible to write programs and never need to use a SET or a nontext file, these data structures can make certain types of data handling much easier. In Pascal, variables of a FILE type can be declared. Every file variable has a **file buffer variable** associated with it. If the file is of type Text, the file buffer for an input file contains the next character or next component to be read. The standard procedures Get and Put can be used with the file buffer to simulate the actions of Read and Write, respectively. It is possible to parameterize procedures that read and write data by sending a file parameter into the procedures. Whenever a file variable is sent into a procedure, it must be sent as a variable parameter. The standard procedures and functions Readln, Writeln, and Eoln are not defined on files of structured types (nontext files).

The SET type in Pascal mirrors the concept of a set in mathematics. A **set** is an unordered collection of **elements** or members. In Pascal, we can declare sets of any simple type, as long as the maximum number of elements in the set is less than or equal to the implementation-dependent limit. Set variables may be assigned values, and may be manipulated using the set operations + (set union), * (set intersection), and − (set difference). Each of these operations must be given two sets as the operands. All of the relational operators are defined between sets. In addition, the IN operator takes an element and a set type and tells whether the element is in the set.

New Terms

file buffer variable	intersection	Get
set	set difference	Put
elements	FILE	IN
union	FILE OF Text	SET

EXERCISES

1. Write appropriate type and variable declarations for the following set variables, and initialize the sets to the proper values.

   a. LowNums   the nonnegative numbers less than 25
   b. Odds   the nonnegative odd numbers less than 25
   c. Primes   the prime numbers less than 25
   d. EvenPrimes   the set difference of the Primes and Odds
   e. Evens   the nonnegative nonodd numbers less than 25
   f. Days   the names of the days of the week
   g. Weekdays   a subset of Days
   h. Colors   all the colors that you can think of
   i. Rainbow   a subset of Colors

2. Write procedures to print values of set variables of the three different set types declared in the previous problem.

3. Write a program that formats text on a page. The program should take an input file with text and commands, and format the text according to the commands. The program should

justify text, or insert spaces between words and after punctuation so that both right and left margins are even. Example:

```
Write  a  program  that  formats  text  on  a  page.  The  program
should   take   an   input   file   with   text   and   commands,   and
format   the   text   according   to   the   commands.   The   program
should at least  be  able  to  justify  text,  by  inserting  spaces
between   words   and   after   punctuation   so   that   both   right
and  left  margins  are  even.
```

The program should also be able to read commands to set the left margin, the right margin, the page size, and the spacing (single, double, or triple). The commands will all contain a period in the first column of text on a line.

. LM 10	left margin set to column 10
. RM 70	right margin set to column 70
. PS 56	56 lines per page
. SP 2	double spacing

You could extend this to deal with centering titles, skipping lines, or turning off the justification.

4. Write a program that reads two files of records, merges them, eliminates duplication, and writes a third file. Assume one file is sorted, so you could use a binary search to find occurrences of the records of the unsorted file in the sorted file.

5. Telephone or satellite communications often pick up random noise, which enters the stream of data. To eliminate random noise from a file, three versions of the file were transmitted. Write a program that reads all three versions of the file character by character and produces a fourth file, which is the majority vote of the other three. In the unlikely event that all three files disagree on a particular character, give the context and give the user a chance to decide.

6. Write a function called `Size`, which takes a set variable as a parameter and returns the number of elements in the set. Will this work for any set variable? Why or why not?

7. Rewrite the dating program that begins on page 436. Instead of using an array of booleans to build an individual's responses to any given question, use a set. Write a function that determines how many elements are in a set of this type. Evaluate a couple's compatibility by comparing the ratio of the intersection of their response sets to the union of their response sets for each question. If they have close to the same number of elements in both the union and intersection, then they are a good match on that particular question. Determine a consistent scoring algorithm that makes use of this fact.

8. Write a program that colors a map in such a way that no two territories that share a common boundary are the same color. The input file will be a list of each territory's neighboring territories. For example, if the input file begins:

```
2 3
1 3 7
1 2 8
```

territory number 1 shares a boundary with territories 2 and 3, and so forth. The output should indicate the color that each territory must be. Four colors should be enough to color any map, but your algorithm may not be efficient enough to find the solution.

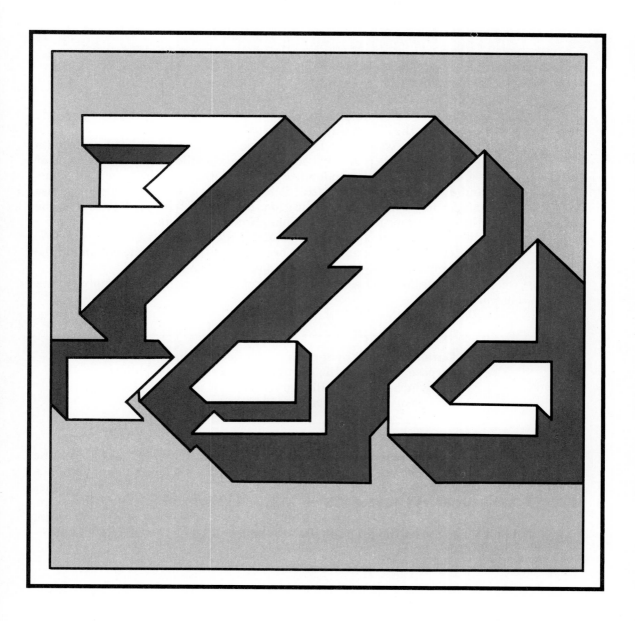

WRITING AND DOCUMENTING LARGE PROGRAMS

If, after finishing this first programming course in Pascal, you go on to write useful programs, the chances are good that they will be longer than most of the programs you have written so far. You have seen the power of Pascal's data structure, and you have probably become aware of applications for your home or business. Because of the expandability and flexibility of both the control structures and data structures, in Pascal it is easy to write tailor-made data base programs for any conceivable application. Because of the specific needs of the users, these programs are often very long. However, long programs can be written methodically and in a way that makes debugging a fairly quick process. We will break down the program-writing process into two parts, the writing of the control structure and the writing of the data structure.

This discussion applies to many types of programs, and not simply to data base programs.

> **Data base (DB) program:** Any program whose chief purpose is to organize, manipulate, search, and sort data, and which has the ability to receive new data and print out listings of stored data.

DB programs can perform simple calculations, but their main purpose is the organization of data. A program that generates address lists or mailing labels or a telephone book would be an example of a DB program. Other examples include a library card catalogue program, a stock portfolio program, a grading program for teachers, a college selection program, a grocery inventory program, and a computer dating program. For each of these examples, the bulk of information about the problem is stored in the data bases, which the control structures manipulate.

Data Structure and Stepwise Refinement

In a data base program, designing the data structure is usually one of the most important parts of the program design. A good data structure can save a lot of time and code by making data easy to find and manipulate. For example, here are two possible data structures for an address list.

```
TYPE     Person1 = RECORD
                 Name : Word;
                 Address : AddressType;
         END;

         List1 = ARRAY [1..Max] OF Person1;

         Person2 = RECORD
                 FName, LName : NameType;
                 Address : AddressType;
                 ZIP : ZipType;
         END;

         List2 = RECORD
                 Lis : ARRAY [1..Max] OF Person2;
                 Len : Integer;
         END;
```

These two record structures store the same amount and type of information. Each stores a person's name and address. However, the second structure is probably better. Why? Because specific information is easier to access. When you are writing your data structure, think about the types of things you are going to want to do with it. You will probably want to be able to sort the array somehow. How will you sort it? In the second data structure, the last name is separated from the first name, which facilitates sorting the list alphabetically by last names. If two last names are the same, we can go to the first names. With only one data structure for the name, it would be difficult because finding the last name wouldn't be simple. Or, if the last name occurred first in the array, then writing out the first name followed by the last name would be difficult.

We should note a second change between the first and second versions: the second version contains space for the ZIP code that is separate from and supplemental to the address, which also contains the ZIP code. The separate space for the ZIP code is designed entirely for sorting. Suppose we want to sort the list by town or location. The easiest way to do this is to sort ZIP codes. This will ensure that the names of all people in the same area will appear together on the list. This is another example of letting the applications determine and refine the data structure.

In general, determining the data structure will be a multistep process. Refinement will continue as you write the procedures that will manipulate the data structure. The advantages of using records for the individual components will soon become very clear as the data structure grows in complexity and size.

As an example of data structure refinement, let's create the data structure for a grading program for a class of students. At the first level of refinement, we have:

```
TYPE    Class = RECORD
```

Now let's think of all the types of information we will want to store in this class.

```
TYPE    Class = RECORD
                Name : Word; (* name of the class *)
                Instructor : Word; (* instructor's name *)
                NumStudents : Integer;
                Students : StudentArray;
        END;
```

Since we will have many students, we'll need to declare an array that will hold each student's data.

```
StudentArray = ARRAY [1..MaxStuds] OF Student;
```

For each student we will need to know a hodgepodge of information, so chances are good that the record structure is the way to go.

```
TYPE    Student = RECORD
                FName, LName : Word;
                Scores : ScoreArray;
                Total : Real;
                Grade : GradeType;
        END;
```

This is a good start. We need to declare `ScoreArray`, which shouldn't be too hard once we decide if the scores will be entered as integers or as real numbers. Let's opt for integers right now; we can change it if we must.

```
TYPE    ScoreType = Integer; (* for ease of changing *)
        ScoreArray = ARRAY [1..MaxScores] OF ScoreType;
```

This looks like it may hold us for a while. We can wait to decide on `Word` and `GradeType` later; they are not crucial to the shape of the data structure. Here is what we have so far.

```
        ScoreType = Integer; (* for ease of changing *)
        ScoreArray = ARRAY [1..MaxScores] OF ScoreType;
        Student = RECORD
                FName, LName : Word;
                Scores : ScoreArray;
                Total : Real;
                Grade : GradeType;
```

```
      END;
      Class = RECORD
              Name : Word; (* name of the class *)
              Instructor : Word; (* instructor's name *)
              NumStudents : Integer;
              Students : StudentArray;
      END;
```

Now, as we begin to write the code, we'll spot some problems. How should the `Total` be calculated? Should each score be worth the same percentage of the final grade? Will all tests have a maximum of 10 points? 100? Perhaps we should add some more fields to the class record.

```
Class = RECORD
        Name, Instructor : Word;
        NumStudents : Integer;
        Students : StudentArray;
        MaxValues : ScoreArray; (* maximum value for
                                             each score *)
        Weighting : ScoreArray; (* %weight for each score *)
END;
```

These additions make weighted averaging possible; instructors can weight assignments differently.

It might occur to us to add another feature, a class rank for each student. Because we will be able to calculate each student's total, we can sort the students by total from highest to lowest to obtain class ranks for every student. Class ranks could aid in grade determination.

```
      Student = RECORD
              FName, LName : Word;
              Scores : ScoreArray;
              Total : Real;
              Rank : Integer;
              Grade : GradeType;
      END;
```

The point of this exercise is to demonstrate how a large and useful data structure may be built up from an increasing understanding of the problem. You will notice how the development of a data structure parallels the top-down development of the code, the strategy we have been employing throughout the text. Some aspects of the needs of the data structure may be obvious immediately; others will become apparent only after outlining the control structure. Usually, when the code dealing with a certain data structure becomes clumsy and convoluted, it is time to reevaluate the data structure. Often, refinements can greatly simplify the code.

One final advantage to having one huge record containing all the various pieces of information needed for the problem: parameter passing is easy. There are no extraneous variables to pass around, just one huge record that contains everything. When parts of the structure, such as one student's record or one set of scores, are being examined, these can be sent out. In the larger procedures, the entire structure can be passed as a parameter very neatly.

Finally, the question of permanent data storage becomes important. With all of the data in this huge data base, it will be necessary to store the data in a permanent structure for use at a later time. A file will be necessary. The size of the file and requirements of the program will help you determine what type of file is necessary, a text file or perhaps a file of a structured type. As your data structure grows, the importance and convenience of structured files increase.

SELF TEST
Design a data structure for use in a data base program used by a travel agent to book airline reservations. Think about the different data needed and choose the best way to organize the data.

Control Structures and Stepwise Refinement

No matter how much interpretation is stored in the data structure, the control statement of your large programs will no doubt be extensive. Because of the emphasis on procedures and procedural breakdown, you have been writing programs with many short procedures. That is good, and you should continue to do so. One temptation when writing long programs is to write long procedures. *A long procedure in a long program may be worse and more difficult to read than a long procedure in a short program.*

Often the most difficult part of writing a huge program is knowing how to begin. It may even be difficult to write the main program without spending a little time thinking about what it is going to do. Rather than trying to write a main program or pseudocode first, spend some time brainstorming the types of things your program will be doing with the data structure you currently have in mind. For example, will you be

sorting? by name? total amount? score? ZIP code? call number?
searching? by name? by subject? by author? by index number?
reading a list from an input file?
writing a list to an output file or terminal?
reading an item from the terminal?
summing? averaging? performing other calculations?
adding and deleting items in a list?
copying items from a list?
transferring items in a list?
printing a histogram?
charting or graphing values?
altering fields within a record?
correcting or updating records?

For each action you want your program to carry out, give a one-word name to that action and a three- or four-line description of the action. The word will quite possibly become a procedure name, and the description a procedure comment.

Assigning action names and descriptions is crucial and should not be over-looked. It is through this process that we really begin to understand what our program is going to do. As we write out the comments, fuzzy thinking is revealed. If we can write precise comments for each action or procedure, then we are a long way toward the solution of the problem. Examples:

> SumScores: This procedure takes each student's scores and calculates a weighted average for each student. This is done by summing, for each score, Score/MaxScore * Weighting. The final Total has a maximum of 100, since the weights are in percentages (10 percent, for example). The procedure returns the class of students with totals calculated for each student.
>
> SortByAuthor: This procedure sorts a list of books by the name of the author. Last names appear first, and capitalization is ignored. The procedure returns the sorted list.

Once the rough breakdown has occurred, it is time to think of a global control structure to pass off control to each of the various procedures. As mentioned, a CASE statement inside an indefinite loop works very well because it is an expandable control structure in much the same way as a record is an expandable data structure. At any time in the future, new commands may be added and the CASE expanded.

```
REPEAT
        Prompt;
        Command : = GetCommand;
        CASE Command OF
                'A' : Append (...);
                'C' : Change (...);
                . . .
        END;
UNTIL (Com = 'Q');
```

This command-oriented control structure implements a menu from which the user is allowed to pick commands and actions. The menu is common and is used in sophisticated software packages today because of the flexibility and expandability it affords the programmer. The commands needn't be limited to one letter; they might be declared as an enumerated type. The procedure Get-Command can be as simple as reading a character or number or as complicated as necessary to allow the programmer to type words or phrases as commands. Often, certain commands may take an argument; the possibilities for increasing complexity are endless.

SELF
TEST

Write a main program control structure for the airline reservation program mentioned on page 502. Does thinking about the procedures necessary to complete this program change or add to your understanding of the data structure required? How?

The Trade-Off: Control and Data Structures

In any problem, a trade-off exists between the amount of information stored in the data structure and the amount of information stored in the control structure. Although we don't often think about information being stored in a control structure, information is stored there. When we have a problem to solve, the data—the numbers, names, facts, and dates—usually go into the data structure. This needn't be the case. We could write a program to sum and average the scores of a class of students that uses no data structure at all. The program would be ugly and very inefficient to write or modify. For example:

```
PROGRAM AverageScores (Output);
BEGIN
        Writeln (Output, 'The average is'
                (92 + 45 + 73 + 89 + 100 + 37 +
                41 + 33 + 71 + 68 + 95 + 78 +
                49 + 51 + 67 + 93 + 44 + 68 + 54 +
                98 + 21 + 33 + 44 + 68 + 54 + 37 +
                41 + 33 + 17 + 95 + 90 + 50)/32:1:1);
    END.
```

No variables were used. In a sense, all the data were stored in the code itself. *This is a foolish way to write programs.*

On the other hand, we often think that the rules we use to help us process the data should go into the control structure. This is true for most programs, like the correct version of AverageScores:

```
PROGRAM AverageScores (Input, Output);
VAR Score, Sum, NumScores : Integer;
BEGIN
        Sum := 0; NumScores := 0;
        WHILE NOT Eof (Input) DO BEGIN
                NumScores := NumScores + 1;
                Read (Input, Score);
                Sum := Sum + Score;
        END;
        Writeln (Output, 'The average is', Sum/NumScores:1:1);
    END.
```

The data are stored in the variables, but the manipulations needed to achieve the desired result are stored in the code: the WHILE loop, increasing NumScores by increments, the summing statement, and the calculation for the average.

However, in some cases, it makes sense for the data structure to hold more data so that the control structure is easier to write. Examine the following two definitions of type Word and the corresponding ease with which they are used in the procedure WriteWord.

```
(* The first definition of Word *)
TYPE    Word = ARRAY [1..MaxChars] OF Char;

PROCEDURE WriteWord (VAR OutFile: Text; W : Word);
VAR     i : Integer;
BEGIN                      (* Assume W padded with spaces*)
        i := 1;
        WHILE (W[I] <> ' ') DO BEGIN
                Write (OutFile, W[i]);
                i := i + 1;
        END;
END;


(* The second definition of Word *)
TYPE    Word = RECORD
                Txt : ARRAY [1..MaxChars] OF Char;
                Len : Integer;
        END;

PROCEDURE WriteWord (VAR OutFile : Text; W : Word);
VAR i : Integer;
BEGIN
        FOR i := 1 to W.Len DO
                Write (OutFile, W.Txt[i]);
END;
```

The second procedure is a lot more straightforward because of the inclusion in the data structure of the length of the word. In general, this is a good programming trick. If you have an array that will have a variable number of filled locations, put it inside a record whose other field is the number of filled locations. This facilitates checking for a full array. This also demonstrates how it may be possible to improve the efficiency and readability of your code by selectively increasing the amount of information stored in the data structure. We could get carried away and write a program that has *all* the information about the problem in the data structure. This is essentially what a Pascal compiler or interpreter is—a set of programs whose input file (the Pascal program) contains all the information about the problem and whose output is the solution of the problem. This is the extreme. Hopefully, we won't have to write our own Pascal compiler, so we can stop short of this end of the spectrum.

Programming Example 17.1

Assignment: Write a general data base manager program. It should be general enough to allow the user to create a record structure and to name the fields in each record. It should handle text as well as numeric fields. It should be able to do most of the things in the list on page 502.

Solution: This is going to be a big project. When this program is finished, it could be put on a floppy disk and sold for lots of money, because people all over the country are beginning to use programs like this in their businesses. We will not write the entire program, because we have already done much of the necessary programming. After we have written a major outline of the data and control structures, the rest should be fairly routine.

Let's think a little about the data structure first. The first place to begin would be at the top.

```
TYPE    DBArray = ARRAY [1..MaxRecords] OF RecType;
```

Now all we have to decide is what one record looks like. In general, a single record is going to look more like an array than a record, because it simply contains a number of identically structured fields—the fields will look different once they receive values. This is true because we want the user of the program, and not the programmer, to decide what the fields will be called and how they will be formatted. Suppose, for example, that each RecType were simply an array of FieldRecs, where we define FieldRec as a variant record. The type of data we want to store in each field determines the values that the record will hold.

```
TYPE    ...
        FieldRec = RECORD
            Name : Word;
            Size : Integer;
            CASE Which : FieldType OF
                Txt :       (W : Word);
                Numeric :   (Value : Real);
                Formula :   (W : Word; Value : Real);
                Bool :      (Value : Boolean);
        END;

        RecType = ARRAY [1..MaxFields] OF FieldRec;
```

This obviously demands a type declaration for FieldType, which will be an enumerated type. We can also look into the definition of Word, a simple record structure.

```
TYPE      Word = RECORD
              Txt : ARRAY [1..MaxChar] OF Char;
              Len : Integer;
          END;

          FieldType = (Txt, Numeric, Formula, Bool);
```

The list for `FieldType` results from thinking a little while about possible applications. One nice feature, besides simply storing numbers and words, is to store formulas, using other fields in the record and calculating values of complex expressions. For example, if there are fields in the record for scores, there might be another field in the record that always contains the sum of all the scores. This type of program feature is used extensively in spread-sheet programs for microcomputers. Perhaps not immediately but at some time in the future it might be fun to add this capability to our data base program.

Another feature is the ability to store boolean data. This is especially useful when selecting a portion of the records in the data base. Depending on the particular usage, a boolean field could be used to indicate that a book is checked out or overdue in a library, or to indicate in a club's newsletter data base whether a person is an active member of an organization.

At this point we have a fairly good idea of the data structure we will use. We may find that more modifications of the data structure are necessary later, but it should be easy to do that when the need arises. It is easier to think through the data structure of an all-purpose data base program after having written some data base programs for specific uses.

The next step is to outline some of the basic tasks that we want our data base program to perform. We can begin this outline after outlining the data structure only because we knew when we wrote the data structure what we would need to accomplish. Now we must specify those main tasks and briefly outline the subtasks involved in performing each task. For example, one main task that any data base program needs to accomplish is the reading and altering of data. This is a large task that can be broken down into smaller subtasks that should be able to execute independently of one another. The following are command names and brief command summaries for most of the reading and altering commands.

Structure   used to initialize field names and sizes. Structure allows the
              user to specify the structure at the terminal or directs the computer
              to read the structure from a file.
ReadData   used to read records into an array for random access, quick
              changes, and updates. The user can enter the data for each record at
              the terminal or direct the compiler to read from a file of records.
Append   used to allow the user to append a single record to the existing
              data base.

Delete   used to delete a single record or multiple records from the data base array. Does not change any file of records unless the array is written to the file. Verifies the intention of the user before deleting.

Alter   used to alter the values in a single record or multiple records. Prompts the user for each field or allows the user to specify which fields are to be altered.

Modify   used to modify the structure of one or all of the records in a file, changing the names, sizes, or types of the fields in any or all of the records.

In order to add a little more organization to this program, we will call the procedures used to implement these commands Module 1.

Module: A group of related and often dependent procedures and functions in a program.

A module is usually not an entire program but a large segment of the program that is grouped as a single logical unit.

Another necessary set of operations is composed of those operations required to print the data base to a terminal or to an output file. Furthermore, we are going to want to have a variable format because the same program may be used to make invoices and address labels. A library data base program may be used to print catalogue cards indexed by subject, or author, or title; the format would be different in each case. The following list gives a few of the printing commands, which we frame together as Module 2.

DefineFormat   used to store information that enables the computer to print each record. DefineFormat specifies the "template" that the printer will use when printing each record. For example, the user could define the following template for an address label.

```
<Title> <First Name> <Last Name>
<Address>
<City>, <State> <ZIP Code>
```

Browse   used to allow the user to examine the contents of individual or multiple records using either sequential or random access.

Print   used to print individual records, portions of the data base, or the entire data base, using any defined template or printing format.

These procedures cover the basics of getting data into the data base, changing it, and getting it out. But other things can be done with the data base as well. One main task would involve reordering the data base, or selecting a subset of the data base for inspection, printing, or other tasks. Module 3 contains these procedures:

Select   used to trim down the full data base to consider subsets of the whole. For example, it could be used to select all of the records where the last name begins with a C, or where the call number is between HA0040 and HA0065, or where the Smoker flag is TRUE.

Search   used to find an individual record in the array. It could implement a binary search if the array is sorted by the appropriate key, otherwise, it implements a sequential search. Any field in the record could be used as the key. Multiple searches on the same key move sequentially through the list, eventually finding all occurrences of the desired key.

Sort   used to sort the array of records by any field in the record or even by multiple fields. For example, when last names are the same, the sort will encompass the first name. The sort will be alphabetical or numerical, depending on the field type of the key. Sort allows both low-to-high sorts and high-to-low sorts.

Merge   used to merge two sorted files of records and to create a third file, which is in the correct order. Will compare any field as the sort key, but if the files are not sorted beforehand, the merged file will not be sorted.

If we are able to implement all of these facilities, then we really have a useful program. However, after these are implemented, we will probably think about more powerful utilities, especially in the areas of manipulation and format. Module 4 contains these utility procedures:

Calculate   used to calculate sums, averages, standard deviations, and so forth which use the numerical data in the data base.

Histogram   used to create a histogram of the values in any selected numeric field from either part of or the entire array of records.

Index   used to generate and print an index of the array of records, using any field as the key. Could be used to generate author, title, and subject indices, for example.

At this point, we are probably ready to begin writing pseudocode. Notice that we have done a lot of work to clarify and understand the problem before we begin even to write pseudocode. The pseudocode for the main program is:

DataBase Manager:
    Introduce program
IF the user wants help, give help

> Loop until the user quits:
> > Read a command
> > Execute command
> Conclude session

Obviously, the bulk of the work will be in Execute command. This will, no doubt, be simply a CASE statement with a lot of procedure calls. The values the case expression assumes will be the values returned by the GetCommand procedure, possibly characters or enumerated types. Perhaps at the beginning it is just as easy to write GetCommand so that it returns the commands as character variables, and change it to allow more mnemonic command names later. What happens when commands like Append and Alter or Search, Select, and Sort begin with the same letter?

Without getting into the specifics of how a command is going to be given, let's look at an example of a command procedure to see how this type of procedure will be structured. We will examine the procedure Structure, which initializes field names and sizes and allows the user to specify the structure at the terminal or directs the computer to read the structure from a file. A simple pseudocode version of what we have described is:

> Structure:
> > Determine from what file to read the structure
> > IF from input file
> > > THEN read entire structure
> > > ELSE prompt user for structure

This simple outline converts quickly to Pascal, although the bulk of the work remains in the two new procedures it calls.

```
BEGIN
        Writeln (TermOut,  'Do you want to structure the',
                           ' data base at the terminal');
        Writeln (TermOut, 'or from a file? (T, F, or A',
                           ' to Abort command)');
        Readln (TermIn, Ans);
        Ans := Cap (Ans);
        IF (Ans='F')
            THEN GetFileStruct (Struc)
            ELSE IF (Ans='T')
                THEN GetTermStruct (Struc)
                ELSE Writeln (TermOut, 'Command aborted.');
END;
```

So it is necessary to turn to GetFileStruct and GetTermStruct. Get-FileStruc is fairly easy, because we will assume that the file the structure is sitting in is a FILE OF RecType. Therefore, once we read the file name and open the file for reading using Reset, then we can simply read the entire structure with a single Read statement.

```
PROCEDURE GetFileStruct (VAR Struct : RecType);
(* used to read the record structure from a file     *)
(* rather than from the terminal.                    *)
VAR     FileName : Word;           (* read from terminal *)
        StrucFile : FILE OF RecType;
BEGIN
        Writeln (TermOut, 'What is the file name ',
                          'containing the structure?');
        ReadWord (TermIn, FileName);
        Reset (StrucFile, FileName.Txt);
        Read (StrucFile, Struct);
END;    (* GetFileStruct *)
```

In writing large programs, it is very easy to misplace small procedures that are used in other procedures. GetFileStruct is an example of a small procedure that will only be used by Structure. Therefore, we will declare GetFileStruct as a subprocedure of Structure. We have used subprocedures before, although with shorter programs it probably isn't necessary. However, this program, when completed, may have more than 100 procedures in it. If we don't nest some of those procedures, then reading the program will be difficult.

The next procedure we need to write, which again will be a subprocedure of Structure, is GetTermStruct. This procedure will not be as easy to write as the previous one, and so we should take time to outline it.

> GetTermStruct:
> Explain to user how to quit the loop
> Loop until record is filled or user wants to quit:
> Prompt for field name
> Prompt for field size
> Prompt for field type

We must design a way to allow the user to leave the loop before all fields have received name, size, and type. One cumbersome way to do this is to ask whether the user is finished after every field. A more elegant method allows the user to quit simply by typing a blank line when there are no more fields to be entered. In order to do this, the first prompt must be given before the loop test is executed, and then the test for end of line can be made. If the user typed anything, then it will be read as usual. If not, the loop will terminate. Here is the Pascal version of this algorithm:

```
PROCEDURE GetTermStruct (VAR Struct : RecType);
(* used to read from the terminal the record         *)
(* structure for the desired implementation.         *)
VAR     FieldCntr : Integer;      (* FOR loop counter  *)
```

```
BEGIN
    Writeln (TermOut, 'You will be prompted by field',
                    ' numbers. Enter a blank line for');
    Writeln (TermOut, 'the field name when you are',
                    ' finished. ');
    FieldCntr := 1;
    WITH Struct DO BEGIN
        Writeln (TermOut, 'Field No. 1 Name==>');
        WHILE (FieldCntr<MaxFields) AND
            NOT Eoln (TermIn) DO BEGIN
            WITH Fields [FieldCntr] DO BEGIN
                ReadWord (TermIn, Name);
                Writeln (TermOut, 'Size (#)==>');
                Readln (TermIn, Size);
                GetFieldType (FieldCntr, Which);
                FieldCntr := FieldCntr + 1;
                Writeln (TermOut, 'Field No. ',
                        FieldCntr:1, ' Name==>');
            END;
        END;
        NumFields := FieldCntr - 1;
    END;
END;      (* GetTermStruc *)
```

This procedure is straightforward and is simple to read and write, with the exception of GetFieldType, which does for a variable of FieldType what ReadWord does for a variable of type Word. Notice that the WITH statement helps keep the variable names short and enables us to group statements around a particular record variable.

GetFieldType looks like the version of GetCommand that you have seen before. Because enumerated types cannot be read from a text file, it is necessary to have the user type characters, which are then converted via the CASE statement to values of FieldType.

```
PROCEDURE GetFieldType (Cntr : Integer;
                        VAR Which : FieldType);
(* This procedure is used by the GetTermStruct to read*)
(* the field type of each individual FieldRec.         *)
VAR    Ch : Char;
BEGIN
    Writeln (TermOut, 'Field No. ', Cntr:1, ' Type?',
                    'T, N, F, B or H for Help');
    Readln (TermIn, Ch);
    WHILE NOT (Ch IN ['T', 'N', 'F', 'B']) DO BEGIN
        IF (Ch <> 'H')
            THEN Writeln (TermOut, 'Illegal response');
        HelpFieldTypes;
        Writeln (TermOut, 'Field No. ', Cntr:1,' Type?',
                    'T, N, F, B or H for Help');
```

```
        Readln (TermIn, Ch);
    END;
    CASE Ch OF
        'T' : Which := Txt;
        'N' : Which := Numeric;
        'F' : Which := Formula;
        'B' : Which := Bool;
    END
END;
```

Again, because we have continually broken down the procedures into short fragments, it is easy to see what is going on here. HelpFieldTypes is a simple procedure that writes information about the possible field types and how to respond appropriately.

As you can tell, this is going to be a long program. But most of the procedures, when broken down carefully, will be straightforward. You may want to get fancy and add terminal graphics, using a set of procedures that put text anywhere you want on the screen. But the read and write procedures are little different than the read and write procedures we have written previously. The sorting and searching procedures will be a little more complicated because they are now sorting and searching any of the fields in the record. But through the use of variables, one procedure should be able to search or sort for any key in any field. Figure 17.1 shows the module tree for DataBaseManager.

Common Errors and Debugging

1. **Writing program code without thinking about data structure at all.** This can lead to very sloppy code, and you won't rely on the data structure enough to solve the problem. Spend some time thinking about all the information you have to solve the current problem. Which of it should be in the data structure? How should it be organized? Which should go in the control structure? How should that be broken down?

2. **Writing program pseudocode that specifies data structure too soon.** Early in the problem-solving process, your procedural breakdown and rough pseudocode should not depend on the fine details of your data structure. It is while you are writing these procedure outlines that you refine your ideas about data structure. Suppose you received a brainstorm and totally reorganized your data structure. How much work would be wasted? Not too much if you tackle data structure after some procedural breakdown.

3. **Casting data structures in concrete.** You may find that you are having to write several gruesome procedures in order to deal with your pet data structure. Perhaps the procedure is not to blame; it may be time to change your data

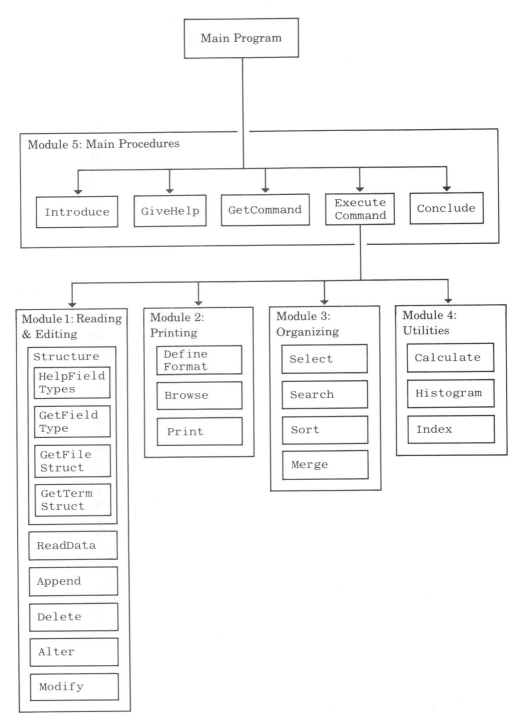

Figure 17.1: Module Tree for DataBaseManager

structure. This is often the case when it seems as if you need several extra variables to handle one procedure's task. Perhaps all of the hassle can be eliminated by adding one more field in the record, or by removing an enumerated type. Be willing to evolve; it is the secret to survival.

4. **Writing code without writing comments.** This is probably the most common programming error in the world, and one of the most fatal, in the long run. Everyone is guilty of this at times, even teachers and authors of programming textbooks. When you sit down to write a program, the purpose of each procedure and variable may be clear to you at the time, but you never know when you'll work on it or modify it. Even a week later, everything begins to fade in your memory, and reconstructing your original intent may be difficult. Furthermore, the comment is one of the most underrated programming tools—it can be useful to you as you attempt to clarify the problem.

SUMMARY

Some of the most useful types of programs on the microcomputer market are the extremely flexible data base programs, which organize and manipulate large quantities of structured data for a wide variety of uses. In any large program and especially in data base programs, the manner in which the data is structured plays an important role in the ease with which the program handles the data and performs its task.

The problem of designing a data structure that efficiently contains all the relevant data is not unlike that of designing an algorithm for solving a problem. The design will probably be a multistep refinement process, for the data structure will alter as the problem and the process of solving it becomes better understood.

The breakdown of a large problem into smaller tasks and subtasks that are easily solved is the advantage of stepwise refinement. Before you write any Pascal code, and often before you write even a detailed outline of the main program, you should give tasks and subtasks precise English descriptions. This ensures that you understand what you are trying to accomplish with each of the procedures that you will eventually call and write. A useful means of organizing the control structures in large programs is to group the procedures into **modules,** which contain related procedure and function declarations. Another means to program organization is to nest procedures by declaring specific procedures as subprocedures of the procedures that use them.

For any given problem, a trade-off exists between the amount of information stored in the data structure and that stored in the control structure. The goal of data-structure design is to produce a data structure that has enough information to ensure a simple, elegant control structure without the data structure becoming cumbersome or inefficient.

New Terms

data base program	module

EXERCISES

1. Write a pseudocode outline for a chess program with an accompanying data structure. If you don't know chess, consider any board game: backgammon, checkers, even tic-tac-toe. What types of information that are not normally represented on the board (the "data structure") might serve better as part of the data structure than as part of the control structure? Write the pseudocode for the main control structure and include comments for each of the procedures it calls.

2. Write a pseudocode main program, data structure, and procedure comments for a grocer's inventory program. Brainstorm the type of data needed and the best way to handle it. The program should alert the grocer when inventory is low, allow price comparisons of different brands of the same item, and allow the grocer to calculate amount owed to any or all of the wholesalers that supplied the goods.

3. Write a pseudocode main program, data structure, and procedure comments to store statistics. Pick statistics about your favorite sport; the stock market; TV programs; medical, law, or business school admissions; life support systems; or statistics about a field that interests you. Propose a data structure and a control structure that will read independent values and calculate all dependent values. Calculate means and standard deviations where appropriate and useful.

4. Take the data structure and control structure outlines given in the programming example in this chapter and finish enough of the procedures to yield a limited but working general-purpose data base management program. How did your data structure or control structure evolve as you learned more about the tasks and the problems inherent in them?

5. Pick one of the outlines of problems 1 through 3 and write the complete program. Did you need to alter your proposed data structure as you wrote your program? Were there parts of your control structure that could be simplified by adding complexity to your data structure?

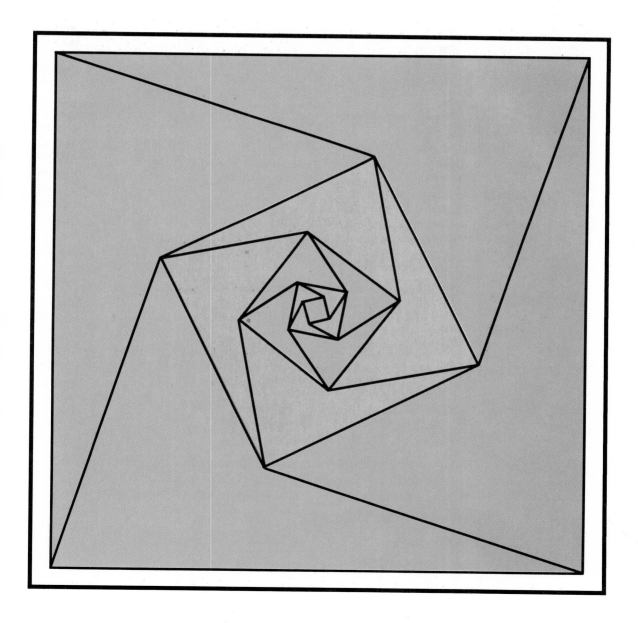

RECURSION

The most common type of control structure we have used in this book (except for procedures) has been some sort of looping structure: the FOR, WHILE, or REPEAT loops. This is not surprising. In general, doing things repeatedly is where the computer excels. Once a program is written to make one calculation, it can make 10,000 calculations in relatively little additional time. The way we have chosen to repeat segments of code is through a strategy called iteration, introduced in Chapter 7. Iterative repetition is not the only form of repetition, however. We can also use **recursion** to execute statements repeatedly. Let me give you an example by defining recursion.

> **Recursion:** The process of defining statements recursively.

You might complain about this definition because it violates the normal rules of definition; it uses a form of the defined word in the definition. However, this is exactly what recursion is all about.

Single Procedure Recursion

To help demonstrate the difference between iteration and recursion, let's look at another example. Suppose we want a mathematical algorithm to calculate any X^n, where X is any real number, and n is a nonnegative integer exponent. X^n means

$$X^n = \underbrace{X \times X \times X \ldots \times X}_{n \text{ times}}$$

If we were writing an iterative solution, we would write:

```
FUNCTION Power (X : Real; N : Integer) : Real
VAR     Result : Real;
BEGIN
        Result := 1.0;
        FOR i := 1 TO N DO
                Result:= X * Result;
        Power := Result;

END;
```

The value of Result is the value we are looking for, X^n. However, we could think of the problem in a different way altogether. Our desire is to calculate X^n. If we knew the value of X^{n-1}, then we could simply multiply X^{n-1} by X to find the value of X^n.

$$X^n = X \times X^{n-1}$$

This algorithm can be stated formally as:

$$X^n = 1, \text{ if } n = 0$$
$$X^n = X \times X^{n-1}, \text{ if } n > 0$$

This algorithm can be encoded into Pascal as:

```
FUNCTION Power (X : Real; N : Integer) : Real;
BEGIN
        IF (N = 0)
                THEN Power := 1.0
                ELSE Power := X*Power (X, N-1);
END;
```

The recursion enters into the definition of Power in that the function may call itself in order to calculate the result. The fact that this executes many multiplications for a large N is not obvious because no iterative looping mechanism is being used. However, as many multiplications occur in the recursive solution of Power as in the iterative solution. Let's look in detail at how it works. Suppose we want to write out the value of 5^3. We can see this calculated as follows:

```
Writeln (Output, Power (5.0,3));
```

The write statement executes a call on the function Power.

```
Level 0: Writeln (Output, ...)
    Level 1: Power (5.0,3) = 5.0*
```

```
        Level 2: Power (5.0,2) = 5.0*
            Level 3: Power (5.0,1) = 5.0*
                Level 4: Power (5.0,0) = 1.0
                Level 3: Power (5.0,1) = 5.0*1.0 = 5.0
            Level 2: Power (5.0,2) = 5.0*5.0 = 25.0
        Level 1: Power (5.0,3) = 5.0*25.0 = 125.0
Level 0: Writeln (Output, 125.0)
```

Therefore, after all the calculations are made, 125.0 is written to the output file. You will notice that each calculation of Power was suspended until the second half of the multiplication had a determined value. After Power (5.0,0) had been calculated, then Power (5.0,1) could be calculated.

What do you suppose the result would be if the line had read:

```
Writeln (Output, Power (5.0, -1));
```

In this case, the calls to Power would look like this.

```
Level 0: Writeln (Output, ...)
    Level 1: Power (5.0,-1) = 5.0 *
        Level 2: Power (5.0,-2) = 5.0 *
            Level 3: Power (5.0,-3) = 5.0 *
                Level 4: Power (5.0,-4) = 5.0 *
                    . . .
```

The recursion never quits, because the terminating condition, N = 0, is never satisfied. It would be necessary to either rewrite the function Power or to ensure that it is never called with a negative value for N.

SELF TEST

Write a function called NegPower, which recursively calculates the correct value for X^n, where X is a real number and n is a negative integer.

Are you beginning to see how recursion works and why it can be useful? After you have gotten into the habit of thinking iteratively, it is sometimes difficult to switch gears. Even if you understand it, the last example might seem stupid because the nonrecursive solution was significantly less complicated. Let's look at a problem where the recursive solution is a lot simpler than the iterative solution. Suppose you are reading in a line of characters and you want to write them out in reverse order. To obtain the iterative solution, you need to implement an array.

```
PROCEDURE Reverse;
CONST    MaxChars = 80;
VAR      Line : ARRAY [1..MaxChars] OF Char;
         I, NumChars: Integer;
```

```
BEGIN
        NumChars : = 0;
        WHILE NOT Eoln (Input) AND
                        (NumChars < MaxChars) DO BEGIN
                NumChars : = NumChars + 1;
                Read (Input, Line [NumChars]);
        END;
        Readln (Input);
        FOR I : = NumChars DOWNTO 1 DO
                Write (Output, Line [I]);
END;
```

This is a fairly straightforward procedure, but long. An easier version of Reverse is:

```
PROCEDURE Reverse; (* reverses a line of type *)
VAR Ch: Char;        (* holds the character at the
                        current level of recursion *)
BEGIN
        Read (Input, Ch);
        IF NOT Eoln (Input) THEN Reverse;
        Write (Output, Ch);
END;
```

Can you convince yourself that this recursive procedure does what it says it can do? Let's examine how the procedure deals with a sample input line.

```
TYPE A LINE > ABC DEFG
Level 0: Call Reverse
   Level 1: Ch = 'A'; not Eoln, call Reverse
     Level 2: Ch = 'B'; not Eoln, call Reverse
       Level 3: Ch = 'C'; not Eoln, call Reverse
         Level 4: Ch = ' '; not Eoln, call Reverse
           Level 5: Ch = 'D'; not Eoln, call Reverse
             Level 6: Ch = 'E'; not Eoln, call Reverse
               Level 7: Ch = 'F'; not Eoln, call Reverse
                 Level 8: Ch = 'G'; Eoln is true; write 'G'
               Level 7: Write 'F'
             Level 6: Write 'E'
           Level 5: Write 'D'
         Level 4: Write ' '
       Level 3: Write 'C'
     Level 2: Write 'B'
   Level 1: Write 'A'
Level 0: done
GFED CBA
```

Two questions for you to consider: In the example above, how many storage spaces were created? How many were created for the iterative solution? With the iterative solution, an entire array was declared, with 80 storage spaces, the maximum number of characters on a line. *In the recursive solution, each call of* Reverse *creates one local character variable.* The procedure was called eight times, so eight local variables were created. The recursion assured that all letters on a line would be read and stored before any were printed out, and then they were printed in reverse order. The use of recursion made Reverse a very simple procedure to write.

A visual way to think about recursion is to see it as stacking and unstacking plates. Each call to the procedure Reverse is like a plate. Each plate has space on it to store one variable, a character. Each time procedure Reverse is called, another plate is set on top of the stack of plates. (See Figure 18.1.) By the time Eoln is reached, there is a stack of as many plates as there are characters on the line. As the procedure calls are completed, the plates are taken off the stack in reverse order until finally the first plate on the stack is removed. (See Figure 18.2.)

How does one go about writing recursive procedures? The process can be broken down into two steps:

Recursion Steps: Every recursive solution involves

1. determining a means of breaking down the problem into one single step and a simpler but similar problem, and
2. determining an end point to the process.

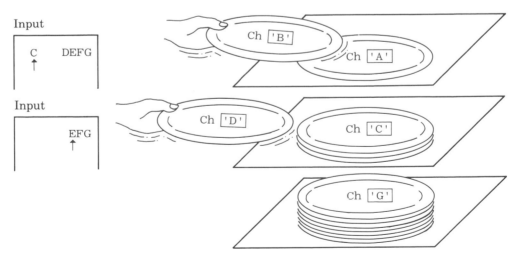

Figure 18.1: Recursive Calls Are Like Stacking Plates

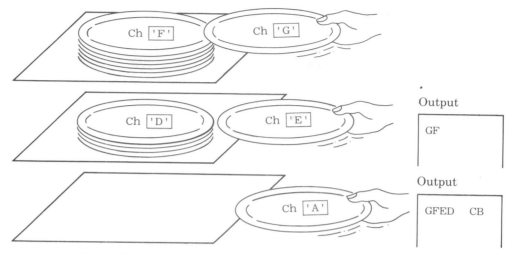

Figure 18.2: Returning From Recursive Calls Is Like Unstacking Plates

The problem breakdown corresponds to the statement

```
Power := x*Power (x,n-1)
```

Here the solution to the original problem is seen as a single multiplication of x and the result of a simpler problem, just as finding the solution to X^{n-1} is simpler than the solution to x^n because it involves one fewer multiplication. The **end point** of the recursion is when n is zero. At this point, the function no longer recurs, and values are returned. Take care to ensure that the simplification makes the end-point condition an inevitability; otherwise, an infinite loop may occur—as we saw in the case of the call Power (5.0, -1). This condition is analogous to conditions for the proper use of a WHILE or REPEAT loop.

SELF TEST

Describe what happens and what should be done about each of the following situations.

1. Write (Power (0.5, -3));
2. FUNCTION Power2 (x: Real; n: Integer): Real;
   BEGIN
           IF (n = 0)
                   THEN Power2 := 1
                   ELSE Power2 := Power2 (x,n);
   END;
3. PROCEDURE Reverse;
   VAR   Ch : Char;

```
BEGIN
        Read (Input, Ch);
        Reverse;
        Write (Output, Ch);
END;
```

As you can see, if the recursive procedure lacks either the end point or the simplification of the problem, the recursion is likely to continue until the computer runs out of memory space or the programmer runs out of patience.

Programming Example 18.1

Assignment: Write a recursive procedure that reads a word into an array, positions the word at the rightmost point, and justifies the preceding text to fit. Assume Eoln ends the word to be read.

Solution: This will look something like the procedure Reverse. The trick is that we won't know in what position to put each character in the array until we read the last character on the line. We could use an interative algorithm.

```
ReadNRightJust:
        Initialize Cntr to 0
        Loop until Eoln:
                Increment Cntr
                Read char into array
        Loop from Cntr down to 1:
                Shift char in array
```

But this interative algorithm wouldn't give us a chance to practice recursion. The recursive algorithm is shorter and simpler, though perhaps not as obvious.

```
ReadNRightJust:
        Read a character
        If Eoln, then initialize index
                Else ReadNRightJust
        Store character
        Decrement index to array
```

The reason this algorithm works is that the index is not initialized until the Eoln marker is reached. At this point, the index is initialized to the maximum index in the array. When the character is stored, it is stored with this index, and then the index decreases by decrements. If Eoln is not reached, then the recursive call is made, and upon the return from the recursive call, the value of the index is calculated from the procedure. To convert this simple algorithm into Pascal:

```
PROCEDURE ReadNRightJust (VAR W : Word;
                          VAR Index : Integer);
(* This procedure reads a word from the input file and   *)
(* stores it in the W array, but it is right justified in *)
(* the array. The procedure is recursive, calling itself  *)
(* until the end of the line is encountered, which         *)
(* signifies the end of the word.                          *)
VAR     Ch : Char;
BEGIN
        Read (Input, Ch);
        IF Eoln (Input)
                THEN Index := MaxChars
                ELSE ReadNRightJust (W, Index);
        W[Index] := Ch;
        Index := Index - 1;
END;
```

Programming Example 18.2

Assignment: Here is the puzzle known as The Tower of Hanoi. In a temple in the town of Hanoi, there were supposedly three poles on a golden platform and 64 disks. Each disk had a hole in the center and each disk was a different size. The Buddhist priests were given the task of moving the 64 disks from one pole to a second pole. The disks had to be on one of the three poles at all times. This doesn't seem like a terribly difficult task, except that the following simple rules must be followed:

1. Only one disk may be moved at a time.
2. A disk must be moved from the *top* of one pole to the *top* of another pole.
3. A larger disk may never be placed on top of a smaller disk.

The assignment is to write a program that would perform the priests' task in a puzzle involving fewer than eight disks. The initial situation for a problem with six disks is shown in Figure 18.3.

Solution: In general, the way to think about moving N disks from pole A to pole C is to break the process down into three steps:

Move N disks from A to C:
    Move the top N-1 disks from A to B

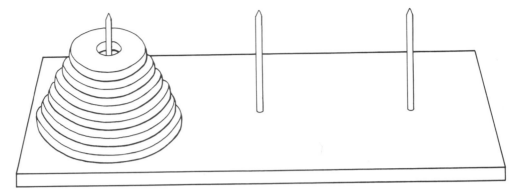

Figure 18.3: The Tower of Hanoi

Move the Nth disk from A to C
    Move the N-1 disks from B to C

This general algorithm will work for any value of *N* greater than 1, to and from any poles A, B, or C. When *N* equals 1, the solution is trivial.

Move N = 1 disks from A to C:
    Move the Nth disk from A to C

This can be programmed if we imagine writing a procedure that will do what is specified in the algorithm above. The main block of the program is simple.

```
BEGIN
        Writeln (Output, 'Welcome to the Tower of Hanoi.');
        Writeln (Output, 'How many disks are there?');
        Readln (Input, NumDisks);
        MoveDisks (NumDisks, 'A', 'C', 'B');
END.
```

PROCEDURE MoveDisks takes four parameters: the number of disks, the "from" pole, the "to" pole, and the extra pole, which will be used for temporary storage. PROCEDURE MoveDisks will write out the move lines one disk or more at a time. Let's look at MoveDisks:

```
PROCEDURE MoveDisks (NumDisks: Integer;
                     Init, Dest, Extra: Char);
BEGIN
        IF (NumDisks = 1) THEN
                Writeln (Output, 'Move disk #1 from ',
                                 Init, 'to', Dest, '.');
```

```
        ELSE BEGIN
                MoveDisks (NumDisks - 1, Init, Extra, Dest);
                Writeln (Output, 'Move disk # 'NumDisks:1,
                            'from', Init,'to', Dest,'.');
                MoveDisks (NumDisks - 1, Extra, Dest, Init);
        END;
END;
```

Examine the output when the problem contains four disks.

INTERACTIVE SESSION

```
Welcome to the Tower of Hanoi.
How many disks are there?
4
Move disk #1 from A to C.
Move disk #2 from A to B.
Move disk #1 from C to B.
Move disk #3 from A to C.
Move disk #1 from B to A.
Move disk #2 from B to C.
Move disk #1 from A to C.
Move disk #4 from A to B.
Move disk #1 from C to B.
Move disk #2 from C to A.
Move disk #1 from B to A.
Move disk #3 from C to B.
Move disk #1 from A to C.
Move disk #2 from A to B.
Move disk #1 from C to B.
```

SELF TEST

How many move operations are performed when NumDisks = 2? NumDisks = 5? NumDisks = 10? How many times is MoveDisk called when NumDisks = 4? What do you think would happen if NumDisks were given a value of 25?

In order to avoid generating hundreds of pages of results—which would happen when NumDisks gets large—we will add a precaution to the main program.

```
BEGIN
        Writeln (Output, 'Welcome to the Tower of Hanoi.');
        Writeln (Output, 'How many disks are there?');
        Readln (Input, NumDisks);
        IF (NumDisks > 0) AND (NumDisks < MaxDisks)
            THEN MoveDisks (NumDisks, 'A', 'B', 'C')
            ELSE Writeln (Output, 'Number must be between',
                    ' 1 and ; MaxDisks:1');
END.
```

A programming trick that makes recursively generated output easier to read involves indenting the output according to the level of recursion. For example:

```
PROCEDURE Tab (HowMany : Integer);
(* This procedure prints HowMany spaces on the output line*)
BEGIN
        Write (Output, ' ':HowMany);
END;


PROCEDURE MoveDisks (NumDisks: Integer;
                     Init, Dest, Extra: Char);
(* This recusively defined procedure moves NumDisks disks *)
(* from the initial pole to the destination pole by        *)
(* using the extra pole to store all but the bottom        *)
(* disk, then moving the bottom disk, then moving those    *)
(* disks on the extra pole back to the destination.        *)
BEGIN
        IF (NumDisks = 1) THEN BEGIN
            Tab ((MaxDisks-1)*2);
            Writeln (Output, 'Move disk #1 from ',Init,
                            ' to ', Dest,'.');
        END ELSE BEGIN
            MoveDisks (NumDisks - 1, Init, Extra, Dest);
            Tab ((MaxDisks - NumDisks)*2);
            Writeln (Output, 'Move disk #', NumDisks:1,
                    ' from ', Init,' to ', Dest,'.');
            MoveDisks (NumDisks - 1, Extra, Dest, Init);
        END;
END;
```

The following is the output for a problem in which NumDisks = 5.

INTERACTIVE SESSION

```
Welcome to the Tower of Hanoi.
How many disks are there?
5
                Move disk #1 from A to B.
              Move disk #2 from A to C.
                Move disk #1 from B to C.
            Move disk #3 from A to B.
                Move disk #1 from C to A.
              Move disk #2 from C to B.
                Move disk #1 from A to B.
          Move disk #4 from A to C.
                Move disk #1 from B to C.
              Move disk #2 from B to A.
                Move disk #1 from C to A.
```

```
          Move disk #3 from B to C.
              Move disk #1 from A to B.
          Move disk #2 from A to C.
              Move disk #1 from B to C.
      Move disk #5 from A to B.
              Move disk #1 from C to A.
          Move disk #2 from C to B.
              Move disk #1 from A to B.
          Move disk #3 from C to A.
              Move disk #1 from B to C.
          Move disk #2 from B to A.
              Move disk #1 from C to A.
      Move disk #4 from C to B.
              Move disk #1 from A to B.
          Move disk #2 from A to C.
              Move disk #1 from B to C.
          Move disk #3 from A to B.
              Move disk #1 from C to A.
          Move disk #2 from C to B.
              Move disk #1 from A to B.
```

Notice that the output is easier to read and the patterns can be identified more easily.

SELF
TEST

What is the output of the following program? Identify the two components of recursive solutions in PROCEDURE Laugh.

```
PROGRAM Test (Output);
PROCEDURE Laugh (Num : Integer);
BEGIN
        IF (Num <> 0) THEN BEGIN
                Laugh (Num-1)
                Write (Output, 'Ha ');
        END;
END;
BEGIN
        Laugh (8);
END.
```

FORWARD Declarations

In rare situations, it may be necessary to write a pair of procedures in which each procedure calls the other. In this case, it is necessary to deal with the fact that one must be declared first, but both are dependent on each other. The way to do this is to make one declaration a FORWARD declaration.

```
PROCEDURE A (VAR x,y,z: Real);
        FORWARD;
PROCEDURE B (VAR i,j,k: Integer);
VAR     . . .
BEGIN

        . . .
        A (Tom, Dick, Harry);
        . . .

END;


PROCEDURE A (* no parameter list here *);
BEGIN

        . . .
        B (Huey, Duey, Louie);
        . . .

END;
```

A FORWARD declaration allows multiple procedure recursion. You might use a FORWARD declaration when reading commands from the terminal, for example.

```
PROCEDURE GetCommand (VAR Com: Char):
        FORWARD;
PROCEDURE Error (VAR Com: Char);
(* produces an error message if an incorrect command *)
(* was given                                         *)
BEGIN
        Writeln (Output, 'You typed an illegal command.');
        Help; (* writes out legal commands *)
        GetCommand (Com);
END;
PROCEDURE GetCommand (* VAR Com: Char *)
(* notice comments around parameter list *)
BEGIN
        Read (Input, Com);
        IF NOT (Com IN LegalCommands)
                THEN Error (Com);
END;
```

Multiple procedure recursion can often be awkward and more difficult to read than the same code written iteratively. However, it sometimes becomes necessary, especially when dealing with pointers, as we'll see in the next chapter. Because the FORWARD declaration of a procedure is usually not near the actual code of the procedure, it is good to get in the habit of putting comments around what would be the formal parameter list in the heading of the actual code of the procedure, as we did with GetCommand.

When Not to Use Recursion

One result of a recursive call is that the computer must set up an entirely new procedure environment. When we execute the recursive version of Reverse on a line of 50 characters, only 50 variables are set up, as opposed to 80 character variables (1 × 80 array of characters) for the iterative solution. Yet with the iteration, the procedure `Reverse` is only entered once. With recursion, it is entered once for each character, or 50 times. This initialization of a procedure environment is somewhat costly in terms of computer time and space. In general, every problem that can be solved recursively can be solved iteratively, and vice versa. Most of the time, the iterative solution is more straightforward, cheaper, and more efficient. Use iteration unless you see a very elegant or efficient recursive solution, as with `Reverse`. Do not overuse recursion, because it is expensive.

Programming Example 18.3

Assignment: Write a program to evaluate arithmetic expressions that are on an input file. The expressions will have the familiar arithmetic operators +, -, *, /, as well as an exponentiation operator, ∧. You should also take parenthetical expressions into account and follow standard precedence rules.

This program is not difficult, but it requires us to think recursively. We will be off to a good start if we understand the way computer languages like Pascal evaluate precedence in order to deal with any level of complexity. Recursion is what allows a programming language to handle unlimited nesting of parentheses.

In order to see the recursive structure in this problem, let's look at the precise definition of the syntax of an arithmetic expression:

expression: a sequence of one or more simple expressions separated by the arithmetic operators + or -.

simple expression: a sequence of one or more terms separated by the arithmetic operators * or /.

term: a sequence of one or more signed factors separated by the exponentiation operator ∧.

signed factor: a factor with an optional + or - in front of it.

factor: a number or a parenthesized expression.

number: a valid integer or real number in Pascal.

The way to read this is like a series of dictionary definitions. In order to complete the first definition, it is necessary to know what a simple expression is. Each line in the string of definitions uses something that is defined in the following line. This is true of every line but the last two. The definition for *factor* is that it is either a number, which is defined as you would expect, or a parenthesized expression. So, you see, this definition refers to itself, indirectly, and hence *could* go on forever.

Solution: The solution to this problem is to convert the specifications of the arithmetic syntax to a Pascal program. Recursion occurs because the code that

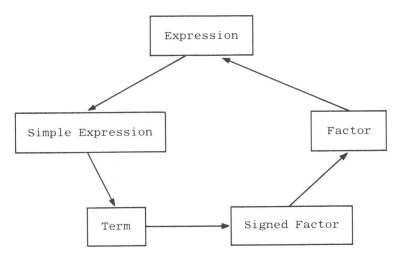

Figure 18.4: Expression Syntax Interdependence

calculates Expression must be called by a procedure that it calls. Let's examine the problem more closely.

Suppose we declare functions to calculate Expression, SimpleExpression, Term, SignedFactor, and Factor. Each of these functions will be short, but they will all be related to each other. Their interdependence is demonstrated in Figure 18.4.

Let's take a look at the function Expression, which will return the value of the expression after calculating it according to the above syntax rules.

```
FUNCTION Expression (VAR Error : Boolean) : Real;
VAR      E: Real;
         Opr: Char;
BEGIN
         E := SimpleExpression (Error);
         WHILE (Input^ IN ['+','-']) DO BEGIN
             Read (Input, Opr);
             CASE Opr OF
                 '+': E := E + SimpleExpression (Error);
                 '-': E := E - SimpleExpression (Error);
             END;
         END;
         Expression := E;
END;     (* Expression *)
```

You will notice that it uses another function called SimpleExpression, and calls it according to what is in the input file buffer variable. If the input file contains a simple expression followed by a plus or minus sign, then the value of another simple expression is retrieved and added or subtracted from the first.

The next function, `SimpleExpression`, is almost identical.

```
FUNCTION SimpleExpression (VAR Error : Boolean) : Real;
VAR      S: Real;
         Opr: Char;
BEGIN
         S := Term (Error);
         WHILE (Input^ IN ['*','/']) DO BEGIN
            Read (Input, Opr);
            CASE Opr OF
               '*': S := S * Term (Error);
               '/': S := S / Term (Error);
            END;
         END;
         SimpleExpression := S;
END;     (* SimpleExpression *)
```

This time the function to be called is `Term`. `Term` looks like the first two, except it scans for only one operator, the exponentiation operator, rather than two.

```
FUNCTION Term (VAR Error : Boolean) : Real;
VAR      T: Real;
BEGIN
         T := SignedFactor (Error);
         WHILE (Input^ = '^') DO BEGIN
            Get (Input);
            T := Exp (Ln (T) * SignedFactor (Error));
         END;
         Term := T;
END;     (* Term *)
```

`SignedFactor` eliminates a possible plus or minus sign from the input, and calls the function `Factor`. `Factor` is looking for either a number, signified by a digit in the input file buffer variable, or a left parenthesis to begin the definition of a nested expression. This is where the recursion comes in.

```
FUNCTION Factor (VAR Error : Boolean) : Real;
VAR      F: Real;
BEGIN
         IF (Input^ IN Digits) THEN BEGIN
            Read (Input, F);
         END ELSE IF (Input^ = '(') THEN BEGIN
            Get (Input);
            F:=Expression (Error);
            IF (Input^ = ')')
               THEN Get (Input)
               ELSE Error := TRUE;
         END ELSE Error := TRUE;
         Factor:=F;
END;     (* function Factor *)
```

Therefore, because `Factor` calls the procedure `Expression`, while the procedure `Expression` calls procedures that eventually call `Factor`, we have a need for a FORWARD declaration.

```
FUNCTION Expression (VAR Error : Boolean) : Real
        FORWARD ;
```

Notice also that the only function that changes the value of `Error` is `Factor`, yet in order to parameterize consistently, we must send it in as a variable parameter to all the functions that eventually call `Factor`. We will use the global variable `Digits` as if it were a global SET constant, which cannot be a constant. However, at no time in the entire program does the value of `Digits` change, and in this case, it makes sense to use a global variable that is not included in parameter lists. Here is the final program.

```
PROGRAM RecursiveEval (Input, Output);
(*************************************************************)
(* This program evaluates expressions that are given in    *)
(* the input file, and it writes the values to the output  *)
(* file. If the expression is illegal, an error message    *)
(* is given instead. This program uses recursion.          *)
(*************************************************************)

TYPE    DigSet = SET OF Char;

VAR     Digits : DigSet;
        Value : Real;
        Error : Boolean;

FUNCTION Expression (VAR Error : Boolean) : Real;
        FORWARD ;

FUNCTION Factor (VAR Error : Boolean) : Real;
VAR     F: Real;
BEGIN
        IF (Input^ IN Digits) THEN BEGIN
            Read (Input, F);
        END ELSE IF (Input^ = '(') THEN BEGIN
            Get (Input);
            F:=Expression (Error);
            IF (Input^ = ')')
                THEN Get (Input)
                ELSE Error := TRUE;
        END ELSE Error := TRUE;
        Factor:=F;
END;    (* Factor*)
```

```
FUNCTION SignedFactor (VAR Error : Boolean) : Real;
BEGIN
        IF (Input^ = '-') THEN BEGIN
            Get (Input);
            SignedFactor := -Factor (Error);
        END ELSE BEGIN
            IF (Input^ = '+') THEN Get (Input);
            SignedFactor := Factor (Error);
        END;
END;    (* SignedFactor *)


FUNCTION Term (VAR Error : Boolean) : Real;
VAR     T: Real;
BEGIN
        T := SignedFactor (Error);
        WHILE (Input^ = '^') DO BEGIN
            Get (Input);
            T := Exp (Ln (T) * SignedFactor (Error));
        END;
        Term := T;
END;    (* Term *)

FUNCTION SimpleExpression (VAR Error : Boolean) : Real;
VAR     S: Real;
        Opr: Char;
BEGIN
        S := Term (Error);
        WHILE (Input^ IN ['*','/']) DO BEGIN
            Read (Input, Opr);
            CASE Opr OF
                '*': S := S * Term (Error);
                '/': S := S / Term (Error);
            END;
        END;
        SimpleExpression := S;
END;    (* SimpleExpression *)

FUNCTION Expression (* VAR Error : Boolean *) ; (* : Real *)
VAR     E: Real;
        Opr: Char;
BEGIN
        E := SimpleExpression (Error);
        WHILE (Input^ IN ['+','-']) DO BEGIN
            Read (Input, Opr);
            CASE Opr OF
                '+': E := E + SimpleExpression (Error);
                '-': E := E - SimpleExpression (Error);
            END;
        END;
```

```
                Expression : = E;
END;        (* Expression *)

PROCEDURE Evaluate(VAR Error : Boolean;
                    VAR Value: Real);
BEGIN
        Value : = Expression (Error);
END;        (* Evaluate *)

BEGIN      (* Main Program *)
        Digits : = ['0'..'9'];
        Writeln (Output, 'Type your expression: ',
                            '(Blank line to quit)');
        WHILE NOT Eoln (Input) DO BEGIN
            Error : = FALSE;
            Evaluate (Error, Value);
            IF Error
                THEN Writeln (Output, 'Illegal expression')
                ELSE Writeln (Output, 'Result:',Value:10:2);
            Readln (Input);
            Writeln (Output, 'Type your expression: ',
                                '(Blank line to quit)');

        END;
END.       (* Main Program *)
```

The following sample session shows the limited error checking as well as the ability to use unlimited nesting.

INTERACTIVE SESSION

```
Type your expression: (Blank line to quit)
2^2^2^2
Result:     256.00
Type your expression: (Blank line to quit)
2^(2^(2^2))
Result:   65536.01
Type your expression: (Blank line to quit)
2+3*4+5*6-7/8*9*10
Result:     -34.75
Type your expression: (Blank line to quit)
((2+3)*4+5*6)+7*8
Result:     106.00
Type your expression: (Blank line to quit)
10^0.5
Result:       3.16
Type your expression: (Blank line to quit)
100^(10^0.1)
Result:     329.50
```

```
Type your expression:  (Blank line to quit)
(*2)
Illegal expression
Type your expression:  (Blank line to quit)
(2*)
Illegal expression
Type your expression:  (Blank line to quit)
```

This type of program could be expanded to serve many different uses. By adding some standard functions like Sin and Ln, you could create an on-line calculator program. You could even create a spread-sheet program, like those that are popular for microcomputers.

Common Errors and Debugging

1. **Forgetting actual parameter lists on recursive function calls.** Inside a function, it is tempting to treat the function identifier as a variable identifier. With nonrecursive functions, we must avoid putting the function identifier on the right-hand side of an equation; therefore, we must often use a dummy variable name whose value will be assigned to the function at its end. However, with recursive functions, like Power, we must have the function call on the right side of the equation. Remember that it is a function, with parameters, and not simply a variable.

2. **Putting formal parameter lists on forward-declared procedure definitions.** When you first define a procedure using FORWARD, it may look strange to declare it later without the parameter list. In order to make the code easy to read, include the formal parameter list with the body of the procedure, but put it in comments, so it will be accepted by the compiler. It is also an error to include the function type on a function body on a function that has been declared FORWARD.

3. **Forgetting either of the two essential requirements of a recursive procedure.** If a recursive procedure does not have an end point, then it will continue execution indefinitely or until some kind of arithmetic overflow exists. Overflow occurs, for example, when the computer tries to divide by zero or multiplies numbers larger than it can handle. Likewise, if a procedure has an end point but is not breaking the problem down into simple and smaller parts, then the procedure will never reach the end point, and an infinite loop exists.

4. **Composing faulty recursion.** Recursive programming is difficult because it is not a matter of intuition for many people. It is easy to write recursive procedures that don't work, but it is often not very easy to figure out what went wrong. Use debugging print statements to help you see what is going on with variables and with the program control. You can declare a boolean constant called Debugging which is satisfied when the program is still in the debugging stages and which

is set to FALSE once the program is working. A procedure that writes the values of all the crucial variables can be helpful in determining where the discrepancy between what you want to happen and what is actually happening lies.

```
CONST    Debugging = TRUE;

         IF Debugging
                 THEN WriteVariables (...);
```

5. **Overusing recursion.** Don't use recursion when there is a straightforward iterative solution. Iterative solutions are usually less expensive, because each time a procedure is entered, some memory space must be allocated for the program counter and any local variables. Recursion usually involves many procedure entries. As we saw in The Tower of Hanoi, tabbing the output can be helpful in watching recursion in action.

SUMMARY

Recursion allows a form of repetition that is not explicitly expressed by the control structures, but is carried out through the logic of the program and the recursive procedure calls. Every correct recursive procedure or algorithm involves two essential steps, (1) breaking the problem down into simpler but similar problems and (2) determining an end point or terminating condition for the process.

In rare instances, it is necessary or convenient to write a pair of procedures, each of which calls the other. In this case, a FORWARD declaration of a procedure can be used. The FORWARD declaration allows Pascal to check any occurrence of an identifier in the statement part of the code to ensure that it has been declared before it is used. FORWARD declarations are used to set up multiple procedure recursion.

In general, every problem that can be solved recursively can be solved iteratively. In most cases the iterative solution is more straightforward and is more efficient in its use of computer time and memory space. Only use recursion when it is sufficiently more elegant and straightforward to warrant its use.

New Terms

recursion	end point	FORWARD

EXERCISES

1. Write a recursive procedure that takes a positive integer as a parameter and prints that many asterisks to the output file.

2. Write a recursive function that takes two integer parameters, High and Low, and returns the value of

$$\text{High} \times (\text{High} - 1) \times (\text{High} - 2) \times \ldots \times \text{Low}$$

which is equivalent to

$$\frac{\text{High!}}{(\text{Low}-1)!}$$

Recall that $N!$ is read as "N factorial" and is calculated by

$$N! = N \times (N - 1) \times (N - 2) \ldots \times 2 \times 1$$

3. Write a procedure that recursively sorts an array using the selection sort method described in Chapter 15. The procedure should find the smallest element in the array, move it to the top, and then recursively sort the remaining elements.

4. Any term in the Fibonacci sequence, 1, 1, 2, 3, 5, 8, . . . is defined by the equations

$$f_n = f_{n-1} + f_{n-2}$$
$$f_1 = f_2 = 1$$

Write a recursive function that calculates any nth term in the sequence, when $n <= 20$. Write a program that uses the recursive function and counts how many times it is called. For any n, write out both the Fibonacci number generated and the number of times the function was called. Do you see any correlation?

5. A more general form of the Fibonacci sequence is

$$f_n = f_{n-1} + f_{n-2}$$

$$f_1 = a$$

$$f_2 = b$$

Find another way to generate any term in the Fibonacci sequence recursively. Think of the Fibonacci function as having three parameters, a, the first term in the sequence; b, the second term in the sequence; and n, the index of the desired term. The following recurrence relationships apply.

$$f(a,b,1) = a$$
$$f(a,b,2) = b$$
$$f(a,b,n) = f(b, a + b, n - 1), \text{ for } n > 2$$

Write a recursive function that calculates the nth Fibonacci term. Write a program that keeps track of the number of times the function is called. What is the difference between this recursive function and the one described in the previous problem?

6. Suppose we wanted to calculate the greatest common divisor (GCD) of two positive integers. The algorithm can be expressed recursively as:

$$GCD(a,b) = b, \text{ if a MOD b} = 0$$

$$GCD(a,b) = GCD(b, a\,MOD\,b) \text{ if a MOD b} <> 0$$

Write a function that calculates the GCD of two integers recursively.

7. Write a program that takes as input a file of alphametic, or cryptarithm, problems that are of the form

DONALD
GERALD

ROBERT

DONALD + GERALD = ROBERT is a valid mathematical operation when each letter represents one digit, and different letters stand for different digits. The output for this program is the solution to the problem:

526485
197485

723970

The solution should also print the alphametic assignments.

0	1	2	3	4	5	6	7	8	9
T	G	O	B	A	D	N	R	L	E

POINTERS AND LISTS

In the last chapter we learned about recursion. If you liked recursion, you are sure to love this last topic, because what recursion is to control structures, pointers are to data structures. Let's take a look at some of the reasons why we might need recursive data structures.

A favorite data structure example in the last few chapters has been Word, a packed array of characters. Suppose we want to create a data structure that can store every word in the English language, or at least every word in a large dictionary. At this point, we are going to run into a problem with insufficient space set aside in memory. It would be ideal to be able to organize the data structure in such a way that most of the allocated memory is actually being used. But there is a problem. What should the declaration for Word look like? Well, the easy way would be to declare it as we always have.

```
Word = PACKED ARRAY [1..MaxChar] OF Char;
```

The problem here is the value of MaxChar. Most English words contain six or fewer letters, but there are some that are over twice that. How do we deal with very long words? Do we simply set MaxChar to 15 and hope we do not have to enter words longer than 15 characters? But then most of the spaces for characters in memory will be empty. Or perhaps we declare

```
Dictionary = PACKED ARRAY [1..BigMaxChar] OF Char;
```

and set BigMaxChar to some high value. We could separate words by spaces. But this decreases the flexibility of the data structure and increases the amount of work the control structure must do to extract useful information. For example, finding the 450th word, or a particular word, is a laborious task.

This type of problem is especially common when dealing with large programming applications, when the size of the data structure varies widely. The problem with arrays, or arrays of records, is that the maximum size of a data structure must be set when the program is compiled. Certainly, it is possible to change the limits and recompile the program, but that solution doesn't help if, in the middle of a program execution, all the declared space is used. There should be a way to allocate memory during the execution of the program.

Dynamic Versus Static Allocation

There is indeed a way to allocate memory space during the execution of a Pascal program. The allocation of memory space during execution is called **dynamic allocation.** The alternative method, **static allocation,** fixes memory space at compile time, and that is what we have seen in all the programs we have looked at, with the exception of the recursive procedures we wrote in the last chapter. Dynamic allocation is not fixed but is variable, and the amount of memory space allocated can vary from execution to execution and can vary from one point to another in the same run of a program.

Access to a dynamically allocated memory location is attained through a **pointer. A pointer variable** acts as a name acts for a statically allocated variable, as shown in Figure 19.1.

The difference between Row and a pointer called Ptr is that the name Row always applies to the same memory location inside the scope of the declaration of Row. However, when Ptr is declared, no memory location is originally associated with it. At a later time, Ptr may be given a memory location, and that memory location may change over the course of the execution of the program.

Declaring a Pointer Type

When declaring a pointer type, it is necessary to indicate the type of memory location to which the pointer refers.

```
TYPE     IntegerPtr = ^Integer;
         Color = (Red, Orange, Yellow, Green, Blue, Indigo, Violet);
         ColorPtr = ^Color;
         Word = PACKED ARRAY [1..MaxChar] OF Char;
         WordPtr = ^Word;
```

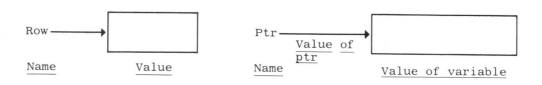

Figure 19.1: Comparison Between Static and Dynamic Variables

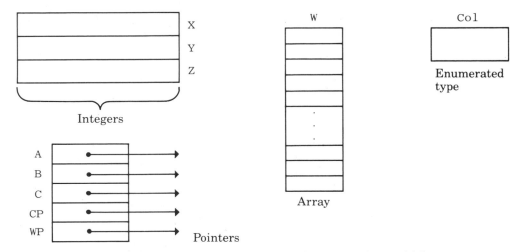

Figure 19.2: Comparison Between Pointers and Other Variables

A pointer itself is not a memory location in which data can be stored. A `ColorPtr` cannot have the value `Red`, it merely points to some memory location that can have that value. Likewise, `WordPtr` is not an array. It merely points to some array in memory. The differences between the different variables declared below are shown in Figure 19.2.

```
VAR     x, y, z : Integer;
        A, B, C : IntegerPtr;
        Col : Color;
        CP : ColorPtr;
        W : Word;
        WP : WordPtr;
```

Lists

At this point, the motivation for the use of pointers might not be obvious. Why have a pointer to an integer variable? It seems as if it creates an unnecessary memory location—one for the pointer as well as one for the value actually stored. That is true. But the pointer is a crucial building block for a very important and powerful data structure: linked lists.

Normally when we declare pointer types, we declare pointers that access records.

```
TYPE    Node = RECORD
                 Value : Integer;
                 Next : ^Node;
        END;
VAR     Head : ^Node;
```

The symbol ∧ before the name of the record type, Node, indicates that Next is a field that is a pointer. Next is not a record, nor is it an integer variable. It is a variable that points to variables of type Node. A better way to declare this would be to rename this pointer type.

```
TYPE    NodePtr = ∧Node;

        Node = RECORD
                Value : Integer;
                Next : NodePtr;
        END;
VAR     Head : NodePtr;
```

This is better because you will probably be passing pointers as parameters (Does that surprise you?), therefore, you need to give the pointer type a legal identifier name. ∧Node is not a legal identifier and cannot be used in a parameter list. You may, however, be wondering if Pascal will let you declare the type this way. The declaration seems to refer to a type called Node, which at this point in the program hasn't yet been defined. That is indeed true, but because Node is a pointer type, the Pascal compiler will not complain, as long as the type is eventually defined in the same block. The record type of a pointer is usually defined in the following line.

It is at this point that we can see how pointers can be used to build recursive data structures. Node was defined as a record containing a value and a pointer to another Node record. Recall the definition of recursion: a form of repetition that is carried out through program logic by procedures that may call themselves. This definition describes control structure recursion. The recursion we see in this chapter is data structure recursion, or the process of defining data structures recursively. The definition of Node is obviously recursive.

The value of all this is that we can create an entire list of linked records and use this list for sequential data storage, in much the same way we use arrays.

Figure 19.3 represents a list of the first 10 positive squares in descending order. Each **node**, or discrete storage structure, is linked to the next by means of its pointer. The record that Head points to consists of two boxes, a value (100) and a pointer. Head∧.Value equals 100, Head∧.Next points to a second record in the list. To reference different elements of the list, we can simply build up the name until we find the desired location.

```
Head∧.Value = 100
Head∧.Next  is a pointer
Head∧.Next∧  is a record
Head∧.Next∧.Value = 81
Head∧.Next∧.Next∧  is a record
Head∧.Next∧.Next∧.Value = 64
Head∧.Next∧.Next∧.Next∧.Value = 49
```

At this point, the whole thing may still seem rather awkward. But suppose we wanted to insert another value at the head of this list. If we had been working

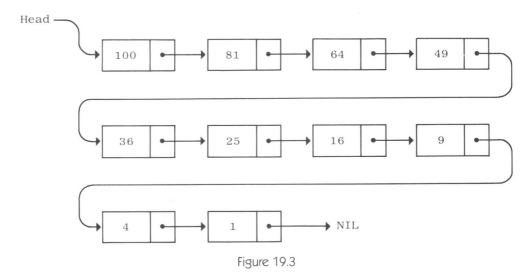

Figure 19.3

with an array structure, this would be difficult. We would have had to move every value down one slot in the array in order to insert a new value at the beginning. With a linked list, it is easy to do. Figure 19.4 shows a picture of what we will do. In order to make the insertion, we simply make the new record point to the head of the old list and the head of the list point to the new record. In Pascal, this is how it would be done.

```
Temp^.Next := Head;
Head := Temp;
```

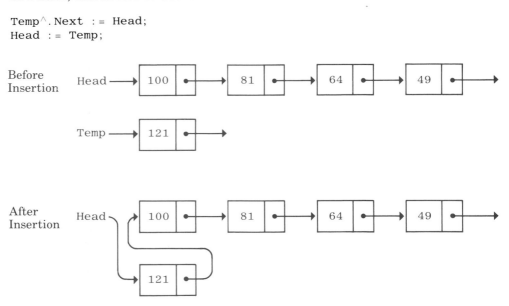

Figure 19.4: Inserting at the Head of a List

This assumes that Temp is a pointer that points to the new record that is to be inserted.

New and Dispose

Perhaps the usefulness of pointers is becoming clearer. Although we have talked about the possibility of allocating storage dynamically, until now we haven't seen a new storage structure actually being created. We need to learn how to set aside new records in memory so that we can build up a list as long as desired.

The way we set aside memory locations in Pascal is by using the standard procedure New. New takes a parameter that is a pointer and gives that pointer a memory location to point to. Pictorially, Figure 19.5 shows what New accomplished. New creates the record to which the assigned pointer parameter points. Therefore, if we wanted to put the value 121 at the head of the list in Figure 19.3, the complete process will look like this.

```
New (Temp);
Temp^.Value : = 121;
Temp^.Next : = Head;
Head : = Temp;
```

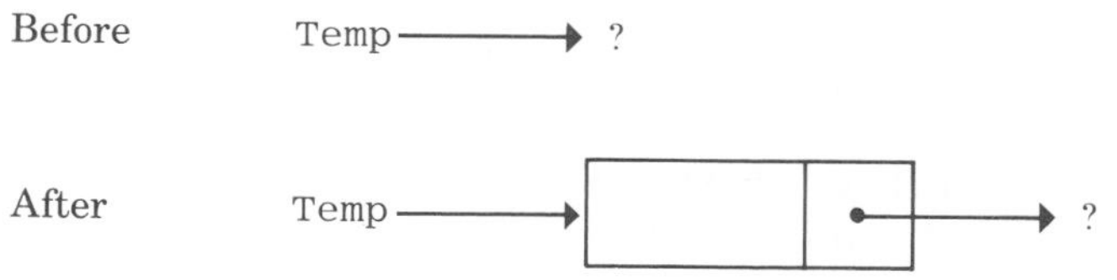

Figure 19.5: New Allocating Storage Dynamically

Suppose, on the other hand, we wish to delete the record containing a certain value from the list. Deleting is almost as easy as inserting. Figure 19.6 demonstrates what happens when an element is deleted. This is what it looks like in Pascal.

```
Temp^.Next : = Temp^.Next^.Next;
```

This assumes that Temp points to the record *before* the one that is to be deleted.

What happens to the value we deleted? Once a pointer is no longer pointing to it, it is totally inaccessible. However, it is still occupying space in memory. In order to free memory space so we don't run out, it is always a good policy to Dispose of a pointer. Dispose is the Standard Pascal procedure that is the counterpart of New: it eliminates the space referenced by the pointer parameter and frees it for future use. Disposing of a pointer is tricky. What would happen if I executed the following?

```
Dispose (Temp^.Next);
Temp^.Next := Temp^.Next^.Next;
```

The problem is obvious. Disposing of `Temp^.Next` means that `Temp^.Next^` no longer exists as a record. The action, in effect, chops off the remainder of the list, making all of the other values inaccessible because no pointer is pointing to them. Here is the proper way to delete from a list and dispose of a deleted record.

```
Old := Temp^.Next; (*assign deleted record pointer to old *)
Temp^.Next := Temp^.Next^.Next;   (*delete the record*)
Dispose (Old); (*please do not litter--dispose of properly*)
```

NIL and Uninitialized Pointers

Suppose we want to write a little loop that prints out the entire list from head to tail. We should be able to use an indefinite loop—a loop because the operations will be repeated; indefinite because we don't know how many elements are in a list.

```
Temp := Head;
WHILE        ?        DO BEGIN
        Write (Output, Temp^.Value);
        Temp := Temp^.Next;
END;
```

When should this WHILE loop end? The objective is to go until the next pointer doesn't point to anything. But how will we know? If we try to access `Temp^.Next` when no value is located there, we will get a run-time error. The solution is to

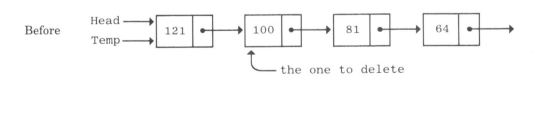

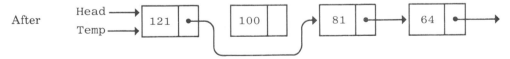

Figure 19.6: Deleting an Element From a List

initialize the pointers to NIL, which is a reserved word in Pascal and corresponds to the integer 0. We could then write:

```
Temp := Head;
WHILE (Temp <> NIL) DO BEGIN
        Write (Output, Temp^.Value);
        Temp := Temp^.Next;
END;
```

If a pointer has not been given a structure to point to, via the New procedure, and if it has not been assigned the value NIL, then the pointer is said to be **uninitialized.** Be careful to initialize pointers that may not receive locations to NIL, so that you can make safety checks before trying to access NIL or uninitialized pointers.

Fundamental List Procedures

When working with lists, there are a few fundamental procedures that most programs will need to use in some modified fashion. These procedures are crucial to the addition and deletion of elements to the head or the tail of a list. We will examine several procedures and how to write them.

Initialization

A list can be initialized very simply by setting the head pointer to NIL. After initialization, insertion can be done correctly.

```
PROCEDURE InitList (VAR Head : NodePtr);
BEGIN
        Head := NIL;
END;
```

Stack Insertion

A procedure that inserts a value to the head of a list can be used to implement a **stack**, which is a list where the last element added becomes the first element to leave the list, in the same way you use a stack of plates. (This type of structure was used in the recursive procedure Reverse discussed in Chapter 18.) Whenever you insert a value into a list, you will need to use the standard procedure New. Don't attempt to store the value in a record that hasn't been created yet. An illustration of what PROCEDURE AddToHead does is seen in Figure 19.7.

```
PROCEDURE AddToHead (VAR Head : NodePtr; Val : Integer);
VAR     Temp : NodePtr;
```

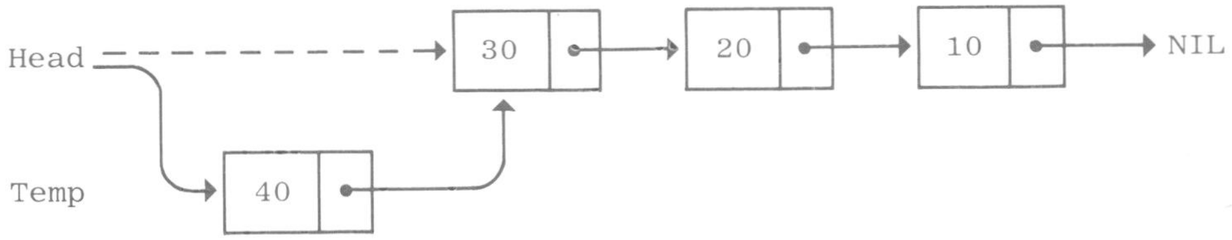

Figure 19.7: AddToHead

```
BEGIN
        New (Temp);
        Temp^.Value := Val;
        Temp^.Next := Head;
        Head := Temp;
END;
```

Queue Insertion

A procedure that inserts a value onto the tail of a list can be used to implement a **queue**, which is a list where the first element added to the list becomes the first element to leave the list. This is how most lines you wait in work—first come, first served. The procedure AddToTail is a little trickier than AddToHead, because it is necessary to find the tail before adding the element. A pseudocode outline of the algorithm would be:

```
AddToTail:
        IF Head is NIL
                THEN Add To Head
                ELSE set Temp to Head
                        Find the last record
                        Make a new record on the tail
                        Assign inserted value to record
                        Set Next pointer to NIL
```

In Pascal, this algorithm can be implemented by the following code.

```
PROCEDURE AddToTail (VAR NodePtr; Val : Integer);
VAR     Temp : NodePtr;
BEGIN
        IF (Head = NIL)
                THEN AddToHead (Head, Val)
                ELSE BEGIN
                        Temp := Head;
                        WHILE (Temp^.Next <> NIL) DO
                                Temp := Temp^.Next;
```

```
                New (Temp^.Next);
                Temp^.Next^.Value := Val;
                Temp^.Next^.Next  := NIL;
         END;
END;
```

Notice the WHILE loop that searches for a NIL pointer. This program fragment appears frequently when working with lists. Figure 19.8 shows how AddToTail works.

Deletion from the Head

A procedure that removes the first element from a list can be used with either of the previous two procedures to implement a stack or a queue. Any procedure that deletes a node from a list must use the procedure Dispose to ensure that the memory space is returned to the reservoir of available space. DeleteHead is essentially the reverse of AddToHead. Remember that if we try to access the record components of a NIL pointer, we will get an error.

```
PROCEDURE DeleteHead (VAR Head : NodePtr;
                      VAR Val : Integer);
VAR      Temp : NodePtr;
```

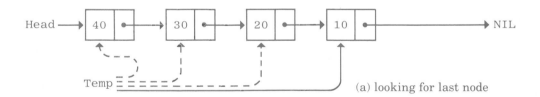

(a) looking for last node

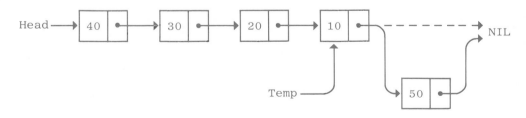

(b) inserting new node

Figure 19.8: AddToTail

```
BEGIN
        IF (Head <> NIL) THEN BEGIN
                Val := Head^.Value;
                Temp := Head;
                Head := Head^.Next;
                Dispose (Temp);
        END;
END;
```

Figure 19.9 shows how DeleteHead works.

Deletion from the Tail

Just for the sake of symmetry, we will look at how to construct a procedure that deletes a node from the tail of a list. This procedure looks somewhat like Add-ToTail, yet it is more complicated because we have two special cases: when Head is NIL, and when Head points to a record whose Next component is NIL. These conditions are equivalent to saying that the list contains no elements or one element. Probably the most confusing aspect of a procedure like this is the fact that the temporary pointer must remain pointing to the record in front of the record we want to delete. This is true because we are going to need to change the Next pointer of the record previous to the deleted node, so that it is pointing to NIL when the procedure is completed. Here is the working procedure.

```
PROCEDURE DeleteTail (VAR Head : NodePtr;
                      VAR Val : Integer);
VAR     Temp : NodePtr;
BEGIN
        IF (Head <> NIL) THEN BEGIN
                IF (Head^.Next = NIL) THEN BEGIN
                        Val := Head^.Value;
                        Dispose (Head);
                        Head := NIL;
                END ELSE BEGIN
                        Temp := Head;
                        WHILE (Temp^.Next^.Next <> NIL) DO
                                Temp := Temp^.Next;
                        Val := Temp^.Next^.Value;
                        Dispose (Temp^.Next);
                        Temp^.Next := NIL;
                END;
        END;
END;
```

The logic of this procedure is illustrated in Figure 19.10.

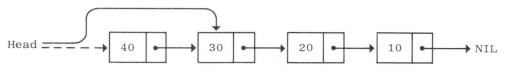

Figure 19.9: `DeleteHead`

Printing a List

The procedure that prints a list in order is easy compared to the procedures we have been working with. No new records are created, and we dispose of none. If the list is empty, nothing is printed.

```
PROCEDURE PrintList (Head : NodePtr);
VAR      Temp : NodePtr;
BEGIN
        Temp := Head;
        WHILE (Temp <> NIL) DO BEGIN
                Write (Output, Temp^.Value:1, ' ');
                Temp := Temp^.Next;
        END;
END;
```

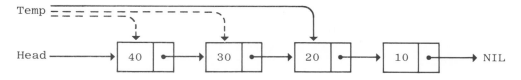

(a) finding the correct node

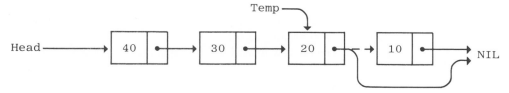

(b) deleting the last node

Figure 19.10: `DeleteTail`

SELF
TEST

Write a procedure like `DeleteTail` that deletes a specific value from the list. The procedure should take three parameters, the `Head` pointer, the value to be deleted, and a boolean flag whose conditions are satisifed only if the value was not found in the list. Make sure you dispose of your litter.

Programming Example 19.1

Assignment: Write a program that takes three input files, each a list of dictionary entries from three different dictionaries. Each file is sorted alphabetically. The program should compile and print a master list that contains all entries but no duplicates. The master list should be in alphabetical order at all times.

Solution: This is a job for a list structure if there ever was one. The task could be accomplished by a rather clumsy three-file merge sort, but the linked list structure is perfect for a growing list of words. We will get a chance to use and modify several of the procedures from the last section.

The data structure looks much the same as the other linked lists we have used in this chapter, except the node contains a word instead of an integer.

```
CONST    MaxChar = 16;
         Blank = '                   ';  (* Used in ReadWord *)

TYPE     Word = PACKED ARRAY [1..MaxChar] OF Char;

         ElementPtr = ^Element;
         Element = RECORD
             Wrd : Word;
             Nxt : ElementPtr;
         END;

VAR      Dict1, Dict2, Dict3 : Text;
         List : ElementPtr;
```

Let's think about what we will be doing. The first task is to read the first file into the linked list structure. Then we will read each of the other files, word by word, while checking to see if the words are already in the list. We will find the place where each word should be, and if a word isn't there, we will insert it into the list at that spot. In this way, we keep the list alphabetized at all times. A very rough outline of this procedure follows.

```
Merge Dictionaries:
    Reset Input files
    Read first dictionary
```

Read and compare second dictionary with first
Read and compare third dictionary with first
Print resulting list

This outline converts very easily, using three procedures we have yet to declare.

```
BEGIN     (* Main Program *)
          Reset (Dict1);
          Reset (Dict2);
          Reset (Dict3);
          ReadDict (Dict1, List);
          ReadNCompare (Dict2, List);
          ReadNCompare (Dict3, List);
          PrintList (List);
END.      (* Main Program *)
```

However, as we think about this outline, we realize that we could write the procedure ReadNCompare in such a way that the procedure ReadDict is not really necessary. We could use ReadNCompare to read all three dictionaries into the computer. Let's take a look at the algorithm for ReadNCompare.

ReadNCompare
        Loop until Eof (InFile):
                Read Word
                Find Correct place to insert
                IF Word is not in the list,
                        THEN Insert it

To translate to Pascal:

```
PROCEDURE ReadNCompare (VAR InFile : Text;
                        VAR List : ElementPtr);
(* This procedure reads an input file word by word and    *)
(* compares each word in the input file with those in the *)
(* list to make sure that only one copy of each word is   *)
(* added to the list. This procedure expects and returns  *)
(* a sorted list.                                          *)
VAR     Temp : ElementPtr;
        W : Word;
BEGIN
        Temp := List;
        WHILE NOT Eof (InFile) DO BEGIN
            ReadWord (InFile, W);
            IF (W < List^.Wrd) THEN BEGIN
                Insert (List, W)       (* alphabetically 1st *)
            END ELSE IF (W < List^.Nxt^.Wrd) THEN BEGIN
                Insert (List^.Nxt, W)  (* alphabet. 2nd      *)
            END ELSE BEGIN
```

```
                         WHILE (W > Temp^.Nxt^.Wrd) AND
                               (Temp^.Nxt^.Nxt <> NIL) DO
                         Temp := Temp^.Nxt;
                    IF (Temp^.Nxt^.Nxt = NIL)
                         THEN Insert (Temp^.Nxt^.Nxt, W)
                         ELSE IF (Temp^.Nxt^.Wrd <> W) THEN
                               Insert (Temp^.Nxt, W);
               END;
          END;
     END;
```

The convoluted part of the procedure—checking to see if the word should be higher than the first two words on the alphabetical list—is necessary because the search process, involving the WHILE loop and the Temp pointer, actually skips the first two words on the list. However, this procedure is fatally flawed, and will cause a run-time error. Can you see how? If the List has fewer than two words in it, as it does when it is first called, it will attempt to access an uninitialized pointer. So we must add another procedure that checks the length of the dictionary and builds it up to at least two words if necessary. This procedure is not too difficult to write.

```
PROCEDURE CheckFirstTwo (VAR InFile : Text;
                         VAR List : ElementPtr);
(* This procedure ensures that the list is at least two    *)
(* elements long, for proper use of ReadNCompare.          *)
VAR     W : Word;
BEGIN
        IF (List = NIL) THEN BEGIN
            ReadWord (InFile, W);
            Insert (List, W);
        END;
        IF (List^.Nxt = NIL) THEN BEGIN
            ReadWord (InFile, W);
            IF (List^.Wrd < W)
                THEN Insert (List^.Nxt, W)
                ELSE Insert (List, W);
        END;
END;
```

All we must do to finish the program is to add a line that calls CheckFirstTwo to the beginning of ReadNCompare, and then write the familiar procedures Insert, ReadWord, and PrintList. The final program is as follows:

```
PROGRAM MergeDictionaries (Input, Output);
(* This program merges three dictionaries into one list    *)
(* alphabetized by words and then prints out the list of   *)
(* words. It does this by reading each dictionary into     *)
(* list, making sure to enter the words alphabetically     *)
(* and eliminating duplicates.                             *)
```

```
CONST    MaxChar = 16;
         Blank = '                  ';

TYPE     Word = PACKED ARRAY [1..MaxChar] OF Char;

         ElementPtr = ^Element;
         Element = RECORD
            Wrd : Word;
            Nxt : ElementPtr;
         END;

VAR      Dict1, Dict2, Dict3, OutFile : Text;
         List : ElementPtr;

PROCEDURE InitList (VAR Head : ElementPtr);
(* This procedure initializes a list to NIL.               *)
BEGIN
         Head := NIL;
END;


PROCEDURE Insert (VAR Head : ElementPtr; W : Word);
(* This procedure inserts a word in a node at the head of *)
(* the list pointed to by Head.                           *)
VAR      Temp : ElementPtr;
BEGIN
         New (Temp);
         Temp^.Wrd := W;
         Temp^.Nxt := Head;
         Head := Temp;
END;


PROCEDURE PrintList (VAR OutFile : Text;
                          Head : ElementPtr);
(* This procedure prints a list of words to the OutFile.  *)
VAR      Temp : ElementPtr;
BEGIN
         Temp := Head;
         WHILE (Temp <> NIL) DO BEGIN
                 Writeln (OutFile, Temp^.Wrd);
                 Temp := Temp^.Nxt;
         END;
END;


PROCEDURE ReadWord (VAR InFile : Text; VAR W : Word);
(* This procedure reads a word from InFile. The word is   *)
(* less than MaxChar characters and is terminated by Eoln *)
VAR      Cntr : Integer;
BEGIN
         Cntr := 0; W := Blank;
         WHILE (Cntr < MaxChar) AND
```

```
                            NOT Eoln (InFile) DO BEGIN
                Cntr := Cntr + 1;
                Read (InFile, W [Cntr]);
        END;
        Readln (InFile);
END;

PROCEDURE CheckFirstTwo (VAR InFile : Text;
                         VAR List : ElementPtr);
(* This procedure ensures that the list is at least two   *)
(* elements long, for proper use of ReadNCompare.          *)
VAR     W : Word;
BEGIN
        IF (List = NIL) THEN BEGIN
            ReadWord (InFile, W);
            Insert (List, W);
        END;
        IF (List^.Nxt = NIL) THEN BEGIN
            ReadWord (InFile, W);
            IF (List^.Wrd < W)
                THEN Insert (List<.Nxt, W)
                ELSE Insert (List, W);
        END;
END;

PROCEDURE ReadNCompare (VAR InFile : Text;
                        AR List : ElementPtr);
(* This procedure reads an input file word by word and     *)
(* compares each word in the input file with those in the  *)
(* list to make sure that only one copy of each word is    *)
(* added to the list. This procedure expects and returns   *)
(* a sorted list.                                           *)
VAR     Temp : ElementPtr;
        W : Word;
BEGIN
        CheckFirstTwo (InFile, List);
        Temp := List;   (* List has at least 2 words in it *)
        WHILE NOT Eof (InFile) DO BEGIN
            ReadWord (InFile, W);
            IF (W < List^.Wrd) THEN BEGIN
                Insert (List, W)      (* alphabetically 1st *)
            END ELSE IF (W < List^.Nxt^.Wrd) THEN BEGIN
                Insert (List^.Nxt, W)   (* alphabet. 2nd    *)
            END ELSE BEGIN            (* find correct location *)
                WHILE (W > Temp^.Nxt^.Wrd) AND
                      (Temp^.Nxt^.Nxt <> NIL) DO
                    Temp := Temp^.Nxt;
                IF (Temp^.Nxt^.Nxt = NIL)
                    THEN Insert (Temp^.Nxt^.Nxt, W)
```

```
                        ELSE IF (Temp^.Nxt^.Wrd <> W) THEN
                              Insert (Temp^.Nxt, W);

               END;
           END;
     END;


BEGIN    (* Main Program *)
         InitList (List);
         Reset (Dict1); ReadNCompare (Dict1, List);
         Reset (Dict2); ReadNCompare (Dict2, List);
         Reset (Dict3); ReadNCompare (Dict3, List);
         PrintList (Output, List);
     END.    (* Main Program *)
```

Sample input files for this program were:

Dict1	Dict2	Dict3
ALPHABET	ANDREW	ABACUS
CADMIUM	BASEBALL	ALABASTER
ELEMENT	FASHION	ANDROID
FRIEND	FRIEND	BASEBALL
LOUSY	GRUESOME	DIAL
MIDDLE	RUSTIC	LAMB
NEW	TAYLOR	MIDDLE
OLD	UNDER	NEW
QUITE		OLD
RUSTY		RUSTY
SMOOTH		ZENITH
TOOLS		
UNDER		
XEBEC		

The output file generated contains the following words:

ABACUS	DIAL	MIDDLE	SMOOTH
ALABASTER	ELEMENT	NEW	TAYLOR
ALPHABET	FASHION	OLD	TOOLS
ANDREW	FRIEND	QUITE	UNDER
ANDROID	GRUESOME	RUSTIC	XEBEC
BASEBALL	LAMB	RUSTY	ZENITH
CADMIUM	LOUSY		

Other Pointer Structures

The pointer makes many different types of data structures possible. The linked list can be used to implement a stack or a queue. As we mentioned briefly, a stack is a data structure where the last element added is the first element to leave (Last In, First Out: **LIFO**). This type of data structure is used by Hewlett–Packard calculators, using reverse postfix notation.

A second and more common type of data structure is the queue, or the line, where the first element added is the first to leave, and new elements are added to the end of the queue (First In, First Out: **FIFO**). The progress of a queue is similar to the progress of a line of people. You usually enter the line at the end and leave the line after you have moved up to the beginning.

Another structure is the circular linked list. Suppose the following structure shown in Figure 19.11 existed:

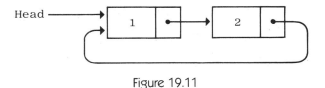

Figure 19.11

The second record's pointer points to the first. If, at this point, a third element were added between the first two, we would have the structure shown by Figure 19.13.

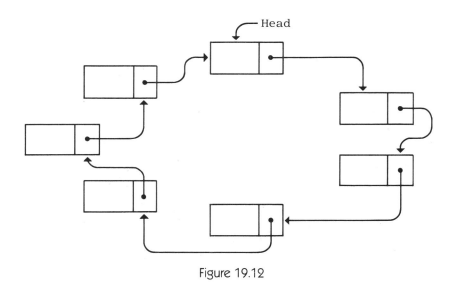

Figure 19.12

Figure 19.13: A Circular List Structure

We have created a **circular linked list,** a list that has a head but no tail. Figure 19.12 illustrates the circular nature of this kind of list.

A fourth type of structure is the doubly linked list. Sometimes it may be necessary to know both the next and the previous elements in a list for any member of it. Perhaps reverse searches or printing the elements in reverse order might be necessary. There is nothing sacred about a node record only having one pointer in it. Figure 19.14 illustrates such a structure.

```
TYPE     NodePtr  = ^Node;
         Node = RECORD;
                 Value : Integer;
                 Next,
                 Prev : NodePtr;
         END;
```

A **doubly linked list** has three compartments in each record, two pointers, and a value. Notice that two extra pointers are needed, one at `Tail` and one at `Head`. Inserting and deleting into this type of structure is understandably more complicated than inserting and deleting into singly linked lists.

The final type of data structure is the tree structure. The tree structure extends our example of a record with two pointers, as Figure 19.15 shows. To translate into Pascal:

```
TYPE     NodePtr = ^TreeNode;
         TreeNode = RECORD;
                 Value : Integer;
                 Left,
                 Right : NodePtr;
         END;
VAR      Head : NodePtr;
```

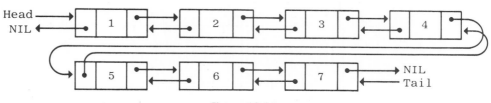

Figure 19.14

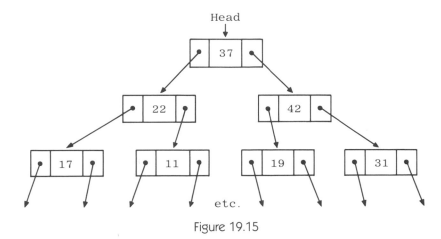

Figure 19.15

For obvious reasons, a linked structure like this is called a **tree structure** in which each node is said to have **branches,** which in turn have nodes with more branches. Figure 19.15 shows a **binary tree,** so called because each node has a maximum of two branches. But trees can have 10 branches per node if desired. For example, the following declarations would define a structure like that shown in Figure 19.16.

```
TYPE    NodePtr = ^Node;
        Node = RECORD
                Value : Integer;
                Next : ARRAY [1..Max]OF NodePtr;
        END;
```

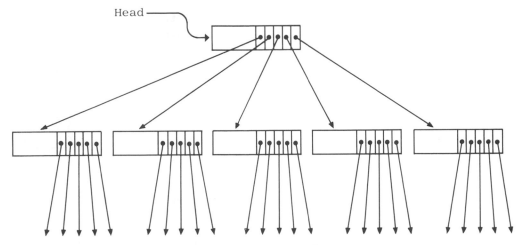

Figure 19.16: A Large Tree Structure

Programming Example 19.2

Assignment: Write a program to count the nodes of a binary tree structure.

Solution: Let's break down the problem into two problems: one to count the nodes on the left half and one to count the nodes on the right half. We now have a couple smaller problems to deal with. This sounds like the beginning of a recursive program. The two necessary steps in recursion are problem breakdown and a definite end point. The breakdown is simple.

> Count binary tree nodes:
> Total = nodes in left branch +
> nodes in right branch +
> 1 (the current node)

The end point comes when the current NodePtr is NIL, meaning that it has no nodes. A tree whose NodePtr is NIL has exactly zero nodes, and then we don't have to break the tree down any further. Suppose we are working with these type declarations.

```
TYPE    NodePtr = ^Node;
        Node = RECORD;
            Value : Integer;
            Left, Right : NodePtr;
        END;
```

Since our desire is to obtain a single number, the number of nodes in the tree, let's define CountNodes as a function. The code is very short.

```
FUNCTION CountNodes (Tree : NodePtr) : Integer;
(* This function recursively counts the number of nodes   *)
(* there are in the binary tree that is passed into it.   *)
(* It counts the number of nodes on the left branch, adds *)
(* to it the number on the right, and adds 1 for the      *)
(* trunk of the tree, the current node being examined.    *)
BEGIN
        IF (Tree = NIL)
            THEN CountNodes := 0
            ELSE CountNodes := 1 + CountNodes (Tree^.Right)
                                 + CountNodes (Tree^.Left);
END;
```

We could add to this a function that sums all the values in a binary tree.

```
FUNCTION SumValues (Tree : NodePtr) : Integer;
(* This function recursively sums the values of nodes *)
(* in a binary tree that is passed into it.  It sums  *)
```

```
(* the values of the nodes on the left branch and adds to *)
(* it the values of the nodes on the right. It also adds  *)
(* the value of the current trunk of the tree.            *)
BEGIN
        IF (Tree = NIL)
            THEN SumValues := 0
            ELSE SumValues := Tree.Value +
                            SumValues (Tree^.Right) +
                            SumValues (Tree^.Left);
END;
```

We could then write a simple function that calculates the average of all of the values in a tree.

```
FUNCTION TreeAve (Tree : NodePtr) : Real;
BEGIN
        TreeAve := SumValues (Tree) / CountNodes (Tree);
END;
```

Common Errors and Debugging

1. **Referencing NIL or uninitialized pointers.** Two steps will save you from this error. First of all, initialize all pointers that haven't received a value by assignment or through the procedure New to NIL. This will allow you to test their values later. Secondly, whenever accessing a field in the record of some pointer, make sure that the pointer is not NIL. Reference the pointer in the WHILE loop test before moving the temporary pointer. For example:

```
WHILE (Temp^.Next <> NIL) DO
        Temp := Temp^.Next;
```

2. **Attempting to use a pointer as the value to which it points.** Remember, it is impossible to read, write, or assign values to pointers. Pointers need the symbol ^ in order to reference their data. It is only valid to assign pointer variables to other pointer variables.

3. **Attempting to store data in an uninitialized pointer.** Each new pointer must receive a memory location through New before the pointer can be used to store information. Nothing is in the memory locations before initialization.

4. **Deleting incorrectly.** When deleting from the middle of a list, it is necessary to have a temporary pointer that points to the record before the record to be deleted. It is the previous record's Next pointer that will be changed. If the

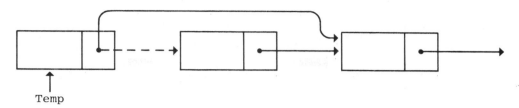

Temp

Figure 19.17

temporary pointer refers to the record to be deleted, it is impossible to alter the list correctly. Figure 19.17 illustrates a proper deletion.

5. **Counting down a list incorrectly.** When a temporary pointer is used to count down the list, take care that no changes are made to the list. The following commands do *not* have the same effect.

```
Temp := Temp^.Next;      (*correct*)
Temp^.Next := Temp^.Next^.Next;   (*incorrect, destroys the list*)
```

SUMMARY

Pointers allow the **dynamic allocation** of variable memory space, so programs can compile and execute correctly without knowing ahead of time how much storage space is necessary. An integer pointer variable has as its value the memory location where an integer value can be stored, but to try to store an integer in a pointer variable produces an error. Pointer variables are most often used in the form of linked lists, which are lists of records, or nodes, each of which contain some useful information and a pointer to the next node in the list.

Lists can be manipulated more easily than arrays in certain respects. It is very easy to add or delete nodes at the beginning of a list; it is much more difficult to do the same with array structures. The standard procedures New and Dispose must be used to allocate and dispose of memory locations assigned to pointer variables. It is an error to try to access the record fields of an uninitialized pointer. Pointers without memory locations should be initialized to the value NIL. You can then use the pointers when searching for the end of a list when printing the entire list or deleting the final element.

Procedures for adding and deleting elements at the head and the tail of a list can be used to implement a **stack** (**LIFO**) or a **queue** (**FIFO**). When deleting elements, take care to use Dispose to eliminate the deleted record without eliminating access to the rest of the nodes in the list.

Other common pointer structures are the **circular linked list,** the **doubly linked list,** and the **tree.** In a tree structure, each node has two pointers or more, which point to other nodes with other pointers. A node is said to have **branches** because of the shape of a pictorial representation of this type of structure. Probably the most common type of tree is the **binary** tree, in which each node has a maximum of two branches.

New Terms

dynamic allocation	queue	tree structure
static allocation	LIFO	branches
node	FIFO	binary tree
uninitialized	circular linked list	New
stack	doubly linked list	Dispose

EXERCISES

1. Given the list shown in Figure 19.18, tell the result of each of the following operations as they appear in the sequence. Any changes in the list affect the following operations. Note any errors.

    a. `Temp := List`
    b. `Temp := Temp^.Next`
    c. `Temp^.Value := Sqr (Temp^.Next^.Value)`
    d. `Write (Output, Temp^.Next^.Value)`
    e. `Write (Output, Temp^.Next)`
    f. `Temp^.Next := Temp^.Next^.Next`
    g. `Temp^.Next^.Next := Temp^.Next`
    h. `Temp := Temp^.Next`
    i. `Write (Output, Temp^.Value)`
    j. `Temp := Temp^.Next`

2. Find the error in each program fragment.

    ```
    a. FUNCTION SumList (P : ^Node) : Integer;
       VAR      Temp : Integer;
       BEGIN
               Temp := 0;
               WHILE (P <> NIL) DO BEGIN
                   Temp := P^.Value + Temp;
                   P := P^.Next;
               END;
               SumList := Temp;
       END;
    ```

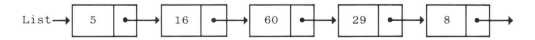

Figure 19.18: List to Be Used With Exercise 1

b. PROCEDURE FindPrevious (P : NodePtr;
                           Which : Integer;
                           VAR Prev : Integer);
 BEGIN
        WHILE (P^.Next<>NIL) AND
               (P^.Next^.Value<>Which) DO
            P := P^.Next;
        IF (P^.Next^.Value=Which)
            THEN Prev := P^.Value;
 END;

c. PROCEDURE PrintList (P : NodePtr);
 BEGIN
        WHILE (P<>NIL) DO BEGIN
            Writeln (Output, P.Value);
            P^.Next := P^.Next^.Next;
        END;
 END;

3. This chapter introduced five important procedures: `InitList`, `AddToHead`, `AddToTail`, `DeleteHead`, and `DeleteTail`. Rewrite the procedures to accommodate a doubly linked list.

4. Rewrite the five procedures to accommodate a binary tree structure.

5. Write an airport runway control program. Assume that it takes a plane about 3 minutes to take off, 2 minutes to land, and that, on average, about 10 planes take off and land every hour, although the arrivals and departures are random. Build a queueing program that monitors the airplanes trying to land and those trying to take off. Operate on a strict queue at first, and then improve your program to give priority to planes in the air, since it costs much more to keep a plane aloft than it does to keep it on the ground. Is this airport's runway too busy?

6. Rewrite the functions that appear on page 563, `CountNodes` and `SumValues`, to accommodate tree structures in which each node has an array of `Max` nodes. Write a function that calculates the average of all of the nodes in the tree.

7. Write a program that allows the user to enter the values of a tree into the data structure. Allow the user to determine the number of branches each node will have, and to see the results of the tree at any time. Represent the tree as an attractive pictorial display, and use the functions developed in the previous exercise to perform simple operations. Allow the user to snip branches of the tree, or to insert into the tree structure.

8. One efficient algorithm for sorting a list of numbers uses a binary tree data structure. This binary tree sort is handled as follows: The first number in the list is placed at the trunk of the tree, the first node. The second number is read and placed in the left branch of the first node if it is less than the first number. If it is greater, it is placed in the right branch. Each successive number is placed on the left if it is less than the current node, and to the right if it is greater. The tree is built up as is shown in Figure 19.19. Write a procedure to build up this type of a list from an input file of integers.

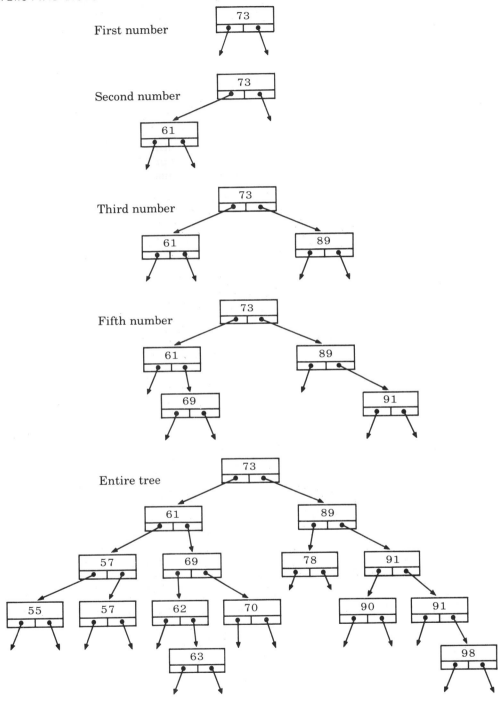

Figure 19.19: Binary Tree Sort

9. The sorted binary tree is printed in order by a simple recursive algorithm.

    Print Tree:
        Print Tree (right branch)
        Print Node value
        Print Tree (left branch)

    Write a recursive function to implement this algorithm. Make sure you include a stopping condition so that the recursion will not continue forever or encounter uninitialized pointers. Combine this function with your last procedure to make a program that reads in a list of numbers and writes out the sorted list.

APPENDIX 1
THE GOTO STATEMENT

The GOTO statement in Pascal is used as a GO TO statement in BASIC; it transfers program control from one statement to another. The GOTO reserved word is followed by a label (an integer between 1 and 9999) and the statement to which the program control is transferred must be identified by the given label. Any labels used in a program must be declared in the block in which they are used. If a label declaration occurs in a block, it must occur before any constants, types, or variables are declared.

For example, suppose the detection of an error would make it desirable to terminate execution of a program.

```
PROGRAM ShowGOTO (Input, Output);
LABEL  999;

PROCEDURE TestData;
VAR    Sum, Cntr, Num : Integer;
BEGIN
       Sum := 0;
       FOR Cntr := 1 TO 100 DO BEGIN
           Readln (Input, Num);
           IF (Num <> 0)
               THEN Sum := Sum + Num
               ELSE GOTO 999;
           Writeln (Output, Sum, Sum/Num);
       END;
END;

BEGIN
     TestData;
999:     Writeln (Output, 'That''s all!');
     END.
```

Of course, this program could be written very easily without the use of a GOTO by using a conditional looping structure, and in general, the statement should be avoided. Especially you former BASIC programmers: eliminate this control structure from your vocabulary.

APPENDIX 2
TURBO PASCAL

The TURBO Pascal system is a compiler/editor system designed to aid in the development of Pascal programs. The editor available in the TURBO system is designed like the popular WordStar word processing program available for personal computers, and the compiler is efficient and well-extended for personal computer usage.

There are many extensions in the TURBO system that can be very useful to the experienced or learning programmer. Furthermore, most of the programs written in this book could be executed with only slight modifications in the area of file handling. Let's first examine some of the major extensions and tools for programming in TURBO Pascal, and then we'll catalogue the differences between the programs written in this book (in Standard Pascal) and those TURBO Pascal will comprehend.

TURBO Pascal's Extended Vocabulary

TURBO Pascal includes a number of additional reserved words and standard identifiers (constants, types, procedures, and functions). First of all, there are several additional reserved words that act as boolean or arithmetic operators in TURBO Pascal.

XOR   eXclusive OR. This boolean operator takes two boolean values and returns TRUE if either of the two values is TRUE. If neither is TRUE, or if they both are TRUE, then the resulting value of the expression is FALSE.

SHL   SHift Left. This arithmetic operator treats the first operand as if it were a binary number. The second operand in the expression is the number of places the binary number should be shifted to the left. For example, 12 SHL 3 means shift the binary number 1100 three places to the left, which produces 1100000, or 96.

SHR   SHift Right. This arithmetic operator is the reverse of SHL; the binary number is shifted the desired number of digits to the right.

Also, a number of the regularly understood operators have extended usages in TURBO Pascal. For example, AND, OR, XOR, and NOT can all be applied to arithmetic operands as well as to boolean operands. Arithmetic operands are converted into binary numbers and a digitwise operation is carried out. For example:

12 AND 22   equals   10110 AND 1100

which is 00100, or 4. Likewise,

12 OR 22   equals   10110 OR 1100

which is 11110, or 30.

12 XOR 22   equals   26

Another reserved word that has been given a new usage is the ELSE clause, which can be used in a CASE statement. The discussion in the book mentioned how the CASE statement was often extended with some allowance for encountering cases that are not explicitly mentioned in any of the CASE value lists. For example:

```
CASE Command OF
     'A' : AddRec (DataBase);
     'D' : DeleteRec (DataBase);
     'O' : Sort (DataBase);
     'P' : Print (DataBase);
     'Q' : Quit (DataBase);
     'S' : Save (DataBase);
     'H' : Help;
     ELSE BEGIN
         Writeln ('Illegal command.');
         Help;
     END;
END;
```

String Handling in TURBO Pascal

Another reserved word new in TURBO Pascal is the type identifier STRING. The STRING data type is essentially equivalent to the Standard Pascal declaration

```
TYPE    String = PACKED ARRAY [1..StrLen] OF Char;
```

In TURBO Pascal, however, this declaration is illegal because STRING is a reserved word. This is used in declarations as follows:

```
CONST    WordLen = 16;
         LineLen = 80;
TYPE     Word : STRING [WordLen];
         Line : STRING [LineLen];
VAR      W : Word;
         L : Line;
```

The maximum length of a STRING type is 255. A variable of type STRING can be given a value by the Readln standard procedure. For example:

```
Readln (Input, W, L)
```

will put the first WordLen characters on a line into W and put the remaining characters (or the next LineLen characters) into the variable L.

TURBO Pascal includes a number of handy string manipulation procedures, functions, and operators. The concatenation operator is easy to use.

```
W := 'Hello' + ' ' + 'Jordan';
L := W + ', how are you?' + ' I''m fine.'
Writeln (Output, L);
```

The value of W would be 'Hello Jordan' and the output line would read:

OUTPUT   Hello Jordan, how are you? I'm fine.

The remaining string procedures and functions are best handled by Table A.1.

For example, let's try to reverse the order of names in a string of the format:

```
Mr. Richard Lamb
```

to be written:

```
Lamb, Richard
```

This type of procedure might be used to prepare a list of names for alphabetization.

```
PROCEDURE Reformat (VAR Name : StringType);
(* This procedure reformats a standard address label to   *)
(* contain last name first, for ease in alphabetization.  *)
VAR      First : StringType;
BEGIN
         Readln (Input, Name);   (* in address label format *)
         Delete (Name, 1, Pos (' ', Name));
                 (* deletes up to and including first space *)
         First := Copy (Name, 1, Pos (' ', Name));
                 (* makes a copy of the first name          *)
```

Name	Syntax	Action
Delete	Delete (St, Pos, Num)	Removes a substring containing `Num` characters from `St` beginning at position `Pos`.
Insert	Insert (Obj, Target, Pos)	Inserts the string `Obj` into the string `Target` at the position `Pos`.
Str	Str (Value, St)	Converts the numeric value of `Value` into a string and stores the result in `St`. `Value` must be written as if it were in a `Write` statement, for example: `Num:5`. The resulting string (if `Num` = 987) would be `' 987'`.
Val	Val (St, Var, Code)	Converts string `St` into an integer or real `Var`. If the string does not represent a legal value, `Code` is given the position in the string where the error occurs.
Copy	Tmp := Copy (St, Pos, Num)	A function that copies a substring from `St`, beginning at `Pos` and containing `Num` characters, into a string variable `Tmp`.
Length	Write (Output, Length (St))	A function that returns the number of characters in the string expression `St`.
Pos	Num := Pos (Obj, Target)	A function that scans the `Target` to find the first occurrence of `Obj`. If `Obj` is not found, then the result is 0.

Table A.1. String Procedures and Functions

```
      Delete (Name, 1, Pos (' ', Name));
              (* deletes first name from string       *)
      Name := Name + ', ' + First;
              (* adds comma and first name to end      *)
END;
```

Here are some examples of the other functions and procedures:

```
      Str1 := 'Hello, Jennie.'
      Str2 := 'ABCDEFGHIJKLM';
      Delete (Str1, 10, 4);       (* Str1 = 'Hello, Jen' *)
      Delete (Str2, 10, 200);     (* Str2 = 'ABCDEFGHIJ' *)
      Insert ('Alex and ', Str1, 8);
                          (* Str1 = 'Hello, Alex and Jen'*)
```

```
I := 497; X := 429.8630;
Str (I:5, Str2);              (* Str2 = '  497'       *)
Str (X:10:2, Str2);           (* Str2 = '    429.86' *)
I := Length ('Person hours worked = ' + Str2);
                              (* I = 32 *)
```

Input and Output File Handling in TURBO Pascal

The Pascal standard file Input will be understood in one of two ways in TURBO Pascal, neither of which is exactly like the input file used in this text. Normally, Input refers to information that is typed at the keyboard, and the input is buffered, or stored temporarily, one line at a time. This allows the user to edit the typed line of input before entering it with a carriage return. The problem is that this buffering causes the Eoln and Eof functions to work incorrectly and text data will be read improperly.

The second way to use Input is to reset a compiler setting in TURBO Pascal by means of the "comment," {$B-}. This is called a compiler directive, and it tells the computer not to buffer the input when it is typed from the keyboard. That means that Eoln and Eof will work correctly, although the user will not be able to edit the input line before typing a carriage return.

If any other files are desired, either hard-copy output or batch mode input files, then the programmer must specify the file name using an Assign statement:

```
Assign (InFile, 'Data1.Txt');
Assign (OutFile, 'Report.mss');
```

An Assign statement must precede the Reset and Rewrite statements for each file. If the user needs to designate the name of the input or output file, the program can request the file name.

```
Writeln (Output, 'Type data file name');
Readln (Input, InFileName);
Writeln (Output, 'Type report file name');
Readln (Input, OutFileName);
Assign (InFile, InFileName);
Assign (OutFile, OutFileName);
```

Before the program terminates, any open files should be closed to prevent the loss of the data.

```
Close (InFile);
Close (OutFile);
```

Screen Control Commands

TURBO Pascal provides a number of simple screen control procedures that facilitate the use of screen-oriented interaction between the user and the computer. With the current level of understanding of Pascal, we have never been able to produce output in any way other than a line at a time. When working with a screen, rather than simply a line, it is easy to produce attractive and easy-to-read dialogue between the user and the computer. Here are some of the procedures and functions and what they do.

ClrEol	Clears all characters from the cursor to the end of the line without moving the cursor.
ClrScr	Clears the screen, places cursor at upper left-hand corner.
DelLine	Deletes the line containing the cursor and moves lower lines up one line.
InsLine	Inserts an empty line at the cursor position. Bottom line on screen scrolls off.
GoToXY	GoToXY (X, Y)—moves the cursor to the Yth row, Xth column, where the upper left corner is (1, 1).
LowVideo	Sets screen printing to dim characters.
NormVideo	Resets screen printing to normal brightness.
KeyPressed	This boolean function returns TRUE if a key has been pressed at the console, and FALSE otherwise.

An example program that uses these procedures to implement a screen-oriented menu is given below.

```
PROGRAM ScreenMenu;
(* This program prints a menu on the screen and allows    *)
(* the user to choose from among the options by moving    *)
(* the cursor up and down until the desired choice is     *)
(* found. Then the selection is made.                     *)

CONST    MaxChoices = 10;
         MaxChars = 20;
TYPE     Word = String[MaxChars];
         ChoiceArray = ARRAY [1..MaxChoices] OF Word;

CONST    Choices : ChoiceArray = ('Red', 'Orange',
                   'Yellow', 'Green', 'Blue', 'Indigo',
                   'Violet', 'Magenta', 'Mauve', 'Black');
```

```
VAR        Selection : Word;

PROCEDURE Flash (X, Y : Integer; S : Word);
(* This procedure flashes word S on the screen at    *)
(* position (X, Y). The flashing is terminated when  *)
(* the user presses a key at the console.            *)
VAR        Blink : Boolean;
BEGIN
     HighVideo; GoToXY (X, Y); Write (S);
     Blink : = TRUE;
     REPEAT   GoToXY (X, Y);
              IF Blink THEN HighVideo ELSE LowVideo;
              Write (S);
              Delay (200); (* Delays .2 seconds        *)
              Blink : = NOT Blink;
     UNTIL KeyPressed;
     LowVideo;
END;


PROCEDURE GiveMenu (Choices : ChoiceArray);
(* This procedure prints the menu of choices given in *)
(* the Choices array.                                 *)
CONST   Indent = 8;    (* Indent 8 spaces from left  *)
        TopLine = 4;    (* Top line of menu           *)
VAR     RowCntr, ChoiceCntr : Integer;
BEGIN
        RowCntr : = TopLine; ChoiceCntr : = 0;
        WHILE (ChoiceCntr < MaxChoices) DO BEGIN
           GoToXY (Indent, RowCntr);
           ChoiceCntr : = ChoiceCntr + 1;
           IF (Choices [ChoiceCntr] <> '') THEN BEGIN
              Write (Output, '- ', Choices [ChoiceCntr]);
              RowCntr : = RowCntr + 2;
           END;
        END;
END;


PROCEDURE SelectMenu (Choices : ChoiceArray;
                      VAR Selection : Word);
(* This procedure allows the user to select one of    *)
(* choices available. The Selection is returned.      *)
CONST   Indent = 8;    (* Indent 8 spaces from left  *)
        TopLine = 4;    (* Top line of menu           *)
VAR     RowCntr, ChoiceCntr : Integer;
        Ch : Char;
BEGIN
        GoToXY (2, 1);
        Write (Output, 'Type U for up, D for down, ',
                       'and S to make a selection,');
```

```
        RowCntr := TopLine; ChoiceCntr := 1;
        GoToXY (Indent, RowCntr);
        Read (Kbd, Ch);  (* read command from keyboard *)
        WHILE  (Ch <> 'S') DO BEGIN
            IF (Ch = 'D') THEN BEGIN
                RowCntr := RowCntr + 2;
                ChoiceCntr := ChoiceCntr + 1;
                If (ChoiceCntr > MaxChoices) THEN BEGIN
                    ChoiceCntr := 1;
                    RowCntr := TopLine;
                END;
            END ELSE IF (Ch = 'U') THEN BEGIN
                RowCntr := RowCntr - 2;
                ChoiceCntr := ChoiceCntr - 1;
                IF (ChoiceCntr < 1) THEN BEGIN
                    ChoiceCntr := MaxChoices;
                    RowCntr := TopLine + 2 * (Max Choices-1);
                END;
            END
            GoToXY (Indent, RowCntr);
            Read (Kbd, Ch);
        END;
        Selection := Choices [ChoiceCntr];
END;


BEGIN
        REPEAT  GiveMenu (Choices);
                SelectMenu (Choices, Selection);
                ClrScr;
                Flash (22, 13, Selection);
                ClrScr; HighVideo;
        UNTIL (Selection = 'Black');
END.
```

APPENDIX 3
CHARACTER SETS

Two different character sets have been referred to in this text. The American Standard Code for Information Interchange (ASCII) and the Extend Binary Coded Decimal Interchange Code (EBCDIC) are the two most common standard character sets. Each character set also includes nonprintable characters (like the bell and control characters) which are not printed in these tables. The ordinal number for each character can be calculated by multiplying the row number (the left digit) by ten and then adding the column number. The blank is shown as a ⌴.

ASCII										
Column:	0	1	2	3	4	5	6	7	8	9
Row 3:			⌴	!	"	#	$	%	&	'
4:	(	)	*	+	,	-	.	/	0	1
5:	2	3	4	5	6	7	8	9	:	;
6:	<	=	>	?	@	A	B	C	D	E
7:	F	G	H	I	J	K	L	M	N	O
8:	P	Q	R	S	T	U	V	W	X	Y
9:	Z	[	\	]	^	_	`		a	b	c
10:	d	e	f	g	h	i	j	k	l	m
11:	n	o	p	q	r	s	t	u	v	w
12:	x	y	z	{			}					

EBCDIC

Column:	0	1	2	3	4	5	6	7	8	9
Row 6:					□					
7:					¢	.	<	(	+	|
8:	&									
9:	!	$	*	)	;	-	—	/		
10:							^	,	%	–
11:	>	?								
12:			:	#	@	'	=	"		a
13:	b	c	d	e	f	g	h	i		
14:						j	k	l	m	n
15:	o	p	q	r						
16:			s	t	u	v	w	x	y	z
17:								\	{	}
18:	[	]								
19:				A	B	C	D	E	F	G
20:	H	I								J
21:	K	L	M	N	O	P	Q	R		
22:							S	T	U	V
23:	W	X	Y	Z						
24:	0	1	2	3	4	5	6	7	8	9

GLOSSARY

activation   the range within a program where an identifier is understood as a specific class and type.

actual parameter   a variable that occurs in the parameter list in a procedure call.

actual parameter list   the list of variables or expressions to be evaluated that is given to the procedure being called.

algorithm   the systematic process or plan used to solve a problem.

algorithmic refinement   the process of program design that begins with an abstract solution and successively refines it by defining each of the subtasks in greater detail.

allocate   to set aside memory space for variables. See **dynamic allocation; static allocation.**

alphanumerics   characters that are either letters or numerals.

argument   the input parameter to a function. See **parameter.**

arithmetic operator   a special symbol or reserved word used in numerical expressions to denote an arithmetic operation producing a numerical result. Examples: +, −, *, /, DIV, MOD.

array   sequential storage locations in memory that bear a common name differentiated by numbers or subscripts.

ASCII   American Standard Code for Information Interchange, a common character code assigning computer-readable codes to alphanumeric and control characters.

assertion   a statement occurring in the form of a comment that the programmer believes to be true in all cases at the point where the assertion occurs.

assignment   the act of storing a calculated or specified value in a memory location.

base type   the type of the individual components that make up an array.

BASIC interpreter   a program that takes a BASIC program as input and executes the statements as directed by the BASIC code.

batch processing   the mode of program execution in which user interaction is not necessary. Input is from a file, and the output is written to a file. Compare **interactive processing.**

binary infix operator   an arithmetic or logical operator that occurs in an expression between two operands.

binary search   a search algorithm that compares the middle element in a sorted array to the element being sought. Each successive comparison is made with only half of the current array.

binary tree   a linked structure in which each node has two pointers that point to other nodes. This structure is different from a doubly linked list in that no pair of nodes are doubly linked by pointers.

bit   a BInary digiT (either 0 or 1) used to store information in a computer. Bits are grouped into bytes and words.

block   a unit of Pascal code consisting of a declaration part (which may be empty), followed by the executable statements, surrounded by a BEGIN-END pair.

boolean arithmetic   the system of evaluating an expression so that it has a value of either TRUE or FALSE.

boolean operator   an operator that combines boolean expressions using boolean arithmetic. AND, OR, and NOT are the three boolean operators.

boolean variable   a variable that assumes only one of two possible values: FALSE or TRUE.

branch   (1) one of several options in a conditional execution statement, (2) a subtree in a binary tree structure.

bubble sort   a sorting algorithm whose passes become shorter and shorter as it drops sorted elements from each successive pass.

buffer variable   See **file buffer variable.**

bug   an error. There are three types of errors: compiler, execution, and intent.

call   a statement that transfers the control of execution to a defined procedure or function.

cardinality   the total number of possible values in any ordinal type.

CASE statement   a Pascal statement allowing for multiple-branch conditional execution. A generalized form of the IF statement.

central processing unit   (CPU) the part of the computer that recognizes and executes instructions and allows communication between the other parts of the computer.

character set   the set of machine-understood characters encoded according to an encoding system such as ASCII.

character string   a string of alphanumeric characters delimited by single quotation marks.

chi-square   a value that indicates the degree to which the given data distribution is statistically unlikely to be random.

circular linked list   a list that has a head but no tail, where each node points to exactly one other node in the list.

class   an attribute of an identifier that indicates whether the identifier is a constant, type, variable, procedure, or function identifier.

code   (1) a computer program or a program fragment, (2) to write a computer program; to convert an algorithm into a program.

comment   a portion of the program ignored by the compiler but included to aid human understanding of the program.

compiler   a program that translates a source code program into a machine language program that can be executed by the computer.

component   a part of a data structure. The component of an array is the element that, by repetition, makes up the array.

component type   See **base type.**

compound statement   a set of zero or more Pascal statements inside a BEGIN-END pair of delimiters.

computer   a machine that has the ability to store, process, and retrieve numerical data and the ability to be programmed, allowing automatic control of the operations performed on the data.

condition   a boolean expression used to determine the action of a conditional execution or repetition statement.

conditional execution   the selection of one action among two or more actions based on the existence of certain conditions.

conditional repetition   repetition of a block of code an unpredetermined number of times.

constant   a memory location referenced by an identifier that stores a value that cannot be changed during a program's execution.

control character   a character at the beginning of an output line that determines the amount of vertical spacing before a printed line.

control structure   a statement that alters in some way the normal sequence of executed statements in a Pascal program.

control variable   the variable used by a FOR loop that controls the cycle of repetitions; may be of any scalar variable type.

CPU   central processing unit.

dangling ELSE   the ELSE clause left over after an IF statement has been prematurely terminated by a semicolon.

data abstraction   the ability to remove from the usage of a data type any specific knowledge about how it is stored or manipulated.

data base program   any program whose chief purpose is to organize, manipulate, search, and sort data and which has the ability to receive new data and print out listings of stored data

data structure   a system of organizing data for ease of storage, processing, and retrieval.

debugging   the systematic removal of errors from a computer program.

declaration   a statement that defines identifier(s) to be of some specific class and type.

default value   an assumed value used by the computer when no value is specified by the user or the programmer.

defensive programming   the strategy of carefully and systematically writing programs to decrease the number of initial syntax, execution, and intent errors.

documentation   any part of the program code that improves readability, modifiability, or usefulness, including comments and well-chosen identifier names as well as specifications and descriptions of the algorithm.

doubly linked list   a list whose nodes use two pointers to enable moving forward and backward from node to node along the list structure.

dynamic allocation   the allocation of memory space after the compilation stage and during the execution stage of a program run. The amount of memory allocation is variable, dependent on run-time conditions.

editor   a program that allows programs or data to be entered into the computer's memory and allows the information stored in memory to be updated and corrected.

element   a value of a simple type that is found in a set of that type.

empty set   a set with zero elements in it.

empty statement   a legal Pascal statement resulting when two semicolons or a semicolon and an END delimiter are used consecutively.

end-of-file marker   the character that indicates the end of an input file.

end-of-line marker   carriage return-line feed (CLRF), which indicates the end of a line of input.

enumerated type   a user-defined type in which all the legal values are legal identifiers and are listed in sequence.

environment   the set of constants, variables, and procedures that is defined at a given point in the program. The environment of a procedure includes all global identifiers as well as any locally declared identifiers.

error   See **syntax error; execution error; intent error.**

execute   to carry out the instructions specified by a Pascal program.

execution error   an error detected in the execution stage of the program-debugging process, usually causing the execution to terminate, or crash.

exponential notation   the method of expressing a number as a value (the mantissa) multiplied by 10 raised to the power indicated by the exponent.

expression   a sequence of variables, function calls, constants, and operators of an appropriate type that is evaluated during the execution of the program.

Fibonacci sequence   a sequence where any number is the sum of the two previous numbers, and the first two numbers are both 1.

field   an individual component of a record variable.

field width   the number of spaces allocated to print a value of a variable or expression.

FIFO   first in, first out. See **queue.**

file   a Pascal data structure that allows sequential but not random access of values.

file buffer variable   a variable that contains the value of the next character or component in a file to be read or written.

fixed field   a field in a variant record variable whose existence is not dependent on the tag field value—it is present for all values of the variant record variable.

flow of control   the order in which each line or part of a program is executed. Normally, flow of control is sequential.

FOR **loop**   the Pascal control structure that implements definite repetition.

formal parameter   a variable that is declared and used inside a procedure, whose value is associated with another variable outside the procedure.

formal parameter list   the list of the variables and their types used as formal parameters inside a procedure.

format   the visual cues a program gives to the reader about its structure and logic.

function   a Pascal subtask that calculates and returns a single value.

global identifier   an identifier that is declared in the main program block. Compare **local identifier.**

GOTO   a Pascal statement that unconditionally alters the flow of control by sending the control to a labeled statement

hardware   any part of the machinery involved in operating a computer, as well as the CPU and memory of the computer itself. Compare **software.**

histogram   a graphical representation of the relative frequencies of values or the ranges of values in a data set.

host type   the base type from which a subrange type is taken.

identifier   a name given as any sequence of alphanumerics. The first character in the sequence must be a letter.

implementation dependent   describes any feature of a language that is not fixed but varies with different computers.

index   the value of the label of a specific component in an array.

index type   the type of the values that specify the index of an array component.

index variable   See **control variable.**

infinite loop   a piece of program code that loops on a condition that will never change or allow the loop to terminate.

initialize   to assign an initial value to a variable before its use.

input file   a sequence of characters in memory that contains data needed to calculate or determine the results of a program.

integer   any whole number, including negative numbers.

intent error   an error caused by faulty logic or by the use of a faulty algorithm. A running program may be structured incorrectly and therefore does not produce the desired result.

interactive processing   the mode of program execution in which the user plays an important role in the program's completion. Input is gathered from the terminal keyboard and output is sent to the user at the terminal screen.

intersection   the set operation producing a set containing only elements occurring in both of two sets.

invariant assertions   a statement about a loop whose validity does not change as the loop progresses.

I/O device   input/output device; a component of a computer system that allows communication between humans and computers.

iteration   repetition in which the variable of the FOR loop is used in the statement(s) under its control.

label   an integer in the range of 1 to 9,999 declared in a label declaration and used to refer to a particular statement. See GOTO.

library function   See **standard function.**

LIFO   last in, first out. See **stack.**

local environment   a procedure's set of locally declared identifiers: constants, variables, procedures, and so forth.

local identifier   a variable that is declared inside a procedure. Compare **global identifier.**

logical operator   See **boolean operator.**

loop   a control structure that allows the repetition of statements until a termination condition is achieved.

machine language   a computer programming language that specifies instructions that the CPU can execute. Programs written in machine language are virtually impossible for humans to read.

memory   the part of the computer where instructions and data are stored for use and processing by the CPU.

merge sort   a sorting algorithm that takes two sorted data sets and merges them into a single sorted data set.

modularity   the degree to which a procedure is modular, or complete on its own with no outside (global) references.

module   a group of related and often dependent procedures and functions in a program.

multidimensional array   an array with two or more index types where both are needed to specify a single component in the array.

nested repetition   repeating a series of repeated actions.

NIL   a Pascal constant used to initialize a pointer variable before it is given a structure to which to point.

node   a discrete storage structure, usually a record, in a linked list or tree structure.

operator   a special symbol or reserved word specifying an arithmetic or logic operation to be performed.

ordinal type   any simple type whose values can be ordered and counted; that is, any simple type except Real.

output   the results of the calculations of a program, usually sent to an output file.

packed array   an array that stores the most information into the least amount of space. Accessing individual elements becomes less efficient than in a regular array, but space allocation is more efficient.

parameter   See **actual parameter; formal parameter; value parameter; variable parameter.**

passed-by-reference parameter   See **variable parameter.**

passed-by-value parameter   See **value parameter.**

perfect number   a number whose exact divisors, excepting itself, sum to equal the number. For example, $6 = 1 + 2 + 3$.

portability   the degree to which a procedure is portable, able to be moved into another environment without affecting its ability to perform its given task.

postcondition assertions   assertions that indicate what the programmer thinks will always be true after the execution of the code.

precedence   an arithmetic hierarchy that determines the order of operations in an expression with more than one operator.

Order of Precedence of Operators

```
NOT, - (negation)
*, /, DIV, MOD, AND
+, -, OR
=, <>, <, >, <=, >=, IN
```

precondition assertions   assertions that indicate the conditions that must be true for the code to work properly in all cases.

predecessor function   the Pascal function, Pred, that takes as a parameter any ordinal value and returns the value that immediately precedes it.

prime number   a number whose only exact divisors are 1 and itself.

procedure   a block of Pascal code that handles a single task, usually a part of the overall task of the program. The syntax of a procedure is nearly equivalent in structure to an entire program.

procedure call   a statement that directs the program control to execute a subtask located elsewhere in the program; the statement that invokes a procedure.

procedure declaration   the block of code that defines the actions that the computer takes and the variables needed for a procedure.

programming code   the programming commands used to direct the actions of the computer. The first programmers used the word code because programs used to be very difficult to read.

programming language   a set of vocabulary, symbols, and rules used to control the operations of a computer.

pseudocode   "false code," an abbreviated form of a solution to a programming problem that includes programming language vocabulary together with English words in an informal structure.

queue   a list where the first element added to the list becomes the first element to leave the list (FIFO).

random access the process of storing and retrieving elements in a data structure where individual elements may be examined in any random order.

random number a number generated by a seemingly unordered and unpredictable algorithm. More appropriately named pseudorandom number.

range the specification of the smallest and largest allowable values in a subrange declaration or an array index declaration.

real number a number with a fractional part or an exponent.

record a structured type that can contain elements of different simple types or other structure types.

recursion a form of repetition that is carried out through program logic by procedures that may call themselves. Recursion is the process of defining statements recursively.

reference parameter See **variable parameter.**

relational operator a binary infix operator that takes two arguments of any simple type and evaluates the defined relationship between the values of the arguments.

Relational Operators

Operator	Meaning
=	Equal to
>	Greater than
<	Less than
> =	Greater than or equal to
< =	Less than or equal to
<>	Not equal to

repeat statement a conditional repetition control structure.

reserved word a word in Pascal that has a set definition and use and cannot be altered.

round-off error errors in numerical computations that occur because of the computer's limited ability to store decimal numbers accurately.

scalar variable any variable that has values that can be counted and listed. Given one value of a scalar variable, it is always possible to calculate the next value in the sequence.

scope the range of statements within a program in which an identifier is given meaning by the compiler.

selection See **conditional execution.**

selection sort a sorting algorithm that sorts an array by selecting the largest or smallest element in the array and placing it at the top of the list and then doing the same with the remaining unsorted list.

semantics   the formal rules defining how valid constructions in a language are to be understood.

sequence   an ordered list of numbers that shows relationship.

sequential access   the process of storing or retrieving elements in a data structure where individual elements must be examined in the order in which they are stored. Examples: linked lists and files.

set   an unordered collection of elements or members.

set difference   the set operation producing a set containing all the elements in the first set that are not in the second set.

simple type   any unstructured type, including Pascal types Real, Integer, Char, and Boolean, as well as user-defined enumerated and subrange types.

software   a computer program. Compare **hardware.**

source code   the program code that a compiler translates into a machine language program.

special symbols   special one- and two-character symbols that act as abbreviations for computer operations or that separate and organize other parts of a Pascal program.

stack   a list where the last element added becomes the first element to leave the list (LIFO).

standard function   a predefined function that operates on a given argument to return a result dependent upon the argument and the definition of the function.

statement   a legal instruction in a programming language.

static allocation   the allocation of memory spaces to variables during the compilation stage of program execution. The amount of memory allocated is fixed at compile time.

stepwise refinement   algorithmic refinement.

structured programming   a method of constructing and designing programs that emphasizes readability, modifiability, and ease of debugging. See **top-down programming.**

structured type   any type composed of more than one element or one memory location.

style   the format and internal documentation of a program; the features of a program that make it easy (or difficult by their absence) to read, modify, and use the program.

subrange type   a type defined to be a subset of any ordinal type.

successor function   the Pascal function, Succ, that takes as a parameter any ordinal value and returns the next value.

syntax   the formal rules defining valid constructions in a language.

syntax error   an error caused when the rules that govern the construction of a program have been broken. Also called compiler errors, because the compiler spots them.

tag field   the field in a variant record variable that determines which variable fields will be included in the variable's structure.

top-down programming   a strategy of program design using algorithmic refinement. The "top" is an abstract definition of the problem and the "bottom" is a highly detailed solution.

tracing execution   simulating the actions of the computer in order to discover an error or bug; a debugging strategy.

transfer function   a function that translates values given as arguments from type Real to type Integer.

tree structure   a linked data structure where each node uses two or more pointers to point to other branches of the tree.

turtle graphics   a simple graphics strategy where commands are like those we would need to give a turtle with a pen attached to its stomach.

type   the specification of the legal values of a simple type or the structure of a structured type.

type compatibility error   occurs when a variable is assigned a value that is not of the appropriate type.

unary function   a function that takes a single variable or value as an argument and returns another single value.

unary operator   an operator requiring only one operand, such as NOT or unary negation, -.

uninitialized pointer   a pointer that has not been given a structure to point to and has not been assigned the value NIL.

union   the set operation producing the set containing all the elements in either or both of two sets.

user-defined type   See **enumerated type; subrange type.**

user-friendly   describes a program that is easily used by a person who is unfamiliar with the program.

value parameter   a formal parameter whose initial value is given by an evaluated expression or variable in the actual parameter list; any changes made to the formal parameter do not affect the value of the corresponding actual parameter.

variable   a location in memory in which information is stored and from which it can be retrieved.

variable field   a field in a variant record structure whose existence depends on the value of the tag field.

variable name   the identifier that is associated with the location of a variable memory cell.

variable parameter   a formal parameter that is identical to the actual parameter to which it is assigned. Any changes made to the formal parameter inside the procedure correspond to changes made to the actual parameter.

variant record   a record structure that utilizes different fields depending on the value of one field, called the tag field.

SELF TEST SOLUTIONS

Chapter 1

Page 17
1. The batch program is better for handling large amounts of data because the data can be typed in or generated and stored in a permanent input file. It would take a long time for the user of the program to type in 100 values.
2. The interactive program allows the user to find the average of two numbers quickly. Creating an input file with two numbers in it is more trouble than it is worth.

Chapter 2

Page 26
      VAR is a reserved word. VARIABLE, A1235, POBOX10106, and Number9 are legal identifiers. 'VARIABLE', '123.', and 'Number' are legal character strings. 123.5 and 000.123 are legal real numbers. VAR., A123.5, and P.O.Box10106 are not legal identifiers (or any other building blocks) because of the illegal characters in each. 123. is not a legal number because there must be at least one digit on each side of the decimal point.

Page 28
1. Semantic error—The sentence contains a subject, a verb, and an object in the proper sequence, but it doesn't make any sense.
2. Syntax error
3. Syntax error
4. Semantic error

Chapter 3

Page 44
1. 68
2. −122
3. 34

Page 45   1. 0
2. 0.5
3. 3
4. 171
5. 0

Page 47   5 * 4 - 3 * 3 =   15

Page 49
```
PROGRAM TwentyOneYearOld (Output);
CONST    NumDaysInYr = 365.25;
BEGIN
         Writeln (Output, 'A person who is ',
                 'celebrating her 21st '
                 'birthday has lived ',
                 NumDaysInYr * 21, ' days.');
END.
```

Page 53   a = 21, b = 19, c = 32, d = 64, and e = 117

Chapter 4

Page 75   A procedure call interrupts the flow of control, telling the computer to execute the statements included in the declaration of the procedure declared. An assignment statement does not interrupt the flow of control of the program.

Page 77   There is no inherent difference between a procedure identifier and a variable identifier. The differences between a program declaration and a procedure declaraction include:
1. procedure declarations cannot include input or output file identifiers
2. the initial reserved word is different: PROGRAM versus PROCEDURE
3. the program declaration ends with a period while procedure declaration ends with a semicolon

Page 84   1. 1
2. 2
3. 3
4. 10
5. 1

Page 91   1. A procedure declaration defines a new identifier, which when found in a procedure call, tells the computer to begin to execute the statements defined inside the section of code labeled by the identifier. A procedure call may be found in the main block of a program while a procedure declaration cannot. Both calls and declarations can occur inside other procedures.
2. A local variable is one that is declared inside a procedure, in the declaration part of that procedure. A global variable is one that is declared before any procedures are declared, in the declaration part of the main program. It is usually impossible to tell them apart by their name alone; it is necessary to find their declarations to distinguish them.

Chapter 6

Page 125
1. too many arguments in actual parameter list
2. correct
3. type conflict of argument (X is integer, both should be real)
4. correct
5. correct
6. correct
7. too few arguments in actual parameter list

Page 128   The output will be the following:

```
19.0  24.0  21.0  17.0
21.8  20.8  22.7  21.3
```

Page 135
1. the global variable of type Integer
2. the local procedure Dick
3. a constant equal to 1.414
4. points A and B
5. point B

Chapter 7

Page 154
```
PROCEDURE Xponenent (X : Real; N : Integer);
   (* This procedure calculates and prints the value of X to  *)
   (* the Nth power. X is assumed to be any real number and    *)
   (* N is assumed to be a nonnegative integer.                *)
   CONST   Dec = 2; (* # of decimal places, could be changed *)
   VAR     Result : Real;    (* the calculated value           *)
           Cntr : Integer   (* the FOR loop counter           *)
   BEGIN
           Result := 1.0;
           FOR Cntr := 1 TO N DO
                   Result := Result * X;
           Writeln (Output, X:1:Dec, ' to the ',N:1,'th power',
                        ' is equal to ', Result:1:Dec);
   END;
```

Page 159
1. The test for the completion of the FOR loop is not satisfied until the 11th time the test is made.

```
FOR Cntr := 1 TO 10 DO
        Writeln (Output, Sqrt (Cntr):1:3);
```

2. The number printed would be 15, right-justified in a default field width of 12 spaces.

Page 162   The only change that is needed is in PROCEDURE MakeLine.

```
PROCEDURE MakeLine;
(* makes a line of Size images for each of two boxes *)
VAR       Col : Integer;
BEGIN
        FOR BoxCntr := 1 TO 2 DO BEGIN
                FOR Col := 1 TO Size DO
                        Write (Output, Image);
                Write (Output, ' ');
        END;
END;
```

This procedure could be improved slightly by adding a character constant called Background which is assigned to ' ', and perhaps by adding a constant NumHorizBoxes, assigned to the value 2, in case we wanted to alter the program to print out a row of horizontal boxes.

Page 163   We can turn the previous right triangle on its head by using a DOWNTO in the FOR loop

```
FOR Row := Size DOWNTO 1 DO BEGIN
        FOR Col := 1 TO Row DO Write (Output, '*');
        Writeln (Output);
END;
```

Chapter 8

Page 200
```
PROCEDURE WeightPredictor;
(* This procedure asks the user to give her or his sex    *)
(* and height and then calculates a very crude estimate   *)
(* of the user's weight.                                   *)

VAR     Sex : Char;            (* of the user *)
        Weight,                (* of the user *)
        Height : Integer;      (* of the user *)
BEGIN
        Writeln (Output, 'Hello, I am going to guess ',
                         'your weight.');
        Writeln (Output, 'Please type your sex (M or F)');
        Readln (Input, Sex);
        Writeln (Output, 'Please type your height in ',
                         'inches.');
        Readln (Input, Height);
        If (Sex = 'F') THEN Weight := Round (Height * 1.88)
                ELSE Weight := Round (Height * 2.43);
        Writeln (Output, 'I guess your weight to be ',
                         Weight:1, ' pounds.');
END;
```

Page 205   1. PROCEDURE OldEnough;
```
          (* This procedure asks for the user's age and returns    *)
          (* whether or not she or he is old enough to attend       *)
          (* school, drive, vote, or purchase alcoholic beverages.  *)
          (* This procedure works as it is structured only for      *)
          (* states where the drinking age is greater than the      *)
          (* voting age, which is 18.                                *)
          CONST    SchoolAge = 5;
                   DriveAge = 16;
                   VoteAge = 18;
                   DrinkAge = 21;
          VAR      Age : Integer;
          BEGIN
                   Writeln (Output,'I will determine what you are',
                                   ' able to do at your age.');
                   Writeln (Output, 'Please type your age.');
                   Readln (Input, Age);
                   IF (Age < SchoolAge)
                      THEN Writeln (Output, 'You are too young even',
                                            ' to read this sentence.')
                      ELSE IF (Age < DriveAge)
                      THEN Writeln (Output, 'You can attend school.')
                      ELSE IF (Age < VoteAge)
                      THEN Writeln (Output, 'With a license, you ',
                                            'can drive a car.')
                      ELSE IF (Age < DrinkAge)
                      THEN Writeln (Output, 'You are old enough ',
                                            'to register to vote.')
                      ELSE Writeln (Output, 'You are old enough ',
                                            'to purchase alcohol.');
          END;
```

2. PROGRAM CompareNumbers (Input, Output);
```
        (* This program asks for three numbers from the user and  *)
        (* compares them to determine which is largest.           *)

        VAR     One, Two, Three, Largest : Integer;

        PROCEDURE FindLargest (First, Second, Third : Integer;
                               VAR Largest : Integer);
        (* This procedure evaluates three integers and determines *)
        (* which of the three is the largest, and returns it.     *)
        BEGIN
                IF (First > Second) THEN BEGIN
                   IF (First > Third)
                      THEN Largest := First
                      ELSE Largest := Third;
                END ELSE BEGIN    (* Second >= First *)
```

```
                IF (Second > Third)
                    THEN Largest := Second
                    ELSE Largest := Third;
            END;
    END;

    BEGIN
            Writeln (Output, 'Type three integers');
            Readln (Input, One, Two, Three);
            FindLargest (One, Two, Three, Largest);
            Writeln (Output, Largest:1, ' is the largest of',
                              ' the three integers.');
    END.
```

3.
```
PROGRAM GetLegalDate (Input, Output);
(* This program asks the user to type in a legal date and *)
(* tests it to determine if it is indeed legal. This could*)
(* be used in a larger program requiring the use of dates.*)
VAR     Day, Month, Year : Integer;
        Legal : Boolean;

PROCEDURE CheckDate (Month, Day, Year : Integer;
                     VAR Legal : Boolean);
(* This procedure validates that the 3 integers given it   *)
(* represent a legal date in this century. Legal is        *)
(* returned TRUE if that is the case.                      *)
CONST   MonthMax = 12;
        DayMax = 31;
        YearMax = 99;
BEGIN
        Legal := (Day > 0) AND (Day <= DayMax) AND
                 (Month > 0) AND (Month <= MonthMax) AND
                 (Year > 0) AND (Year <= YearMax);
        IF Legal THEN BEGIN
            IF (Month = 2) THEN BEGIN
                Legal := (Day <= 28) OR ((Day = 29) AND
                          (Year MOD 4 = 0));
                END ELSE IF (Month = 4) OR (Month = 6) OR
                          (Month = 9) OR (Month = 11)
                    THEN Legal := (Day <= 30);
        END:
END;


BEGIN
        Writeln (Output, 'Type three integers to represent',
                          ' a legal date (M/D/Y).');
        Readln (Input, Month, Day, Year);
        CheckDate (Month, Day, Year, Legal);
```

```
                    IF Legal
                        THEN Writeln (Output, Month:1, '/', Day:1, '/',
                                      Year:1, ' is a legal date.')
                        ELSE Writeln (Output, Month:1, '/', Day:1, '/',
                                      Year:1, ' is not a legal date.');
        END.
```

Page 210 1. FALSE
          2. FALSE
          3. FALSE
          4. TRUE
          5. TRUE

Page 216 1.
```
FUNCTION OldEnoughToVote (Age : Integer) : Boolean;
(* This function takes the prospective voter's age and   *)
(* determines whether or not the person is old enough to *)
(* vote.                                                  *)
CONST   VoteAge = 18;
BEGIN
        OldEnoughToVote := (Age >= VoteAge);
END;
```

          2.
```
FUNCTION InDescOrder (Num1, Num2, Num3 : Integer) : Boolean;
(* This function takes three integers and returns TRUE if *)
(* they were given in descending order, FALSE otherwise.  *)
BEGIN
        InDescOrder := (Num1 > Num2) AND (Num2 > Num3);
END;
```

          3.
```
FUNCTION ValidDate (Day, Month, Year : Integer) : Boolean;
(* This function takes integer values for day, month, and *)
(* year (1-99) and returns TRUE if the three values       *)
(* represent a valid date in this century.                *)
CONST   MonthMax = 12;
        YearMax = 99;
        DayMax = 31;
VAR     TempValidDate : Boolean;
BEGIN
        TempValidDate := (Day > 0) AND (Day <= DayMax) AND
                         (Month > 0) AND (Month <= MonthMax) AND
                         (Year > 0) AND (Year <= YearMax);
        IF TempValidDate THEN
            IF (Month = 2) THEN BEGIN
                TempValidDate := (Day <= 28) OR
                    ((Day = 29) AND (Year MOD 4 = 0))
            END ELSE IF (Month = 4) OR (Month = 6) OR
                        (Month = 9) OR (Month = 11)
                    THEN TempValidDate := (Day <= 30);
        ValidDate := TempValidDate;
END;
```

Page 220
```
FUNCTION RandNum (Low, High : Integer) : Integer;
(* Returns a random number between Low and High, *)
(* inclusive. Uses Round instead of Trunc.       *)
    VAR Num : Integer;   (* Dummy variable for RandNum *)
BEGIN
        Num := Round (Random (Seed) * (High - Low + 1));
        IF (Num = High - Low + 1)
            THEN RandNum := Low
            ELSE RandNum := Low + Num;
END;
```

Chapter 9

Page 242
```
PROCEDURE AddOdds;
(* This procedure adds the odd numbers until the sum is  *)
(* greater than 1985, and then writes the final number   *)
(* summed, the sum and the square root of the sum.       *)
CONST    Target = 1985;
VAR      Odd, Sum : Integer;
BEGIN
        Sum := 1; (* include the first odd, 1, initially  *)
        Odd := 1;
        WHILE (Sum <= Target) DO BEGIN
                Odd := Odd + 2;
                Sum := Sum + Odd;
        END;
        Writeln (Output, 'The sum of the odd numbers from ',
                '1 to ', Odd:1, ' is ', Sum:1);
        Writeln (Output, 'The square root of the sum is ',
                Sqrt (Sum):1:0);
END;
```

Page 247
```
PROGRAM Encode (Input, Output);
(* This program encodes a text input file by translating  *)
(* every letter to another letter in the alphabetic       *)
(* sequence. The letters are shifted by a fixed amount,    *)
(* which can be changed by changing the constant Shift.    *)
(* The output file produced is the encoded text.           *)
CONST    Shift = 1;
VAR      Ch : Char; (* The character read from input file  *)

FUNCTION IsALetter (Ch : Char) : Boolean;
(* This function returns TRUE if the character in          *)
(* question is either an upper or lowercase letter.        *)
BEGIN
        IsALetter := ((Ch >= 'a') AND (Ch <= 'z')) OR
                     ((Ch >= 'A') AND (Ch <= 'Z'));
END;
```

```
FUNCTION ShiftChar (Ch : Char) : Char;
(* If a letter is given as input, then the resulting   *)
(* value will be a shifted letter (including wrap around *)
(* from Z back to A). If the character is not a letter,  *)
(* no change is made.                                    *)
VAR        TempChar : Char; (* Dummy variable, value of fn *)
BEGIN
         IF IsALetter (Ch) THEN BEGIN
            TempChar := Chr (Ord (Ch) + Shift);
            IF NOT IsALetter (TempChar) THEN
                TempChar := Chr (Ord (Ch) + Shift - 26);
         END ELSE TempChar := Ch;
         ShiftChar := TempChar;
END;


BEGIN    (* Main Program *)
         WHILE NOT Eof (Input) DO BEGIN
                WHILE NOT Eoln (Input) DO BEGIN
                        Read (Input, Ch);
                        Write (Output, ShiftChar (Ch));
                END;
                Writeln (Output);
                Readln (Input);
         END;
END.     (* Main Program *)
```

Page 260
```
PROGRAM CapitalizeFile (Input, Output);
VAR     Ch : Char;

FUNCTION Cap (Ch : Char) : Char;
(* This function capitalizes a character if the character *)
(* is a lowercase letter. Otherwise, it doesn't change it *)
BEGIN
         IF (Ch >= 'a') AND (Ch <= 'z')
                THEN Cap := Chr (Ord (Ch) + Ord ('A') -
                                Ord ('a'))
                ELSE Cap := Ch;
END;

BEGIN    (* Main Program *)
         REPEAT
                REPEAT
                        Read (Input, Ch);
                        Write (Output, Cap (Ch));
                UNTIL Eoln (Input);
                Writeln (Output);
                Readln (Input);
         UNTIL Eof (Input);
END.     (* Main Program *)
```

In order for this program to work correctly, there must be at least one character on each line and at least one line in the input file. Otherwise, either a read operation error would result or a blank line would be read as a single space.

Chapter 10

Page 286

```
PROGRAM DisMerge (Input, OutFile1, OutFile2);
    (* This program decodes two messages given in a single   *)
    (* file. The messages were merged together and therefore *)
    (* every other character belongs to the same message. The *)
    (* program breaks the single input file into two output  *)
    (* files, containing the two messages, which are assumed *)
    (* to be the same length.                                 *)
    VAR   Ch : Char;  (* Character read from input file       *)
          FirstFile : Boolean; (* TRUE when character should*)
                               (* be put in the 1st file.    *)
    BEGIN   (* Main Program *)
            FirstFile := TRUE;
            WHILE NOT Eof (Input) DO BEGIN
                WHILE NOT Eoln (Input) DO BEGIN
                    Read (Input, Ch);
                    IF FirstFile
                        THEN Write (OutFile1, Ch)
                        ELSE Write (OutFile2, Ch);
                    FirstFile := NOT FirstFile;
                END;
                Writeln (Output);
                Readln (Input);
            END;
    END.    (* Main Program *)
```

Chapter 11

Page 307

```
PROCEDURE RainbowWrite (VAR Color : Integer);
    (* This procedure reads a value from the input file      *)
    (* between 1 and 7 and writes one of the seven colors of *)
    (* the ROYGBIV rainbow to the output file.               *)
    (* Color is returned with the value of the number read.  *)
    BEGIN
            REPEAT Writeln (Output, 'Type a number between 1',
                                    ' and 7.');
                   Read (Input, Color);
            UNTIL (Color >= 1) AND (Color <= 7);
            CASE Color OF
```

```
                         1 : Writeln (Output, 'Red');
                         2 : Writeln (Output, 'Orange');
                         3 : Writeln (Output, 'Yellow');
                         4 : Writeln (Output, 'Green');
                         5 : Writeln (Output, 'Blue');
                         6 : Writeln (output, 'Indigo');
                         7 : Writeln (output, 'Violet');
                 END;
         END;
```

Page 312 1. a CASE statement
          2. an IF statement
          3. a CASE statement
          4. a nested IF structure

Chapter 12

Page 326 1. TYPE   HairColors = (Red, Blond, Brown, Black);
          2.   Sex = (Male, Female);
          3.   MaritalStatus = (Single, Married, Separated,
                                           Divorced);
          4.   HouseholdRodents = (Mouse, Rat, GuineaPig,
                                           Hamster);

Page 331 1. FUNCTION DayBefore (Today : Day) : Day;

```
             (* This function takes a value of type Day and returns   *)
             (* the day in the week immediately preceding it. It also  *)
             (* handles Sunday correctly.                              *)
             BEGIN
                 IF (Today = Sunday)
                         THEN DayBefore := Saturday
                         ELSE DayBefore := Pred (Today);
             END;
```

          2. FUNCTION ColorDro (Which : Integer) : Color;

```
             VAR     Temp : Color;
                     Cntr : Integer;
             BEGIN
                 Temp := Red;   (* initialize to 'zero' *)
                 FOR Cntr := 1 TO Num DO
                         Temp := Succ (Temp);
                 ColorDro := Temp;
             END;
```

3. FUNCTION FavPod : Pod;
    (* This function asks the user for her or his favorite   *)
    (* Pod and then returns the value of the corresponding   *)
    (* enumerated type.   *)
    VAR   Ch : Char; (* Character user types   *)
    BEGIN
            Writeln (Output, 'Indicate your favorite pod by ',
                             'typing its first letter.');
            Writeln (Output, 'Your choices are: Arthropod');
            Writeln (Output, '   Brachiopod');
            Writeln (Output, '   Cephalopod');
            Writeln (Output, '   Gastropod');
            Writeln (Output, '   Pelecypod');
            Readln (Input, Ch)
            IF (Ch = 'A') OR (Ch = 'B') OR (Ch = 'C') OR
               (Ch = 'G') OR (Ch = 'P') THEN BEGIN
               CASE Ch OF
                   'A' : FavPod := Arthropod;
                   'B' : FavPod := Brachiopod;
                   'C' : FavPod := Cephalopod;
                   'G' : FavPod := Gastropod;
                   'P' : FavPod := Pelecypod;
               END;
            END;
    END;

Page 335   First, some of the possible women's clothing sizes:

```
TYPE      DressType = 6..16;
          ShoeType = 5..10;
          PantsType = 5..14;
          ShirtType = 5..14;
```

Of course, you could have gone crazy and declared all of these with declared constants for both bounds. Next, some men's sizes:

```
TYPE      SleeveType = 28..37; (* in inches *)
          NeckType = 14..17;   (* in inches *)
          ShoeType = 6..14;
          WaistType = 30..42;
          InseamType = 28..38;
          CoatSize = 32..50;
```

The procedure to fit a person might use a small function and look something like this:

```
FUNCTION LegalVal (Val, Lo, Hi : Integer) : Boolean;
(* This function returns TRUE if the Val given is between *)
(* Lo and Hi, inclusive. If the value given is illegal, a *)
(* message is given to the user.                          *)
VAR       TempLegal : Boolean;
```

```
         BEGIN
                 TempLegal := (Val >= Lo) AND (Val <= Hi);
                 IF NOT TempLegal
                     THEN Writeln (Output, 'Value should be between',
                                     ' ', Lo:1, ' and ', Hi:1,'.');
                 LegalVal := TempLegal;
         END;

         PROCEDURE WeddingFit (VAR Sleeve : SleeveType;
                     VAR Neck : NeckType; VAR Shoe : ShoeType;
                     VAR Waist : WaistType; VAR Inseam : InseamType;
                         VAR Coat : CoatSize);
         (* This procedure fits a male for an entire suit, as used *)
         (* in a wedding. Included are measurements for shirt,      *)
         (* pants, coat and shoes.                                  *)
         VAR     Legal : Boolean; (* True if legal value given      *)
                 Num   : Integer;
         BEGIN
                 REPEAT  Writeln (Output, 'Type your sleeve length');
                         Readln (Input, Num);
                 UNTIL LegalVal (Num, 28, 37); Sleeve := Num;
                 REPEAT  Writeln (Output, 'Type your neck size');
                         Readln (Input, Num);
                 UNTIL LegalVal (Num, 14, 17); Neck := Num;
                 REPEAT  Writeln (Output, 'Type your shoe size');
                         Readln (Input, Num);
                 UNTIL LegalVal (Num, 6, 14); Shoe := Num;
                 REPEAT  Writeln (Output, 'Type your waist length');
                         Readln (Input, Num);
                 UNTIL LegalVal (Num, 30, 42); Waist := Num;
                 REPEAT  Writeln (Output, 'Type your inseam length');
                         Readln (Input, Num);
                 UNTIL LegalVal (Num, 28, 38); Inseam := Num;
                 REPEAT  Writeln (Output, 'Type your coat size');
                         Readln (Input, Num);
                 UNTIL LegalVal (Num, 32, 50); Coat := Num;
         END;
```

Page 339   The preceding program fragment uses LegalVal to prevent read operation errors.

Chapter 13

```
Page 351    TYPE    Days = (Sun, Mon, Tue, Wed, Thu, Fri, Sat);
                    AccidentType = ARRAY [Days] OF Integer;
            VAR     Accidents : AccidentType;
```

Page 354
```
CONST    Max = 100;
TYPE     ScoreArray = ARRAY [1..Max] OF Integer;
FUNCTION ValueFind (VAR SA : ScoreArray;
                         Value: Integer) : Boolean;
VAR      Cntr : Integer;
BEGIN
         Cntr := 1;
         WHILE (Cntr < Max) AND
                 (Value <> SA[Cntr]) DO
                 Cntr := Cntr + 1;
         ValueFind := (SA[Cntr] = Max);
END;
```

Page 356
```
TYPE     Days = (Sun, Mon, Tue, Wed, Thu, Fri, Sat);
         AccidentType = ARRAY [Days] OF Integer;
PROCEDURE AccidentCount (VAR Acc : AccidentType);
(* This procedure counts the number of accidents *)
(* occurring on any given day of the week. The   *)
(* array is assumed to be initialized.           *)
VAR      Ch : Char;
BEGIN
     WHILE NOT Eof (Input) DO BEGIN
         Read (Input, Ch);
         CASE Ch OF
           'S': BEGIN
                 Read (Input, Ch);
                 IF (Ch = 'u') THEN
                   Acc [Sun] := Acc [Sun] + 1
                 ELSE Acc [Sat] := Acc [Sat] + 1;
               END;
           'T': BEGIN
                 Read (Input, Ch);
                 IF (Ch = 'u') THEN
                   Acc [Tue] := Acc [Tue] + 1
                 ELSE Acc [Thu] := Acc [Thu] + 1;
               END;
           'M': Acc [Mon] := Acc [Mon] + 1;
           'W': Acc [Wed] := Acc [Wed] + 1;
           'F': Acc [Fri] := Acc [Fri] + 1;
         END;
         Readln (Input);
     END;
END;
```

Page 360
1. The indices to NumArray should be J and J-1, not I and I-1.
2. Same as 1.
3. When I = J = 1, the subscript J-1, which equals zero, will produce an array index out of bounds. The indices should be J and J+1.
4. The indices to the NumArray should be J and J+1, not J and I.

Page 368   For it to work correctly, the last line of the WHILE loop should read:

```
ELSE Top := Midpoint + 1;
```

Because it does not, this procedure will only find a number if it is the first number in the array. The Bottom value will decrease until it is finally equal to the Top, which will never change. Otherwise, a value which should be found will be reported not in the array.

Page 371

```
PROCEDURE ReadWord (VAR W : Word);
(* This reads a word until a non-alphanumeric *)
(* character is encountered.                  *)
VAR Cntr : Integer;
    Ch : Char;
    Legal : Boolean;      (* true when character *)
                          (* is alphanumeric     *)
BEGIN
    Cntr := 0;
    REPEAT     (* assume at least one char *)
        Read (Input, Ch);    (* on line      *)
        Cntr := Cntr + 1;
        W [Cntr] := Ch;
        Legal := ((Ch >= 'A') AND (Ch <= 'Z')) OR
                 ((Ch >= 'a') AND (Ch <= 'z')) OR
                 ((Ch >= '0') AND (Ch <= '9'));
    UNTIL Eoln (Input) OR NOT Legal;
    IF NOT Legal THEN W [Cntr] := ' ';
END;
```

Chapter 14

Page 398

```
TYPE    MatrixType = ARRAY [1..Max, 1..Max] OF Integer;
PROCEDURE Invert (VAR Mat : MatrixType);
VAR Temp,
    I, J : Integer;
BEGIN
    FOR I := 1 TO Max DO
        FOR J := I TO Max DO BEGIN
            Temp := Mat [I, J];
            Mat [I, J] := Mat [J, I];
            Mat [J, I] := Temp;
        END;
END;
```

Chapter 15

Page 426
1. Yesterday is an array variable, requiring an index, not a field.
2. Correct
3. Mail is a type identifier, and is not a variable.
4. Today is an array expecting an index of type Times, not of type Integer.
5. Correct
6. Correct
7. Letter is a record, requiring a field, not an index.

Page 429
1. Integer variable
2. Player, a record
3. Word, an array of characters indexed by integers (the team name)
4. Integer
5. A single character in the player's name.

Page 436
```
PROCEDURE SelectionSort (Arr : ArrType;
                Bottom : Integer;
                VAR Swaps, Comps : Integer;
(* This procedure counts the number of swaps  *)
(* and comparisons a selection sort algorithm *)
(* makes on an array. It leaves the array     *)
(* unchanged.                                  *)
VAR Top, First, ThisOne : Integer;
BEGIN
    Swaps := 0; Comps := 0;
    FOR Top := 1 TO Bottom - 1 DO BEGIN
        First := Top;
        FOR ThisOne := Top TO Bottom DO
            IF (Arr [ThisOne] < Arr [First])
                THEN First := ThisOne;
        Comps := Comps + Top - Bottom + 1;
        Swap (Arr [First], Arr [Top]);
        Swaps := Swaps + 1;
    END;
END;


PROCEDURE BubbleSort (Arr : ArrType;
                Bottom : Integer;
                VAR Swaps, Comps : Integer;
(* This procedure counts the number of swaps *)
(* and comparisons a bubble sort algorithm   *)
(* makes on an array. It leaves the array     *)
(* unchanged.                                  *)
VAR I, J : Integer;
```

```
BEGIN
    Swaps := 0; Comps := 0;
    For I := Bottom - 1 DOWNTO 1 DO BEGIN
        FOR J := 1 TO I DO
            IF (Arr [J] > Arr [J+1]) THEN BEGIN
                Swap (Arr [J], Arr [J+1]);
                Swaps := Swaps + 1;
            END;
        Comps := Comps + I;
    END;
END;
```

Chapter 16

Page 475
```
IF (Input^ = 'A')
        THEN Readln (Input)
        ELSE Read (Input, Num);
```

Page 476   The letter 'h' would be written to the output file.

Page 477
```
PROCEDURE ReadWord (VAR W : Word;
                    VAR InFile : Text);
(* This procedure reads a word until Eoln *)
(* from any input file.                   *)
VAR Cntr : Integer;
BEGIN
    Cntr := 0;
    WHILE (Cntr < Max) AND
            NOT Eoln (InFile) DO BEGIN
        Cntr := Cntr + 1;
        Read (InFile, W [Cntr]);
    END;
END;

PROCEDURE WriteWord (W : Word;
                     VAR OFile : Text);
(* This procedure writes a word to any *)
(* output file.                        *)
VAR Cntr : Integer;
BEGIN
    For Cntr := 1 TO Max DO
        Write (OFile, W [Cntr]);
END;
```

Page 484   1. Eight values of this set are possible: { }, {0}, {1}, {2}, {0, 1}, {0, 2}, {1, 2}, {0, 1, 2}
2. 2^n

Chapter 17

Page 502

```
CONST    MaxChars = 25; ShortMax = 3;
         MaxFltsTrip = 10;
         MaxFlights = 100;

TYPE     Word = PACKED ARRAY [1..MaxChars] OF Char;
         ShortWord = PACKED ARRAY [1..ShortMax] OF Char;
         StatusType = (Reserved, Ticketed, Paid, Cancelled);
         SeatClass = (First, Coach);

         Customer = RECORD
           Name : Word;
           Num : Integer;
           CredCardNum : Integer;
           Street : Word;
           CityStateZIP : Word;
           AmtPayable : Integer;
         END;

         PersonsFlight = RECORD
           Carrier : ShortWord;
           Number : Integer;
           DepartCity,
           ArriveCity : ShortWord;
           DepartTime,
           ArriveTime : TimeType;
           Date : DateType;
           Class : SeatClass;
           Seat : ShortWord;
         END;

         FlightArray = ARRAY [1..MaxFltsTrip] OF
                             PersonsFlight;

         Itinerary = RECORD
           TheFlts : FlightArray;
           Price : Real;
           CustNum : Integer;
           Status : StatusType;
         END;

         SeatArray = ARRAY [SeatClass] OF Integer;

         AnyFlight = RECORD
           Carrier : ShortWord;
           Number : Integer;
           DepartCity,
           ArriveCity : ShortWord;
```

```
                      DepartTime,
                      ArriveTime : TimeType;
                      Date : DateType;
                      Seats : SeatArray;
                    END;

                    AllFlights = ARRAY [1..MaxFlights] OF AnyFlight;
```

```
Page 504   BEGIN      (* Main Program *)
                      Introduction;
                      StoreGlobalData (Flights, Customers);
                      GetWorkingItineraries (Itineraries);
                      REPEAT
                          GetCommand (Command);
                          CASE Command OF
                              EditCust : EditCustData (Customers);
                              EditItin : EditItinerary (Itineraries);
                              PrntTics : PrintTickets (Itineraries,
                                                       Customers);
                              EditFlts : EditFlights (Flights);
                          END;
                      UNTIL (Command = Quit);
           END      (* Main Program *)
```

The main program structure indicates that the customer data should be distinct from the itinerary data, because the customer data should only need to be entered once for each customer, while several different itineraries may be created for a single customer.

Chapter 18

```
Page 520   FUNCTION NegPower (X : Real; N : Integer) : Real;
           (* This function calculates X to the N where X  *)
           (* is a real number and N is a negative integer.*)
           (* This function does not work if N is positive.*)
           BEGIN
               IF (N = 0)
                   THEN NegPower := 1
                   ELSE NegPower := NegPower (X, N + 1) / X;
           END;
```

Page 523 1. An infinite recursion occurs, because the end point is never satisfied. (N becomes increasingly negative, but never reaches zero.)
2. If n does not equal zero initially, then an infinite recursion occurs, because n is never decreased by the function. There is no simplification of the problem.
3. An infinite recursion occurs, because the logic of the program never allows for an end condition.

Page 527 Three move operations are performed when NumDisks = 2. When NumDisks = 5, 31 operations are performed. In general, the number of moves is equal to one less than 2 raised to the number of disks. Theoretically, the program would be able to handle a value of 25 for NumDisks, but the time to run and print all the calculations, even at 100 per second, would be about 100 hours.

Page 529 The output would read:

Ha Ha Ha Ha Ha Ha Ha Ha

The simplification is in the parameter pass of Num-1 into the procedure. The end point is satisfied when Num becomes 0.

Chapter 19

Page 554
```
PROCEDURE DeleteValue (VAR Head : NodePtr;
              Val : Integer; VAR Error : Boolean);
(* This procedure takes a list and a value and *)
(* returns the list with the value deleted     *)
(* from the list. If the value is not found,    *)
(* then Error is returned as TRUE.              *)
VAR      Temp : NodePtr;
BEGIN
    IF (Head <> NIL) THEN BEGIN
        IF (Head^.Val = Val)
            THEN DeleteHead (Head, Val)
            ELSE IF (Head^.Next = NIL)
                THEN Error := TRUE
                ELSE BEGIN
                    Temp := Head;
                    WHILE (Temp^.Next^.Next <> NIL)
                      AND (Temp^.Next^.Val <> Val)
                      DO Temp := Temp^.Next;
                    IF (Temp^.Next^.Val = Val)
                        THEN Temp^.Next :=
                            Temp^.Next^.Next
                        ELSE Error := TRUE;
                END;
    END;
END;
```

Index of Selected Defined Indentifiers

The following defined identifiers are used in programs appearing in the text.

AddToHead, 549
AddToTail, 550
ArrayEqual, 386
Average, 127
AverageNumbers, 155
AverageScores, 166, 261, 306

BigLetters, 408
Blank, 370, 554
BlankVerse, 487
BoxDimensions, 59
BubbleSort, 357

CalcNumDays, 309
CalculateInterest, 65
CalculateTax, 337
Cap, 209, 246, 487, 492
Capitalize, 142, 209, 356
CensusCount, 256
ChiSqu, 377
CodingArray, 351
Color, 341
Colors, 326, 351
ConvertAngles, 138
Cube, 141

DataBaseManager, 514
DateType, 392
Day, 326, 327, 329

DayOfBirth, 309
DaysInMonth, 304, 309
Debugging, 214
DeleteHead, 551
DeleteTail, 552
DeprecSchedule, 176
Dice, 220
Dictionary, 395

Encode, 357
ESPTester, 80, 97, 238

Finished, 362
Fold, 381
FormLetters, 292
FreqArray, 351, 356, 388
Fruit, 326
Future, 340, 392

GasFigures, 121
Geometry, 46, 50, 53
GetCommand, 451, 456
GradingCurve, 181

Help, 462
Histogram, 375
Hourglass, 172, 174

IsALetter, 356, 357

LargePrimes, 251
Legal, 334

LettersOnALine, 491
LetterType, 332

MakeChange, 62
MakeLargeBoxes, 161
MakePattern, 75
MakeThreeLetters, 82, 97
MatchMaker, 433, 445, 471
MathTutor, 226, 237
Maxint, 23, 248
MergeDictionaries, 556
MergeSort, 480
MoveDisks, 526
MoviePatrol, 202, 215

NumGuess, 266

Person, 438
PlayOneGame, 316
PlusNMinus, 402
Pods, 326
PokerHand, 326
PrimeCheck, 250
PrintInBlocks, 288
PrintList, 553

Rand, 227, 229, 237, 267

RandNum, 220, 227, 267, 317
ReadDict, 395
ReadNCalc, 400
ReadNRightJust, 525
ReadPerson, 431, 439
ReadWord, 354, 370, 395, 433, 477, 557
RecursiveEval, 534
ReportScore, 317
RoundTo, 144

Search, 362, 365
SearchCardNums, 365
SelectionSort, 436
Shapes, 447
SkipSpaces, 245, 476, 477, 484, 487
Swap, 359, 371, 422, 436

TextArray, 351, 387
TurtleDraw, 457

WantsToPlay, 214, 272
WantsToQuit, 262, 269, 315
WeekDays, 332
WeightVal, 307
WriteSet, 490
WriteWord, 505

Subject Index

Activation, 135
Actual parameter, 124
Ada, 7
Algorithm, 10, 57, 60, 85
Algorithmic refinement, 10
Alphametic, 540
Alphanumeric, 24
AND, 207
Argument. *See* Parameter.
Arithmetic expression, 43
   syntax, 531
Arithmetic operator, 43
Array, 347
   binary search, 360–367
   comparison to BASIC, 388
   comparison to records, 427
   declarations, 348–351
   errors, 353, 385–387, 410
   index, 350
   index out of bounds, 467
   multidimensional, 394–398
   noninteger indexing, 356
   packed, 368
   reading and initializing, 351–353
   sequential search, 353
   sorting, 358
   syntax, 350
Array of records, 426–429
   limitations, 474
   using, 429–434
ASCII, A3-1
Assertions, 205–207, 247–248
Assignment, 42
Astrophysics research, 376
Atanasoff, John V., 3

ABC. *See* Computer, Atanasoff-Berry.

Base type. *See* Component type.
BASIC, 18–19
   arrays, 388, 412
   conditional repetition, 273
   CLOSE, 297
   FOR-NEXT, 188
   IF, 232
   IFEND, 234
   global variables, 146
   GO TO, 92, 240
   GOSUB, 92
   input, 65, 297
   key words, 34
   ON-GO TO, 320
   OPEN, 297
   PRINT, 297
   remarks, 34
   RETURN, 92
   style, 112
   variables, 65
   WEND, 275
   WHILE, 275
Batch processing, 14
BEGIN-END, 27, 154–156
Binary search, 360–367
Binary tree, 562
Blackjack, 470
Block, 90, 133–136
Boolean
   constants, 210
   errors, 229
   expression, 198, 207
   functions, 214

Boolean (continued)
    operators, 207
    variables, 210
Branches, 562
Brian, 123
Bubble sort, 358–360
    compared to selection sort, 436

Call. *See* Function, Procedure.
Capitalization, 26, 102
Cardinality, G-2
Carriage control character. *See* Control character.
Carriage return-line feed, 25
CASE statement, 304–307
    compared to IF, 311
    compared to ON-GO TO, 320
    compared to records, 503
    errors, 319
    expression, 305
    extensions, 312
    syntax, 305
    value list, 305
Cathode-ray tube, 5
Central processing unit, 5
Char, 141–142, 167–168
Character input of numbers, 484
Character set, A3-1, G-2
Character strings, 24
Chicken dinner, 9
Chi-square, 376
Chr, 142
Circle
    area, 192
Circular list, 561
Comment, 26
    as a programming tool, 105, 503, 515
    rules, 105
Compiler, 13
Compiler errors. *See* Execution errors, 41
Component access rules, 427
Component type, 349
Compound statement, 154, 196
Computer
    Atanasoff-Berry, 3
    components, 6
    definition, 2
    ENIAC, 3
Computer dating services, 436
Condition. *See* Test.
Conditional execution, 196
    CASE, 304
    IF, 196–200

Constant, 48
    character string, 370
    style, 104
Control character, 29
Control structure, 74. *See also* CASE, FOR, GOTO, IF, REPEAT, WHILE, WITH.
    compared to data structures, 504–505
    stepwise refinement, 502
Correctness of programs. *See* Assertions, Tracing execution.
CPU, 5
CRLF, 25
CRT, 5

Dangling ELSE, 203
Data, 5
Data abstraction, 340, 392
Data base program, 498
Data structure, 346, 474
    compared to control structures, 504–505
    design, 499
    stepwise refinement, 499
Data type, 340. *See also* Type.
Debugging, 31
    aided by subrange types, 339
    arrays, 385–387
    boolean, 229
    CASE, 319
    definition, 31
    files, 295
    FOR, 187
    functions, 145
    IF, 229
    input, 271
    multidimensional arrays, 410
    parameters, 145
    pointers, 564
    records, 467
    recursion, 537
    REPEAT, 271
    sets, 493
    tracing execution, 183–187
    variables, 63, 145
    WHILE, 271
Declarations
    constant, 48–49
    forward, 529
    function, 140–141
    label, A1-1
    procedure, 75–77
    type, 324–326, 332–334
    var, 40–42

Declaration section, 27, 40, 48, 75, 325
Delimiters, 28
Design. *See* Program.
Dice rolls, 389
Digitized image, 321
Direct access. *See* Random access.
Dispose, 547
DIV, 43–44
Documentation, 34, 100
DOWNTO, 157
Dynamic allocation, 543

E, 24
EBCDIC, 153
Eckert, J. P., 3
Editor, 12
Efficiency, 216
Elegance, 101
Elements, 482
ELSE, 196
   dangling, 203
Empty set, G-4
Empty statement, 30
Encryption, 248, 300, 351
End of file. *See* Eof.
End of line. *See* Eoln.
ENIAC, 3
Enumerated types, 324–331, 332
   delarations, 324
   ordering, 331
   reading and writing, 341
Environment, 90
Eof, 242–246
Eoln, 242–246
Errors
   execution, 31
   intent, 31
   memory size, 411
   round off, 177, 188, 231
   syntax, 31
   type compatibility, 43, 64
ESP, 77
Execute, 14
Execution errors, 31
Exponential notation, 24
Expressions
   arithmetic, 43
   boolean, 198, 207
   evaluation of, 43–45, 198, 208

Factorial, 188–189, 539
Fibonacci sequence, 193, 218, 238, 539
Field width

default, 46
   user defined, 108
Fields, 423
   fixed, 448
   tag, 448
   variable, 448
FIFO, 560
Files, 12
   buffer variable, 475, 484
   components. *See* Files, structured.
   errors, 295
   input, 49
   multiple I/O, 283–286
   merge sort, 479
   parameters, 288–289, 477
   structured, 477–479, 502
   text, 475–477
   variables, 284
Fixed fields, 448
Flow of control, 74
Folding algorithm, 376
FOR statement, 152–154, 156–159
   common errors, 183
   compared to WHILE and REPEAT, 261–262
   increment, 156
   syntax, 153
Form letters, 84, 289
Formal parameter, 123
Format, 100
FORTRAN, 7
Functions
   boolean, 214
   call, 54
   errors, 145
   numerical standard functions, 55
   pred, 329
   recursive, 519–520
   standard, 54
   succ, 329
   transfer, 56
   unary, 54
   user-defined, 140

Games
   Blackjack, 470
   Bridge, 470
   Chess, 516
   guessing, 263–271
   parlor, 300
   Rock, Paper, Scissors, 315
   Solitaire, 472
   trivia, 417

Get, 476
Global variable, 90
GOTO statement, 240
Grading curve, 177
Graphics
  simple, 169
  turtle, 449
Greatest common divisor (GCD), 539
Greco-Latin square, 415

Hardware, 5
Histogram, 371, 376
Host type, 332

Identifier, 25
  length of, 25
  meaningful, 103
  scope of, 133–135
  style, 103
IF statement, 196–200
  compared to CASE, 311
  efficiency, 216–218
  errors, 229
  nesting, 200
  style, 216–218
  syntax, 196
Implementation dependent, 23
IN operator, 483
Income tax, 335
Index type. *See* Component type.
Indentation, 101
  guidelines, 102, 161
Infinite loop, 242, 272
Initialization
  of arrays, 351–353
  of pointers, 548–549
  of variables, 42
Input, 5
  errors, 271
  file, 49
Intent errors, 31
Integers, 23
Interactive processing, 14
Interactive program, 17, 53, 59, 62, 80,
  117, 138, 226, 288, 315, 406, 441, 457,
  487, 491, 510, 534
  guidelines, 111
Interpreter, 18
Intersection, 483
Invariant assertions, 247–248
Iteration, 162–163, 519
I/O device, 6
I/O procedures, 282–283

Jordan, 123

Label declaration, A1-1
Large data structures, 429
Latin square, 415
LIFO, 560
Lists, 544–547
  circular linked, 561
  deletion, 551–552
  doubly linked, 561
  initialization, 549
  insertion, 546
  printing, 553
  queue insertion, 550
  stack insertion, 549
Local variable, 90
Loop. *See* Control structures, FOR,
  REPEAT, WHILE.

Machine language, 14
Machine representation, 41
Magic cube, 416
Magic square, 414
Map coloring, 495
Mauchly, J. W., 3
Maxint, 23
Mean, 178
Memory, 5
Merge sort, 479, 554
MOD, 43–44
Modularity, 131
Module, 508
Morse code, 414
Multidimensional arrays, 394–398
  comparison to BASIC, 411–412
  declarations, 394–397
  errors, 410

Nested loop, 159
Nesting
  array declarations, 396
  compound statements, 154
  FOR statements, 159
  IF statements, 200
  parentheses, 45
  WITH statements, 432
New, 547
NIL, 549
Node, 545
NOT, 207
Numerical errors. *See* Roundoff errors.

Operator

arithmetic, 43
assignment, 43
binary infix, 43, 208
boolean, 207
precedence, 44, 208
relational, 199
set, 483
unary prefix, 208
OR, 207
Ord function, 142
Output, 5
file, 29
readable, 47
style, 108–110

Packed array
comparison, 369
errors, 369
Page procedure, 290
Palindrome, 390
Parameter, 122
actual, 124
formal, 123
file, 286, 288–289
errors, 145
list, 123–124
with records, 431
value, 122–125
variable, 126–128
variable vs. value, 132
Pascal, Blaise, 7
Pascal's Triangle, 389
Pass-by-reference, 132
Phase, 376
Pointers, 543
accessing, 544–545
allocating, 547
declarations, 543–544
disposing, 547
errors, 564
NIL, 548
uninitialized, 549
Portability, 131
Postcondition assertion, 206
Postfix notation, 208
Precedence, 44
Precondition assertion, 206
Pred function, 329
Prime numbers, 248–253
Procedure
call, 73
declarations, 75–77
definition, 73

I/O, 110
recursive, 518–524
short, 107
style, 106
syntax, 76
Program
compiling, 13
data base, 498
declaration, 27
design, 499
documentation, 100
editing, 12
execution, 14
heading, 33
indentation, 101–102
interactive guidelines, 111
limitations, 445
modularity, 131
portability, 131
robustness, 271
spaghetti, 131
style, 101–108
syntax, 27
tracing, 183–187
user-friendly, 111
user-hostile, 112
verification, 205–207, 247–248
Programming
code, 7
defensive, 32
language, 7
structured, 7
top-down, 12, 85, 94
Pseudocode, 12, 513
Put, 476

Queue, 550

Random
number, 218
number generator, 220
particle interactions, 392, 416
Read statement, 50, 243
Readln statement, 51, 244
Real numbers, 23
printing, 108–109
Records
arrays of, 426–429
compared to arrays, 427
compared to CASE, 503
components, 422
declarations, 422–424
errors, 467

Records (continued)
  fields, 424
  fixed fields, 448
  in memory, 423
  parameter passing, 431, 501
  syntax, 449
  tag field, 448
  using WITH, 431–432
  variable fields, 448
  variant, 446–449
Recursion, 518–524
  calls, 522
  compared to iteration, 521
  data structures, 544–547
  end point, 523
  errors, 537
  functions, 537
  overuse, 531
  steps, 522
Relational operators, 188–189
REPEAT statement, 259–260
  compared to FOR and WHILE,
    261–262
  errors, 271
Reserved words, 22
    Reset procedure, 284
    Rewrite procedure, 284
    Robustness, 271
    Round function, 56, 143, 219
Run-time errors. *See* Execution errors.

Scalar type. *See* Simple type, Enumer-
    ated type.
Scaling, 313
Scope, 135
Searching
  binary, 360–367
  sequential, 353
Seed, 219
Selection sort, 435–436
  compared to bubble sort, 436
Self-documenting, 103–106
Semantics, 28
Separators, 26
Sequential searching, 353
Set difference, 483
Sets
  base type, 482
  errors, 493
  initialization, 482
  membership, 483
  operations, 483
Side effects, 146
Simple type, 41

Simplified Integrated Modular Prose,
    322, 416
Software, 5
Sorting
  bubble sort, 358
  merge sort, 479, 554
  selection, 435–436
  using a binary tree, 567–568
Source code, 13
Spaghetti programs, 131
Special symbols, 23
Stack, 549
  of plates, 522
Standard deviation, 178
Standard Pascal, 158, 313, 547
Standard procedures
  Dispose, 547–548
  Get, 476
  I/O, 110, 282
  New, 547–548
  Page, 290
  Put, 476
Statement. *See also* Control structure, 28
  assignment, 42–43
  compound, 154–156
  empty, 30
Static allocation, 543
Stepwise refinement, 12, 499–504
String. *See also* Character string, Packed
    array.
  assignment, A2-3
  concatenation, A2-3
  constant, 370, A2-1
  pattern finding, A2-4
  substrings, A2-4
Structured programming, 7
Structured type, 348
Style, 100
  errors, 112
  IF statement, 216–218
  output, 108–110
  program, 101–108
  rules, 113
Subrange types, 332–334, 339
Subtask, 72
Succ function, 329
Syntax, 27

Tag fields, 448
Test, 196
Text, 283–284
Top-down programming, 12, 85
Tower of Hanoi, 525
Tracing execution, 183–187

Tree, binary, 562
  sorting using, 567
Triangle number, 192
Trunc function, 56, 220
Turtle graphics, 449
Types
  as documentation, 342
  base, 349
  compatible, 64, 339–340
  component, 349
  errors, 340–341
  index, 350
  pointers, 543
  simple, 41
  structured, 348, 422
  user defined, 332

Uninitialized pointers, 548
User defined
  constants, 48
  types, 325–326, 332–334
User friendliness, 111, 117

Value parameters, 122–125
Variables, 40
  assignment, 42–43
  character, 141, 167
  control, 153
  declarations, 40–42
  file, 284
  errors, 63, 145
  global, 90, 159
  index, 153
  local, 90
  local vs. global, 128
  name, 41
  parameters vs. global, 129
  pointer, 543
  Scalar, 153
Variable fields, 448
Variable parameters, 126–128
Variant records, 446–449

WHILE statement, 241–242
  compared to FOR and REPEAT, 261–262
  errors, 271
  syntax, 241
Wirth, Niklaus, 7
WITH statement, 431
  nested, 432
Write statement, 46
Writeln statement, 29